CONTENTS

Foreword, by Miguel León-Portilla	xi
Preface	xix
Acknowledgments	xxvii
Part 1. Essays	
Nahuatl Plays in Context, by Barry D. Sell	3
Death and the Colonial Nahua, by Louise M. Burkhart	29
Nahuatl Catechistic Drama: New Translations, Old Preoccupations, by Daniel Mosquera	55
Instructing the Nahuas in Judeo-Christian Obedience: A *Neixcuitilli* and Four Sermon Pieces on the Akedah, by Viviana Díaz Balsera	85
Part 2. Plays	
Transcription Guidelines	115
The Three Kings	118
The Sacrifice of Isaac	146
Souls and Testamentary Executors	164
Final Judgment	190
How to Live on Earth	210
The Merchant	242
The Life of Don Sebastián	268
Appendixes	305
References	321
Index	331

FOREWORD

Fernando Horcasitas (1924–1980) and Nahuatl Theater

Miguel León-Portilla

New Spain's various forms of theater in Nahuatl have attracted the attention of a good number of researchers. Thanks to them we know that such theater owes its existence to the efforts of Franciscan friars. In some ways this theater came to take the place of the feasts and performances of pre-Hispanic times. Only a few years after the conquest of the Mexican metropolis of Mexico Tenochtitlan (now Mexico City), some Franciscans, with the invaluable help of their native assistants, chose subjects mostly from the Holy Scriptures and also from texts already existing in Spanish or Latin, then prepared scripts, had them translated into the Nahuatl language, and organized performances.

Accounts left by some Franciscan and Indian chroniclers recall how intensely the natives enjoyed such performances, which were usually held in the open air. I myself, as an eyewitness, can testify how in our time many people have similarly enjoyed attending the staging of one of these old theater pieces. The staging was put on by a professional, Miguel Sabido, and his company, which includes Nahuatl-speaking actors. The performance also took place in the open air, near the pyramid of Tlatelolco to the north of Mexico City; there have been other performances at the sumptuous Palace of Fine Arts in the heart of the metropolis.

We owe to the Franciscans Toribio de Benavente Motolinia, Gerónimo de Mendieta, and Juan de Torquemada the first vivid accounts of how these plays were presented, as early as the 1530s at places such as the same Santiago Tlatelolco or in the atrium of the cathedral of Mexico City. Their extant scripts, mostly copies of the original texts, are preserved at various archives and libraries in Mexico, the United States, and Europe and permit careful appreciation of the plots, dialogue, and other stylistic attributes of the plays we know today as pieces of this early theater. A very good example of what can be done is offered by this book in which seven pieces are rendered (some for the first time) in English, translated directly from the Nahuatl language by Louise M. Burkhart and Barry D. Sell.

The recent "discovery" of what may be the oldest extant original Nahuatl text of this genre, dating to about 1591—entitled "Miércoles Santo" or "Holy Wednesday" and published by Louise M. Burkhart—demonstrates that the field is open to further progress in the study of what is indeed the earliest form of Euro-Indian theater in the Americas (Burkhart 1996). The recording, translation, and publishing of some of these plays has a rich history, in which a very significant role was played by Fernando Horcasitas Pimentel, to whose memory the *Nahuatl Theater* set is dedicated.

Predecessors in Research on Nahuatl Theater

I will briefly recall some of Fernando's most distinguished predecessors in the field. Two Mexican scholars deserve particular attention. One is the well-known bibliographer and editor of several sixteenth-century chronicles, Joaquín García Icazbalceta (1825–1894). He wrote a well-documented study on this subject, "Representaciones religiosas en México en el siglo XVI," published in 1877, as an introduction to the *Coloquios espirituales y sacramentales* by Fernán González de la Eslava. García Icazbalceta also made several references to the same matter in his *Bibliografía mexicana del siglo XVI* (1886 and 1954). His contributions in this field called the attention of scholars to these compositions conceived as an instrument for the conversion of the Indians and as a genre within the literary productions of colonial Mexico.

Francisco del Paso y Troncoso (1842–1917) is the other Mexican scholar who made important contributions related to Nahuatl theater. He was well versed in the Nahuatl language and an assiduous researcher in the main documentary repositories of Europe. He was the first to publish the Nahuatl texts and his own translations into Spanish of five pieces of this genre (Paso y Troncoso 1899, 1900b, 1902, 1907). He also wrote "Comedies en langue nahuatl: Une petite vieille et le gamin, son petit fils," a paper presented at the twelfth International Congress of Americanists, held in Paris (1900a, 309–16). Thanks to Paso y Troncoso's publications, examples of Nahuatl theater became widely accessible for the first time.

Two North Americans who spent a large part of their lives in Mexico, John H. Cornyn (1875–1941) and Byron McAfee (1880–1962), also became attracted by these plays. In 1944 they introduced and published the Nahuatl text and an English version of a composition entitled "Tlacahuapahualiztli (Bringing Up Children)," preserved at the Library of Congress (Cornyn and McAfee 1944, 314–51). This play does not have, as several others do, a biblical subject. Its theme is the Christian education that is to be offered to indigenous youth. As noted by its two editors, to achieve its purpose, ideas and forms of expression in the play were derived from some *huehuehtlahtolli*, testimonies of the "old word."

To the same researchers is due the study and English translation of another play, entitled "Souls and Testamentary Executors." A copy is preserved at the National Library of Anthropology and History, housed in the Museum of Anthropology in Mexico City; an English translation was published by Marilyn Ekdahl Ravicz (1970, 211–34). This is another example of a play with a nonbiblical plot, as it deals with the misdeeds perpetrated by a widow, helped by the executors of her dead husband's will. Instead of ordering masses for his soul, she used the inherited riches to foolishly enjoy life.

Byron McAfee translated another play into English, also catechistical, but like "Souls and Testamentary Executors" of a nonbiblical nature. Its plot has to do with the avaricious dealings of a *pochtecatl* or "merchant" who loses his soul in punishment for his misdeeds. McAfee's English version of this play has been published by the same Marilyn Ekdahl Ravicz (1970, 99–118). To the same McAfee, in collaboration with the short-lived but well-known Mexicanist Robert H. Barlow (1918–1951), is owed the publication and translation of another production, *Un cuaderno de Marqueses* (1947), a good example of popular theater whose plot has to do with the conquest of Mexico.

Angel María Garibay K. (1892–1967), the chief exponent in contemporary research on Nahuatl literature, included indigenous colonial theater among his many concerns. To it he dedicated a whole chapter in his *Historia de la literatura náhuatl* (1953–1954, 2:121–59). There he makes a pertinent observation on how "it was not possible that the Mexicans, once they fell under the burden of the Conquest, would lose their [essential] nature. Being a people inclined to live in the open air, they required the constant presentation of various forms of spectacles in their feasts during the year" (1953–1954, 2:122).

Garibay continued his discussion on what he calls "the catechistical theater," describing the pieces published by Paso y Troncoso and others of whose existence he knew. Commenting on an article by Fernando Horcasitas, "Bibliografía descriptiva de las piezas teatrales en lengua náhuatl" (Horcasitas 1948), he states that "it is the most complete attempt ever done on describing the known materials in this area of literary production. Therein thirty four pieces are included there" (1953–1954, 2:129). If in his chapter on "the catechistical theater" Garibay could not encompass all of what is known today about this dramatic genre in Nahuatl, it is at least true that he offered a well-informed comprehensive synthesis of it, as well as some excerpts of his own translations into Spanish of several of those plays.

Theater in Nahuatl, in a different key, is exemplified by the piece edited and translated into English by William H. Hunter, *The Calderonian Auto Sacramental El Gran Teatro del Mundo* (1960). This piece was originally adapted into Nahuatl by the priest Bartolomé de Alva Ixtlilxochitl, a brother of the well-known Tetzcocan chronicler don Fernando de Alva Ixtlilxochitl. In his publication Hunter discusses the historical background, paying attention to the development of various forms of theater in New Spain and in particular to the genre known as *auto sacramental*, to which this piece by Calderón belongs.

In his appreciation of the work done by Alva Ixtlilxochitl, Hunter states that Alva "demonstrates good judgment in refraining from any attempt to render into Nahuatl the sonorous intricacies of the Calderonian verse" (1960, 150). Hunter acknowledges the considerable help he received from Garibay and McAfee.

I have mentioned already the name of Marilyn Ekdahl Ravicz. Although not a scholar concerned directly with the Nahuatl language and culture, she produced a book entitled *Early Colonial Religious Drama in Mexico: From Tzompantli to Golgotha* (1970), with an ample preface in which she also deals with the pre-Hispanic background and the colonial context of religious drama. She offers English translations of the versions prepared by Paso y Troncoso of "The Sacrifice of Isaac," "The Adoration of the Kings," and "The Destruction of Jerusalem."

She includes three more pieces in her book. These are: "The Merchant," "How the Blessed Saint Helen Found the Holy Cross," and "Souls and Testamentary Executors." In doing this she took advantage of the translations into English done by McAfee, who, according to her, authorized their publication. In only one case, that of "Souls and Testamentary Executors," had McAfee prepared his translation in collaboration with Cornyn. The main merit of Ravicz's book is its calling attention once more to the existence of this colonial literary genre.

The authors we have considered published their works years before the more comprehensive contribution by Fernando Horcasitas. Several of them profited from Fernando's bibliographical essay on Nahuatl theater that appeared in 1948. Here I will just add that, after the publication of Horcasitas's *El teatro náhuatl* in 1974, others have continued research on various aspects of the same subject, although—with the exception of Louise M. Burkhart (1996)—no one has edited and translated another piece originally in Nahuatl. The names and works of those researchers are María Sten, *Vida y muerte del teatro nahuatl* (1974, 1982) and Othón Arróniz, *Teatro de evangelización en Nueva España* (1979). They both continued along the lines first proposed by José Rojas Garcidueñas as early as 1935 in his *Teatro de la Nueva España en el siglo XVI*, in which no in-depth research was done to approach directly the compositions in their Nahuatl originals.

Fernando Horcasitas's Distinguished Career as a Nahuatl Scholar

Born in Los Angeles, California, on September 26, 1924, and registered by his parents as a Mexican citizen, Fernando grew up in an environment influenced by two cultures. In the milieu of his family he became rooted in Mexican tradition. While attending grammar school and later Loyola High School, he was at the same time exposed to Anglo-American culture. So it was that his background was bicultural and bilingual. He could express himself, with equal proficiency and elegance, in both Spanish and English.

When his parents returned to Mexico in 1944, putting an end to their voluntary political exile, Fernando settled in the country's capital. He then enrolled in the Department of Philosophy and Letters of the National University. There he became deeply interested in studies of a humanistic nature, mainly history and linguistics. Two years later he joined the National School of Anthropology, concentrating on the fields of ethnology, archæology, and Nahuatl culture.

At those two institutions he met Robert H. Barlow; it was an encounter that profoundly influenced his professional career. In 1947, at Barlow's request, he began to serve as secretary for *Tlalocan,* a journal of source materials on the native cultures of Mexico. Many years later, in 1977, he wrote in the same magazine an article entitled "Para la historia de *Tlalocan,*" in which he described the origin of this journal, conceived, as he stated, by Barlow, "one of the most brilliant anthropologists attracted by the cultures of Ancient Mexico" (Horcasitas 1977, 15).

Under the guidance of professors as distinguished as Pablo Martínez del Río and Wigberto Jiménez Moreno, he obtained in 1953 his master's degree in anthropology summa cum laude. His dissertation, entitled "An Analysis of the Deluge Myth in Mesoamerica," was presented at the institution then known as Mexico City College, the predecessor of what is now the Universidad de las Américas. At the same college he began his teaching activities, which embraced a rather large number of subjects including the ethnohistory of Mesoamerica, the Nahuatl language, and a seminar on folklore narrative.

Among his first publications the one already mentioned on Nahuatl theater, published in the *Boletín Bibliográfico de Antropología Americana*, stands out, as it signaled the revival of active interest in this genre of Nahuatl literature and the beginning of Fernando's valuable contributions in the area. His activities as secretary of *Tlalocan* intensified following Barlow's death in 1951, and he took on the task of publishing the journal as one of his most cherished responsibilities until the end of his life.

In *Tlalocan* and in other journals such as *Mesoamerican Notes, Estudios de Cultura Náhuatl*, and *Anales de Antropología* he published a good number of articles, several of which dealt with oral tradition and theatrical pieces performed in some contemporary Nahuatl-speaking communities such as, for example, "Textos de Xaltepoxtla" (1962), "Los xoxocoteros, una farsa indígena" (1967), "El entremés del Señor de Yencuictlalpan, una farsa en náhuatl" (1972a), and "La danza de los tecuanes" (1980).

In 1963 Fernando Horcasitas became a full-time research professor at the National University. There he taught Nahuatl in the Department of Summer Courses. Becoming a member of the same university's Institute of Historical Research, of which I was director, he played a significant role in the creation there of a Department of Anthropology. The seventeen years he worked at the university, in particular those since the transformation of said department into the Institute of Anthropological Research in 1968, were particularly fruitful in his life. He prepared and published several other contributions while working there. Two had to do with oral narratives he had collected from a very distinguished native speaker of Nahuatl, doña Luz Jiménez (1897–1965), native of the town of Milpa Alta in the southern part of the Federal District of Mexico.

In one he presented the remembrances of doña Luz, expressed in Nahuatl, about the last years of the dictatorship of Porfirio Díaz and subsequent happenings during the Mexican Revolution of 1910–1920. Emiliano Zapata occupies an important place in her narrative. Horcasitas accompanied the Nahuatl text with a Spanish translation and an ample introduction. He asked me to write a prologue, which I did, stressing the significance of the publication. The book, *De Porfirio Díaz a Zapata. Memoria náhuatl de Milpa Alta* (Horcasitas 1968), aroused wide interest and was also published in an English version, translated by Horcasitas himself (Horcasitas 1972b).

Another contribution, also based on oral narratives by doña Luz Jiménez, was entitled *Los cuentos en náhuatl de doña Luz Jiménez* (Horcasitas and O. de Ford 1979). In it a good number of legends, tales, and other accounts were also presented in the original Nahuatl, accompanied by Fernando's translation into Spanish.

Horcasitas was very interested in the sixteenth-century work of the religious chroniclers and in several indigenous early colonial codices (books of paintings) with Nahuatl glosses. One manifestation of this interest was the preparation—in collaboration with Dr. Doris Heyden and with an extensive introductory study, copious notes, and an index—of an English version of what can be described as the ethnographic work of the Dominican friar Diego Durán, *Book of the Gods and Rites and the Ancient Calendar* (1971). His extensive introductory study is particularly valuable because of the information he gathered about the author and his work. Once again, Fernando asked me to prepare another prologue, which was for me an honor and a pleasure.

As for the codices, I will only mention two examples that had been previously unpublished: "Anales jeroglíficos e históricos de Tepeaca" (Horcasitos and Simons 1974), and "El Códice de Tzictepec, una nueva fuente pictórica indígena" (Horcasitas and de Magrelli 1975). The first is a pictorial chronicle with text in Nahuatl covering the years 1524–1645. It deals with natural phenomena held as omens, with epidemics, the arrival of viceroys, the building of churches, the execution of criminals, the construction of an aqueduct, and a plague of grasshoppers. The other document belongs to the group known as Techialoyan codices. It is interesting how in this codex there is emphasis on the bonds that the village of Tzictepec (near Toluca) had with Tlacopan in the period of the Triple Alliance and also during colonial times.

His Main Contribution

Busy as Fernando was with these and other publications, he continued his research on the subject he cherished so much: Nahuatl theater. In 1974 he succeeded in offering the first part of what he entitled *El teatro náhuatl: Épocas novohispana y moderna*.

As he put it in an introductory note to *Teatro náhuatl*:

The aim of the present work, of which the first part appears in this volume, is offering something little known to researchers of the language and culture of the Nahuas: a corpus of dramatic pieces in that language. We will take as a point of departure the catechistical productions of the first half of the 16th century, proceeding to those which continue to be represented in our towns. (Horcasitas 1974, 13)

In what is entitled "Preliminary Study" Horcasitas describes "the universe of the feast" and theatrical representations in several indigenous languages of the New World, particularly in Nahuatl. He points to what is known about pre-Hispanic representations, as one antecedent, and also discusses theatrical performances in Europe, mainly in Spain, during the Middle Ages and in the sixteenth century.

Concentrating on missionary theater he investigates its origins and purpose, giving also a chronology of its development. To facilitate an understanding of how such theater was staged he describes people's participation in it, the scenery and costuming, the music that accompanied it, and how the actors were chosen and taught.

Of much interest to the discussion in this volume is the attention he gives to the causes of the decline of this theater, as well as to the literary merit of the compositions, the reactions of the natives, and the results the friars obtained with these performances. The preliminary study, ample enough, is followed by an "Anthology of the Dramatic Pieces," in which he presents thirty-five of them, offering whenever available their Nahuatl text accompanied by a translation and a relevant commentary.

Fernando described in a "Note" at the beginning of his book what were the other dramatic compositions he intended to publish, in addition to those he labeled "ancient missionary theater," that is, the ones included as a first part in his published volume. The second part of Horcasitas's work should embrace pieces of moral content, dealing with themes not taken from Holy Scripture. A third part would be composed of the "Marian Theater," those about the Virgin Mary. Part 4 was to be dedicated to "Courtly Theater," also in Nahuatl, which would include adaptations from the Spanish classical theater. Pieces related to the conquest of Mexico and to the battles between Moors and Christians, and others in which the apostle Saint James played a key role, were to make up the fifth part. A last part was to be concerned with what he described as "Village Theater," a miscellaneous corpus of popular compositions, several of them still performed in modern times.

Of this vast project Fernando succeeded in publishing only the first part, dedicated entirely to missionary theater in Nahuatl. The materials he had assembled to be incorporated into the other five parts, in accordance with his plan, are preserved today at the Latin American Library of Tulane University in New Orleans, depository of his personal archives.

In the present book, three of the pieces published and studied by Horcasitas are rendered into English: "The Sacrifice of Isaac," "The Three Kings," and "Final Judgment." As to the other four pieces included here, Fernando knew about those published in *Tlalocan*, that is, "Yn Animastin Yhuan Alvaceasme" (Souls and Testamentary Executors) and "Yn Pochtecatl" (The Merchant). He was aware also of the Nahuatl texts that Paso y Troncoso had published and of others entitled "La Pasión del Domingo de Ramos," which is preserved at the Middle American Research Institute of Tulane University, and "La conversión de San Pablo," which was in a manuscript belonging to the bibliographer and historian Federico Gómez de Orozco. In addition, he listed and described, with the support of reliable sources, others pieces reaching—as noted—a total of thirty-five compositions.

Fernando Horcasitas Pimentel has left us a rich legacy of works related to the culture and language of the Nahua people. He guided and helped a good number of students and colleagues, and even when he had to interrupt his teaching activities due to illness, he kept his spirits up until his last days. Proof of this is provided by a report he wrote a few months before his final departure on the precise date of his fifty-sixth birthday, September 26, 1980. In this report he stated that he had reached the final stage of what would be the second volume of his *Teatro náhuatl*. He wrote also that "in view of the very poor situation regarding the publication of Mexican folklore texts and of serious studies on them, I plan to dedicate time to the publication of a collection of them" (Horcasitas in León-Portilla 1982, 36).

I just will add that it has been an honor and a pleasure for me to join here Louise M. Burkhart and Barry D. Sell in dedicating this book to Fernando's memory. He opened many new doors into the treasure trove of literary productions in Nahuatl, conceived indeed as a part of universal literature, produced by men and women of all times and in all places.

PREFACE

Louise M. Burkhart and Barry D. Sell

In the entire western hemisphere the only extant colonial plays in any Native American language are those in Nahuatl, the principal indigenous language of Central Mexico. In the decades following the Spanish conquest, Roman Catholic friars taught Nahua students to write their own language using the roman alphabet. As the Nahuas already had pictographic writing and tremendous respect for the written word, they enthusiastically adopted the new technique. European genres of discourse and text were transposed into hybrid Nahua-Christian forms.

As early as the 1530s, friars began to use theatrical performances as a tool of evangelization. Theater, like other performative modes of Christian devotion, appealed to the Nahuas, whose traditional religious activities focused more on collective rituals than on preaching or private devotions. A native theater developed, based on Spanish models but with native actors and sponsors. Scripts were authored by friars, in collaboration with literate Nahuas, and also by Nahuas themselves—with and without priestly oversight—and were sometimes based on Spanish scripts and sometimes invented for the local context.

The purpose of this and the other three volumes in the *Nahuatl Theater* set is to bring together and disseminate scripts and scholarship on this first truly American theater. By publishing a series devoted to Nahuatl theater we aim to establish the place of these dramas in the literary canon of the Americas, approaching them not just as an evangelization technique (as they have often been treated) but also as subaltern literature, as symbolic capital, as transcripts of intercultural dialogue, as primary linguistic data, and as artistic products.

We build especially on the work of the late Mexican anthropologist Fernando Horcasitas, whose *El teatro náhuatl* of 1974 is still the classic book on the subject. To this groundwork we bring a quarter-century of advances in the study of Nahuatl grammar and translation; current understandings of the colonial history of Mexico, and of colonial historical processes more generally; grounding in contemporary cultural and literary theory; and familiarity with the broader context of Nahuatl written expression, both civil and ecclesiastical.

The field of colonial Nahua studies has seen tremendous advances since the mid-1970s, with the publication of excellent modern grammars of the language such as J. Richard Andrews's in 1975, and Michel Launey's in 1979; the 1982 completion of Arthur J. O. Anderson and Charles E. Dibble's translation of the *Florentine Codex*, a Nahuatl-language encyclopedia of traditional Nahua culture produced under the direction of the sixteenth-century Franciscan fray Bernardino de Sahagún; and studies of Nahuatl civil and historical documents by James Lockhart, Sarah Cline, Susan Kellogg, Susan Schroeder, and others. This growing body of work has begun to approach (in sophistication if not in size) that done on early Euro-Americans.

Colonial religious literature in Nahuatl has not received equivalent attention, but significant contributions include Louise Burkhart's works (1989, 1996, 2001), Barry Sell's 1993 dissertation, Arthur J. O. Anderson's translations of some of Sahagún's doctrinal writings (Sahagún 1993a, 1993b), and Sell and John Frederick Schwaller's critical edition of a seventeenth-century confession manual (Alva 1999). Burkhart's *Holy Wednesday: A Nahua Drama from Early Colonial Mexico* (1996) examined in great detail one native-authored Nahuatl drama and its Spanish source. Similar work has not yet been published on other Nahuatl dramas; secondary studies continue to rely on limited sources and outdated translations.

Our volumes will bring the remaining corpus of Nahuatl dramas up to current standards of research. While the anthology format does not permit us to devote as extensive and consistent a descriptive attention to the texts as Burkhart did in *Holy Wednesday*, we engage the material at a similar level of intensity. We have made this a collaborative project involving scholars from different academic disciplines, in order to encourage a broader range of insights. Our work also complements and, we hope, will contribute to ongoing research by scholars in Mexico, such as the group working with Professor María Sten at the Universidad Nacional Autónoma de México, who recently produced a volume on Franciscan-Nahua theater (Sten et al. 2000).

The four volumes of *Nahuatl Theater* will include transcriptions and translations of all surviving colonial Nahuatl plays, some related Nahuatl texts, and scholarly essays by the volume editors and by outside scholars. We will use colonial-era scripts as much as possible. We will also avail ourselves of the copious material translated and composed by Faustino Chimalpopoca Galicia, a nineteenth-century Nahua scholar who was a speaker of the language.

Our transcriptions of the Nahuatl texts are meant to be useful to students and scholars of Nahuatl who need access to the dramas in their original language for their own translation studies and exercises. Our transcriptions will also support studies of language usage and variation across time and, to some degree, space. For example, linguists may use this extended corpus of documents to investigate Spanish influence on Nahuatl (use of loanwords, appearance of calques and syntactic changes), aspects of style (for example, the use of the reverential system, parallel constructions, traditional metaphors), and dialectical variation.

Our readable English translations are intended to allow both specialists and nonspecialists to understand the content of the plays and, thus, the wide range of dramatic themes and plots surviving from the Nahua past. How was life represented on the Nahuatl stage? How did playwrights working in Nahuatl go about their work? How were European texts and ideas adapted to the Mexican context? What multiple messages were conveyed by the plays? What staging techniques were used? Students of colonial social history and historical ethnography, of evangelization and religious history, of theater history, and Spanish American and Native American literature will find these translations a useful resource for investigating a variety of issues. Texts such as these should find an expanding audience among nonspecialists as contemporary Mexicans and Mexican Americans, including people of Nahua ancestry, increasingly seek to understand and recover their ethnic history.

These dramas speak to issues of multiculturalism not just because they come from another culture but because they are by nature multicultural, products of the hybrid zone between Spanish and Nahua cultural worlds. Theater too is by nature ambivalent, engaging two simultaneous realities: the imagined reality of the drama and the everyday world beyond the stage. Colonial dramas are particularly fascinating in that they display, in the microcosm of the theatrical event, the author's and actors' collective representation of what the colonial order is or should be, thus commenting on the "real" world. But this representation, presented in Nahuatl but stemming from European discourses, is never univocal but always conflicted and subject to different interpretations, native and other subaltern readings differing from those of the dominant Spaniards.

The project is organized into four volumes, of which you hold the first in your hands. A summary description of the individual volumes in the series follows.

Volume 1, *Death and Life in Colonial Nahua Mexico*, coedited by Barry D. Sell and Louise M. Burkhart, contains seven Nahuatl dramas dating roughly from the first half of the seventeenth century. Six of these plays have been previously published in now-outdated editions; one is presented here for the first time. Five are morality plays emphasizing death, judgment, moral reform, and punishment for moral failures; two are *autos* derived from biblical narratives (the story of Abraham and Isaac and the story of the three wise men). In the accompanying essays, Burkhart examines the plays' prominent themes of death and the care of the dead in the context of other Nahuatl writings on these topics; Sell examines the colonial social context of the plays and, through a close examination of the manuscripts, establishes their likely dates; Daniel Mosquera contributes a more theoretical piece on the plays' theological and catechistic aspects; and Viviana Díaz Balsera compares the dramatic treatment of the Abraham-Isaac story to its use as a moral *exemplum* in Nahuatl sermons. A foreword by Miguel León-Portilla, the senior Mexican scholar of Nahuatl literature, reviews the contributions of Fernando Horcasitas and other early scholars to the study of Nahuatl theater. A detailed discussion of the manuscripts—their present location, size, provenience, and peculiarities—can be found in the first half of Sell's essay.

In volume 2, entitled *The Virgin of Guadalupe*, we turn to the history of the Mexican devotion to Our Lady of Guadalupe, the country's principal religious focus. This devotion is the subject of much attention and controversy, witness the recent debates over the canonization of Juan Diego, the legendary Nahua hero of the apparition story, and the long historical debate over the authenticity of the apparition tradition. While the earliest (1649) Nahuatl version of the apparition legend has been published in a recent critical edition (Sousa et al. 1998), the later development of the Guadalupan tradition in Nahuatl remains little known, despite the central place this devotion came to occupy in native as well as nonnative Mexican religious life. Stafford Poole, C. M., one of the leading experts in the world on the history of the apparition, will be coeditor with Burkhart and Sell. Here we are concerned not with the historicity of the apparition legend but with its historical and literary development and dissemination.

Two colonial dramatizations of the apparition story are known. Nineteenth-century copies of both, made by the Nahua scholar Faustino Chimalpopoca Galicia, are in the New York Public Library. The first play, with three acts, is called *Coloquios de la aparición de la Virgen Santa María de Guadalupe* ("Colloquies of the Apparition of the Virgin Saint Mary of Guadalupe"); both Fernando Horcasitas and the Mexican scholar Ángel María Garibay Kintana attributed it to the early eighteenth century. A second and earlier copy of this play, made by or for the Mexican priest and scholar José Pichardo (1748–1812) in the late eighteenth century, is in the National Library of France. The other play, comprising one act in verse, is titled *El portento mexicano, comedia famosa, y la primera en verso Mexicano* ("The Mexican Portent, Famous Drama, and the First in Mexican Verse"); Fernando Horcasitas tentatively dated it to about 1690.

As companion material for the two dramas, in order to provide context on the Guadalupan devotion of the late seventeenth and early eighteenth centuries, we will include transcriptions and translations of some other previously unpublished Nahuatl Guadalupan materials, such as prayers and praise songs.

Volume 3, *Spanish Golden Age Drama in Mexican Translation,* on which the noted Hispanist Elizabeth R. Wright joins Burkhart and Sell as coeditor, will be truly bicultural, focusing on three Golden Age Spanish plays and a comic intermezzo (over seventy folios total length) that were adapted into Nahuatl by don Bartolomé de Alva Ixtlilxochitl around 1640. Alva's work survives in the Bancroft Library of the University of California at Berkeley. Alva was Spanish on his father's side but on his mother's side was descended from one of the Aztec Empire's royal dynasties. He was a native speaker of Nahuatl and one of very few men of either native or mixed blood to be ordained into the Roman Catholic priesthood. Thus, he was perfectly positioned to be a cultural broker between native and Spanish worlds.

The Spanish plays are *El Gran Teatro del Mundo* ("The Great Theater of the World") by Pedro Calderón de la Barca, the great master of eucharistic drama; *La Madre de la Mejor* ("The Mother of the Best"), about the conception and birth of the Virgin Mary, by Félix Lope de Vega Carpio, the most famous of all Spanish playwrights; and *El Animal Propheta y Dichosa Patricida Don Julián* ("The Prophet Animal and the Blissful Patricide, Don Julian"). A chapbook version of the latter play circulated under Lope de Vega's name, and Alva attributes it to him, but it was written by Antonio Mira de Amescua, a reasonably well-known playwright who was strongly influenced by Lope; this issue of authorship is itself of interest in studies of Golden Age drama.

An English translation of Alva's Calderón adaptation was published by William A. Hunter in 1960, before all the more recent advances in Nahuatl scholarship. The other two have never been published. This only known case in which classic works of the Spanish theater were rendered into Nahuatl provides a unique opportunity to see how metropolitan "hits," so to speak, played in the colonial provinces. The

Spanish plays, with English translations, will be presented along with Alva's work. This will allow the kind of controlled comparison between Spanish model and Nahuatl adaptation that Burkhart was able to carry out in *Holy Wednesday*, with an extra advantage in that we know the precise identity of the Mexican author.

In addition to their significance as local adaptations of Spanish masterworks, Alva's dramas are important for Nahuatl linguistic studies. Alva devoted his work to Father Horacio Carochi, the Jesuit linguist who produced the most important colonial grammar of Nahuatl (1645) and who developed a system for using diacritical marks to indicate long vowels and glottal stops, essential features of the language usually ignored by earlier grammarians. Intermittently, but nevertheless to a useful extent, Alva or someone familiar with Carochi's diacritics applied these marks to his translations. Our work will reproduce these revealing diacritics and analyze how they were used. In directing his theatrical translations to the Jesuits, Alva intended them for linguistic study and training rather than for performance since Jesuits ordained in Mexico were required to study Nahuatl. Thus while it is possible that Alva's work was performed, we do not assume this was the case and will treat the plays as having primarily been texts for private study.

Volume 4, *Nahua Christianity in Performance*, is still in the planning stages. We intend to include all other extant colonial and nineteenth-century Nahuatl plays, including a Passion play recently discovered in Mexico, works copied or composed by Faustino Chimalpopoca Galicia in addition to the Guadalupan dramas, and two pieces held by the John Carter Brown Library.

Our principal goal is to present the dramas with meticulously accurate transcriptions, up-to-date and readable translations, and supporting documentation on dating, authorship, and context. Our secondary goal is to offer interpretations of the historical, literary, religious, and linguistic significance of the materials through the supplementary essays.

The process by which a set of volumes such as this is produced and the general guidelines that are followed may be of some use to those interested in undertaking similar projects or in extending the work we have begun here. Briefly stated, they can be organized into five categories: identification of sources, establishment of authoritative texts, transcription, translation, and interpretation.

Locating and identifying sources is fundamental to our work. Much of the extant corpus of colonial Nahuatl dramas is fairly well established but surprises occur: the "Holy Wednesday" drama was discovered in 1986 and a Passion drama was recently discovered in Mexico. The original manuscript of three plays in our volume 1, lost according to some scholars, resides contentedly in the Clements Library of the University of Michigan; some other "lost" texts may also reappear. The text currently held by the Academy of American Franciscan History, "The Life of Don Sebastián," was unknown until very recently.

Establishing an authoritative text is often trouble free. In most cases, only one copy of a Nahuatl drama survives. However, one exception is a drama in our volume 1, for which a second copy follows the first in the Library of Congress manuscript. We transcribed both but translated only the first, noting all meaningful discrepancies in wording between that version and the second copy. Another exception is the

"Colloquies of the Apparition" Guadalupan drama, for which two versions survive. Using both versions in tandem, we will produce as authoritative a reconstruction of the original as possible, documenting the discrepancies between the two extant versions.

The issue is much more complex for the Spanish dramas in volume 3, as these circulated in various manuscript and chapbook versions before or alongside more "authoritative" editions. For our work to be a valid contribution to studies of Golden Age drama, we must give serious attention to identifying the correct texts. We are in the process of determining (from date and content) which of the extant versions of the Spanish plays were the likeliest candidates to have been used by Alva as the basis for his Nahuatl adaptations. These, rather than any now-standard editions, are the relevant sources for the *Nahuatl Theater* set. This task requires extensive archival research in multiple repositories: the National Library in Madrid, the Archive of the Indies in Seville, the Spanish theater archive in Almagro, the British Library, and the University of Pennsylvania Library.

Meticulous transcriptions form the foundations of accurate translations and interpretations. Working from originals or microfilms, we digitally transcribe the dramas. Transforming handwritten Nahuatl into digital format is always somewhat problematic, as scribes used various abbreviations, diacritics, and punctuation marks that cannot always be reproduced exactly. Some standardization of diacritics is inevitable, but we include all such features and mirror them as closely as possible. The orthography of the original is reproduced exactly. Following established practice, we do insert spaces between words and eliminate spaces within words (Nahua scribes tended to write in phonological units rather than words; line endings frequently bisect words). When one person has completed a transcription, another checks it thoroughly, marking corrections. A third—and in some cases, a fourth—complete check is also made. Some microfilms are clear enough that all features are easily visible. When this is not the case, transcriptions made from films are also checked against the original manuscripts.

The most accessible part of the primary sources are the English translations, and they have been prepared with the utmost care. The colonial Nahuatl (urban, written) of these sources differs substantially from contemporary spoken Nahuatl. Our collective translation experience from our work with other colonial texts and our familiarity with European religious texts provides the best preparation for translating these plays. Our procedure was that one person completed a draft translation. A second person went over it thoroughly and offered corrections and suggestions. The first person incorporated these, the second reviewed the text again, and a third person may also have reviewed the work. Passages that can be translated only tentatively have notes stating as much; alternative readings for ambiguous passages are also noted. The translations of the Spanish dramas into English will be a collaborative effort by Elizabeth Wright and Daniel Mosquera, with review by Burkhart and Sell.

No text, especially for those unable to directly read the original, speaks for itself. A critical part of presenting Nahuatl theater to a broad scholarly audience is to provide interpretative essays. These essays are not meant to exhaust all avenues of investigation but to elucidate the scripts from a variety of disciplinary perspectives and, we hope, to inspire further studies of them. Of particular interest are issues of translation; the negotiation of power and authority between Nahuas and the colonial church; colonial Nahua religious understandings and practices; issues of authorship, literacy, and text production; and Nahuatl linguistics.

None of the above would be possible without the difficult and groundbreaking work done by our predecessors, first the Nahuas and the priests who wrote the plays and later those who copied, rearranged, and commented upon them. Priest-grammarians of the later colonial period would look back—with much justification—at the first half of the colony as a golden age of Nahuatl written expression. No subsequent period could hope to equal the time when the most original, germinal, and innovative texts (including the plays) were created, but the present could be considered another kind of golden age, one in which a great deal of previous lore and knowledge has been reclaimed for future generations, native and non-native alike. If the period up to circa 1650 was the "Golden Age of Production" of Nahuatl texts, the time from circa 1970 to the present could be considered the "Golden Age of Recovery" of that rich and varied corpus. That such is possible for Nahuatl plays is due above all to Fernando Horcasitas, whose *El teatro náhuatl* (1974) was so many years ahead of its time.

ACKNOWLEDGMENTS

This volume and the entire *Nahuatl Theater* set were prompted by the generosity of Gregory Spira. While working in the Hispanic Manuscripts Division of the Library of Congress he spontaneously offered to provide Barry D. Sell access to the Nahuatl texts held there. He then provided photocopies to Sell of three of the plays presented in this volume. Spira also checked the initial transcriptions against their originals. No less helpful was making his apartment available so that Sell was able to visit the Library of Congress and see the texts for himself. Such an auspicious start encouraged Sell to seek out other early Nahuatl dramas and to think of a more comprehensive effort. With that idea in mind and the first few transcriptions in hand, he approached Louise M. Burkhart with a request and a challenge: would she like to dramatically extend the work she began in her standard-setting *Holy Wednesday: A Nahua Drama from Early Colonial Mexico* (1996) by becoming the coeditor of a large Nahuatl Theater project? She quickly accepted. This took matters from wishful thinking to practical reality. And it all began with an unexpected act of generosity.

The institutions holding the manuscripts that are transcribed and translated here are greatly appreciated for preserving and making available these unique texts. The Library of Congress greatly facilitated the examination of their three plays. The Academy of American Franciscan History graciously shared a previously unknown early Nahuatl drama in their collection and granted permission to reproduce it. The William L. Clements Library, University of Michigan, which holds three of the most widely known early pieces, provided an exceptionally clear microfilm and allowed us to publish the texts.

We would also like to thank James Lockhart for his thorough review of a draft of our translations, as well as John Frederick Schwaller and an anonymous reviewer for the University of Oklahoma Press for their helpful comments. Our acquisitions editor at the University of Oklahoma Press, Jo Ann Reece, saw this project through a lengthy review process with unflagging persistence and enthusiasm. We also thank our in-house editor, Marian J. Stewart, and our copyeditor, Pippa Letsky, for working efficiently and enthusiastically with a cumbersome, multi-authored bilingual manuscript.

Subvention funds for this volume were generously provided by the University of Oklahoma Foundation, the Department of Anthropology at the University at Albany, State University of New York, and the New York State/United University Professions Professional Development Committee.

Last, we make special mention here of the contributors to this volume: Miguel León-Portilla, Viviana Díaz Balsera, and Daniel Mosquera. They participated when this volume was just a hope. Their efforts and their confidence in our project are greatly appreciated.

PART I

Essays

NAHUATL PLAYS IN CONTEXT

Barry D. Sell

The readers of this first volume of the Nahuatl Theater set hold in their hands some unusual texts. In the entire western hemisphere, the only extant colonial plays in any Native American language are those in Nahuatl ("Aztec"), the language spoken by the Nahuas ("Aztecs") of Mexico. Their rarity is hardly unexpected.

Colonial Mexico was the one area in all the Americas where a large number of alphabetical texts in native languages were produced. This was due both to native precedent and to European encouragement. Unlike other First Peoples of the Americas, many Mesoamericans already had a tradition of recording information by making symbols on paper.[1] The prestige attached to traditional writing eased the transition from local to intrusive modes of record-keeping. The Spanish variant of Europeans had their own reasons for encouraging a familiar literacy. Businesspeople and administrators alike benefited from the assistance, collaboration, and guidance provided by literate Christianized natives.

Native youngsters learned to write their languages with the characters of the Spanish alphabet. As the critical target group of Spanish colonization, the Nahuas were the first to adopt the new writing tradition; by the 1530s the first extant documents in alphabetical Nahuatl appeared.[2] Mayas, Mixtecs, Zapotecs, Tarascans, and others would follow suit decades later. However, the Nahuas' early head start, greater numbers, and wider geographical spread gave them an overwhelming advantage even among Mesoamericans who were culturally predisposed to the new mode of writing. Thus it is no surprise that most alphabetical native-language texts from 1500 to 1800, not only in Mesoamerica but throughout the Americas, are in Nahuatl.

The sheer bulk of the extant Nahuatl corpus is impressive but largely unknown to the general public. Ten thousand printed pages, most church-related, are dwarfed by ecclesiastical manuscripts; one in a Mexico City archive has 888 pages all by itself. Larger yet is civil documentation, which in spite of its present mass is but a fraction of its original size due to the unsparing vicissitudes of changing times and circumstances. Like its counterparts in other Mesoamerican tongues, the Nahuatl corpus includes sermonaries, confessional manuals, books of Christian doctrine, testaments, land titles, civil and criminal proceedings, bills of sale, and so on. Size does make a difference, though, for it allowed for more variety, and among the items particular to the Nahuatl corpus are plays.

There is an inherent difficulty in presenting these dramas to a broad audience. Except for the obstacles posed by deciphering the idiosyncratic scrawl of hurried notaries, colonial texts in Spanish can be directly consulted with relative ease by those who know modern Spanish. Not so with Nahuatl. The gap between colonial and current Nahuatl is significantly wider because Spanish influence on it has been profound. Hence critical or skeptical readers—including the vast majority of modern speakers of Nahuatl—will in most cases be unable to verify for themselves the validity of a transcription, the accuracy of a translation, and the soundness of the subsequent interpretation and analysis. Helping to bridge that gap at the beginning of the twenty-first century is the function of the essays in this and succeeding volumes of the Nahuatl Theater set.

The Manuscripts

A brief review of the texts should help orient the reader. They are described in the order in which they appear in this volume. The Clements Library of the University of Michigan holds three texts bound together: "The Three Kings" (1r–23r), "The Sacrifice of Isaac" (23v–36r), and "Souls and Testamentary Executors" (36v–52r). A set of four bound pieces is held by the Library of Congress (LC): "Final Judgment" (1r–10v), two versions of "How to Live on Earth" (11r–28v [the basis of the English translation included here], 29r–43v), and "The Merchant" (44r–53v).[3] The Academy of American Franciscan History owns a previously unknown play: "The Life of Don Sebastián" (29 pages).

Long-established conventions for titling in Spanish and English have been followed in four of the seven cases. "The Life of Don Sebastián" is presented here for the first time. One of the two translators of this piece, Louise M. Burkhart, chose the title from the opening words of the main text, "Moral example which speaks about the life of Don Sebastián" (p. 5). "How to Live on Earth" was originally presented by John H. Cornyn and Byron McAfee in *Tlalocan* 1.4 (1944) as "Tlacahuapahualiztli (Bringing Up Children)." Burkhart decided that the present title, derived from an early speech in the play, would be more appropriate. "The Three Kings" was presented in transcription and translation first by Francisco del Paso y Troncoso in his *Biblioteca Náuatl* II (1900b) and later by Fernando Horcasitas in his *El teatro náhuatl* (1974, 256–79). Both of these noted Mexican scholars referred to it as "La adoración de los reyes." In the absence of anything resembling a title at the beginning of the drama, both editors think the present designation is more in accord with the opening lines.

Fundamental to analyzing these dramas is the task of establishing their authorship, dates of composition or copying, and provenience. There are several scattered clues to these pressing concerns. Prefatory remarks in "The Merchant" indicate that what follows is an

Edifying example that speaks about a merchant. I am writing it today; it is my property. My name is Don Joseph Gaspar and I am a resident here in San Juan Bautista Tollantzinco. I am setting down the day and year: today is Saturday, 15 November, of the year 1687. (36r)

There are later references to the *altepetl*[4] of Xochimilco and Tepeyacac, and to purchasing land "three years ago in the year 1627" (48r–v).

Also helpful is the following from the end of "The Sacrifice of Isaac":

Finis. Laus Deo. This moral example was prepared in the year 1678. It was copied today, Friday, the first of February of the year 1760. And as to whether in truth I worked on this moral example, [I affix my signature]: Bernabé Vázquez. (36r)

Some useful information can be found as well in "The Life of Don Sebastián." The first words read "Praise Play in Nahuatl" and "From Huaxtepec" (1). Near the end are the following remarks: "Finis. Laus Deo. Amen. This moral example was finished today, the first of April of the year one thousand, six hundred, ninety and two" (27).

There is no overt indication of whether the plays are Nahua translations of Spanish or Latin pieces or simply ad hoc creations composed by some combination of clerics and literate Nahuas. The two named individuals are little known. If Bernabé Vázquez was indeed the copyist of "The Sacrifice of Isaac," then he can be assigned the same role regarding "Souls and Testamentary Executors" since both are bound together and are in the same hand. He was most probably a Nahua notary, given his practiced hand and facility in the language, although his names were not the Spanish appellations most common among Nahuas. His status could not have been very high because he lacked the (by then) increasingly common "don."

Sporting the title when it had a more lofty connotation was don Joseph Gaspar of San Juan Bautista Tollantzinco who claimed to have written, or finished writing, "The Merchant" on Saturday, November 15, 1687. The references cited above to "three years ago in the year 1627" and to Xochimilco and Tepeyacac (most likely the *altepetl* of the same names that neighbored Mexico City to the south) put the play in a time and place I consider more propitious for its creation, that is, in the capital when Franciscan scholarship was at the height of its influence during the sixteenth and early seventeenth centuries. It should be added that Franciscans ministered to Tollantzinco (Spanish *Tulancingo*) and Xochimilco. Don Joseph was almost certainly not the writer nor even the copyist; colonial conventions called for the author of record, patron, or supervising editor to take full credit for producing a text.

Additional considerations point to a less direct role by don Joseph. In two notarial documents from Tollantzinco dated October 7, 1687, and Wednesday, November 3, 1687, don Joseph Gaspar appears as a witness, his formal authority deriving from his position as an *alcalde* or member of the Hispanic-style town council.[5] As with so many other Tollantzinco records, the notary of the *cabildo* (Spanish-style town council), don Joseph de la Cruz, wrote the entire text and apparently signed for everyone. Don Joseph Gaspar did not sign his own name, nor did he add his own distinctive rubric. The notary simply added the very same undistinguished rubric to don Joseph's and several other names. This does not prove that don Joseph was unable to write, but it does not speak well for the possibility.

The dates support my working assumption that all the plays have been through a process similar to that which produced two copies of "How to Live on Earth," each in a different hand and with a similar, though not identical, content.[6] "The Merchant" was created or copied in 1630 and then (re)copied on Saturday, November 15, 1687.[7] "The Sacrifice of Isaac" is explicitly said to have been copied on Friday, February 1, 1760, from a 1678 version that itself may have been derived from an even earlier text. The same dates may also apply to one of its two companion dramas ("Souls and Testamentary Executors") since it is in the same hand and literary style. The seventeenth century surfaces also in "The Life of Don Sebastián," which was finished on April 1, 1692.

Miscellaneous clues from "The Life of Don Sebastián" strengthen the church connection but leave the place of composition or copying still undetermined. The proclamation at the beginning, that what follows is a "Praise Play in Nahuatl," strikes me as a typically clerical formulation. Nahuas had infrequent occasion to speak of their cultural or ethnic entirety in terms of "Nahuas" (for the people) and "Nahuatl" (for the language) in texts written by and for themselves. Clerics had rather more, so these terms are usually found in ecclesiastical Nahuatl texts (see Sell 1993, 129–36). Unfortunately for our purposes, the names of early Mexican *altepetl* sometimes repeat, so it is unclear just which "Huaxtepec" is referred to on the first page of "The Life of Don Sebastián."[8]

Hence, little is securely known about such basics as dates of composition or copying. Previous scholarship on Nahuatl theater has at times erroneously indicated more secure dating of texts than is actually possible, and inherited errors continue to plague the study of these dramas. A pointed example is provided by something as simple as the dating of "Final Judgment." Fernando Horcasitas asserts (1974, 564) that in contrast with many other works described in his collection, "de *El juicio final* sí poseemos un manuscrito antiguo . . . fechado 1678 (aunque seguramente ésta es la fecha de la copia solamente)" (concerning *Final Judgment* we do indeed possess an ancient manuscript . . . dated 1678 [although surely this is only the date of the copy]). Until recently I myself thought the same (Sell 1988, 4).[9] Put simply: "Final Judgment" is undated, and there is no overt sign of any kind that it was newly composed or translated, an original or a copy.[10]

Proceeding, then, with caution, I turn to a consideration of some revealing aspects of the plays. These include the writing habits of the scribes, the types of loanwords present, the nature of the Nahuatl sociopolitical terminology used, and the pervasive if somewhat uneven presence of traditional Nahuatl formal speech.

It often seems that nothing that originated in the Spanish-speaking world remained completely unchanged once the Nahuas made it their own. The art of writing Nahuatl with the Roman characters of the Spanish alphabet is no exception. Yet even specialists in Nahuatl studies can little appreciate much of the strongly Nahua cast of the plays under consideration. James Lockhart regards Fernando Horcasitas's *El teatro náhuatl* as

> a vast contribution to Nahuatl philology . . . [that] brings together a substantial portion of the existing theatrical corpus in transcription and Spanish translation,

some of it published in the late 19th and early 20th centuries by Paso y Troncoso, and some of it published for the first time. As Horcasitas realized, TN is far from definitive. The transcriptions mainly modernize the orthography, with consequent loss of distinctions, although some idiosyncrasies of the originals are retained; division into words is often highly inconsistent, punctuation is arbitrary, and typographical errors and misreadings are rife. Horcasitas' texts are sufficient for many purposes, and for the most part I have used them without further recourse to the originals (which are themselves nearly all posterior copies, some of them unreliable modern transcriptions). The translations improve on their predecessors and give a generally adequate notion of the content, but errors abound, and much improvement is needed. In due course an updated, more complete, and much more critical edition of the corpus will be required. (1992, 595–96 no. 97)

The present critical edition attempts to build on the strengths of Horcasitas's work and rectify its weaknesses. The editors had access to the colonial originals of the seven texts in this book and used them as the basis of our final transcriptions.[11] We strenuously attempted to reproduce as far as possible all the original spelling, punctuation, and capitalization[12] although spacing follows current practices.[13] Consequently there are thousands of differences between the present transcriptions and those published earlier. Yet in fairness to Horcasitas and others, the reader should understand that these latest productions are no more sacrosanct than their predecessors. There are inevitable divergences between any handwritten manuscript and its modern typographic variant, in part due to the preferences and training of the transcribers. Future presentations of the same materials may include complete photoreproductions of the originals (not possible here), or utilize information technologies currently unavailable. Nonetheless the present transcriptions are enough of an advance over former renderings and are sufficiently suggestive of the originals that they supersede all previous versions. If nothing else, this latest round of transcriptions may encourage more direct personal examination of the texts. The editors would welcome that increased interest and scrutiny.

A direct comparison of transcriptions will help to demonstrate the contrast between the present renditions and earlier ones. Some of the spacing between lines has been adjusted to allow for easier reading of both selections. Horcasitas's version of "Juicio Final" begins :

JESÚS
Nexcuitilmachiotl motenehua Jucio Final
I
Tlapitzaloz. Motlapoz ilhuicac. Hualmotemohuiz San Miguel.

San Miguel: Dios itlachihualtzitzihuané, ma xicmatican inhuan ca tel ye anquimati, ca ipan ca in iteotenehuatiltzin in totecuyo Dios, ca quimotlamilliz, quimopolhuiz, in oquimochihuilitzino in itlazomahuiztatzin Dios in cenmanahuactli. Ca quimopolhuiz, quimotlamilliz, in ixquich in oquimochihuilitzino, in nepapan totome, i nepapan yoyolime, ihuan in amehuantin. ¡Ca namechmopolhuiz, in ancemanahuactlaca! (Horcasitas 1974, 568)

Our rendering of the same text from f. 1r of the LC manuscript:

+

Nexcuitilmachiotl. motenehua Juiçio final—
tlapitzalos motlapoz yIh.^{c} hualmotemohuiz S.^{n} mig.^{l} =

S.^{n} miguel = v Dios ytlachihualtzitzinhuane. ma xicmatican. yhuan Ca tel ye anquimati. Ca ypan Ca yn iteotenahuatiltzin ȳ tt.^{o} D.^{s} Ca quimotlamilliz quimopolhuis yn oquimochihuilitzino. yn itlaçomahuiztatzin Dios. ȳ Senmanahuactli. Ca quimopolhuis. quimotlamilliz. yn ixquich yn oquimochihuilitzino. ȳ nepapan totome. y nepapā yoyolime. yhuan yn amehuantin. Ca hamechmopolhuis. yn ansemanahuac tlaca.

There are many noticeable differences in just these two small samples. More relevant to our purposes than the substitution of *JESÚS* for a cross is that Horcasitas added accent marks where there were none, drastically changed formatting, transformed notarial markings into a colon, resolved standard abbreviations, imposed current notions of capitalization and punctuation to create sentences, regularized most spelling according to his own lights, and added textual divisions (scenes) that did not exist in the original. Elsewhere he forces blocks of text into paragraph form. His changes conformed to the scholarly standards of his time and place, yet it is precisely the deviations from European-style norms that are of interest here. His "corrections" go a very long way toward eliminating precisely those features typical of Nahuatl documents.

Consider simply one aspect of the changes in punctuation. When left to their own devices Nahuas applied alphabetical writing to the elements discernible in speech—that is, letter/sound segments, syllables, and the phonological phrase—rather than to the European-style units of word, sentence, and paragraph with their relatively standardized spellings, punctuation, and spacing. Lockhart has accurately noted that the phonological phrase "consisting of a nuclear nominal or verbal stem with its affixes and its adverbial or other modifiers, is a far more obvious, detectable entity in Nahuatl than either the 'word' or the complete utterance (sentence)" (1992, 338–39). He later adds that, while the use of spaces to indicate phonological phrases is debatable, it is undeniable that in some instances Nahua writers used "a period (a dot at least) between phrases" and that this clearly shows their tendency "to think in terms of a phrase type quite foreign to European languages" (1992, 339). I concur. This clue to the identity of the writer is obscured in Horcasitas's version, and obvious in the present one.[14]

Certain features of the seven plays (eight texts) are now more readily apparent. Overall, there is intrusive *n* as well as the loss of *n* in all the expected environments; idiosyncratic capitalization that sometimes appears patterned; heavy punctuation in one part of a text that is seemingly abandoned in another; an indifference at times to the notion of standardized spelling; the presence of assimilation, loss, and gemination that might provide clues to the speech habits of the scribes;[15] the frequent use of *y* rather than *i* at the beginning of a phrase; and so on. All this within the framework of great variance among the texts. If I were to place the texts on some sort of continuum, it would go from those produced more independently by Nahuas to those generated under clerical supervision. Somewhat impressionistically, I would place the two copies of "How to Live on Earth," "Final Judgment," and "The Life of Don Sebastián" on the more independent end of the spectrum, the other four on the more supervised.

Nonetheless all the texts occasionally but persistently defy easy assumptions. Judging by the handwriting, six of the eight documents are by different scribes; only "The Sacrifice of Isaac" and "Souls and Testamentary Executors" come from the same well-trained hand. Yet all eight are in what I judge to be more or less skillfully rendered variants of the clear italianate hand taught by Franciscan *nahuatlatos* (experts in Nahuatl; translators) to their Nahua pupils in the first decades after the conquest. In some respects, such as the standardization of spellings, the two aforementioned plays hew more closely to European norms than almost any of the others. But then there is a distinctive anomaly, like their very nonstandard rendering of Nahuatl *ceppa* (in *oc ceppa* "again") as *cecppa,* with its outrageously impossible-to-pronounce consonant cluster *cpp*.[16] Such similarities and anomalies are to be expected from the general run of civil and ecclesiastical Nahuatl texts.

The original lettering tentatively provides additional clues to dating. Very early in the development of alphabetical Nahuatl writing there was some hesitation about how to represent the affricate [tˢ]. By mid-sixteenth century the digraph *tz* became the settled convention in most Nahuatl writings, especially those associated with the church. Alternative solutions from an earlier period of evolving standards are infrequent. Among the early manuscripts and imprints that contain such alternates is the anonymously authored Dominican *Doctrina cristiana* of 1548. The handwritten copy that provided the basis of the book was already rather dated because the by-then-dominant *tz* is a rarity in this book of Christian doctrine (for one of the few examples, see f. 13v). It is written variously *c, tc,* and *tç,* the latter two predominating (see ff. 6v, 11v, 30r, 124v, 129r, and passim; it is possible that *tc* is a print-shop error for *tç*). An even earlier Nahuatl text from circa 1540 uses *ç* and *z* in place of *tz* (Cline 1993). There are occasional later examples.[17] None of these notably early or nonstandard forms replaces *tz* in any of the plays in this volume.[18]

During much of the sixteenth century prevocalic [w] was variously represented as *v, u,* and *hu.*[19] A sampling from the mid-sixteenth century contains the following representative examples: *yvan/yuan, civatl/çivatl, peua, yehuatzin, vecauh, vel/uel, cavitl,* and *quavitl/quauitl* (Sell and Kellogg 1997, 341–49; *Doctrina cristiana* 1548). By the end of the sixteenth century, *hu* became the prevailing standard, again especially in church-related texts. Hence such items as *yvan/yuan* usually would be spelled *yhuan, vel/uel* as *huel,* and *quavitl/quauitl* as *quahuitl.*[20] There are thousands of instances where prevocalic [w] appears before *a, e,* and *i* in the eight pieces. With only one exception, there is always *hua,* never *va* or *ua*; always *hue,* never *ve* or *ue*; always *hui,* never *vi* or *ui.*[21] The relentless representation of prevocalic [w] as *hu* and [tˢ] as *tz* establishes beyond reasonable doubt that whatever the plays' original dates of composition, their extant versions cannot be earlier than the last quarter of the sixteenth century.

Another period-specific change occurred during the last quarter of the following century. Orthographic *s* began to appear where *z* would earlier have been expected.[22] Narrowing the possible environments down to that of verbal complexes yields results that are both expected and unexpected. "The Life of Don Sebastián," with its self-admitted dating of April 1, 1692, has *s* for *z* in 61 unspoken (i.e., stage and other directions) and 229 spoken (i.e., speaking parts) instances. This will serve as a baseline for what follows. "Final Judgment" has been touted to be very old but it has 62 unspoken and 110 spoken instances, fixing the present copy at a time probably no earlier than the late seventeenth century. A mild surprise is offered by "The Three Kings." Its traditional language is much too old for a late-seventeenth- or early-eighteenth-century date of composition, yet it contains 73 unspoken and 125 spoken instances. This speaks directly to the diachronic layering of the plays with their complex mix of features from different periods. "The Merchant" contains four unspoken and one spoken instances of *s* for *z*. Since I take it to be a 1687 copy of a 1630 text, this strongly indicates that the earlier date is the more operative one. In this case, the scribe copied fairly exactly an older text with spelling that probably differed from his, a practice that is reflected in some of the other plays in this volume. Between "Souls and Testamentary Executors" and "The Sacrifice of Isaac," there is exactly one unspoken instance of *s* for *z* in a verbal complex. Both texts were apparently copied in 1760 from 1678 versions, which themselves were surely much older, given the type of Nahuatl used. A real surprise is the first version of "How to Live on Earth." Here there are five unspoken and no spoken instances, all in a hand different from that of the main text. This and other features would place it sometime during the first half of the seventeenth century rather than the eighteenth as I had thought at first. This also highlights the differences I have observed between those parts of the eight texts intended for and worked on by scribes, the unspoken written instructions, and those shared by all members of the community, the spoken dialogues. Nonspoken parts tend to have more later-colonial features.

The above evidence suggests the seventeenth century as a central point around which the texts were composed or copied. This holds true as well for the types of loanwords present in the seven plays. Some years ago, Frances Karttunen and James Lockhart pointed out the diachronic patterning of loan acquisitions in their *Nahuatl in the Middle Years: Language Contact Phenomena in Texts of the Colonial Period* (1976). Subsequent work has refined and supported their initial judgments (see especially Karttunen 1982, 1985; Lockhart 1992, ch. 7, 1999, ch. 8).

They postulate three stages of Nahuatl's relationship and reaction to Spanish. Stage 1 was very brief. It lasted from Spanish contact to circa 1540. During this time, routine daily contact between the great mass of Nahuatl- and Spanish-speakers was almost nonexistent. Hence meaningful direct verbal communication was severely constrained because both sides lacked the requisite language skills. Only a tiny number of Spanish nouns were borrowed. Stage 2 lasted from approximately 1540 to 1650. This was a time of significantly more interaction between selected individuals and groups, leading to a greater capacity on both sides to communicate orally with each other. The overwhelming result was the passage of many Spanish nouns into the Nahuatl lexicon. These newly acquired items were accommodated to Nahuatl speech habits and they supplemented rather than displaced native vocabulary. There were also a few scattered anticipations of what was to come. Stage 3 begins circa 1650 and continues to the present day. A whole range of significant adaptations to Spanish occurred: unfamiliar sounds were acquired; a strategy for borrowing verbs devised; particles incorporated; Nahuatl syntax altered; portions of the native lexicon displaced; and idioms more readily adopted. These changes flowed from a deepening one-on-one interaction that had created a critical mass of bilingual Nahuas who served as a conduit for bringing more of the Spanish-speaking world into Nahua life. My own extensive reading of colonial Nahuatl writings confirms this schema.²³

The seven translated dramas in this volume contain over two hundred Spanish and Latin phrases and words. There are a number of possible stage 3 items or features in the unspoken sections. The most notable is the Nahuatlized Spanish verb *trasladar* (to copy) in "omotrasladoro" at the end of "The Sacrifice of Isaac" (see f. 36r). However, I consider the central and more resistant-to-change original core of the plays to be that which the actors spoke and the audience heard—that is, the dialogues. There the picture is quite different. The loans shrink drastically in half, to 111. There are no examples of borrowed verbs using the Nahuatl verbalizing suffix *-oa* (see above). There are none of the Spanish particles used by post-1650 Nahua writers such as *sin, como, para, hasta, pero,* and *mientras*. There are no Spanish-style dependent clauses introduced by the Spanish particle *que* or by its back translation into Nahuatl *tle* and *inin*. There are no instances where the Nahuatl terms for close kin and the cardinal directions are replaced by their Spanish counterparts. There is not even one example of a Nahuatl inanimate noun being pluralized based on the Spanish model. On the contrary, all 111 items are of a type compatible with stage 2 although several may have come into Nahuatl in stage 3 (refer to Appendixes 1–4 for the discussion that follows).

The speaking parts draw most of the 111 loans from a small pool of older church items. The name or title *Dios* is by far the most frequent. It alone accounts for fully 317 spoken occurrences in the seven plays' total of 784 occurrences (or some 40 percent of the total). *Dios* ranges from a low of 18.6 percent of the loan frequency in "The Three Kings" to highs of 55.8 percent in "The Sacrifice of Isaac" and 62.8 percent in "How to Live on Earth."²⁴ It is one of the oldest, with attested first appearances in 1548.²⁵ The five most frequently spoken loans—*Dios, ánima, misa; Jesucristo,* and *Lucifer*—account for 412 occurrences out of 784 (some 52.5 percent) and appear in Nahuatl documents no later than 1552. I judge 16 of the 20 most frequently used items to be primarily ecclesiastical. Those 16 come to 537 occurrences out of 784 (68 percent of the total), and all appear in various types of Nahuatl texts no later than the early seventeenth century.

The church bias is stronger yet when the more mundane loans are taken into account. By my reckoning there are approximately one hundred total occurrences of such items in the seven plays. These include terms for money (*peso[s]* and *tomin[es]*), measurements of time (*domingo* and *hora*), legal terms and posts (*juramento, justicia, juez, testamento, testigos, escribano,* and *escritura*), designations of rank and function (*alcalde, conde, marqués, rey[es],* and *emperador*), and Spanish-style objects (*puerta* and *mesa*). Fifty-four of those occurrences are in "The Merchant." In some cases this one play contains all, or almost all, of the most frequently used. "The Merchant" has sixteen out of seventeen total occurrences in the seven plays of *pesos* and ten out of thirteen occurrences of *tomín,* as well as all occurrences of *tomines* (6), *testamento* (5), *peso* (4), *escribano* (2), and *escritura* (2). The already strongly ecclesiastical tone of the other six plays would be intensified if this play were excluded.

Focusing on the spoken loans reduces drastically the number of names being bandied about. Traditional social mores discouraged the use of individuals' names in direct address. All eight occurrences of the name Isaac in "The Sacrifice of Isaac" are about him, not directed to him personally. Nonetheless there was no absolute prohibition either. Once, in the same play, the slavewoman Hagar speaks of Abraham to her son Ishmael. However, the other four instances are in direct address: God the Father repeats Abraham's name twice in rapid succession, and his angel later does the same. Evidently this was a standard attention-getting device. Perhaps it was also permissible in these circumstances because social superiors (and who could be higher in a Christian-conceived social hierarchy than God and His angels?) were addressing a social inferior.

In "The Three Kings," ten out of seventeen spoken occurrences of Herod's name are in direct address, nine times by the three kings or Herod's priests, the tenth by Herod himself (unique in all the plays). Herod never addresses Casper, Melchior, or Balthasar by name but only in exalted and respectful terms. From a Nahua perspective, this pattern marks Herod as a vile character lower in status than the visiting kings. Although not a precise time-delineating marker, this usage would be more typical—or perhaps it would be more accurate to say stronger and more prevalent— earlier in the colonial period rather than later.

Many dimensions of loan meanings cannot be fully examined here. One that merits some attention is the use of *Jesús* less as a name or title than as an exclamatory indication of strong emotion. Out of nine occurrence only two are shorthand for Jesus Christ: 1 of 1 occurrence in "The Merchant" and 1 of 4 occurrences in "The Life of Don Sebastián."[26] The other seven all convey some combination of astonishment, dread, and bewilderment: 1 of 1 occurrence in "Souls and Testamentary Executors," 2 of 2 occurrences in "Final Judgment," 1 of 1 in "How to Live on Earth," and 3 of 4 in "The Life of Don Sebastián" (see ff. 44r, 4v, 18v, and pp. 17, 21). It is repeated in rapid succession in "Final Judgment" ("Jesus! Jesus!") and almost the same in "The Life of Don Sebastián" ("Jesus, what are you saying, Jesus!"). This more idiomatic usage (from a Hispanic standpoint) would be expected by the seventeenth century but not earlier.

A few of the loans have no dates of first appearance or present other minor problems of placement. Nonetheless, given the sometimes unusual references, this has more to do with hit-or-miss usage in very specialized Nahuatl genres or my lack of access to a broader database. There are also no problems presented by unanalyzed borrowed strings of words like *obra de misericordia*. These are typical of colonial Nahuatl texts. There is one such item, however, that I do not ever expect to find in the general corpus. The Latin phrase *surgite mortui venite a judicium* in "Final Judgment" was meant to be a high-sounding if meaningless (to the average Nahua parishioner) jumble of sounds (see f. 6v; the Latin means "Arise, O dead, and come to judgment"). These very same words, carved in stone, are prominently displayed on one of the processional chapels in the courtyard of the Franciscan church complex of San Andrés Calpan, Puebla. The processional chapel was completed circa 1550. It forms part of a dramatic rendering of the Last Judgment. Christ sits on his throne and beneath him is this stirring Latin phrase which was publicly exposed over decades and centuries to the Nahua parishioners of San Andrés Calpan. However, there is no compelling reason why even the few local notaries (who eventually learned to write both Nahuatl and Spanish) would have learned it and written it down in their documents. The sculpted images accompanying the meaningless words conveyed the essential information quite effectively, and besides, if anyone were curious about their meaning the local priest would have offered explanations in Nahuatl or Spanish. Hence finding an attestation for this Latin passage in any Nahuatl document (even in San Andrés Calpan) borders, in practical terms, on the impossible (see photograph, page 40).

There is one notable calque in mixed Spanish/Nahuatl form. There are eight occurrences of the loanword *cuenta,* not with the more common meaning of "rosary bead(s), rosary," but with the sense of "accounting," as in "to give or make an accounting of [something to someone]." Seven of the eight occurrences use the Nahuatl verb *maca,* "to give," in a rather straightforward calque based on Spanish *dar cuenta de,* "to give an accounting of [something to someone]" (see "How to Live on Earth," f. 21v; "The Life of Don Sebastián," p. 19; and "Final Judgment," ff. 2r, 3r, 5r [twice], and 7r). The eighth uses Nahuatl *chihua* "to make" as part of the related Spanish idiom "to make an accounting of [something to someone]" (see "Final Judgment," f. 7r). They appear in "Final Judgment" (6), "How to Live on Earth" (1), and "The Life of Don Sebastián" (1).

This is one of the few fully attested anticipations of stage 3. Undeniable confirmation of its stage 2 authenticity appears in the so-called *Diario* of Chimalpahin, the greatest Nahua annalist of the colonial period. In his entry for Saturday, January 21, 1612, he goes on at length about a troublesome—and apparently troubled—priest, fray Jerónimo de Zárate. He ruminates a bit about the cleric's questionable activities, perhaps consoling himself somewhat with the thought that "ma çan icel yc quimomaquiliz cuenta in totecuiyo Dios" (he alone will have to give an accounting of it to our lord, God). A few lines later he adds that when Zárate dies, "yc cuenta quimomaquiliz" (he will have to give an accounting of it to him; Chimalpahin 1965, 2:103). Added support comes from the published Nahuatl translation of the life of Saint Anthony of Padua by fray Juan Bautista and Agustín de la Fuente (1605). Here *cuenta* appears once as part of the calque and then in the general sense of "accounting": "quimmacaz melahuac cuenta in Officiales) (he will give a true accounting [of it] to the [king's] officials) and "Xiccuilican, xiccelilican, cuenta inin tlacatl" (take and receive an accounting [of this matter] from this person; Bautista 1605, 49r).

The general tenor of the loans suggests a stage 2 origin for the plays. Nonetheless there are at least two borrowings that smack of early stage 3. During his fulminating at the priests in "The Three Kings," Herod twice uses *judiazos* and *chicharrones.* The former contains the derogatory augmentative suffix *-zo* and is correctly inflected for the masculine plural *-os.* The latter is correctly inflected for the plural *-es.* Spanish as the language of insult is well attested among Nahuatl speakers today so this usage per se is not in question (see Hill and Hill 1986, 118–20). However, I intuitively feel that on balance this may imply a greater knowledge of the subtleties of Spanish than perhaps even Chimalpahin or Agustín de la Fuente possessed at the beginning of the seventeenth century, and it may be more appropriately associated with the period around 1700.[27]

Whenever appropriate the loans are Nahuatlized in ways typical of the time. One of the most interesting examples is *pexotli,* which can be found in a nonspeaking portion of "Final Judgment" (f. 6r). A tiny group of very early Spanish loan nouns bear what has been called the Nahuatl "absolutive suffix." In this particular case, the absolutive suffix *-tli* is attached to Spanish *peso,* "weight; scales." This attests to its very early entry into Nahuatl as well as to the (usually) unmarked glottal stop present in every borrowed Spanish noun that ended in a vowel.[28] The presence of orthographic *x* for *s* is probably a clue to its actual pronunciation by Nahuatl speakers, who early on would have substituted the affricate [š] for the Spanish sibilant.[29]

Sociopolitical terms also provide some clues to dating. Lockhart has correctly stated that, with regard to "political organization and kinship" as well as to "social rank," circa 1650 "proves to be a watershed in the evolution of vocabulary and concepts" (1992, 117). For example, such traditional terms for town council officeholders as *teteuctin*, "lords," and *pipiltin*, "nobles," are nonexistent or rare in eighteenth-century documents (1992, 49). He has not seen *tlatoani*, "dynastic ruler," used in that sense after 1661 (1992, 132). Wherever there is occasion to use such terminology in the plays, there is a decided bias toward the pre-1650, rather than the post-1650, period. This again speaks to probable dates of composition and/or copying that center on the seventeenth century, in particular the first half.

The traditional Nahuatl high rhetoric called *huehuetlatolli*, especially evident in pieces like "The Sacrifice of Isaac" and "The Three Kings," is also much more common prior to 1650.[30] There is a very precious and revealing detail of the *huehuetlatolli* in these plays that throws light on the entire group of plays and suggests some concrete, if tentative, conclusions about their origins.

The largest collection of explicitly prehispanic-style *huehuetlatolli* is contained in what is known today as book 6 of the twelve-book *Florentine Codex*. The entire work began in the late 1540s and went through various revisions and versions over the next thirty years. The editor of record was fray Bernardino de Sahagún. During the sixteenth century, the expertise in Nahuatl of this prominent Franciscan was equaled or surpassed only by a fellow Franciscan, fray Alonso de Molina, who had learned it as a small child and had native-speaker fluency. Notwithstanding Molina's preeminence in the language of everyday life, the Franciscan *nahuatlato* fray Jerónimo de Mendieta would aver that in "los secretos y antigüedades de la lengua ha alcanzado más que él ni otro ninguno" (the subtleties and ancient usages of the language [Sahagún] has achieved more than [Molina] or anyone else).[31] Sahagún directed a large and able group of Nahua collaborators, some his former students literate in Nahuatl, Spanish, and Latin.[32]

Another collection of *huehuetlatolli* pertains to the circle of the greatest colonial grammarian of Nahuatl, the Jesuit *nahuatlato* Father Horacio Carochi. The text is known today as the *Bancroft Dialogues*. They can be appreciated in a critical edition by Frances Karttunen and James Lockhart (1987). Two sections of those dialogues (one rather lengthy) closely parallel parts of chapter 10 of book 6 of the *Florentine Codex*. These borrowings establish beyond reasonable doubt that the mid-seventeenth-century Jesuit had access to the precious fruits of earlier Franciscan and Nahua scholarship (Karttunen and Lockhart 1987, 11–13).[33] No less certain is a similar connection between two sections of "The Three Kings" and the same chapter 10 of book 6 of the *Florentine Codex*.[34] Intriguingly, both the *Bancroft Dialogues* and "The Three Kings" borrow from the same pages (Sahagún 1950–1982, 6:47–49). The chapter is devoted to the installation of a new ruler and lamentations on the death of the old one. The three texts are noticeably close at times, but they are not identical. Compare the following excerpts from Sahagún's work and the play:

auh in aoc nane, in aoc tate in cujtlapilli, in atlapalli, auh in aoc ixe, in oc nacace, in aoc iyollo in atl, in tepetl: in ma iuh nontica, in amo naoati, in amo tlatoa in ma iuhquj quechcotontica.
(And the vassals no longer possess a mother, no longer possess a father. And no longer doth the city have the able, the prudent. They are as if mute; they speak not; they talk not; they are as if beheaded.) (Sahagún 1950–1982, 6: 47)

auh canel aocmo nane aocmo taye in cuitlapilli in atlapalli Auh canel aocmo ixxe in aocmo nacaçe in iuhqui nontiticac in amo nahuati in amo tlatohua innniuhqui quechcotonticac.
(And truly the tail, the wing [i.e., the vassal] no longer has a mother, no longer has a father. And truly it no longer has eyes, it no longer has ears [i.e., it lacks prudence]. It is as if it stands mute. It does not speak, it does not talk. It is as if it stands beheaded.)[35]

In his prologue to the *Sermonario* of 1606, fray Juan Bautista wrote that he and Agustín de la Fuente had compiled a three-volume collection of plays, which they intended to publish. They had already published a collection of elegant *huehuetlatolli* in 1600 that was based on work from sixty years before. Bautista explicitly acknowledged that they drew from the works of many eminent Nahua and Franciscan writers including Sahagún. They included parts of Sahagún's sermons in their sermonary. Their entire trajectory speaks of reviewing an extensive corpus of the best and most varied older writings, and then copying and revising them in preparation for publication. The three volumes of plays are among several works that unfortunately never left the press.

Given the above, I tentatively conclude that most or even all of the plays in their present form came from the texts gathered for Bautista and de la Fuente's three unpublished volumes of Nahuatl plays. The Franciscan *nahuatlato* and his trilingual Nahua coauthor—like no one else before or since—had the motivation, opportunity, training, and support needed to collect such materials and work them up. The textual ties to Sahagún in "The Three Kings" and the Franciscan jurisdiction where "The Merchant" was copied reinforce my supposition. The less-author-specific clues mentioned above point to circa 1600 (when Bautista and de la Fuente were active) as a time of likely copying and rearranging. Since I judge that some or all of the plays passed through—rather than originated at—their hands, there is the strong possibility that many arose in some fashion before, perhaps even well before, 1600.[36]

Caution is necessary in attribution, given the types of clues found in the texts themselves. It is further required since we can only appreciate these writings in their now-extant forms; most, perhaps all, can with varying justification be said to be later copies of older originals. The reader should thus regard the following as suggestions rather than ironclad conclusions. I consider "The Sacrifice of Isaac," "Souls and Testamentary Executors," "The Three Kings," and "The Merchant" in their currently known colonial versions as the most probable yields of the Bautista and de la Fuente collaboration. I deem "Final Judgment" and "How to Live on Earth" to be less certain products of their hands. I judge "The Life of Don Sebastián" to be the least certain, and in fact it may be a genuine product of the late seventeenth century. In any case, now that the plays are in more reliable transcriptions and their originals all located, a new round of scholarly analysis can more precisely verify or disprove these tentative assertions.

Life in the *Altepetl*: The Setting of "The Merchant"

Other contributors to this volume comment far more knowledgeably than I could on some of the otherwordly aspects of the dramas. I will discuss some of their more mundane features with a special focus on "The Merchant." Here as elsewhere the emphasis is on drawing out characteristics of the plays that may not be obvious to the general reader.

The arena in which the plays' Nahua characters, Christian supernaturals, and biblical figures mingle and interact is the *altepetl*. The term is a quasi-compound derived from the metaphorical doublet *(in) atl (in) tepetl* (the water, the hill), which refers to two essentials of community life. Postcolonial scholars have variously rendered it as tribe, village, empire, city, city-state, people, settlement, nation, and kingdom. My own preferences run to characterizing it most often as an ethnic city-state of greatly varying size.[37] This sociopolitical entity and its subdivisions are the overwhelming referent in the notarial corpus when Nahua scribes referred to unit identity. Its infrequent appearance in the dramas belies its importance. It is only within the framework of *altepetl* roles and expectations that the characters are most fully understood.[38]

A prime example is provided by the use of the term *tlatoani* (plural *tlatoque*), the traditional dynastic ruler of the altepetl and one of its defining features. The main thrust has to do with someone in charge who says things, that is, "Speaker" rather than "speaker," hence "one who issues commands, who gives orders," hence "ruler, governor." Since colonial times it has often been translated *rey*, "king." Indeed in "The Three Kings," Nahuatl *tlatoque* is paired a number of times with the Spanish loanword *reyes*, "kings."[39] Here the more neutral designation "ruler" has been chosen to avoid too easily casting Nahua *tlatoque* into the role of exotic "Indian kings." The word is present in all the plays. It is used in several ways typical of the 1540–1650, or stage 2, period: as a title of the ruler of an *altepetl* (Abraham), as one of the most frequently used epithets of the Christian deity (God), and in the more general sense of an important person who is not a ruler or even of noble birth (the avaricious merchant).

The *tlatoani* stood in a distinctly non-European relationship to the *altepetl*. Named subunits called *tlaxilacalli* (etymology uncertain) or *calpolli*, "big house," were the building blocks of the late prehispanic and colonial *altepetl*. They stood in relationship to each other in accordance with what Lockhart has termed a cellular or modular type of organization. *Altepetl* were created by the "aggregation of parts that remain[ed] relatively separate and self-contained, brought together by their common function and similarity, their place in some numerical or symmetrical arrangement, their rotational order, or all three" (Lockhart 1992, 436; brackets mine). He adds that this contrasts with the more urban-centered and nucleated Spanish municipality, which "stretched from a dominant center in the city to subordinate parts in the country" (1999, 100).

It is not surprising that Spaniards considered the area encompassing the residence of the current *tlatoani*—the central marketplace, nearby miscellaneous clusters of dwellings lying in distinct *tlaxilacalli*, and the main church (often the former site of the temple dedicated to the *altepetl*'s patron deity in prehispanic times)—as a *cabecera* (head town) and outlying *tlaxilacalli* or parts thereof as *sujetos* (dependencies; subject settlements). From their perspective, the early colonial *tlatoani* and his successor, the *gobernador* ("governor," or head of the local Spanish-style town council), was or should be in command of this so-called *cabecera* and its supposedly subordinate parts. However, from the Nahua perspective (at least for quite some time), this alleged urban center had no special status or name. *Tlatoque* and their later colonial counterparts were first and foremost based in their various *tlaxilacalli* and represented them. Ideally the highest-ranking members of these subunits rotated the post of *tlatoani*/governor according to some fixed order.

None of this is obvious in any of the plays, even in "The Merchant," which is the most naturalistic drama and the one on which I will focus below. "The Three Kings," with its emphatic use of late prehispanic forms of speech and social terminology, quite unselfconsciously pairs Nahuatl *tlatoque* with Spanish *reyes* (see above). This pairing may mislead the unwary reader. However, I take this usage to be no more or less expected than the many other shifting functional equivalencies that are rife within the extant Nahuatl and Spanish corpus when either party talked about the other. Each side long operated within its own conceptual framework and assumed that the other thought as it did (Lockhart [1992, 445] calls this process Double Mistaken Identity; for a current restatement of his position, see also 1999, 98–119). When communicating across cultural/linguistic borders, the tendency was to strive for pithy analogues rather than unwieldy longwinded definitions that took into account every conceivable similarity and difference. Both the Nahua and Spanish personages in question had power and authority over others, played vital roles in group unity and identity, and in other ways were essential parts of early modern Nahua and Spanish society.

The inhabitants and routines of the colonial *altepetl* are most fully represented by "The Merchant." In order of appearance, the cast comprises an unidentified speaker giving the prologue, Merchant, Old Man and Old Woman (an elderly couple), Young Woman, two sick people, Lowly Servant, Mature Man (married), Lord, an unidentified group of servants, Mother (accompanied now or later by nonspeaking children), Notary, Alcalde, Constable, Priest, Doctor, Sick Man (Merchant in his final agonies), Nobleman, several demons, the Merchant/Sick Man's wife, Guardian Angel, and two noblemen. Here we can see some of the rich complexity of Nahua society: the old and the young, those of varying degrees of wealth and poverty, men and women, nobles and commoners, people who are single or widowed or married, employers and employees, crucial *altepetl* officials, the healthy and the sick, members of various occupations (although farm folk and petty craftspeople are mostly implied), and even the presence of non-Nahuas, such as Priest. If one subtracts the obligatory opening speech, three quarters of the play passes in selected worldly pursuits before the first supernatural being makes his appearance. Customary activities include bargaining, borrowing and lending money, engaging the services of municipal officials, creating documents, and so on. The only comparable piece is "Souls and Testamentary Executors."

Lockhart suggests that these two dramas imply a subgenre (1992, 597n.120). There is a definite tilt in these two instances toward the confessionals' detailed presentations of the seventh commandment against stealing than toward the oftentimes more abstract offerings found in doctrinals and sermonaries.

Given a lingering popular conception that Spaniards overwhelmed and controlled passive native subjects, it is noteworthy that the few non-Nahuas in the plays have ineffectual powers of persuasion and nothing more. The priest in "The Merchant" is completely unsuccessful when he tries to persuade Merchant to show mercy to Mother and her two children, or when he pleads with Merchant's metamorphosed self, Sick Man, to make the true confession that will spare him the torments of hell. The cleric in "Final Judgment" is shocked by Lucía's confession but can do nothing beyond registering shock and horror. The priest in "Souls and Testamentary Executors" enjoys no real success with the spouse of don Pedro, for she is already observing all necessary Nahua and Christian protocols. In short, these church-sponsored dramas seem to undercut the moral stature of priests by denying them an authority they allegedly possessed.

Nahua *altepetl* often enjoyed considerable autonomy, survived in admirable fashion catastrophic imported epidemics that took off perhaps 95 percent of their numbers by the beginning of the seventeenth century, and seemingly always bedeviled their official spiritual advisers with their non-Christian beliefs and behaviors.[40] Among many pertinent colonial comments is the following marginal note (or lamentation?) from the Bautista and de la Fuente sermonary of 1606: "*La facilidad con que los naturales se juntan con Mestizos, y Españoles para contra su ministro, y padre*" (the ease with which the natives join with mestizos and Spaniards against their minister and priest; Bautista 1606, 617). Earlier marginalia drive home the point that "base and vile people" provoke damaging testimony against priests, and later marginalia almost wistfully enjoin Nahua parishioners to follow the lead of Saint Francis by loving and revering their spiritual fathers (Bautista 1606, 49, 616; cited in Sell 1993, 225n.219, 226n.225, respectively). Bautista's dismal view of Nahua treatment of the clergy is echoed decades later by the secular cleric (and mestizo) don Bartolomé de Alva [Ixtlilxochitl] in his confessional manual of 1634. Regarding taking the name of God in vain, Alva asks: "Perhaps some bad Spanish Christian paid you so that you would take an oath against a priest or some other honorable person, or someone who is a representative of the devil—through and because of you—wants to dishonor him, just taking his revenge and anger out on him?" (Sell and Schwaller 1999, 91–93).

The plays make no mention of one profound reality of early modern Nahua life: the nonclerical and nonroyal "mestizos and Spaniards" who evidently formed a considerable part of the "base and vile people" who set Nahuas against God's representatives on earth. The absence of ethnic, racial, or national diversity is perhaps the single most serious omission in the plays. The human landscape of Nahua Mexico has been reduced to a purist version of Nahua-only communities served by presumably Spanish priests. The contradiction between dramatized impression and recorded fact is stark in "The Merchant." The brief remarks in Nahuatl at the beginning of this play place it in Tollantzinco in 1687. Ten years later, the noted Franciscan chronicler fray Agustín de Vetancurt would write that Tollantzinco, ministered to by his order, contained more than fifteen hundred natives and more than six hundred Spaniards and mestizos (Vetancurt 1982,

63). Furthermore, the natives were not purely Nahuas: Tollantzinco was also home to Otomis, a people of distinct culture and language who were marginalized by the Nahuas in central Mexico (Lockhart 1991, 26–27). Interaction was intense among people of differing backgrounds and status in provincial capitals like Tollantzinco and the kinds of places where the plays would have been performed.

Operating within an increasingly variegated colonial context that is scarcely mentioned in the play, the chief protagonist of "The Merchant" is easy enough to recognize from the Nahuatl notarial record. Rebecca Horn's work provides a salient example close to 1630 when the play may have been copied or composed. (The following is drawn from Horn 1998, 75–76; Horn 1997b, 115, 135, 206; and from the testament of Juan Fabián that she used and that can be found in transcription and translation in Anderson et al. 1976, 58–63). Juan Fabián lived in Coyoacan, a large altepetl in the Valley of Mexico southwest of Mexico City. He made his testament in 1617. This well-to-do Nahua commoner traded in the native fruit called *zapotl* ("zapote"), probably grown on the orchard he possessed. He also owned a substantial amount of other land, at least one parcel of which had been purchased. He employed local Nahuas including carpenters. He had a horse, several mules, and sacks and pack gear. He very actively lent money to, and borrowed money from, both Nahuas and Spaniards. Neither this real-life example of a Nahua merchant nor Merchant from the play was overwhelmed by commerce, monetary dealings, or the market economy.

Many routine economic activities largely escape Nahuatl documentation.[41] Even when they do appear, we often see only a part of the process. The initial contracting of obligations like debts is infrequent in the extant record.[42] Mention of such financial dealings is most recurrent in testaments, because the obligations remained outstanding and needed to be satisfied by heirs or testamentary executors. Yet even while one often finds details about amounts, names, and circumstances,[43] there are rarely any particulars regarding fixed schedules of payment of specific amounts of principal and interest. Therefore, a discussion of the details of Merchant's financial dealings is in order before proceeding to a consideration of how typical or atypical the general circumstances were, as well as whether they contain welcome clues to how such financial transactions were structured. For ease of presentation, I will follow the order in which they appear in the play.

Merchant's first transaction involves Old Man and Old Woman. They need ten pesos so their son, now in police custody, will not be bound over to a textile manufacturing shop. Merchant charges ten pesos at 50 percent interest, that is, four *tomines* for each peso lent (since each peso equals eight *tomines*). They are to pay within fifteen days. If they fail to meet the two-week deadline, they are to pay twenty pesos, that is, interest plus penalty will equal 100 percent of the principal. When the fifteen days have passed, Merchant sends an underling to collect the money. Lowly Servant threatens them with jail or seizure of their property if they do not immediately make payment. Evidently they were successful in meeting the deadline for they hand Lowly Servant the full amount due.

Young Woman asks for a loan of twenty pesos so she can take care of her ailing parents, and she offers some personal items as collateral. She promises to make restitution in twenty days. She makes no mention of paying interest. Merchant cackles that he is not about the business of lending money to a crying pretty woman like herself but rather seeks an increase of his wealth. He proposes as absolute conditions that she pay 50 percent interest, that is, the twenty pesos principal plus ten pesos in interest, and that he might knock a little off the interest if she services him sexually. She indignantly refuses.

The two sick people who beg alms of Merchant mention no specific amounts before they are run off by his servants. Given the didactic character of the play, I would guess that a token amount such as a *tomín* or two was implied. This particular transaction is one of the instances that are most obviously gauges of the Merchant's propensity for shortchanging the spiritual side of his transactions.

Mature Man approaches Merchant with a request. He is going to Guatemala to get his spouse. He asks Merchant to guard one thousand pesos for him until his return. Four months pass. Mature Man reappears and asks for his money back. Merchant greets him politely enough but claims to know nothing about the entrusted amount. Mature Man asks him to take an oath on a cross and affirm that he does not, indeed, have the money. Merchant complies by laying his hand on the cross, swearing a false oath, and taking the name of God in vain. The episode ends with Merchant's servants driving Mature Man away with severe blows. This is another egregious instance of Merchant shortchanging himself spiritually.

Merchant deals quite differently with Lord. This high nobleman requests a loan of four thousand pesos for one month. Merchant agrees immediately, merely adding that Lord will need to pay four hundred pesos, that is, ten percent interest, on the principal. Lord agrees.

The last episode is the most complicated. Mother asks Merchant to give her the testament of her deceased husband (perhaps held in trust or against some incurred debt) so that she and her two children can lay claim to his estate. Merchant denies he has such a document. He claims that he bought the land and fields she mentions from her spouse, and that he knows nothing of any money and gems. He then insultingly speculates that perhaps she herself dissipated the items in question, or that her late husband did not make a testament, or that she and some unnamed companion (perhaps an illicit lover?) squandered the property. He calls her a drunk, urges her to sleep it off, and peremptorily bids her farewell. She once again appeals to his compassion only to be rudely rebuffed for a second time. He then summons Notary to create a false document (the testament mentioned below?), backdated three years, that supports his theft. Notary asks to be paid for his counterfeit paper trail and Merchant promises recompense.

Meanwhile, Mother appeals to Alcalde, who sends Constable to bring Merchant to him. Merchant comes before this representative of the local *cabildo*, once more lays his hand on a cross, swears an even stronger false oath, inviting the devil to take him if he lies, and again takes the name of God in vain. Notary produces the sham document, which alleges that Merchant paid one thousand pesos for the husband's house and fields. He further substantiates Merchant's lies by asserting that he witnessed both the money changing hands and the making of the dead man's testament. Alcalde dismisses Mother's claims.

Priest makes a final effort at moral persuasion but Merchant is adamant. This series of compounded transgressions against God and man evidently shifts the balance of Merchant's spiritual account too far into debt. Merchant becomes Sick Man, who in short order falls deathly ill. His ill-gotten earthly goods now do him no good. Just before he is strangled by demons, the once arrogant merchant calls in two noblemen to make his testament and take charge of distributing his spiritually worthless wealth. God's justice has been served.

Of this wealth of details concerning typical behaviors and attitudes, I will mention only a few. Merchant twice swears a false oath on the cross, taking the Lord's name in vain. The second time he adds for effect that if he is lying let it be God's will "that the devil take me." This clearly violates the second commandment: "HAVE you sometime falsely sworn the honored name of God? You did it on a cross? You took an oath, by means of swearing, and you verified what you know is not true?" (Sell and Schwaller 1999, 91).[44] Taking oaths on the cross was widespread although not always recorded. In a civil suit in Tlaxcala in 1568, a group of witnesses were required to swear in the name of God and Saint Mary, with their right hands on the cross, which they had kissed, that they would answer truthfully. If they lied, the devil would punish them; if they told the truth, God would have mercy on them (Sullivan 1987, 125). In a Tlaxcalan criminal case of 1565, several witnesses were deposed in similar fashion, although there was no mention of diabolical punishment or divine mercy (Sullivan 1987, 308–9, 310–11, 314–15).

Alcalde hears Mother's complaint against Merchant. Alcaldes ranked higher than *regidores* (city councilmen) in colonial Nahua municipal government, just the opposite of what was true in Spanish *cabildos* (Lockhart 1992, 36–37). They were *cabildo* members, judges, and high-ranking members of their *altepetl*. Alcalde's ultimate collusion with Merchant's nefarious schemes, even if unwitting, is perhaps already suggested by the good relations enjoyed between Merchant and Lord. I find no hint that Merchant is anything more than a very wealthy commoner who has successfully parlayed his financial success into something approaching equality with the local high-born.

Other sorts of incidents would have little reason to appear in the Nahuatl notarial record. Merchant treats Old Man and Old Woman with active disdain when they appeal to him in their time of great need. This goes against the fifth commandment: "Did you honor your mother and your father, your elder brothers, the elderly men and women who were born first?" (Sell and Schwaller 1999, 101). More specifically, dutiful Nahua Christians were instructed: "Did you honor elderly men and elderly women? Or did you hold them in no regard? Did their miseries not inspire compassion in you? Did you not help them?" (Molina 1984, 30r).[45] This closely accorded with traditional Nahua notions concerning respect for the elderly as recorded in a collection of traditional *huehuetlatolli*. A young person of high station who is traveling is given instructions on how to properly greet commoners of advanced age. An old man is to be greeted with "Nottatzine nocoltzine, notlatzine" (O my father, O my grandfather, O my uncle) and an old woman with "Nonantzine, nocitzine" (O my mother, O my grandmother), to be followed by "ma ihuiyan ma icemel xommohuicatiuh, ma cana tommohuetziti" (May you be going along calmly and happily, may you not fall down somewhere; Bautista 1600b, 51v–52r).

A thread of physical violence runs through the plays. "The Merchant" contains some of the more explicit scenes. Merchant's servants run off the two sick people.

Later they run off Mature Man, "severely beating him." Near the end of the play, one of the demons strangles Merchant/Sick Man to death. Herod might be physically threatening the Jewish priests when he drives them away in "The Three Kings." Aside from the obvious close call in "The Sacrifice of Isaac," there is a threat of implied violence when Second Nobleman speaks of running off Hagar and Ishmael. Near the end of "Souls and Testamentary Executors," there is possible torture by the demons of the condemned. Don Sebastián murders his wife in "The Life of Don Sebastián." Woman walks along berating her son, Little Child, and slapping his face in "How to Live on Earth." Little Child speaks of seizing her by the hair. While in the forest, Third Youth speaks of beating and slapping his parents and seizing them by the neck. He is apparently killed by a fierce beast while his companions sleep. Death "kills" Lorenzo and his wife by shooting arrows. At the end of the play, Christ tells the demons to take Condemned One to the fiery cavern where he is to be hung, beaten, and broken to bits. Lucía in "Final Judgment" suffers at the end from her fiery apparel. Shortly thereafter, stage directions twice indicate that she is to be beaten by demons as they drive her into hell.

Familial-, gender-, and age-based violence is to some extent addressed in the questions standard in confessional manuals. Under the fourth commandment, to honor your father and your mother, are the queries: "Did you repeatedly beat them when you were drunk? Did you slap them in the face? Do you repeatedly kick them? . . . Perhaps you pulled out their facial hair or grabbed them by their hair as you are wont to do?" (Sell and Schwaller 1999, 101). Spouses were to be properly treated under the same commandment (Molina 1984, 29v). Physical abuse directed against the young was placed within other contexts such as drunkenness and the failure to treat one's family properly. When a drunkard comes home in a rage, "he beats his wife and children, kicking and kicking them, throwing earth at them" (Sell and Schwaller 1999, 121). This is apart from the equation made between abortion and murder in the fifth commandment (Molina 1984, 31v; Sell and Schwaller 1999, 103). Less routine types of violence get some play in the Nahuatl notarial record. There are several such incidences in the largest single collection of colonial Nahuatl testaments. These documents were generated in the *altepetl* of Culhuacan and almost all are from the years 1579–1589. One was an attack on a peace officer and another an interethnic assault, a black man who gravely wounded a Nahua (Cline and León-Portilla 1984, 136–37, 220–21).[46]

Old Man and Old Woman need their loan so they can free their son from what is evidently a stint of forced labor in an *obraje* (textile manufacturing shop) to pay off debts or a serious crime. Old Woman later remarks with some urgency to Old Man that the same could happen to them if they do not repay the merchant on time. She had heard in the marketplace that another couple suffered this very fate. Their fear of *obrajes* was well founded. From a business angle, *obrajes* had "high start-up and operating costs, modest profits, and low prestige" (Horn 1997b, 219). Since the resulting low wages were not sufficient to attract enough free workers, forced laborers like slaves and prisoners were often employed. They were literally locked up inside these notorious establishments (see Horn 1997b, 218–20, for more details on the presence and operation of *obrajes* in Coyoacan). Conditions were so bad that a manual for confessors of 1600 advised dealing leniently with Nahuas who worked in *obrajes* and stole from their owners. This was one of the few situations where the need to make restitution under the seventh commandment was relaxed: "Y comoquiera que no pueden restituir pues son alli perpetuos deudores y esclauos, no tienen obligacion de restituyr" (But inasmuch as they cannot make restitution since there they are perpetual debtors and slaves, they are not obliged [by the church] to make restitution; Bautista 1600a, 14r, brackets mine).

Going into debt to satisfy judicial penalties and paying or working off the debt thus incurred were accepted practices. There are two typical examples from the above-mentioned testaments of Culhuacan. In a testament of August 25, 1580, the widow María states that "my late second husband named Francisco Quauhtli and I borrowed a peso belonging to the ward heads so that we could leave jail when we were both imprisoned" (Cline and León-Portilla 1984, 79).[47] She then tries to make arrangements to discharge this financial burden. In the testament of February 12, 1581, of Luis Tlauhpotonqui, a *pochtecatl* or merchant like Juan Fabián mentioned previously, there again is a debt pending by "Miguel Huelilhuitl[:] ... nine pesos.... And as to the three pesos which he paid, he just worked at our home to pay it. With this money he got out of jail, because he broke the head of Juan de San Miguel when he was *alguacil mayor*. And he is to pay this promptly" (Cline and León-Portilla 1984, 137).[47] It was also acceptable in some cases to compel people to work to pay off their transgressions. The Tlaxcalan *Actas* (town council minutes) for November 4, 1547, decree that a pay scale is being set for those Tlaxcalans "arrested for drunkenness and hired out as punishment" (Lockhart et al. 1986, 35).[48] The pay scale varies from two *tomines* to one peso per month depending on whether the labor is common or skilled, the work is in [Nahua] Tlaxcala or [Spanish] Puebla, and the employers are Tlaxcalans or Spaniards. Other instances of forced labor can be found in the *Actas* (Lockhart et al. 1986, 42 [item 54] and 45 [item 72]).

While the ten pesos requested by Old Man and Old Woman and the twenty pesos solicited by Young Woman are more or less within the upper range of similar dealings in Nahuatl testaments, the one thousand pesos entrusted to Merchant by Mature Man, the four thousand pesos loaned by Merchant to Lord, and the one thousand pesos supposedly paid to Mother's deceased husband by Merchant are unusually large sums. For comparison, I cite an instance recorded in the Tlaxcalan *Actas*. The minutes for May 1, 1562, state that the *altepetl* of Tlaxcala is borrowing four hundred pesos from the *altepetl* of San Andrés Calpan (located in the present-day state of Puebla). Somewhat in the fashion of Young Woman's initial proposal, they give no interest rate but pledge *altepetl* assets against the debt and promise to pay it back in ten months (Lockhart et al. 1986, 118–19). This is in response to ongoing financial difficulties and represents one of the largest strictly monetary sums in the twenty-year run of these town council minutes. An even larger sum is mentioned on December 18, 1553. The *altepetl* has formed a company with Juan Ruiz, "a Spaniard," and, as part of the deal, the *altepetl* has bought thirty oxen, the cost so far coming to about eight hundred pesos (Lockhart et al. 1986, 90).[49] Horses and mules, high-value commodities in native communities, are assigned values from five to forty pesos (Cline and León-Portilla 1984, 105, 137, 155, 189, 275; Anderson et al. 1976, 60–63).

Other cash amounts mentioned in wills tend to be small, frequently measured in *tomines* rather than pesos. A debt of only four pesos caused considerable distress for one Joaquín Matlalacan of Culhuacan, who in his 1585 testament charges his executors with recovering the sum from his debtor, Gerónimo de San Mateo Tlalxopan: "Let the executors ask him for them in order that masses be said for me; many times I asked him for them, but he almost killed me over them" (Cline and León-Portilla 1984, 237). In Tollantzinco in 1582, the local church needed a bell, so the *altepetl* obtained a loan of one hundred pesos from a local Spaniard. After two and a half years, only half of the debt had been paid back. The Spanish creditor then took vigorous legal action. Part of the town's *cabildo* ended up in jail. All this over fifty pesos! (Lockhart 1991, 28–29). These amounts pale in comparison to the one thousand and four thousand pesos mentioned in the play. This strongly suggests that the amounts were exaggerated in order to increase their dramatic and didactic impact.

The one real surprise in the entire play is the emphasis on moneylending and the details concerning schedules of payment of principal and specified interest. Mention of usury in the ecclesiastical Nahuatl corpus is typically brief compared to the relatively copious amounts of ink spent on drunkenness and idolatry.[50] In the rather extensive section devoted to the seventh commandment against stealing in fray Alonso de Molina's confessional manual of 1569, almost lost among folio after folio of detailed questioning is the following: "Did you sometime loan at interest, did you perhaps lend things, so that you would be given [back] much more?" (Molina 1984, 41r).[51] Molina's book of Christian doctrine includes under the seventh commandment an equally brief mention of merchants who are moneylenders (Molina 1578, 37r).[52] Other references are usually just as brief.[53]

Usury receives more attention in the two-volume handbook on confession prepared by fray Juan Bautista and Agustín de la Fuente. In this 1600 imprint they write:

¶ En muchas partes desta nueua España, se vsan logros, prestando vna persona a otro vn peso, y rescibiendo despues dos, o poco menos y finalmente siempre mas de lo principal que se presta, ora sea en dineros, ora Mayz, o en otras semillas. Y muy pocos se acusan deste peccado, y asi sera bien que los predicadores de quando en quando prediquen contra el y los confessores pregunten a los Mercaderes o Indios ricos, si han dado a logro: para mandarles restituyr lo que asi vuieren lleuado. Ay proprio vocablo de logro, que es, tetech tlaixtlapanaliztli, tetech tlamieccaquixtiliztli, y para dezir diste a logro? Cuix tetech otitlaixtlapan, cuix [te]tech otitlamieccaquixti?

In many parts of this New Spain money is lent at interest, one person lending another one peso and afterwards receiving two or a little less, but in any case always more than the principal lent, whether it be in money or maize or other seeds. And very few confess to this sin, and so it would be good if once in a while preachers preached against it and the confessors question the merchants or rich Indians as to whether they have lent at interest with the aim of ordering them to make restitution of what they would have made. There is appropriate terminology for lending at interest which is tetech tlaixtlapanaliztli, tetech tlamieccaquixtiliztli. And in order to say "Did you lend money at interest?" [one says] "Cuix tetech otitlaixtlapan? Cuix [te]tech otitlamieccaquixti?" (Bautista 1600a, 15r–v; all brackets mine)

In 1713 the Augustinian fray Manuel Pérez commented on usury in his *Farol Indiano*, a technical religious manual aimed at helping priests minister to Nahuas. In his view, although in general confessional inquiry about usury was best avoided so as not to teach bad behaviors, Nahuas of Mexico City did lend money at interest with the understanding that "mientras dura el no bolver the principal, esta el deudor dando cada semana vn tomin al acreedor" (as long as the principal has not been repaid the debtor gives a tomin each week to the creditor; Pérez 1713, 187). He adds that he has heard of such practices both in confession and out of it from both creditors and debtors. Fifty years later appeared the combination grammar–dictionary–confessional manual (1765) of Bachiller Don Jerónimo Tomás de Aquino Cortés y Zedeño. This secular cleric in the bishopric of Guadalajara asks if the confessee has lent three *reales* in order to receive four *reales* back (33 pecent interest), or lent four pesos in order to get four pesos and four *reales* back (12.5 percent interest). He next asks if the confessee has made loans in kind of such goods as maize, beans, and wheat, expecting to receive more back than he lent (Cortés y Zedeño 1967, 169–70).

These testimonies suffice to establish that moneylending at interest was practiced by Nahuas, at least to some extent, and hence there was some context for a didactic play in which it is a featured sin. Details of the practice—both in the play and in the statements cited above—vary considerably; the inconsistencies in Merchant's behavior may, thus, be compatible with native practice even while the size of some of the loans is highly exaggerated.

As in so much else, this play like the others ultimately offers very few surprises or unusual challenges to researchers already familiar with the colonial Nahuatl corpus in both its civil and ecclesiastical components. The texts are skewed to serving Christian didactic ends, distorting and/or illuminating in ways that are often predictable and expected. This should not detract from their intrinsic value to the interested reader. Here is early Nahua culture and language presented in a fairly lively fashion in a genre unique among Native American alphabetical texts.

Notes

1. Mesoamerica is a culture area comprising much of what is now modern Mexico and northern Central America.

2. I am thinking here of the Nahuatl censuses of the Morelos region. For a representative sample in transcription and translation with commentary, see Cline 1993.

3. Due to last-minute considerations of space, the second version of "How to Live on Earth" will appear in Volume 4.

4. This fundamental sociopolitical unit of Nahua life will be discussed in some detail below, but for now the reader should be aware that contemporary Spaniards often translated the term as *ciudad* (city) and *pueblo* (people, settlement).

5. I first became aware of these documents from Lockhart (1992, 50). The originals are in the Special Collections Department of the University of California at Los Angeles.

6. Some of the plays have additions/corrections/changes in a hand different from that of the main text, suggesting that they were still works in progress.

7. The observant reader will note that the earlier reference to a Tollantzinco notarial document written on *Wednesday*, November 3, and this reference to *Saturday*, November 15, both in 1687, do not jibe.

8. The most prominent would be Oaxtepec, Morelos. The Dominicans built a church complex there, which can still be appreciated today.

9. Imagine my surprise when I inspected the original several years ago at the Library of Congress and could find no date whatsoever! My chagrin was somewhat lessened upon discovering that my coeditor repeated in good faith the same error (see Burkhart 1996, 282 n. 8).

10. Inaccuracies can be extremely hardy. The same faulty dating continues to appear in recent scholarship.

11. I gratefully acknowledge a deep debt to Fernando Horcasitas, John H. Cornyn, and Byron McAfee. I began in some cases with digitized versions of their transcriptions, which speeded my initial progress and also helped me realize just how different the new transcriptions were. I also twice personally consulted the four texts housed in the Library of Congress (LC) and doublechecked them against our evolving transcriptions. None of this would have been possible without the help of Greg Spira, who also helped with the first drafts of the LC transcriptions.

The four texts from the University of Michigan's Clements Library and the Academy of American Franciscan History were consulted via microfilm (exceptionally clear) and hard copy, respectively. Once digitized, all transcriptions were fully checked three (in some cases, four) times by Louise M. Burkhart and Barry D. Sell, over a period of two years. Inevitably there must be outright errors, but the editors have worked hard to minimize them.

12. At times it is a very subjective and frustrating exercise trying to settle on an individual scribe's intent (or lack thereof) regarding capitalization. The same is true of spacing.

13. Speaking only for myself, I generally follow the usages of fray Juan Bautista and Agustín de la Fuente. Their published work (1599–1607) anticipates modern norms in many particulars.

14. The second version of "How to Live on Earth" is the other play most like "Final Judgment" in this respect.

15. I am in general agreement with Lockhart (1991, 122–40) on the phoneticity of Nahuatl texts.

16. See "The Sacrifice of Isaac" for "oc cecppa" (28v) and "Oc çecppa" (30r). "Souls and Testamentary Executors" has even more examples: "oc çecppa" (39r, 40r, 51v), "ocecppa" (39v), and "oc cecppa" (43r). Although bound together with them, "The Three Kings" not only is written in a different hand but lacks this telltale marker.

17. A document from Xochimilco in 1572 uses *tç* for *tz*, apparently reflecting the influence of the renowned *nahuatlato* fray Bernardino de Sahagún who had been stationed there. The text can be found in Karttunen and Lockhart 1976, 94–96.

18. While I have conscientiously tried to verify this last statement, there may be one or two examples I have inadvertently missed. Given other considerations below, my first impression would be scribal error.

19. I have very occasionally encountered *hv*, which admittedly may contain nothing more than a stylized *u*. For some examples, see Karttunen and Lockhart 1976, 105.

20. Exceptions can be occasionally found such as in a 1572 document from Xochimilco (Karttunen and Lockhart 1976, 94–96). Sahagún's influence on the Nahua notary involved can be seen in the use of *ho* or *o* for prevocalic [hu] as in "mochihoaz" for *mochihuaz* or "nicpeoaltia" for *nicpehualtia* (94). Even published clerical texts contain examples. Many can be found in Sahagún's own *Psalmodia christiana* (1583) and Arthur J. O. Anderson's critical edition of same (Sahagún 1993b).

21. The one exception can be found in "The Life of Don Sebastián" (p. 21): "Otlapopol*ui*s" [italicization mine]. I regard this as simple scribal error. Here the Find command of my word processor (Word 5.1 for the Mac) was invaluable. I searched for and examined every single possible occurrence of *va/ua/hua*, *ve/ue/hue*, and *vi/ui/hui*.

22. The question of whether this orthographic shift implies changes in actual speech deserves a separate discussion.

23. For the sake of brevity I am oversimplifying. I urge the interested reader to consult Karltunen's and Lockhart's works directly.

24. From this point forward, unless otherwise indicated, "How to Live on Earth" refers to the first version, which forms the basis of the English translation included in this volume.

25. Those relatively few Nahuas living primarily among Spaniards at a very early time— the live-in Nahua pupils of the friars and full-time servants of Spaniards—surely recognized, and were using, *Dios* even before the appearance of alphabetical Nahuatl texts in the late 1530s.

26. See f. 52r and p. 13, respectively. My impression is that the use of *Jesús* gradually increases from the sixteenth to the eighteenth centuries.

27. For the circa 1700 period, I am thinking of the sorts of annals of which a representative sample can be found in Karttunen and Lockhart 1976, 114–15. Alternatively, Burkhart suggests (personal communication dated January 17, 2001) that perhaps this is an attempt to make Herod appear "ethnically Spanish in contrast to the Nahua (and so culturally superior) Magi." She adds that the author "may have imitated insults he heard Spaniards using, or asked a Spaniard to suggest appropriate terms." This may well be on the mark.

28. If written according to some colonial and current conventions, it would thus read (minus diacritics to indicate vowel length) *pexohtli*.

29. Regarding this and other very early loans with the absolutive suffix, consult Karttunen and Lockhart 1976, 21–22; Lockhart 1992, 295, 565n.82; and Sell 1993, 75–76. This and similar letter substitutions that correspond to actual Nahuatl speech provide another indication that native speakers wrote, copied, and rearranged the plays.

30. It would not be entirely correct to add that there were no late colonial attempts at writing down at least elements of early colonial *huehuetlatolli*. The well-read Jesuit *nahuatlato* Father Ignacio de Paredes admired it. He tried to use bits and pieces of it in the four publications that appeared under his name in 1758 and 1759.

31. Mendieta 1988, 558. Wayne Ruwet of the UCLA Library System first alerted me to this source. This translation differs somewhat from that in Sell 1993, 118.

32. See Sell 1993, 39–56, for the important role that literate Nahuas played in producing manuscripts and publications that rarely acknowledged their assistance.

33. Carochi also borrowed from the *Florentine Codex* in his grammar of 1645 (see Carochi 1983, 124v). The two parallel passages are compared side by side in Sell 1993, 45.

34. See Burkhart's notes in the translation of "Three Kings," ff. 17r–v, 19r–20r.

35. See ff. 17r–v and the facing translation of "The Three Kings" in this volume. Small changes were made here to fit the context.

36. The sermonary of 1606 by Bautista and de la Fuente included large chunks of Sahagún's 1548 sermonary (originally written in 1540). Their *huehuetlatolli* publication was based largely on the late 1540s work of the Franciscan *nahuatlato* fray Andrés de Olmos. In both cases, the team of Bautista and de la Fuente published texts that were first written fifty or more years before the publications appeared. Perhaps portions of some of the plays go back as far, although how to prove this remains a difficult task in the absence of relevant new primary sources.

37. For those not familiar with the specialized literature on the altepetl, a good beginning would be the relevant chapters and sections of Lockhart 1991, 1992, 1999.

38. The term itself appears once in "The Sacrifice of Isaac" and "The Merchant," twice in "The Life of Don Sebastián," and fifteen times (plus two unspoken) in "The Three Kings."

39. Every time *reyes* is used, it is paired with *tlatoque* (four times in spoken dialogue, three times in unspoken sections) and bears the Nahuatl pluralizing suffix *-me*. The Nahuatl term

always comes first. During the early colonial period, such a pair was probably interpreted by the average Nahua listener as "*tlatoque,* [what Spanish-speaking people would call] *reyes.*"

40. The seemingly endless campaigns against idolatry, along with the manuscripts and books written to aid priests in those efforts, attest to the survival of non-Christian beliefs and practices. See Sell and Schwaller 1999 for a recent critical edition of one such work.

41. A point well made by Lockhart: "Since the routine of daily life consists of an almost infinite number of discrete small actions and strategies, its elements must have seemed individually too insignificant (as well as too obvious or presupposed) to deserve space on the written page. . . . Nahuatl writing is never merely discursive but always for a specific purpose; in mundane Nahuatl documentation, that purpose is generally to claim or protect rights or possessions that might be legally challenged. In the sphere of marketplace activity, the crafts, and the production, sale, and consumption of agricultural commodities, challenges apparently did not reach the level of legal action within the altepetl framework" (1992, 176).

42. Intent to borrow is mentioned in the Tlaxcalan *Actas* (*cabildo* minutes), to be discussed later.

43. This is true of Juan Fabián's testament (Anderson et al. 1976, 58–63) and that of another Nahua merchant, Luis Tlauhpotonqui (in transcription and translation in Cline and León-Portilla 1984, 134–43).

44. This is standard fare in confessional manuals directed toward Nahuas. For an earlier example, see Molina 1984, 25v.

45. The Nahuatl reads: "¶ Cuix otiquimmahuiztili yn veuetque, yn ilamatque: acaçomo tle ypan tiquimittac, acaçomo mitztlaocoltia, yn intlayhiyohuiliz, acaçomo tiquimpalehui?" The facing Spanish reads: "¶ Honraste y reuerenciaste a las personas ancianas: o dexaste de tenerles el deuido respecto, no teniendo compassiõ de sus miserias, dexandolos de ayudar?"

46. The third case is in Cline and León-Portilla (1984, 237) and is mentioned below.

47. By "ward heads," she literally means those in charge of the *tlaxilacalli,* or the "tlaxillacalleque" (Cline and León-Portilla 1984).

48. A transcription and translation of this portion of the minutes can be found in Anderson et al. 1976, 118–21.

49. Another large sum, 300 pesos for two chasubles, is the next item of business mentioned.

50. For the latter two topics, Bartolomé de Alva, 1634 (Sell and Schwaller 1999) is one example among many.

51. This is my translation of the Nahuatl. The Nahuatl and facing Spanish read: "¶ Cuix yca tetech titlayxtlapan, cuix noço ytla tictetlacuilti, ynic oc ye cenca miec timacoz?" / "¶ Diste alguna vez algo a logro, o prestaste alguna cosa, para que te la boluiessen con crecida ganancia?"

52. The main text is in Nahuatl with headings and indexes in Spanish. The Nahuatl reads: "Auh in ampuchteca, macamo tetech xitlaixtlapanacā, macamo tetech xitlamieccaquixtican."

53. For some examples, see Molina's small confessional manual of 1565, 15r; Bautista 1599, 32v; and Lorra Baquío 1634, 73r.

DEATH AND THE COLONIAL NAHUA

Louise M. Burkhart

In his study of death in sixteenth-century Spain, Carlos Eire writes: "[D]eath was the unique moment, common to all, when the church could make the ultimate claim over each individual and over society as a whole; it was arguably the consummate Catholic experience, the ultimate expression of a society's beliefs, and also the ultimate opportunity for shaping and controlling a society's behavior" (1995, 5). Pious Spaniards sought not only to live good lives but to die good deaths. They were in the latter endeavor aided by a plethora of guidebooks as well as such exemplary models as Philip II and Teresa de Ávila (Eire 1995). Preconquest Mexicans held very different beliefs about the dissolution of the self at death and the dispersal of its components, which included multiple animating essences. Becoming colonial and becoming Christian demanded considerable accommodations in the views and practices associated with death, including adjustments to the mass deaths brought about by Old World infectious diseases.

The Church's intrusion into the emotional experience of bereavement and the social realignment brought about by the loss of a family and community member can be seen as one strategy for "shaping and controlling" indigenous behavior in ways that furthered the hegemony of Spanish religious and legal institutions. Colonizing death helped to colonize the living as well, although, as with all colonial introductions, Nahuas manipulated the new ways of dying for their own purposes.

The plays "How to Live on Earth," "The Merchant," "Final Judgment," "The Life of Don Sebastián," and "Souls and Testamentary Executors" all focus on human moral behavior and its punishment or reward. These morality plays, with their graphic representations of the soul's fate, were intended to persuade Nahua audiences to accept and conform to Catholic moral teachings, principally by displaying the frightful posthumous consequences of disobedience. The five plays share a common—and bleak—moral vision, one of human frailty, demonic temptation, angelic despair, and sudden death. Demons bear some of the blame for humanity's dire state, but they, like Death, are subject to divine authority and are only doing their job. The human characters are responsible for their own fates. They repent, too late to save themselves but in time to warn others. The obligation to care for souls in purgatory is a recurring theme, as is the infernal fate of recalcitrant sinners. The five plays can be considered a subgenre of Nahuatl drama, and they may be a remnant of a much larger corpus of morality plays that circulated among colonial Nahua communities.

The purpose of this essay is to situate these five morality plays within a wider universe of discourse on death in the colonial Nahua setting, examining how Christian concepts of death and the afterlife were presented to and by Nahuas in other contexts. To gain some understanding of how Nahua audiences would have received and interpreted these dramas, it may be useful to examine what they were likely already to know about the topics they saw dramatized. Space does not permit a fuller explication of either the European or the indigenous cultural background, but I hope that the material I do present here will enhance readers' understanding of the five dramas.

Souls and Bodies

Teaching about death is one area in which we might expect the contradiction between indigenous monism and Christian dualism to be highlighted. At death, according to Christianity, the human person bifurcated itself into earthly body and immortal, immaterial soul, with the soul proceeding to an immaterial world beyond, its destination depending on the moral condition of the deceased. The sloughed-off earthly coil, despised in Catholic doctrine as an enemy of the soul for its carnal temptations, met its deserved fate in decay. While the fates of preconquest souls were not wholly divorced from the condition of their owners, as some deities chose certain people to join them in their afterworlds, notions of personal moral responsibility, with the promise of heavenly reward for good deeds and the threat of damnation for bad, were colonial introductions, difficult for priests to inculcate (Burkhart 1989). Souls did not belong to another world but were part of this world, manifested in visible, natural phenomena (Furst 1995).

The soul that most closely corresponded to the Christian notion was the *-yolia*, a life force housed in and closely associated with the heart *(yollotl)*, which was the seat of various cognitive as well as emotional processes (López Austin 1984, 1:207, 252–57).[1] The *-yolia* was considered a shadowy double of the person, though it could also manifest itself as a bird or a butterfly, as a stone, and as breath (Furst 1995). This was the one soul that retained an individual identity after death and also passed on to an afterworld, usually the shadowy *mictlan,* or underworld "place of the dead." Furst suggests that a pallid bird- or butterfly-shaped pattern that forms on the upper back of a corpse when the blood settles into the tissues was seen as a physical manifestation of the *-yolia* leaving the body (1995, 40–41). But the *-yolia* did not necessarily depart immediately or completely. In burials it was represented by a stone that was interred with the body or remains and that lent animating force to the bones (Furst 1995, 54, 59–61).

Friars introduced their own concept of the soul (Spanish *ánima,* Latin *anima*) by linking their word with *-yolia;* in colonial Nahuatl texts, the terms are used interchangeably and are often paired in a diphrase. While doctrinal texts pay much attention to the moral condition and fate of these essences, delineations of their precise nature and origin are lacking, allowing Nahuas to perpetuate their own beliefs and simply adopt *ánima* as a synonym for *-yolia*. In the texts quoted in this paper, I translate *-yolia* as "spirit" and *ánima* as "soul."

In the dramas, souls in the form of human actors are seen to leave their bodies, walk about, and talk, carrying on the deceased's identity and relationship to the living (speaking, for example, of "my wife" or "my relatives"). The souls of Lorenzo and his wife in "How to Live on Earth" are played by children; the actors playing the souls of several of the corrupt characters are to wear black clothing and/or makeup. It is unlikely that preconquest Nahuas thought of their *-yolia* in quite this way, but beliefs that the *-yolia* retained an individual identity and could appear as a double of the body provided precedents for these portrayals. Immorality, if not explicitly linked with the color black, was associated with dirtiness and bad odors, which the smell of the explosives used in the dramas might invoke. It is possible that Nahuas dressed the children playing the good souls as angels, which fit the *-yolia*'s identification as a bird. And these dramatized souls certainly appear as concrete beings manifested in this world, not as part of any ethereal beyond.

Nahuatl also lacked any term corresponding precisely to "body" (Spanish *cuerpo*, Latin *corpus*). The term usually used in colonial texts is *-nacayo*, or a person's *nacatl*, "meat or flesh," which is what I translate as "body" in the texts quoted below. This term properly referred to the soft tissues of the body, exclusive of the bones. These were the parts that decayed into the earth after death (or were burned away in cremation), leaving the bones, which retained something of the individual's vital forces (López Austin 1984, 1:176–77). The diphrase *in -tlallo in -zoquiyo,* "(one's) earth, (one's) mud," that appears in the dramas can substitute for *-nacayo*; it also suggests putrescible flesh rather than enduring bone. Thus, whereas European Christians considered the body a unit, Nahuas may have continued to make a meaningful distinction between soft tissue and bone. The former returned to the earth, the latter remained.

Bones figure in two of the plays. "How to Live on Earth" makes several references to the "bones and tibias" of the dead, which, for Nahuas, may serve not only as reminders of dead forebears but as manifestations of their ongoing essence. In "The Life of Don Sebastián," the character Death (Miquiztli) plunks the skulls of the dissolute nobleman's parents onto the table before him, a memento mori that was also a confrontation with parental authority. Death appears as a character also in "How to Live on Earth" and "Final Judgment." Probably costumed to look like a skeleton (Lucifer addresses him as "bones" in "The Life of Don Sebastián"), he too embodies the enduring life force of bones.[2] As Christ's constable, Death is a positive—not a fearsome—character in the plays, consistent with a distinction between fleshly decay and osseous vitality. Ideas about bones retaining a vital essence and having regenerative power might have informed native interpretations of the resurrection of the dead, enacted in "Final Judgment."

Preconquest Nahuas associated soul loss not with the *-yolia* but with the *tonalli*, an animating essence located in the head and associated with the sun's heat (López Austin 1984, 1:243–47). Even so, this idea that a soul could leave and return to the body was a precedent for the near-death experiences that colonial Nahuas occasionally reported, in which their spirit temporarily departed into the kind of afterworld presented to them in Christian preaching and dramas. Friars, seeing these reports as evidence of their own success, inscribed some of them in their chronicles. The scenarios vary: Mary, saints, friars coming to console the dying person (Mendieta 1980, 459–60; Dávila Padilla 1955, 146); a quick trip to hell, then to heaven, with instructions to confess in order to come there (Motolinia 1979, 95); black creatures dragging a young man off to a dark place of torments until he calls on Mary for help (Motolinia 1979, 95–96); demons put to flight by an angel (Dávila Padilla 1955, 615–16). One man from a town near Tlaxcala reported that he was brought to judgment, where he saw demons who wanted to take his soul, while angels defended it, until Saint James drove off the demons and the man regained consciousness (Mendieta 1980, 464). A woman of Culiacan, reviving as her body was about to be carried to church, told of appearing at judgment before an angry Christ, who sent her back to warn the people of her province to listen to the word of God and obey it (Mendieta 1980, 465).

In some cases the person's actual death was scheduled in the course of these visions. This is a European motif, seen for example in a Nahuatl narrative, based on a story recorded by Saint Gregory, of a garrulous young girl to whom the Virgin appears with a promise to take her to heaven in a month if she will stop talking so much (*Sermones y santoral en mexicano* n.d., 315r–v; Burkhart 2001). Other Nahuas also predicted their deaths, sometimes first preaching to relatives or neighbors to reform their sinful ways before it was too late for them (Mendieta 1980, 454–57). One young girl of Mexico City, apparently healthy, insisted on confessing to fray Alonso de Escalona, for her guardian angel had told her she would die that day, which she did, after foretelling, accurately, that her sister would die the next day (Mendieta 1980, 456). Such experiences, however much they resemble European models (and in the friars' retelling they may be molded further), suggest an attempt to exert control over the new, Christian representations of death and souls. At the same time, divine figures who tell a person when he or she will die also recall the traditional belief that deities such as the rain gods chose people to join them.

Death in Nahuatl Doctrinal Texts

Priests preaching in Nahuatl placed great emphasis on sin and its punishment, often presenting a simple dichotomy between heavenly reward and infernal torment. The seven mortal sins, the ten commandments of God, and the five commandments of the Church were to be memorized, and confession manuals organized their moral examinations around these lists. Hell is described sometimes in graphic detail, with its fires and its stenches, with its demons who, like Lucifer with his "metal warping frame" in "Final Judgment" and his sword in "The Life of Don Sebastián," torture the damned with assorted metal implements (Burkhart 1989, 54–56). On earth these demons are ever ready to tempt the unwary. The Augustinian fray Juan de la Anunciación warns of how they use food, pulque, women, and other temptations as bait, just like a fisherman uses a worm on a hook to deceive a fish (1577, 43v). When someone thinks about going to church, the demon comes to inspire bad thoughts, telling the person that going to church will serve no purpose and he or she will be hungry, thirsty, and cold (1577, 35v–36r). Demons beset women on their way to church in "The Life of Don Sebastián" and "Souls and Testamentary Executors."

As Lorenzo's wife in "How to Live on Earth" reminds her husband, Ash Wednesday was an occasion when priests encouraged people to contemplate their mortality. On this occasion, the Franciscan ethnographer fray Bernardino de Sahagún explains to his listeners that contemplation of death works like a medicine to keep them from sinning. He urges parents to admonish their children as follows:

> O my precious child, always remember that your life will come to an end, that you will die, and you do not know when, perhaps tomorrow, perhaps the day after. You will not remain here on earth for long. And when you die, if you lived well here on earth, and if you did penance on account of your sins, you will rest, you will rejoice in the home of God. But if you did not live well, if you die in your sins, when you die then your suffering will begin, so that you will suffer forever there in the place of the dead. (Sahagún 1563, 29r)[3]

He goes on to explain how death came to humanity as punishment for the sin of Adam and Eve. Later in the sermon, incorporating the day's biblical text from Genesis 3:19, Sahagún explains that the purpose of the ashes is "so that you will remember your being judged, your being sentenced, your death, for your mother Holy Church says to you, 'You person, you who are my child, may you remember that you are dust, and you will become dust again'" (29v). Everyone is made of earth, and all must humble themselves and do penance. The listeners are told that they should not love their bodies, for they are just earth, the food of worms; instead they should care for their souls (30r).

Fray Juan de la Anunciación, in his Ash Wednesday sermons, urges people to do penance during Lent; the ashes are to remind them that they themselves are earth and mud. Even one who is high-ranking and noble will become earth at death and should consign his or her body to the earth, for it will become the food of worms. The soul is what should be treasured, for it is not ash and earth but the image of God (1577, 39v). The Franciscan fray Alonso de Escalona, on the same occasion, tells sinners that God is angry at them because of their sins. They must turn toward God so that he will save their spirits *(-yolia)* from his judgment *(itetlatzontequililiz)* (n.d., 156v). As long as they are still alive, the demon cannot take them, and they still have a chance to turn their lives around and do penance for their sins. We should judge ourselves on earth so that we are not judged when we die, for sinners who do not save themselves from God's judgment while they still live on earth are sentenced to the fires of *mictlan* (Escalona n.d., 157v, 158v).

The souls of saints were sometimes observed to proceed directly to heaven, as do the souls of Saints Francis and Martin of Tours in Sahagún's *Psalmodia christiana* (1993b, 308–9, 334–35). But ordinary Nahuas virtuous enough to escape damnation could not expect so immediate a reward. A sojourn in purgatory was their more likely fate. To this place, as the mestizo priest don Bartolomé de Alva succinctly states:

> go the souls of those baptized Christians who did not provide satisfaction here on earth [with] their penance, for they are still to bring it to a conclusion. God gives them a penance of fire, there to quickly prepare and purify themselves during the time He has set down for them. (Sell and Schwaller 1999, 87)[4]

Mural painting of purgatory from the open chapel of the Augustinian establishment at Actopan, Hidalgo. Souls languish in the flames, while a fortunate few depart with the assistance of angels. Photograph by Louise M. Burkhart.

Visual representations of purgatory seemingly were rare in colonial Mexico, but an example from the open chapel at Actopan, Hidalgo, shows the souls in flames. Ladders lead up from the flames, along which angels convey souls fortunate enough to have earned their release.

In his sermon on the Passion of Christ, Sahagún provides a more detailed exposition on the soul's fate after death. In Christ's case, the demon was waiting to carry off his soul, thinking that Christ was only a man, not a deity. But when Christ's soul emerged, his divine nature was visible, and the demon realized who he was and became frightened. Christ then seized him and chained him up in his home in the place of the dead (Sahagún 1563, 51r–v). This differs from an ordinary person's experience:

> All of us, when our soul emerges, the demon is waiting for it. And our soul, when it sees him, is very frightened, very scared, because the demon is very frightening, very scary. But our lord there comforts and strengthens his precious ones, his friends. And when our soul has emerged then it is taken before the Justice (*Justicia*) of God, in order to be accused, in order to be judged. And as for the Justice of God, it is very frightening. There is absolutely nothing like it. It overlooks absolutely nothing, even if it is just a little sin, called venial. It arranges the punishment of everything. Thus our soul is very frightened and scared when it is taken before the Justice of God. (51v)

A specific punishment is ordained for each particular sin, great or small. But then Jesus Christ speaks on behalf of his followers, saying: "'My suffering, which I endured, I assign to them, in order that they be rescued from the Justice of God. If it is necessary that they be flogged, that they be slapped in the face, on account of their sins, I myself was flogged, I was slapped in the face.' The suffering of our lord becomes the payment for his friends, his precious ones." (51v) When someone dies who has confessed a mortal sin but has not completed the assigned penances, he or she must go to purgatory:

> On account of each mortal sin he or she will do penance for seven years. Such is the command that the Justice of God established. On account of all of his or her sins, perhaps it will be 400[5] years. But to the Holy Church, by God's order, belongs Indulgence. Indulgence derives from the Passion, the suffering of our lord, which is the foundation stone of the Holy Church. Thus he or she will not go to purgatory. Thus it is evident how greatly he helps people, he consoles people with his Passion, with his death. So it is necessary that we be very grateful, and that we remember it every day. (52r)

This Passion-oriented account presents Christ as the principal intercessor on behalf of the dead, before an impersonalized "Justice." People are obliged to carry out penances in purgatory, but the text notes how indulgences can lessen one's term there.

However, it was Mary rather than Christ who was most often represented as the sinner's advocate, beseeching a judgmental Christ to have mercy on people's souls. The Tridentine reformed breviary of 1568 codified her role in the drama of death by standardizing the last line of the Hail Mary prayer as "pray for us sinners now and at the hour of our death" (Graef 1963–1965, 1:230–31). This was rendered into Nahuatl in different ways, including "may you speak for us sinners now and when our life on earth is about to end" (Anunciación 1575, 232–33) and "we sinners beseech you, may you speak for us before God now and when we are on the verge of death" (Sahagún 1993b, 24–25). She appears in this intercessory role on behalf of the dead in "How to Live on Earth," "The Life of Don Sebastián," and "Souls and Testamentary Executors." In "How to Live on Earth," it is to Mary that Lorenzo and his wife direct their prayers on behalf of the dead, prayers that may be understood to be rosaries, as later in the play Christ describes these good dead as people who pleased him by praying the rosary.

The anonymous Dominican *doctrina* of 1548, in a sermon on souls, describes the four sections of *mictlan* as being like huge houses (*yn iuhqui cenca ueuei calli*). These are the inferno of the damned (represented as a house in "The Life of Don Sebastián" and "Souls and Testamentary Executors"), the limbo of unbaptized children, purgatory, and the now-vacant limbo of the Holy Fathers (*Doctrina* 1944, 120r–22r). The third "house" is described as follows:

> There go those who sinned on earth, who did not keep the commands of God, but because of their sins they were very sad, they wept very much, and they confessed their sins before the heart-straightener.[6] Or perhaps they did not confess because it was not possible, but they wanted very much to straighten their hearts. Or they did not complete their penances here on earth. Therefore they go there to purgatory. Our great ruler, God, casts them there in order that there they complete what they did not do on earth on account of their sins. (121r)

In purgatory these souls must endure great suffering, but people on earth can help them by performing works of mercy, by fasting, and by praying for them.

> And the thing that is most helpful is the mass, when mass is said for them, perhaps one, or perhaps two, or perhaps many of the masses that are said for the souls in purgatory. The reason why it is a very great prayer, the mass is quite surpassing, is because our precious rescuer, Jesus Christ, who is truly God and truly man, is there when mass is said. And when we help the dead we will act prudently, for first we will help our fathers, or perhaps our mothers or perhaps our children, our wives, our grandfathers, or perhaps our relatives, our uncles, our aunts, or perhaps our friends and others who were baptized here on earth. (121v–122r)

However, one should not waste one's effort trying to help those who were never baptized, for they cannot be saved (122r).

This passage neatly summarizes the needs of the dead and the obligations of the living, an important theme in "How to Live on Earth" and "Souls and Testamentary Executors." The idea that it is useless to pray for the damned appears also in a miracle narrative in which an abbess who has been praying for the soul of her niece, a nun, is taken by Mary on a tour of hell. She sees her niece's soul being tortured in hell because of failure to confess a sexual sin; the aunt then prays for her no more (*Doctrina* n.d., 22v–24r; Burkhart 1999, 99–100).

Service to the dead was also taught through the fourteen works of mercy, comprising seven corporal and seven spiritual acts, which some Nahuatl catechisms list. The seventh corporal work of mercy is to bury the dead, an act the two good youths in "How to Live on Earth" perform for Lorenzo and his wife. Fray Juan de la Anunciación (1575, 204) describes this as an obligation not only to bury the dead but to join any funeral procession one sees and pray for the deceased's soul. One must not perform any old-time, non-Christian acts on the grave. The friar then declares that death is with everyone and draws one toward the tomb every day. Some live a long time and some do not, but everyone's life will end. Death "is not some omen, or something that is seen in a dream, nor is it something alive, nor is it like you see it painted, and it is not a cranium, a skull; death is with each person" (205). Friars considered the introduction of Christian burial rites a fundamental aspect of evangelization, as fray Diego Valadés suggested by placing a funeral procession in his idealized depiction of the Franciscan mission.

The seventh spiritual work of mercy, though it could be simply stated as an obligation to pray for everyone (*Códice franciscano* 1941, 45), more often was elaborated to encourage prayers for the dead (Anunciación 1565, 38v; Anunciación 1575, 207; and 1577, 263v). Fray Pedro de Gante's 1553 *doctrina* states that, even more than for the living, we should pray for the dead, whose souls God placed in purgatory, so that God will have mercy on them and take them up to heaven (Gante 1981, 63r). In the Dominican *doctrina*, Nahuas are told to help living people to know and serve God, but also to help the dead. Purgatory is here described as a prison and a place of suffering greater than that caused by syphilis, leprosy, or any other sickness on earth. Fires here on earth are like painted pictures compared to the fire of purgatory. The

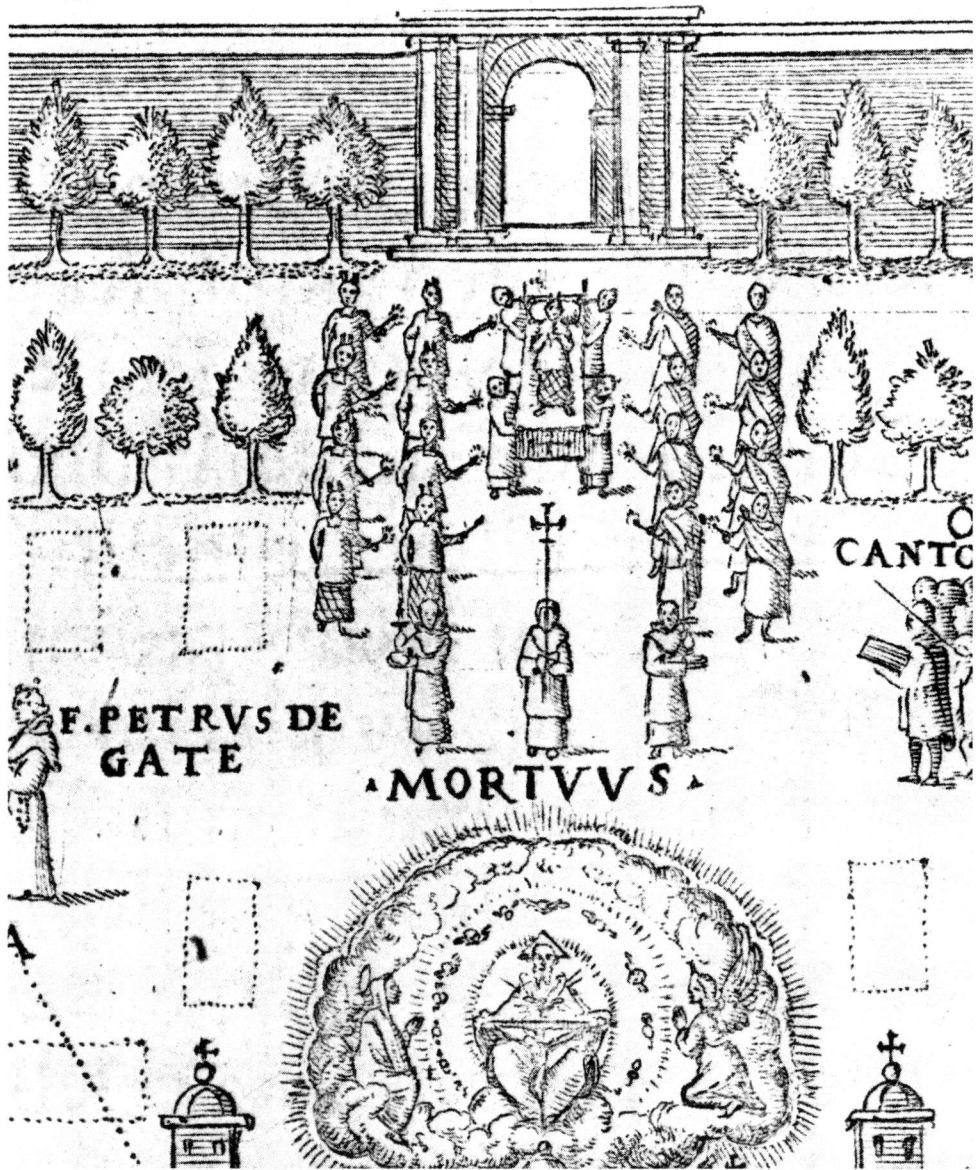

Detail from an engraving by fray Diego Valadés showing Franciscans and native Mexicans within an idealized church *atrio*. Here, a funeral procession enters the churchyard. Courtesy of the John Carter Brown Library at Brown University.

passage ends, "Therefore, oh my precious children, may you help the dead so that you may be helped" (*Doctrina* 1944, 118v–19v).

Fray Juan de la Anunciación (1575, 207–8) explains that, in regard to the dead, one should pray only for those who died in baptism and good deeds of the faith, whose souls may be doing penance in purgatory for their sins. One should not pray for innocent baptized children or for saints, for they are already in heaven. "Likewise," he adds, "one must not pray to our lord God for the people of long ago, the idolaters, who were your ancestors, who died in their blindness. They were not baptized, nor did they know the faith of our lord God. They went straight to the place of the dead, to make their homes there forever" (208–9). Unbaptized children cannot be released from the darkness of limbo (209). He then explains that purgatory is a place of torment where go the souls of believing Christians who did not do all the necessary penance for their sins. Purgatory means "the soul's place of complete purification" (*ycenquizcachipahualoyan yn anima*), where souls are purified so they can go to heaven. The souls in that fiery place can be helped through various good deeds, prayers, offerings, masses, and works of mercy, which diminish the suffering and help the souls get to heaven (209–10).

Friars sought to extend to Nahuas the benefits of papal jubilees—plenary indulgences occasionally granted to anyone who performed a specified series of devotional acts, including fasts, prayers, alms, confession, and taking communion. These eliminated whatever debt of time in purgatory the person had accrued up to then. In his *confessionario mayor*, fray Alonso de Molina provides two sets of instructions for attaining these plenary indulgences (1984, 95v–98r). Fray Juan de la Anunciación (1575, 148–52) provides one set, preceded by an explanatory discourse on purgatory. Here the friar notes that no one knows how much time he or she will have to spend in purgatory. In order that one may escape it entirely, the Church keeps "what in a sacred way is a very great treasure, a benefit for people, which is the suffering and merits of our lord Jesus Christ, which he earned as a human man, also the penances of the Saints. It is the privilege and boon of the Holy Father to assign and grant these to people" (150). Whenever he does so, by carrying out all the pope's commands one can gain full remission of punishment for all sins that have been absolved in confession.

The Franciscan fray Juan Bautista Viseo, in collaboration with the Nahua scholar Agustín de la Fuente and probably other Nahuas as well, produced a Nahuatl version of the *contemptus mundi* as well as a work entitled "Book of the Misery and Brevity of the Life of Man." The latter was published in 1604; the former survives, with eighteenth-century annotations by the Franciscan fray Agustín Vetancurt, in the John Carter Brown Library. As such esoteric works of otherworldly contemplation would have found a more limited audience than the sermons and catechisms cited above, I restrict my comments to a few observations on the published volume.

Its five treatises guide the reader on a contemplative journey through the miseries of human life, death, the final judgment, the torments of hell, and eternal happiness in paradise. The treatise on death emphasizes the frightening nature of death, the tomb, the dead body, and all that happens to the dying and dead person. By contemplating death one may gain the wisdom to govern one's life, the resolve to abandon sin, and the foresight to prepare for a good death (*inic qualli yectli ipan micohuaz*, "so that one will die in the good, the proper" [Bautista 1604, 38v–45r]). Just as soldiers drill for battle, so should we examine the pathways we will follow in death, "for no one can see death, and the road that is followed is very dark, quite dangerous, quite rocky, as we all know, and full of destruction and danger. One who falls will not be able to rise again, but will go falling into the abyss, the place of the dead, Hell" (44v). When the soul comes out from the body, it follows an unknown road to a new land, beset by frightening things and the shadow of death, dependent for help on its guardian angel, threatened by wild beasts (70r–v). Even more frightening is the judgment it will undergo, in the presence of judge, accusers, and defenders, as each deed is recounted and the sentence is pronounced (70v–72r). How will it be, the text asks, if you are condemned forever? You will know great pain and suffering. "But how your enemies will rejoice, will delight, will consider it a festival, will celebrate a festival. They will really gloat over you, they will laugh at you" (72r).

Texts on the Final Judgment

The Final Judgment drama presents another afterlife scenario, enacting what happens when Christ returns, the dead come back to life, and people are consigned to their permanent destinations. Christ's return as judge was proclaimed in the seventh Article of Faith pertaining to Christ's humanity, *Inde venturus est judicare vivos et mortuos* (whence [from heaven] he will come to judge the living and the dead). Nahuas would have learned of the final judgment principally from explanations of this article, which was part of the basic catechism. It was also the subject of a number of Indo-Christian artistic works—in both relief sculpture, as on a *posa* chapel at San Andrés Calpan, Puebla, and mural painting, as in the large open chapel at Actopan, Hidalgo.

The 1548 Dominican *doctrina* (*Doctrina* 1944, 126v–28r), explaining the seventh article of faith, describes how at the end of the world everyone will die but will then come back to life in the bodies that they have now. Everyone will gather in the Valley of Jehosaphat, near Jerusalem, to be judged.[7] Jesus Christ will come down in his human form to judge the good and the bad. "And he will interrogate each one, and he will inquire as to what they did, and what they said, and what they thought, what they coveted, and what they neglected through laziness while they still lived here on earth" (127r). He will start with the popes and work his way down through the ecclesiastical hierarchy, then the rulers and lords and their wives, those who are indigenous people (*nican tlaca*, "people here") and Spaniards and people from everywhere in the world, and then the common people from all over the world. All the sins everyone did—and all the good things everyone did—will be revealed. He will take the good people to his royal home in heaven, body and soul, and the bad ones he will cast into the place of the dead, or hell, body and soul.

Gante's 1553 *doctrina* (1981, 30r–32v) tells how Christ will give all people what they deserve, in accordance with their deeds, although here he does not interrogate them. The people will be divided into four groups, two to be damned and two to be saved:

> The first ones to be judged are those who just took the faith in vain, who just believed in our lord God in vain, who did not carry out with their lives what they said, "I believe in our lord Jesus Christ, who is our precious rescuer, our deity, our ruler." And even though they said this with their mouths they did not live according to his sacred commands, they were like bad Christians. Even though sometimes they did good things, they died in mortal sin. The way they will be judged is that they will be scorned, they will be cast into the place of the dead. The second ones who will be judged are the true Christians, who lived according to what is good and proper, who worried about their sins, who died in penance and penitence. They will be judged with compassion, they will be rescued, they will be given eternal happiness in heaven.

Native artist's relief sculpture on one of the *posa* chapels at the Franciscan establishment of San Andrés Calpan, Puebla. Christ sits in judgment, flowers to his right and sword to his left, flanked by angels and attended by Mary and John the Baptist. The dead rise from their graves. Photograph by Louise M. Burkhart.

The third group contains those hopeless cases who never even believed in Christ, while those in the fourth group are so good that they will judge others rather than being judged themselves. To these privileged souls Jesus Christ said, "You will place yourselves with me on twelve golden thrones so that you also will judge the people of Israel."[8] Christ will invite the two good groups to take the eternal happiness that has been waiting for them since the world began. But to the accursed he will say:

> "You accursed ones, you never believed in me, and you did not serve me. And you died in your sins, your wickedness. Go, so that you will never see me. Get away from me, you accursed ones. You will be tied up forever there in the fiery oven, in the middle of the fire. You will never rest. May you fully take your utter suffering, your burning, which will never ever come to an end. You will never be able to escape. You will always remain shut up there with the demons whom you served, whom you obeyed. May you suffer with them. Suffering is waiting for you there."

Detail from a mural painting of the Final Judgment in the open chapel at Actopan, Hidalgo. While an angel blows a trumpet, dead people rise from their graves. In the foreground, one is accosted by a demon while an angel attends another. Photograph by Louise M. Burkhart.

Then the earth will stretch open its mouth and swallow up the damned with the demons.[9] Christ will lead the saved ones to heaven, accompanied by music and song.

In his 1575 *doctrina* (54–66), fray Juan de la Anunciación describes how God will come to examine *(quimmotlatemoliliquiuh)* all people about what they said, did, thought, and desired in regard to the sacred commands, rewarding those who kept his commands and punishing those who did not. He distinguishes between the individual judgment *(tetlatzōtequililiztli yn tetech pouhtica)* that everyone undergoes when his or her soul has departed and the final, universal judgment *(tecentzonquizcatlatzon tequililiztli)*, when all people will die and be judged in front of one another. All will be assembled and Christ will descend from heaven to the place of judgment, up in the air. He will have the angels place the good on his right hand and the bad on his left.[10] To the good he will explain how all the kind acts they performed for the poor, sick, or hungry were also done for him. He will escort them to heaven; a description of its delights follows. Then he will return to harangue the bad, with specific reference to works of mercy that they failed to perform:

> How wretched you are! You have failed, you have cursed yourselves, you have destroyed yourselves with sin. Listen to your blind deeds. Truly you joyfully

pursued earthliness, and you obeyed your bodies, you did anything that demanded you to sin, you served the worthless demons. And you did not keep my commands for me, nor did you obey my admonitions. I went about among you naked, but you did not clothe me with pity, and I went about starving, but you did not feed[11] me with pity, you did not give me water with pity, and I was sick, I was imprisoned, but you did not visit me with pity, so my heart did not rest through your consolation, and when I was a vagabond you did not house me with pity. (60–61)

A similar reproach appears in "The Life of Don Sebastián." Then Christ will consign them to hell. The earth will break open in their midst and they will roll down, bumping from crag to crag, until they reach their fiery home in the place of the dead. A description of hell completes the exposition of the article.

The same fray Juan de la Anunciación presents a slightly different account in the catechism appended to his 1577 *Sermonario* (238v–39v). He tells how a great fire will purify the earth. Then (as in Luke 21:25–26) the sun will go dark, the moon will cease to shine, the stars will fall from the sky, and the people will fall into great dismay. By the power of God all will revive to be judged. Those who had good lives will be pure and will outshine the sun; the bad will be frightful and blacker than the night. Even though each of us is judged individually when we die, unwitnessed by other people, this judgment will be done publicly. But rather than describing an interrogation, this friar says "our lord God will create, will make, a light, which very quickly will reveal everything that each person thought, everything he or she said, everything he or she did, all the time that he or she lived." Then Christ will judge everyone, giving rulership in heaven to the good people who had pity on the poor and kept his commands. The bad will be cast into the place of the dead to burn forever in the fires.

Churchgoers also heard priests sermonizing about the end of the world on the first Sunday in Advent, for which the Gospel text was a passage in Luke (21:25) where Jesus speaks of the signs in the heavens and turbulence on earth that will precede the coming of the Son of Man in glory and the redemption. Sahagún, in his sermon for this week, tells how the people will revive and be divided, the good at Christ's right hand and the bad at his left. He will invite the good ones to take their kingdom and they will enter heaven. The bad ones he will consign to the flames of the place of the dead (Sahagún 1563, 1v). Fray Juan de la Anunciación describes the destruction of the world in considerable detail, then the individual sinner's frightening experiences: the gaping mouth of hell will be trying to suck you in, demons will prepare to throw you down into the fire, you will see all your sins and bad deeds threatening you and accusing you before God. No one will be able to help you, nor will you be able to hide: you will have to stand by yourself before God. Anunciación then urges his listeners to look ahead and prepare themselves for judgment (1577, 3v–4r).

Fray Juan Bautista and his Nahua collaborators wrote three sermons on this gospel text (Bautista 1606, 121–248). The first two deal with the signs of the end of the world, while the third recounts in detail, with many parables and biblical references, the coming of Christ as judge and the final judgment. The sermon compares the last judgment to a court trial on earth, with judge, accused, accusers, witnesses, and a place for the trial to occur. Fortunately for humanity, the judge will be Christ, who will be merciful. All people will come back to life, even if they died very long ago, and all their good and bad deeds will be manifested. No one will be able to hide from the judge. Accusers and witnesses will include each person's own conscience (*ineyoliximachiliz*, "knowledge of one's heart"), all of God's creations, everyone's own sins, and Lucifer and the other demons. The good will be placed at Christ's right hand and he will call them to take possession of the kingdom of heaven. The bad will go to his left, and in anger he will consign them to the fires of *mictlan*. The torments of hell are detailed, including the demons' delight in causing their prisoners to suffer in the stinking, black, and dirty fires. It will be the angels who carry out Christ's judgment, and even the Virgin Mary will be unable to intercede on behalf of the condemned. The end of the sermon stresses that knowledge of this final reckoning leads prudent people to avoid sin.

Bautista also devoted the third treatise of his contemplative work "Book of the Misery and Brevity of the Life of Man" to the final judgment (1604, 72v–102v). The treatise has four chapters. The first focuses on the frightful nature of the judgment, the second (like the first two sermons in his 1606 book) on the signs that the day is coming, the third on the destruction of the world and the resurrection of the dead, and the fourth on the coming of the judge and the judgment itself, with its accusers and witnesses.

Nahuatl Wills

Separation of the self into spirit and flesh was emphasized when people dictated their last will and testament. This activity, highlighted in "Souls and Testamentary Executors" and "The Merchant," was considered an essential component of a good death. Colonial Nahuas' participation in this custom resulted in a large corpus of documents, which is enormously important for reconstructing many facets of colonial Nahua social and economic life (Cline 1986; Cline and León-Portilla 1984; Horn 1998; Kellogg 1998; Lockhart 1992; Wood 1991, 1998). Perhaps as much as or even more than formal preaching, will-making familiarized Nahuas with Catholic practices and discourse related to death. Friars provided model wills in Nahuatl, such as the published examples offered by the Franciscan fray Alonso de Molina in his *confessionario mayor*, first published in 1565 (Molina 1984; see Cline 1998) and the Dominican fray Martín de León in his 1611 *Camino del cielo* (1611); native notaries mastered the proper formulas for recording them. As statements of faith, wills are somewhat problematic: notaries tended to write down similar standardized pious formulas that may not correspond to actual declarations by the dying person, and elaborate invocations may index elite display rather than intense indoctrination (Cline 1998, 24–25; Lockhart 1992, 251–54). However, more personal statements do appear, and even the most formulaic wills indicate that people were conversant with the concepts and considered their inscription appropriate and necessary.

Testamentary statements related to beliefs about death fall mainly into two categories: the encommendation (Eire 1995, 36), in which testators' consign their souls to God and their bodies to burial; and a subsequent statement, in which they bequeath money or goods to pay for masses for their souls in purgatory. Some also make arrangements for their funerals. The basic formula for the encommendation imposes a dualist division between soul (called *-yolia, ánima,* or frequently both) and body (*-nacayo,* "flesh," or the "earth, mud" diphrase) as the components of the human self relevant in the context of death. Fray Alonso de Molina's model testament suggests the following wording for this part:

> First of all, I place my soul in the hands of our lord God, for he made it, and I beseech him to have compassion for me, to pardon my sins for me, to take me to his home in heaven (when my soul has left my body). And my body I consign to the earth for thence it came. It is earth, it is mud. And I want only a mantle with which it will be wrapped in order to be buried. And I want it to be buried there in our church of Saint Anthony of Padua, where the priest will indicate for me my sepulcher, my tomb, my burial place (Molina 1984, 61v; Cline 1998, 28).

Fray Martín de León's model proposes the following:

> Now first of all I leave my soul in the hands of our lord Jesus Christ, because he made it, he rescued it with his precious blood, with his death on the holy cross. And my trunk,[12] my body, I consign to the earth, because thence it came, of it it was made. I also command that when God wants me to die, my earthly body will be buried there in the church-home of God, in the home of Saint N. here in the altepetl N. wherever my priest will bury me, in my burial place. And so that I will be buried there I make an offering of N. peso(s). (1611, 139v)

Most Nahuatl wills will have some statement analogous to these. Some samples will indicate the range of variation.[13] One of the earliest Nahuatl wills yet published is that of Mexico City's María Tiacapan, from 1561, who stated, "And I say that my deity, my ruler made my soul and I go place it in his hands and I say that all my children, you who are here beside me, I order you not to forget me. May you always pray to our lord on behalf of my soul" (Reyes García et al. 1996, 282). The 1566 will of don Julián de la Rosa, a Tlaxcalan nobleman, gives a more formulaic statement:

> First I entrust my soul to God, the all-powerful, who created it, who rescued it with his precious blood. And my body I give to the earth because thence it came. If this is a sickness from which my body will die, I want to be buried there in the church of Saint Mary in Tlaxcala, in front of the crucifix. (Anderson et al. 1976, 44–45)

Martín Jacobo's 1577 will from Mexico City states, after the customary invocation of the Trinity:

> The first of my words that I say is that if I die I place my spirit, my soul, entirely in his hands. May he take it for it is his creation, it is his rescued thing. May he carry it to his home in heaven. And my body is earth, is the food of worms. And when I have died I will be buried here in [the church of] Saint Mary in the barrio of Quauhtepec. (Reyes García et al. 1996, 170)

This statement by Miguel Chimaltecuhtli, from 1580, is typical of the corpus of sixty-five wills from Culhuacan:

> First I say that I give my spirit, my soul, to our lord God because he made it and he came to rescue it with his blood here on earth. And my body I give to the earth because thence it came. And when my soul has come out my body will go to be buried at our church of Saint John the Evangelist. (Cline and León-Portilla 1984, 46–47)

However, fellow Culhuacan resident Juana Tiacapan, also dying in 1580, did not distinguish her spiritual from her physical fate: "When I die, may our lord God carry me to himself, because he is the rescue of my soul, it is his image. And may my angel, my guardian, carry me before God" (Cline and León-Portilla 1984, 66–67).

In 1596 Juana Mocel of Mexico City dictated:

> First of all I go place my soul in the hands of our lord God for he made it. And I beseech him to pardon me my sins with which I offended him all the time that I lived here on earth, so that he will come to carry me to his home in heaven when my soul has abandoned my body. (Reyes García et al. 1996, 274)

A will from 1617 gives this statement:

> And now our lord God has placed his justice (*justicia*) upon me. My name is Juan Fabián, my home is here in San Bartolomé Atenco, still of my own will I establish my testament, since my earth, my mud has grown old. I am just waiting for the word of my precious father, God, when he will pass judgment on me, so that I will leave the earth. If our lord God destroys me I place my spirit, my soul, in his hands because it is his rescued thing, he rescued it. And my earth, my mud belongs to the earth because thence it came, for I will become earth and mud. May our lord God just take my spirit, my soul, for I give it entirely to him. (Anderson et al. 1976, 58–59)

Justina Xochicuetzin, a Tlaxcalan colonist in San Esteban de la Nueva Tlaxcala (now in Coahuila), planned this death in 1627:

> First of all I place my soul in the hands of our lord God and I beseech him to have compassion for me, to pardon me for my sins. May he take me before him in heaven when my soul has abandoned my body and I beseech the eternally maiden Saint Mary to speak for me before her precious child when I am on the verge of death, also Saint Peter, Saint Paul, and Saint Francis, so that they will speak for me before God. And my body I consign to the earth for thence it came, it is earth, it is mud, and I want just a mantle with which it will be wrapped in order to be buried. Where I used to sit [in church?], there my body will be buried. (Offutt 1992, 426–27)

Don Agustín Miguel, from San Bartolomé Capuluac in the Toluca Valley, shows even more concern for his soul in his will, dictated sometime after 1634. He prays that he may happily receive what God has sent him, "your scorpion, your nettle," that is, his illness. He continues:

> I place my spirit, my soul, entirely in his hands. May he receive it happily, for I am a sinner, I have offended him with many things, I am a great, 400-times sinner, which they (devils? angels?) will remember about me. So that he will love me, truly I will repay God's death. Now it is time, now it is the moment that my accounting *(notlapoal)* arrives, by which I will go to give an account *(cuetan)* to God. As for my earthly body, at the feet of my precious father Holy Saint Bartholomew I will be buried. (Wood 1998, 104–5)

In 1661 Agustina Juana of Coyoacan declared:

> God has placed his justice *(justicia)* upon me, a sickness. My earth, my mud is quite heavy, but there is nothing wrong with my soul. If my ruler, God, wants me, I place entirely in his hands my spirit, my soul, since it is his creation, his rescued thing. . . . When I have died I will be buried at the foot of my precious father Saint John the Baptist [the main Coyoacan church]. I will be buried there in front of Our Lady of the Transit. (Horn 1998, 78)

As late as 1776, Nahuas such as don Felix Martín Ramos of San Esteban produced wills with similar formulas:

> This is first of all, that I leave my soul in the hands of our lord God, since it is his creation and through [his] death he rescued it on the holy cross. And my earthly body I consign to the earth for from it it was made. I also declare that when God wants me to die I request that my earthly body be buried in the church-home of our lord God Saint San Francisco, in front of the altar of our precious and honored mother of the Conception, wherever there will be a place. (Offutt 1992, 438–39)

Many Nahua testators refer to their soul by the Nahuatl as well as the Spanish term. Death is attributed to God. Some see their sickness or death as God's "justice" or judgment upon them; some express concern over sin. Being carried before God, even being judged and having to provide an "accounting" of oneself, are motifs in the morality plays that have also found their way into wills.

In the model wills, the above statements are followed immediately by bequests to help the deceased's soul shorten its stay in purgatory. Molina's model provides for a vigil and one or more masses "for the sake of the helping of my soul," to be said when the body is buried or, if not possible then, the following day (1984, 61v). León's testator, "in regard to the helping of my soul," leaves money for masses, the number to be specified in each case, and for the *teopan tlaca,* or native church attendants. These are to pray three *responsos,* or responses for the dead (chanted during "Souls and Testamentary Executors"), as they take the body to church and also "they will say vigil *(Vigilia)* over me" (1611, 139v). These requests follow Spanish custom under which testators often specified a certain number of pauses or *posas* on the way to church, when the pallbearers could rest and the clergy would intone a response (Eire 1995, 124–25). For the vigil, people gathered around the dead body to pray for a period before burial (Eire 1995, 121).

Nahua testators typically provide for their burial and masses through cash bequests or, more frequently, by ordering that certain property be sold to raise the needed funds. Juana Mocel ordered a house sold and a debt collected, assigning a total of ninety-five pesos to her burial and masses (Reyes García et al. 1996, 275). Other individuals whose wills are quoted above sought to help their souls with cash and the sale of fine clothing, a horse, a donkey, building stone, and crops in the field. María Tiacapan financed no masses but left money for three responses to be said for her in the main Tlatelolco church, encharging district officials present at her deathbed with seeing that this was done; annotations on her will indicate that it was. She also provided candles for all of her grandchildren to carry at her funeral, a shirt and a maguey-fiber shroud for her body, and money for the church singers and other funeral expenses (Reyes García et al. 1996, 282–83). Some testators left money to pay for the tolling of bells; for example, both Juan Fabián and Agustina Juana left money for the bells to be rung at four different churches (Anderson et al. 1976, 58–59; Horn 1998, 78–79). This tolling of bells for the dead appears in "Souls and Testamentary Executors." Martín Jacobo left fifteen pesos to buy masses for his parents and twenty pesos in alms for local churches, but he must have depended on his heirs to finance masses for his own soul (Reyes García et al. 1996, 171).

Such death-related bequests represented a significant transfer of property from indigenous families to the Church. People must have considered the financing of masses for their souls a serious obligation. Although requiem masses might also serve as commemorative rites and a source of prestige, people presumably understood that the masses' principal purpose was to benefit the soul in purgatory, and thus in dictating their wills people assumed that their souls would pass through this place rather than proceeding directly to heaven or undergoing damnation. Otherwise, there was little point in imposing this financial burden on their heirs. These requested masses were, indeed, not always performed, whether as a result of greed, indifference, poverty, or a feeling that "the dying man or woman had overdone it in the moment of extremity" (Lockhart 1992, 214). Still, to have at least one mass said was seen as a serious obligation, although sometimes even this was not carried out as quickly as the deceased might have wished, the executor sometimes dying beforehand and financing the neglected masses through his or her own will (Lockhart 1992, 214; also León-Portilla and Cline 1984, and Anderson et al. 1976, 64–65). *Fiscales*, the highest-ranking indigenous religious officials, often served as executors and were also responsible for receiving the payments for the masses; overzealous execution of this office could lead to conflicts over the handling of estates (Lockhart 1992, 213–15).

Care of the Dying and the Dead

A proper Spanish death was attended by a priest, who would administer the sacrament of extreme unction, exhort and pray for the dying person, and help to keep at bay the demons who were thought to lurk about the deathbed (Eire 1995, 29–32). Most Nahuas, however, probably died without a priest at their bedside. Cline observes that none of the Culhuacan wills were witnessed by any of the local Augustinians (1986, 21). During the early years, the friars were too busy ensuring that the most vital sacraments were delivered, but eventually the sacrament of extreme unction (or the last rites) did become available to Nahuas who requested it—and who lived close enough to a priest to be able to call one to a loved one's deathbed or carry the sick person to the church (Mendieta 1980, 307).

Some Nahuatl catechisms mention this sacrament only briefly (*Códice franciscano* 1941, 39; Anunciación 1565, 28v; Gante 1981, 58v; Sahagún 1993b, 30–31). Fray Juan de la Anunciación's 1577 catechism explains that it is to be administered to adults who are in danger of dying (260v–61r). His 1575 version (162–65) explains that God places goodness *(qualtiliztli)* in the sacrament, with which peoples' souls are helped. The priest anoints with holy oil each of the sick person's five senses. The sick person, after confessing, must ask the priest for the sacrament humbly, saying, "O my precious father, if my sickness increases, if I become very ill, may your heart grant that you will give me as my gift the sacrament, the sacred anointing and marking *(teoyotica teoçaliztli temachiotiliztli)*." It is the responsibility of people in the sick person's household to bring him or her to the church; this implies that the Augustinians did not make house calls.[14] An admonition to console the sick person encourages him or her to trust in God, who does not want his or her soul to be lost but to take it to heaven, even if it is not deserving, and to receive his or her approaching death gladly. Don Bartolomé de Alva's 1634 confession manual presents a similar admonition, in which the dying person is encouraged to be brave and to be sure to confess anything that is troubling him or her so as not to present God with a dirty soul (Sell and Schwaller 1999, 153).

But even Nahuas who faced this crucial moment without priestly attention were given some resources to assist them in their passage. The Franciscan fray Pedro de Gante (1981, 151r–58v) and the Dominican fray Martín de León (1611, 141r–54v) adapted the *Ars moriendi*, or guidebook for dying well, into Nahuatl, with admonitions, questions, and prayers for the dying and instructions on the treatment of the dying person and the corpse.[15] Such guidebooks supplement will-making by introducing additional European death customs into Nahua homes.

Gante's guide, a section of his widely used *doctrina* of 1553, is titled, "Here is how each person who is a true Christian will prepare, when he or she is sick, so that he or she will die in the service of our lord Jesus Christ" (151r). Gante begins by recommending that whoever is caring for the person ascertain whether he or she has been baptized, and instructions on how to carry out this rite, which a lay person could perform in time of extremity, follow. Then additional questions verify the person's Christian beliefs, contrition for sin, desire for pardon, and so forth; the proper answer, "yes," is printed after each question. The final questions ask if the dying person prays to Mary and all the saints to speak for him or her before God, whether he or she asks that the Holy Church and all true Christians pray for him or her and help him or her before God, and whether he or she lays his or her death and suffering in the illness as an offering before God. There follows a series of prayers for the dying person to make to Christ, then a prayer to Mary, who is asked to ensure that the dying person will see Christ and will hear the angels calling to his[16] soul to come out and rejoice with them, and to help him so that his enemies—that is, the demons—will not afflict him.

Gante urges repetition of these prayers, the catechism, and the Passion of Christ. The latter could be done using the texts for the canonical hours printed elsewhere in Gante's book (132r–44r). An image of Christ should be placed before the dying person, holy water should be sprinkled about, and a candle that has been blessed should be placed in the person's hands when death is near. Those present should kneel and recite a long litany beseeching God to save the person and requesting the intercession of Mary and a list of other saints. Referencing non-Christian native practice, Gante cautions them not to kneel before or call to the dead "as is done in confusion" (that is, idolatry or heresy), or to make offerings to them "as it used to be done long ago." Anyone who does this will fall into serious sin (158r–v). The body will be wrapped in a white mantle. When they are about to bury it, a cross will go in front, before which they will kneel and pray the prayers Our Father and Hail Mary as offerings to God on behalf of the deceased's soul.

Fray Martín de León's bilingual *Arte de bien morir,* which follows his will-making instructions in the 1611 *Camino del cielo,* was intended for use by Nahuatl or Spanish speakers. It begins with four admonitions to the dying, urging acceptance of mortality, gratitude for the opportunity to prepare for death, acceptance of the attendant suffering as penance for sin, and the renunciation of earthly cares in order to focus on the divine. He or she should ask all those present to pray to God to have mercy on his or her soul, and should pray to Mary and to all the angels and saints, especially his or her own guardian angel and Saint Mary Magdalene, that they pray to God on his or her behalf. A series of questions follows. A priest is to be called if the person has any unconfessed sins. One question concerns the disposal of the person's goods and payment of debts and is to be followed by the making of the will. Then there is a series of prayers, to Christ, Mary, the angels, and any saint to whom the person was particularly devoted. Other instructions include the bringing of a crucifix, which the dying person is to kiss; signs of the cross made over the eyes, mouth, ears, nose, and heart to guard against demonic deceptions; the provision of a blessed candle with the seal of Our Lady; and other procedures required for certain indulgences (such as the Santa Cruzada). León also provides instructions for the proper arrangement and disposal of the body, emphasizing that whatever masses and alms the dead person provided for in the will should be carried out quickly so that he or she will not remain long in purgatory. God will punish negligent relatives and executors with suffering in hell—a threat that gets carried out in "Souls and Testamentary Executors."

Colonial Nahuas participated avidly in religious confraternities—voluntary sodalities that carried out devotional and charitable activities and provided leadership opportunities for indigenous men and women (Lockhart 1992, 218–29). Confraternities offered indulgences to their members in exchange for the execution of specific devotions. To Nahuas, gaining these indulgences may not have been a major motivation for joining a confraternity, but once they had done so they were drawn further into the Catholic system of toting up release time from purgatory. For example, members of the confraternity of the Most Holy Sacrament in Tula gained papal indulgences by attending, candles in hand, a special mass on the first Sunday of each month and on five Marian feast days and the feasts of Saints Joseph and Francis (Schwaller 1989, 241).

The copious papal indulgences enjoyed by members of the popular confraternity of the rosary were publicized in Spanish through local editions of such works as the

Dominican Hierónimo Taix's *Institución, modo de rezar, y milagros e indulgencias del Rosario de la virgen Maria* of 1576,[17] but also in Nahuatl. A 1572 translation of rosary indulgences into Nahuatl, by fray Alonso de Molina, was about to be published by the printer Pedro Ocharte when he was arrested (for other reasons) by the Inquisition; the work survives in a handwritten copy (*Doctrina* n.d., 108v–15v; Fernández del Castillo 1982, 85–141; Schwaller 1991, 313–15). Compilations of miracles associated with the rosary promised other death-related rewards. In one Nahuatl series (*Sermones y santoral en mexicano* n.d., 322v–28v), a young woman who belongs to the confraternity, after being attacked by a wolf, survives long enough to confess and receive the last rites, thus accomplishing a good death. Another young female confraternity member returns to life after drowning, once her mother reminds the Virgin that the girl was a rosary devotee and vows to join the confraternity herself. And another young woman devoted to the rosary, a poor shepherdess, enjoys a splendid death attended by the Virgin and other heavenly maidens. One local legend held that the Dominican fray Domingo de la Anunciación, by praying the rosary, was able to call back from death a man from Tepetlaoztoc who had died before the friar could come to confess him; after confessing, he died again (Dávila Padilla 1955, 615–16).

Confraternities assisted the dead and dying in more immediate ways as well. The Nahuatl statutes from Tula (Schwaller 1989, 241–43) call for a draped litter and two processional crosses to be used for any member's funeral. All members of the sodality, summoned by fifteen chimes of the church bell, are to march in the funeral procession. Spanish members (who did pay higher fees) are to receive vigils, masses, and responses at confraternity expense. Nahuas who wanted these things had, presumably, to pay for them themselves. For twice the normal membership fee, a dying person could join the confraternity and receive the death benefits and indulgences. But the confraternity also buried destitute residents of the community, whether or not they were members. Confraternity officers were to ensure that any sick member confessed and received communion, so that he or she would be prepared for a good death.

The 1619 statutes of San Miguel Coyotlan's confraternity of Our Lady of Solitude (Sell 2000, 354) call for similar attention to the dead and dying. When a member is ill, confraternity deputies must fetch a priest to hear his or her confession. Members must provide candles for the funerals of poor members and finance two low masses for them. The latter obligation extends even to poor people who do not belong to the sodality: members must pay for a mass if the person would otherwise receive none. That Nahua confraternities typically took seriously the obligation to provide masses for dead members is also indicated by the well-preserved colonial confraternity records from colonial Tecamachalco, which contain careful annotations regarding the masses performed for deceased members and the money spent on these (Annette McLeod, personal communication, 2000).

Some confraternities were explicitly dedicated to death and the dead. The Augustinians founded confraternities for the souls in purgatory at all of their establishments in Mexico; these sponsored weekly masses on Mondays for the souls of all the dead (Grijalva 1624, 72v). By the late seventeenth century, confraternities of the souls were common at Franciscan establishments as well, in some cases separate ones for Spaniards and natives (Vetancurt 1982). In 1710 the Jesuits founded a branch of their Good Death Society, dedicated to preparing its members for death through a well-regulated life, among the Nahuas of Mexico City; membership in this sodality also brought indulgences (Schroeder 2000).

Good Deaths and Bad

Most of the deaths that occur in the five plays, on or off stage, are disastrously bad deaths. The disrespectful youth in "How to Live on Earth," the greedy and lecherous protagonist of "The Merchant," and the widow and executors in "Souls and Testamentary Executors" are actually killed by demons, having sunk so low as to be beyond redemption. Doña Juana is murdered by her husband who, unshriven of this mortal sin, is then stoned to death. Lucía in "Final Judgment" does not die but receives eternal punishment at judgment time for failing to confess her sins before it was too late. All of these characters go to hell. Thus, on the whole the plays emphasize negative examples, modeling frightful fates that the prudent observer will strive to avoid. The torments enacted by demons visually reinforce teachings about hell delivered in sermons and catechism lessons.

The behaviors for which these characters earn such dire punishment were acts that most Nahuas already disapproved of. Even if some Nahuas in the audience did not consider the merchant's usury inherently sinful, they would have objected to his theft of a widow's property. Murder, adultery, promiscuity, drunkenness, and disrespect for parents were, like theft, sanctioned under preconquest as well as colonial moral codes. To colonial Nahuas familiar with wills, failure to arrange the masses funded by a dead person's will was also a serious breach. So, the moral lessons were not in themselves particularly rigid or alarming, even if the punishments were severe. To feel morally superior to the bad characters in the plays, and thus expect to avoid their fate and end up, at the worst, in purgatory, might not have seemed all that difficult, despite the bleak tone struck by many of the heavenly and allegorical characters.

Lorenzo and his wife of "How to Live on Earth" and don Pedro of "Souls and Testamentary Executors" die good deaths and proceed to purgatory. Don Pedro dies offstage, apparently just after he goes to church and makes his last confession, but the deaths of Lorenzo and his wife are staged. They die with no one to attend them, but even so their deaths have features of the good deaths prescribed by Gante and León. They have just confessed and they are at peace with one another and accepting of their fate. An angel calls to them and other souls come to help, bringing the candles that the dying person is supposed to hold and ushering the emerging souls to purgatory.

Aside from their participation in the sacrament of confession, the principal pious behavior attributed to these three characters is their own renunciation of earthly wealth in favor of service to the dead in purgatory. Lorenzo and his wife forego seeking a living in order to pray for their dead relatives; don Pedro and his wife sell their house to raise money for the dead. Upon his death, don Pedro joins the soul of the corrupt widow's husband, who laments the squandering of his property that should have gone to finance masses to shorten his confinement, and other souls who complain of people's neglect. Don Pedro's widow has little left to spend on her husband's soul, the two of them having expended their resources on other dead, but the priest assures her that she can help him with her prayers and tears. Lorenzo and his wife do gain admittance to heaven, while in the other play Christ promises Mary that he will help don Pedro and his companion souls. The emphasis, in these two plays, on the worthy dead as a focus of attention for the living is a more instructive model than the simple sanctions against greed, lust, and murder. A good person is not simply one who avoids serious sin but one who actively serves the dead. These plays reinforce the cultural attention to the dead introduced into colonial Nahua practice through will-making, confraternities, indulgences, and funerary rites.

Four of the five plays (all except "The Merchant") feature courtroom drama, with Christ sitting in judgment as others testify regarding the moral fitness of the human characters. These scenes vary in regard to who conducts the interrogations and what questions are asked, and more variations are found among the doctrinal texts discussed earlier. Given this variability, people may have formulated quite different notions of how their judgment and sentencing would proceed. However, the general idea that one would appear before Christ and undergo questioning or provide an accounting of oneself may have been widely disseminated. The Nahuatl and Spanish words used for this accounting—*cuenta* in Spanish, words based on *pohua*, "to count," in Nahuatl—support a notion of enumeration, how many good and how many bad things one did, rather than some more abstract testimony of faith.[18] Since, in general, priests had great difficulty eliciting "good" confessions from Nahuas or inducing a fear of hell among them, the idea of the judgment of the soul may not have worked very well as a tool for policing and disciplining the self. Nahuas may have seen it simply as a frightening thing that had to be endured on the way to purgatory, like the obsidian winds and clashing mountains that afflicted their ancestors' *-yolia* en route to the place of the dead.

Nowhere in the dramas is sinful behavior, or the failure of the humans to heed the admonitions of angels, connected explicitly to indigenous identity—it is the people of earth in general who are in this sorry state. There is a universality to these representations of sin and death. And yet, by depicting death and the afterlife in such concrete manners, the plays may actually have reinforced rather than challenged the this-worldly orientation of Nahua religiosity. Hell is described as an abyss and represented theatrically as a substage area or a house. Heaven is revealed behind doors or curtains, and one can climb there on a ladder. When souls leave their bodies they are visible, portrayed by children or other actors. Christ, Mary, demons, and angels appear in visible, concrete form, and so do abstractions such as Death himself, a distinct and morally positive, not evil or fearsome, character. The souls—or, at the world's end, the living people and the resurrected dead—appear before Christ as before a judge at court or a priest at confession. The world after death does not seem like an utterly unknown and immaterial world beyond. This aspect may have helped to make these and similar plays persuasive, if not in substantially changing people's moral attitudes or behaviors, at least in forming their images of their posthumous fate and encouraging people to seek a good death through participation in Christian sacraments, confraternities, prayers, and the making of wills with bequests for masses.

Notes

1. The term *-yolia*, like those referring to other body parts, is obligatorily possessed, always appearing in texts with a possessive prefix, never as an absolutive noun. In this it differs

from the other animating essences, *tonalli*, "heat," "fate," "day," and *ihiyotl*, "breath," which were less tied up with individual identity.

2. This figure may have recalled both the day-sign *miquiztli*, represented by a skull, in the traditional 260-day ritual calendar, and the deity Mictlantecuhtli, or Lord of the Place of the Dead, whom colonial texts sometimes identify with Lucifer but who was represented as a skeleton and was not evil. However, as use of the ritual calendar and memories of preconquest deities lapsed in the colonial era, such connections may have been relevant only for the first generation or so after the conquest, at least in urban areas.

3. All translations are my own unless otherwise noted.

4. Translation by Barry D. Sell and John Frederick Schwaller.

5. In the Mesoamerican vigesimal system, this is an ideal number (twenty counts of twenty) used to represent the idea of a large quantity.

6. One of the Nahua terms applied to sacramental confession, based on a preconquest rite of purificatory confession, was *yolmelahua* or "to straighten (one's or someone's) heart." Another commonly used term was *yolcuitia*, literally "to cause (someone or oneself) to take heart," which I translate as "confess."

7. Josaphat in the text; this placement derives from the Book of Joel (3:2), where this valley is the site of a prophesied final battle between God and his enemies (Stafford Poole, personal communication, 2000).

8. In Matthew 19:28, Jesus tells his disciples that "in the regeneration when the Son of man shall sit in the throne of his glory, ye also shall sit upon twelve thrones, judging the twelve tribes of Israel."

9. This passage recalls the "hellmouth" motif common in medieval art and drama, which represents the entrance into hell as a gaping mouth in the earth.

10. The right and left hands had, respectively, positive and negative associations for Europeans that did not necessarily carry over into the Nahua context. For preconquest Nahuas, the left side, based on the sun's viewpoint when crossing over the sky, was associated with winter (when the sun rose and set toward the south), the dry season, and warfare, but not evil. Indeed, for a ruler to place someone on his left hand was a compliment, as seen in the figure of speech "I will place you on my left, in my obsidian sandals" (Sahagún 1950–1982, 6:259).

11. Text repeats *oannechycnotlaquentique*, "you clothed me with pity," but *oannechycnotlaqualtique* was probably intended.

12. *Tlactli*, the trunk of the body and, by extension, the body as a whole. Use of this term reflects the fact that Nahuatl lacked a term corresponding precisely to *cuerpo*.

13. These examples come from published transcriptions and translations of the wills; I have adapted the translations to my own style.

14. This was, indeed, a point of contention between the regular and the secular clergy; the latter accused the former of laziness for not going out to people's homes to administer this sacrament (Stafford Poole, personal communication, 2000).

15. Neither of these approaches the length of a manual composed for use with Spanish speakers, part of the *Directorio para confesores* issued by the Third Mexican Provincial Council of 1585 (*Directorio del Sancto Concilio Provincial Mexicano celebrado este año de 1585*, MS in Biblioteca Nacional, Madrid; I thank Stafford Poole, C.M., for this information).

16. Vocative suffixes are used but the text could be easily adapted by a female speaker. This prayer is in Burkhart 2001.

17. Spanish-language summaries of indulgences for other confraternities were also published in Mexico. For example, a 1584 publication relating to the confraternity of the Most Holy Sacrament (*Sumario de las Indulgencias*, 1584) enumerates generous indulgences for those who, at certain times or intervals, pray sets of five Our Fathers and one Hail Mary in reverence to that sacrament.

18. Sell's essay (this volume) discusses this usage of the Spanish loan *cuenta*.

NAHUATL CATECHISTIC DRAMA

New Translations, Old Preoccupations

Daniel Mosquera

A few years ago while I was working at the National Archives in Mexico City, a friend—knowing about my interest in Nahuatl drama—inquired why anyone would spend so much time studying it. After all, he insisted, there were histories, treatises, relations, religious doctrine and teachings, and heaps of Nahuatl legal documentation under continuous scrutiny that could be more pertinent to a student of Mesoamerica. His reasoning was based partly on the belief that catechistic drama written and performed in Nahuatl was largely an extension of Spanish devotional and sacramental plays, with an added dimension of "disorientation." He noted that, when judged against Spanish *autos, loas,* and *farsas,* Nahuatl drama seemed imperfect and simplistic, and that it could scarcely provide any new substantial information on Nahua contact with Christianity. Although I found his argument uninformed, it left me with the feeling that I had already encountered, partially and in various guises, similar deliberations. This quandary brought to my attention the difficulties in assessing the character of this drama while analyzing the expansion, expression, and performance of Christianity.[1]

There is not a pooled or detailed colonial record, Spanish or Nahua, of the process involved in the overall production of the dramas, although some recent analyses have furnished very valuable findings.[2] How did the dramas arrive in the continent and what use did they receive after arrival? Who was responsible for their adaptation into Nahuatl and what methods were employed? How were the dramas enacted and what kind of affinities developed between neophytes and performances? Who supervised their organization and performances and what concrete effect did they have on the transmission and settlement of Christian doctrine and practices? Did the dramas play a significant social role in the arrangement of popular Christianities and the diffusion of distinctive cults, and did participants affirm any type of Nahua Christian identity?[3] Can devotional and catechistic spectacles and practices in colonial Mexico and medieval and early modern Spain offer insights about each other? In the past twenty years, questions posed by diverse scholars about agencies, especially Nahua agencies, during the first two centuries of Spanish colonization have provoked a general reassessment of the Christianizing campaign. The study of Mesoamerica has much profited from this situation, as more translations of Nahuatl records and discerning scholarship come to fruition. In light of a series of new translations of Nahuatl texts—this volume embodying but one such undertaking—and to the extent that they afford supportive interpretations, I would like to endeavor in this essay a plausible approach to some of the questions contemplated here.

Although Spanish religious drama before the late fifteenth century is to this day still a partial mystery, some observations are feasible by looking at legal documentation, Councils, medieval laws, and city and township records. Clerical culture in New Spain undoubtedly had access to numerous sources of doctrine and biblical lore; *sermonarios* and compilations of *exempla* and *autos* may have often traveled with some of the friars. I will start by examining in a comparative way the historical contexts for Nahuatl catechistic drama, to the degree that they can be localized, and by hazarding some ideas about the intricacies of continuity and transformation tied typically to any act of exchange between cultures. I will then look at each piece individually and in relation to other dramas, especially in connection with the practice of penance and confession, venturing some observations about "radicalized spectacles" that may help us to reevaluate Nahuatl drama.[4]

Catechistic Drama and Popular Culture: A Comparative Analysis

Nahuatl drama reflects a complex interplay of social, religious, and political negotiations between, for the most part, transmissible beliefs and attitudes, some of fascinating adaptability.[5] A similar interplay could be said of Catholicism as it has evolved in many parts of Latin America today. Like most Nahuatl writing, catechistic drama discloses elements that go beyond simple emulation and instruction. Hence, reducing any interpretation of Nahuas under Spanish rule and instruction to a mere trade-off between resistance and conversion is, as James Lockhart has underscored in his work, to miss the mark (1991, 10; 1992, 2–3, 203). In connection to the Nahua, the questions then arise: what of either Spanish or Nahua extraction survives, or "continues," and how has it been shaped by the evolution of religious, social, or political practices? Recent answers to these questions have challenged many of the earlier assumptions, and the methodologies that address the former have emphasized different sources, hence resulting in often contradictory conclusions.[6] This section will be concerned partially with the question, What of Spanish extraction survives? by comparing what characterizes the interaction between popularized and intractable Christian tenets in Spanish and postconquest Nahua settings.

At first sight, this query may seem oversimplifying, even unorthodox, but reaching out to medieval studies may facilitate understanding. If we accept Aron Gurevich's claim that coexisting traditions within Christianity are applicable to medieval Spain, we may begin by asking how New Spain compares. Although circumstances were far from analogous, we might hazard some generalizations. Christianization was administered in both continents to proselytes and followers in different stages using an assortment of tactics, sometimes by force and often by instruction. In Europe, Christianizing forces proved unable to eradicate "folkloric culture" and instead were compelled to interact with it, to the extent that "in both cultures earthly and supernatural, material and spiritual planes merged" (Gurevich 1993, xvi).[7] The popularization of Christian doctrine in Europe inevitably brought the transformation of Christianity, although, Gurevich argues, "in the sphere of hagiography the adjustment of the requirements of theology to the requirements of the masses remained under the Church's control: the legend, the *vita* and the 'miracles,' whatever their folkloric sources may have been, flowed out of the clergy's pen" (1993, 78). The early medieval scriptural tradition to which Gurevich refers comprised penitentials, confession handbooks, and casuistry guides for priests, all of which assisted the Church in dealing with popular traditions "not only about saints, but also in a much wider circle comprising beliefs, perceptions and practices, in order to subordinate these to the demands of official religiosity" (1993, 78).

Colonial Mexico, we must recall, abounded in precisely these types of texts.[8] Addressing the issues of what official religiosity assimilated and how both cultures interacted in this process becomes central to any study of popular religious practices. In reconciling what is "penned" with what is learned, a new problem arises as we then try to gauge what exactly is the result. The example of the story of the Virgin of Guadalupe and the miracles she performed in Mexico seems to have had precisely this sort of trajectory. Although reaching no definitive conclusion about *how* Laso de la Vega's Nahuatl version *(Huei tlamahuiçoltica)* came into being, Sousa et al. illustrate a composite of strategies revealing official and nonofficial mediation throughout. The hypotheses proposed in the preliminary study suggest a compound agency in the production of the text. The sudden late popularity of the cult, the possible manifestation of graphic and textual influences, the probable mediation of Nahua aides, even the possibility of material circulating orally and affecting the outcome and transmission of the story unveil a very intricate scenario (Sousa et al. 1998, 1–47). In a sense, the Christian icon through hagiography becomes a kind of sponge with various performative functions. For the Church the most important of these would be to appropriate the forces comprising "gentile" or pagan religion (Gurevich 1993, 102).

Drawing from his extensive experience with Nahuatl texts and community records, Lockhart presents an argument about Spanish-Nahua interaction that could well be applied to the medieval situation described by Gurevich. Let us consider his ideas at length:

> Change went on constantly, and it occurred precisely because of contact with Spaniards. Increasing degrees of contact with the numerically growing and territorially expanding Hispanic population caused successive general waves of indigenous structural readjustment. The Spaniards represented, however, more the fuel than the motor of the development. They did not, by themselves, either individually or en masse, determine the nature of change; *change was a transaction between two groups and two cultures. . . . it was the nature of Nahua culture in relation to Spanish culture that determined the shape (as opposed to the tempo) of change.* (Lockhart 1992, 21; my emphasis)[9]

Although cognizant of these cultural transactions, the Church did not always ignore this mutual adaptation of cultures, in particular when it dealt with public displays of devotion and religiosity that did not resemble official practices. Both in Europe and

New Spain, there were repeated official attempts to control the proliferation of doctrinal material and its dramatic production in situations that were perceived by the Church as being suspect. In fact, from the beginning the Church was mistrustful of any type of "translation," in general, as became manifest in the various councils that regulated the number of feasts, religious dramas, and the participation of the populace.[10]

Without mentioning religious drama per se or referring specifically to the New World, the Council of Trent (1545–1563) advocated strong regulation of doctrinal and liturgical matters and of their diffusion. This concern prompted, among other Councils, the Council at Salamanca in 1565 to require strict revision of the material used in Nativity plays (demanding local ecclesiastical supervision of performance and texts for approval) and the Council of Toledo to prohibit completely any performance of plays and dances during religious services (Harris 1992, 193). Attempting to solve this problem, the general amendment Urban VIII authored in the Council of 1642 (*Universa per Orbem*) regulated the number and quality of feasts.[11]

In 1555, midway through the Council of Trent, the First Concilio Provincial in Mexico was under way. Here the preoccupation about "translation" was naturally more literal and the overall concern toward the intactness of doctrine more crucial. The first *Capítulo* censures Spaniards and Nahuas alike—the former probably because of the frequent insufficiency of native language knowledge to impart doctrine; the latter because of the belief that Nahuas were by definition inadequate to translate, least of all transmit, complex theological ideas:

> Que no se den a los yndios sermones en su lengua y que ninguna doctrina se traduzga en lengua de indios si no fuere examinada por clérigo o religioso que entienda la lengua en que se traduze.—Muy grandes inconvenientes hallamos que se siguen de dar sermones en la lengua de los indios, así por no entender como por los herrores y faltas que hazen quando los trasladan; por ende statuimos y mandamos que de aquí adelante no se den sermones a los indios para trasladar ni tener en su poder; y los que tienen se les tomen y recojan.

> That no sermons be given to the Indians in their language and no doctrine be translated into Indian languages without being examined by a cleric or friar who knows the language in question.—We have discovered grave mistakes that continue to be preached in Indian languages, either from not understanding or not having translated things well; we require and state by law that from now on no sermon be given to Indians to translate or keep in their power; and if any Indian has any it must be confiscated. (Cited in Llaguno 1962, 167–68).[12]

This passage suggests as well that cleric-inspired sermons may have circulated unsupervised among Nahuas, who in turn utilized them to preach their own understanding of Christianity. This general official unease with the management of religiosity included also the authority to allot divine powers to objects, people, and phenomena, and the access natives had to liturgical ritual objects: "[S]tatuymos y mandamos que se tenga muy gran cuidado por los ministros que no permitan ni consientan que [los indios] traten las cosas sagradas ni que en su poder aya hostias, porque de tenerlas se an seguido escándalos y cosas muy sospechosas . . . por lo cual mandamos a los dichos curas y clérigos que no permitan a los dichos yndios thener en su poder y a su dispusiçión las dichas hostias ni el olio ni crisma" (We order and require that great care be taken by ministers not to allow that [the natives] deal with sacred things nor that they have access to wafers, since, were they to have them, suspicious and scandalous things may occur . . . because of this we order the aforementioned priests and clerics not to allow the Indians to have access to the said wafers nor the consecrated oils; Llaguno 1962, 168). There was continuous anxiety about precisely how the natives were voicing and practicing their Christianity, although no remedy ever contemplated prohibiting dramatic performances altogether.

The provisional synod of 1565 proscribed any written material from the Holy Scriptures from falling into native hands, except for catechisms properly supervised by the prelates (Ricard 1966, 56–57). The Third Concilio Mexicano of 1585 speaks of supervising the use of masks ("máscaras y ynsignias") and controlling dances within the churches, recommending instead that the dances be performed outside: "donde se vea lo que hazen y se pueda oyr y entender lo que cantan; y en los dias de ffiesta no se hagan hasta después de misa mayor por la mañana" (where we may see what they do and hear and understand what they sing; and they are not to do it during feast days until after high Mass in the morning; Llaguno 1962, 286). This Council issued an edict to curb the propagation of profane dances and *representaciones* during religious festivities, demanding that only if they adhered to doctrine and "useful devotion" could they receive authorization from the archbishop at least a month before the performance (García Icazbalceta 1968, 353). Later, in Europe, Urban VIII expressed alarm in 1625, 1631, and 1640 in connection with the unofficial proliferation of hagiographic material, as the Church sought to normalize the rise of miracles, the multiplication of saints, and the like (Rubial García 1997, 56).

The performance of religious plays inside the churches and in public spaces also worried the Church. References dating back to the first Fathers reveal a growing discomfort with dramatic performances in general. From the fifteenth through the eighteenth centuries, ecclesiastical authorities in Europe struggled for control over the use made of sacred material during feasts and celebrations. Spain was no exception. National and provincial Councils in Aranda (1473), Gerona (1475), and Toledo (1565) condemned and censured excesses, "abusos y profanaciones," deriving from more direct participation of the townspeople in religious *representaciones* (Cotarelo 1904, 16).

Medieval Spanish dramas, specifically liturgical and religious drama, are scarce, resulting in a variety of scholarly conjectures about origins and transformations. The often-quoted fourteenth-century *Siete partidas* suggests that there was a drama based on biblical motifs, "que mueven a los homes a facer bien et haber devocion en la fe . . . et demás porque los homes á hayan remembrança que segunt aquello fueron fechas de verdat" (that move men to do good and to be devotedly faithful . . . and besides so that men will remember that they were made of truthful [events]; Cotarelo 1904, 16). What is most remarkable of Alfonso X's law (34, tít. 6, *Partida I*), though not surprising, is that the performances are restricted to the big cities where there are bishops and archbishops who can supervise them: "et non lo deben facer en las aldeas, nin en los lugares viles, nin por ganar dineros con ello" (and they must not be performed in villages, nor vile places, nor for profit; 16). Stern has suggested that given the

Church's endorsement of Nativity and Easter plays in the document, such dramas must have been known at least in Castile (1996, 76).

Echoing Gurevich's analysis of the penitentials in the early Middle Ages, Stern offers an assessment that resonates with views of Nahuatl drama as interpreted in this essay. She contends that official Latin writings treated the relationship between pre-Christian and Christian worldviews as sequential, whereas the Latin hagiographies, visions of the otherworld, and penitentials validated the belief that Christianity had assimilated much of the pre-Christian world: "Thus the two cultures coexisted and interacted in complex and contradictory ways" (Stern 1996, 72).

Although just over two centuries after the believed performance of "Final Judgment" in Tlatelolco, a case dating to 1768 and investigated by the Inquisition in Mexico seems to present a telling example of this type of situation. News came to the Holy Office that in the town of Ozumba, parish of Tlalmanalco, a play representing the Passion of Christ "en disposición cómica" (in a comical fashion) was presented annually on Easter Sunday. The documents allege that the performance of the play included an irreverent Judas and a naked native Christ who also consecrated the Host during the Last Supper:

> y saliendo al teatro el que hace el papel de Jesucristo desnudo públicamente con grande indecencia y escándalo con la gravísima circunstancia de que cuando se hace la Cena simula éste que consagra y alza una hostia y se hincan todos a adorarla; y finalmente, que a todo esto preceden los ensayos que para su ejecución se hacen y empiezan desde mediada la Cuaresma, los que se ejecutan de noche, convidando la gente para que asista a son de caja, que salen tocando por las calles y plaza desde la oración hasta las nueve de la noche, que dan principio al ensayo, el que se finaliza a más de la medianoche.[13]

> and appearing in the play (is) the one who plays Jesus, naked in public and with great indecency and scandal, adding the grave circumstance that when they enact the Last Supper he simulates the consecration, raising a wafer, after which everyone kneels to praise it; and finally that all of this is preceded by rehearsals done at night which start from mid-Lent, inviting the people to come using drums, which they play in the streets and plazas from the Prayer until nine o'clock when they start the rehearsal, ending past midnight.

A *Comisario*, notary, and priest were assigned to this and other locations in the province of Chalco to look into the allegations, resulting in over a hundred folios. The legal process included interrogations of members of the community who had played different roles over the years and the subsequent confiscation of plays written in Spanish and Nahuatl. The copies that were confiscated probably represented similar versions of the text of the Passion cycle.

This may not have been an isolated case, however. Nahuas had organized their own confraternities since the sixteenth century, starting in the bishopric of Mexico with the confraternity of Santiago in Tlatelolco, Veracruz in Xochimilco, and Santo Cristo de Burgos in Culhuacan (Bazarte Martínez 1989, 46). Confraternities soon multiplied in the seventeenth century with natives joining in with Spaniards ("cofradías mixtas" such as Santísimo Sacramento and Ánimas Benditas) or forming their own assemblies. The confraternities in Mexico had a cohesive influence on the preservation of communities, but, most important, they offered a platform against which the community itself could protect and hoist its own cults. "Su objeto principal, a pesar de los curas y párrocos, no fue la difusión del catolicismo sino la fiesta del santo patrón" (their main objective, in spite of priests and friars, was not the dissemination of Catholicism but the feast of the patron saint; Bazarte Martínez 1989, 44). There is abundant documentation that reveals much activity with *retablos* and *representaciones* made for festivities related to sanctioned cults; other attempts were persecuted or penalized, though the plays in question are not mentioned. For instance, one Juan Rivera from Tepecoacuilco was summoned, to be later absolved, for having presented a *comedia* to the Indians of Tuxpan in the presbytery of the church.[14] Although there is no description of the type of play, it is likely that it had some religious content. The province of Chalco represents one among many examples that has auspiciously been documented, in which ecclesiastical authorities tried to control the circulation of popular religious devotion.

The Dramas

Described often by the friars as a persecutory mobilization against the devil, the Christianizing campaign had a very concrete effect on the social life of the natives. A massive and expanding campaign was deployed, staging a series of instructional negotiations that served, in different degrees, to establish a Christian presence in New Spain without eradicating local traditions and beliefs. As has been noted by historians of early America, this was a double-edged attempt. On the one hand, the early friars sought to understand better the very customs they wanted to eradicate. On the other hand, they modeled a frequently erratic catechization on those documented Nahua beliefs.

Among the various strategies of Christian didacticism, catechistic drama stood out and was very instrumental in attracting Nahuas to Christian practices, at least initially those drawn more by spectacle and festivity. We can surmise that among the main didactic goals was to transport the natives back to a mythical origin, in this case biblical, the backdrop against which social, moral, and sacramental notions were implemented. I locate catechistic drama in New Spain in a period of intense religious induction, unparalleled in the history of religious campaigns. If early chronicles are nearly accurate, in New Spain catechistic drama spills over into other territories of everyday life. It is echoed in daily doctrine, narrated in stories and histories, and reenacted constantly in sacramental practices. This analysis examines catechistic drama in the context of cultural and religious transformation. While looking at Nahuatl dramas that promoted specific ideas, I also engage native and Christian notions of recollection, penance, exemplarity, and eschatology.

In a letter dated November 17, 1532, and directed to the King Charles V of Spain, fray Martín de Valencia (1474–1534) describes in succinct and poignant words the extent of the friars' involvement in the religious matters of the indigenous peoples. This Franciscan led the spiritual expedition of the first twelve missionaries arriving in Mexico in 1524 at the behest of Hernando Cortés: "y una de las cosas por donde se conoçe que a nuestro gran Dios le plega que esta nación se salbe, es *averles mostrado el castigo por la ofensa pasada, y darles remedio para escapar de la que obieran incurrido* (and one of the ways whereby we know that God is hopeful for this nation to be saved, is *having shown them (the natives) the punishment of their past offenses and giving them remedy to escape from what they would have done*; Cartas de Indias 1980, 1:54; my emphasis).

A complaint about various judicial and territorial injustices of many of the Spanish colonizers, most of whom participated in the *encomienda* system, this letter is also a summary of some of the processes of transculturation and religious instruction to which the natives were subjected. In this letter, fray Martín refers not only to the former belligerent behavior of some of the Indians (the revolt against Cortés's advances; the constant threat of the Chichimecas, for example) but also to the counteracting attitudes of a good number of elders and *caciques* in the different communities. These beliefs may simply be echoes of the skepticism with which the Nahua leaders were said to have met the twelve Franciscans and their doctrine in 1524.[15] To this scenario is added the quick decimation of the indigenous populations owing to epidemics, which lasted well into the late sixteenth century, overwork, and taxation. The deployment of catechistic drama in the sixteenth and seventeenth centuries meets native responses to Christianization precisely in this crossroads between disinclination and devotion.

"How to Live on Earth" is a drama with many preconquest overtones (Horcasitas 1974, 53).[16] It is a moral and didactic piece with several fictional characters whose good or bad behavior is addressed in terms of restitution. Directed at "all sinners," the drama begins with a calling to those who will honor and serve Jesus:

> God's beloved mother places before us her sadness. Reverently, humbly she places before us her sadness, her weeping swoon. But as for us, we just waste her precious and honored tears, which here on earth lie flowing on account of our sins. And likewise here on earth the precious blood of our beloved honored savior, our lord Christ, has been wasted. Today he gives and shows to all of us sinners his precious and honored passion (11r–v).[17]

"How to Live on Earth" stands out for its insistence on the admission of sin and the need for timely repentance. This insistence is placed at the beginning of the drama, when the newly wed and Christianized Lorenzo voices his concern about how he and his wife will live on earth and whether it is wise, in God's eyes, to seek wealth and personal property (12r). This may be consonant with *contemptus mundi* beliefs exemplified and much emphasized by the early Franciscans. The transactional nature of purgatory as represented during the Middle Ages becomes apparent in this first exchange, as Lorenzo expresses distress about "debt" related to his dead parents and the mediating influence of the Virgin Mary: "Do they owe something to someone here on earth? If only we had for their sake repaid the goods, the silver and gold, precious things, jades, for here on earth they come to an end" (12r–v). Associated not only with material debts inherited from the parents, this bond verbalizes as well a debt to interceding divinities.

First Angel lays emphasis on perseverance and honoring a bond ("a precious cord of heaven") that is vulnerable to the deceptions of the *tzitzimitl* (12v; see below for a discussion of this term), whereas a rather eloquent First Demon identifies the negation of Christian rites as his locus of action (13r–v). In fact, much of what is demanded from the characters stresses a proper exchange in which listening plays a major role and much is submitted to judgment, both divine and demonic. Praying for the dead before God and the Virgin becomes initially a point of contention between Angel and First Demon. The demon, by placing emphasis on inappropriate Christian behavior, defines his world of action in terms of dissidence and deviation in an interesting strategy. This economics of penance in which the living help the dead—and themselves by atoning for the latter—may teach Christian contempt toward the accumulation of material goods and their obsolescence in God's kingdom, but it also directs attention to valuations of debt. Deliverance is presented then in the context of a tributary religious and social affiliation. The subsequent appearance of a mother scolding a child concentrates on obedience and going to church, although the general theme of praying for others remains pivotal.

This affiliation through penance also signals an apprehension over Christian retributive rites, announcing a type of reckoning that graduates the "new economy" in a scale of transactional values (such as gold and silver, property, debt, and so on), all or part of which will level off with continuous prayer and remembrance. It is a reminder and reenactment of a bondage whose symbolic power may effect radical change. The verbal clash of demons and angels—the latter of which continually, according to First Demon, rob him of his servants—addresses this possibility as well. The drama calls attention to valuations of indigenous reality in connection to Christian penitential and retributive observances, emphasizing vassalage and subjugation to diametrically opposed forces: to devils and to God. A double effect is conceivable, in terms of the series of expectations produced by angels and devils, since both had the role of portraying for the audience specific behavioral examples while eliciting fear.

In a way, the drama was directing attention to the preconquest reluctance to confess sins immediately after they happen, waiting instead until the moment of death. We know that the natives considered confession a final option, expecting absolution and clearance from the law for crimes such as adultery or for other transgressions (Soustelle 1955, 234–35). In "How to Live on Earth," early confession is rewarded, as First Angel proclaims to the devil, stressing the need for recollection: "You declare that they do not cry out to me, that they do not remember me" (13r). During this exchange, First Demon recalls the original sin by offering a short summary of the Fall (15r), an event that should evoke specific images to a Nahua audience that had been exposed to Christian doctrine for several decades. As in medieval drama, maintaining interconnectedness among the various plays and themes was an important feature here made more significant by the reminder of what was probably one of the earliest Nahuatl plays.[18] The play is in any case inhabited by references to remembrance and accounting, repayment, retribution, and confession, in connection with the living and the dead.

Other characters appear in the drama, including several in their formative years. They exemplify choices that reflect similar concerns over proper observances such as confession (17v–18v). In the character's final reckoning, several "souls" approach the dying one, Lorenzo, as the heavenly gates open. This episode is followed by insistent petitions on the part of these helping souls "to repay [Lorenzo and his wife's] love," to repay the sadness and pity they endured, and in turn to pray for those who will soon join God (25v). In a drastic change of scenes accompanied by trumpets, a Christ figure imparts judgment as he reminds the Virgin about her sufferings and his final torment (26v–27r); again, this is reminiscent of other biblical passages the audience had probably seen enacted before. The final moments contain as much violence as can be expected of any medieval play related to the Final Judgment, as orders direct the demons to hang, beat, and tear to pieces the disrespectful one. Condemned leaves, crying to the spectators, "You who bring up children, you who raise children, do not be idiotic, as if you were not rational. Open your ears! Listen to the sermon and the exemplary model. You are not going to fall into the fiery crag like I am now about to do!" (28v). The moral illustration of this drama is intensified by the violence of the final scene.

In an excellent study on medieval drama and violence, Jody Enders has concluded that there is a strong connection, inherited from the classical rhetorical era, between torture and truth. Showing that "the medieval understanding of torture both enabled and encouraged the dramatic representation of violence as a means of coercing theater audiences into accepting the various 'truths' enacted didactically in mysteries, miracles, and even farces" (1999, 2–4), Enders concludes that much of this cruelty was, and continues to be, fundamental to rhetoric (232). We may not deem as fully reliable Motolinia's and others' enthusiastic descriptions of natives' participation in Nahuatl dramas, but we can surmise a remarkable growing devotion that owed as much to the language's ability to transmit powerful emotions as to the natives' adherence to signs that verified some sense of continuity.

The friars' recurring insistence on the natives' pre-Christianity may, therefore, have had a wider application than has been documented in the dramas. It not only infiltrated the religious fabric of the community but also instituted a consciousness of restitution for a series of offenses perhaps unknown until then. When the act of atonement for a newly defined "sin" then becomes public—for example, renunciation of idolatrous customs, various penitential and retributive offerings—the whole community participates in this act and is thus subjected to a new chain of events. Catechistic drama epitomizes the most elaborate link in this chain, since it serves the purpose of both instituting a presumed new order and inviting collective participation in its transmission.

Even so, the practice and ritualization of confession were not foreign to the Mesoamerican experience but are, in fact, among the many similarities between Nahua and Christian religions that were noted and documented, with distinct ideological intentions, by several of the early chroniclers. Striking in one of Las Casas's descriptions of this practice is his observation of native inclination to extreme dramatism when carrying out penitential acts. These were done, according to Las Casas, for reasons of a mythical-cosmic value or because a transgression had been recognized by them. In several ways, this capacity in the natives for doing penance, in the context of Christian purgatorial rites, had profound implications. Las Casas further explains:

> todos guardaban inviolablemente aquestas cerimonias, porque allende que si se sabía que alguno algo dellas quebrantaba, era ásperamente castigado, tenían vehementísimo temor que de cierto habían en breve de morir, según estimaban

ser gravísimo ese pecado, y sábese por los nuestros religiosos que comúnmente acaecía así, o porque el demonio (permitiéndolo Dios), les causaba la muerte con obras que para ello hacía, para tenellos más devotos y ligados en aquella penitencia y cerimonias de su servicio, o porque *la imaginación de haber cometido pecado que tenían por tan grave, solía ser tan vehemente que de pura tristeza se morían.* (1967, 2:215; my emphasis)

All of them kept to these ceremonies inviolably, because if any part were to be broken, the person would be severely punished, producing such terrible fear that they anticipated death on the spot, if the sin was estimated to be very serious, commonly known by our clergy to be the case, or because the Devil (God permitting), caused them to die, in order to instill in them more devotion and to keep them fastened to penitence and rites to his service, or because *the thought of having committed a sin they considered to be terrible was so vehement that they would die of sadness.*

This dynamic of guilt becomes, in fact, a conditioning factor almost in a psychosomatic way: the ritual of retribution finds expression through the suffering of the body.

In addition, doing penance is described both as an act of contrition and regret and as a fundamental part of many sacrificial rites; yet, what is most significant in Las Casas's description is the identification of the natives' capacity to acquire a consciousness of guilt through an act of re-creation ("la imaginación de haber cometido pecado" [the imagination of having committed a sin]). In the context of New Spain's incipient Christianity, this retribution also may have acquired material and spiritual value and was much exploited in catechistic drama in the attempt to infuse an ideology of continence and retribution. The drama exploited this disposition in the natives by emphasizing the anguish of mental and spiritual distress that medieval drama exploited so consistently.

Through the verbal act of penitence and confession the individual becomes, in a personal and social sense, confronted with, and often divorced from, portions of his past.[19] The drama moves from the genesis of the defiled individual (the First Fall, for example, or the institution of sacramental religion) to the representation of a dislodgment patent in the suffering of the body. "Yn Pochtecatl" ("The Merchant"), another Nahuatl drama centered on timely repentance and proper management of goods, presents the suffering of the body as the result of a transgression that translates into a specific sin.[20]

"The Merchant" represents a continuation of the medieval religious drama that instructed by dramatizing didactic narratives. These constructions would concentrate, primarily, on a single occurrence traversing in a linear fashion: from the acting out of a particular experience of sin or transgression to the moment of judgment or retribution, which would end in either salvation or damnation. "Everyman" and "Mankind" are good medieval examples—both morality plays in which a collective humankind, the principal character, is ultimately saved from damnation by personified Christian abstractions such as Good Deeds and Mercy.[21] Although proper and honest deeds are apparent throughout this play, "The Merchant" lacks the allegorized elements of such morality plays, focusing instead on the torments of perdition and the inability to receive timely forgiveness through either repentance or retribution.[22]

"The Merchant" reflects, moreover, Franciscan and Nahua preoccupations about the restitution of goods and timely repentance. The drama has a simple plot, and its main character could be seen as an extension of the Herodian figure, a medieval example of great pride, blindness, and greed. The first words spoken by Merchant at the very beginning of the Nahuatl drama certainly exemplify this view: "No one can equal me in all my power, in all my goods and property, the gold and silver, the jades and emeralds, the precious pearls. No one can equal me in all the diverse precious things that are my pleasures" (44v).[23] "The Merchant" begins with a prologue announcing the character of the drama. It is about a moneylender who did not return the wealth and property taken from others, oppressing others with his dealings, "what happened to his body and his soul was very frightening and very terrifying" (44r). The drama follows a series of encounters between Merchant and several stock figures, dramatizing Merchant's disrespect toward doing penance and his fall into the sins of avarice and "cobdicia." The play ends by expressing concern about spiritual regeneration, implied in Christian salvation.

The emphasis on the refusal to grant mercy even after penitential conditions are met introduces a stringent view of redemption. Bevington recognizes, concerning medieval morality plays, that placing emphasis on penitential scourging and good deeds as the only means to salvation may have had to do with the assumption of "some urgency in the context of the late fifteenth century, when abuses among the clergy and disaffection among worshippers were on the increase" (1975, 939). In sixteenth- and seventeenth-century Mexico, disaffection among worshippers may have provided this tone and context. Without losing sight of the dogma of salvation, "The Merchant" transforms these concerns into instruments of fear. The specific sin around which this drama is constructed is usury, and the context in which this sin is dramatized suggests the existence of tributary relationships in which Merchant exerts control over Notary and Alcalde, and "weak-minded" women and men of various ages.[24] From the early ideographic prayers and primers to doctrines, sermon books, and confessionaries, catechistic and instructional material dealt with the Christian dogma of sins, some of which may have invited performances.[25] Predictably, the evangelizing campaign had at its disposal a wide range of dramatic images to reassert continuously paradigms of exemplarity and suffering. The sin around which this play is built may speak to Spanish preoccupations about native behavior and may address possible Nahua unease over Spanish abuse of authority.

Merchant's continual breaking of the Ten Commandments and the Commandments of the Church is accompanied by repeated references to bodily pain and punishment, threats of dismemberment, imprisonment, and torture.[26] The most revealing episode related to this last point occurs when Merchant demands Notary's help to forge some documents in order to procure a woman's property and money (48r–v). The woman is a widowed mother, whose husband had left his wealth and property for Merchant to keep (47v). Merchant is summoned as soon as the complaint reaches the judge. When he appears in court he swears in vain, breaking the First Commandment. Priest then reminds Merchant of the futility of accumulating material goods: "know that when you die you will not take any of your goods and property with you . . . help yourself [for] no one else can help you" (49v–50r). This exchange between Mother, Merchant, and

Priest includes the flouting of a specific Christian law framed by the dispossession of material goods, as God's kingdom comes nearer.

Strikingly relevant, and indicative that this drama may have addressed Spaniards as well as natives, is that the play was perhaps attending to a growing problem in Nahua communities, that of land titles and inheritance, as has become evident in much of the work done on testaments, wills, and other legal documents. As Spaniards' and *criollos'* numbers increased, Nahua communities saw their lands diminish and conflicts increase regarding property that was inherited (or not). Many of the testaments attest to pervasive confusion and dishonesty, as the different communities responded to changes imposed by Spanish officialdom, many of which reassigned political value to rulers and communities (see Lockhart 1992, 28–47). The impositions served to advance Nahua as much as Spanish geopolitical organizations.

When the demons make an entrance, the sick man recognizes himself as a defiled body: "My soul is about to perish and my earthly body is very mired down" (51v). The struggle that ensues between forces of angels and demons is both a summons to confess and a calling to renounce association with the devil and a life of sin. The priest stresses precisely this need, as he advises the now too-late repentant sick man: "[God] wants you to save yourself so that you merit and attain his royal home, for you are likely to die when you least expect it. And now he concedes to you time to save yourself by confessing" (52r). At the end, Merchant is made the victim of terrible suffering in hell. He endures further pain at the hands of devils—they choke him to death. His death and the departure of his soul are represented with the "blackened soul" and the sound of rockets. It appears that the Mexicans had grown very fond of pyrotechnic elements used in the dramas, and fireworks served also to announce the fall into hell by one of the boys in "How to Live on Earth" (Horcasitas 1974, 127). The sound effects may have echoed preconquest ones. The sight of the tormented body as the character is led to the place of the dead *(mictlan)*, in the midst of pyrotechnic sounds, must have certainly generated amusement and perhaps fear. It still remains a mystery how color played a part in such effects.

The enigmatic ending of "The Merchant" is accompanied by the words of Guardian Angel. It is a warning to prevent the community going astray from the righteous path of a presumably rediscovered Christian life. The words are also a reminder of the loss of a Judeo-Christian link in the distant, biblical past. The drama, however, makes manifest a strong correlation between the human and the social body in terms of acknowledging—through the drama and in a very real sense before Nahua and maybe Spanish authorities—participation in a defiled polity.

Religious allegiance and realignment entrenches itself in the individual and communal performance of guilt. Guilt is also elicited in the context and symbolism of payment and transaction. As Friedrich Nietzsche suggested more than a century ago, there is a close relationship between guilt and pain, both of which occur in the sphere of contracts, debt, and legal obligations (1956, 194–95).[27] It is for this reason that the language of pledge and compensation is frequently present in catechistic dramas.

The drama "Yn Animastin Yhuan Alvaceasme" ("Souls and Testamentary Executors") shares with "The Merchant" the enactment of a final reckoning in terms of payment, debt, and expressions of allegiance. In addition, confession appears as the opening toward the reconciliation of that debt. The staging of several of the dramas such as "The Merchant," "Souls and Testamentary Executors," and "Final Judgment"—all of which included hells and fiery scenes—identified fever and sickness as divine responses to sin and lack of proper penance. Physical experiences of thirst, fire, and dryness came to be associated with fire and condemnation, evident in this example from "The Merchant":

> If your lips are so dry with just a little illness, if you are so thirsty, how can you suffer the fires of hell and the dried cracking of lips in hell which have no other cure? They will make you drink molten lava, which is very hot, very painful and very heart-rending. (52v–53r)

Thirst is well known in Christian tradition as a metaphor, particularly in the mystics, for the need for (and receptivity to) Christian love (agape). In this drama, sickness and the dualities of dryness and wetness, of hot and cold, may have addressed Nahua as much as Christian cosmic values. Ortiz de Montellano (1990, 8) and López Austin (1988, 380–85) noted that the natives treated disease completely on a supernatural plane; that is, on a plane that was in accord with the animistic view of the universe. López Austin further asserts that the supernatural "was judged to be material, potentially visible, tangible, and audible" (1988, 383). So there was a causal connection between the different planes of the gods and the earth. The friars capitalized on the coincidence of sickness and native religious beliefs, attempting to equate one with the other and attributing both to divine retributive intervention.

According to Christian Duverger, the expression of these dualities in penitential acts was related to the Nahua *tonalli* (1978, 184). The *tonalli* was connected with the maintenance of balance, in particular if it included penitential offerings (184). In other words, the offering of blood (bloodletting) created a direct link, inscribed in the individual since the moment of birth, between the individual and the divinity; the offering's sole purpose was the sustenance and continuance of a cosmic order that gave the community its balance (184–85). In the eyes of the clergy, this manifestation of the natives' need to maintain a cosmic balance through suffering and chastisement became an indication of a certain messianic symbolism. Catechistic representations of penance documented and employed this symbolism in the guise of accountability.

The beginning of "Souls and Testamentary Executors" illustrates this inclination.[28] Don Pedro, one of the central characters, speaks to his wife of his distress over the dead: "I go about discontent before God concerning the unfortunate dead people. They have already given an accounting to him, already been examined before him concerning their deeds, the various sins, and already been judged" (36v–37r). This drama exhibits an infernal setting that emphasizes the horrors of suffering and pain in the context of demon-affiliation. Lucifer's introductory speech and complaint to the five demons addresses issues of property and payment (or the lack thereof): "Do not uselessly lose it through neglect; really go after those in whose hands the dead left themselves. Go, induce them to dissipate absolutely all the property of the dead so that the souls they are to take from us will not escape from our hands" (38r).

Evidently, the sense is that salvation is at stake for those in purgatory and for those involved in the spectacle of retribution. Recalling the Commandments and remembering the dead also play prominent roles in the play.[29] There is repeated emphasis on dismemberment and torture. At the sound of fireworks, the second executor declares why he is condemned, as he responds to the first executor's cry of despair, "Woe to us who are sinners!" The second executor counters, "It is your fault that we are punished and made to suffer here for I said to you that the goods and property of the souls with which they will be helped should be entered into the church. That is why these things are happening to us now" (47v). Material goods become tangible in the context of retributive cleansing and sin, with clear litigating implications regarding property, its loss and possible recovery.[30]

Confession and the dislodgment of material goods was a transactional phenomenon documented in Motolinia's *Memoriales* (written roughly between 1527 and 1541), where we find extensive descriptions of the presumed results of confession. Motolinia dedicates eight chapters to this sacrament, three of which emphasize the aspect of material retribution. According to Motolinia the practice of the Christian sacrament of penitence started in 1526 (1996, 243). He also pays special attention to the docility and devotion manifest in the natives' approach to Christian confession and penance (243–67). Of particular importance are chapter 32 ("Como los yndios rrestituyen lo que son a cargo porque no se les niegue la absoluçión e vn enxemplo a éste proposito" [How the Indians make restitution of what they have in order to gain absolution and an example concerning this]), and chapter 35 ("Como dan libertad a sus esclauos e rrestituyen lo que no poseen con buen título" [How they free their servants or make restitution of what they do not own through good title]). Both chapters present descriptions of material restitution and specific, short, exempla-like narratives that not only serve as possible testimony of Nahua penitential behavior under colonial rule but also provide us with invaluable anecdotal information about commingling patterns of retribution and penance in sixteenth-century Mexico.

Sahagún describes a penitent Indian in connection with the penance dictated by a Nahua priest or mediator *(tlapouhqui)* (1990, 1:20). When he had finished, the priest imposed on the man a penance that would vary in severity: short or lengthy fasts, scarification of the tongue (which might be pierced through and have as many as eight hundred thorns or straws pushed through the wound), sacrifices to *tlazolteotl*, and various other austerities. Once the man did penance, he could no longer be punished upon this earth (1:20–21). This schema of retribution may find a parallel enactment in the catechistic dramas mentioned in this chapter. Perhaps the most salient characteristic is the repeated voicing of regret and admission of guilt. This admission becomes tangible in the context of Christian salvation or damnation. The last words of Widow in "Souls and Testamentary Executors" attest to this:

> Oh! Oh! Oh! You who will have fasting garments, mourning clothes, do not regard them as frivolous for you are ordered to it through penance, prayers and fasting, and communion will be taken each month. I did not do this and now I am paying the penalty. Let everyone take an example from me. (52r)

She and the executors are carried off to hell by demons in the midst of violent cries and threats of dismemberment. "You who are the house of hell, swallow us up once and for all," cries the second executor. "Let us not look at you [the condemned]. As for you devils, just rip us to shreds once and for all" (52r). This "exemplary sign" or *neixcuitilli* takes the form of a public confession that calls for collective repentance and emulation. In addition, this calling also attempts to generate a consciousness of debt, a radically distinct emphasis from that of preconquest restitution of cosmic order. Sins were not believed to be inherent and could assume independence from the individual, in a metaphorical sense.

Catechistic drama may have had a stronger effect on an audience in the context of broadening the scope of the sin to include, for instance, all those whose "consciousness" of transgression had not yet matured to produce a proper Christian penitential act. Two good examples are "Souls and Testamentary Executors," in which honoring the dead demands constant prayers and vicarious acts of negotiation, and "The Merchant," in which material goods are to be "given back" in time to achieve salvation. In these two cases, salvation does not materialize for the main characters, whose penitential acts of contrition have been either too late in coming or substantially insufficient. The "debt" incurred by the transgression has overridden any supernatural intervention other than that of the devils, all of whom have been reduced in these dramas to inflictors of pain and torture or to mere agents provocateurs with no voice in the legislating process.

This depiction of devils is by no means distant from European models. Much medieval and early modern iconography has devils continuously pestering good and erratic Christians, as becomes evident especially in *exempla*. In New Spain, devils (translated into Nahuatl sometimes as *tzitzimitl* [pl. *tzitzimime*], but most often as *tlacatecolotl* [pl. *tlatlacatecolo*]) seem to be limited generally to vicarious assistants who inflict or threaten to inflict bodily pain and suffering after the Last Judgment or after death. As is to be expected, there were testimonies against the friars and their teachings using terms similar to the ones the friars used to portray devils in the Nahua community.

A significant example of this is the case of a native called Martin Ucelo (Ocelotl). Evidence in Sahagún and in Inquisition records shows that Ucelo, after more than a decade of exposure to Christian ideas and to preaching, had begun to use his knowledge of these ideas to discredit Christian indoctrination to his own advantage. Residents of Tecalco who knew Ucelo report that he preached against the friars, using doctrinal ideas pertaining to the end of the world. Ucelo refers to the messengers of punishment who will cause destruction (León-Portilla 1974: 26; *Procesos de indios idólatras y hechiceros* 1912, 19–21). Ucelo is reported to have said that the friars would descend turned into "chichimicle" (cf. *tzitzimime*): "si no se pudiese sacar lumbre, que habría fin el linaje humano, y que aquella noche y aquellas tinieblas serían perpetuas . . . y que de arriba vendrían y descenderían los *tzitzimime*, que eran unas figuras feísimas y terribles y que comerían a los hombres y mujeres" (if no fire could be drawn, then there would be the end of the human race, and that the night and darkness would be perpetual . . . and *tzitzimime* would descend, creatures that were very ugly and terrible and would eat humans, men and women; cited in León-Portilla 1974, 27).

Ucelo's imprecations directed attention to the grim nature of Christian eschatology that was manifest in the practices and teachings of the friars. The residents of Tecalco declared that Ucelo had said that "esta ley de los [crist]ianos, no sabéis que nacimos para morir, é que después de muertos no hemos de tener placer ni regocijo; pues por qué no nos folgaremos mientras vivimos" (this Christian law, you do not know we were born to die, and after death we will have no joy nor pleasure; so why not take advantage while we live; *Procesos de indios idólatras* 1912, 27). León-Portilla comments on this same passage, noting that Nahua critiques of the friars recognized, in spite of apparent similarities, a certain absurdity in Christian teachings (1974, 27), which reminds us of similar descriptions found in Muñoz Camargo.[31]

Burkhart describes Nahua fatalism as a felicitous discovery by the friars as they promoted Christian doctrine (1989, 79). The Nahua lacked any notion of punishment after death but they believed that human actions could be responsible for a final destruction, and Burkhart argues that the friars may have found it more effective to associate punishment for sin with the end of the world rather than with individual death (79). This method, she argues, could have coincided more with Nahua views of collectivity and may have deemphasized individual salvation (79); yet salvation was still central in the instructional process that came to be epitomized by the Last Judgment, and several plays ended with raucous and violent renditions of it.

"Nexcuitilmachiotl. motenehua juiçio final" ("Final Judgment") has been hailed as one of the most distinctive of the surviving Nahuatl dramas, with as yet no direct European referent (Horcasitas 1974, 567). It dramatized at a collective level an elaborate and complex event around which much Christian doctrine was erected. The drama represented a heightened convergence of past, present, and future times. In other words, a temporal origin partakes of the collapse of history as we know it, tracing the biblical timeline from the Adamic myth of exile, the Augustinian *felix culpa* of much medieval thought, to the alignment of the Last Judgment in which God would mete out punishment or salvation for the living and the dead, including those in purgatory. This judicial event of converging times reenacts therefore a dramatic sequence of recollection. In a very concrete sense, the Last Judgment is centered on acts of remembrance.

Like Motolinia's plagues in his *Historia de los Indios de la Nueva España*, "Final Judgment" is part of European and New World eschatology, a mode of experience and interpretation that anticipates or references the end of times.[32] In both cases, an act of chastening confirms the power of a divinity, reestablishes a causal relationship between states of defilement and cleansing, and tempers any future transgression by promising salvation. In Spain, for example, the theme of divine judgment and redemption enjoyed much popularity, showing a long and varied trajectory. The judgment of humankind and the harrowing of hell were, if not central to, at least ingredients of several Spanish *autos*. Examples of this eschatological drama are the plays "Aucto de la redención del género humano" (Play about the redemption of mankind) and "Aucto de la acusación contra el género humano" (Play about the accusation made against mankind; Rouanet 1979, 2:449, 4:47).[33] For a medieval audience, the moment of the Final Judgment demanded self-examination and connected eschatological readings with the liturgy of Advent and its penitential practices (Bevington 1975, 2). The idea of a Second Advent played a significant role in much of the Franciscan campaign of evangelization, especially in their adaptation of Christian eschatology to Nahua indoctrination.

The mapping of eschatological signs, we have come to realize, had idiosyncratic ritual manifestations in Nahua and Christian cultures. The friars paid close attention to Nahua fatalism and were often quick to draw parallels that accentuated Christian eschatology (Burkhart 1989, 77, 79). Muñoz Camargo explains how God, as a gesture of mercy to the natives, fought the devil and rectified the signs he had truncated and used to mislead the natives by sending new signs along with messengers (1986, 179). The friars equally acknowledged other coincident structures and events.[34] In the context of varied eschatologies, "Final Judgment" is a catechistic drama that represents and promotes more than a simple sacramental sensibility. It reproduces the Christian inferno, acknowledging Nahua fatalism and practices concerning death, yet insisting on specific Catholic practices sanctioned in *doctrinas* and sermons.[35] New Testament condemnation meets indigenous responses to calamity and tribulation.[36]

The drama incorporates a total of seventeen characters that deliver lines, including personified abstractions distinctive of medieval miracle and morality plays, in order of appearance: Saint Michael, Penance, Time, Holy Church, Death, Lucía, Priest, Antichrist, First Living Person, Christ, First Angel, Second Angel, First Dead Person, Second Dead Person, Second Living Person, Third Dead Person, Second Demon, Satan, First Demon, and the Condemned. The structure of the drama follows a linear trajectory, divided into sections that dramatize different exchanges of the Last Judgment.

The Christian theme of the drama belongs to the New Testament, Luke 21:25–33 and Matthew 25:31–46 (Horcasitas 1974, 567), although the theme of rewarding people according to their past behavior populates the Old Testament, apocryphal texts, and all sorts of divinatory lore. In Matthew, we find a reference to the Second Coming, the reenactment of judgment, and the subsequent congregation of living and dead before Christ and his retinue of angels. Luke speaks of a judgment day when the Son of Man will be revealed. Horcasitas speculates that the drama was performed with a general mass (567).

Although the episode of the Antichrist echoes John's Apocalypse, as Horcasitas explains, there is no direct European antecedent to the Nahuatl drama (1974, 567). He cites, as a possible partial source to the Nahuatl Antichrist, the twelfth-century German *Antichristus,* a drama that apparently used also a great number of actors or participants (567). Horcasitas is probably referring to the *Ludus de Antichristo,* the "Play of Antichrist," which McGinn describes as worthy of a Hollywood production because of its immense cast and grand subject matter (1994, 134). In this play, paganism (Gentilitas) and Judaism (Synagoga) enter into dispute with the Christian Church over political and spiritual control of the world, with the subsequent victory of the German emperor, who then fulfills his "apocalyptic function by laying down his crown in Jerusalem" (134). The second and last parts of the play deal with the entrance of the Antichrist, accompanied by Hypocrisy and Heresy; his investiture as false king; and a final refutation that prompts the conversion of the Jews and the collapse of the Antichrist. As with several other Antichrist figures throughout history, he is here identified with theological and political dissent and reformation. Insofar as the Antichrist was considered an evil principle in constant war with Christ, his appearance or fancied personification evoked the end of time and the liberation of the righteous. The Antichrist was an apocalyptic motif connected then with the loosening of Satan and a collective anguish that anticipated a renewal of divine leadership.

Spanish apocalyptic motifs were, as in the rest of Europe, popular during the Middle Ages, and their popularity had continued in spite of successive failed predictions of the end of the world. Those motifs were accentuated by the ideas of apocalypticists like Joachim de Fiore, monastic and secular millenarianism, epidemics, and popular ardency for fatalism. In the thirteenth century, Berceo wrote *Signos que aparecerán antes del Juicio Final*, a narrative poem that listed the fifteen signs that would anticipate Judgment Day. Different narratives about these fifteen signs proliferated in Europe and were associated with pre-Christian Sibylline oracles translated at some point into Latin and inserted into various *Signa judicii* (Ramoneda 1980, 22–23). Supposedly echoing a sermon by St. Jerome, Berceo's narrative addresses the social and religious corruption of his time, imploring for penitence and warning that God will see and judge all "en medio del mercado" (in the middle of the marketplace; 1980, 148, line 70).[37]

"Final Judgment" belongs to the tradition of homiletic and visionary apocalypticism. It is a general exhortation to remember the sins committed and to repent, to revise religious allegiances, and to accept the destiny that Christian divinity affords at the final judgment. The drama is also an allegorization of New Spanish paganism that deploys significant aspects of Christian instruction such as respect for the sacraments of matrimony, penitence, and confession and for the notions of death and the Church as promoted by Tridentine Catholicism.

Although individualized by sins and gender, the Nahua character of Lucía may represent neophytes who have not converted, who have only partially converted, or who have already embraced as lawful the Christian liturgy. The friars measured catechization at any level, we must recall, in terms of expressions of devotion and daily participation in Christian ritual practices, whether they knew them to be genuine or not. In this drama, abstract symbols adopt recognizable human (Nahua) faces resulting in a simple and categorical vision of a final tribulation.

The drama begins with wind instruments to indicate the use of music, "Heaven will open" to refer to the manipulation of space and to signal a spatial hierarchy, and ends with "Saint Michael will descend" to confirm the hierarchy but also to acknowledge a metaphysical distinction. Saint Michael comes from above, and a Nahua audience would therefore perceive him as a messenger of a divinity. The archangel's address, resembling the functional *loa* or introductory address of Spanish *autos*, is equally appealing:

> O creations of God! May you know, and indeed *you already know, for it is in the sacred commands*, that he will finish off, he will destroy the world that his precious and honored father, God, made. He will destroy, he will finish off all that he made, the various birds, the various living creatures, along with you. He will destroy you, you people of the world. But be certain that the dead will revive. The good and proper ones who served the just judge, the sentencer, God, he will take to his royal home, the place of eternal and utter bliss, glory, the place of utter bliss of all the male and female saints. But the bad ones who did not serve our lord God, may they be certain that they will merit suffering in the place of the dead. So then, weep, *remember it*. (1r; my emphasis).

The emphasis on remembering highlights several issues of Franciscan perception of the Nahua. It accentuates doctrine taught on a constant basis and reemphasizes the idea that the Nahua had a partial knowledge of God's laws, a suggestion much encouraged in ecclesiastical sixteenth-century chronicles of New Spain. In particular, it was important to place these notions in a context of remembrance. From Gonzalo Fernández de Oviedo (1478–1557), among other chroniclers, we know that the natives had a special capacity to memorize "las cosas pasadas e antiguas" (past and ancient things; 113–14).[38]

By presenting a Nahua audience with this idea of remembrance, the drama is also trying to generate parallels between some religious predispositions and Christian doctrine. The drama is not, in fact, giving the impression of teaching something new but is trying to help the audience evoke a knowledge many of the evangelists assumed natives already had. The "you already know" of the exhortation's beginning signals a different act of remembrance from the decree of the end, "remember." The two could be complementary, however, in the sense that both acts direct attention to recalling and then maintaining a covenant.

Arróniz ventures an interpretation that deserves consideration, although it may, in a superficial sense, assign too much importance to the friars' campaign without recognizing also the active role played by the Nahua in translating the new doctrine. From the reports given by different chronicles, we have gathered that the drama caused much commotion and excitement among the audience. We have also come to recognize in these descriptions a Franciscan fervor that crystallized often in hyperbolic descriptions of conversion and optimism. At the same time, we should keep in mind that spectacles like this and "The Conquest of Jerusalem" may have been large-scale productions that involved on occasion local settings and more often than not collective participation. In this light, Arróniz wonders what in "Final Judgment" could have caused such excitement and wonderment in the natives of Tlatelolco (1979, 20).

As Arróniz discerns, the exemplary nature of the drama served to instill terror toward a God who was inflexible—in this case about unmarried promiscuity. We should remember that the drama is named *Nexcuitilmachiotl*, a word derived in part from *nexcuitilli* meaning "example we take from others," and not from *temachiyotiliztli*, which means "example we give to others" (Molina 1977, 96v). This semantic distinction in Nahuatl between exemplary agent and target, Arróniz argues, was indicative of a people used to ritualizing victory and defeat (1979, 22). As a continuation of examples of victory, "Final Judgment," then, promotes a model to be first evoked, adopted, and remembered.

The personifications of Penance, Time, and Death continue to emphasize remembrance. First, Penance denounces all world inhabitants for their sins *(intlatlacol)*, which they are unable to avoid (1v). Accusations that prophesy death follow this admonition, denouncing how blind and deaf the Nahua are, and lament their forgetfulness of God (1v). It is Time who next pronounces itself a herald of God and reminds the audience (we imagine a very dramatic and authoritative appeal) of their need to remember God and to show remorse and serve Him: "I am crying out into their ears so that they will remember their creator, their maker, the deity, the ruler, God" (2r). Time's words echo Saint Michael's earlier mention of the coming of the Last Judgment and inculcate again the importance of recollection, of summoning Nahua past actions in order to face God's Judgment. Holy Church then takes the general calling for remembrance and redirects it around the sacrament of matrimony, appealing to the audience to cry and feel remorse.

Sweeping continues, declaiming that many of the Nahua have yet to confess or have not confessed in sufficient measure.[39] The emphasis is again on recollection, on rendering an account of "how they lived on earth" (3r). This mental collection of so-called sinful actions took many forms as the friars tried to promote the belief that much of Nahua ritual life was defiled. We recall Motolinia's description of some early attempts at extracting confessions, in which the Nahua would bring "escriptos" (writings) of their sins (1996, 261). Many of these participants were, Motolinia explains, Nahua women married to Spaniards. He also commends the Indians for their willingness to discipline themselves by public flagellation (260). Self-disciplining occurred frequently too, every Friday, and during Lent three days a week (260). Sweeping's urging for penitence, fasting, and purification of heart assumed that, in the natives' memories, there were fresh references of Christian commendation and instruction.

Death closes the circle of exhortation begun by Penance by making the first reference to hell, which the friars often translated as *mictlan* in Nahuatl, the place where the sinful will fall. Sahagún is known to have questioned the adoption of certain Nahua terms to translate Christian notions to the natives. He insisted that *tlacatecolotl*, another term used to translate "diablo," was inadequate although it referred to necromancy, apparitions, and the underworld (1990, 1:267).[40]

Burkhart has argued, using as an example the lack of such references in Sahagún, that some friars were less inclined to read eschatological signs in New Spain. They concentrated, instead, on daily observances (1989, 82). Individual salvation remains a more common theme, with the Nahua's "collective orientation," Burkhart explains, "focus[ing] upon patron saints and community festivals" (82). Daily observances called for purification and cleansing of hearts, although not in as strident a fashion as that of "Final Judgment." In the drama, the appeal acquires an immediate dramatic referent with the appearance of Lucía, an Indian woman verisimilar enough to represent an individual case while maintaining the metonymic value suggested by a collective responsibility.

Lucía appears when Death and Confession leave the stage accompanied by the sound of trumpets. She makes an entrance announcing how distraught she is at the coming of Judgment and how she needs to be confessed (4r–v). The character of Lucía could signal a converted or partially converted member of the Nahua community whose sacramental behavior has been partial to Christian doctrine, suggesting, as many Nahua believed, that a confessor could remedy this imbalance and help to purify the defiled person.

In the drama, the priest and confessor reacts with much exasperation, and his imprecations to Lucía serve only to heighten the sense of doom. He expresses how terrible—"four hundred times"—are the sins committed by Lucía and how the devil is responsible for her distancing herself from God and from the sacrament of matrimony (4v). Lucía is left alone, recognizing her terrible sin. She repents to save her life, albeit too late, calling herself a great sinner.

Portrayed as a false god, Antichrist appears, raising a left hand and wearing a "mantle of wickedness." He speaks to his "children" and then vanishes while fireworks proclaim the entrance of Christ. The directions describe the opening of the skies as Christ descends in the company of Saint Michael, who is carrying the scales of justice. After the singing of "Christus Factus Est," Christ declares the end of the world in terms of cleansing: "As I set down in my sacred commands, I will sweep things, I will purify heaven and earth" (6r).

The drama continues with the gathering of the living and the dead and a continuation of Lucía's condemnation before Christ. Categorical condemnation extends to other characters among the living and the dead, who are brought in by Saint Michael. As the condemned enter, devils torture and pester them. Christ interrogates each one in connection with the sacraments (matrimony, for Lucía), proclaiming punishment and reminding them of the torment they will endure. This torment, Christ proclaims, includes also a type of recollection of sins and vices that will be paraded before her (8r–v).

By linking Lucía's religious affiliation with service to earthly vices, Christ is presenting this as a crucial cause of her proscription. Because this is a physical act of eviction, it may recall the myth of expulsion from Eden, a theme many evangelized Nahua knew in some variety. The Nahua, personified here by Lucía, are reminded of Edenic life via accounting of transgressions. The "perfect symbol for centrality and order" often associated by the friars with the Nahua "heaven" *Tlalocan* (Burkhart 1989, 70) becomes indirectly an instrument of coercion. Lucía's late recognition is met with violence and torture, as she faces demons who push her violently into a steaming hell.

Instead of the word *mictlan*, the composite expression *temazcalli* is used here to designate this place of suffering.[41] Sahagún explains that the *temazcalli* was associated with the curing of diseases and with the cleansing of impurities (1990, 1:461, 2:904). The friars may have tried to link the curative symbolism of the *temazcalli* with the purgatorial elements usually associated with hell and purgatory, an association that could extend to the *tlachpanaliztli* that promotes cleansing and confession. Although *mictlan* was not a place of fire, fire played prominently in the ritual of the New Fire, which celebrated a new calendar round. Fire was related intimately with the gods Huitzilopochtli and Tezcatlipoca, reported obsessively by the friars as horrible manifestations of the devil.

It is difficult to know what kind of perception the audience entertained when these associations of Nahua symbols and Christian valuations intermingled. The New Fire ritual of renewal included certainly a fear of destruction and a great anxiety that translated into a multiplicity of wondrous expectations (such as, pregnant women turning into animals, for example; Burkhart 1989, 73). To mention fire in connection with hell—a house of torture and pain—was surely an unintended attempt to mix preconquest and Christian manifestations of dread. The devils may have been perceived as *tzitzimime* as well, in the event that the ritual of the New Fire did not draw fire: "If fire could not be drawn, then the Tzitzimime would descend from the heavens to consume humankind" (Miller and Taube 1993, 87).[42] Like the *tzitzimime*, the devils in "Final Judgment" may have suggested supernatural characteristics and the power to "consume," as alimentary metaphors become manifest in their speech.

Perhaps this is what Second Demon and Satan imply, after several demons gather instruments of torture:

> Second Demon: Grab up the fiery chains and the fiery metal staff with which we will beat them and tell our ruler, Lucifer, that we are taking his servants over there. Let him quickly send the fiery metal warping frame there where we will take his servants.
>
> Satan: I am bringing everything right here with which we will tie them up so that not one will flee from our hands. *Now we have our drink and our food,* there in the depths of the place of the dead. We exerted all our efforts so that our servants fell into our hands. (8v–9r; my emphasis)

The insinuation is that devils can devour their victims, an act that could easily summon images of *tzitzimime* under certain changes in the skies, such as solar eclipses. The *tzitzimime* were also thought to descend headfirst from above (Miller and Taube 1993, 176), a belief the friars may have echoed in New Spanish iconography of the devil. Examples of descending devils abound in medieval iconography. Illustrations of this iconography in New Spain appeared in open chapels and churches and were surely replicated in iconography and plays. Plates 8 and 10 of Muñoz Camargo's *Descripción de la ciudad y provincia de Tlaxcala* also give an idea of the type of iconography that informed the plays in general. Devils resemble medieval devils as either descending on Christian icons (plate 8) or running from fire (plate 10). The devils in the drama play a role that promotes fear of pain and agony, using images that have, moreover, strong preconquest associations.

"Final Judgment" dramatizes scenes taken from biblical scripture, and it probably epitomizes in New Spain—granted we understand the collective staging of the drama in the context of massive didacticism—the *sensus allegoricus* Zumthor identifies with medieval religious drama. Most of the medieval drama that revolved around the cosmic struggle between God and the devil, Zumthor argues, implied a figuration of the two (1972, 438).[43] The devils belong to the array of characters the friars tried to associate with preconquest apparitions (of priests, of supernatural beings, for example) and to the cosmology of an anti-Christian world that threatens to substitute Christian worship and *ordo*. It may be that this event of the Last Judgment was for the Nahua just another *prodigio*, a portent with no sweeping importance beyond the spectacular.

At this point, it would be fitting to conclude with Muñoz Camargo's description of *prodigios* (portents) from his *Historia de Tlaxcala*. He explains how the native Tlaxcalans responded to events that carried eschatological symbolism. Referring to the sign of fire that would mark an end to the world, with a ball of fire and universal death, Muñoz Camargo retells how the Nahua interpreted the arrival of the Spanish to be precisely this sign. He ventures the following account:

> Tienen por muy cierto que ha de haber otro fin, que ha de ser por fuego y que la tierra ha de tragarse a los hombres, que todo el universo mundo se ha de abrasar y que han de bajar del cielo los dioses y las estrellas, que, personalmente, han de destruir a los hombres del mundo y acaballos, y que las estrellas han de venir en figuras salvajes. Este es el último fin que ha de haber en el mundo. Cuando los nuestros llegaron a esta provincia, como atrás lo dejaremos tratado, entendieron que era llegado el fin del mundo, según las señales y apariencias tan claras que veían.

They hold as true that there will be another end, that it will come in fire and that the earth will swallow humankind, that the entire universe will be in flames and that gods and stars will descend from heaven. They will destroy all humans, will finish them off, and the stars will resemble savage figures. This is the last end in the world. When our ancestors arrived to this province, as was explained earlier in this treatise, they perceived that it was the end of the world, according to the clear signs and apparitions they saw. (1986, 170–71)

According to Muñoz Camargo, these signs of calamity provoked dread and concern and occasioned collective expressions of pain, cries, and rituals of bloodletting (180). We must still wonder what type of response Nahua catechumens had to the devotional and apocalyptic motifs that the friars, and especially the Franciscans, popularized. Certainly, a changed consciousness of renewal and of end times may have settled in, and Judgment Day played a role in that readjustment. Perhaps for the Nahua this cognitive process of reading apocalyptic signs was in some fundamental ways similar to that of a medieval member of the laity. The medieval mind read visually when confronted with a text, as Bevington explains, and "textually in terms of narrative and moral lesson, when confronted with an image" (1975, 6).

"Final Judgment" was the text and subtext that the friars were constantly teaching to the Nahua in sacramental practices, in the primitive liturgy of catechism, and its power derived from persistent visual reading. Its exemplary nature and its didacticism came after the visual fact. The need to designate the territory of conflictual reality, as it becomes manifest in the geography of texts I have studied, is unavoidable. "Nahuatized Christianity" certainly favors the belief in a Nahua active response whereby Christianity was reformulated along with Nahua beliefs, generating what could aptly be termed popular Christianities. The deployment of Christian doctrine meant to instill a belief in inherited defilement and to "amend" cultural traditions of self and society. As Adorno discerns, Amerindian peoples learned from discourses of sin and the Commandments a social code of behavior that helped to determine relations between races, dominant and dominated (1990, 31). And yet, Nahuatl drama reverberated in many other experiences of Christian dogma such as miracles, exempla, and anecdotes—stories and modes of telling that gave birth to multiple experiences and perceptions of Christian doctrine, toppling the millenarian expectation of a homogeneous Christian state.

Notes

1. The adequacy of the qualifier "catechistic" for Nahuatl drama may draw some attention. That didactic and Christian elements present in Nahuatl drama tried to promote specific ideas and types of behavior consonant with Catholic indoctrination is not a matter of dispute. However, a distinction must be drawn between specific texts or performances that were grafted onto the evolving identity of a community and those that had an initial catechistic intention. When some of the *autos* were first introduced, they had, we assume, specific objectives besides bringing as many neophytes together as possible: the teaching of sacramental practices (marriage, confession) and other aspects of Christian doctrine such as belief in the Devil, Hell, defilement by sin, divine intervention (as in miracles) and punishment, to name a few. The continuation of these performances resulted eventually in the reenactment of dramas

whose proselytizing goal was no longer a primary attribute. Needs to reassert local cults, to please or appease local divinities (or saints), and perhaps even to excel in both presentation and importance of the *altepetl* or the community, may have infused the performances with much distinctiveness.

2. Dramatizations of catechistic and edifying plays must have started as early as the 1530s (Ricard 1966, 195; Horcasitas 1974, 562–63; Burkhart 1989, 80). Fernando Horcasitas had a pioneering interest in Nahuatl drama and his published volume *El teatro náhuatl* (1974) gathered an impressive array of examples. The second volume, yet to be published, is now under the guidance of Dr. María Sten in Mexico City. With the publication of Louise Burkhart's *Holy Wednesday* (1996) and the advent of new research on devotional material using Nahuatl sources, there has been renewed interest in Nahuatl drama. For a compressed bibliography on work done on Nahuatl theater, consult Burkhart 1996 (281–82). Vivid although probably suspect descriptions of the plays come from the early friars such as Motolinia and Las Casas. Chimalpahin mentions that in 1533 there was in Santiago of Tlatelolco a representation *(neyxcuitilli)* of the end of the world (1998, 2:187) and mentions Passion plays being represented in 1583 and 1587 in Mexico City (2:257, 263). More *representaciones* are mentioned in other Nahua chronicles. I will revisit these descriptions later in the essay.

3. My use of the phrase "popular Christianity" in reference to colonial Mexico will be explored below.

4. By "radicalized" is here meant the permutation undergone by any cultural model in the process of becoming, consciously or not, a defining instrument of identity. In a concrete sense, the term is linked with the semantics of root or "rooting," which would connote also a process of making something a foundation, a base, in a sense of inhabiting and appropriating a space. In Spanish the verb *radicar* means also to be the inhabitant of a place. In the case of colonial Mexico, the situation is especially complicated by the diversity of agents and motives acting upon a "knowledge" presumed by the friars and church officials to be unchangeable and homogenizing; and also by the different degrees and nature of catechesis. Nahuas, it appears, accepted Christian ways mostly as a means to order, reorder, and preserve what to them were acceptable and Nahua-consonant lifestyles, in spite of the various displacements they underwent after the conquest (Lockhart 1992, 208; 1991, 10). At the same time, Nahuas preserved many of the core traditions of official religiosity. One must wonder what the pope would see if he visited a church in a local Tzotzil community in Chiapas, whether his unspoken discomfort with popular Catholicism would find reconciliation only in the numbers.

5. This is by no means an original idea. The background Burkhart lays out in *Holy Wednesday* (1996, 14–36) opens up a wide range of interpretations and possibilities, calling for an appraisal of Nahuatl drama that emphasizes Nahua agency (42–48): "Colonial Nahuatl theater was a literary and performance genre that developed separately from Spanish colonial drama. Plays were performed in the Nahuatl language, by Nahua authors, and for a principally Nahua audience" (42). Her belief that Nahuatl drama resembles biblical and hagiographic earlier Spanish *autos* rather than Golden Age *comedias* and *autos sacramentales* (42) is by now indisputable. Luis Weckmann has also discussed issues of continuity in his seminal work on the medieval heritage in Mexico, also in the context of popular religiosity (1984, 248–72).

6. The most often cited work is Robert Ricard's *La "conquête spirituelle" du Mexique* (1933; published in English in 1966), an influential work in ecclesiastical history stressing the belief that the Christian campaign had been for the most part, if equivocal in some cases, still a successful and sweeping endeavor. His interpretation relied heavily on the accounts of the early friars, some of whom, like fray Toribio Motolinia, fray Bernardino de Sahagún, and fray Andrés de Olmos, had developed an extensive knowledge of Nahua culture, language, and history. This interpretation has found echoes in many other works, including Georges Baudot's *Utopie et histoire au Mexique* (1976). See Sarah Cline's "The Spiritual Conquest Reexamined" (2000), Lockhart (1992, 2–6), Klor de Alva (1982, 345; 1993, 175), and Burkhart (1996, 59–61) for reassessments and critiques of Ricard's interpretation.

7. The term *folkloric* has had a variety of uses and may not be adequate to designate Mesoamerican civilizations with complex and sophisticated religious, political, and social

systems, lest we be faulted for romanticizing Nahua responses to religious colonialism. The same caution would apply to the term *popular culture*, which even Gurevich has limited to the early Middle Ages, "when the overwhelming majority of the population were peasants and their style of thinking necessarily affected the totality of social consciousness" (1993, xix). The equation of popular and Nahuatized Christianity is a qualitative and useful one, however. *Popular* is neither conceived as a vulgarized version of Christianity (a prejudice that has determined much medieval scholarship to this day) nor is *Nahuatized* seen as a partial or primitive expression of it. I would like to ask for the reader's indulgence in the hope that this analogy will later become clearer. To my understanding, the term *Nahuatized* was first developed by Klor de Alva, under the premise that Christianity for the Nahua meant a continuation rather than a break of their own religion(s) (1993, 175). The idea of Nahuatization, however, is evident in earlier works by Lockhart and Burkhart.

8. Most of the texts written in Nahuatl were made up of doctrines, confessionaries and catechisms, and what we could term casuistry guides. Ruiz de Alarcón's treatise on superstitions written in 1629 may be considered one such guide, meant to catalog the perceptions and practices that its future readers intended to change or eradicate. For studies of Nahuatl printed books, see Ascensión H. de León-Portilla's *Tepuztlahcuilolli: Impresos en náhuatl: Historia y bibliografía* (1988), Barry D. Sell's *Friars, Nahuas, and Books: Language and Expression in Colonial Nahuatl Publications* (1993), and "The Classical Age of Nahuatl Publications and Don Bartolomé de Alva's *Confessionario* of 1634" (Sell and Schwaller 1999). Sell 1993 includes a listing of books by genre.

9. An earlier version of this text was first published in 1990 in *Estudios de Cultura Náhuatl* 20.

10. Sahagún, and later Molina, were known to have had problems with the translation of doctrinal material, although fray Maturino Gilberti's seventeen-year trial (1559–1576)—because of his translation into Tarascan of the *Diálogos de doctrina cristiana*—has been more widely documented (Ricard 1966, 58–60).

11. This predicament of the Spanish ecclesiastical authorities was by no means ever settled. In the eighteenth century, fray Benito Jerónimo Feijóo was still writing about the need to control religious festivities in his *Teatro crítico universal* (vol. 6, para. 2): "La multitud de días festivos, perjudicial al interés de la República, y nada conveniente a la Religión (On the plethora of feasts, harmful to the Republic, and not at all suitable to Religion). Advocating control over the "abusos" and "profanaciones" that had so much infiltrated religious festivities, Feijóo presents a summarized account of many of the Councils, especially in Spain, that dealt with this issue, including the Council of Cambray (1565) and Burdeos (1583) (6:147–52).

12. The texts of the *Junta de 1544* and the *Concilio Provincial Mexicano* of 1555, 1565, and 1585 appear reprinted in Llaguno's *La personalidad jurídica del indio y el III Concilio Provincial Mexicano (1585)* (1962). This and subsequent translations are mine, unless otherwise noted.

13. "Las representaciones teatrales de la Pasión," *Boletín del Archivo General de la Nación* (1934): 332–56. Louise Burkhart informed me that this case had in fact been documented in the *Boletín*. The volume of *Fondo Inquisición* from which this text was extracted is 1182. I located a similar though more extensive description of this incident in volume 1072, folios 195–294. A friend in Mexico informed me that the case the *Boletín* transcribes (dated June 18, 1770) is a summarized account of the 1768 case. The 1934 paleography includes a portion of a play dealing with Pontius Pilate's dictate after the Jews have condemned Jesus, but it does not offer transcriptions of full-length confiscated passion plays that appear at the end of the 1768 corpus I identified. Horcasitas relies on the *Boletín's* 1934 publication for his short analysis (1974, 425–30). On eighteenth-century Passion plays of presumed earlier Nahua authorship, see Juan Leyva's *La Pasión de Ozumba*, a compact and well-research study and edition of one of two Ozumba Passion plays taken from the plays confiscated by the Inquisition in 1768. This incident deserves further scrutiny in the hope of shedding more light on the dynamics of Nahua Christian religiosity as it evolved into the eighteenth century. A full study of the case, including paleography of the plays, is under preparation for future publication.

14. *Archivo General de la Nación*, Fondo Tierras, vol. 2778, exp. 2, 25 (1680).

15. The famous *coloquios* attributed to Sahagún and his Nahua aides was subjected to revisions ("limóse") in order to reflect an exchange more or less determined by the catechistic zeal (Sahagún 1986, 20).

16. From Nahuatl *tlaca(tl)* (person) and *huapahu(a)* (to raise children) (Karttunen 1992, 81, 253; Molina 1977, 116r). No longer the only rendering from Nahuatl, "Tlacahuapahualiztli" has been translated here as "How to Live on Earth." It was translated by John H. Cornyn and Byron McAfee as "Bringing Up Children," a translation followed by Ravicz. Both McAfee and Cornyn place its conception and possible performance after the fall of the capital of Moctezuma, between 1521 and 1530 (316); whereas Horcasitas, who translated the title as "La educación de los hijos," believes it was conceived and performed between 1540 and 1550 (1974, 79). One of the play's themes is the disposition of material goods after death, which indicates prolonged exposure to Spanish ecclesiastical and legal proceedings and expectations concerning the aftermath of death. The first decade after the arrival of the twelve Franciscans is surely too early for this play to have been written or enacted.

17. Translation courtesy of Louise Burkhart. Translations of dramas discussed in this essay are courtesy of Louise Burkhart and Barry Sell and can be found in this volume.

18. Our knowledge of the myth of the Fall in Nahuatl drama starts with "La caída de nuestros primeros padres" (The Fall of Our First Parents), although earlier ideographic renderings were certainly used to transmit the story. According to Motolinia, this *auto* was performed outdoors by native Tlaxcalans honoring the feast of Easter. The Tlaxcalans assisted Cortés in his victory over the Mexicans and in the occupation of Moctezuma's city in 1521. Motolinia described a performance of this play in his *Historia de los Indios de la Nueva España* (1985, 200–202). García Icazbalceta published this and other descriptions appearing in Motolinia in his "Representaciones religiosas de México en el siglo XVI" (1968, 313–37). There are short references to this drama in Las Casas, who cites Motolinia's description (1967, 1:329–31), and in Torquemada (1986, 3:231); but they do not contribute any new information. Horcasitas has shown that the dialogue partially resembles one found in the *Doctrina cristiana en lengua española y mexicana por los religiosos de la orden de Santo Domingo* (1548) (Horcasitas 1974, 176, 179–83). Not much else can be derived from other sources.

19. Early Christian and medieval books of penance (some of which acquired differing shapes in the New World in the form of catechisms and confessionaries) were employed in facilitating a transition from paganism to Christianity; they provided, as well, an ordered and elaborate series of questions and descriptions with the intention of regulating religious and social behavior (McNeill and Gamer 1990, 3). The "Penitential of Silos," which describes penalties for and descriptions of sacramental and social transgressions, is a good Spanish example (285–90). Penitentials existed therefore to exercise control, which would in turn ensure the purification of the Christian community (Tentler 1977, 12). Braswell points out that in many ways the medieval sinner stood alone, in isolation, at least until confession was ended and an order had been issued to do penance and "sin no more" (1983, 13). An interesting difference arises between the medieval sinner, whose sense of collectivity in sin comes only by way of sharing a doctrinal and sacramental knowledge with others, and the Nahua sinner, who had to simultaneously internalize this knowledge, redefining the nature and context of transgression, and to realize his or her position in the face of authority, penitence, and the reestablishment of order.

20. Horcasitas believes that some of these dramas were directed at both colonizers and colonized alike, emphasizing different aspects of didacticism (1974, 170). In my view, this drama belongs to the didactic representations in the tradition of the seven sins, with direct admonitory intentions directed in this case primarily at the natives: to teach retribution and repentance of specific sins in the context of Christian salvation, with a clear emphasis on the symbolic value, or lack thereof, of material goods and property.

21. As Bevington explains in his prologue to "Everyman," however, Good Deeds refers not only to a series of charitable acts that will pave the way to salvation and grace, but also to issues affecting the Church, such as the prescription of proper penitential rites and scourging (1975, 939).

22. Personifications of abstractions were very popular in pre-Renaissance Spanish drama, evident in the variety and number present in the "autos viejos." Catechistic drama presents few examples, of which Holy Church, Death, Penance, and Sweeping each make a salient appearance, all in the apocalyptic drama "Juicio Final." Some of the names of these personifications differ from Horcasitas's translation (1974, 561–93), where Confession and Penitence are used instead.

23. Translation of this play courtesy of Barry Sell.

24. For a view of the historical context of the sacrament of penitence and the dogma of sins, see Lu Ann Homza's article "The European Link to Mexican Penance" (1999).

25. See, for instance, the "Oración del Padre Nuestro en jeroglífico," published in Cuevas 1928, 1:186.

26. Observing days of penance (as in fasts), along with hearing mass, and going to confession at least once a year—all these were part of the Precepts of the Church, or Commandments of the Church.

27. The idea of guilt as a contractual construct has been identified in connection with practices of penance, particularly in the context of the medieval Christian world. Mary C. Mansfield, for instance, finds similar associations in thirteenth-century France: "Penance in the most general sense was obviously about reconciliation: the payment of a moral debt, the restoration of social relations, the reinstatement of the excommunicant, the renewal of peace" (1994, 289). Maureen Flynn's essay "The Spectacle of Suffering in Spanish Streets" connects this retributive "exchange" in terms of the body, and its capacity symbolically to transfer its suffering and pain, "circulating as a costly currency in the purchase of spiritual goods" (1994, 161).

28. Translation courtesy of Barry Sell. Fernando Horcasitas speculates that the creation or performance of this play occurred between 1540 and 1550 (1974, 79). This drama is one of the most apocalyptic of all, along with "Final Judgment." Although its main subject is the teaching of respect for the dead and the Christian notion of purgatorial suffering in connection with the prayers and honoring for the dead (by way of masses, etc.), it encompasses didactic material such as it is found in *Doctrinas* (for example, the Sacraments and the Ten Commandments, a Last Judgment scene with a wheel of fire, and an underworld).

29. Another play, entitled "The Life of Don Sebastián," also introduces the Commandments at the end of the play. In "Souls and Testamentary Executors," this exchange occurs between Saint Michael and Lucifer, whereas in "The Life of Don Sebastián" it is between personified Death and Lucifer and several demons. Saint Michael presents them as commands whereas Death interrogates one of the demons.

30. In her commentary on this drama, Ravicz discusses why a woman, and not a man, is the protagonist of chastisement and reckoning. She believes it was easier to present a woman as a symbol of negative values since "the fear of God and divine retribution is traditionally more easily instilled into women than men" (1970, 233). Although she makes no mention of the extension of medieval Christian misogyny and the tradition of portraying women as "naturally" weaker and as instruments of the devil, Ravicz does present the possibility that some of the evangelistic dramas used women as protagonists in some instances because, in Nahua culture, women had a certain responsibility in the instruction of children and in the preservation of sanctity in the home (1970, 233–34). Lucía in "Final Judgment," Hagar in "The Sacrifice of Isaac," and Widow in "Souls and Testamentary Executors" are vivid portrayals of this possible meaning.

31. Any student of colonial historiography must acknowledge also certain Nahua interpretations. Initially, one responds to New World narratives with a certain incredulity, finding a range of gestures that often smack of absurdity. Muñoz Camargo confirms that many natives had precisely this kind of response when they saw the friars preach: "Cuando predicaban estas cosas, decían los señores caciques: 'Qué han estos pobres miserables? Mirad si tienen hambre y, si han menester algo, dadles de comer'" (When they preached these things, the lord chiefs said: "What is the matter with these miserable beggars? See if they are hungry and, if they want something, feed them"; 1986, 177). Other Indian nobles and priests identified those foreign gestures simply as signs of sickness or madness: "Estos pobres deben de ser enfermos o estar

locos. Dejadlos vocear a los miserables, tomádoles a su mal de locura. Dejadlos estar [y] que pasen su enfermedad como pudieren" (These beggars must be sick or mad. Let them rave, such poor people with their madness, and let them deal with their sickness however they may; 1986, 177). The newcomers, carriers of wondrous words and objects, often seemed fools in need of attention.

32. Its first line, "Nexcuitilmachiotl motenehua juiçio final," translates into "Exemplary sign called Final Judgment." Below, the lines "y tetlatzontequilizylhuitl" provide another reference to the Day of Judgment (Horcasitas 1974, 564). Translations of this play are courtesy of Louise Burkhart.

33. Eschatological themes appear in several other dramas, such as the several *autos* and *farsas* on the Resurrection (Rouanet 1979, 4:66, 3:1, 2:514) and Adam and Eve (4:1, 2:133, 216, 243) Even *farsas sacramentales* such as "Desafío del hombre" (challenge of man; 3:513) echo eschatological sentiments, as a worried Church declares that man's prayer and penitence, with God's guidance, are needed for salvation (3:527). Prayer and Penitence are also characters in this play, in conflict with Lucifer, Lies, and Pride. Another interesting example is "Farsa sacramental de la residencia del hombre" (sacramental farce about man's residence [on earth]), in which Man comes before Justice and Conscience to be sentenced for his sins (1:153–54).

34. The myth of Xochiquetzal was associated with Eve in Eden, and echoes of Noah and the biblical flood were identified with floods of a previous Nahua age (Burkhart 1989, 77).

35. See Burkhart's article in this volume. Her study of the dramas and translations provides a clear and general idea of how the Nahua understood death and how catechistic drama attempted to reorient perceptions and responses to this final event, legally, socially, and theologically.

36. Historians have referred to "Final Judgment" at different lengths. Garibay speaks of a "Juicio Universal," a drama performed supposedly in 1535 that he, like García Icazbalceta, attributes to Olmos, who had arrived in New Spain in 1528 (1987, 2:131). Garibay believes this "Juicio" to be the same as the twenty-one-page manuscript located at the Library of Congress, the same on which Horcasitas bases his translation into Spanish. Horcasitas is one of the first to study this drama in some detail and to provide a summary of what the early chroniclers wrote (1974, 562–67). John Cornyn and Byron McAfee's 1932 translation was published in Ravicz's *Early Colonial Religious Drama in Mexico* in 1970. Othón Arróniz studied the drama in some detail, providing useful interpretations and historical background, in his book *Teatro de evangelización en Nueva España* (1979). In 1992, Jerry Williams published a study of colonial drama in Mexico that deals briefly with this piece (1992, 50–55). Susan McMillen Villar provided a synthetic background of the drama and a more extensive analysis than Horcasitas did, in her dissertation "Drama and the Theater in the Millenarian Project of the Franciscans in New Spain" (1993). The drama is referenced in chronicles and in most historical studies of evangelization in New Spain, which suggests the possibility that several reenactments occurred at least in Tlatelolco and Mexico City between 1531 and 1539.

37. The association of commerce and trade to official religiosity did not escape the watchful eyes of the Mexican councils. Chapter 4 of the Provincial Council of 1555 warns against the "mercados y tianguez" (market places) set up by the natives, on saints' days or on Sundays, because they distracted them and kept them from mass, sermons, and festivities celebrated in their own towns (in Llaguno 1983, 188–69).

38. See Las Casas (1995, 1:23–6; 1967), Motolinia (1985, 113), and Torquemada (3:122) for views about a native pre-Christianity

39. Given that the exhortation here centers on confession, Horcasitas has translated *Tlachpanaliztli* as Confession. Burkhart has opted to maintain the literal meaning of "acto de barrer" (act of sweeping; Molina 1992, 117v) in order to preserve the Nahuatl sense of cleaning.

40. See Burkhart for a discussion of Sahagún's responses to the use of Nahua terms by the friars to designate Christian ideas (1989, 41–45).

41. *Temazcal* is a Hispanicized version of Nahuatl *temazcalli*. Molina identifies this as the name of a kind of public bath, a furnace with vapors where the Nahua bathe or clean themselves (1977:97v).

42. See the discussion above on *chichimicle* or *tzitzimime*, dealing with Martin Ucelo's apocalyptic use of the name in connection with the friars

43. Zumthor's notion of "ordo" derives from his analysis of the *Jeu d'Adam* as *Ordo representaciones Adae*, a name given to the play by the copier (1972, 438). Zumthor's ideas about religious medieval drama ("prédication par personnages" [preaching through characters]) are applicable to catechistic drama in New Spain precisely in the context of allegorization. Allegorization was for the friars both a "réalité ultime" (final reality) and a didactic mechanism that appealed, as in Zumthor's dramatized Scripture or hagiographic *legenda* (legends), to audiences' sensory perceptions (439).

INSTRUCTING THE NAHUAS IN JUDEO-CHRISTIAN OBEDIENCE

A *Neixcuitilli* and Four Sermon Pieces on the Akedah

Viviana Díaz Balsera

In this essay I will compare the *neixcuitilli* "The Sacrifice of Isaac" with exegeses of the Akedah episode (the binding of Isaac) in four sermons from the beginning of the seventeenth century. The sermons are by three of the most distinguished *nahuatlatos* (experts in Nahuatl; translators) in New Spain at that time. A basic assumption of the article is that cross-cultural colonial contexts of reception alter, hybridize, and multiply semantic possibilities as messages are translated into indigenous languages and cast into the target culture's modes of conception and expression. The effects of hybridization that are produced as beliefs and practices from the foreign colonizing culture are imposed on the target culture can be more or less unexpected, more or less unpredictable. Frequently they may produce what Miguel León-Portilla calls "cultural nepantlism," or straddling the border between the two cultures, with the old ways obfuscated and the new ones not yet assimilated (León-Portilla 1974, 24, 33). Or these effects may paradoxically contribute to the survival of the old in spite of attempts to implement the new. They may even result in the alteration of the new by the traces of the old. And although it is sometimes impossible to know how certain messages were actually received by the intended colonial audience (without any direct contemporary testimonies about the matter), it is worthwhile to explore the apparent ambiguities, contradictions, and problems the texts present, if only to the modern reader. This gives us a better sense of the difficulties involved in the colonization of the imaginary (Gruzinski 1988), and a better sense of the possibility that the colonizer might not have always been totally present to himself, and in full control of his discourses, as he strove to reshape and control the will and desire of the colonized-to-be.

The representation of the Akedah episode to a Nahua audience presents two main issues to the modern critic, regarding the admixture and hybridization of cultural discourses in the colonization of the imaginary. The first issue is to explore how this foundational episode is depicted to a community that in its own not-so-remote precontact past had practiced human sacrifice as part of its essential duty to feed the gods and conserve the world. This fact must have been integral to how the audience read the episode of Abraham's obedience and thus must have affected the universality of its meaning as posited by the colonizer. Second, and closely related to the first issue, there is the interest in exploring the problems inherent in presenting this episode to the Nahuas in order to establish radical differences between the precontact gods, so harshly condemned by the spiritual colonizers, and the new colonial deity they should obey. These issues taken together dramatize in an exemplary way some of the uncertainties, ironies, and ambiguities of the Spanish spiritual colonization, which imposed a new god in the lands of Anahuac, but whose discourses were never powerful enough to eradicate the old.

In the first part of the article I will outline briefly the important place allotted to the episode of the Akedah in the religious traditions of the spiritual colonizer, Christianity, and in Judaism. In the second part of the article, I will examine how this controversial episode is depicted to the Nahuas in the *neixcuitilli* "The Sacrifice of Isaac." I will bring some aspects of the prehispanic religious practices of the audience to bear in my discussion, in order to show the similarities and differences that the text produces between such practices and the Akedah episode. These similarities and differences produce hybridization effects whereby the episode acquires new and unanticipated meanings, which make it slightly other to itself. In the third part of the article, I will examine the exegesis of the Akedah episode in sermons by fray Juan Bautista, fray Juan de Mijangos, and fray Martín de León. We will see how the interpretations of this controversial episode involving human sacrifice, although articulated from the perspective of clearly authoritative Christian voices, did not fully differentiate themselves from the cultural memories of prehispanic religiosity that they sought to obliterate.

Abraham in the Judeo-Christian Tradition

Abraham is a key figure in Judaism, Christianity, and Islam. His name comes either from the Babylonian *Abam-rama*, "he loves the Father," that is, God, or from the Canaanite name *Ab-ram*, "the Father is exalted" (*New International* 1:76). The name Abraham signifies "father of a multitude" and was given by God himself to the patriarch-to-be in Genesis 17:5. Because of Abraham's unwavering belief in the seemingly implausible promises of Yahweh, his faith was counted for righteousness and thus he was the man with whom God sealed a covenant that changed the course of history. The extraordinary promises that would be the basis of Abraham's life figure in Genesis. Being one hundred years old and having a wife who was ninety, he was promised a son and descendants that would be as numerous as the grains of sand on the seashore (Genesis 17:19–22, 22:16–18). God pledged to Abraham, a foreign nomad and wandering shepherd, that his descendants would inherit the rich land of Canaan (17:8) and, although he came from an insignificant tribe, that all nations would be blessed through him. Abraham's faith was manifested in a life of utter obedience. He left his father's house and constantly moved from one place to another at God's command. Most important, he was tested "to see whether in his person the people of God would esteem God enough to be willing to offer human sacrifice" (*New International*

1:76), and he was thus asked to sacrifice the beloved son that had been finally granted to him in a supernatural way. The ultimate act of obedience that was the binding of Isaac at Mount Moriah moved God not only to promise but to actually take an oath to bless Abraham and all his descendants. The stature of Abraham is thus of epic proportions for Judaism. He is the great mediator, the patriarch and father of Israel and of multitudes. He is the first man to have left behind the cult of false gods. He is the one who, if stood by, guarantees that God will not go back on his promise (Kuschel 1995, 19). God saw in Abraham "the innermost reality of the human soul" (Buber 1968, 42) and he was the first man in Scripture to whom God let himself be seen (43).

The Christian tradition had to come to terms with the figure of Abraham early on because of his central importance in Jewish theology. In his Epistle to the Galatians, Paul notes that Abraham justified himself through his unwavering faith, not through the Law, which came later. This allowed him to extend the promise of salvation and of the covenant to the Gentiles. In his letter to the Romans, Paul reiterates this call to the universality of the structure of Abraham's faith, "hoping against all hope, not doubting in the promise of God" (Kuschel 1995, 88), in the belief that Christ is the son of God and that he was in fact resurrected from the dead. He did not exclude Israel because of her unfaithfulness in Christ (she remains "loved by God, for the sake of the fathers" [Romans 11:28]), but with the advent of Christ, Israel is no longer the exclusive mediator of humanity for salvation. God's promise to Abraham has been fulfilled in Christ and Abraham remains the father of the Jews, but in faith. For his part, Matthew the Evangelist insisted on the carnal descent of Christ from Abraham, thus emphasizing that salvation and blessings for humanity would indeed come from the patriarch's lineage. However, Matthew, still without excluding the Jewish community, starts broaching the topic that carnal descent is inferior to spiritual kinship and that "a purely formal appeal is nothing to God" (Kuschel 1995, 94). In this sense, God's covenant with Abraham has not been derogated by Christ: it has been fulfilled by him in a faith that is the true essence of Israel.

James's epistle differs from Paul's in that he considers deeds to be a necessary evidence of faith. If there is faith, it will show in works, but faith alone will not be enough for salvation. James refers to Abraham, "our father" (2:20–24), in order to support his argument that faith and works are inseparable. James's position not only seeks to redefine Christianity vis-à-vis Judaism (actually not too difficult considering the Jewish stance on faith and acts) but also considers the offering of Isaac on the altar as a deed: "Was not Abraham our father justified by works, when he offered his son Isaac upon the altar?" (2:21) Much like Philo of Alexandria (c. BC 20–50 AD), James thinks that, although the sacrifice was not carried through, Abraham's acts—of taking Isaac up to Mount Moriah, tying him up, and drawing the knife—were already complete acts, not merely an internal disposition to do something (this will be important for our discussion of "The Sacrifice of Isaac" later on).

In John's Gospel, the relationship between Judaism and Christianity starts to break apart. John declares there cannot be knowledge of God without Christ (8:31–59). Thus the Jews, because of their hardness of heart and desire to kill him who had come from God and who had existed before Abraham was born, and in spite of being carnal descendants of the patriarch, were not his real children but children of the devil. As Jeffrey Siker observes: "The Jews who staked a special claim on their self-designation as 'descendants of Abraham' conceded by John, find themselves abandoned in the Fourth Gospel" (1991, 142). This will be the beginning of the exclusion of the Jews from the Christian ecumenical community, and the appropriation of Abraham as son of Christ.

With Augustine's theology of Abraham three centuries later, John's seizure of the father of Judaism would be consolidated, backed up by the patriarchs of the early Christian Church—Barnabas, Ignatius, and Justin. In book 16:32 of the *City of God*, Augustine treats the episode of the sacrifice of Isaac as God's temptation of Abraham to prove his obedience not to him, but rather to the world. In perhaps not the most convincing argument, Augustine states that "Of course Abraham could never believe that God delighted in human sacrifices; yet when the divine commandment thundered, it was to be obeyed, not disputed. Yet Abraham is worthy of praise, because he believed all along that his son, on being offered, would rise again" (1950, 554). That is, Abraham obeys God's awful command, represented by Augustine as a "not blameworthy temptation," knowing that God does not desire human sacrifices, and always believing that his son would be restored to him once offered. On this count, Augustine openly incorporates Hebrews 11:17–19. Augustine then reads Isaac as a type of Christ, as Isaac carries to Mount Moriah the wood upon which he is to be sacrificed, and once Isaac's father is forbidden to smite him, the ram then typifies Christ, who is sacrificed for the sake of humanity. According to Saint Augustine, in this figural relationship that anticipates Christ, the promise to Abraham (in terms of the blessing of the nations through his seed) is fulfilled. In terms of the old covenant between Abraham and God, Augustine follows John in stating that it has been superseded by the advent of Christ. The only reason for the existence of the Jews is the fact that their scriptures give testimony of the truth of Christianity (Kuschel 1995, 127). Insofar as Jews refuse to do this or misunderstand it, they are excluded from the plan of salvation. This position regarding Abraham and Judaism was passed on through Church tradition up to the twentieth century. And certainly, it was the prevailing one in Mexico during the sixteenth and seventeenth centuries.

"The Sacrifice of Isaac" and the Violence of Obedience

Critics are in agreement that the Nahua theater of evangelization had a clear didactic function from the perspective of the spiritual colonizers (Horcasitas 1974, Burkhart 1996, Lopétegui y Zubillaga 1965, Arróniz 1979, Williams 1992). This theater was supposed to teach the Nahuas regarding the new deities and narratives of origin they were henceforth supposed to believe in and claim as truth. The codification of the term *neixcuitilli* or "something that sets an example" (Burkhart 1996, 46) to refer to this dramatic colonial genre indicates that the Nahuas certainly did not miss the point of the friars' edifying intent.

Although the friars never elaborated on why they chose theater as a technology of evangelization, it may be posited that the religious dramatic tradition that had emerged in Europe since the tenth century helped to persuade them that spectacle was a great supplement to the verbal doctrine regularly received by the faithful from the pulpit.[1] The friars must have realized the vital role public rituals held in preconquest society. As is well known, the Nahuas believed in a large pantheon of gods. Scholars of Aztec studies have identified at least 128 major deities, making regular yet overlapping appearances, to whom worship was rendered (Nicholson 1971, 408–10). Each of the eighteen months of their solar calendar was dedicated to one or several deities, to whom a specific ceremony had to be carried out in order to influence their supernatural activities or to guarantee their survival.

These ceremonies or rituals were not merely a random group of religious activities. They followed an elaborate script meticulously overseen by priests. They would generally be celebrated in open public places such as the temple plazas and platforms. Often an individual, usually the sacrificial victim, wore the regalia of the deity in question and enacted a sacred narrative, supported by priests, penitents, and the more or less active participation of the people. Thus, as Ángel Garibay has suggested, it might well be that the friars felt compelled to transplant some of Spain's own traditions of public religious celebrations in order to fill the void created by suppressing the busy calendar of prehispanic pagan festivities (1953–1954, 2:155–56). Perhaps, to attract large masses of Nahuas to the new religion, "the most effective—indeed, the only—way . . . was through the use of song, dance, plays, processions, and their accompanying pageantry and paraphernalia" (Burkhart 1996, 43).

The Nahua theater of evangelization may have been conceived to introduce the new religious discourses, without breaking away from the prehispanic public ways of worship, as long as these ways were not incompatible with Christianity. The Nahuas themselves were in charge of the mise-en scène of the actual performances of the *neixcuitilli*, and even of a good deal of the commitment to paper of the dramatic scripts, which underscores the fact that the theater of evangelization, albeit an idea coming from the spiritual colonizer, could not possibly have been realized without active Nahua collaboration. This theater must be studied therefore from a double perspective: from the point of view of the colonizer, as an evangelization device whose realization largely depended on prehispanic ways of constructing spectacle, and as a theater that legitimized the colonized-to-be (Burkhart 1996, 48) by the display of their great capacity to appropriate the new gods, a capacity that harked back to precontact times, as Sahagún pointed out in his exasperated comments in the prologue to the *Arte adivinatoria* (in García Icazbalceta 1954, 382–83).

Furthermore, as James Lockhart has pointed out, given the understandable problems of the friars' linguistic competence in Nahuatl, it is difficult to know how much of the dramatic texts in the extant *neixcuitilli* they actually composed. Lockhart speculates that perhaps the Spanish ecclesiastics actually wrote in Spanish and the Nahua amanuensis would then translate into Nahuatl. An isolated unfinished phrase in Spanish that appeared in a sixteenth-century manuscript playlet entitled "Holy Wednesday" suggests to Lockhart that the Nahua aide did not understand what it meant but copied it down anyway. Several misspelled words in Spanish lead Lockhart to propose that the dramatic script was never again supervised by the friar: "It is as though the directing Spaniard, although in a sense probably deserving to be called the author of the play, never looked at it again once he had given it to a Nahua to translate and realize as he saw fit" (1992, 403). Needless to say, this hypothetical situation implies, at the material level of the dramatic script itself (not to say of the theatrical performance), enormous possibilities for inflecting the authority of the colonizing discourses.

There are some unsettling ambiguities brought about by the way in which the Akedah episode is represented to the Nahua audience in the *neixcuitilli* "Del naSimiento De iSaac del Sacrificio q.e habrahan Su Padre quiso por mandado de Dios hazer."[2] The 1760 extant manuscript of "The Sacrifice of Isaac" attests that it was copied from a 1678 "original." Fernando Horcasitas, the Mexican translator of many of the extant plays of the Nahua theater of evangelization, proposes that the date of composition of this specific *auto* must probably be located in the first half of the sixteenth century. He argues that Motolinia mentions in his *Historia de los indios de la Nueva España* the representation of an *auto* of this title in Tlaxcala in the religious festivities of 1539 and that no other chronicle mentions it again. The metaphorical language and certain speech patterns of the play seem to hark back to prehispanic usage. The inclusion of the episode of Ishmael and Hagar would indicate for Horcasitas an interest on the part of the friars in fighting the institutionalized polygamy that then prevailed among the Mexica nobility (1974, 191).

Of the three arguments supporting an early sixteenth-century composition of the play, the latter is perhaps the weakest, since the fact that Ishmael was Abraham's son is never directly stated (Williams 1992, 73). It can only be inferred through an oblique allusion to Ishmael's birth in a scene between Hagar and Ishmael.[3] Although the other two arguments may also be contestable, still there is some good reason to treat in this essay the *neixcuitilli* as if in fact it preceded the sermon pieces. The *neixcuitilli* does not show the theological refinement, discernment, and precision of the sermons, and herein lies the crux of some of its fascinating problems. Such "shortcomings" may certainly be from a problem of genre, or even from a contingency of composition, but it is not unreasonable to situate the less sophisticated text temporally before others showing more complexity, so without any decisive evidence to the contrary, we will proceed with what seems the most sensible scenario.

"The Sacrifice of Isaac" is clearly divided in two parts.[4] The first deals with the expulsion of Hagar and Ishmael from Abraham's household and, following the biblical episode, represents a banquet offered in honor of Isaac. Although there are several important moments of cultural translation that make this first part more readable and familiar to a Nahua audience, I will focus only on the representation of the controversial episode of God's demand for the human sacrifice of Isaac in the play's second part. If the dates of the *neixcuitilli* are the ones proposed by Horcasitas, it could be hypothesized, as many critics have done, that "The Sacrifice of Isaac" may possibly have been intended to show the Nahua audience the difference between the recently repudiated prehispanic deities, who demanded human sacrifices, and the new Judeo-Christian one, who did not (Horcasitas 1974, 198–99; Potter 1986, 312; Williams 1992, 73–74). If the play was written at a later period and was aimed at new Nahua generations, raised under the strict prohibition of human sacrifices, the urgency to establish such a difference might not have been so great. In either case, however, "The Sacrifice of Isaac" shows features that can seem inconsistent with the representation of the Christian God as truthfully good precisely because he does not desire human sacrifices: "The true God that we preach to you because he is good he loves well the Christian people and you too if you'd like to be his friends; and for all of this he does not want you to kill your children nor your slaves . . . . nor that you improperly shed your blood (Córdoba 1988, 35; translation mine). This statement appears in fray Pedro de Córdoba's *Doctrina cristiana*, printed in Mexico in 1544. Thus, it can be reasonably assumed that the Nahuas had already been introduced to this basic difference between the Christian and prehispanic deities by the first half of the sixteenth century, if not soon after the Twelve set foot in Mexico and human sacrifices were prohibited in 1525 (Motolinia 1951, 99).[5] But in the attempt to secure the continuing subordination of the indigenous audience to the authority of the Christian god, the latter will be portrayed in the *neixcuitilli* in a very different light. Far from being depicted as a merciful "Father who does not want to sadden us, who does not want to afflict us, but who wants to gladden us" (Sahagún 1993a, 137; translation mine), He is represented as demanding a total obedience and subjection similar to those rendered to the prehispanic deities by the Nahua ancestors.

The second part of the play opens with the dramatic figure of God the Father. He claims to have properly prepared all things of heaven and earth and declares that "all people on the Earth" will obey his consummate will ("Sacrifice," 31v). Abraham then comes onstage, politely and earnestly praying for Isaac's fate, since he is very worried his son will not obey God as he should. Abraham conveys a strong fatherly concern for the fulfillment of his son's religious duties, and great fear and deference to his God. In answering his prayers and devoted concern, however, God the Father calls on Abraham and requires him to sacrifice his beloved Isaac: "If it is true that you can carry out my sacred commands, seize your child named Isaac whom you greatly love and take him to the top of the mountain in the place named Moriah. There you are to kill him. If truly you carry out my sacred command my heart will be satisfied." (32r)

The violence of the demand being put forth by the Judeo-Christian god can be orthodoxically explained away as a test of obedience of an evidently righteous man. Abraham's instant acquiescence is thus represented in the *neixcuitilli* as part of the *pilli*/patriarch's exemplary faithful demeanor: "I will carry out your command. I intend to do it for you, the All-powerful, whose words I hear, are eternally worthy of being believed" (32r). This accords with the Jewish theology of Abraham as a faithful and honorable man, "deeming that nothing would justify disobedience to God and that in everything he should submit to his will" (Josephus 1.225, quoted in Siker 1991, 23). It also conforms with the Pauline conception of Abraham as father of all those who have faith in God (Romans 4:16–19) and all those who never doubt his promises.

In the colonial context of sixteenth- or even early seventeenth-century Mexico, however, this demand for a human sacrifice by the Christian god acquires unexpected, hybrid meanings, because it resembles the former exaction of human victims by the Nahua prehispanic deities as enacted in the old calendrical rituals. Abraham's piety as shown in his acquiescence to sacrifice his son to his God would not have been particularly extraordinary or new in the lands of Anahuac. In the first treatise of Motolinia's *Historia*, where he will later refer to the 1538 Corpus Christi festivities and to the only recorded performance of a "Sacrifice of Isaac," the friar discusses the feast celebrated in honor of Tlaloc, god of rain and water, to whom the Nahuas sacrificed children:

> Once a year when the corn was a palm high, a feast was held in the towns where the chief lord resided and where his house was called a palace. On the appointed day the Indians sacrificed a boy and a girl about three or four years

of age. *These were not slaves, but the children of chiefs, and the sacrifice was performed on a hill out of reverence to the idol who,* they said, was the god of water and who gave them the rain, and whom they invoked when there was lack of water. (Motolinia 1951, 118–19; emphasis mine).

Later on, Motolinia states that as the corn grew higher, children up to seven years old would also be sacrificed, the idea being that there was a correlation between the height of the corn and that of the children. However, he specifies that the older children were the sons and daughters of slaves, whereas the younger ones were the children of noble men and women, as if to imply a greater sacrificial value during the initial stages of the corn cycle. Contemporary anthropologists have not been able to verify Motolinia's claim on the noble provenance of the little children sacrificed to Tlaloc (Román Bellereza 1987, 139). Nonetheless, it is significant that he brought up the issue, even if erroneously, because of the many coincidences broached for the Christian imagination between this sacrifice and Isaac's—who, although not the son of a nobleman, was nonetheless the son of a prominent free one. The fact that, in the *neixcuitilli*, Abraham's social status is raised from that of a desert seminomad to that of a *pilli*, "nobleman," (and sometimes even *tlatoani*, "ruler")[6] suggests that the coincidences brought up by Motolinia's passage were being alluded to in the play.

On the other hand, Isaac's age goes unmentioned in the first and second parts of the play. In the opening scene, Sarah refers to him as "a young fellow" who has been raised up with her breast milk (24v). So he is already weaned, although we are not given a clear clue as to how recently. Inga Clendinnen has observed that the Nahuas usually weaned their children by age three (1991, 188–9). We could thus surmise that the "young fellow" Isaac must be at least four years old or more. It is not mentioned whether the banquet celebrated in Isaac's honor is to commemorate his weaning, as in the case of the biblical story. Also, in that story, Isaac seems to be around thirty years old when he goes to Mount Moriah to be sacrificed. Abraham opens the second part of the play with his worries over his child Isaac not carrying out his proper duties to God, and God the Father also refers to Isaac as "your child." This might suggest that Isaac is the same age in the first part of the play as in the second. Only at the moment of the representation, however, would the audience be able to discern his age, from the physical stature, voice inflection, and so on, of the actor playing that role. Needless to say, the smaller the child, the more likely he could be associated with the little children sacrificed to Tlaloc on the mountaintops, according to Motolinia the offspring of noblemen and noblewomen.

A couple of scenes later, Abraham, as a Nahua *pilli* or nobleman, arrives on the hilltop with his beloved Isaac. Much like the people crying for the little children taken to be slaughtered for Tlaloc (according to Sahagún 1989 1:107–8), the disconsolate lord sheds copious tears as he explains to Isaac that God has asked for his death in order to see if the people would really obey His orders. He then adds, "Now receive death with great humility, for he speaks thusly: I will be able to raise the dead for I am eternal life everywhere in the world" (33v).

In this exhortation to Isaac we may see a reference to Hebrews 11:17–19 and to Saint Augustine's claim that Abraham had unwavering faith that God would fulfill His promise of numerous descendants even as he demanded the sacrifice of the only beloved son. However, in spite of such faith, the depiction of Abraham's immense sorrow (an *amplificatio* of the biblical story) also reveals the inordinate suffering provoked in Abraham by the violence of the deity's command. In the pain inflicted upon loyal worshippers, the god of the spiritual colonizers seems to resemble the arbitrary god Tezcatlipoca, about whom it was said that "he was the only one who ruled the world, and that only he gave prosperity and wealth, and that only he took them away whenever he pleased. . . . That is why he was greatly feared and respected, because they believed it was in his hand to raise and bring down" (Sahagún 1989, 1:38; translation mine).

Similar to the biblical story, it is only when the sword is already falling over Isaac, when Abraham has started to slaughter his son, that an angel finally appears to seize his hand. The angel explains that God "has thus seen how you love him and carry out his sacred commands so that you do not violate them" (34v). The angel declares that Abraham must sacrifice a lamb instead, which is never represented dramatically. Horcasitas points out that the restatement of the Franciscans' prohibition of human sacrifices would explain the dissimulation of the animal sacrifice (1974, 189). With the angel's intervention to stop the slaying of Isaac, the friars may indeed have intended to proclaim to the Nahua public that the Christian god rejected human sacrifice.[7] They seriously overlooked the fact that, as Robert Potter points out, "the original story implicitly credits the idea of sacrifice, as a fitting response to a divine command" (1986, 312).[8] Moreover, as though God were not content with Abraham's initial disposition to perform the sacrifice, only at the very moment that the slaughter is to be consummated is it finally interrupted. As Abraham slowly walks to and climbs up Mount Moriah, as he dutifully cuts the firewood and ties and blindfolds Isaac, as he draws the knife, in his heart and imagination Abraham has already slaughtered his beloved son not once, but over and over again. This is what Philo of Alexandria saw when he stated that Abraham's sacrifice "though not followed by the intended ending, was complete and perfect" (*De Abrahamo* 62–68, quoted in Siker 1991, 23), and what James the Apostle meant when he considered the offering of Isaac on the altar as works that justified Abraham, along with his faith (James 2:21–22).

In the biblical episode, a deeply moved Yahweh sends the angel back to tell Abraham that he has sworn by himself, that is, by the highest being that he can conceive, that because Abraham has not withheld from him his only son Isaac, his seed will bless all the nations on earth (Genesis 22:18). But in the play God takes no oath at all. The character of Abraham is rewarded only by being released from his son's execution at the very last moment. As they descend from the peak of Mount Moriah, Abraham admonishes Isaac:

> Now may the honored name of the All-powerful, God the Father, whose compassion is very great, be eternally praised everywhere in the world. If all we people of the earth would carry out his precious sacred commands we would greatly please him. And as for you, my beloved child, you have seen how he saved you from death. Now as long as you live, always love him with all your heart and do not take in vain the name of God, and love your neighbors. Such are his orders. (35r–v)

There is no sense that Abraham has accomplished anything extraordinary, unique, and irreversible for all the peoples of the world. He is represented as having only fulfilled—albeit remarkably well—his duty to obey God's command. Although there is mention of Isaac as a prefiguration of Christ in an angel's passage at the very beginning of the play, the paramount epic dimension of the covenant between the patriarch of the Jews and of all nations and Yahweh is all but suppressed in the rest of the *neixcuitilli*.[9] With his act in extremis, Abraham generates only authority enough to establish himself as an example of obedience for Isaac and for the Nahua audience. And if the passage was intended to show the audience that although Abraham's ordeal was onerous, the orders spelled out to Isaac to follow from that moment on would be easy and nongrievous, the *neixcuitilli* gives no reason to think that such commandments were entirely new. Abraham had already mentioned to Isaac in the first part of the play that there were three things he should always follow and remember.[10]

Abraham's model behavior seems to be underscored in the dramatic text by the angel's ambiguous closing admonishment to the audience:

All of you who are here have now heard this *marvelous thing*. And as for you, may you live entirely according to his sacred commands, may you and your children not violate a single one. Take good care that they will not go about playing and wasting time, so that they will serve with goodness our lord, God, and so that they will also merit the kingdom of heaven. May it so be done. (35v–36r; emphasis mine)

Although the angel defines what the audience has seen as a "marvelous thing," something that causes admiration, it is impossible to determine what such a marvelous and unheard-of thing refers to specifically. It could as easily be God's order to sacrifice Isaac, Abraham's willingness to carry out such a command, God's sparing of the human victim, or all of the above. The angel then edifies the audience by saying that the marvelous thing they have witnessed in the *neixcuitilli* has instructed them to keep God's commandments. But by linking the undecidable marvelous thing to the exhortation to obey the divine commandments and to keep children from playing and wasting time, the angel's passage certainly does not give much indication of anything exceptionally achieved for ages to come. Such a link between the marvelous and the ordinary opens up the possible interpretation that any of the spectators could be required to undertake and readily submit to Abraham's horrific ordeal. This didactic exemplariness of "The Sacrifice of Isaac" dangerously splits the Judeo-Christian God's unique, tremendous, perhaps most controversial request in the Scriptures into an iterative, duplicable one. Thus, with the loss of the epic dimension of the Akedah episode, the God that emerges in the dramatic text of "The Sacrifice of Isaac" becomes Nahuatized, hybridized, somewhat other to itself.[11] By being depicted as not having given up forever the demand for human sacrifice, if only just to test the obedience of his creatures, He is not *radically* differentiated from the violent, frightening prehispanic deities of the audience to whom all had also to be offered unhesitatingly in order to keep cosmic time alive. In this sense, the friars involved in the production of the dramatic text of "The Sacrifice of Isaac" partially betrayed the difference between the violent Tlaloc, the arbitrary Tezcatlipoca, and the all-loving, benevolent Christian god they proclaimed in their writings, in their pulpits, and in the very prohibition against human sacrifice that had been issued in 1525.

Along with many critics of the play, one may argue that, in spite of any similarity with the prehispanic deities, the God of "The Sacrifice of Isaac" is ultimately posited to the audience as not desiring human sacrifice (Horcasitas 1974, 189; Cornyn, quoted in Horcasitas 1974, 198–99; Ravicz 1970, 97; Williams 1996, 73–74; Potter 1986, 312). However, it should be recalled that, particularly for Christians, an act does not necessarily need to be fully performed in order either to be sinful or to bring blessings. In fact, the possibility that lustful thoughts and yearnings may be already sinful, independently from their materialization, is one of the constitutive aspects of the Christian moral subjectivity that the missionary agents were assiduously trying to implant in the Nahuas.[12] Christ's warning that whosoever looked lasciviously at a woman had already committed adultery with her in his heart (Mat: 5:27–28) clearly reflects this point. What is relevant to "The Sacrifice of Isaac" about such a specific mode of sinfulness and the interiority that it broaches is that the *neixcuitilli* indeed shows this new Christian form of subjectivity to the Nahuas while ironically creating strong continuities with their religious past. The *neixcuitilli* displaces the utter materiality of the final, external act of human sacrifice, but it retains as desirable the thought and internal disposition to perform it. It emphasizes that Abraham was ultimately spared of having to execute the actual immolation of the human body. But the violence and the yoke of having to submit to such a command is not lifted. For only by his unquestionable readiness to surrender to such an atrocious demand (not unlike the Nahua ancestors' obligation to perform human sacrifices), only after having carried out all the necessary steps for the slaughter, was Abraham rewarded by being freed from acting.

The Nahuatization of Abraham and of the colonial god that our reading has suggested may not only be imputed to the ardent desire of domination of the friars conceiving of "The Sacrifice of Isaac." It may have also been an effect of the participation of the Nahua scribes, as was mentioned above. The erasure in "The Sacrifice of Isaac" of the radical difference between the violent Tlaloc, the arbitrary Tezcatlipoca, and the all-loving, benevolent Christian god championed by the friars may have been a subversive intervention by the scribes to signal to the audience that the colonial god did not utterly condemn the prehispanic practices of human sacrifice. Or, such an erasure and hybridization may have been the result of an unwitting cultural projection through which the Nahua aides made sense of the new by making it look familiar to the known. Or finally, the omissions that hindered the epic transcendence of the Akedah episode as well as the weakness of the text's formulation of Isaac as a prefiguration of Christ may point to "the large field of Nahua discretion and independence in translation, extending to numerous adaptations and additions" (Lockhart 1992, 403), that in this case perhaps resulted in a less adequate grasp of the foreign theology's subtleties.

In any case, by not breaking decisively with the religious violence of the prehispanic past, "The Sacrifice of Isaac" transformed Abraham's seminal act of total surrender to the deity into something less than extraordinary for the Nahua audience. After all, the men and women in Anahuac had also been capable of sacrificing the most precious and beloved to their gods, believing these gods to be true. And from a Christian perspective, it may be argued that the *neixcuitilli* hybridized the

Akedah episode by portraying God the Father as expecting from the Nahua masses a form of absolute surrender that in the Judeo-Christian tradition had been demanded only from Abraham, Jesus, and Mary.

Abraham Revisited by a Star Team of Early Seventeenth-Century *Nahuatlatos*

Sermons by three of the most prominent *nahuatlatos* of the seventeenth century—fray Juan Bautista, of the Franciscan order; fray Juan de Mijangos, an Augustinian; and fray Martín de León, a Dominican—provide commentaries to the Akedah episode.[13] Bautista's and Mijangos's texts were carefully revised by the outstanding Nahua *letrado* and trilingual teacher at the Colegio de Santa Cruz in Tlatelolco, Agustín de la Fuente.

It may be perhaps more than an exceptional coincidence that these three salient contemporaries would have written exegeses on the binding of Isaac for the edification of the Nahua faithful around the same period of time. Besides the *neixcuitilli* and some occasional references to Abraham sprinkled in sermons here and there, the Akedah episode is not commented on much by any other friar-*nahuatlato* in print.[14] Were exegeses on the binding of Isaac shunned by less audacious spirits—both before and after Bautista, Mijangos, and León—because of fears of possible misunderstandings by the Nahua audience of the thorny issue of the demand for human sacrifice by the Judeo-Christian God? Needless to say, much archival work and research must still be done in order to venture any hypothesis on why this prominent trio of *nahuatlatos* decided to take on the Akedah episode during the first two decades of the seventeenth century, other than it being merely a fortunate coincidence or collegial theological rivalry. It could very well be the case that future scholars may find in presently unknown manuscripts of devotional literature exegeses of the binding of Isaac spread throughout the colonial period. Until such new evidence is found we will have to work with what we have, which already offers interesting possibilities for textual analysis. For one thing, such analyses of the commentaries will show how the exacting and controversial demand for a human sacrifice by the Judeo-Christian God was represented by these friars' official voices, and how the Nahuas were expected to think about it. In each sermon piece we will see how the didactic thrust of the episode mirrors discursively in one way or another the violence of the ordeal portrayed. And as with the *neixcuitilli*, we will be able to appreciate that the violence of the depicted Christian sacred in these sermons was not totally alien to that of the prehispanic past.

Bautista and the Violence of God's Favors

Fray Juan de Bautista is considered by some to be perhaps the most eloquent, influential, and prolific *nahuatlato* of his time. According to Ángel Garibay, "nobody in his time . . . took the Castilian language to the heights to which fray Juan Bautista elevated the Mexican one" (Garibay 1953–1954, 2:171; translation mine). Since Bautista was associated during the last decades of the sixteenth century with the trilingual Colegio de Santa Cruz, and he was published in the seventeenth century, Ascensión H. de León-Portilla considers Bautista an important figure of transition (1988, 1:51). The extant imprints of his work, although only a part of his total output, are notorious both for the wide range of topics they cover and because of their impressive volume. His extant imprints are the trilingual *Advertencias para los confesores de los naturales* (1600a); a book of *huehuetlatolli* associated with fray Andrés de Olmos, which Bautista edited (1600b); a book of ascetic meditations entitled *Libro de la miseria y brevedad de la vida del hombre y de sus cuatro postrimerías* (1604); a life of Saint Anthony of Padua (1605); and his monumental *Sermonario en lengua mexicana* of 1606. This sermonary contains sermons only for the four Sundays of Advent[15] and the feast days of Saint Andrew and the Conception of Our Lady. Thus it has only a fraction of what Bautista intended to publish and is, according to Sell, the longest single extant Nahuatl publication (1993, 31n.110).

I now turn to two short sermon sections that refer to the Akedah episode in Bautista's massive *Sermonario*. In order to make the sermons more manageable and useful for many occasions, there was the long-standing practice of dividing long sermons into pieces or units that could be read independently from each other. Since there was no fixed length, either for the sermon or for each of its constituent units, it is difficult to know how many sections were read to the faithful in a single occasion. The piece to which our section on the Akedah episode belongs is the second sermon written for the feast of the Apostle Saint Andrew.[16] This feast belongs to the calendar of saints,[17] and not to the principal cycles of the life of Christ, but it falls on November 30 and is thus part of the Advent period. The (tenuous) connection between Saint Andrew's feast and the treatment of the Akedah episode is established through a commentary on Matthew 4:18, where the evangelist talks about Jesus walking along the shore of the Sea of Galilee and calling upon Andrew and Simon to become fishers of men. The point that Bautista highlights to the Nahua brethren is how saints have a clear memory of the circumstances of their calling: "Because those who are saints take good care of and remember well, not only what mercies are done to them that they receive, with which people are benefited, but likewise where, in what place, the time, when, in which they received them" (Bautista 1606, 288). The ancient saints remembered in similar fashion, Bautista continues, and he then brings up Abraham the patriarch as an example of the proper way to remember God's favors.

The Christian God that fray Bernardino de Sahagún portrayed to the Nahuas in his *Apéndiz a la Postilla* as a good father who never wanted to afflict people (1993a, 135–37) is very different indeed from the one who, in this sermon, orders Abraham "to lay out an offering of, to make an offering of, his beloved son, his firstborn . . . Isaac" (Bautista 1606, 288). Abraham obeys and after he has everything ready for the sacrifice, has bound Isaac, and has drawn the knife to slay him, God finally stays his hand in order to prevent the slaughter, saying: "That is enough, O Abraham, let that be all, for the people of the earth have already seen, are already satisfied, that you are most obedient" (Bautista 1606, 288).

This representation of Abraham's obedience as evidence to be shown to the people rather than to God is a reference to Saint Augustine's interpretation of the Akedah episode in the *City of God*.[18] But Bautista's particular take is not so much that Abraham was tested by God to show the world an unimaginable proof of piety, but rather that the people of the world needed to be convinced of Abraham's unfaltering obedience. Once they were persuaded he would actually carry out the slaying, the execution could be stopped. Although there is no further elaboration on this point, the people's satisfaction with the Akedah would suggest it is their standards of maximum obedience (rather than or not only God's) that have been met. And the insinuation that they were (just) convinced of Abraham's piety by his offering of Isaac rather than profoundly impressed or shocked would imply that the people's expectations of total submission to the deity were severe in the extreme. The communal aspect of the people's criterion adds then to its harshness, since Abraham's proof of utmost obedience is now not something unique, generated within the inscrutable realm of the sacred, but rather something over which there is a human consensus and an expectancy: something not utterly unimaginable, but heard of, and talked about. There is then an erosion of the stature of Abraham's act. It is admirable and worthy, yes, but the fact that it is within the bounds of people's standards situates it below the marvelous, below what is almost humanly unbearable. In this downgrading of the patriarch's exceptional act—by making it meet human expectations of the proper measure of extreme piety—we may find a similarity with the *neixcuitilli* on "The Sacrifice of Isaac," which also lessened the uniqueness of Abraham's act, albeit by the implication of its possible repeatability.

In contrast to the *neixcuitilli*, the sermon does bring out the epic dimension of Abraham's act: "By my praiseworthy name I promise you that from your beloved child your lineage will emerge as a mercy to the people of the world" (Bautista 1606, 288). The passage gives a clear sense that God's solemn promise to Abraham will have important consequences for the whole of humanity. But rather than underscoring the greatness of the patriarch's act that moved God to take an oath, the emphasis shifts to the favors God imparts upon Abraham: "And so that Abraham would always remember the very great favor our Lord, God, had done for him there, he named the top of the mountain where he would have made an offering of his child: *Dominus videt*. It means: our Lord watches" (Bautista 1606, 289). It is important to point out that, whereas Saint Augustine fully acknowledges the Genesis passage in which the causal relationship between Abraham's act and God's oath is established,[19] Bautista downplays the merits of the former by focusing only on God's promises and mercy, as if they had been freely bestowed upon Abraham, as if Abraham had not done anything to deserve such favors. In this second moment of lessening the merits of Abraham's perfect yet terrifying obedience there is a violence not totally dissimilar to the downgrading of his act in the *neixcuitilli* from the singular and unique to the merely exemplary. Bautista then shifts points of view and takes on Abraham's perspective:

> It means: our Lord watches. It is as though it means that our Lord, God, saw that quickly, right away, I obeyed him, I did what he ordered me to do. And so he was merciful to me, he had pity on me and on my child when he ordered me not to kill him, not to make an offering of my child. Most especially he favored me by declaring to me a belief in the Savior of the world, that he will be my descendant. (Bautista 1606, 289)

Bautista's *inventio* of Abraham's monologue evidently sidesteps the agony inflicted on the patriarch by God's awful demand. For the Lord allegedly did *not* see right away, quickly, that Abraham would obey, as the sermon claims he thought out loud. The Lord waited and watched how Abraham woke up that fateful morning and walked with Isaac for three long days until they reached Mount Moriah. God looked on as they slowly climbed the mountain, as Isaac was burdened by the wood he carried. God saw how Abraham tied up the lad and blindfolded him, and how the disconsolate father finally drew the knife to stab him. Not until the very last possible moment, not until there was no hope left that he would give up on his command did he finally feel pity and stay Abraham's hand. There is then a great deal of rhetorical violence in declaring that God saw immediately that Abraham would obey and in defining as merciful the patriarch's release from his gruesome imperative.

Because the sermon is more theologically precise than the *neixcuitilli* in representing the universal scope of the Akedah episode, the so-called favors conferred to Abraham are not limited to the physical restitution of Isaac. The promise that the Savior of the world will come from his lineage is something exceptional indeed, although not wholly incommensurable with or unrelated to the patriarch's singular piety. The sermon winds up by reminding the audience that, as the patriarch remembered where and when he had been shown favor and mercy, so the Nahua faithful should always be mindful to acknowledge gratitude to God because of the constant benefits he bestows upon them. The displacement of God's oath and covenant with Abraham by the Christian economy of grace, favors, and mercy moves the patriarch's willingness to sacrifice his son from the realm of the meritorious and relocates it in that of the due. The lack of emphasis and recognition of the immensity of Abraham's act as motivating the promise of the Savior would seem to suggest that, in the Christian religion, everything God does for his creatures is ultimately a favor and a gift, independent of people's acts. It is ironic, however, that in this sermon piece this incommensurate economy of gifts, mercy, and favors becomes more oppressive than that of the superseded reciprocity of the covenant and the law. For Abraham, in spite of his extraordinary act in extremis, is represented as not entitled to receive anything in return except his eventual salvation, on the condition that he always keeps obeying God.[20] The life of Isaac and the promise of the Savior as his descendant are not depicted as things Abraham either earned or deserved. They are represented as favors that the Lord freely and mercifully conferred upon him, and that he could have just as easily withheld without any detriment to his justice. The sermon section then concludes with its initial reference to Saint Matthew and his insistence on retrieving the circumstances of the calling of the apostles.

The second sermon fragment from fray Juan Bautista also deals with the Christian economy of love and favors, but its interpretation of the Akedah episode is very different from the first. This fragment is part of a long sermon based on the Epistle of the Second Sunday of Advent, Romans 15:4–13. The exegesis of the Akedah episode is inspired by Romans 15:9: "So that the gentiles might glorify God for his mercy." The point of the sermon piece will be to persuade the Nahua brethren of the gratitude they owe God, since as Gentiles they have been given the Savior for free: "We who are gentiles did not earn it, we were not promised it, wherefore it is very necessary that we be grateful and thankful" (Bautista 1606, 346). Bautista brings in as contrast the children of Israel, whose father Abraham had to do "a great many things" (346) in order to receive the promise of the Savior. The Franciscan then relates in detail the story of Abraham, closely following the biblical version. He represents how God tested the patriarch by calling upon him to offer his beloved firstborn, and how Abraham dutifully obeyed, preparing an ass, cutting wood for the holocaust, and going off very early in the morning with two servants and Isaac. Bautista narrates how, while they climbed the mountain God had singled out, Isaac asked where the offering was and a devastated Abraham answered that the Lord would provide the lamb. Bautista tells how Abraham bound the hands and feet of his beloved son, how he drew the knife "in order to decapitate his child" (347), and how the angel finally prevented him from continuing. Bautista departs from the biblical episode at this point, as he elaborates on the great docility and subjection of Isaac, who, in spite of being thirty years old, in no way tried to prevent or dissuade his father from carrying out the offering:

> Nor did he say to him: O my father, look. Perhaps you are fooling yourself or you are deceiving yourself . . . for God is not giving you [such] orders. Perhaps it is just that your fasting and vigils are making your head faint and confused. Has someone [else] killed, has someone [else] made an offering of his only child, his firstborn? Absolutely no one! He [Isaac] absolutely did not respond in that fashion. (347)

The driving force of the arguments Isaac could have raised but never did, according to Bautista, is based on the horror of what Abraham was willing to do in obedience to the deity. In sharp contrast with the *neixcuitilli* and with the earlier fragment analyzed, in this section Bautista focuses on the singularity of Abraham's act. He emphasizes how the patriarch's unheard-of obedience was the high price paid for God's oath to have the Savior of the world, God's own beloved son, come from Abraham's lineage.[21] But whereas this sermon section fully acknowledges Abraham's great merits, it also reveals that the violence of the test he was subjected to by God was almost beyond human endurance, and hence the great promise made to the patriarch, and through him to the children of Israel, in exchange for his great act.

The sermon then picks up again the theme of the gratitude owed by the Gentiles, since they did not do any penance, did not pay any price in order to receive the grace of Jesus Christ. The piece concludes by exhorting the Nahua brethren to be patient and receive consolation from the divine words, which oblige the Nahuas to consider all the good they have received from God, having been delivered from the false "people-eating beasts of hell" their ancestors not so long ago worshipped (Bautista 1606, 349). Whereas in the *neixcuitilli* the exhortation to the Nahua audience to emulate Abraham's obedience could be (mis)read as a demand to be ready and willing to offer up a son if God would so command, in this sermon piece it is clear that the Nahua faithful will never be required to undergo Abraham's onerous ordeal in order to receive the Savior's gifts. As Gentiles, they have received the latter under the superabundant economy of grace, in which things circulate freely and not as payment or expenditure.

By reminding the audience of the concrete historical iniquity of their not-so-remote ancestors, the sermon may also have reminded Nahuas of the annihilation and destruction that came upon them as they were delivered from their supposed servitude. Thus, in focusing only on the spiritual participation of the Nahuas in this Christian universal economy of superabundance, favors and release, there is great violence in dismissing the material reality of the millions of lives that were lost as the Nahuas received the redeeming Word. Abraham had to pay the cost of slaughtering Isaac for the sake of the deity, whereas the price the Nahuas paid for being freed from eating and drinking their own "bodies, their blood and their hearts" (Bautista 1606, 349), was the actual loss of legions of Isaacs, most precious jewels, in the great sixteenth-century *cocoliztli* (diseases; epidemics) that God had sent, not so long ago, together with the arrival of Christianity. The great gifts, favors, and mercies of God as depicted by Bautista in his two sermon fragments on the Akedah, allegedly free, actually came with a high price tag for humanity, perhaps not totally unlike the toll paid by the Nahua worshippers for the prosperity and affluence conferred by the prehispanic deities.

Mijangos and the Appeasement of God

Our third sermon piece comes from another outstanding *nahuatlato* of the early seventeenth century, the Augustinian fray Juan de Mijangos. His two major works are the *Espejo divino*, published in 1607 and reprinted in 1626, and a sermonary published in 1624. Both of these works are extremely long,[22] and their explicitly intended audiences were clerics and literate Nahuas (Sell 1993, 75). Both books fall under the genre of devotional and ecclesiastical literature, widespread in Spain during the first half of the sixteenth century but closely watched by an increasingly suspicious Inquisition after 1559 (Nalle 1999; Bataillon 1966).

The voluminous *Espejo divino* is noteworthy because it is written as a dialogue between a father and his son. This is remarkable because it weds European and Nahua cultural traditions. The *Espejo* harks back to the dialogue form that was characteristic of the humanistic spiritual literature of the sixteenth century widely diffused by the printing press,[23] as well as to the oratorical prehispanic genre of the *huehuetlatolli* or "words of the elders." Both genres had in common the intention of edifying their audiences in the art of proper social and religious conduct. As Barry Sell has pointed out: "Mijangos explicitly states in his prologue that he wrote the book in this form in order to make it more understandable to his Nahua readers" (Sell 1993, 75). This desire to make spiritual advice and reflection accessible and real to a secular, literate, and cultivated readership is precisely what had moved reformers and, later, counterreformers, to adopt the lively dialogue form.

Trying to engage the Nahua readership to which the *Espejo* is directed, Mijangos makes extensive use of the vintage figural language of the *huehuetlatolli*, employing characteristic metaphorical doublets and many stock idioms and expressions. In the sermon fragment dealing with the Akedah, this characteristic figural language of the prehispanic genre is further complemented, wittingly or unwittingly, by casting the mediation of Christ the Savior in terms that resonate with prehispanic ways of relating to the sacred. The sermon fragment opens with an invitation to the reader to understand God's ways and works "in the time of the ancient way of living" (262). But first, Mijangos tackles the issue of Christ's redeeming role in the very present time of the reading audience:

> First know that how today in our time . . . we lay out and make an offering to our Lord, God, of the honored body and of the precious blood of his beloved honored child, our Lord Jesus Christ, in mass, it is as though with it we appease, we calm, our deity and ruler, God, if he is angry with us because of our great sins, because there [i.e., in mass] is remembered how for our sake he was crucified, how he was made to suffer burning pain because of our sins and faults, our great and abominable sins. (262)

The doctrine of transubstantiation, which proclaims that the bread and wine are transformed into the body and blood of Christ when consecrated by the priest in the mass, is surely what allows Mijangos to say that the people make an offering in the mass in order to placate God the Father's anger for their sins.[24] By alluding to the iterative nature of Christ's sacrifice that is implicit in this doctrine, the terms "offering," "blood," "sin," and "appeasement of the deity" are linked together in the passage in ways not totally alien to the sacrificial economy of prehispanic times. As scholars of Aztec studies have pointed out, the people of Mesoamerica believed there had been a time of "intranscendent existence of the gods" (López Austin 1984, 1:68; my translation), a time that was interrupted by a violent, creative mythical period when the deities sacrificed themselves and destroyed each other in order to give birth to the different suns, the last being the fifth, under which humans currently lived. This turbulent mythical or creative time of the gods did not cease with the creation of humankind: it constantly impinged on human time, but now according to cycles, patterns, and rotations, which were fixed by the calendar devised by the primeval pair of humans or semi-divine entities, Oxomoco and Cipactonal (Sahagún 1989, 1:233–35; Nicholson 1971, 398; López Austin 1984, 1:264–65). Rituals had the important function of reenacting this mythical time in a controlled way, so that its thrust would be beneficial to the community rather than deadly (López Austin 1984, 1:70; Matos Moctezuma 1984, 135). Prehispanic gods were given steady ritual service by human beings in order to appease, feed, and placate them and thus ensure "the return of reproduction through the channels that human beings needed for living" (López Austin 1977, 244).

For her part, Louise Burkhart explains that, for the Nahuas, sin or *tlatlacolli* was conceived of not so much as a state of internal degradation (as in Christianity), but more as the material effect of damage brought about "by any sort of error or misdeed . . . from conscious moral transgressions to judicially defined crimes to accidental or unintentional damage" (1989, 28). *Tlatlacolli* could also be damage caused by breaches of the all-important rituals, by improper sexual conduct, by stealing, intoxication, and even unintentional acts that spoiled something. All of the above sins were forms of disruptions of order that destabilized and upset the delicate cosmic balance. These disruptions, in their turn, could cause the anger of the gods, or the unmanaged unleashing of their influences, which could be harmful to the individual and to the community. Lockhart argues that during prehispanic times there was the belief that the anger of the gods or supernatural beings was the basic cause for disease (1992, 259), which was a dreaded form of damage and imbalance affecting human beings. Taking all this into account, we can conjecture that in prehispanic times there was a systematic relation between blood offerings and the placating of the destructive anger or hunger of the gods; the rupture of this relation was a form of sin that could be fatal to the individual and to the human community at large.

In Mijangos's passage, the relations between the offering, sin, and the appeasement of the deity are not ordered in the same way as in the Nahua prehispanic system, but the relation among the three terms is nonetheless present. Thus, the blood of Christ appeases the anger of God that has been aroused by the awful sins of the human community. It is as if the sins did not give God his due, what belongs to him, what he expects as creator of the universe. This offends him, stirring his anger and his desire to make his creatures suffer. This is why it is said that Christ "was made to suffer burning pain because of our great sins" (Mijangos 1607, 262), that is, a pain commensurate with the grave transgressions of humanity, which otherwise would be inflicted on the creatures themselves.[25] The difference is that, whereas in the prehispanic system the divine anger may be conceived of in terms of hunger (see Read 1998), in the Christian system the anger is markedly moral. And whereas in the prehispanic system divine anger is likely to be aroused by the sin of a sacrifice improperly performed, in the Judeo-Christian system the sacrifice is offered so as to placate the wrath caused by sin.

Mijangos proceeds to discuss the sacrificial practices of "our fathers and our grandfathers [i.e., our ancestors]" (262). The Nahua readers must thus understand their ancestors to be Judeo-Christian as well as Mesoamerican, an identification quite unlikely to take place in the context of this sermon. The practice that Mijangos discusses as belonging to the "time of the ancient way of living" was the spilling of the blood of a lamb in order to placate God's anger for the sins committed by people. Although also propitiatory, according to the passage this ancient sacrificial economy involved no human sacrifice. Mijangos then declares that when Christ was tormented and crucified such "ancient usage" came to an end, and "our consummately good way of making offerings" (262) emerged, which is the mass: "There we lay out and make an offering to our Lord, God the Father, of the honored precious body and precious blood of his beloved child, our Lord Jesus Christ" (263). It is ironic that, since this new, superior Christian sacrificial economy is clearly centered on human sacrifice, it would seem closer to the prehispanic system than to the Jewish one left behind. However, since such human sacrifice is constantly reenacted in a highly mediated way, namely, in the transubstantiating ritual of the mass, it also evidently implies significant differences with the Mexican sacrificial economy. In any case, once Mijangos has established how the old sacrificial practices were superseded by the new Christian way of making offerings, he brings in the episode of the Akedah.

Thus the Lord orders Abraham to cut the neck of his child Isaac on top of the mountain, where he will show him a miracle. As Abraham is ready to strike his son, the angel appears and stops the slaughter, saying: "Now he knows that you truly love him . . . and that you want to please him, for you do not want to make him angry, you do not want to bother him" (265). The angel's representation of Abraham's act in extremis as just a desire to please, as a desire not to make angry or to bother God, although compatible with Nahua standard linguistic usage, is nonetheless an understatement, to say the least. As in the *neixcuitilli*, the epic dimension and awful singularity of Abraham's act is reduced to the ordinarily devout, to not wanting to upset the deity. Again, there is no sense here of something transcendental, never heard of, as we saw in the second sermon fragment of Bautista analyzed above. The great violence of God's test in the biblical story is further increased in the sermon with the lessening of the patriarch's extraordinary act into the familiar and the quotidian.

But in contrast to the *neixcuitilli*, Mijangos will not try to exhort the Nahua readers to take Abraham as an example to follow. A lamb appears in a thicket, which Abraham will be able to offer in lieu of his son: "It is just as though with the lamb he paid the price for, he bought, and saved his beloved honored only child Isaac, whom our Lord, God, had ordered him to make an offering of to him, so that he did not die, so that his throat was not cut" (265). The miracle promised by God was, then, to allow Abraham to perform the awful sacrifice he had demanded with a lamb that he himself provided, so that, in the end, Isaac could go free. A wonder of a bargain indeed! Mijangos interprets Isaac as the "very sign and example of our Lord Jesus Christ" and the lamb as the "sign and example" of the sinner (265). It is relevant to point out that Saint Augustine interprets both Isaac and the ram as figures of Christ.[26] Mijangos clearly takes a different exegetical route in order to illustrate God's love for humankind through a dramatic reversal of the Akedah story:

> Thus it is clear how very much the deity and ruler, God, loves us, for that we will escape, that we lousy sinners defend ourselves, he cast and left his beloved only child, his beloved honored son, in the hands of the utterly wicked and very oppressive Jews. . . . He was made to suffer [so that] finally he was hung on the cross, crucified. Thus the deity and ruler, God, greatly favored and had mercy on us for if his beloved honored son would not have suffered for our sake, would not have died for our sake, if not: we would suffer, we would be killed. (265–66)

That is, if in the Akedah episode the lamb is sacrificed in lieu of Isaac, with Christ's crucifixion it is the beloved son who is sacrificed so that the lambs (i.e., the sinners) may go free. Clearly, in contrast with the great pain inflicted on Abraham by God's test, this astonishing reversal should show the readers evidence of God's great love for humanity. Still, the sacrifice of Jesus does not abolish or supersede the violence of God the Ruler, or the economy of debts, payments, and retributions that He presides over and enforces, according to the sermon. It is as if God's wrath, once aroused, had necessarily to be appeased in one way or another. And rather than hurting or killing the lambs who kindled his anger with their sins, he enigmatically (incomprehensibly?) chose to spare them by upgrading the offering and having his own son, who was also himself, be sacrificed to him.

The violent cosmic economy of sacrifice, debts, payments, and retributions upon which Mijangos founds his exegesis in this sermon is not something he draws only from the Nahuas, if he does at all. It is a tradition received from apocalyptic Judaism by Paul, the authors of the Synoptic Gospels, and the Fathers of the Church (Daniélou 1964; Lachowski 1967, 851; Cilveti 1977, 67–94, and 1989). Origen, Saint Gregory of Nisa, Saint Leo the Great, and even Saint Augustine concede to the devil a certain juridical entitlement over humanity (Cilveti 1977, 71). With original sin, humankind became indebted to God and enslaved to the devil, and thus the Prince of the World gained rights over humankind.[27] And indeed, there is a clear reference to these teachings in our sermon fragment when Mijangos writes how "with his precious blood he saved us, he paid the price for us, since we were the slaves, the captives of the devil" (262).

This is, however, the only mention of the devil in the sermon piece. Although Mijangos is alluding to this Jewish-Christian tradition of debts, payments, and sacrifice, his emphasis is not so much on how Jesus sacrificed himself in order to liberate humankind from the devil. Rather, the focus is on how Jesus appeased God the Father's anger with his blood and then on how the Father allowed his beloved son to be crucified by the Jews (not the devil), so that the people would not be killed. This shift of emphasis could be explained as Mijangos's desire to downplay the notion of Christ's sacrifice as ransom for humanity to the fallen angel. The patristic notion was dramatic and moving indeed, but it risked transforming the devil into a stupendous power that God the Ruler and his beloved son seem almost forced to satisfy in order to save humanity.[28]

With the shrouding of the role of the devil in this Judeo-Christian economy of debts, payments, and sacrifice, the prehispanic sacrificial regime all of a sudden does not look so utterly alien. For when Mijangos emphasizes God and not the devil as the supernatural entity to whom payments are due, the demand for blood sacrifice is not portrayed as something expected only by evil forces. Here we should note again that even though the sermon identifies the ancestors of the Nahuas as those who practiced animal sacrifices, such an identification carries little rhetorical force. The most outstanding commonality between the Akedah and the Crucifixion episodes is human sacrifice, and human sacrifice was much more readily associated with precontact religious practices than with Jewish ones, as any minimally educated Nahua would know.

The representation of God's pleasure over Abraham's disposition to slay his son as a proof of his devotion, the representation of the human sacrifice of the honored precious Christ as what saved sinful humankind from being killed, and finally, the representation of the mass as a new mode of repeatedly offering the son's flesh and blood in order to placate the Lord's wrath, may not necessarily have been interpreted by the Nahua readers as a radical break with their ancestors' sacrificial universe, in which the anger of life-giving deities had also to be appeased with offerings and entreaties, and in which the constant enactment of sacrifice by gods and humans is what spares time from destruction. What Mijangos's sermon certainly suggests is that the Christian "consummately good way of making offerings" was superior and more efficacious than any other sacrificial regime that had come before. But the need to placate the anger of the deity with the most precious offering of blood and flesh lest great misfortune befall people (not totally unlike the Nahuas of prehispanic times had believed) had not been abolished. Thus, wittingly or unwittingly, in Mijangos's exegesis of the Akedah episode and of the Crucifixion, a violent hybrid cosmic economy emerged in which prehispanic conceptions of the relationship between humanity and the sacred, although greatly modified by the colonial present, had not been fully left behind.

The Virgin Mary as the New Abraham

Our last sermon piece comes from the most prominent Dominican *nahuatlato* of the early seventeenth century, fray Martín de León. In 1611 he published the first devotional manual of the seventeenth century, entitled *Camino del cielo en lengua mexicana*.

This manual contains also a cathecism, a calendar of the prehispanic year, and a guide for the dying (León-Portilla 1988, 1:83). His second published work, to which our sermon piece belongs, is a long sermonary in Nahuatl with sermons for Sundays and holidays running from the first Sunday of Advent to Holy Week. The sermonary was originally conceived in four parts to cover the whole year, but only the first was published (León-Portilla 1988, 2:228). His other important work was a short manual published in 1614 entitled *Manual breve y forma de administrar los Santos Sacramentos a los indios universalmente*. Its three reprints in 1617, 1640, and 1669 are evidence of its widespread use in Mexico.

The piece concerning us here is conceived as part of Christ's farewell to his mother, Mary, the Wednesday before his death. This episode has no basis in the Gospels, canonical or apocryphal. It was conceived by a thirteenth-century Franciscan from San Gimignano named Giovanni da Cauli (Peck, quoted in Burkhart 1996, 25) as part of a book of meditations about the life of Christ, appropriately entitled *Meditationes vitae Christi*. The episode in question takes place in Mary Magdalene's house. The Virgin implores Jesus to stay with them for Passover, since she realizes that her son's intent to go to Jerusalem and thus bring redemption to humanity actually means his death (26). In a somewhat chauvinistic way, Jesus rebukes her, claiming that he must follow his father's desire. The overwhelming pathos and potential beauty of da Cauli's episode made it a likely candidate to be borrowed and rewritten by ecclesiastical writers, playwrights, and preachers dealing with Holy Week.[29]

In our sermon piece by fray Martín de León, Jesus's riposte to the Virgin's entreaties also displays the patriarchal privileging of the Father's will and the placing of it over the mother's. Jesus brings in Abraham, who was ordered by God to offer him Isaac, as an example for the Virgin to follow. Jesus emphasizes the horror of Abraham's test by pointing out how he carried in his own hands the very knife with which he would slay Isaac "and the fire with which he would be burned" (León 1614b, 316r). Jesus admonishes his mother to consider how Abraham utterly disregarded his agony in order "to comply fully with the wishes of God the father" (316r). He then tells her that "if God the father had wanted you yourself to kill him, thus your great love would have been revealed. But such was not necessary. God just wants you to endure patiently" (316r). The violence inherent in Mary's ordeal is augmented by the suggestion that God is requiring less from her than from Abraham, since she is only expected to witness the horror of her beloved son's death rather than actually carrying it out. Finally, however, Jesus concedes that just by willingly offering her child (that is, himself) to God, "you greatly surpassed Abraham's obedience and love" (316r), for, contrary to Isaac, we should add, her beloved son did indeed die.

The image of God the Father as a frightening deity who expects total and uncompromising submission from humankind is reinforced in León's passage, since God is represented as having demanded the sacrifice of a beloved son for a second time. In spite of the acknowledgment that God's command has caused Abraham anguish and will be terribly painful for the Virgin, the focus is clearly on the necessity to obey unquestioningly, regardless of the enormous personal cost his commands may entail. And if the Nahua faithful felt that these exacting demands were made by the colonizer's god only to the most pious and loving saints of Christianity, namely Abraham and Mary, and would no longer be required of them, maybe they would remember with secret satisfaction that these insuperable deeds of obedience were not that different from what their ancestors had also been capable of doing for their gods, who in exchange for their absolute submission had for a long time showered the lands of Anahuac with much food, wealth, and prosperity.

Conclusions

The Akedah is an episode that speaks about something beyond reason and even beyond the ethical. It speaks of the uncanny mysteries of faith that perhaps only those within the Jewish and Christian communities can fully grasp and understand. Yet, it is also an episode that exalts the capacity of human beings to defy their own earthly nature and give up what they cherish most for the sake of an otherly divinity. As soon as the focus of the episode shifts to this profound human dimension of Abraham's deed, the enormous spiritual violence of the Akedah comes to the fore.

In these readings of "The Sacrifice of Isaac" and the sermon pieces on the episode of the Akedah, I have focused primarily on the severity, not only of the enunciated story, but also of the different positions the Nahua audience is expected to take on the Judeo-Christian episode of the ultimate test of the human soul. Of all the pieces analyzed, perhaps the *neixcuitilli* is the most problematic, since the audience is asked to model behavior on Abraham while scarcely considering the singularity of the patriarch's perfect deed of obedience. The demands made on the Nahua faithful by the sermon pieces vary, as we have seen. But all of them coincide in representing God the Father's awful request as something righteous, which ought not to be questioned but only accepted. There is nothing theologically improper in these pieces, even when the emphasis on the episode may change depending on the moral lesson the friar intended to transmit to the faithful. All four sermon pieces, even Mijangos's, could conceivably have been addressed to a Spanish audience. Yet, the episode of the Akedah could never have meant the same culturally for a Spanish audience as it did for a Nahua one. And by thus meaning something different, these representations put into question the posited universality of the Judeo-Christian Word. This is where the forces of hybridization come into the play.

By representing the Akedah episode to the Nahua audience as a model to follow, as exemplary of the colonial God's difference, and as harbinger of a new cosmic economy of human sacrifice, the episode acquired meanings it did not have before. Far from its representing a decisive break with the prehispanic past, there is little that the Nahuas could have learned from the Judeo-Christian patriarch's epic piety that their ancestors' devotion to their gods had not already taught them. True, at the very end of the episode, God stopped the offering of Isaac, which indeed marked a significant difference from the prehispanic deities. Human sacrifice was no longer portrayed as being essential to the preservation of the world, as was believed during prehispanic times.

And yet, even if no actual material sacrifice ever took place, the Judeo-Christian God's demand for human sacrifice presupposed an expectation of utter service and obedience that was not incongruent with the unquestioning submission required of the Nahua ancestors by their prehispanic gods. If to this onerous expectation of obedience we add the downplaying of God's absolute commitment to bless Abraham and his descendants that we see in the *neixcuitilli* and in several of the sermon pieces discussed, an even more pronounced degree of mixture and hybridization becomes apparent. By scaling back God's oath into merely an expression of satisfaction with the fulfillment of his commands, the spiritual colonizers emphasized even more the severe expectancy of unconditional submission, thus Nahuatizing even further the figures of Yahweh and Abraham from what could be argued was already available in the biblical episode of the Akedah.

Thus, as Homi Bhabha has observed about colonial discourse, "Hybridity intervenes in the exercise of authority not merely to indicate the possibility of its identity but to represent the unpredictability of its presence" (1994, 114). In their ardent desire to subject the Nahua audience to Christianity by parading Abraham as an example of obedience, the spiritual colonizers partially betrayed the difference between their Judeo-Christian God and the prehispanic deities. As a result, they may also have unwittingly opened up a space for the audience to accommodate memories of the old prehispanic disposition to sacrifice the most precious to the gods, in order to placate divine anger and prevent the onset of misfortune. This is not to say that the Nahuas thought the Judeo-Christian God to be a Tlaloc or a Tezcatlipoca in disguise. Instead, as William Taylor has suggested, the great site of continuity between prehispanic and colonial Nahua religiosity may have lain "in habits of conception—in ways of representing and entering the sacred" (1996, 5). With "The Sacrifice of Isaac" and these four sermon pieces, rather than showing the way to break away decisively from these prehispanic forms of relating to the sacred, the friars may well have contributed to their preservation in the brave new world of Spanish colonialism.

Notes

1. It has long been held that medieval religious drama was born in the tenth century with the liturgical tropes *Quem quaeretis?* and the *Visitatio sepulchri*. These were short dialogues in Latin, interpolated in the Easter mass, in which an angel appeared to the three Marys in order to announce to them Christ's resurrection. Little by little, this simple dialogue would grow with the addition of characters and more complex scenes.

2. These are the opening words of "The Sacrifice of Isaac" (23v).

3. This scene occurs as Abraham's servants are preparing a banquet to introduce Isaac to his blood relatives. Says Hagar: "Today the great ruler Abraham has yet again invited people to a banquet because of the great esteem he has for his child. But as for us, since we are lowly servants, we are held in no regard. And as for you, my child, you are doubly luckless. Would that I could find relief in you, that you could give relief to all my earthly torments, for in truth your birth and your lot are eternal weeping" (28v). Although Hagar's sense of being wronged by Abraham's neglect toward her and her child would seem to indicate that Abraham's relationship to Ishmael was more than that of a master, the point is not made sufficiently clear and is not ever mentioned again in the play. Thus, it is difficult to claim that the *neixcuitilli* was taking an open stance against polygamy. What will be emphasized is Hagar's ineptitude for bringing up her son properly.

4. I am using the translation in this volume, and I will adopt the abbreviated title, "The Sacrifice of Isaac."

5. The destruction of temples and idols commenced in 1525, a year after the first Twelve arrived in Mexico (Motolinia 1951, 99; Mendieta 1980, 226–30). According to fray Juan de Zumárraga's letter of June 1531, already five hundred temples and twenty thousand idols had been destroyed (Israel 1975, 7–8). Although scholars have questioned these numbers and accounts

as being inflated by a partisan interest in promoting the evangelizing achievements of the orders (Lockhart 1991, 204), it seems that the Mexica priesthood and human sacrifice were eliminated almost immediately (Gibson 1964, 100).

6. This class upgrading is pointed out in John Cornyn's preliminary notes on "Sacrifice" (Horcasitas 1974, 198–99).

7. These are the positions of Jerry Williams (1992, 73–74) and Marlyn Ravicz (1970, 97).

8. Potter then adds that "having established this, the story decrees . . . the end of human sacrifice in the tribe of Abraham, and the forging of a new relationship with divine power" (312). But then, in the next paragraph, he arrives at the conclusion that by dramatizing these events for the Nahua audience the anonymous playwright "recapitulates . . . [the] message of hope—that divine power has ceased to exact such sacrifices from its subjects" (312). This was only partially the case, and herein lies the striking contradictions of the position of this play vis-à-vis the practice of human sacrifice.

9. The passage reads as follows: "Listen, you people of the world: in the example of this child Isaac will be seen everything that will happen to the beloved son of God when he will save people everywhere in the world, for through his blood and his death he will open up heaven where sits his beloved honored Father. But meanwhile, before it happens to the son of God, it will first happen to the precious and blessed child Isaac" (25r–v). The passage is ambiguous. Since ultimately Isaac's blood will not be shed, it is not clear what those things are that will happen to Isaac and that the audience must take as an anticipation of those that will happen to Christ.

10. Abraham declares to his son in the first part of the play that God's commands are three, and that Isaac should not violate a single one ("Sacrifice," 27v). These commands are not specified in the passage, nor is it clear why the playwright chose the number three instead of ten (for the commandments) or two (for the commands all Christians must follow). However, the number does coincide with the three commands represented to Isaac as he and his father walk back home after the gruesome episode.

11. I have written more extensively about the *neixcuitilli* "The Sacrifice of Isaac" in "A Nahua Yahweh or a Judeo-Christian Tlaloc? Domination, Hybridity and Continuity in the Nahua Theater of Evangelization," *Colonial Latin American Review,* 2001.

12. Here I turn once more to Sahagún's additions to the *Postillas*, or the gospel and epistle commentaries to be said in Mass every Sunday of the year. Writes Sahagún: "Y sabe que cuando andas pensando en algún pecado mortal, aunque no consientas en que lo cometas, pues tan sólo te alegre el pensar en ello y en tu más íntimo ser bien sepas que no lo deseas cometer, pues tan sólo el pensar en él te da placer, ya has pecado" (And know that when you are thinking about some mortal sin, even if you do not consent to commit it, just because by thinking about it you become happy, and in your innermost being you know well that you do not desire to commit it, just because by thinking about it you receive pleasure, you have already sinned; Sahagún 1993a, 43, translation mine).

13. I am grateful to Barry Sell for his generosity in allowing me to use for this article his unpublished translations of the Bautista and Mijangos sermon fragments on the Akedah. I also thank Louise Burkhart for permitting me to use her translation of León's fragment, which is published in Burkhart 2001, 94.

14. I owe Barry Sell the valuable information that, from his examination of many imprints and manuscripts of the sixteenth and seventeenth centuries, he has found no further mention of the Akedah episode. Among the key imprints he has examined besides Bautista's and Mijangos's works are fray Juan de la Anunciación's *Sermonario* (1577), fray Juan de Gaona's *Colloquios de la paz y la tranquilidad Christiana* (1582), and Sahagún's *Psalmodia christiana y sermonario de los sanctos del año* (1583). He has found nothing, either, in the work of the eighteenth-century Jesuit Father Ignacio de Paredes (email, December 8, 2000).

15. Advent is the period that precedes the festivity of Christmas or the Nativity. It commences with the Sunday closest to November 30 (Nacar Fuster and Colunga 1961, 16) and ends on December 25. It is supposed to be a time of expectancy and of spiritual preparation.

16. I owe this information also to Barry Sell, who as translator of these sermon pieces has had firsthand access to Bautista's imprint, and thus to the organization and distribution of the

sermons among the four Advent Sundays and among the calendar of saints corresponding to the Advent period.

17. The calendar of saints was incorporated into the liturgical year by the Church soon after the cycles of the Nativity and Easter were established, which commemorated the principal events of the life of Christ. The calendar of saints is divided into four hierarchical categories according to their importance. The feast of Saint Andrew belongs to the second category, which includes the less principal feasts of the lives of Christ and of the Virgin Mary, the lives of the Apostles, and of other significant saints (Nacar Fuster and Colunga 1961, 15–19).

18. "Among other things, of which it would take too long time to mention the whole, Abraham was tempted about the offering up of his well-beloved son Isaac, to prove his pious obedience, and so make it known to the world, not to God" (Saint Augustine 1950, 554). Saint Augustine's canonical exegesis of the Akedah must have been an indispensable intertext of our three star *nahuatlatos*' sermon pieces on the subject, and this exegesis will be important in this article also as an authoritative point of reference against which to compare the different inflections given to the episode by Bautista, Mijangos, and León.

19. "And the Angel of the Lord called unto Abraham from heaven the second time, saying, By myself have I sworn, saith the Lord; because thou hast done this thing, and hast not spared thy beloved son for my sake; that in blessing I will bless thee, and in multiplying I will multiply thy seed as the stars of heaven, and as the sand which is upon the seashore" (Saint Augustine 1950, 556).

20. "Paul insists that man does not earn reward in the same full and fundamental sense in which he earns punishment. He merits in a lesser, secondary sense, since the graces that make him holy and move him to do good are a gift: 'The wages of sin is death, but the gift of God is life everlasting in Christ Jesus Our Lord' (Romans 6:23)" (Most 1967, 674). In other words, according to this economy of grace and gifts, Abraham is owed nothing by God because the patriarch's willingness to sacrifice his son is already a gift that will eventually obtain him salvation, unless he were to decline such a gift to do good in the future, not repent about his refusal, and thus be punished.

21. "Right because of me, for my sake, I make an oath because after you did it you did not destroy your beloved child, your firstborn, on my account. Behold, I will favor you, thus I will show you mercy. I will multiply your lineage, such that it will be . . . like the sand lying spilled on the seashore" (Bautista 1606, 348).

22. The *Espejo divino* has "7 preliminary pages + 552 numbered p. + 3 final ones" and the *Primera parte del Sermonario y santoral* has "15 preliminary pages without numbers + 564 numbered p. + 93 with tables and misprints" (León-Portilla 1988, 2:275; translation mine).

23. In fact, the famous dialogues of *De los nombres de Cristo* by the renowned Augustinian fray Luis de León (published in Salamanca in 1583 with four subsequent editions in 1585, 1587, 1595, and 1603) may have been a humanist model for fray Juan de Mijangos, along with fray Juan de Gaona's *Colloquios de la paz y tranquilidad en lengua mexicana*. Mijangos's emphasis on the elegance and style of the Nahuatl as a vernacular language would seem to emulate fray Luis de León's efforts in elevating the Castilian language. Fray Bermúdez Pedraza, a contemporary of fray Luis, declared that "[he] wrote the books *Del nombre de Dios* [sic] and *La perfecta casada* with such a chaste and graceful language that they may be useful to learn phrases, rhetorical colors and soft ways of speech" (quoted in Cuevas García 1982, 63; translation mine). The Ciceronian style of fray Luis de León's dialogues in which one speaker-master develops his thoughts in long doctrinal arguments without being interrupted by his interlocutors (Cuevas García 1982, 53) are quite in line with the monological style of the *huehuetlatolli*. Most important is perhaps fray Luis's invitation (to those who felt up to the task) to write in the vernacular about things closely related to the Scriptures, since the Church had prohibited reading the Bible in the vulgar languages (Cuevas García 1982, 37). We should remember that Mijangos was quite intent on defending the richness of Nahuatl for expressing the subtleties of scriptural thought. Just like the *Nombres* and the *Perfecta casada*, "the *Espejo divino* is a series of meditations inspired by the Bible and by the teachings of the Fathers of the Church" (León-Portilla 1988, 2:275; translation mine). According to Robert Ricard, the learned friar Alonso de la Veracruz

had been a close friend of fray Luis (Ricard 1991, 12). Fray Alonso was elected provincial of the Augustinian province four times (Grijalva 1985, 402). He founded the Colegio de San Pablo and its library. He was professor of Scriptures in the Universidad de México (Grijalva 1985, 179–80; 396–403). When fray Luis de León was incarcerated by the Inquisition for his propositions, fray Alonso declared (albeit not publicly) that he was in agreement with them (Grijalva 1985, 400). Although fray Alonso died only one year after the *Nombres* and the *Perfecta casada* were published, it can be surmised that copies of these books were received in Mexico, and that the renowned and now-vindicated fray Luis de León would be widely read (and emulated) by his Augustinian brothers.

24. This doctrine had been reaffirmed by the Council of Trent on October 11, 1551, in chapter 4 of session 13: "It has always been the conviction of the Church of God, and this holy Council now again declares, that by the consecration of the bread and the wine a change takes place in which the entire substance of the bread is changed into the substance of the body of Christ our Lord and the entire substance of the wine into the substance of His blood. This change the holy Catholic Church fittingly and properly calls transubstantiation" (quoted in Vollert 1967, 260). Now, the way Mijangos presents the offering of Christ—as a way to placate God the Father whenever he is angry with the sinner—underscores the iterability of the actual sacrifice of flesh and blood, which is what transubstantiation means, and not its one-time occurrence.

25. Later in the sermon piece, Mijangos writes: "Thus the deity and ruler, God, greatly favored and had mercy on us for if his beloved honored son would not have suffered for our sake, would not have died for our sake, if not: we would suffer, we would be killed" (265).

26. Saint Augustine writes: "In order, then, that the children of the promise may be the seed of Abraham, they are called in Isaac, that is, they are gathered together in Christ by the call of grace" (1950, 555). Later on, Saint Augustine establishes a similarity between Isaac carrying the wood for his execution and Christ carrying the cross. Since Isaac was not slain, after all, but the ram: "What then did he [the ram] represent but Jesus, how, before He was offered up, was crowned with thorns by the Jews?" (555).

27. "The Synoptics further described sin as resulting in slavery to the devil, an idea that entered into their concept of guilt. Thus, Christ's victory over the devil led to freedom from sin and guilt" (Lachowski 1967, 851).

28. This may possibly be why the theologian L. Lercher calls the Church Fathers' quasi-dramatic representation of humanity's liberation from its servitude to the devil "minus convenientium," that is, less convenient (quoted in Cilveti 1977, 70n.4).

29. Burkhart (1996) analyzes a sixteenth-century Nahuatl adaptation of a Spanish play that dramatizes and elaborates on this episode.

PART 2

The Plays

TRANSCRIPTION GUIDELINES

The editors of *Nahuatl Theater* have attempted to reproduce as closely as possible the spelling, punctuation, capitalization, and other orthographic features of the original Nahuatl manuscripts. This practice extends to including expected marks like crosses (often resembling plus signs above or in proximity to the word for cross) as well as unexpected marks like those resembling equal signs whose function is unclear. In order to make the transcriptions as suggestive as possible of the handwritten originals, later additions to the main text, typically written in smaller charcters above or below the main text, are placed in corresponding superscript or subscript positions. This is reflected in the formatting of the corresponding English. The growing number of those studying early Nahuatl will find the foliation of the transcriptions included in the English translations, which will facilitate matching the longer Nahuatl passages with their English interpretations.

While there will always be some differences between handwritten manuscripts and their modern printed counterparts (like those in this set), we hope that our renditions will be of great help to those searching for reliable versions of these early Nahuatl writings. One of the more obvious minor areas of disputed interpretation will be our resolution of characters of various sizes into lower- or upper-case letters. Sometimes the intentions of the original scribes were unclear, at least by current orthographic conventions, so our decisions may be legitimately disputed by those who compare the originals with our versions.

Our one major departure is in the spacing of letters into the familiar units of "words." Here our practice generally follows that established by fray Juan Bautista and the Nahua teacher Agustín de la Fuente in their extensive published corpus (1599–1606); fortuitously, it usually anticipates and coincides with current scholarly norms. Notwithstanding our approach, most of those who wrote early Nahuatl texts thought more in terms of those elements most obvious in speech, i.e., the syllable and the utterance, than of the word and the sentence. Thus transcriptions and translations are closely linked since our renderings of the originals ultimately reflect our understanding of what we think the authors of the texts meant to say. There should be little dispute most of the time given the content of the plays and the relative brevity and formulaic nature of much of the dialogue, but extended speeches always involve deciding what is more—or less—probable given what preceded and followed a dubious passage. This is further complicated by Nahuatl's complex system of affixes: in certain cases does a particular syllable end one item or begin a new one? While we are confident that the majority of our choices will stand the test of time, there will inevitably be advances in the study of early Nahuatl and Nahuas that will render some of our decisions less probable.

Present Location
William L. Clements Library, University of Michigan
Ann Arbor, Michigan

[1r]
+

Nican pehua nican tzinti inninnemilitzin[1] in yeintin tlatoque Reyesme in quenin Oquimotlapalhuitzinoque in tlaçomahuisteopiltzintli yn ipiltzin D.^{S} in toteCuio. Jesu x$\overline{p}$o in onpa Ohualeuhque in iquiçayanpa in tonatiuh Auh nican pehua nican motlalia i nexcuitilmachiotl in quenin omochiuh huallehuasque in yeintin tlatoque reyesme onpa in iquiçayanpa in tonatiuh quihualyacantias in intitlan in inteyacancauh yhuan Citlali Oc achi huel tlayacanas. auh in icuac ye hualaçisque in yeintin tlatoque reyesme in ixtlahuacan inahuac yn iAltepeuh in ERodes motlatis in [1v] Citlali auh niman onca tlatos in

Gaspar = Ye huecauh in nontlachixtiuh in aocmo nicnotilia in mahuistic Citlali in tomahuisteyacancatzin in ixquich cahuitl in techmoyacanilia huel iuhqui nicmati iuhqui niquilnamiqui Ca ye otaçico in canpa Omotlacatilitzino in mahuistic piltzintli in tictotemolia Ca huel nelli Ca iscatqui in huey Altepetl in Jerusalem ca ninomati ye otictonextilique in tlein tictotemolia = Auh xihualauh in tehuatl in titotetlayecolticauh Xonyauh Xoncalaqui in ipā huey Altepetl Jerusalem iuhqui xiquilhui Xicmelahuili in canpa Otihualeuhque iquisayanpa in [2r] tonatiuh auh ca çentzonpa ticontēnamiqui[2] in imatzin in icxitzin ma techmomaquili in itlatocahuelitzin inic huel tictixpantilitihue in tlein tonetequipachol auh i ni=can ixtlahuacan in ihueyAltepetzin Jerusalem nican ticonchie in itlatocahuelitzin inic huel onpa tonyasque tictixpantilitihue in tlein tonetequipachol—

Titlantli = Ma nicneltili in amotlatocatlanahuatiltzin ma nicchihua in annechmonahuatilia Canel namotlacauhtzin—

Yas in titlantli yquiahuatempa in ERodes quitlapalos in Calpixqui quilhuis

Titlantli = Tlatohuanien ma mitzmochicahuilican in teteo Oticmiyohuilti [2v] ma xicmomachilti ca nintetlayecolticauh in yeintin tlatoque—Reyesme—

---

1. inninnemilitzin: read *in innemiliztzin*.
2. ticontēnamiqui: standard *tocontennamiqui*. Here and below can be found *ticon-* for standard *tocon-* and *xicon-* for standard *xocon-*. See Carochi 1983, 42v–43v.

The Three Kings
Translated by Louise M. Burkhart, with assistance from Barry D. Sell

[1r]

Here begins, here commences the life[1] of the three rulers, kings, how they greeted the precious and wondrous sacred child, the child of God, our lord Jesus Christ. They came from the east.[2] And here begins, here is placed the exemplary model, how it happened that the three rulers, kings, came from the east. Their messenger, their guide comes leading them. And the star goes a bit ahead. And when the three rulers, kings, are about to reach the plain next to Herod's altepetl,[3] the star will be hidden. [1v] *And then speaks*

CASPER: I have been looking around for quite a while. I no longer see the wondrous star, our wondrous guide, that has been leading us the whole time. What I really think, what I reckon, is that we have reached the place where the wondrous child whom we are seeking was born. Truly indeed, here is the great altepetl of Jerusalem. I think that we have now found what we are seeking. But come, our servant. Go forth, go enter into the great altepetl of Jerusalem. Tell him, explain to him, that we came from the east [2r] and that we kiss his hands, his feet, four hundred times.[4] May he give us his royal authorization so that we can go put before him what our problem is. And here on the plain of his great altepetl of Jerusalem, here we await his royal authorization so that we can go there, we can go put before him what our problem is.

MESSENGER: Let me carry out your royal command, let me do what you command me, since I am your servant.

(The messenger goes to Herod's door. He greets the steward. He says to him:)

MESSENGER: O ruler, may the deities[5] give you health.[6] Greetings.[7] [2v] Know that I am the servant of three rulers, kings.

---

1. The term is used as if this were a biographical story, such as a saint's life.
2. Literally, "where the sun comes out." The biblical basis for the story is in Chapter 2 of the Gospel according to Saint Matthew. It begins (verse 2:1): "Now when Jesus was born in Bethlehem of Judea in the days of Herod the king, behold, there came wise men [Magi in the Vulgate] from the east to Jerusalem." Matthew states that there were three gifts but does not specify the number of wise men. According to Farmer (1992, 312 13), since the time of Origen (third century) they have traditionally been numbered at three and were subsequently given the names Casper or Jasper, Melchior, and Balthasar. An iconographic tradition represents one as an old man, one as middle-aged, and the third as young. The practice of depicting one as a dark-skinned African dates from the fifteenth century.
3. altepetl: the largest sociopolitical unit to survive Spanish conquest and colonization. During colonial times the word was translated in many ways including *ciudad* (city) and *pueblo* (people, settlement).
4. Here and below, *four hundred* is a common idiom in the vigesimally based traditional counting system for "countless, innumerable." Where it occurs in the phrase "four hundred times" it could be construed as meaning "countless or many times over."
5. Here and below, the messenger is the only character in the play who professes belief in multiple deities.
6. Here and below, formulaic statement about—or inquiry into—someone's health (literally, "strength") that forms part of polite greetings, similar to statements in the *Bancroft Dialogues* (Karttunen and Lockhart 1987).
7. Formulaic polite greeting, literally, "You have expended breath on [unspecified object]" or "You have fatigued yourself."

Calpixqui = Ma nican tihuitz nocniuhtzinē ma te[l?] huel huey in monetequipachol huel mixco nestihuitz—

titlantli = Tlacatlen tlatohuanien ma mitzmochicahuilican in teteo – Oticmiyohuilti ma xicmomachilti ca onpa nihualehua in iquiçaianpa in tonatiuh auh ca onpa noChantzinco in itocayocan Prençia auh yeintin tlatoque Oniquinhualnoyacanili auh nican ononaçico in ipan in mohueytlatocatlaltzin auh in mohueytlatocauh in ERodes ma ixpan xinechmohuiquili Ca intencopatzinco in tlatoque in pipiltin inic nicnotlapalhuico— [3r]

Calpixqui = Ca ye cualli nocniuhtzinen ma oc nican Xinechie ma oc nicnotili oc nicnolhuili in tlatohuani ERodes—

Auh niman yas tlecos in Calpixqui ixpan in ERodes quicopinas in insombrero yexpa motlancuacolos El fragmento agrega: auh ixpan motlanquaqueztietzi çe ynca ytlanquateuh, auh nima etc[3] auh niman quitos—

Calpixqui = ^{Totecuiyoyē} Tlacatlen tlatohuanien teuctlen huel ye nohuianpa Oquis oaçic Omoteneuh O^{n}caquistia in motenyo in momahuisyo in ixquich in mohuelitilis in ixquichtin Cm̄c tlaca Pipiltin tlatoque teteuctin mitzmimacaxilia^{n} mitzmomahuistililia^{n} Auh Çe huey^{n} tlamahuisolli^{n} in ^{axcan} topam quimochihuilia^{n} in toteotzin totla^{to}catzin in nican motecpanchantzinco motlatocachantzinco Ohualla [3v] intitlan in yeintin tlatoque Reyesme huel çenca hueca in ohualquisque Ohualeuhque ca niman ayac iuhqui hualmaxitia in ipan in motlatocaAltepetzin huel Çentlamantli in itlatol huel tlaque yn ixayac auh ninomati ca tlateotocani^{me} auh mixpantzinco tlatosnequi Onca quiahuac quichie^{n} in motlatocatlanahuatiltzin Cuix nicnotzas Cuix calaquis Cuix mixpantzinco neçi(quiuh)$^{\text{(quihui)}}$—

ERodes = huey tetzahuitl huey tlamahuisolli^{n} in tinechtenehuilia^{n} ma calaqui ma nixpan neçiqui inic nicmatis Canpa^{n} agrega inchan, campan in Ohualeuh tlein quinequi—

temos in calpixqui quinotzas ^{auh} **in titlantli——expan motlanquacoloz yn ixpan Erodes——namiquilis**[4] **in iman in icxin nima huallemos**[5] **in calpixquin quitos** [4r]

Calpixqui = Ma ximocalaquitzino nocniuhtzinen Ca mitzmonochilia^{n} in tlatohuani in ERodes—

titlantli = Ca ye cualitzin nocniuhtzinen =—

yxpan yas in ERodes——in titlantli motlacuaquetzas

titlantli = tlacatlen tlatohuanien ma xinechmomaquili in momatzin in mocxitzin in nimotlacauhtzin $^{\text{inic nictennamiquis}}$—

Yc moquetzas in ERodes oc cecpa[6] **motlalis—**

---

3. Here and below, the superscript additions/corrections/changes appear to be in a different hand.
4. namiquilis: read *quitennamiquiliz*.
5. huallemos: evidently to be read *hualtemoz*.
6. oc cecpa: here and below can be found this and other variants of standard <u>oc ceppa</u>.

STEWARD: Welcome, O my friend. Your problem must be very great, as it is quite evident on your face.

MESSENGER: O personage,[8] O ruler, may the deities give you health. Greetings. Know that I come from the east. And my home is there in the place called Persia. And I have led here three rulers. And I have arrived here in your great and royal land. And as to your great ruler, Herod, take me before him. By order of the rulers, the noblemen, I come to greet him. [3r]

STEWARD: Very well, O my friend. Wait for me here for a bit. Let me see and tell the ruler, Herod.

(And then the steward goes, going up[9] before Herod. He takes off his hat. He bends his knees three times. The fragment adds: and before him he kneels on one knee, and then, etc. And then he says:)

STEWARD: O our lord, O personage, O ruler, O lord, in all places has your fame and your renown gone out, arrived, been declared, been pronounced. You are all-powerful. All the people of the world—nobles, rulers, lords—fear and respect you. But our deity, our ruler is performing a great wonder upon us today. Here to your palace, your royal home has come [3v] the messenger of three rulers, kings, who have come, who have ventured here from very far away. Absolutely no one like this has come [before now] to your royal altepetl. His speech and his face are quite distinct.[10] And I think that he is an idolater.[11] And he wants to speak before you. There in the doorway he awaits your royal command. Shall I summon him? Shall he enter? Shall he come appear before you?[12]

HEROD: It is a great omen, a great wonder, that you declare to me. Let him enter, let him come appear before me so that I will find out where add: his home is, where he came from, what he wants.

(The steward goes down. He summons the messenger. And he bends his knees three times before Herod. He kisses his hands, his feet. Then the steward comes down. He says:) [4r]

STEWARD: Do enter, O my friend. The ruler, Herod, summons you.

MESSENGER: Very well, O my friend.

The messenger goes before Herod. He kneels.

MESSENGER: O personage, O ruler, give me your hands, your feet, so that I, your servant, may kiss them.

(Thus Herod stands up. He sits down again.)

---

8. Literally, "O person," or "O human being," this term was used frequently in formal speeches as a vocative and title denoting respect for the addressee (see the *Bancroft Dialogues* [Karttunen and Lockhart 1987, 34–35] and the *Florentine Codex,* book 6 [Sahagún 1969]).

9. Stage directions suggest that the set for Herod's palace has an upper and a lower level, with Herod's hall or throne room raised above the stage.

10. Tentative translation. The speech is distinct; the face is *huel tlaque* [?].

11. Emendation in text makes this plural, referring to the kings as well, but it probably should remain singular, referring only to the messenger.

12. Here again, text is emended to plural, as if to include the kings, but it should refer only to the messenger.

titlantli = — Ma xicmiyohuilti pilen tlatohuanien in titlacatl in tiERodes ma mitzmoChicahuilican in teteo ma xicmomachilti ca onechhualmotitlanique in yeintin tlatoque pipiltin in nican ixtlahuacan ynahuac in mohuey^{n}Altepetzin Omaxitico auh ^{ca} Onca nechmochielia^n [4v] Onpa Ohualquisque $^{ynyn\ campa}$ in iquisayanpa in tonatiuh huel Çenca hueca ^{auh} Çentzompa^n qui(hual)tennamiqui quitennamiqui solamte in momatzin in mocxitzin ^{auh} çenca necnoma(ti)^{chi}listica mitzmitlanililian $_{mitz(hual)}$falta ^{hual}motlatlauh(tilia)^{tiliyan} ma xiquinmomaquili in motlatocahuelitilitzin inic mixpantzinco neçiquihue mitzmixpantiliquihue in tlein intequipacholtzin $^{tlacatle\ tlatohuanie.}$

ERodes = Nocniuhtzinen ic otimaxitico ma mitzmochicahuili in totecuio D.^{s} tiquinmolhuilis in moteachcahuan in motlatoca^{ycniuh}tzitzinhuan in moteucyohuan Ca çentzompa nictlasocamati in intlatocamahuistetlaçotlalitzin inic Oquimomahuistililico in noAltepeuh in nochan in nocalitic ma nican hual[5r]mohuicacan $^{ma\ hual}$mocalaquican ca yntlatocachantzin ma nicnomaçehuis in inMahuisXayacatzin ma nicmatis in tlein innetequipacholtzin ca niquinnochielia—

titlantli = Ca ye cualitzin tlatohuanien nopiltzintzinen—

Auh niman (quinotzas) ^{quinnahuatiz7} **in ipilhuan ERodes**

ERodes = Auh yn amehuantin in antlatoque in anpipiltin in anteteuctin Xihuian Xiquimonamiquiliti Xiquinçiauhquetzacan tlapitzalos netotilos Xiquinmahuistililican XiquinXochitican Ca nican niquinnochielia—

Auh niman yaS in titlantli (quinnotzatiuh in tlatoque in ixtlahuacan Altepetenco) Variante auh niman yaz in titlantli yhuan tennamiquisque yn ipilhua Erodes ycan xochitl yhuan tlapitzalin achtopa yaz yn titlantlin quitoz_____

[5v]

titlantli = Ononaçito in canpa Oannechmotitlanique ixpan Ononneçito in ERodes in huey pilli in huey tlatohuani auh Ca huel Çenca quitlaçocamati in amotetlaçotlalitzin Ca quimitalhuitzinohua ma hualmocalaquican ma hualmohuicacan ma moçehuitzinoqui yn incalitictzinco Ca mochi intlatquitzin Ca mochi intetzinco pohuis in quexquich noaxca notlatqui—

Achitzin nenemisque in—tlatoque hualtemosque—ȳpan yn iCaballohuan—auh onca tlapitzalos quinXochitisque ^{auh} **in ERodes** $^{niman\ hual}$=**temos quintlapalos ymixpam motlanquacolo^{tie}s quitos Erodes**_____ [6r]

ERodes = Anquimiyohuiltique in oanmaXitico in oanhualmohuicaque in anmahuistililonime in anteteuctin in antlatoque Ma amechmochicahuilitzino in teotl in tlatohuani totecuio D.^{s} Cuix achitzin amechmochicahuilia in tloque nahuaque D.^{s}—

---

7. To the right in the margin: *auh*. It is unclear whether this was meant to be included in the text.

MESSENGER: Be welcome,[13] O nobleman, O ruler, you personage, Herod! May the deities give you health! Know that three rulers, noblemen, have sent me as a messenger. They have arrived here on the plain next to your great altepetl. And they are waiting for me there. [4v] They came from the east, very far away. And four hundred times they kiss your hands and your feet. And very humbly they ask of you, they beseech you, may you give them your royal authorization so that they may come appear before you, they may reveal to you what their problem is, O personage, O ruler.

HEROD: O my friend, welcome.[14] May our lord God give you health. You are to tell your masters, your royal friends, your lords, that I thank them four hundred times for their royal and wondrous affection, with which they have come to honor my altepetl, my home, the inside of my house. Let them come [5r] here, let them enter their royal home, let me be deserving of their wondrous faces, let me learn what their problem is. I await them.

MESSENGER: Very well, O ruler, O my nobleman.[15]

(*And then Herod summons gives orders to his noblemen.*)[16]

HEROD: And, you rulers, you noblemen, you lords, go, meet them, greet them! Wind instruments will be played. There will be dancing. Honor them, adorn them with flowers! I wait for them here.

(*And then the messenger goes to summon the rulers on the plain at the edge of the altepetl. Variant: And then the messenger goes, and Herod's noblemen[17] go, to meet the others with flowers and flutes. The messenger goes first. He says:*) [5v]

MESSENGER: I reached the place you sent me to. I appeared before Herod, the great nobleman, the great ruler. And he is most grateful for your affection. He says: "Let them enter, let them come, let them rest inside their house, for everything is their possession, for everything will belong to them, whatever is my property, my possession."

(*The rulers move on a bit. They get down from their horses. And then wind instruments are played. They adorn them with flowers. And Herod then comes down, greeting them, going on bended knee before them. Herod says:*) [6r]

HEROD: Greetings! You have arrived, you have come, you honored ones, you lords, you rulers. May the deity, the ruler, our lord God, give you health. Does the Lord of the Near, the Lord of the Nigh, God, give you a little health?

---

13. This is an optative statement, literally, "May you have expended breath on [unspecified object]" or "May you have fatigued yourself," the pragmatic thrust (probably uppermost in a typical Nahua's mind) being a formulaic polite greeting.

14. Welcome: literally, "so you have come to arrive."

15. The possessed form of *pilli* normally means "child" rather than "noble" (see Carochi 1983, 9v–10r). However, the doubling of the honorific suffix here, as in later speeches by Casper and Balthasar, indicates that "my noble" is the intended meaning (Karttunen and Lockhart 1987, 39–40). This can also be found in Molina 1977, 73v: "Nopiltzintzine. a señor. vel. o señor. vel. señor. [dize el que habla con persona de calidad]" (Nopiltzintzine. Ah Lord, or O Lord, or Lord [says one who speaks with a person of high rank]).

16. Literally, "his children," in this case meaning the high-born subordinates of Herod.

17. See previous note re "his children."

Melchor = Ma ximehuiltitie tlacatlen tlatohuanien in tiERodes Ca çenca ticmahuiço-hua in motetlaçotlalitzin Otlacauhqui in moyolotzin Ca in timotlacahuan in timo-maçehualhuan Ca achitzin Otictomaçehuique in techiCahualistli Ca çenca ticontennamiqui in motlaçomatzin in motlaçoicxitzin—

ERodes = Ma ximotlecahuican yn a[6v]mochantzinco in amaltepetzin ma Ximo-calaquican anmotlacualtisque Canel amochantzinco in anmaxitico—

Calaquisque in tlatoque moçehuisque huel Çenca quinmahuistilisque———

ERodes = = Ma xicmitalhuican in anteteuctin in antlatoque in anmahuistililonime in anpipiltin tle ica in ixquichica in anhualmohuicaque Çenca nicmahuiçosnequi in amotetlaçotlalitzin—

Melchor = Ca çenca Otictomaçehuique Çenca otitechmocnelili tlacatlen tlatohuanien ERodese Canel tipilli Ca titlatohuani—Ca tiquinmomahuistililia in mo[7r]tlahuan auh ma xicmomachilti Ca ye huecauh in inmacpa in toColhuan in ye huecauh hue-huetque Oquimopielique in çenca huel ye huecauh in huey in huey tlamatini Oquicahuilitehuaque y.n achtopaittalistli auh yn achtopaitohuani itoca catca Balan Auh Oquimitalhuitzino in tetatzin Jacob tlacatis Çe mahuistic Çitlali itech isRael tlecos moquetzas hueyas Çe pilli Çe tlatohuani quinmococolhuis quinmotlatza-cuiltilis in itlayacancahuan in mohuap quinmoçenpolhuis in ipilhuan Çet auh in achtopaittalistli Ca huel Oquimoyolotique in huehuetque in tocolhuan inic huel quimochielisque in pilli in [7v] tlatohuani ihuan in iCitlaltzin inic machos mahuiçolos in iquin maxitiquiuh in machiotl in tetzahuitl in anoço Citlali in ipan in ilhuicatl Oquixquetzque in toColhuan in matlactin omome ixtlamatque hue-huetque tepeticpac Çemicac yesque iquiçayanpa in tonatiuh itztiesque in iquin mahuiçolos in mahuistic Citlali. Auh in axcan ye nauhtzonXihuitl in ye quimochielia Cemicac tepeticpac tlachieloya auh in axcan ye quesquilhuitica in oquimonequilti in ipalnemohualoni in tloque in nahuaquen totecuiotzin yohual-nepantla in icuac ye nohuianpa Cochihualoticatqui in Altepetl Auh Oquimotilique çe huel mahuistic Çitlali. in matlactin omome huehuetque [8r] huel pepetlaca in Çitlali huel quiçenpanahuia in tonatiuh in nohuianpa Otlanes Otonameyotic ihuan çenca huel huey tlamahuiçolli in itic in Çitlali in oquimotilique Ocatcaya çe huel mahuistic chipahuac Çenca ylehuiloni in piltzintli in itic Ocatcayaya Auh niman nochantzinco Onmehualtique Omotlaloque Onechmoxitilito Auh inniscate[8] in tla-toque in pipiltin nonahuac Ocatcayaya Onechmotlapalhuito auh niman Oniquin-notz Oniquimixiti Otictotilique in Çitlali auh in mahuiztic teopiltzintli Ca iuhquima Otechmoyolehuili Ca niman Otitoyecnonotzque Otitocohuanotzque Oti-tochichiuhque Otitotacatique Auh Auh niman Otli otictopehualtili[9][8v]que inic tic-totemolisque in piltzintli Auh in mahuistic Çitlali ca niman Otechhualmoyacanili

---

8. inniscate: read *in iz cate*.
9. In anticipation of the following page: *que*.

MELCHIOR: Do remain seated, O personage, O ruler, you who are Herod. We marvel greatly at your hospitality. Your heart has been generous. We are your servants, we are your vassals. We have enjoyed a bit of health. We fervently kiss your precious hands and your precious feet.

HEROD: Ascend to [6v] your home, your altepetl. Enter. You are to eat, since it is at your home that you have arrived.

(The rulers enter. They rest. They treat them with great honor.)

HEROD: Tell, you lords, you rulers, you honored ones, you noblemen, why you have come all this way. I want very much to honor your affection.

MELCHIOR: We have been very fortunate. You have shown us great favor, O personage, O ruler, O Herod. Since you are a nobleman, you are a ruler, you honor your [7r] uncles. And know that our grandfathers long ago, the elders of long ago, kept in their hands a prophecy that the great sages of ancient times bequeathed to them. And the name of the prophet was Balaam. And he said that from father Jacob would be born a wondrous star; that from Israel would ascend, would arise, would grow a nobleman, a ruler, who would wound and would punish the leaders of Moab, who would destroy the children of Sheth.[18] And the elders, our grandfathers, took much to heart this prophecy by which they would await the nobleman, the [7v] ruler, along with his star, by which he would be known, he would be noted, when a sign, an omen, or a star would appear in the sky. Our grandfathers appointed twelve prudent elders to be always on a mountaintop in the east, to be watching for when the wondrous star would be observed. And now it has been sixteen hundred[19] years that they have been waiting continuously for the star in the observatory on the mountaintop. And now some days ago He by Whom All Live, the Lord of the Near, the Lord of the Nigh, our lord, wanted it to happen, in the middle of the night, when people were asleep everywhere in the [various] altepetl. And the twelve elders saw a very wondrous star. [8r] The star was shimmering so brightly that it surpassed the sun. It was bright everywhere, full of rays, and it was a very great wonder that within the star they saw that there was a quite wondrous, pure, very appealing child who was inside it. And then they set forth, they ran to my home, they went to wake me up. And the rulers, the noblemen who are here were with me, had gone to greet me. And then I summoned them, I woke them up. We saw the star. And it was as if the wondrous, sacred child inspired us. Then we came to an agreement, we dined together, we adorned ourselves, we gathered our provisions. And then we took to the road [8v] in order to search for the child. And

---

18. Balak, ruler of the Moabites, engaged the seer Balaam to curse the Israelites, who were traveling through his land during their exodus from Egypt. But Balaam saw that the Israelites were blessed by God and he defied Balak. The prophecy recounted here, which Christian exegetes applied to Christ, is from Numbers 24:17: "I shall see him, but not now: I shall behold him, but not nigh: there shall come a Star out of Jacob, and a Sceptre shall rise out of Israel, and shall smite the corners of Moab, and destroy all the children of Sheth." As a prophecy attributed to an ethnic group other than the Israelites, it could be assigned to the non-Jewish ancestors of the Magi.

19. In the traditional vigesimally based Nahua counting system this is literally "four units of four hundred," that is, 4x(20x20). This has a distinctly ideal ring to it within the framework of prehispanic Nahua culture. In the cellular or modular structure characteristic of *altepetl* and song/poetry (among others), one finds a tendency for Nahuas to construct symmetrically balanced wholes out of four pairs.

Oticualitztiaque auh nican Otihualaque Otonaçico in ipan in moAltepetzin Jerusalem Otictopolhuique in tomahuisteyacancatzin in aocmo tictotilia Auh ipampa in axcan Oticmatque aço nican ipan in mohueyAltepetzin tictonextilisque in tlein tictotemolia Çentzompa teuctlen tlacatlen ERodesen ca timitztotlatlauhtilia ma xitechmolhuili—in canpa Omotlacatili in canpa mohueztica in intlatocauh in Judiosme Ca ye nelli ca ye Oticquitaque[10] in iÇitlaltzin in ompa in iquiçayanpa in tonatiuh Auh ca Otihualaque Otictoteotitzinoco ixpantzinco[11] [9r] Otitopechtecaco Otictomahuistililico—

ERodes = = Tlatohuanie Cuix timotlapololtia tlein ticmotenehuilia aquin tlatohuani aquin intlatocauh in Judiosme intlacamo nehuatl Onechmotlauhtili in tlatocayotl in Roma Enperador Çesar de Agusto Cuix amo nohuaxca Cuix amo notlatqui Cuix amo nitlatohuani Cuix amo nitlatocati Cuix ye onipoliuh Cuix ye Onimic Cuix ye onitlan Cuix acmo nicmati Cuix amo—niERodes Cuix acmo nipilli aquin nopan tlatocatis in axcan ^{ma} içiuhcan ~~An~~nechmelahuiliqui in ~~an~~noteyacancahuan in ~~an~~Judiosme in ~~an~~noteopixcahuan in ~~an~~tlamatinime in a~~ma~~moxhuaque[12] in teoyotica pipil[13][9v]tin in teoyotica tepachohuanime ma nechmelahuiliqui in tlein Citlali tlein piltzintli tlein tlatohuani in quimote^{ne}huilia in tlatoque iÇiuhcan Ca ye nimiquiznequi ye niçotlahuas iyoyahuen ninotolinia Ay Ay Ay—

Calpixqui = Ca ye cuallitzin tlatohuaniē ma niquinnotza macamo Ximotequipachotzino—

niman yas in calpixqui quinnotzatiuh in teopixque————

Calpixqui = = Ca ye huitze tlatohuanien macamo titotlapololtican in tixquichtin timotla^{ca}huan in timomaçehualhuan in tiJerusalem tlaca—

1° teopixqui = = Ma mitzmochicahuili in Çe nelli teotl tepachohuani D.^{s} tlacatlen tlatohuanien ERodes^e~~tzin~~[14] [10r] [~~ma~~] ca mitzinco tontlachie in timotla^{ca}huan Ca çenca tipaqui titotlamachtia titoyolalia Ca neçi ca mitzmochicalia[15] in totecuio D.^{s} ma xitechmomaquili in momatzin in mocxi.tzin ma tictennamiquican tlein ticmonequiltia ma ticoncaquican ma timitztotla^{ca}machiti^{li}can—

---

10. Oticquitaque: standard *otiquittaque*.
11. In anticipation of the following page: *O*.
12. The preceding crossed out subject prefixes (second-person plural) anticipate dialogue by Herod that appears on 10r.
13. In anticipation of the following page: *tin*.
14. In anticipation of the following page: [~~ma~~].
15. mitzmochicalia: read *mitzmochicahuilia*.

the wondrous star then led us in this direction. We came along watching it. And we came here, we reached your altepetl of Jerusalem. We lost our wondrous guide. We no longer see it. And therefore we now have realized that perhaps here in your great altepetl we will discover that which we seek. O four-hundred-times lord, O personage, O Herod, we beseech you, tell us where the ruler of the Jews was born, where he is seated.[20] For it is true that we have seen his star there in the east. And so we have come, we have come to worship him, [9r] we have come to bow down before him, we have come to honor him.[21]

HEROD: O ruler, are you confused? What are you talking about? Who is the ruler? Who is the ruler of the Jews if not I? The Emperor of Rome, Caesar Augustus, granted me the rulership. Is it not my property? Is it not my possession? Am I not the ruler? Do I not rule? Have I already perished? Have I already died? Have I already been finished off? Am I no longer mentally competent? Am I not Herod? Am I no longer a nobleman? Who will rule over me? Now let my Jewish leaders, my priests, the sages, those who keep the [sacred] books, those who are noblemen in regard to sacred things, [9v] those who are governors in regard to sacred things, come quickly to explain it to me. Let them come to explain to me what star, what child, what ruler the rulers are talking about. Quickly, for I am about to die, I am about to faint! Alas! I am afflicted! Ay! Ay! Ay![22]

STEWARD: Very well, O ruler. Let me summon them. Do not be anxious!

(Then the steward goes to summon the priests.)

STEWARD: They are coming now, O ruler. Let us not become confused, all of us, we who are your servants, we who are your vassals, we people of Jerusalem.

FIRST PRIEST: May the one true deity, the governor, God, give you health, O personage, O ruler, O Herod. [10r] We gaze into your face, we who are your servants. We are very joyful, we are happy, we are contented for it appears that our lord God gives you health. Give us your hands and your feet that we may kiss them. What do you want? Let us hear it, let us obey you.

---

20. "Seated" with the connotation "in all his authority and majesty." Alternatively, "where he is fallen [to earth, or from the womb?]."

21. Parallels Matthew 2:2, in which the wise men say to Herod: "Where is he that is born King of the Jews? For we have seen his star in the east, and are come to worship him."

22. Matthew 2:3–4: "When Herod the king had heard these things, he was troubled, and all Jerusalem with him. And when he had gathered all the chief priests and scribes of the people together, he demanded of them where Christ should be born."

ERodes = Yn amehuantin in anJudiosme in anteopixcatlatoque in antlamatinime in amamoxhuaque Ça çentzompa antetlapololtique teca anmocaca^{ya}uhtime[16] çenca anteistlacahuitinemi in neltilistlatolli aocmo anquiximati in aocmo antenehualo Cuix amo çemicac namechilhuitinemi Ca namotlatocauh huel annechtlaçotla quenin huel amistlacati Ca in yeintin tlatoque Oma[17][10v]xitico Ohualeuhque ompa in iquiçayanpa in tonatiuh inchantzinco Onpa yohualnepantla Oquitaque in Citlali quilmach in Citlali in intlatocauh in Judiosme ca ye Otlacat aquin piltzintli aquin tlatohuani in nopan tlatocatis içiuhcan Xinechmelahuilican Cuix amo anquitaque in yancuic Citlali Cuix çeçenyohual in ancochi Cochmiquinime tlatziuhque pitzome Cuix amo anquipohua in maytines in yohualnepantla Judiasos Diablo ipilhuan iÇiuhcan xontlatemocan xinechyolpachihuitican amo namechçenpopolos tlahueliloqueyen—

2.º teopixqui = Macamo ximocualanalti totecuioyen tle çan nen Camo tomachispan camo totlatlacol [ma in?] mo[11r]chihua ma ticmomachiltis Ca in totecuio Otechmotenehuilili Ca techmomaquilis in quemanian in itlaçopiltzin in D.^s in nican tlalticpac in quihualmihualis in topanpa monacayotitzinoquiuh auh intla ye Ohualmohuicac Cuix tictoquixtililisque in iteotlanequilitzin · Cachtopaittalistli[18] Oquimotenehuili Oquimotecpanili in tetecuio[19] D.^s—

ERodes = Xontlatemocan tlahueliloqueyen in teoamoxpan canpa in tlacatis in amotlatocauh yes isquime[20]—

1.º teopixqui = Xicanati in teoamoxtli ma tontlatemocan ma techmonextilili in D.^s aquin quimotemolia in piltzintli ic moyolçehuis in tohueytlatocauh ERodes—[11v]

3.º teopixqui = = Ca iscatqui ma tontlatemocan ma techmonextilili in tlacatl

oncan tlatemosque ipan in teoamoxtli in Judio teopixque———

1.º teopixqui = tlacatlen Erode^{es}~~tzinen~~ ca nican quimitalhuia in achtopaittohuani Ysayas capitulo in inelhuayo in çenquiças ixhuas moscaltis Çe tlacatl tlatocapilli auh ixhuas cueponis çe mahuistic Xochitl ic necis Ca pilli ca tlatohuani ipan tlacatis ca itech pohuilis in itlacamecayo in David—

ERodes—Ye nicmati tlahueliloqueyen in titlapaltontli Ca itech pohuis yn itlacamecayo in David canpa in tlacatis tlein ipan Altepetl içiuhcan xontlatemocan xinechmelahuili[12r]can amo namechichinos namechxipehuas chicharones namechcuepas Judiasos—

---

16. teca anmocacayauhtime: read *teca anmocacayauhtinemi* or *teca anmocacayauhtique*.
17. In anticipation of the following page: *Xi*.
18. Cachtopaittalistli: read *ca achtopaittaliztli*.
19. tetecuio: scribal error; standard *totecuiyo*.
20. isquime: see note in translation.

HEROD: You Jews, you priestly rulers, you sages, you keepers of the [sacred] books, four hundred times you have confused people. You go about mocking people, you go about deceiving people greatly. You no longer recognize truthful words, you are no longer acclaimed. Am I not forever going about telling you that I am your ruler? You sure do love me. How well you do lie! Three rulers have arrived, [10v] have come from the east. In their home there in the middle of the night they saw a star. It is said that the star is[23] the ruler of the Jews who has been born. Who is the child? Who is the ruler who will rule over me? Quickly, explain this to me! Didn't you see the new star? Are you asleep every night? Sleepyheads! Lazy ones! Pigs! Don't you recite matins[24] in the middle of the night? Rotten Jews,[25] children of the devil, quickly, go find out, satisfy me, and I will not destroy you, O scoundrels!

SECOND PRIEST: Do not be angry, O our lord. What's the use? What is happening is not our concern nor our fault. [11r] Know that our lord declared to us that he will someday give us God's beloved child. He will send him here to earth. He will come to take on flesh for our sake. And if he has come, are we to tamper with[26] his sacred will? Our lord God declared and established the prophecy.

HEROD: Go look up, O scoundrels, in the sacred book, where he will be born, the one who will be the ruler of all of you.[27]

FIRST PRIEST: Go get the sacred book. Let us look it up, may God reveal to us him whom they seek, the child, so that our great ruler, Herod, will be appeased. [11v]

THIRD PRIEST: Here it is. Let us look it up, may the personage[28] reveal it to us.

(*At that point the Jewish priests will search in the sacred book.*)

FIRST PRIEST: O personage, O Herod, here the prophet Isaiah, chapter,[29] says: "From his root will emerge, will sprout, will grow, a certain royal child. And a wondrous flower will sprout, will blossom." By this it would appear that the nobleman, the ruler, will be born from and belong to the lineage of David.

HEROD: I already know, O scoundrels, you pip-squeak, that he will belong to the lineage of David. Where will he be born? In what altepetl? Quickly, look it up, explain it to me, [12r] and I won't singe you, flay you, turn you into pork rinds, rotten Jews.

---

23. That the star indicates that this ruler has been born may be the intended meaning.
24. An anachronistic reference to the observance of the canonical hours, a series of eight daily offices of devotion practiced by friars, monks, and other pious Catholics, including the indigenous students at the Franciscan College of the Holy Cross in Tlatelolco. The first hour, matins, falls at midnight.
25. *Judiazos*, here and below literally means "big Jews," an augmentative Spanish loanword with deprecatory meaning.
26. *Tictoquixtililisque*: tentative translation; literally, "we will cause it to go out in regard to him (honorific applicative of *quixtia*)."
27. The last word in this speech is *isquime*, a plural form of "all." Logically, this would refer to the priests, or Jews in general, but it lacks the *am-* subject prefix it should have. Tentative translation.
28. That is, God.
29. No chapter number is given. The playwright may be mimicking priests' readings of weekly Bible lessons at church services. The prophecy cited is Isaiah 11:1–2: "And there shall come forth a rod out of the stem of Jesse, and a Branch shall grow out of his roots: And the Spirit of the Lord shall rest upon him," interpreted by Christian exegetes as a reference to Christ's birth from the lineage of Jesse's son David.

3.º teopixqui = Ma techmopalehuili in totecuio D.ˢ ma techtolini in tlatohuani ca huel cualani axcan techichinos chicharrones techcuepas—

2.º teopixqui = Yn timahuistic titlatohuani in çenca tiylehuiloni in tiERodes iscatqui yn oquimotecpanili in totecuio D.ˢ in ticmotemolia Auh Xicmomachilti in tlein quimitalhuia in achtopaitohuani in tehuecapaittani Meçias in ipan Çe capitulo auh in tehuatl tiBelem in tiJudiatlalpan Camo titepiton in ipan yn iteyacancahuan in pipiltin in in Judia huel motechpa quisas in teyacanqui in tepachohuani tlatohuani—[12v] in teoyotica quinpachohua yn iAltepeuh isrrael ic neçis in tlacatl tlatohuani ca onpa Otlacat yn ipan in Betlem in Judiatlalpan ma onpa contemoti intla ticmonequiltia—

ERodes = Ypan Betlem xontlatemocan tlahueliloqueen axcan namechichinos quenin aic annechilhuique pitzome diablo ypilhuan

oJo niman oncan quintocas in ERodes in Judio. teopixque Oc Cecpa onca quiçocohuasque[21] in teoamoxtli oJo

ERodes = YSiuhca xinechtlalcahuican oncan niquinnonotzas in tlatoque—

Calaquisque in teopixque auh in ERodes inhuicopa mocuepaS in tlatoque huel mocnomatis—[13r]

ERodes = Yn çenca anmahuistililonime in anteteuctin in antlatoque ma xinechmotlapopolhuilitzinocan Çenca tepitzin Onomnocualanalti amixpantzinco intechcacopan in nopilhuan yeicca[22] amo Onechmelahuilique in quenin tlamahuiçoltica mochihuas Auh in axcan ca huel çenca namechnotlatlauhtilia ma xinechmolhuilican ye quexquich cahuitl in ones in omotac in Citlali in onpa amochantzinco in oanquimotilique Ma xinechmolhuilican Ca çenca namechnotlatlauhtilia—

Gaspar = Tlatohuanien nopiltzintzinen in timahuiztic titlatohuani in tiERodes ma xicmomachiltitzino macamo timitztocualantilisque amo motechtzinco toncualani Ca ye Oticma[13v]huiçoque in motetlaçotlalitzin auh amo timitztostlacahuilizque in Çenca timahuistililoni in titlatohuani ma xicmomachiltzino Ca ye matlactli yhuan yeiltica huitica in otictotilique in çe mahuiztic Citlali in onpa in iquiçayanpa in tonatiuh amo huecauhtica inic Oticualtotilitiaque Auh in axcan yohuatzinco Otictopolhuique in tomahuisteyacancatzin inic nican icalaquian in moaltepetzin Jerosalem Çentzompa teuctlen ERodesen—

ERodes = hoannechmocnelilique in anteteuctin[23] in antlatoque Otlacauhqui in amoyolotzin in axcan ma ximohuicacan in onpa in huey Altepetl Betlem Camo hueca Ca çan nican inahuac in Jerusalem Ma çenca [14r] huel yca in piltzintli Auh in iCuac anquimotilistique Ma annechmolhuilitiquiçasque inic no nehuatl in nicnotlapalhuitiuh nicnoteotitiuh in teotl in tlatohuani nicnotlatocatitiuh ma onpa ximohuicacan—

---

21. quiçocohuasque: read *quiçoçohuasque*.
22. yeicca: read *yehica*.
23. There is a written indication of some kind above the letter *c* but its intent is not clear.

THIRD PRIEST: May our lord God help us! May the ruler [not] torment us! He is really angry. Now he will singe us, he will turn us into pork rinds.

SECOND PRIEST: You honored one, you ruler, you very appealing one, Herod, here is what our lord God established, which we are seeking. And know what the prophet, the seer Micah says, in one chapter: "And you, Bethlehem, you land of Judea, you are not small among the governors and nobles of Judea. From you will come the leader, the governor, the ruler [12v] who in a sacred way will govern[30] the altepetl of Israel."[31] By this it would appear that the personage, the ruler has been born there, in Bethlehem, in the land of Judea. Let them go look for him there, if you wish.

HEROD: In Bethlehem! Go look it up, O scoundrels! Now I will singe you! How can it be that you never told me, O pigs, children of the devil?
(Note Then at that point Herod drives out the Jewish priests. Note: Again they open the sacred book.

HEROD: Leave me at once! Then I will consult with the rulers.
(The priests enter. And Herod turns toward the rulers. He is very humble.) [13r]

HEROD: Pardon me, you very honorable lords and rulers. I got a bit angry at my noblemen[32] in front of you because they did not explain to me that it would happen in such a wondrous manner. And now I fervently beseech you, tell me how much time it has been since the star appeared, was seen, when you saw it there in your home. Tell me, I fervently beseech you.[33]

CASPER: O ruler, O my nobleman, honored one, ruler, Herod, be informed of it. Let us not make you angry. We are not angry at you. For [13v] we have marveled at your hospitality. And we will not lie to you. You are very honorable, you are a ruler. Be informed that it has been thirteen days since we saw a wondrous star there in the east. It was not long ago that we came along watching it. But this morning we lost our wondrous guide here at the entrance to your altepetl of Jerusalem, O four-hundred-times lord, O Herod.

HEROD: Thank you, lords, rulers. Your hearts have been generous. Now, go to the great altepetl of Bethlehem. It is not far away. It is right here close to Jerusalem. May it be very [14r] well with the child. And when you have seen him, come by to tell me so that I too may go to greet and to worship the deity, the ruler, I may go to take him as a ruler. Go there.[34]

30. Verb is present tense but future is presumably intended.
31. In Matthew 2:5–6 the priests' response is as follows: "And they said unto him, In Bethlehem of Judea: for thus it is written by the prophet, And thou Bethlehem, in the land of Juda, art not the least among the princes of Juda: for out of thee shall come a Governor, that shall rule my people Israel." The Nahuatl text gives the prophet's name as Meçias, or "Messiah," but the text in Matthew derives from the book of the prophet Micah (Spanish Miqueas, Latin Michaea), verse 5:2: "But thou, Bethlehem Ephratah, though thou be little among the thousands of Judah, yet out of thee shall he come forth unto me that is to be ruler in Israel."
32. Literally, "my children," in this case meaning the high-born subordinates of Herod.
33. Matthew 2:7: "Then Herod, when he had privily called the wise men, inquired of them diligently what time the star appeared."
34. Matthew 2:8: "And he sent them to Bethlehem, and said, Go and search diligently for the young child; and when ye have found him, bring me word again, that I may come and worship him also."

Balthasar = Ma motlaçonahuactzinco mocauhtzino in tlamatcayelistli ihuan ma mitzmochicahuili~~ean~~tzinocan in tloque nahuaque in ipaltzinco nemohualoni in totecuio D.ˢ nopiltzintzinen teuctlen tlacatlen tlatohuaniē Ca ticontennamiqui in momatzin ihuan in mocxitzin Ca ye titohuicatihui tlatohuanien nopiltzintzinen—

Niman quincahuatiuh in ERodes, in tlatoque tlatzintla icaltenpa. [14v] auh niman yasque calaquisque ᵃᵘʰ ⁱᵖᵃ̄ **theopan ixpan quinextisque in Cjtlali niman tlatos in Balthasar huel quimotetzahuis** ʸᵗˡᵃⁿ ᵃʳᶜᵒ **in Citlali quitos———**

Balthasar = honotlaçoicniuhtzitzinhuanē ma xiconmitilican in otechhualmoyacaniliaya in tomahuisteyacancantzin in mahuistic Citlali Ca ye no cuel techmoyacanilia ho tla xiconmotilican notlaçomahuisicniuhtzitzinhuanen—

Melchor = Ma çemca ic titopapaquiltican yeica ca ye Otictonextilique Otechmonextililitzino in tloque nahuaque in ipaltzinco nemohualoni in tomahuisteyacancantzin in quenin Ohualmelauhtia ye moquetza ye motzicohua [15r] yn ipan Çe xacalçolli Omoquetz Omotzico itech Omopacho auh tlein quitosnequi Cuix amo çe huey tecpancalli itech mopachosquia in niCan Altepetl icalaquian—

Melchor = = Xihualauh in tehuatl in titotetlayecolticauh xoncalaqui xontlachie xontlatemo tlein tlamahuiçolli Onca quimopielia in totecuioitzin in totlatocatzin—

titlantli = Ca ye cualitzin tlatoqueyen ma oc noncalaqui ma oc nontlachie—

**OnCan calaquis in theopan in titlantli tlachietiuh oc çecpa hualquisas quitos—
Oraçion**

BALTHASAR: May peace be with your precious self, and may the Lord of the Near, the Lord of the Nigh, He by Whom All Live, our lord God, give you health, O my nobleman, O lord, O personage, O ruler. We kiss your hands and your feet. Now we are going to go, O ruler, O my nobleman.

(Then Herod escorts the rulers below, outside of his house.[35] *[14v] And then they go, they exit. And in in front of the church they discover the star under the arch.*[36] *Then Balthasar speaks. He is quite astonished at the star. He says:)*

BALTHASAR: O my beloved friends, look! Our wondrous guide that led us this way, the wondrous star, is leading us again! Oh, do look, O my beloved honored friends!

MELCHIOR: Let us be very joyful for this! For we have found it! The Lord of the Near, the Lord of the Nigh, He by Whom All Live has revealed to us how our wondrous guide came straight in this direction. Now it is stopping, now it is halting. [15r] It has stopped, it has halted, above a shack. It has drawn near to it. But what does it mean? Would it not draw near to a great palace, here at the entrance to the altepetl?[37]

MELCHIOR: Come, our servant. Go in, go look, go find out what marvel our lord, our ruler is keeping there.

MESSENGER: Very well, O rulers. Let me go in, let me go look.

(At that point the messenger enters the church. He goes and looks. He comes out again. He gives a speech.)

---

35. That is, he will escort the Three Kings down to the lower level of the stage setting representing his palace, seeing them off.

36. The phrase "under the arch" appears in the manuscript in the margin after the verb *quimotetzahuiz*, but it would seem to refer to the placement of the artificial star, which could have been suspended from an arch. The stage directions indicate that the actors move the drama right into the church building. Upon leaving Herod's palace, which could be a stage set erected in the churchyard or open chapel, the kings may go into an "offstage" space, then come out again and ride to the church. The "shack" is probably meant to be represented not by the church building itself but by a manger scene set up inside of it. According to the Franciscan chronicler fray Gerónimo de Mendieta, indigenous people customarily erected such crèches, with statues of Mary, Joseph, the infant Jesus, and shepherds, in their churches from Christmas to Epiphany (Mendieta 1980, 432). As Mary and Joseph do not speak in the drama, they may be represented by the statues rather than by living actors.

37. Matthew 2:9–10: "When they had heard the king, they departed; and, lo, the star, which they saw in the east, went before them, till it came and stood over where the young child was. When they saw the star, they rejoiced with exceeding great joy."

titlantli = Yn antlatoque in āReyesme ca onicchiuh in tlein Oannechmonahuatilique Ca onontlachieto auh ca niman [15v] atle iuhqui niquitoz ca niman atlein iuhqui nicnenehuiliz in ononcalac in onontlachix Ca huel çenca tlanestoc huel iuhqui in ye hualquiças in tlanextli in tonameyotl in nohuianpa quiquistoc auh Onicnotili çe tlaçomahuistic Çenquiscatlateochihualichpotzintli quimonapalhuitica çe tlaçomahuistic tlateochihualpiltzintli Auh ynahuactzinco mohueztnoticatqui Çe huehuetlacatzintli Auh quimoyahualhuiticate in tlaçomahuispipiltzitzintin aastlacapaleque auh Onca inahuactzinco cate Omentin manenencatzitzintin Auh yn ilhuicac tlaçoÇihuapilli Ca huel quimoçenpanahuilia yn ixquich nepapan tlaçoXochitl y nestic in costic in tlaçoXochitl Camopalpopoyauh[16r]tic ye mochi in nepapan tlaçoXochitl in tlauhqueCholtic in onpa quiquistoc Auh in tlaçomahuistlateochihualpiltzintli in itlaçomahuizÇenquiscatlaçomahuizqualtilispepetlaquilisXayacatzin Ca huel Çenquizcachipahuac Auh in itlaçomahuisÇenquiscatzomtzin yuhqui in Costic teocuitlatl inic pepetlaca in anoço iuhqui in çepayahuitl inic chipahuac Auh ca huel ÇenquiscaCualcan in omotlacatilitzino Çacaxacaltzinco in omotlacatilitzino in tlaçomahuizteopiltzintli Auh tlatoqueyen Ma tihuian ma tictotlapalhuiti ma tictomahuistililiti ma ixpantzinco titocnomatiti ma ixpantzinco titopechteca^{can}[24] tlatoqueyen—

_____[25] [16v]

Melchor = Ma çemicac yectenehualo in tomahuizteotzin in totlatocatzin D.^{S} Ca ye Otictonextilique in tictotemolia ma ticalaquican tlatoqueyen nocniuhtzitzinhuanen ma tictoteotitzi.noti ma ixpantzinco titopechtecati ma tictotlahuenchihuililiti—

onca motemohuisque in tlatoque inpan yn icaballohuan moCalaquis[26] **in teopan huel mocnomatisq^e tlatocanenemisque motlācuaquetzatihue Altar itzintla in canpa mochihua in Missa yhuā ipan Euangelio tla otlan in Credo quimotlapalhuitzinosque in tlaSomahuisteopiltzintli**—[17r]

ÇeÇenyacan yca Oraçiones tlapehualtis in

---

24. The three superscript letters, *can*, were themselves overwritten with *ti=*. This seems to anticipate the "titopechtecati" uttered by the next speaker, Melchor, on the following page.
25. In anticipation of the following page: *Melchor*.
26. moCalaquis: read *mocalaquizque*.

MESSENGER: You rulers, you kings, I have done what you commanded me. I went and looked. And I cannot [15v] describe it at all, I cannot compare it with anything at all. I went in, I observed. It is very bright. It is like when the light, the sunlight, is about to come forth. It is issuing out in all directions. And I saw a precious, wondrous, and utterly blessed maiden holding in her arms a precious, wondrous, and blessed little child. And next to her is seated an elderly person.[38] And surrounding them are precious and wondrous little children with wings. And there beside them are two animals. And the heavenly precious[39] noblewoman greatly surpasses all the various precious flowers, ash-colored and yellow precious flowers, deep-purple-tinted ones, [16r] all the various precious flowers, like roseate spoonbills, that lie issuing forth there.[40] And the precious, wondrous, utterly precious, wondrous, good, and shimmering face of the precious, wondrous, and blessed child is utterly pure. And his utterly precious and wondrous hair is like gold, the way it shimmers, or like snow, it is so pure. And the precious and wondrous sacred child was born in an utterly good place, he was born in a hut. And, O rulers, let us go, let us go greet him, let us go honor him, let us go humble ourselves before him, let us bow before him, O rulers! [16v]

MELCHIOR: May our wondrous deity, our ruler, God, be forever praised! We have found what we are looking for. Let us enter, O rulers, O my friends! Let us go worship him! Let us go bow before him! Let us go make offerings to him!
(At that point the rulers get down from their horses. They enter the church. They humble themselves quite a bit. They proceed in a regal manner. They go and kneel at the foot of the altar where mass is being performed, and in the Gospel, when the Creed is finished,[41] they will greet the precious and wondrous sacred child, [17r] one at a time, with orations. He begins:)

---

38. Joseph, elderly according to a medieval tradition based on apocryphal gospels, which by the sixteenth century coexisted with a newer interpretation that regarded him as a young man.
39. precious: also has the connotation "high-born."
40. Filling Christ's birthplace with flowers is a Nahua innovation seen also in the *Psalmodia Christiana*'s Christmas text (Sahagún 1993b, 372–73) and the *Cantares Mexicanos* (Bierhorst 1985, 254–57); the latter work also compares the flowers to roseate spoonbills. The *Psalmodia Christiana*'s Epiphany text adds many types of flowers to the gifts brought by the three kings, elaborating upon a Latin antiphon that speaks only of gifts and tribute (Sahagún 1993b, 40–41).
41. These stage directions suggest that the drama is integrated into the church service.

Gaspar = Tlacatlen toteCuioyen tlaçochalChihuitlen quetzalen teoxihuitlen maquistlen ca ye nican Otihualmohuetzititzino in nican Omitzhualmotlalilitzino in motlaçotatzin D.ˢ tloq̄yen nahuaqueyen ipaltzinco nemohualonien Ca ye nelli ye oyaque Omotecato in motechicatzitzinhuan[27] in machcocolhuan in prophetasme in patriarcasme in ye nechca onmatihui in tlacatl in tlatohuani David Auh in tlacatl ⱶ in tlatohuani Abraham Oconcauhtehuaque Oconquetztehuaque in caCaxtli in tlatconi in tlamamaloni in Çenca yetic in amo Ehualistli = in amo huel ixnamiconi Can mach [17v] oc qualmati[28] oc quihualytta in imicanpa in intepotzco Can mach Oqualmati[29] in imauh in intepeuh in ye iuhtimani in ye iuh inencauhyan mochihua Can mach Oc quihualmati in çequi Cuauhtla Sacatla inon çeçenmantiuh in tlatconi in tlamamaloni auh canel aocmo nane aocmo taye in cuitlapilli in atlapalli Auh canel aocmo ixxe in aocmo nacaçe in iuhqui nontiticac in amo nahuati in amo tlatohua inᵐniuhqui[30] quechcotonticac in ayocac. itzonteco mochihua in iyacac onicatiuh yn axcan Noteotzinen Notlatocatzinen in titlaçomahuisteopiltzintli Ca tehuatzin ticonmanilitzinos momactzinco mocahuas in itequipanolocatzin in motlaçomahuistatzin D.ˢ yhuan ca mixpantzinco nicnoCuitia ca ye ixquich [18r] Cahuitl in

---

27. motechicatzitzinhuan: read *motechiuhcatzitzinhuan* (as below).
28. qualmati: read *quihualmati* (as below).
29. Oqualmati: read *oc quihualmati* (as below).
30. inᵐniuhqui: read *in iuhqui*.

CASPER[42]: O personage, O our lord, O precious jade, O quetzal plume, O fine turquoise, O bracelet! You have seated yourself here. Your precious father, God, has placed you here, O Lord of the Near, O Lord of the Nigh, O He by Whom All Live. It is true that your progenitors, your great-grandfathers, the prophets, the patriarchs have gone, have gone to lie down, and the personage, the ruler, David, and the personage, the ruler, Abraham, who go along further back. They left behind, they set aside the carrying frame, the instrument of carrying, the instrument of bearing,[43] which is very heavy, which cannot be lifted, which is unbearable. [17v] Is it possible that they still come to know, that they still come to see what is behind them, in back of them? Is it possible that they come to frequent their water, their hill,[44] which lies now as in the beginning,[45] which now is becoming like his[46] desolate place? Is it possible that they still frequent some forest or grassland, where the instrument of carrying, the instrument of bearing lies scattered?[47] And truly the tail, the wing[48] no longer has a mother, no longer has a father. And truly it no longer has eyes, it no longer has ears.[49] It is as if it stands mute. It does not speak, it does not talk. It is as if it stands beheaded. No longer is there anyone who is its head, who goes in front of it.[50] Now, O my deity, O my ruler, precious and wondrous sacred child, it is you who will grasp, in your embrace[51] will remain the work for your precious and wondrous father, God. And I confess before you that up until now [18r] I was living in darkness, in gloom, since I did not know you. But

---

42. Casper's speech, through the word "beheaded," closely parallels the beginning of the *Florentine Codex* oration for the installation of a new ruler (Sahagún 1950–1982, 6:47). After greeting the new sovereign, the speaker notes the passing of the rulers of old who will return no more and laments the sad plight of the leaderless vassals. The playwright inserts Old Testament leaders for the departed rulers. The plight of the vassals becomes the plight of all humanity, awaiting Christ's arrival. The texts are not identical, but they are so similar that the playwright must have had access to this text or a close cognate. There is also a similar speech in the *Bancroft Dialogues* (Karttunen and Lockhart 1987, 133).

43. Metaphor for government: the common people are "carried" by their rulers like a burden (Sahagún 1950–1982, 6:246; Karttunen and Lockhart 1987, 54).

44. their water, their hill: here and below, a metaphorical diphrase that often appears as the quasi-compound *altepetl*, the largest sociopolitical unit to survive Spanish conquest and colonization. During colonial times it was translated in many ways including *ciudad* (city) and *pueblo* (people, settlement).

45. The *Florentine Codex* here has *iooatimanj*, referring to darkness. *Iuhti* refers to the original condition of something. See Siméon 1977, 212, entries for *yuhti* and *yuhticaua*.

46. In the *Florentine Codex* this place belongs to "our lord" (Sahagún 1950–1982); the possessor is not specified here.

47. That is, the city has reverted to a wild state in the absence of rulership.

48. Tail(s), wing(s): prevalent metaphor for common people or vassals. There are numerous references to this in colonial Nahuatl texts. The following Spanish gloss by the famed Nahua Latinist, don Antonio Valeriano, appeared in fray Juan Bautista's sermonary of 1606 (559–60): "Cuitlapiltin, atlapaltin (cuitlapilli, *es la cola*, atlapalli, *el ala del aue, y junto* cuitlapiltin, atlapaltin, *en el singular*, cuitlapiltin, atlapaltin, *en el plural, significa la gente menuda plebeya, y comun*)" [cuitlapiltin, atlapaltin (cuitlapilli *is the tail and* atlapalli *a bird's wing, and together* cuitlapilli atlapalli *in the singular and* cuitlapiltin atlapaltin *in the plural mean the lesser, plebeian and common folk*]. See also Molina 1552, 204r: "Pueblo de menudos. cuitlapilli, atlapalli. ytconi, mamaloni. maceualtin" and 240v: "Vasallos o gente plebeya. per metaphoram. cuitlapilli, ha,tlapalli. ytconi. mamaloni. quiltica nemi. quauhtica nemi. yn haualnecini ycochca yneuhca. ycemiluitica. yomilhuitica." Note that *cuitlapilli atlapalli* is the first diphrase in the Molina entries, as if indicating that it is the most widely used and accepted.

49. That is, with no one to govern them, the people lack prudence.

50. That is, the people lack a leader.

51. embrace: here and below, tentative translation.

tlayohuayan mixtecomac Oninemia Canel amo Onimitzniximachilitzinoaya auh in axcan ca Oticmotlanextililitzino in noyolia in noaniman ihuan in ixquichtintzitzin in ilhuicatl itic monoltitoque in motlachihualtzitzinhuan in otiquinmotlanextililitzinoco Auh noteotzinen Ca huel nimitznotlatlauhtilitzinohua ma huel xicmoçelilitzino in noyolia in noaniman ihuan in nonemilis inic huel mochihuas ynic nimitznohuenChihuililitzinohua inin Copaltzintli itocan inÇiençio Ma huel xicmoçelilitzino Noteo[31] notlatocatzinē = **oncan tlācuanenemis quimotlahuenchihuililitzinos ihuan quimomotennamiquiliz**[32] **in tlaçomahuisteopiltzintli oc çecpa hualtzinquisas qui**[33] **[18v]**

Gaspar = Auh noteotzinen notlatocatzinen ca no mixpantzinco nicnocuitia Ca tinelli titeopixcatzintli tinelli tiSaçerdote ca ticmocuitlahuitzinos in itlayecoltilocatzin in motlaçotatzin D.[s] Auh noteotzinen ihuan Ca timonomahuenchiuhtzinos ytech in Cruz inic ticmoyolçehuilitzinos in motlaçotatzin D.[s] Auh notlatocatzinen noteotzinen tloqueē nahuaqueē ipaltzinco nemohualonie ma huel xicmoçelilitzino in noyolia in noaniman ihuan in nonemilis—

Melchor = Notlaçomahuisteotzinen notlatocatzinen in tihuel nelli Oquitzintli in tihuel nelli teotzintli Ca moch ica in noyollo nimitznoneltoquititzinohua Ca oticmochihuilitzino Oticmoyocolilitzino in ilhuicatl in tlaltic[19r]pactli in ittalo in amo ittalo Ca huel tehuatzin motetzinco ca in tlatocayotl inic ticonmoyacanilis in Cemanahuatl inic ticonmopachilhuis auh. in ixquichtin motlachihualtzitzinhuan Ca ixquich cahuitl in timitztochielitzinohua ye ixquich cahuitl mohuicpatzinco tonelçiçiuhtinemi Ca ye Otimaxitzinoco ca ye Otihualmohuicatzino in omitzhualmihuali in motlaçomahuistatzin D[s] auh ca tehuatzin mopantzinco Oya in iyotzin in itlatoltzin in motlaçomahuistatzin D.[s] Auh Ca oc tehuatzin tonmetiçihuitis Auh Ca oc tehuatzin itlan tonmaquiltis in cacaxtli in tlamamalli Canel Omitzmotenehuilitiaque in motechiuhcatzitzinhuan in machcocoltzitzinhuan ȳ Patriarcasme in Prophetasme [19v] in

---

31. Noteo: given the context, evidently scribal error for *noteotzinen*.
32. quimomotennamiquiliz: read *quimotennamiquiliz*.
33. In apparent anticipation of the following page: *tos yn*. However, this does not repeat on the following page so it properly belongs to the last item on 18v, to be read: *quitos yn*.

now you have illuminated my spirit, my soul, along with all those who live in heaven, your creations, whom you have come to illuminate. And, O my deity, well do I beseech you, receive well my spirit, my soul, and my life, so that it may be done, so that I may make an offering to you of this copal called incense. Receive it well, O my deity, O my ruler.

(At that point he goes about on his knees, he makes the offering, and he kisses the precious and wondrous sacred child. He withdraws again. He says:) [18v]

CASPER: And, O my deity, O my ruler, I also confess before you that you are the true priest, you are the true clergyman. You will look after the serving of your beloved father, God. And also, O my deity, you will make an offering of yourself on the cross in order to appease your beloved father, God. And, O my ruler, O my deity, O Lord of the Near, O Lord of the Nigh, O He by Whom All Live, receive well my spirit, my soul, and my life.

MELCHIOR: O my precious and wondrous deity, O my ruler, you who are a really true man, you who are a really true deity,[52] with all my heart I believe in you. You made, you created heaven, earth, [19r] that which is visible, that which is invisible. You are the one incumbent upon whom is the rulership, by which you will govern the world, by which you will rule it. And as for all your creations, until now we have been waiting for you, until now we have gone about sighing toward you. Now you have arrived, now you have come. Your precious and wondrous father, God, sent you. And it is you upon whom has gone the breath, the words of your precious and wondrous father, God. And you will yet become weary from burdens.[53] And you will yet go putting your effort into the carrying frame, the load. Truly your progenitors, your great-grandfathers, the patriarchs, the prophets, [19v]

---

52. The pairing of *oquichtli* ("man" or "male") and *teotl* was common in Nahuatl in reference to Christ's dual status as human and divinity.

53. Beginning with this sentence and ending with the phrase "No longer," Melchior's speech resembles a later passage in the *Florentine Codex* oration cited above (Sahagún 1950–1982, 6:48–49). The playwright identifies the past rulers with Old Testament figures, the vassals with unredeemed humanity, and Christ's city with the Church. The cross, like the vassals, is a burden Christ must bear.

YsRael tlatoque in teteuctin in omitzmotenehuililitiaque in itechpa Otimoquixti in ye nechca Onmatihui Ca oc tehuatzin tonmotlatquilis ticonmomamalis in moCrutzin +: in temaquixtiloni moCuitlapantzinco ticonmotequilis Auh cuexantzinco[34] momalhuatzinco[35] quimotlalilia in motlaçotatzin D.^S in itcoca ymamaloca in—Cuitlapilli in atlapalli in maquixtilos Ca iuhqui in piltontli monenequi mosuma auh ca Cuel achitzinca Ca huel tehuatzin momacotzinco[36] ticonmotlalilitias in matzin in motepetzin Yn tonantzin Santa Ygleçia Ocuel[37] tehuatzin Ocuel achitzinca ticonmonapalhuis ticonmotlahuitequililis mopan[20r]tzinco Oya in iyotzin in itlatoltzin in motlaçotatzin D.^S tloqueyen Nahuaqueyen Ca omitzmomapilhuili Omitzmixquechili Cuix huel Oc timotzinquixtitzinos Ca niman aocmo Auh yn axcan Notlaçomahuisteotzinen Notlatocatzinen Ma çenquiscayectenehualo in motlaçomahuistocatzin in tinotlatocatzin Ca çenca Onicnomaçehui in momahuiztetlaçotlalitzin Auh tlein inic nimitznoCuepililitzinos Ca mixpantzinco ninopechteca nimitznoteotitzinohua nimitznoçenmacatzinohua nimitznoçenmaquilia in noyolia in noaniman ihuan in nonemilis ihuan inin Costic teocuitlatl Ma huel Xic[20v]moçelilitzino noteotzinen notlatocatzinen Ma xinechmotlapopolhuilitzino = Amen

OnCan tlatennamiquis yhuan tlahuenchihuas aocmo tlein quitos in Melchor Auh niman Oncan tlatos in Balthasar—

---

34. cuexantzinco: scribal error; read *mocuexantzinco*.
35. momalhuatzinco: read *momamalhuaztzinco*.
36. momacotzinco: read *momacochtzinco*; parallels similar wording in the *Florentine Codex* (Sahagún 1950–1982).
37. Ocuel: here and below, read *oc huel*; in parallel passages in the *Florentine Codex* (Sahagún 1950–1982), these are rendered *oc cuel achic*.

the rulers and lords of Israel made you known. Those from whom you descended, who go along further back, made you known.[54] You will yet go to carry something, you will go to bear on your shoulders your cross, the instrument of salvation, which you will place on your back. And in your lap, in your backpack[55] your beloved father, God, places the carrying of, the bearing of, the tail, the wing, who is to be saved. It is as if it is a little child, who has to be cajoled, who becomes angry, but only for a moment. It is indeed in your embrace that you will go place your water, your hill,[56] our mother holy church. Soon you will go carry her in your arms, you will go lull her to sleep.[57] On you [20r] has gone the breath, the words[58] of your beloved father, God, the Lord of the Near, the Lord of the Nigh. He has pointed his finger at you, he has encharged you. Perhaps you can still back out of it? No longer! And now, O my precious and wondrous deity, O my ruler, may your precious and wondrous name be utterly praised, you who are my ruler. I have benefited greatly from your wondrous love. And what will I do for you in return? I bow low before you, I worship you, I give myself entirely to you, I give entirely to you my spirit, my soul, and my life. And this gold, receive it well, [20v] O my deity, O my ruler. Pardon me. Amen.

(At that point he gives a kiss [to the child] and makes an offering. Melchior does not say anything more. And then at that point Balthasar speaks.)

---

54. This alludes to the Old Testament texts interpreted as prophecies regarding Christ.

55. This diphrase refers to responsibility for governing others (Karttunen and Lockhart 1987, 53; cf. Molina 1977, 72v: Nocuexanco nomamalhuazco yeloatiuh. tener el cargo de regir y gouernar a los otros). This *mamalhuaztli* contrasts in vowel length with the name of the constellation *Mamalhuaztli* (Karttunen 1983, 135).

56. your water, your hill: as before, a more high-sounding version of the quasi-compound *altepetl*.

57. The imagery here is of the ruler's city or subjects as a metaphorical child who must be cuddled and coddled. Sahagún's Spanish gloss in the *Florentine Codex* speaks of "making for them the sound so that they sleep" (Sahagún 1950-1982, 6:49n.6). The corresponding Nahuatl verb, *tocontlavivitequiliz* in the *Florentine Codex* and the reverential *ticonmotlahuitequililis* in the drama, literally mean "you will go to beat on things for him/her" (applicative of *huitequi*). Based on Sahagún's gloss, we take this to refer to the making of some rhythmic sound to help a child sleep.

58. A similar phrase occurred earlier in Melchior's speech. Here it parallels wording in the *Florentine Codex* (Sahagún 1950–1982). It has the sense of God appointing him; in other words, "You are the lord's anointed."

Balthasar = tlacatlen tlatohuaniē in ticmopielitzinohua in ilhuicatl ihuan in tlalticpactli in pilotl in tlatocayotl auh ca huel nelli tiD.^{s} tloqueyen nahuaqueyen ipaltzinco nemohualonien Auh Ca ^{ni}mitznoçenneltoquititzinohua moCh ica in noyolia in noaniman ihuan in nonemilis Auh Ca huel tehuatzin topampatica[38] Oticmocahuilitzino in motlaçomahuistla[21r]tocayotzin ihuan in motlaçomahuistlatocaicpaltzin Auh yn axCan Ca topampatica timoCauhtzinos in nican Tlalticp^c timotemachtilitzinos ihuan topampatica Temimiltitech mitzmomailpilitzinosque Mitzmomecahuitequilitzinosque in moyaotzitzinhuan in Judiosme Auh Ca topampatica pinahuistica Cruztitech + Mitzmoma^{ma}çohualtilitzinosque timomiquilitzinos Auh Ca san inpanpa in Cm̄c tlaca auh Canel motlachihualtzitzinhuan momiquilisticatzinco tiquinmomaquixtilitzinos Auh in axcan tlein nel nimitznomaquilitzinos tlein nel ONimitzto̶^{no}huenChihuililitzino̶que̶^{co} Ca niman atlein Ca çan ix[21v]quich nican catqui nimitznohuenChihuililitzinohua Çenca tlaçotli chichic Paatl in ito^{ca} Mirra Auh in icuac tepetla^{a}calco tocos in motlaçomahuisnacayotzin Ca ic quimamatilosque Auh in axcan notlaçomahuisteotzinen tlein nel On̶i̶^{ti}mitzn̶i̶t̶o̶^{to}huenchihuililitzinoco Ca san ixquich in toyolia in toaniman ihuan in tonemilis Ma huel Xitechmotlapopolhuilitzino notlaçomahuisteotzinen = **oncan tlatennamiquisque no quichiuh in GaSpar ihuan in Melchor oc çecpa tzinquiSaS quitos =**

Balthasar = = Auh in tehuatzin tlaçomahuistlateochihualichpotzintlen in aic motetzinco Oaçic in tla[22r]tlacolpeuhcayotl Auh Ca huel Çenquistoc in motlaçomahuisGraçiatzin in onpa in ilhuicatl itic y.huan nohuian Cm̄c in aic tlamis in aic tzomquisas in moÇihuapiltlatocamahuisyotzin[39] Auh tlein nel nimitznohuenChihuililitzinos tlein nel Otimitztomaquilitzinoco Ca niman atlein Ca san ixquich in toyolia in toaniman ihuan in tonemilis Ma huel xitechmotlapopolhuilitzino notlaçomahuisnantzinen Ca ye titohuicatihui Ma iuh mochihua in—Amen Jesus Maria y Joseph =

Niman oncan monextis in Angel quimmonahuatilis in yeintin tlatoque quitos

---

38. topampatica: here and below, standard *topampa* for the early colonial period. However, our initial impression is that this form is occasionally seen in the later colonial period.

39. moÇihuapiltlatocamahuisyotzin: standard *moçihuapillatocamahuizyotzin*.

BALTHASAR: O personage, O ruler, you have in your keeping the sky and the earth, nobility and rulership. And it is indeed true that you are God, O Lord of the Near, O Lord of the Nigh, O He by Whom All Live. And [I] believe in you utterly, with all my spirit, my soul, and my life. And you are the one who, for our sake, has left your precious and wondrous realm [21r] and your precious and wondrous royal seat.[59] And now, for our sake you will remain here on earth, you will teach people, and for our sake your enemies, the Jews, will tie you by the hands to a stone column, will flog you. And for our sake they will shamefully stretch you by the arms on the cross. You will die. And it is just for the sake of the people of the world. And truly, as for your creations, through your death you will save them. And now, what, truly, will I give to you? Of what, truly, have I come to make you an offering? It is nothing at all. It is only [21v] of this here that I make an offering to you, a very precious bitter potion, called myrrh. And when your precious and wondrous body is buried in the sepulcher, they will anoint it with this. And now, O my precious and wondrous deity, of what, truly, have [we] come to make you an offering? It is only our spirits, our souls, and our lives. Pardon us fully, O my precious and wondrous deity.

(At that point he[60] *gives a kiss like Casper and Melchior did. He withdraws again. He says:)*

BALTHASAR: And you, O precious, wondrous, and blessed maiden, original sin never reached you.[61] [22r] And your precious and wondrous grace lies gathered all together there in heaven and everywhere in the world. Your queenly honor will never be finished, will never come to an end. And of what, truly, will I make an offering to you? What, truly, have we come to give you? It is nothing at all. It is only our spirits, our souls, and our lives. Pardon us fully, O my precious and honored mother. Now we are going to be on our way. May it so be done. Amen. Jesus, Mary, and Joseph.[62]

(Then at that point an angel appears. He gives instructions to the three rulers. He says:)

---

59. *Icpalli*: the basketry seats on which indigenous rulers sat; by extension, rulership. Often appears as part of the metaphorical diphrase *petlatl icpalli* "reed mat, basketry seat" (seat of authority, rulership, and so on). A common idiom attested early, for example, in Molina 1555, 131, the last item under "Gouernar" (and one of a number of explicitly marked metaphors for governing) is "petlapan, ycpalpan nica" (I am on the reed mat, I am on the basketry seat). See also Molina 1977, 33v and 81r (Nahuatl-Spanish) and 108v (Spanish-Nahuatl).

60. Verb is plural but singular seems to be intended.

61. A reference, using wording typical of Nahuatl texts, to Mary's immaculate conception, or conception free from original sin.

62. Matthew 2:11: "And when they were come into the house, they saw the young child with Mary his mother, and fell down, and worshipped him: and when they had opened their treasures, they presented unto him gifts; gold, and frankincense, and myrrh."

Angel = Yn antlatoque in AnReyesme oçenquizcatlacauhqui ~~tanquimocnelilitzi~~[22v] noque in tlaçomahuiztlateochihualichpotzintli yhuan in itlaçomahuizpepetlaquiliz Çenquizca Çenteconetzin in ixquichica anhualmohuicaq^e anquimotlapalhuitzinoco anquimotlahuenchihuilitzinoco Auh Ca huel namechnotlatlauhtilia maca acmo onpa ic amocueptzinozque in canpa ic anhualmohuicatzinoque ma oc çe otli inic anmohuicazque inic amo imac anmohuetzititihue in ERodes huey tlahueliloc ca çan amechmoztla^{cahuili} inic oquito Ca no nehuatl niaz nicnoteotzinotiuh Auh ca huel cualani quimomiquiztlatzomtequililiznequi auh ca niman ayānmo inma in momiquilitzinos Ca ac quinmomaquixtilitzinos in C͞m͞c tlacca[40]

yntla otla in MiSSa oncan quimotzatzaliliz n[41] San Joseph quimonahuatiliz in Angel quitoz————[23r]

Angel = = Josephtzinen Josephtzinen Josephtzinē ma xicmochololtilitzino in tlaçomahuizteopiltzintli ca ye huitz in ERodes in tlahueliloc ca quimotemolitinemi ma onpa xicmohuiquilitzino in egipto itzintla in huey Çoyama[~~hui~~?]itl ma onpa xicmotlatilitzino inic amo quimomiquiztlatzomtequililitzino^s[~~quihui~~?] ca ye ixquichtin pipiltzitzintin quinmictitihuitz ma içiuhca ximototoquiltitzino Santo Josephtzinen————————

---

40. tlacca: read *tlaca*.
41. quimotzatzaliliz n: read *quimotzatzililiz yn*.

ANGEL: Rulers, kings, you are most generous,[63] you have shown favor [22v] to the precious, wondrous, and blessed maiden and her precious, wondrous, shimmering, perfect, and only child ever since you came, you came to greet him, you came to make offerings to him. And I do beseech you, do not return the way you came. Go by another road, so that you do not go to fall in the hands of Herod, the great scoundrel. For he just lied to you when he said: "I too will go, I will go to worship him." And he is very angry. He wants to sentence him to death. But in no way is it time yet for him to die. Who will save the people of the world?

(When mass is over, at that point the angel cries out to Saint Joseph, giving him instructions. He says:) [23r]

ANGEL: O Joseph! O Joseph! O Joseph! Flee with[64] the precious and wondrous sacred child! For Herod, the scoundrel, is coming. He is going around searching for him. Take him to Egypt under a large palm frond, hide him there so that he will not sentence him to death! He is coming to kill all the little children! Go speedily, O Saint Joseph![65]

---

63. The word *amoyolloh*, "your hearts," which would complete this idiomatic phrase, seems to be missing here.

64. Literally, cause him to flee.

65. Matthew 2:12–13: "And being warned of God in a dream that they should not return to Herod, they departed into their own country another way. And when they were departed, behold, the angel of the Lord appeareth to Joseph in a dream, saying, Arise, and take the young child and his mother, and flee into Egypt, and be thou there until I bring thee word: for Herod will seek the young child to destroy him." The playwright attributes both warnings to the angel.

Present Location
William L. Clements Library, University of Michigan
Ann Arbor, Michigan

[23v]
Del naSimiento De iSaac del Sacrificio q.ᵉ habrahan Su Padre quiso por mandado de Dios hazer de la Prime=ra Jornada = Hualquiçaz Abraham Yhuan ynamic Saram = = = =

Abrahan = Yn cemicac timohuetznotica[1] in timoçenhuelitiliani in tiDios tetatzin in oticmochihuili in Ylhuicatl in tlalticpac:tli in tonatiuh in metztli yhuan in çiçitlaltin auh in ixquich ittalo yhuan in amo ittalo in nohuian Çemanahuac onoc auh in ixquichtin in Ylhuicac chaneque in çemicac mitzmoyectenehuilia in motlatochantzinco[2] [24r] in Ylhuicatl ytic canel ic otiquinmoChihuili in çemicac moChantzinCo motlamachtizque auh in tehuātin in timotlaChihualtzitzinhuā in otitechmoChihuili in otitechmoyocolili Ca tehuatzin mohueliticatzinco in titotolinia i nican tlalticpac = Auh in tehuatzin notlaçonamictzinen in motechtzinco = oquiz in moconetzin in meezço in motlapallo macamo ytla ic quimoyolitlacalhuiz in iteyocoxcatzin in moçenhuelitiliani Dios tetatzin—

Saran = = Yn titlaçopilli in ye ixquich cahuitl in ye timonemiltia in nicā tlalticpac in omitzmochihuili in ixquich Yhuelitzin in Dios tetatzin Auh in nehuatl in çenca[3] [24v] ic ninotequipachohua in axcan =

oncan choca Yca ce paño ic mixpopohuaz = = =

habraham = Amo çenca ximochoquili tlein mitztequipachohua ma xi=nechmolhuili—

Saram = = Ynic nichoca in nehuatl Ca ytechcopa in nochalChiuhconetzin iSaac in ipepetlaquiliz in itlanexyo in naniman Canel neezyo notlapallo oquinoqui Auh nochichihualayotica nomemeyālotica onicnohuapahuili auh in axcan Ye ixco Ye icpac tontlachie ye chamactzintli aquin huel techilhuiz in Cuix onca tocnopil tomaçehual in itechcacopa = in toconetzin cuix quimotlayecoltiliz in Dios inic nemiz in tlalticpac[4] [25r] acaçomo quichihuaz in itenahuatiltzin in iuhqui ic techmonahuatilitzinohua in titlachihualtzi=tzinhuan intla moztla huiptla Ximomiquili aquin quihuapahuaz aquin quititiz in mahuiztic nemiliztli in Ylhuicac tehuicac—

oncan chocas

Yc choca in nanimantzin ça çan : nenpolihuiz in nochichihualayo in nomemeyallo oc achi qualli macamo nitlacahuapahuani nitlacaChihuani—

= Oncan monextia Angel

---

1. timohuetznotica: here and below, a nonstandard item. Perhaps the intention (in standard orthography) was *timoyetztzinotica*.
2. In anticipation of the following page: *in*. motlatochantzinco: read *motlatocachantzinco*.
3. In anticipation of the following page: *ic*.
4. In anticipation of the following page: *a*.

The Sacrifice of Isaac
Translated by Barry D. Sell, with assistance from Louise M. Burkhart

[23v]
Of the birth of Isaac and of the sacrifice that his father Abraham wanted to make by order of God. Of the first act.
Abraham enters along with his spouse, Sarah.
ABRAHAM: You the All-powerful, God the Father, are eternal. You made heaven and earth, the sun, the moon and the stars, and all that lies seen and unseen everywhere in the world. All the residents of heaven eternally praise you in your royal home [24r] in heaven since for that reason you made them eternally rich in your home. But as for us, we your creatures whom you made and created, we suffer here on earth by your authority. And as for you, O my beloved spouse, out of you emerged your child, your offspring. May he offend in nothing his Creator, the All-powerful, God the Father.

SARAH: You high-born nobleman, whom the All-powerful God the Father made, have been living here on earth for some time.[1] But as for me, I am very [24v] anguished now.
(At that point she weeps. She wipes her face with a cloth.)
ABRAHAM: Do not weep so much. What is bothering you? Tell me.

SARAH: The reason I am weeping concerns my precious child, Isaac, who is the light and radiance of my soul, which gave me my offspring.[2] I raised him with my breast milk, my milk, and now we gaze into his face already a young fellow. Who can tell us whether we are fortunate and deserving concerning our child? Will he serve God while he lives on earth? [25r] Perhaps he will not carry out his commands in the way in which he orders us, his creatures, [to do]. If you die soon, who will raise him? Who will show him the honorable way of living that conducts people to heaven?
(At that point she weeps.)
For that reason my soul weeps. My breast milk, my milk, will have been spent in vain. It would have been better if I had not raised children, if I had not given birth.
(At that point Angel appears.)

---

1. Tentative translation. The entire utterance seems incomplete, as if the Nahua scribe simply left out a line or two of text.
2. Tentative translation. Evidently "neezyo notlapallo oquinoqui" is an unattested metaphorical phrase. It literally means "it/he [soul/Isaac] spilled my blood, my dye," the diphrase "blood, dye" being a metaphor for "offspring" often with connotations of noble birth (e.g., on the Nahuatl-Spanish side of his dictionary see Molina 1977, 93v: "Teeço, tetlapallo. hijo o hija `d nobles cauallleros" and on the Spanish-Nahuatl side, 71r: "Hijo de principal o senador. pilconetl. tecpilconetl. teeço, tetlapallo. teoxiuh. tetlapanca. tetzicueuhca.").

Angel = Ylhuicac ocaquiztic in moneyolnonotzaliz ixpantzinco in ixquich yhuelitzin in Santissima Trinidad Xicaquican in āçemanahuactlaca in itechpa mottaz inin piltzintli iSaac in quexquich⁵ [25v] ypantzinco mochihuaz in Dios itlaçopiltzin inic motemaquixtiliz in nohuian çemanahuac ca yyezçoticatzinco imiquizticatzinco quimotlapolhuiz in ilhuicatl in ompa mehuiltitica in itlacomahuiztatzin⁶ auh in oquic ayāmo mochihua ipantzinco in Dios itlaço=piltzin yehuatl yacachtopa ypan moChihuaz in tlaçotlateochihualpiltzintli iSaac auh in titetatzin in titenantzin ic ximoyollalican—

Polihuiz in Angel

habraham = = Amo cenca ximoyoltequipacho Ca ixquich yhuelitzin ca yehuatzin quimochicahuiliz quimohuapahuiliz in nochalchiuh in nocozticteocuitlapiltzin auh in axcan ma oc ticalaquican ma oc tepitzin titoçehuiti

_____⁷[26r]

Saram = Ma yuhqui mochihua ma ximoCalaquitzino—

v Calaquizq.ᵉ tlapitzaloz hualquiçaz iSmael çan yçel

iSmael = Çenca tonehua chichinaca in nix in noyollo in itechcopa in piltontli in iSaac in çenca huel qualnemiliçe in aic quinequi in nechmocniuhtiz in manoço notlan mahuilti in iuhqui oc çequintin pipiltotontin in titoçepanahuiltia ca in quexquich in quinahuatia yn itatzin in inantzin mochi quichihua in itenahuatil amo tlein = ma ytla quitlacohua auh inin queni huel nicchihuaz tla oc nonnonotza

v Hualquiçaz Demonio = veStido de Angel o de vieJo⁸ [26v]

Demonio = Tlein ticchihua telpochtlen iuhqui nimitzitta çenca huey in monetequipachol—

Ismael Ca quemaca miec in nechtequipachohua auh quen ticmati intla itla onca nonetequipachol ac omitzilhui—

Dem.º = = Amo tiquitta ca ylhuicac niChane onpa onihualyhualoc inic nimitzilhuiz in tlein ticChihuaz in nican tlalticpac—

iSmael = Auh ma niccaqui in motenahuatil—

Dem.º = Xicaqui in axcan inic timotequipachohua ca nican ca Ca yehuatl itechcopa in tlaçopilli iSaac inic huel qualnemiliçe in çemicac quineltoquilia in itenahuatil in itatzin auh iuhqui tiquilnamiqui tiquilehuia inic acmo quitlacamatiz⁹ [27r] yn itatzin in inantzin ca nimitzilhuiz in quenin ticChihuaz—

iSmael = Queni Çenca ninoyollalia in niCaqui in motlatoltzin ma nicnomaçehui in motepalehuilitzin Canel ilhuicac tichane Ca timotepalehui=liani—

Dem.º = Huel xicmoyolloti in notenahuatil xiquitta in axcan Ca yn i=tatzin yhuan ynantzin tecohuanotzatzque Çenca neyolaliloz papacohuaz auh in tehuatl ticcuitlahuiltiz inic quintlalcahuiz yn itatzin yn inantzin inic cana anmahuiltitihue auh intla ça nen omitztlacama ca ic quitelchihuazq.ᵉ in inconeuh in manel huel quitlaçotla—

iSmael = Yuhqui nicChihuaz in motlanahuatiltzin—

---

5. In anticipation of the following page: *y*.
6. itlacomahuiztatzin: read *itlaçomahuiztatzin*.
7. In anticipation of the following page: *Saran*.
8. In anticipation of the following page: *D*.
9. In anticipation of the following page: *y*.

ANGEL: Your concerns have been clearly heard in heaven before the All-powerful, the Most Holy Trinity. Listen, you people of the world: in the example of this child Isaac will be seen everything that [25v] will happen to the beloved son of God when he will save people everywhere in the world, for through his blood and his death he will open up heaven where sits his beloved honored Father. But meanwhile, before it happens to the son of God, it will first happen to the precious and blessed child Isaac. And you who are fathers, you who are mothers,[3] console yourselves with that.

(Angel disappears.)

ABRAHAM: Do not be so anguished, for the All-powerful will strengthen and raise my jade, my golden child. But for now, let us enter, let us rest a bit. [26r]

SARAH: May it so be done. Enter.

(They exit. Wind instruments are played. Ishmael enters alone.)

ISHMAEL: Deep within me there is great burning pain concerning the boy Isaac, who is of very good life. He never wants to make friends with me nor play with me as do the other boys with whom I play. However many orders his father and his mother give him, he carries them all out. He is at fault in absolutely none of their orders. Now then, what can I do? Let me figure this out.

(Demon enters dressed as an angel or an old man.) [26v]

DEMON: O young man, what are you doing? You appear to me to have very great cares.

ISHMAEL: Yes, there is much that worries me. But how do you know if I have some cares? Who told you?

DEMON: Do you not see that I am a resident of heaven? I was sent here from there in order to tell you what you are to do here on earth.

ISHMAEL: Let me hear your commands.

DEMON: Listen, here is what has you so occupied today. It concerns the high-born noble Isaac, who is of such good life. He always gives credence to the commands of his father. But you have been thinking that you want him to no longer obey [27r] his father and his mother. I will tell you how to do it.

ISHMAEL: How very content I am to hear your words. Let me enjoy your help since you are a resident of heaven and you are a helper of people.

DEMON: Take right to heart my commands. Look. Today his father and his mother have invited people to a banquet. There will be great contentment and enjoyment. But you are to oblige him to abandon his father and his mother by you and him going somewhere to play. And if he so ruinously obeys you they will despise their child for it even though they greatly love him.

ISHMAEL: I will carry out your command in that fashion.

---

3. father(s), mother(s): in this order or reversed, a common diphrase that means "parent(s)" A staple of polite speech, it is often not gender specific.

Demonio = Auh in nehuatl Ca ye niauh Yn ilhuicatl itic Ca onimitzyolalico yhuan onimitznahuatico = in tlein ticChihuaz—[10] [27v]

Calaquizq.ᵉ çeçecni huetziz truenos = hualquicaz[11] **Abrahan yhuan ypiltzin YSaac huel hualmoyecchichiuhtiazque—**

Abra.ᵃ Yn tinocozticteocuitlacozqui in tinochalchiuhmacuex in tinoztacteocuitlaneapan tinotlaçopiltzin xihualmohuica çenca noneyolaliztica nimitznahuatia in quen nimitzmalcochohua canel omitzmochihuili in moçenhuelitiliani in Dios teTatzin in ixquich in itlachihualtzin in tlalticpac yn ittalo ihuā in amo ittalo =. Auh xicmocaquiti notlazomahuizpiltzinē, ma nen itla quemanian itla ic ticcatzauh in moyolia in moaniman Ma çemicac Xicchalchiuhmati Xicepyollomati canel ytlachi=hualtzin in Dios auh in itlaçomahuiztlatocatenahuatiltzin in totecuiyo Dios in etlamantli in itlanahuatiltzin macamo çentlamantli tiquitlacoz huel moyollo itech XicquiCuilo Çemicac Xicquilnamiqui Ca onmohuetznotica in motechiuhcatzi[12] [28r] in moteyocoxcatzin in omitzmochihuili in çemicac yectenehualoni Yn ilhuicac in tlalticpac, auh in axcan Xicmomachilti notlaçomahuizpiltzinen Ca nican hualmohuicazq.ᵉ in motlacamecayohuan mitzmotiliquihue yhuan quimatiquihue in quenin çenca nimitznotlazotilia in tinotlaçopiltzin————

ISaac = Yn tinotlaçotatzin in tlalticpac tinotechiuhcatzin ca ye ochicahuac in motlallotzin in moço:quiotzin ixquich tlatequipanoliztli tlamaçe:hualiztli ye nimitznomaquilitzinohua in nican tlalticpac inic ye tinechmohuapahuilia auh tinechmomaquilia in nocochca in noneuhca Auh inic nictlapachohua in notlallo in noçoquio mochi tehuatzin motelaocoliliztlachihualtzin ticmochihuilitzinohua auh cocoliztli temoztli[13] nimitznomaquilitzinohua in tinotlaçotatzin Ca çenca onicnomaçehui in motlaçomahuiztlatoltzin inic tinechmononochilitzino:hua, motzontecontzin nictlapana melchiquiuhtzin niquehuaz notlazomahuiztatzinen Ca[14] [28v] yn ixquich tinechmonahuatilia, ca mochi nicchi=huaz—

Abraham = Ximohuica[15] Xiquinnahuati in notetlayecolticahuan ma yçiuhca tlaçencahuacan in oncan notlaquayan in oncan tepitzin titoyollalizq.ᵉ—

ISaac = Ma niman, niauh nicneltili in motlaçotlanatiltzin[16] notlaçotatzinen————

<u>v</u> Calaquizque in iSaac Yhuan habrahan hualquiça Agar la esclava yhuan iconeuh iSmael = = = = = = = = = = = =

---

10. In anticipation of the following page: *Ca.*
11. **hualquicaz:** read *hualquiçaz.*
12. In anticipation of the following page: *in.*
13. temoztli: standard *temoxtli.*
14. In anticipation of the following page: *y.*
15. Ximohuica: originally written *Ximohuicacan.* The last three letters are obscured by the X that immediately follows.
16. motlaçotlanatiltzin: scribal error; as elsewhere in this text, read *motlaçotlanahuatiltzin.*

THE SACRIFICE OF ISAAC—151

DEMON: As for me, I am going into heaven for I came to console you and to tell you what you are to do. [27v]
(They exit. Thunderclaps sound in various places. Abraham enters along with his son Isaac. They come well dressed.)

ABRAHAM: You my golden jewel, my jade bracelet, my silver necklace, you my beloved child, come. With great contentment I give you orders as well as embrace you since All-powerful God the Father made you, he by whom everything on earth, the seen and the unseen, was made. Listen, O my beloved honored child, do not sometime soil your spirit and your soul with something. Always regard it as a jade, as a precious pearl, since it is a work of God. And as to the precious honored royal commands of our lord, God: his commands are three; do not violate a single one. Inscribe them well on your heart. Always remember them, for there exists your Engenderer [28r] and Creator who made you and is eternally worthy of praise in heaven and on hearth. Now know, O my beloved honored child, that those of your lineage will be coming here to see you and to know how very much I esteem you, my beloved child.

ISAAC: You my beloved father and engenderer on earth, your earthly body has already become old with all the work and penance I give you here on earth raising me. You give me my daily sustenance and what I cover my body with. All are your works of mercy which you do for me. I [do not wish to] make you ill, my beloved father, [with my importunities] for I have greatly profited from the precious honored words with which you counsel me. I [do not wish to] give you headaches and stomachaches [with my bothersome chatter]. O my beloved honored father, [28v] all you order me, all I will do.

ABRAHAM: Go, order my servants to quickly prepare my dining area where we will console ourselves a bit.

ISAAC: O my beloved father, let me go right away to carry out your precious command.
(Exit Isaac and Abraham. Hagar the slave enters along with her child Ishmael.)

Agar = Yn axcan in no cuel oc cecppa[17] tecohuanotza in huey tlatohuani habraan in ipampa in ipiltzin in çenca quitlaçotla, auh in tehuan = Canel titetlannenque atlei ypan tittoni auh in tehuatl in tinoconeuh yn atle mocnopil yn atle momaçehual ma tehuatl motech oniçehuini ma oxicçehuiani in ixquich in nochichinaquiliz tlalticpac canel motlacatiliz momaçehual in çemicac Choquiztli =

v oncan chocazq.e innehuan yn iconeuh = [18] **[29r]**

iSmael = : Yn titonatiuh in çenca huecapan in tica ma xi=techhualtotonili yca in çenca huey in motlanex ic in nohuian, C͞m͞C, inic huel tiquihueltlamachtia[19] in ixquichtin in tlalticpac tlaca Auh in tehuantin, Ca tomextin titolinia in atle tolhuil in atle tomaçehual Auh in axcā xicmomachilti nonantzinen in tlein nicchihuaz in axcan yn iquac intla ye tlaqualo azo huel nicnahualquixtiz inic cana titahuiltitihue ynic quitlacoz in itenahuatil in itatzī inic acmo yca yyollo, quitlaçotlaz—

Agar, = Ca huel qualli in tiquilnamiqui ma yuhqui XicChihua—

oncan hualquiça YSaac =

iSaac = tlein anquichihua nican Cuix ye mochi Omoçēcauh in ixquich in monequiz ma motlali in mesa =—

iSmael = Ca yehuatl in axcan nican ic titononotza macamo ytla itlacahuiz itechpa in tecohuanotzaliztli ma mochintin monotzacan in tlapitzq,e in tlatzotzomque ma mochintin hualhuian—[20] **[29v]**

iSaac = Ma yuhqui mochihua yçiuhca Xitlaçencahuacan

v oncan tlaçencahualo in oncan tlaqualoz motlaliz Sillas mesa = miec xochitl intla otlaçencauh oncan tlapitzaloz tlatzotzonaloz hualquiçaz Abraham = Sara yhuan omentin pipiltin tlatoque tenamiquiz = YSaac = =

iSaac = = Ma nican timohuicatz notlaçomahuiztatzinē yhuan in tehuatzin in tinotlaçonantzin = Auh in amehuantintzitzin in antlaçomahuizpipiltin ma ximoçehuitzinocan ca nican tamechtochieli=ticate———

1.º Pilli = O quenin çenca tetlamachti in inezcaliliz inin telpochtzintli ma oc miec quimomaquili in itechicahualitzin in Cemicac mohuetznotica in Çemanahuac tlatohuani Dios—

2.º Pilli = huel çenca itech neçi in çenca huey in inezcaliliz canel tlazoeztli[21] mahuiztique tlaca in in omoquixti[22]—

Abraham = Ma ximoçehuitzinocan yn antlaçopipiltin =

oncan motlalizque tlatzotzona[23] **[30r] tlapitzaloz oncan ycaz Agar auh in iSmael conmati=lanaz Yn iSaac—**

iSmael = Xihualmohuica, nocniuhtzinen y nocuie[24] neyolalilo ma no cana tontaahuiltiti Cuix aca mitzhualmottilia Cuix can çemicac ticmoteoti=tiez in motatzin in monantzin tihuian ti:toyolaliti intla, oc çequintin topilicnihuā, = =

---

17. oc cecppa: here and below can be found this and other variants of standard *oc ceppa*.
18. In anticipation of the following page: *iS*.
19. tiquihueltlamachtia: standard *tiquinhuellamachtia*.
20. In anticipation of the following page: *ysaac*.
21. tlazoeztli: the first z has a cedilla, a feature I have never noticed in any other Nahuatl text.
22. in omoquixti: perhaps to be read *intech omoquixti*.
23. In anticipation of the following page: *loz,*. However, it does not appear on the following page. Therefore read the item as *tlatzotzonaloz*.
24. nocuie: evidently scribal error for *notecuiyoe*.

HAGAR: Today the great ruler Abraham has yet again invited people to a banquet because of the great esteem he has for his child. But as for us, since we are lowly servants, we are held in no regard. And as for you, my child, you are doubly luckless. Would that I could find relief in you, that you could give relief to all my earthly torments, for in truth your birth and your lot are eternal weeping.
(At that point she and her child weep together.) [29r]

ISHMAEL: You, sun, who are very high up, warm us with your very great radiance everywhere in the world, with which you are able to please all the people of the earth. But as for us, the two of us are suffering. We are doubly luckless. But now know, O my mother, what I will do today when all are eating. Perhaps I can sneak [Isaac] out so that we will go play somewhere. Thus he will violate the orders of his father so that he will no longer love him with his heart.

HAGAR: What you are thinking is very good. Do it so.
(At that point Isaac enters.)

ISAAC: What are you doing here? Have all necessary preparations been made? Let the table be set.

ISHMAEL: That is what we were just talking about here. Let nothing be amiss concerning the banquet. Let all the players of wind instruments and drums be summoned; let them all come! [29v]

ISAAC: May it so be done. Make swift preparations.
(At that point all gets prepared in the dining area. Chairs and a table are placed. Next to them are many floral arrangements. At that point wind instruments are played and drums are beaten. Enter Abraham, Sarah, and two high-ranking nobles.[4] Isaac greets them.)

ISAAC: Please be welcome here,[5] O my beloved honored father, and you, my beloved mother. And as for you high-ranking honored noblemen, do rest, for here we are awaiting you.

FIRST NOBLEMAN: O what a great joy it is [to observe] the upbringing of this young man! May God, ruler of the world who is eternal, give him much health.

SECOND NOBLEMAN: His very great upbringing is readily apparent since he is the high-born offspring [of] the esteemed people whom he takes after.[6]

ABRAHAM: Rest, you high-ranking noblemen.
(At that point they sit down. Drums are beaten. [30r] Wind instruments are played. Hagar is standing there. Ishmael goes pulling Isaac along by the hand.)

ISHMAEL: Come, O my friend, O my lord. All are content. Let us also go somewhere to play. Will someone [important] see you [fooling around]? Are you always to be adoring your father and your mother? Let us get going, let us go enjoy ourselves with our other childhood friends.

---

4. Literally, "two noblemen [who are] rulers" In this instance Nahuatl *tlatoque*, "rulers," is almost certainly not meant literally but to heighten their noble status.

5. Ma nican timohuicatz: see Carochi 1983, 67v, 80r, and Sahagún 1997, 296.

6. Tentative translation.

iSaac = Yn nehuatl, amo nonahuatil in nicnotlalcahuiliz in notlaçotatzin yhuan in notlaçonantzin Xinechcahua, tehuatl moçel ximahuilti—

Oc çecppa tlapitzaloz, auh in iSaac, onmicuaniz itla in = Messa huel mocnomaticaz =

Sara = Yn tehuatzin in titlatohuani in çenca timahuictic[25] in tinotlaçonamictzin çenca nimitznotlatlauhtilitzinohua Yhuan in nican mohuetzticate in çenca mahuiztililoni, ma xicmocaquiltican in nocnotlatol in itechcopa in nochalchiuhconetzin ca yn iquac in timotlaqualtiticaca in[26] [30v] tlaçoÇihuatl[27] yn iconeuh imatitech ocan in motlaçopiltzin ynic oquiquixti quiahuac inic mahuiltizque, Auh huel çenca ic nichoca = yn ahuilli Camanalli ca ic mahuizpolihui in motlaçopiltzin = = =

Abraham = Xihualauh in tehuatl in titlaçotli[28] yhuan in mocone:uh nican Ximomemanacan[29] =—

v oncan momenazq.^e [30] Agar yhuan ismael———

Abraham = Xicaqui in titenan in moconeuh in ticpaccayta in çemicac mahuiltia in amo tictlacahualtia Ca tehuatl motlatlacol Ca moztla huiptla mic=tlan tictzauctiaz——

1.º Pilli = = Melahuac in ticmitalhuia yn ahuilli yn camanalli, huel ypeuhca in tlahuelilocayotl, intlacamo tiquintlacahualtizque in topilhuan Ca tehuantin totlatlacol mochihuaz in moztla huiptla—

Sara = Yntlacamo tiquinmototoquiliz in quitlalcahuizque in totlaçomahuizconetzin ca quimachtizque in ahuilnemiliztli yhuan in atlei ypā teittaliztli—

Abraham = Yuhqui mochihuaz in motlanequilitzin—[31r]

2º Pilli = Ma niman Xiquinmototoquili Cuix yuhqui tlaçotlaloni yn aqualnemiliçeque yuhqui in nantli yuhqui in iconeuh aço mach oanquimitalhuique aço yehuatl itla, qualnemiliztli quittitiz, ye quicuitlahuiltia yn imahuizpopololocatzin in Dios yhuan in amehuantzitzin—

Abraan = Xihuian, xinechtlalcahuican acmo nican namechittaz xictlalcahuican in taltepeuh amo anquinmachtizq.^e yn amaqual:nemiliz in oc çequintin tlaçotepilhuan =—

v oncan chocaz in Agar—

Agar = = Onohueytlahueliltic yn ahuel nitlacahuapahua, in aqualli inic onimitzhuapauh in tinotlahuelilocaconeuh axcan mohuan nictzaqua in motlahuelilocayo omochiuh onotlahueliltic—

v oncan chocazq.^e innehuan in AGar yhuan yn iconeuh iSmael—

1.º Pilli = Xihuian xitechtlalcahuican amo oncan xichocatimanican—[32] [31v]

iSmael = Omochiuh, onotlahueliltic yn atle onechonquixti in noxolopiyo——

v Calaquizq.^e AGar yhuan in iconeuh, Ysmael—

2.º Pilli = Ma ximocalaqui, tlacatlen tlatohuaniē = =

25. timahuictic: read *timahuiztic*.
26. In anticipation of the following page: *tla*.
27. tlaçoÇihuatl: scribal error for *tlaçocihuatl*.
28. titlaçotli: scribal error for *titlacotli*.
29. Ximomemanacan: read *ximomamanacan*.
30. **momenazq.^e**: read *momamanazque*.
31. In anticipation of the following page: *2º*..
32. In anticipation of the following page: *iSmael*.

ISAAC: I am not supposed to leave my beloved father and my beloved mother. Leave me, play by yourself.

(Wind instruments are played again. Isaac moves over next to the table. He stands very humbly.)

SARAH: You, my beloved spouse, are a ruler and very esteemed. I greatly implore you and those here who are very worthy of esteem. May you hear my humble words concerning my beloved child. When you were eating [30v] the child of the slave woman grabbed your beloved child by his hand in order to take him outside that they might play. I weep copiously over the trivialities and jokes, for by them your beloved child is dishonored.

ABRAHAM: Come, you slave, along with your child. Here you two will kneel.

(At that point Hagar and Ishmael kneel.)

ABRAHAM: Listen, you who are a mother. Your child, whom you look at with such approval, is always playing. You do not restrain him; the fault is yours. Soon you will pay the penalty for it in hell.

FIRST NOBLEMAN: What you are saying is correct. Wickedness begins with trivialities and jokes. If we do not restrain our children [their flaws] will soon become our fault.

SARAH: If you do not exile those who will forsake our beloved honored child, they will teach him waywardness and to have no regard for others.

ABRAHAM: Your will be so done. [31r]

SECOND NOBLEMAN: Run them off right away. Are those of a bad way of life such as to be worthy of esteem? Like mother, like child.[7] Will they say you said that perhaps a good way of life will show her something?[8] [However] now it constrains her to dishonor God along with you.[9]

ABRAHAM: Get going, leave us, I will see you here no longer. Abandon our altepetl.[10] You will not teach your evil way of life to the other children of high-ranking people.

(At that point Hagar weeps.)

HAGAR: I am very unfortunate! I am unable to [properly] raise children given the bad way I raised you, my malicious child. Now along with you I pay the penalty for your iniquities. Woe is me!

(At that point Hagar and her child Ishmael weep together.)

FIRST NOBLEMAN: Get going, leave us! Do not lie down there crying! [31v]

ISHMAEL: Woe is me! My stupidity didn't do me any good!

(Hagar and her child Ishmael exit.)

SECOND NOBLEMAN: Enter, O personage, O ruler.

---

7. Literally, "such is the mother, such is her child."

8. That is, that she will make proper amends if given a good example.

9. Tentative translation. Alternative translation for the last two lines: "They say that perhaps you said that a good way of life would perhaps show her something, but the way she dishonors God and you keeps her from it."

10. altepetl: Nahuatl term applied to various kinds of sovereign sociopolitical units; most of those existing in central Mexico at this time were of approximately city-state dimensions During colonial times the word was translated in many ways including *ciudad* (city) and *pueblo* (people, settlement).

Abraham = = Ma yuh mochihua, mahuiztiq^e tlacaen ma tihuian—
Calaquizque mochintin oncā = tlapitzaloz motlapoz in Ylhuicatl hualmoquixtiz in Dios Padre motlatoltiz—
Dios Padre = Ye mochi onicçencauh, Yn ilhuicatl in tlalticpactli auh atle itech polihui auh in ixquichtin in Ylhuicac chaneque in noyectlachihualhuan çemicac nechhueltlamachtia[33] aic qui=tlacohua in notlaçotenahuatiltzin auh canel, yuh nitlanahuatia inic quichihuazque quineltilizque in notenahuatiltzin in quichihuazq,^{e} in ixquichtin, tlalticpac tlaca yn iuhqui quinequi = in noçenquizcatlanequilitzin—
<u>v</u> = oncan hualquizaz Abraan[34] [32r]
Abraham = Yn çemicac timohuetznotica in çenca huecapan in Ylhuicatl itic in nohuian tiquinmotztilitica in ixquichtin in motlachihualtzitzinhuan auh in nehuatl, in nimitznixpantilitzinohua in itechpa in motlachihualtzin in otinechmomaquili, in nican tlalticpac in notlaçopiltzin YSaac ca intla nican nemiz tlalticpac ca yuh ca in nix no:yollo aço mitzmoteopohuiliz acaçomo quichi=Chihuaz in motlaçoteotenahuatiltzin in iuhqui timotlanahuatilitzinohua—
Dios Padre = Abraham, Abraham, nimitzonnotza—
Abraham = Ac tehuatzin, in tinechmonochilia—
Dios Padre = Yntla nelli, in huel ticchihua in noteotlanahuatiltzin xiconana[35] in mopiltzin in çenca tictlaçotla in itoca YSaac = Xichuica in icpac tepetl yn itocayocan Moria ompa ticmictiz ic noyollo pachihuiz intla nelli in ticchihua in noteo=nahuatiltzin—
Abraham = Nicchihuaz in motlanahuatiltzin, ca yuhqui ca in in noyollo, Ca tehuatzin in çemicac tineltoconi in ixquich mohuelitzin in niccaqui in motlatoltzin—[36] [32v]
<u>v</u> **Motzaquaz in Ylhuicatl tlapitzaloz, calaquiz in Abraham oncan Cuicoz, mehuaz te de[37] = laudamoz = hualquicaz[38] in Abraham Yhuan YSaac ihuā omentin, ytlannencahuan =**
Abraham = Yn axcan, xicmomachilti, Ca nimitzhuicaz in icpac in nepa ca huey tepetl ompa titla^{tla}tlauhtitihue—
iSaac = Ma yuhqui mochihua in motlanequilitzin notlaçomahuiztatzinen————
Abraham = Auh in amehuantin Xiqualquixtican in tlatlatilquahuitl, yhuan mecatl yhuan çe teposmacquahuitl = =
1,^{o} Criado = Ca ye qualitzin, tlatohuanien—
<u>v</u> **Niman Yazque quicuitihue çe tlalpilli quahuitl, Yhuan mecatl ihuan alfange tlapitzaloz tepitzin—**
2,^{o} Criado = Ca ye nican, catqui in ticmotlania—
Abraham = Ca ye qualli ma tihuian Xinechhualtocatihuian in canin niaz ompa anyazq.^{e} amo anmoXiuhtlatizq.^{e}—[39] [33r]

---

33. nechhueltlamachtia: standard *nechhuellamachtia*.
34. In anticipation of the following page: *A*.
35. xiconana: standard *xoconana*; see Carochi 1983, 42v–43v.
36. In anticipation of the following page: *Mo*.
37. de: read *deum*.
38. **hualquicaz**: read *hualquiçaz*.
39. In anticipation of the following page: *isaac*.

ABRAHAM: May it so be done, O honored people. Let us be on our way.
(At this point all exit. Wind instruments are played. Heaven opens. God the Father enters. He speaks.)
GOD THE FATHER: I have already prepared all of heaven and earth. Nothing is lacking in them. All the residents of heaven, my good creatures, eternally please me. They never violate my precious commands. And since I have given orders such that they will perform and realize my commands, all the people of the earth will perform them in the way my consummate will wants.
(At that point Abraham enters.) [32r]
ABRAHAM: You who are eternally very high up in heaven see all your creatures everywhere [they are]. But as for me, I make a declaration before you concerning your creature you gave me, my beloved child here on earth, Isaac. I am of the opinion that if he will live here on earth perhaps he will offend you, perhaps he will not carry out your precious orders you have commanded.

GOD THE FATHER: Abraham, Abraham, I am calling you.
ABRAHAM: Who are you that calls me?
GOD THE FATHER: If it is true that you can carry out my sacred commands, seize your child named Isaac whom you greatly love and take him to the top of the mountain in the place named Moriah. There you are to kill him. If truly you carry out my sacred command my heart will be satisfied.
ABRAHAM: I will carry out your command. I intend to do it for you, the All-powerful, whose words I hear, are eternally worthy of being believed. [32v]
(Heaven closes. Wind instruments are played. Exit Abraham. At that point all sing. The te deum laudamus is raised up [in song]. Enter Abraham along with Isaac and two of his lowly servants.)[11]
ABRAHAM: Now know that I will take you to the top of that big mountain that is some distance away. There we are going to pray.
ISAAC: May your will be so done, O my beloved honored father.
ABRAHAM: And as for you, bring out the firewood and rope and a sword.

FIRST SERVANT: Very well, O ruler.
(They go right away, taking a bundle of wood along with rope and a sword. Wind instruments are played a little.)
SECOND SERVANT: Here is what you are requesting.
ABRAHAM: Very well, let us go. Come following along after me. Where I will go, there will you go. You are not to be impatient. [33r]

---

11. While grammatically there is ambiguity, contextually the lowly servants would seem to be those of the father.

iSaac = Ca mochihuaz in motenahuatiltzin yn iuh tinechmonahuatilitzinohua, notlaçomahuiztatzinen =

v Niman tlapitzaloz inic yazq,^{e} in canin ca Tepetl—

Abraham = Ye otaçico in intzintlan tepetl in oncan titlatlatlauhtizq.^{e} Auh in amehuantin nican ximocahuacan amo antechhuicazq.^{e} Xiqualhuicacā in notepozMauhcuauh yhuan in tletl auh in tlatlatilquahuitl Xiquechpanoltican in notlaçopiltzin ca ytech monequiz—

v Tlapitzaloz tepitzin oncan quiquechpanoltizq^e in quahuitl, in iSaac niman, yaz tlecotiaz Yn itech Tepetl niman oncan ^{moquetzaz} in iSaac tlatoz =

iSaac = = = Notlaçomahuiztatzinen, Ca çenca huel, ye nechçianmictia in nichuica ynin tlatlatilquahuitl auh tlein ticmochihuiliz—

Abraham = Ca motech monequiz ic nextli mocuepaz in monacayo ic nimitzhuenchihuaz—

iSaac = Auh notlaçomahuiztatzinen Cuix çan ye^{40}[33v]huatl in tichuenchihuazque in quahuitl yhuan in tletl = =

Abraham = Notlaçopiltzinen, çenca tinechpatzmictilia in noyollotzin ca in tley itlanequilitzin in Dios ca yehuatl mochi mochihuaz canel yuh nechmonahuatilitzinohua ma tihuian—

v Tlapitzaloz. Yatiazque niman quitlaliz in quahuitl, Yn iSaac in habraham oncan tlatoz—

Abraham,^{41} = Xiqualhuicacan in tlatlatil,quahuitl nican Xictemacan—

v Niman oncan quixeloz in habraham in quahuitl—

Abraham = Xihualauh nican ximotlanquaquetza, yuhqui onechmonahuatili in Dios, inic nicchihuaz, in itlanequilitzin—

iSaac = Ma mochihua, in itlatocatlanahuatiltzin in Dios yn iuh quimonequiltitzinohua yhuan in tehuatzin = = = = = =

Abraham = Xicaqui yn axcan, notlaçopiltzinen, ca huel iuh. onechmonahuatili in moçenhuelitiliani, in Dios, ynic neltiz yn itlaçoteotenahuatiltzin inic quiMotiliz intla tictotlaçotilia in titlalticpactlaca intla ticchihua, Yn iteotenahuatiltzin auh ca intlatoca^{42}[34r]tzin in yolque Yhuan in mimicque auh in axcan ma huel monecnomachiliztica Xicçeli in miquiztli = Ca yuh quimitalhuia ca in nehuatl nihuelitiz in niquimizcaliz in mimicque ca in nehuatl çemicac niyoliliztli in nohuian ÇmC auh ma mochi=hua yn itlanequilitzin—

v oncan chocaz in Abraham Yhuan mopitzatz^{43} Missericordia

iSaac = Amo ximochoquili notlaçomahuiztatzinen Ca çenca huel nopaquiliztica in nicçelia in miquiztli, ma mochihua yn itlaçoteotenahuatiltzin, in Dios = Yn iuh omitzmonahuatili—

Abraham = Xiqualhuican in moman nicYlpiz inic amo timoliniz—

v oncan quimailpiz yn itatzin Yn isaac———

---

40. In anticipation of the following page: *huatl.*
41. Here and in two other instances below there is no underlining.
42. In anticipation of the following page: *tzin.*
43. mopitzatz: standard *mopitzaz.*

ISAAC: Your command will be done as you order, O my beloved honored father.

(Wind instruments are played when they get to where the mountain is [located].)

ABRAHAM: We have now arrived at the foot of the mountain, where we will pray. As for you, you will stay here; you will not accompany us. Bring my sword and the fire. As for the firewood, put it on the shoulders of my beloved child, for he will need it.

(Wind instruments are played a little. They make Isaac carry the wood on his shoulders. He immediately ascends the mountain. Once there Isaac stands up. He speaks.)

ISAAC: O my beloved honored father, this firewood that I am carrying makes me extremely tired. What are you going to do?

ABRAHAM: You will need to turn into ashes [for] I am going to make an offering of your body.

ISAAC: But, O my beloved honored father, [33v] are we [not] to make an offering of just the wood and the fire?

ABRAHAM: O my beloved child, you greatly anguish my heart. All that which is the will of God must be carried out since such are his orders to me. Let us be on our way.

(Wind instruments are played. They go along. Then Isaac sets the wood down. At that point Abraham speaks.)

ABRAHAM: Bring the firewood. Lay it down here.

(Once there Abraham splits the wood.)

ABRAHAM: Come, kneel here. God has ordered me to carry out his will in a certain fashion.

ISAAC: May the royal commands of God be done in accordance with his will and yours.

ABRAHAM: Now listen, O my beloved child. The All-powerful, God, has strictly ordered me to [make sure] that his precious sacred commands are realized so that he will see if we people of the earth love him and if we carry out his sacred commands, for he is the ruler of [34r] the living and the dead. Now receive death with great humility, for he speaks thusly: I will be able to raise the dead for I am eternal life everywhere in the world. May his will be done.

(At that point Abraham weeps and the Misericordia is played on wind instruments.)

ISAAC: Do not cry, O my beloved honored father, for it is with very great happiness that I receive death. May the precious sacred commands of God be done as he has ordered you [to do them].

ABRAHAM: Give [me] your hands. I will bind them so that you will not move.

(At that point Isaac's father binds his hands.)

iSaac = Notlaçomahuiztatzinen Ma yhuan xinechmixquimilhui ynic amo ninomauhtiz in iquac ticmacoCuiliz in momatzin⁴⁴ in motepozmacquauhtzin ma xinechmotlapachilhuilili⁴⁵ in nixtelolo—⁴⁶ [34v]

Abraham = Ma yuhqui mochihua, notlaçopiltzinen = = =—

oncan quixquimiloz in habraham in i,piltzin, niman huel cacocuiz, in ialfange in habraham =—

Abraham = Ytencopatzinco in Dios, inic timomiquiliz in tinotlaçopiltzin—

v oncan monextiz Çe Angel q:tzitzquiliz, Yn iman in habraham Ynic ahuel quimictiz Yn ipiltzin isaac—

Angel = Abraham, Abram,—

v Quitzitzquiliz in iman v

Abraham = Ac tehuatzin in tinechmonochilia—

Angel = Yn axcan xiccaquican, yhueli^ticatzinco in Dios, yhuan ytencopatzinco ca ic oquimottilitzino in quenin ticmotlaçotilitzinohua, Auh inic ticchihua yn iteotenahuatiltzin, ynic amo tiquitlacohua ca in motlacopiltzin⁴⁷ in çenca ticmotlaçotilitzinohua in axcan, nican Tepeticpac in otiqualmohuiquili in oticmohuenchihuililico in moçenhuelitiliani, in⁴⁸ [35r] Dios tetatzin, Auh in axcan ytlaçotlanequilizti=catzinco, Ynic onihualla inic nimitznolhuilico ynic ticmocahuiliz inic amo momiquiliz in motlacopiltzin,⁴⁹ YSaac—

Abraham = Ma mochihua Yn itlaçotlanahuatiltzin yn iuh quimonequiltitzinohua = Xihualmohuica Notlaçopiltzinen ca ye otimomaquixti, Yn imacpa in miquiztli—

v = oncan quitomiliz in paño inic oixquimiliuhticatCa Yhuan, in mecatl ic mail=pitica quitotomaz,—

Angel = Auh in axcan xicmomachilti ca in ixiptla in motlaçopiltzin, Ca çentetl, ichcaconetzintli ticchichihuaquiuh Yn iuh quimonequiltitzinohua in Dios, ma tihuian Ca nemechcahuatiuh,⁵⁰ in amochan—

Abraham = Ma yuhqui mochihuan, ma tihuian—

v tlapitzaloz, niman hualtemozq,ᵉ Yn icpac tepetl = =

Abraham = = Yn axcan Ma çemicac moyectenehua y⁵¹[35v]n imahuiztocatzin in moçenhuelitiliani in Dios, tetatzin in nohuian CmC in çenca huey in itetlaocolilitzin intla timochintin in titlalticpactlaca, in ticchihuacan Yn itlaçoteotenahuatiltzin ca çenca ic tictohueltlamachtilizque⁵² = = = Auh in tehuatl in tinotlaçopiltzin otiquittac, in quename ic omitzmomaquixtili yn ihuicpa in miquiztli Auh in axcan yn oquix⁵³ cahuitl timonemiltiz Ma çemicac ticmotlazotiliz = yca mochi moyollo Yhuan amo tictlapictenehuaz in itocatzin in Dios, Yhuan tiquintlaçotlaz in mohuanpohuan yn iuh motlanahuatilitzinohua = = =

---

44. momatzin: perhaps to be read *momactzinco*.
45. xinechmotlapachilhuilili: tentative transcription because the end is obscure due to blotting.
46. In anticipation of the following page: *A*.
47. motlacopiltzin: read *motlaçopiltzin*.
48. In anticipation of the following page: *Dios*.
49. motlacopiltzin: read *motlaçopiltzin*.
50. nemechcahuatiuh: read *namechcahuatiuh*.
51. In anticipation of the following page: *ni*.
52. tictohueltlamachtilizque: standard *tictohuellamachtilizque*.
53. oquix: read *oc ixquich*.

ISAAC: And, O my beloved honored father, wrap up my eyes so that I will not be afraid when you raise up your sword in your hand. Do cover my eyes. [34v]

ABRAHAM: May it so be done, O my beloved child.
(At that point Abraham wraps the eyes of his child, and then Abraham raises his sword right on up.)
ABRAHAM: It is by order of God that you, my beloved child, will die.
(An angel appears there. He seizes the hand of Abraham so that he cannot kill his child Isaac.)
ANGEL: Abraham! Abraham!
(He seizes his hand.)
ABRAHAM: Who are you that calls me?
ANGEL: Now listen up! By the power of God and by his orders, he has thus seen how you love him and carry out his sacred commands so that you do not violate them. For today you brought your beloved child, whom you greatly love, to the top of the mountain here in order to make an offering of him to the All-powerful, [35r] God the Father. Now it is by his precious will that I have come to tell you to leave him alone so that your beloved child, Isaac, will not die.

ABRAHAM: May his precious commands be done as is his will. Come, O my beloved child, for you have now been saved from the hands of death.
(At that point he loosens the cloth with which the eyes are wrapped and he undoes the rope with which the hands are bound.)
ANGEL: Now know that the substitute for your beloved child will be a little lamb you are to make ready. Such is the will of God. Let us be on our way, for I am going to leave you at your home.
ABRAHAM: May it so be done. Let us be on our way.
(Wind instruments are played. They immediately descend from the top of the mountain.)
ABRAHAM: Now may [35v] the honored name of the All-powerful, God the Father, whose compassion is very great, be eternally praised everywhere in the world. If all we people of the earth would carry out his precious sacred commands we would greatly please him. And as for you, my beloved child, you have seen how he saved you from death. Now as long as you live, always love him with all your heart and do not take in vain the name of God, and love your neighbors. Such are his orders.

iSaac = = Ca mochi nicChihuaz, Yn itlanahuatiltzin = in Dios, Yhuan in tehuatzin = Auh ma ximocalaquitzino Ca ye otaçico in tochan, ma oc ximoçehuitzino—
v Calaquizque oncan tlatoz Angel =—
Angel = Yn amixquichtin in nican ancate Ca ye oanqui=mocaquiltique Ynin tlamahuiçolli, Auh in amehuantin ma huel xicmonemiliztican, in iteote[54][36r]nahuatiltzin Macamo çentetl, anquitlacozque yhuan in amopilhuan huel Xiquinmocuitlahuican inic amo ahuilnemizque inic qualyoti:ca inic quimotlayecoltilizque in totecuiyo Dios inic no quimomaçehuizque in Ylhuicac tlatoCayotl Ma yuh mochihua =
v = finis Laus Deo, de 1678 A^s Oçencauh[55] inin Neixcuitilli omotrasladaro axcan Ypan tonalli Viernes 1 de febrero, de 1760 Años, auh inic melahuac nehuatl onictequipano inin Neixcuitilli Bernabe Vazquez [simple rubric]

              JESVS MARIA Y
                  JOSEPH
             NEIXCVITILLI, I
            TECHPA TLATOHua[56]

---

54. In anticipation of the following page: *na*.
55. Oçencauh: read *omoçencauh*.
56. To either side of **JOSEPH** are simple drawings (three to the left, two to the right). At the bottom of the page in a different hand: *pa. Neixkuitilli maxiotl ^{vj} Tlatolmaxiotl (Mol)*.

ISAAC: I will perform all the commands of God and you. Do enter, for we have reached our home. Please rest a while.

(They exit. At that point Angel speaks.)

ANGEL: All of you who are here have now heard this marvelous thing. And as for you, may you live entirely according to [36r] his sacred commands, may you and your children not violate a single one. Take good care that they will not go about playing and wasting time, so that they will serve with goodness our lord, God, and so that they will also merit the kingdom of heaven. May it so be done.

Finis. Laus Deo.[12] *This moral example was prepared in the year 1678. It was copied today, Friday, the first of February of the year 1760. And as to whether in truth I worked on this moral example, [I affix my signature]: Bernabé Vázquez.*
                JESUS, MARY AND JOSEPH.
      MORAL EXAMPLE WHICH SPEAKS ABOUT[13]

---

12. *Finis Laus Deo.:* The End. Praise God.
13. There is no indication why there is such an incomplete and abrupt ending.

Present Location
William L. Clements Library, University of Michigan
Ann Arbor, Michigan

[36v]
YN ANIMASTIN Y:HVAN ALVACEAS:ME, HVALQVIZAZ. IN DON PEDRO I:HVAN INAMIC TLatZOtZONALOZ TLaPItZALOZ—

D. Pedro = Tla xihualmohuica notlaçonamictzinen ca izcatqui in cenca nechtequipachohua ninentlamatinemi in ixpantzinco in Dios yn intechcopa in mimiccatzitzintin in macan,¹ nicalpixcatzin in teotl, tlatohuani Dios Auh ca ye oquimotlapohuililique Ca ye ixpantzinco otlatemoliloque yn itechpa yn intlachihualiz in i nepapan² [37r] tlatlacolli yhuan ye otlatzomtequililoque intla oc cecpa³ nican tp̄c hualani ca techmelahuilizquia in quenin omelauhcatlatzomtequililoque acaçomo çan quexquich, in ipalehuiloca yezquia in animasme Auh in tehuantin Ca ye ticmomachitia Ye ixquich cahuitl in tiquinpalehuia in ica MiSsa yhuan ResponSo = Ca çenca ye icnoyohua tonehua in noyollotzin Yn iquac in niquimilnamiqui, in canpa oquimoyeyantlalili in totecuiyo Dios, Aquin huel quimatiz notlaçonamictzinen, auh in axcan, ye totech pachihui tonehuiztli chichinaquiliztli aocmo hualnezini in tocochca toneuhca tlein ynic ticpalehuizq.ᵉ Auh ma tehuatzin Xicmitalhuitzino, notlaçonamictzinen—

Çihuatl = Notlaçonamictzin in ticmotenehuilia ca no çenca, Ye patzmiqui inaniman⁴ ca nican Catqui in niquilnamiqui ma ticnamacacan in çentetl caltzintli in onca ticate ma yehuatl inic mochihuaz yn inMissatzin in animasme Yehuatl quimati çaço tlein tiquizque Cuix oncate ytlachihualtzitzinhuan in totecuiyo Dios, Canel ayac techmomaquilia in [37v] Dios, ma oc tixpan tomattian mochihua maca tlein tiqualnacazitztiazque in moztla huitlpa⁵ intla, otechmopolhui in totecuiyo Dios—

D. Pedro = Ca melahuac in ticmitalhuia nonamictzinen ma tihuian in teopan Ma tictotlatlauhtilitzinoti, in totecuiyo Dios, Ca ye pehuaz in MiSsa ma ticchihuati Çentetzintli Responso in inpa⁶ in animastin motoliniticate purgatorio inic quinmocnoittiliz in Dios, in campa mohuetzticate—

Çihuatl = Ma yuh mochihua notlaçonamictzin ma ti=huian—

v̱ **Calaquizque hualquizazque albaçeas, quihualhuicazque in Testamento quipohuazque**

1. macan: probably to be read as *ma çan* or *maca çan*.
2. In anticipation of the next page: *tla.* in i nepapan: read as standard *yn nepapan*.
3. oc cecpa: here and below can be found this and other variants of standard *oc ceppa*.
4. inaniman: read *in naniman*.
5. huitlpa: read (as elsewhere in this text) *huiptla*.
6. inpa: if not read as *inpa(h)* "their medicine" then read as *inpan* or *inpampa*.

Souls and Testamentary Executors
Translated by Barry D. Sell, with assistance from Louise M. Burkhart

[36v]
Souls and Testamentary Executors. Don Pedro enters along with his spouse. Drums are beaten, wind instruments are blown.

DON PEDRO: O my beloved spouse, please come.[1] Here is what greatly distresses me. Although I am just a steward of God the deity and ruler I go about discontent before God concerning the unfortunate dead people. They have already given an accounting to him, already been examined before him concerning their deeds, the various [37r] sins, and already been judged. If they were to come again here to earth they would explain to us how they were rightly judged. Perhaps it would be no small help to the souls. As for us, you already know that we have been helping them all this time with masses and prayers for the dead. My heart is very compassionate and suffers burning pain when I remember where our lord God has placed them. O my beloved spouse, who can know [his will/where they are]? Torment and pain now press down upon us and we are miserably poor. With what will we help them? O my beloved spouse, speak.

WOMAN: O my beloved spouse, what you are saying also greatly grieves my soul. Here is what I am thinking. Let us sell the little house where we are and with it let the souls' mass be performed. They know whatever it is we will succeed.[2] Since God has given us no one [that is, children], are there creatures of our lord God? [37v] Let it happen before our eyes and in our time. Let us look at nothing [earthly] with affection since tomorrow or the next day our lòrd God may have effaced us.

DON PEDRO: O my spouse, you speak the truth. Let us go to church to pray to our lord God, for mass is about to begin. Let us go make a prayer for the dead for the sake of the souls who are suffering in purgatory so that God will have pity on them where they lie fallen.

WOMAN: So be it, O my beloved spouse. Let us go.

(They exit. The executors enter bringing a testament. They read it.)

---

1. Concerning the optative/imperative particles *ma* and *tla*: the former is used far more frequently in this text than the latter, reflecting general usage in the colonial Nahuatl corpus. In several instances, I have added "please" to the translation in order to convey the stronger sense of pleading that *tla* apparently imparts. The most complete and authoritative contemporary explanation of these particles is in Carochi 1983, f. 25:

> Este *mā*, es nota de imperatiuo, y de Optatiuo, y suele dexarse en la segunda persona singula[r], y plural del imperatiuo; y mas quando se mande à algun inferior, si no es que se le quiera mostrar amor; y assi el amo à su criado dize, *xitlachpāna* barre; y con el *mā*, parece, que se ruega, ò se anima à que hagan algo; y en lugar del se vsa tambien del *tlā* que aun es mas comedido, que el *mā*, y con el se ruega, ò anima mas que con el *mā*.

2. Tentative translation.

1º Albacea = Notlaçoteycauhtzinen quenin huel mochihuaz in iuhqui oquitotiaque in mimicque inic teopā calaquiz in imaxca in intlatqui inic palehuilozque in oc çequintin, Animas, auh ca nican catqui in oqui=cauhtiaque in teocuitlatl huel çenca ic ninotlamachtia quenin huel mochihuaz—

2º Albacea = Macamo mitzmotequipachilhui, Ca nehuatl nicmati in quenin huel mochihuaz, ca huel mone⁷[38r]qui axcan nictlaliz amatl in ixquich in oquitecpantiaque in mimicque mochi niquiquaniz mopopoloz cannoço⁸ mocuiz inic titoyolalizque—

v Calaquizque hualquizazque Demonios luçifer,———————

Lucifer = Tlen⁹ amay tlein anquichihua yn amo anquimocuitlahuia in tp̄c̄ tlaca, ca ça izquilhuitl ma nen anquixichcauhti ma huel ypan Xitotocacan in intech omocauhtiaque in mimicque ma xihuian ma xiquincuitlahuiltican inic huel mochi quipopolozque in miccatlatquitl inic amo huel tomacpa quiçazque in = Animastin in techquixtilizque ma niman nelti moChihua in notenahuatil—

2º Dem,º = Macamo Ximotequipachotzino ca niman ye tihui axcan inic tiquintlapololtizque—

3º Dem,º = Ma niman tihuian ma tiquimittati in tomaçehualhuan in tocnihuan ma tihuian—

v Yazque itzintla Mesa mo=tlalizque tlacuilozque in Demonios hualquiçazq,ᵉ albaçeas—

1º Albacea = Yzcatqui in niquilnamiqui ma tlaco Xicmo¹⁰[38v]çelili Auh in oc tlaco nicCui ma ytlatzin ie ticonixtlapanacan¹¹ ma çatepan ic palehuilozque in animas, Cuix oc quihualmati Ca ye omimicq.ᵉ—

2º Albaçea = Ynontzin, Çenca huel teyolquima ma yuhqui mochihua intla noço popolihuiz anquin¹² tlatoz Cuix aço çeme oncate yn imezçohuan intlapalohua in techtequipachozque, macamo Ximotequipachotzino notlacoteachcauhtzinen¹³ ma oc titoyolaliti. ma tihuian Ca ye onca in tohuaxca totlatqui yhuan yn iquac omicque Ca ayocac ixpan ca za tehuatzin yhuan in nehuatl—

1º Albaçea = Ca melahuac yn oticmotalhuitzino¹⁴ ma tihuian tipapaquilti notlaçoicniuhtzinē—

v Yazque connamiquizque in Viuda quitlaliz luto quihualhuicazque demonios—

Viuda = Yn amehuantzitzin yn antlaçopipiltin campa in ammohuica ma nicaqui in amotlaçotlatoltzin = = =

1.º Albacea = TlaçoÇihuapillen ca otimitztonamiquilico Canel Domingo in axCan tontahuiltitinemi Auh in tehuatzin campa timohuica ma timitztohuiquilican = = =

Viuda = Ca ychantzinco in tonantzin S,ᵗᵃ Yglesia Missa niconcaquiz¹⁵—[39r]

7. In anticipation of the next page: *qui*.
8. cannoço: read *ca noço*.
9. Tlen: here and below, standard *tlein*.
10. In anticipation of the next page: *çe*.
11. ticonixtlapanacan: standard *toconixtlapanacan*; see Carochi 1645, 42v–43v (in Carochi 1983).
12. anquin: read *aquin*.
13. notlacoteachcauhtzinen: read *notlaçoteachcauhtzinen*.
14. oticmotalhuitzino: elsewhere in this text standard *oticmitalhuitzino*.
15. niconcaquiz: standard *noconcaquiz*; see Carochi 1983, 42v–43v.

FIRST EXECUTOR: O my beloved younger brother, how can it be done as the dead left ordered, that their goods and property would enter into the church in order to help other souls? Here is the gold they went leaving behind. I will be very rich with it. How can it be done?

SECOND EXECUTOR: Do not let it bother you. I know how it can be done. It is very necessary [38r] that now I compose a document [concerning] all that the dead left ordered. I will move all that is to be spent from one place to another. Thus will be taken that with which we will console ourselves.

(They exit. The demons and Lucifer enter.)

LUCIFER: What is wrong with you,[3] you who do not take care of the people of the earth? It has just been a few days! Do not uselessly lose it through neglect; really go after those in whose hands the dead left themselves.[4] Go, induce them to dissipate absolutely all the property of the dead so that the souls they are to take from us will not escape from our hands. Let my command be realized and done.

SECOND DEMON: Do not be anxious for we are going right now in order to confuse them.

THIRD DEMON: Let us go right away to see our subjects and friends. Let us go.

(They go and sit down at the foot of the table. The demons write. The executors enter.)

FIRST EXECUTOR: Here is what I am thinking. You take half [38v] and I will take the other half. Let us lend some out at interest and afterwards the souls will be helped with it. Do they still frequent [the earth]? They are already dead.

SECOND EXECUTOR: That is very greatly pleasing. Let it be so done. If perhaps it comes to ruin: who will speak up? Will one of their offspring bother us? O my beloved older brother, do not be distressed. Let us go console ourselves. Let us go, for it is already our goods and property, and when they died it was before no one but you and me.

FIRST EXECUTOR: What you have said is the truth. O my dear friend, let us go enjoy ourselves.

(They go meet Widow. She puts on mourning clothes. The demons enter.)

WIDOW: You dear nobles, where are you going? Let me hear your precious words.

FIRST EXECUTOR: O dear lady, since it is Sunday we came to meet you. Now we are going about enjoying ourselves. As for you: Where are you going? Let us accompany you.

WIDOW: I am on my way to hear mass in the home of our mother holy church. [39r]

---

3. Tlen amay tlein anquichihua / What is wrong with you (literally, What oh what are you doing): here and below this doublet, and perhaps either half of it, can mean "What is the matter with you?" See Carochi 1983, 116v, "*Tle ōtimāilì? mach huel ōchīchīliuh in mīxtelolo?* que tienes? parece, que tienes los ojos muy colorados" (What is the matter with you? Your eyes seem very reddened) and 124v, "*tle ōtax? aoc ticmati?* . . . que tienes, as perdido el juyzio?" (What is the matter with you? Have you lost your mind?)

4. That is, the executors. Tentative translation.

Dem.º 1.º = Xicahua tlein tiquitohua MiSsa xiccahua xiauh xipapaqui yn intla[16] momecahuan—

2º Albacea = Tla xihualmohuica tla nican totlan ximohuetziti tla nican tonpapaquican =—

v conanaz ymatitech inic ome albaçea motlalizque————————

Viuda = Notlaçotelpotzitzinhuan Ca çenca huel ye nicnoyohuatiuh inic niuah in teopa[17] yehica in axcan Yohualtica oniquittac, yn ipan notemic çenca tlayohuia[18] in nonamic in onpa purgatorio auh nicnequi nicchihuaz Missa yn ipanpa Oc çecppa niquitohua ca tel ayanmo huecauh innomomiquili[19] ma oc motelChihua—

1º Albaçea = Xicmocahuili on, Çihuapillen ca quitohua in tlamatinime = in aquin quinequi yaz teopā ma yauh = auh in aquin quinequi papaquiz tlalticpac ma papaqui ma moyollali yehica Ca moztla huiptla momi=quiliz tla xicmottili Cuix amo ye neltiliztli melahuac auh inin ma oc tonpapaquican—

Viuda = = Ca melahuac in ticmitalhuitzinohua oquichpilli ma tipapaquican—

v tlatzotzonazque auh in teopan[20] [39v] tziliniz miccatepoztli, cuicoz mehuaz Responso—

2º Albaçea = Aquique in oconchiuhque MiSsa ca ontzilin in miccatepoztli auh in tehuatin tlein tay tlein ticchihua—

Viuda = Ca yehuatin inniz[21] tocalepohuan tla oc yehuan quimati ma quipopolocan in intomin ca ymixco=yan ic mochamahua = Auh in tehuantin ma ye ic ōçehui in tix in toyollo—

1,º Albaçea = Ca melahuac in ticmitalhuitzinohua camo[22] totequiuh in MiSsa moztla huiptla intla titomiquilizque Cuix ocecppa tihualazque ma oc titoyolalican—

2,º Dem,º = Ye qualli in anquilnamiqui xiquincahuacan in animas, ma ye Xatlican Xitlaquacan Xitecohuanotzacan ma ximoteicniuhtican ma vinotica Ximoçentlalican macamo ximamanacan—

Viuda = Auh in axcan notelpotzitzinhuan ma oc niccui in nechcahuilitihui in miccatomin ma ic titoçepanyollalican—

1.º Albaçea = Ca ye Cualitzin ma oc ticalaquican ma tihuian = = =

v Quihuicazque in Demonios hual[23][40r]quiçazque D,ⁿ Pedro yhuan, y=namic—

---

16. intla: read *intlan.*
17. niuah in teopa: read *niyauh in teopan.*
18. tlayohuia: here and below, read *tlaihiyohuia.*
19. innomomiquili: read *in omomiquili.*
20. In anticipation of the next page: *tzi.*
21. inniz: read *in iz.*
22. camo: here and below, read *ca amo.*
23. In anticipation of the next page: *qui.*

FIRST DEMON: Leave it. What are you saying? Leave mass. Go, enjoy yourself among your consorts.

SECOND EXECUTOR: Please come and sit down here with us. Let us go on enjoying ourselves here.

(Second Executor takes her by the hand. They sit down.)

WIDOW: O my dear young men, I am going to church in an extremely compassionate mood for last night I saw my spouse in my dreams greatly suffering over there in purgatory. I want to make a mass on his account. Again I say that he only died recently. Let [your invitation] be disregarded.

FIRST EXECUTOR: O lady, leave that, for the wise men say: "He who wants to go to church, let him go, and he who wants to enjoy himself on earth, let him enjoy himself and be consoled, for tomorrow or the next day he will die." Please consider. Is it not a veritable truth? And now, let us go on enjoying ourselves.

WIDOW: You speak the truth, O manly noble.[5] Let us enjoy ourselves.

(They beat drums. [39v] Bells are rung in church. A prayer for the dead is raised in song.)

SECOND EXECUTOR: Who put on a mass? The bells have rung. As for us, what oh what are we doing?

WIDOW: As for our neighbors here, let it be their responsibility, let them spend their money for it is their very own. They brag about it. And as for us, let our spirits be appeased with it.

FIRST EXECUTOR: You speak the truth. Mass is not our business. If tomorrow or the next day we die, will we come back again? Let us still console ourselves.

SECOND DEMON: What you are thinking is good. Abandon the souls. Eat, drink, invite people to feasts, make friends, gather together with wine. Do not get worked up.

WIDOW: And now, O my young men, let me take the dead people's money they left to me. Let us console one another with it.

FIRST EXECUTOR: Good. Let us enter. Let us go.

(The demons accompany them. [40r] Don Pedro and his spouse enter.)

---

5. oquichpilli: this compound is composed of *oquich(tli)* "man" here serving as the adjective "manly" modifying *pilli* "noble." If the reverential suffix *–tzin(tli)* were added it would mean "male child" (see Carochi 1983, 9r).

D.ⁿ Pedro = Notlaçonamictzinen, Çenca otictotlamachtique inic ypan otaçique in inMissatzin animas auh, in axcan çenca nimitznotlatlauhtilia macaic tiquinmolcahuiliz in motoliniticate, Purgatorio, in ahuel monomapalehuia momaquixtia ca yuh ca, in itlatoltzin in totecuiyo Dios, ca in Christiano, yn oc t$\overline{pc}$. monemitia teoyotica mopalehuia tlamaçehualiztica yhuan tlahuenchihualiztica inic huel momaquixtiz yn itech²⁴ in tlayohuiliztli Auh Cuix oc çecppa hualmohuicazque tlamaçehuaquihue in nican t$\overline{pc}$. ca niman amo ca ic çenmayan oquinmocaltzacuilitzino in totecuiyo Dios, auh in tehuantin in oc t$\overline{pc}$. inpampa tihuenmanazque aço quinmocneliliz, anoço amo Ca yehuatzin quimomaChiltia in totecuioyo²⁵ Dios, auh yn axcan ma oc ninoçehui Ca çenca, Yetiye in tlalli Çoquitl—

Çihuatl = Otlacauhqui in motlaçoyollotzin notlaçonamictzin yehica Ca tehuatzin motechtzinco nicanaz in qualtlachihualliztli²⁶ inic tinechmozcaltiliz Ca niuhqui, nimopiltzin yn ipan tinechmomachiltia Ca mochi nicneltiliz in ixquich tinechmonahuatilia ma ximochi²⁷[40v]cauhtzino ma ixquich motlapaltzin Xicmochihuilitzino ma ticalaquican—

<u>v</u> **Calaquizque hualquiçazque albaceas, Yhuan, Viuda, ihuan tercero Demonio—**

Viuda = Yn axcan notlaçotelpotzitzinhuan Ca çenca nipapaqui ninoyollalia ca nican Catqui in onechcahuilitiaque in mimicque ma ic ximoyolalitzinocan tle yez Cuix totonalÇiahuiliz ca niman amo—

1.º Albacea = Ma oncan on, Xicmotlalili auh ma mocui in totech monequiz ynic titotlamachtizque—

2º Albaçea = Ma oc motelchihua noteachcauhtzinen ma oc ticaquiti in temachtilli ca ye inman in pehuaz notlaçoicnihuanen ma tihuian—

3º Dem.º = Ximocahua tlen tiquitohua aocmo oncan molnamiqui Ximotentzaqua—

1.º Albaçea²⁸ = Xitechcahua amo XitechmoÇihui Ca tipacticate oc oncan titoyolalia Cuix amotequiuh, in Sermon noço Xiauh xitechtlalcahui ma xiauh amo motequiuh in = tlein ticChihuazque—

<u>v</u> **tlatzotzonaloz hualquizaz D.ⁿ Pe.º ihuan ynamic—** ²⁹ [41r]

---

24. itech: probably a scribal error because *itechpa* seems more appropriate here.
25. totecuioyo: standard *totecuiyo*. The same item can be found below on 50r.
26. qualtlachihualliztli: because of assimilation and loss (abundantly illustrated in this and other texts) read as standard *quallachihualiztli*.
27. In anticipation of the next page: *cauh*.
28. Here and in one other instance below there is no underlining.
29. In anticipation of the next page: *D.ⁿ Pedro*.

DON PEDRO: O my beloved spouse, we have been so fortunate that we have arrived during the souls' mass. Now I greatly implore you to never forget those who are suffering in purgatory, who cannot help save themselves. For such is the word of our lord God: the Christian who still lives on earth spiritually helps himself through penance and offerings to save himself from suffering. Will they come here again to earth to do penance? Absolutely not! Our lord God has imprisoned them once and for all. As for those of us still on earth, we are to make offerings on their behalf. [Only] our lord God knows whether he will favor them or not. Now let me rest for the earth and clay [that is, my mortal body] is very heavy [with illness].

WOMAN: Thank you, O my beloved spouse, because I take from you the good works with which you raise me, me whom you regard as your child. I will carry out all you order me [to do]. Be strong, [40v] exert all your effort. Let us enter.

(They exit. The executors and Widow and Third Demon enter.)

WIDOW: Now, O my dear young men, I am very happy and content. Here is what the dead went leaving me. May you be content with it. What is it to be? Is it our blood and sweat? Absolutely not!
FIRST EXECUTOR: Set it down over there. Let what we will need be taken so that we will be happily rich.
SECOND EXECUTOR: O my older brother, let it be scorned! Let us go hear the sermon for it is high time for it to begin. O my dear friends, let us go.
THIRD DEMON: Shut up. What are you saying? It is forgotten. Be silent.
FIRST EXECUTOR: Leave us alone. Do not upset us for we are still happy and content there. Is the sermon perhaps your business? Go, leave us. Go, what we do is none of your business.
(Drums are beaten. Don Pedro enters along with his spouse.) [41r]

D.ⁿ Pedro = Notlaçonamictzinen ma yhuiantzin tiatihuian[30] in teopā ynic nicnoçeliliz in itlaçomahuiznacayotzin in totecuiyo Jesu christo Ynyoyahuen canin ye niaznequi canin ye ninotlaça Cuix ahuilpa camanalpa notecuiyoen notlatocatzinen ma xinechmocnoittilitzino ma xinechmopalehuilitzino macamo xinechmolcahuilitzino in nitlacatl in çenca nihuey tlatlacohuani ma xinechmotlaocolili in ica in mohueytetlaocolilitzin in mohueyteicnoittalitzin ma xinechmoyolchipahuili Xinechmopapaquili miecpa Xinechmaltili in itechpa in aqualli ayectli in tliltic Catzahuac in notech ca in notlahuelilocayo in çenca tecatzauh teyçolo in notlatlacol yuhquima Çe huey tlamamalli nechyetiçihuiltia in maca çan huey cacaxtli inic tlalla nechaquiaya ma xinechmocnoytilitzino in nitlatlacohuani totecuiyoyen Diosē = = =

Chocaz =—

Çihuatl = Notlaçonamictzin ma ximochiuhcauhtzino ma yçenmactzinco Ximocauhtzino in toteyocoxcatzin in Dios, ma tihuian in teopan

v Calaquizque hualquiçaz animas hualp[oç?]auhtiaz tlecuecalli[31] inic micuiloz mehuaz Peccata tlananquiliz anima nu[32] [41v] nula es. Responsion =—

3.º Anima = Ay inyoyahuen totecuiyoen Diosē. moteicnoytiliniyen motetlaocolilianien ma xinechmotlaocolilitzino yn ica in motetlaocolilitzin moteopohua in nix = in noyollo, yn ipampa in izquitlamantli onicChiuh in moyolitlacolocatzin, Ca ypampa nichoca, ca onimitznoyolytlacalhuitzino in tinoteotzin tinotlatocatzin ca huel tlapanahuia inic titlaçotlaloni ma xinechmotlaocolilitzino in ayac nechtlaocoliani in nican tp̄c. auh Ca tehuatzin in tinotlaçotatzin in otinechmochihuili innotinechmoyocolili[33] Ca tinotepalehuicatzin tinotemanahuicatzin in tlalticpac ca oniccauh in maxcatzin in motlatquitzin inic nipalehuilozquia atle nomaçehual in nitlatlacohuani amo nechilnamiqui in nohualyoque[34] in oc nemi tlalticpac, ca tehuatzin ticmomachiltitzinohua—

v calaquiz mehuaz Responso hualquizaz Cihuatl quitlaliz Luto, quihualhuicaz Candela xochiqualli = inic quichihuatiuh Missa quihualhuicaz Angel—

Çihuatl = Noteotzin notlatocatzin omochiuh onotlahueli[35][42r]tic[36] inic ça nocel otinechmocahuili inic omomiquili nonamictzin auh macamo nican nihuecahuaz in motlalticpactzinco in axcan ma niauh in teopan ynic nicChihuaz Missa inic mopalehuizq.ᵉ animas—

1.º Angel = Ma ximochicauhtzino ma ixquich motlapaltzin Xicchihua macamo ximocahua ma xiauh Xicneltili in motlahuenmanaliz yn inpalehuiloca, in Purgatorio, Cate macamo Xiquincahua—

v connamiquiz, Demonio Segundo

---

30. ma yhuiantzin tiatihuian: perhaps to be read as *ma yhuiantzinco tiatihuian*.
31. **tlecuecalli:** read *tlecueçalli*.
32. **nu:** apparently anticipates the first syllable of "nula," which immediately follows on the next page.
33. innotinechmoyocolili: read *in otinechmoyocolili*.
34. nohualyoque: read *nohuanyolque*.
35. In anticipation of the next page: *tic*.
36. onotlahuelitic: read *onotlahueliltic*.

DON PEDRO: O my beloved spouse, let us go calmly and peacefully to church so that I will receive the precious honored body of our lord Jesus Christ. Alas! Where am I about to go now? Where will I cast myself now? Will it be in frivolities and jokes? O my lord, O my ruler, have pity on me, help me, do not forget me, very great sinner that I am. Be merciful with me through your great mercy and your great compassion. Purify my heart, scour me, cleanse me many times of the bad and evil things, my black and dirty iniquities, my befouling and besmirching sins,[6] that are in me. It is as though a great burden weighs me down, as though a great packframe plants me in the earth. O our lord, O God, have pity on me, a sinner!

(He cries.)

WOMAN: O my beloved spouse, be strong. Leave yourself entirely in the hands of God our Creator. Let us go to church.

(They exit. A soul enters, coming smoking, painted with tongues of fire. The Peccata[7] is sung. The soul answers. [41v] Nula est responsio.)[8]

THIRD SOUL: Oh, alas! O our lord, O God, O compassionate one, O merciful one! Have mercy on me with your mercy. My spirit is tormented because of all the things I did in offense to you. Wherefore I cry, for I have offended you, my deity and ruler, surpassingly worthy of being loved. Have mercy on me, whom no one else on earth would have mercy on. You my beloved Father, who made and created me, are my aid and defense on earth. I relinquished your goods and property with which I would have been helped. I am an undeserving sinner. You know that my relatives who still live on earth do not remember me.

(He exits. A prayer for the dead is raised [in song]. Woman enters, wearing mourning clothes. She comes bringing candles and fruit with which she will make a mass. An angel accompanies her.)

WOMAN: O my God and ruler, woe is me, [42r] that you left me alone when my spouse died! May I not tarry long here on your earth. Let me go now to church in order to perform a mass with which the souls [in purgatory] will be helped.

FIRST ANGEL: Be strong, exert all your effort. Do not stay, go, make your offerings, which will help those who are in purgatory. Do not abandon them.

(Second Demon meets her.)

---

6. in çenca tecatzauh teyçolo in notlatlacol: although *tecatzauh teyçolo* might be considered transparent metaphors for sin, they are not so treated here or in other texts that I have seen. First, the seemingly redundant *in notlatlacol*, "my sins," is added as if in necessary explanation. Second, in Carochi's treatment of similar items, he explicitly states that "*nopotōnca*, mi hedor" means "por metaphora mis pecados" but not the closely related forms of *tecatzauh* (1983, f49).

7. This is apparently from the Office for the Dead, Psalm 24, the verse that begins with Peccata—"Peccáta iuventútis meæ et delíxcta mea ne memíneris; secúndum misericórdiam tuam meménto mei tu, propter bonitátem tuam, Dómine" (*Breviarum romanum* 1961, 1:242). This is Psalm 25, verse 7, in the King James Bible: "Remember not the sins of my youth, nor my transgressions—according to thy mercy remember thou me for thy goodness sake, O Lord."

8. *Nula est responsio*: There is no response.

2.º Dem,º = Çihuatzintlen campa tiaznequi tlein taiz: in teopan tlein ticchihuaz Cuix onpa neçiz in motech monequiz ca amo Cuix noço ompa timo:tlayecoltiz intla teopan tiaznequi ompa tapizmiquiz macamo ompa Xiauh—

Çihuatl = Ca niman amo nihueliti notlaçotelpotzin Ca niaz ma xinechmocahuili ca ytencopatzinco in Dios, inic niquitlaniz MiSsa—

2º Dem,º = Cuix amo titlacaqui, Çihuatzintlen Ca melahuac atle onca MiSsa = Yhuan ayaque, in teopixque quen huel axcan ompa onihualla ma ximocuepa ca nimitznotza tle ipā tinechmati Xiauh in mochan amo miec ic Xiquintla³⁷[42v]pololti in mohuanpohuan xiauh xiquiça—

1,º Angel = Xiccahua tlacatecolotlen ma^ca mo xicnotza in D.ˢ ytetlayecolticatzin Xiauh camo monemac in ichuic tihualmiquaniz Ca nican nica in nitepixcauh inic mochipa nicnocuitlahuitinemi ma xictlalcahui yn itlachihualtzin Dios,—

v Quitocaz hualtzatziz mictlā,caltenco

2.º Dem,º = Cuix amo nimitznotza Çihuatlen, Xihualmocuepa Ca intla tihualmocuepaz mochi ni=macaz³⁸ Yn ixquich axcaytl tlatquitl inic timoyollaliz tipapaquiz—

1º Angel = Xicahua in Dios, Ytlachihualtzin—

Calaquizque mitoz ReSponso intla omito hualquiçaz teopixqui yhuan Çihuatl—

teopixqui = Notlaçopiltzinen ma çan ypaltzinco in Dios, ma moChipa, Çemicac XiquilnamiquiCa in oamechyaCanque = miquiztica ma amechtlaocoltican in achtopa omomiquilique, ma xiquintlaocolican in ixpantzīco in Dios, Ca çenca tlayohua in ompa nechipahualo³⁹[43r]yan = in Purgatorio ca quihualtemachitoque yn amohuen in ican inMiSsa⁴⁰ = anoco⁴¹ tlatlatlauhtiliztica anoço tlahuenchihualiztica in ye oncan Ca oc tleyin inhueli inic mopalehuizque Ca quichixticate, quitemachiticate in tepalehuiliztli inic huel momaquixtizque auh yn iquac tlaocolilo Ca çenca ic mocnelilmati Çenca quitlaçocamati in imicneliloca, Auh ynintzin yn iuh otinechmolhuili in amo huel neçi in mocochca in moneuhca auh macamo ximotequipacho notlaçopiltzinen macamo ic tiquinxicahuaz in ixquichtin Animas ma motlatlauhtiliztica mochoquiztica ixpantzinco in Dios, xicmotlatlauhtili inic quinmotlapopolhuiliz inic quinmocaxahuililiz in intlayohuiliz yhuan inic amo huecahuazque in Purgatorio Auh yn iquac tlamiz in tp̄c. monemiliz ca no mopan motlatoltizque ynic mitzmocneliliz in Dios, ynic ticmaçehuaz Yn ilhuicac papaquiliztli Gloria—

Çihuatl = Notlaçomahuizteopixcatzin otlacauhqui in moyollotzin otinechmocnelili ma oc nimitznotlalcahuilitzino ca tel oc cecppa nihualaz ma oc ytlatzin nicontemo⁴² inic tiquinmopalehuiliz = in Animas ma oc nimitznotlalCahuilitzino—

---

37. In anticipation of the next page: *po*.
38. nimacaz: read *nimitzmacaz*.
39. In anticipation of the next page: *yan*.
40. ican inMissa: read *ica in inMissa* (as below).
41. anoco: read *anoço*.
42. nicontemo: standard *nocontemo*; see Carochi 1983, 42v–43v.

SECOND DEMON: O woman, where are you about to go? What oh what will you do in church? Will you find what you need there? No! Or will you make a living there? If you want to go to church you will suffer from hunger there. Do not go there.

WOMAN: O my dear young man, I absolutely cannot refrain from going. Leave me, for it is by order of God that I ask for a mass.

SECOND DEMON: O woman, don't you understand? Truly there is no mass and there are no priests.[9] I just came from there. Turn back for I summon you. What do you take me for? Go to your home. Do not confuse [42v] your neighbors with [so] many things. Go, leave.

FIRST ANGEL: Leave her alone, O demon, do not summon God's servant. Go, for you do not deserve[10] to move over here to her for I am here, I her guardian [angel] who always goes about taking care of her. Relinquish God's creature.

(He pursues her, crying out from outside the house of hell.)

SECOND DEMON: Oh woman, am I not summoning you? Turn back, for if you turn back in this direction I will give you everything, all the goods and property with which you will be content and enjoy yourself.

FIRST ANGEL: Relinquish God's creature!

(They exit. A prayer for the dead is said. When it is over Priest enters along with Woman.)

PRIEST: O my beloved child, let it just be through the grace of God that you always and forever remember those who preceded you in death. May those who have died first have mercy on you, and may you have mercy on them before God for they suffer greatly over there in the place of self-purification, [43r] purgatory. They rely on your offerings, through the masses performed for them, or prayers, or the making of offerings. What else is there with which they can help themselves? They are waiting and relying on help so that they can be saved. When mercy is shown they are very grateful for the favors done them, they are very thankful for the benefits shown them. And as for this matter, as you have said to me, that you cannot find enough to eat, O my beloved child, do not be distressed. Do not therefore abandon all the souls [in purgatory]. Before God with your prayers and weeping, implore him to pardon them so that he will relieve them of their burden of suffering and so that they do not tarry long in purgatory. When your earthly life comes to an end they will speak on your behalf so that God will favor you, so that you will enjoy heavenly bliss, glory.

WOMAN: O my beloved honored priest, I give you many thanks for the favor you have shown me.[11] Let me take leave of you for now. I will come again. Let me first go seek a little something with which you will help the souls. Let me take leave of you for now.

---

9. Here used in the plural, the singular *teopixqui* is defined in Carochi 1983 [1645], 52r, as "el sacerdote, o religioso, que guarda lo que toca à Dios." This parellels the abstract collective noun *teoyotl* covered in a footnote below.

10. camo monemac: "*ahmo monemac*—no mereces" (Arenas 1982, 106); "Nonemac. la merced, o don que se me hizo o dio" (Molina 1977, 73r).

11. otlacauhqui in moyollotzin otinechmocnelili: below appear two other variants of this typical doublet of thanks. My phrasing in all three cases is based on Molina 1984 [1569], 118v, "¶ Notecuiyoe tlatohuanie, otlacauhquin moyollotzin otinechmocnelili" / "¶ Señor mio, hagoos muchas gracias, por los beneficios q̄ me aueys hecho." See also the dictionary, Molina 1977, 115v, "Tlacaua noyollo. otorgar a conceder algo." as well as 78r, "Otinechmocnelili. doyte gracias por la merced que me heziste."

teopixqui = Ma mitzmoyacanilitzino in totecuiyo Dios ca tel[43] [43v] nimitznoChieliz notlaçopiltzinen—

v calaquizque hualquiçazque albaçeas yhuan, Viuda————

1,º Albaçea = Yn axcan huel monequi ynic çenca huel tipapaquizque inic amo tlein techtequipachoz auh in tehuatzin ma oc Ximoyollali in tinotlaçoicniuhtzin Auh in nehuatl ma oc niccui in totech monequiz inic tipapaquizque titoyollalizque =—

2.º Albaçea = Ca ye qualli ma tihualmoçihuitiz auh in nehuatl Ca nican catqui in teocuitlatl ynic titoyalalizque[44] Cuix mochipa in tp̄c. ma tihualmoçihuitiz nocniuhtzinen————

Viuda = Auh in nehuatl, notlaçotelpotzin ca no nican calqui[45] in tomin, çan ixquich = Caxtolli pesos = Auh in oc çequi ca notzotzomatzin yc onicouh, Cuix yuhqui teixpan ninemiz—

2º Dem,º = Ca ye qualli ye mahuiztic ca mochi yehuatl om, monequi Cuix mohuaxca motlatqui ma xicpopolocan Xahuiecan xipapaquican—

1,º Albaçea = Ca ye onihualla ca nican catqui, ynic onçehuiz in totlaçoyeliz ma tlatzonalo ma cuico tlen anmaylia tocniuhtzitzihuanen—[44r]

v tlatzotzonazque auh in Viuda coniz = vino yc onmotenpopohuaz in luto çatepan quiquixtiz contlaçaz mesapan onca yez Xochiqualli cui=cazque papaquizq.e oncan tzili=niz animas = auh çan içel in anima quiçaz—

1,º Anima = Ay ma xitechmolnamiquilican yn antocnihuan in oc annemi tp̄c. macamo xitechmolcahuilican in ixpantzinco in totecuiyo Dios, yn antohuayolque in oc annemi tp̄c, ma çan ypampatzinco in Dios, ma çe Pater noSter, çe Ave maria Xiquitocan topampa = = = =

Viuda = Jesus tlen moChihua ma oc ticalaquican ma oc titoçehuiti Ca ye teotlac—

2º Dem,º = Amo Ximotequipachocan ca ytzatziliz in cahuitl inic yauh Yohualli auh camo cocoliztli ma ximoyollalican—

2,º Albaçea = Xicmocahuili matzatzin Cuix motequiuh ca tipacticate—

v tlatzotzonazque oc çepa tzatziz anima çan ye yehuatl quitoz ocpa[46] [44v] cruz + auh motlapoz Yn ilhuica[47] auh in oc çequintin animas motlancuaquetzazque ixpantzinco D,s

2,º Anima = Ay yoyahuen totecuiyoen Diosē, ma xitechmocno=ittilitzino in titoteyocoxcatzin in mochipa çemicac timohuetznoticatqui yn imayeccanpatzinco in motlaçomahuiztatzin Dios, Ca mohuicopatzinco tontzatziticate, in inpanpa in tp̄c. motlachihualtzitzinhuan in oc nemi in aic techilcahua in motlacoixpantzinco[48] in momoztlae, inpampa tlahuenchihua yn ica in intlatlatlauhtiliz inic techilnamiqui macayāmo in ma inic ontlamiz tzomquizaz in tlalticpac in innemiliz ma oc Xiquinmocnoyttilitzino xiquinmotlaocolilitzino = =

= = v= tziliniz animas——

---

43. In anticipation of the next page: *ni*.
44. titoyalalizque: read *titoyollalizque*.
45. calqui: read *catqui*.
46. In anticipation of the next page: *cruz*. It is unclear whether **ocpa** should be read as *oc ceppa* or *oppa*.
47. **ilhuica**: read *ilhuicatl*.
48. motlacoixpantzinco: read either as *motlaçoixpantzinco* or (as several times below) *motlatocaixpantzinco*.

PRIEST: May our lord God guide you. [43v] O my beloved child, I will await you.

(They exit. The executors and Widow enter.)
FIRST EXECUTOR: Now it is very necessary that we will be extremely happy so that nothing will bother us. You, my dear friend, be content. And as for me, let me take what we will need to enjoy ourselves and be happy.
SECOND EXECUTOR: Very well, hurry. As for me, the gold with which we will be happy is here. [Will we live] forever on earth? O my friend, hurry.

WIDOW: And as for me, O my dear young man, there is also money here. It is only fifteen pesos. And as for the rest, I bought my rags with it. Am I to go around in public [dressed] like that?
SECOND DEMON: That is good and estimable, for that is all that is necessary. Is it your goods and property? Squander it, pleasure yourselves, enjoy yourselves!
FIRST EXECUTOR: I have come now. Here is what our precious being will be calm with. Let drums be beaten, songs be sung. O my friends, what is wrong with you? [44r]
(They beat drums. Widow drinks wine, cleaning her lips with the mourning clothes. Afterwards she casts them off, flinging them on the table where there is fruit. They sing and enjoy themselves. Bells ring there for the souls [in purgatory]. A lone soul enters.)
FIRST SOUL: Oh! You our friends who still live on earth, remember us. Do not forget us before our lord God. You our relatives who still live on earth, for God's sake say an Our Father or Hail Mary on our behalf.

WIDOW: Jesus, what is happening? Let us enter, let us go rest for it is already afternoon.
SECOND DEMON: Do not grieve, for it is the cry of time as the night goes. It is not sickness. Be content.
SECOND EXECUTOR: Leave your rags.[12] Is it your business? We are happy.
(They beat drums. The soul cries out a second time, that very one speaking twice [in prayer?] [44v] to the cross. Heaven opens. The other souls kneel down before God.)

SECOND SOUL: Oh, alas! O our lord, O God, have pity on me! You our Creator always and forever sit on the righthand side of your beloved honored Father, God. We are crying out to you on behalf of your earthly creatures. Those who are still alive who never forget us in your royal presence make offerings every day on their behalf, remembering us with their prayers. Let it not be that their earthly lives should come to an end and conclusion yet. Have pity on them! Show them mercy!

(Bells ring for the souls [in purgatory].)

---

12. Tentative translation.

3.º Anima = Ay in tiçenquizcahuecapanoloni in titotemaquixticatzin in tiJesu x̄p̄o = Ca titocnoitohua in motlatocaixpantzinco = ma xitechmotlahuel,caquitilitzino ma çan ypanpatzinco in moMiSericordiatzin xiquinmotlaocolili in ixquichtin tlalticpac techmolnamiquilia in techquixtilia in Santa Bula, yhuan in yca in inMiSsa = yhuan ReSponso inic mixpantzinco tlahuēmana auh intla moztla huiptla Xiquinmotlatzom⁴⁹[45r]tequilili totecuiyoen Diosē, aquiq.ᵉ techpalehuiz aquiq.ᵉ in oc techicnoittazque Ca niman ayac Xpiano in tp̄c̄. inic topan tlahuenchihuazq.ᵉ in mixpantzinco ma oc : xiquinmocahuilitzino in ixquichtin tp̄c̄. tlaca

v̄ = = tziliniz animas = = = v̄

4.º Anima = Ay in timºçenquizcateicnoittilitzinohuani in timotetlaocoliliani ma çan ipanpatzinco in motlaçomahuiznantzin Santa Maria, inic omitzmotlacatililitzino yhuan in ica yn imemeyalotzin inic omitzmohuapahuilitzino ma xiquinmocnoyttilitzino in tlalticpac oniquīhualcauhtehuac inic nopan tlatohua in ica in neçahualiztlaquemitl ynic qualyotica quichihua in tohuanyolque yhuan inic ÇeÇenmetztica tlaçelia ma çan, no yuhqui Xiquinmotlaococolilitzino⁵⁰ = = = = = = = =

v̄ = tziliniz, animas = = =

5º Anima = Ay MiSericordia ynYoyahuen totecuiyo Diosē, quenin Çenca nitetlaocolti nitechocti in yca in ayac nechilnamiqui onoçentzomtlahueliltic inic ayac nechiximati in tlalticpac, aço notatzin nonantzin, aço noteachcauh, aço noteicauh, aco⁵¹ nohueltihuatzin aço huecapan nohualqui⁵² inyoyahuen noteyocox⁵³[45v]catzinen ma çan ipanpatzinco in moMiSericordiatzin xitechmocnoittilitzino in tiçenquizcatlateochihualYchpochtzintli ma xitechmolnamiquilitzino in timotlachihualtzitzinhuan yn ayac techylnamiqui ma çan ipampatzinco in motlaçoRoSariotzin in motlatlauhtilocatzin. Ca yn oc tp̄c̄. ninemia aic onimitznolcahuili ma ye Xinechmopalehuilitzino in ninotolinia tlalticpac oniqualcauhtehuac in no=namic acmo nechilnamiqui, amo nictlaocoltia aoctle onca nopalehuiloca in mixpantzinco ma çan huel çe MiSsa, anoço tlatlauhtiliztica ye nechilnamiqui auh in oniqualcahuilitehuac in nopalehuiloca mochihuaz axcan mochi, cahuilquixtia auh in neçahualiztlaquemitl in luto çan ipan xocomictinemi momecatitinemi Cahuilquixtitinenemi ma ixquich ma tlami ma tzomquiza in tp̄c̄ ynemiliz Ca çenca ye miec inic mixtzinco mopactzinco⁵⁴ nemi—

v̄ — Motlapoz Ylhuicatl—

S,ᵗᵃ M,ᵃ = Yn tinotlaçomahuizçenteconetzin in tiJesu x̄p̄o, ca mixpantzinco ninixtlapachtlaça yn inpanpa in motlachihualtzitzinhuan in tlayohuiticate in tetlechipahualoyan = Purgatorio = ma xiquin⁵⁵[46r]mocnoittilitzino Xiquinmotlaocolilitzino notlaçomahuizconetzin ma yehuatl xicmottilitzino = in nochoquitzin nixayotzin notlaocoltzin Ca in oc tlalticpac onenque notlaçomahuizconetzin aic omitzmolcahuilique Cm̄C omitzmotepotztoquilique Ca yn iquac quilnamiquia yn ipampa in motlayohuilitzin ynic otiquinmomaquixtilitzino—

49. In anticipation of the next page: *te*.
50. Xiquinmotlaococolilitzino: standard *xiquinmotlaocolilitzino* (as above and below in this text).
51. aco: read *aço*.
52. nohualqui: read *nohuanyolqui*.
53. In anticipation of the next page: *ca*.
54. mopactzinco: here and below can be found this variant and others of standard *mocpactzinco*.
55. In anticipation of the next page: *moc*.

THIRD SOUL: Oh, you our savior Jesus Christ, perfectly exalted, we humbly speak in your royal presence! Listen with approval and grant us that just because of your compassion you have mercy on all those on earth who remember us, who get holy bulls for us, and with their masses and prayers for the dead make offerings before you. O our lord, O God, if it be tomorrow or the next day, judge them. [45r] Who will help us, who will still have pity on us? For there are no Christians at all on earth who will make offerings on our behalf before you. Abandon all the people of the earth!

(Bells ring for the souls [in purgatory].)

FOURTH SOUL: Oh, you the perfectly compassionate one, you the merciful one! Let it just be on account of your beloved honored mother, Saint Mary, who gave birth to you and who nurtured you with her milk, that you have pity on those whom I left behind on earth so that they would speak on my behalf with fasting garments, so that our relatives would do things virtuously and take communion every month. May you likewise have mercy on them.

(Bells ring for the souls [in purgatory].)

FIFTH SOUL: Oh mercy! Alas! O God our lord! How very much I aroused grief and tears because no one remembers me. I am unfortunate four hundred[13] times over that no one knows me on earth, whether it be my father and mother, or my older brother or my younger brother, or my older sister or my more distant relatives. O alas! O my Creator! [45v] Have pity on me just because of your compassion. You the perfectly blessed maiden, remember us your creatures whom no one [else] remembers. Let it just be because of your precious rosary and prayers to you. While I still lived on earth I never forgot you. Help me. My spouse, whom I left on earth, no longer remembers me, I do not make her sad. There is no longer any help for me before you. Let [my spouse] just remember me [with] one complete mass or through prayers. All of what I left behind to [my spouse] to become a help for me [in purgatory] she now sells for cash, and the fasting garments, the mourning clothes—[my spouse] just goes about in them drunk and taking lovers, selling them to raise cash. Enough![14] Let [my spouse's] life on earth come to an end and conclusion for she offends you in many things.

(Heaven opens.)

SAINT MARY: You, Jesus Christ, my beloved honored only child, I cast myself down before you on account of your creatures who are suffering in the place where people are purified by fire, purgatory. [46r] O my beloved honored child, have pity on them, show them mercy. See my weeping and tears and sorrow, for while they still lived on earth, O my beloved honored child, they never forgot you, they always followed you for at the time they remembered it was on account of your suffering that you saved them.

---

13. The number *four hundred* is a common idiom in the vigesimally based traditional counting system for "countless, innumerable." When it occurs in the phrase "four hundred times," it could be construed as meaning "countless or many times over."

14. ma ixquich: "*no mas*—ma ixquich" (Arenas 1982, 88).

X̄p̄ō = = Çemicac, ychpochtzintlen notlaçonantzinen macamo inpampa Ximochoquili in motetlayecolticatzitzinhuan yehica in oc tlalticpac nemiaya ca mochipa notech mo^(tla)canequia notech motemachiaya manahuilozque palehuilozque maquixtilozque notemanahuilitica yhuan oquiximachilique in notlaçotatzin Dios, auh in iquac nechmotzatzililizque ca niquinhualcaquiliz in intlatlatlauhtiliz yn iquac moyolteopohuazque in atlamatizque in imelel açiz auh in nehuatzin niquinyollaliz niquintēyotiz niquinmahuizyotiz niquinhuecapanoz Çemicac nemizq.^e yollalilozque niquinnextiliz in nopapaquilitzin Gloria = = =

S,^ta M,^a = Ma xicmocnoytilitzino, notlaçoconetzin inic motlaçohuicopatzinco hualmotzatzititicate ma xiquinmo⁵⁶[46v]tlahuelcaquililitzino in motolinia in motlachihualtzitzinhuan—

<u>v</u> : = tlatzotzonazque no tziliniz = animas =

3º Anima = Ay omochiuuh⁵⁷ onotlahueliltic ma xitechilnamiquican yn oc tlalticpac annemi in antocnihuan macamo xitechcahuacan in ixpantzinco in totecuiyo = Dios, Ay Ay intla mochi tlacatl in quenin huel titotolinia ynic titlatlaticate titlayohuia Ca huel nelli ca techtlaocolizquia aquin amehuantin yn antohuayolque, Cuix monequi antechilcahuazque macamo itla ic Xitechilcahuacan aquin techtlaocoliz ma icnoyohua yn amoyollotzin ma xitechtlaocolican ca çenca titotolinia inyoyahuen totecuiyoyen Diosē, ma y=çiuhcan xiquinmotlatzomtequilili in tlalticpac, otiquinhualcauhque in totepantlatocahuan yezque in motlatocaixpantzinco, auh amo techilnamiqui ca tlaqualtica atica quinenquixtia in otiquinhualcahuilitehuaque ma xicmonequiltitzino inic içiuhca nican mixpantzinco neçizque totecuiyo Jesu x̄p̄ōe =

x̄p̄ō = Yn tehuatzin in tiSan Miguel archangel ma ximotlanahuatili inic hualyoltiazq.^e in t̄p̄c̄ tlaca—[47r]

Sn Mig,^l = Ma mochihua in motlatocatlanahuatiltzin ma Xihualquiçacan in mictlan antlan antlatelchihualtin motlanahuatilitzinohua in melahuacamotetlatzomtequililiani = Jues = inic hualyoltiazque inic anquihualhuicazque yn ipanpa miccatlatquitl tlaixquetzaltin inic oquipopoloque in imaxca intlatqui in animas in motoliniticate in onpa = Purgatorio inic aocac quimilnamiqui = = = =

<u>v</u> hualquiçaz Luçifer ihuan in oc çequintin = Demonios =

Luçifer = Otlacauhqui in mo in moyolotzin⁵⁸ otechmocnelilitzino ma tihuian ma tontocacan tocnihuanen = = =

3,º Dem,º = Ma yçiuhca, tiquimanati in totetlayecolticahuan tocnihuanen, ca motlanahuatilia in totecuiyo Dios—

Calaquizque mochintin calitic quimanatihue nacateme in Viuda tliltic yez mochintin tzatzizque, = tlacueponiz in iquac hualquizazque albaçeasme = =—
= anima = [47v]

1,º Albaçea = Ay omochiuh onotlahueliltic, Ay Ay Ay omochiuh ototlahueliltic in titlatlacohuanime—

---

56. In anticipation of the next page: *tla*.
57. omochiuuh: standard *omochiuh*.
58. in mo: repeats in the manuscript.

CHRIST: O maiden eternal, O my beloved mother, do not cry for your servants because while they still lived on earth they always trusted in me, relied on me. They will be defended, helped and saved with my protection, and they recognized my beloved Father, God. When they cry out to me I will hear what they say, their prayers when their hearts are anguished, when they are unwise and in great pain and affliction. As for me, I[15] will console them, make them famous, honor and exalt them. They will live forever, content, and I will reveal to them my bliss, [glory].

SAINT MARY: O my beloved child, show pity when they are crying out to your precious [personage], listen with approval to [46v] those of your creatures who suffer.

(They beat drums. Bells also ring for the souls [in purgatory].)
THIRD SOUL: Oh! Woe is me! You our friends who still live on earth, do not forget us, do not abandon us before our lord God. Oh! Oh! If everyone suffered as we are suffering, burning and languishing, they would certainly have mercy on us. [Where] are you our relatives? Is it necessary that you will forget us? Do not forget us for anything. Who [else] will have mercy on us? Let your hearts be compassionate, have mercy on us, for we are greatly afflicted. Alas, O our lord, O God, quickly judge those on earth. We left them to be our intercessors before your royal presence but they do not remember us. They waste with food and drink what we left them. O our lord Jesus Christ, let it be your will that they promptly appear here before you.

CHRIST: You, Saint Michael the Archangel, order that the earthly people come hither alive. [47r]

SAINT MICHAEL: Your royal command be done. Come out, you accursed ones of hell! The just sentencer, the judge, orders that they will come hither alive, that you will bring them hither because they—as the ones encharged with the property of the dead—used up the goods and property of the souls suffering over there in purgatory such that there is no longer anyone who remembers them [with offerings].

(Lucifer enters along with the other demons.)
LUCIFER: We give you many thanks for the favor you have shown us.[16] O my friends, let us go, let us be on our way.

THIRD DEMON: O our friends, let us quickly go seize our servants for [so] orders our lord God.

(They all enter the house. They go seize the [condemned?].[17] Widow is in black. All cry out. There are fireworks when the executors and a soul enter.) [47v]

FIRST EXECUTOR: Oh! Woe is me! Oh! Oh! Oh! Woe to us who are sinners!

---

15. I: the Nahuatl reads "nehuatzin" (46r), that is, *nehua(tl)+–tzin(tli)*, the intent being the first person singular reverential. This seems to violate traditional Nahua cultural norms. See Carochi 1983, f. 7, where he discusses the uses of *–tzin(tli)* and adds, concerning this very usage, that it cannot be employed "en la primera de reuerencia, y estimacion, porq̃ nadie deue mostrar estima de si mismo" (7v).

16. In the original Nahuatl "in mo" repeats; this may be no accident. See Sell essay in *Nahuatl Theater, Volume Three*.

17. nacateme: here very tentatively translated as "condemned," it also appears in "Final Judgment," tentatively translated there as "fully fleshed." As far as we know this item appears nowhere else.

2.º Albaçea = Ca tehuatl motlatlacol inic nican titla^{tza}cuiltilo in titlayohuiltilo ca onimitzilhui inic teopan calaquiz in imaxca in intlatqui in animasme inic opalehuilozquia yn iuhqui axcan yc topan mochihua—

1.º Albaçea = tlacatecoloÇihuatlen ca tehuatl motlatlacol inic oticahuilquixtique in teaxca tetlatqui ca mochi tehuatl ^{motlatlacol} in tiquiyohuia—
Viuda = Ay omochiuh onotlahueliltic macamo titlacatini ynic amo iuhqui topan omochihuazquia, in temamauhti teyzahui in axcan topan mochi=hua—
Luçifer = Xitotocacan Cuix quin oanquilnamique in amotlatlacol acmo onca ca ye antohuaxcahuan ye antotlatquihuan—
v **Yazque in ixpantzinco in x͞p͞o, = oncan quiçohuazque in imamauh, Lucifer yhuan mochintin in Dem,^{os} motlaquaquetzazque**
Luçifer = Yn tiçenquizcamelahua^{c}tl, Jues in timotetla^{59}[48r]tzoomtequililiani^{60} Ca nican mixpantzinco otiquinhualhuicaque in çenca huey tetlayecoltique in amo omitzmotlacamachitique in amo oquichiuhque in motlanahuatiltzin maçonelihui motlaçoezçoticatzinco otiquinmomaquixtilitzino in tlahueliloque in yollopoliuhque in aic omitzmolnamiquilitzinoque ma xiquinmotlatzomtequilililitzino ca totech pouhque yehica ca çemicac Otelchihualoque auh in teoyotl mochi oquitecococamatque atle ypan oquittaque in motlayecoltilocatzin izcatqui in intlatlacol ma xicmottili=tzino in intlachihual, Ma xicmopohuilitzino in tehuatzin tiAngel in intlatlacol—
S,^{n} Mig,^{l} = Yzcatqui in itenahuatiltzin yn içel teotl in Dios, in matlactetl, in etetl, in itechtzinco pohui in imahuiztililocatzin in yehuatzin Dios, auh in chicontetl itech pohui in intlaçotlaloca in tlalticpac tlaca—
S,^{n} Mig,^{l} = Ynic Çentetl, ticmotlaçotiliz in içel teotl D,^{s} ica mochi moyollo—
Luçifer = Ca niman aic Omitzmotlaçotilique in nican mani, aic omitzmoteotitzinoque—
S,^{n} Mig,^{l} = Ynic ontetl, amo tictlapictenehuaz in itocatzī in Dios,—[48v]
Lucifer = Mochipa Juramento quichiuhtinemia omitzmotlapictenehuilitinemia ypan in imahuil in intlaelpaquiliztlatlacolpa =—
S,^{n} Mig,^{l} = Ynic yetetl, in Domingo, yhuan Ylhuitl ipan atle taiz çan tiquixcahuiz in titlateomatiz—
Lucifer = Yn ixquich cahuitl, in oc tlalticpac nemia aic omitzmoteomachiltique aic omitzmolnamiquilique auh in ilhuitl ipā ye quintequipachohuaya^{61} in innemecatiliztlatlacol oquichihuaya—
S,^{n} Mig,^{l} = Ynic nauhtetl, ticmahuiztiliz in motatzin in monantzin—
Lucifer = Quenin quimahuiztilizq.^{e} in tehuatzin otiquinmomaquili in qualli yectli yhuan Otiquinmochihuili in īpanpa Cruztitech otimomiquili amo omitzmomahuiztililique, in çan mixtzinco mocpatzinco onenque = Auh yequene in oc çequintin tetahuan quinyacantinemi quinhuicatinemi yn inpilhuan yn ocnamacoyan, Vinocalcohui in inpilhuan in çan nequiza = in motlanahuatiltzin. totecuiyoyē Diosē,—

---

59. In anticipation of the next page: *tzom*.
60. timotetlatzoomtequililiani: standard *timotetlatzontequililiani*.
61. quintequipachohuaya: given the context this must be scribal error; read *quintequipanohuaya*.

SECOND EXECUTOR: It is your fault that we are punished and made to suffer here for I said to you that the goods and property of the souls with which they will be helped should be entered into the church. That is why these things are happening to us now.

FIRST EXECUTOR: O devilish woman, it is your fault that we sold other people's goods and property for cash. It is all your fault that we are suffering.

WIDOW: Oh! Woe is me! Would that we had not been born so that the frightening and scandalous things now happening to us would not have happened.

LUCIFER: Run along. You just now remembered your sins? No longer anything for it, for now you belong to us.

(*They go before Christ. There they spread out their document. Lucifer and all the demons kneel down.*)

LUCIFER: You the perfectly righteous judge, you the sentencer, [48r] here before you we brought those who greatly served [us] and did not obey you. They did not carry out your commands even though through your precious blood you saved [these] scoundrels and lunatics who never remembered you. Judge them. For they belonged to us because they were eternally despised. And as for that which pertains to God,[18] they regarded it all as torment and had no regard for service to you. Here are their sins. Look at their works. You, angel, read their sins.

SAINT MICHAEL: Here are the ten commands of God the only deity. There are ten. Three pertain to the honoring of God and seven pertain to the loving of the people of the earth.

SAINT MICHAEL: First, you shall love God the only deity with all your heart.

LUCIFER: Those who are here absolutely never esteemed you, never regarded you as a god.

SAINT MICHAEL: Second, you shall not take the name of God in vain. [48v]

LUCIFER: They used to go about taking oaths all the time, speaking vainly and falsely about you in their useless idleness and in their sins of filthy carnal delight.

SAINT MICHAEL: Third, on Sundays and feast days you shall just occupy yourself in spiritual pursuits.

LUCIFER: All the time while they lived on earth they never acknowledged you as god, never remembered you. On feast days what used to preoccupy them was their sinful love affairs that they used to carry out.[19]

SAINT MICHAEL: Fourth, you shall honor your father and your mother.

LUCIFER: In what way did they honor them? You gave them good and virtuous things, you made them, you died for them on the cross. They did not honor you for that but just showed you disrespect. Moreover, other fathers go about leading and taking their children to the place where pulque is sold, go to the house of wine. O our lord, O God, your command is just in vain!

---

18. teoyotl: depending on context this has many meanings including "that which pertains to the divine cult" such as mass, Christian doctrine, and the sacrament of marriage; see Carochi 1983, 52v–53r.

19. Tentative translation.

S.n Mig.l = Ynic macuiltetl, ayac momac miquiz in teyolia—

Luçifer = Quenin. ayac in imac miquiz Ca huel miec teaniman [49r] oquixpoloque inic otetlatlacolcuitique inic nezia tp̄c. ca qualnemiliçeque Ca miecpa otemiquizylehuique = = =

S.n Mig.l = Ynic Chiquaçentetl, amo taahuilnemiz in tlaticpac[62] =—

Luçifer = Ca huel axcan ypan in oanoloque in imahuilpapaquiliz in innemecatiliztlatlacol—

S.n Mig.l = Ynic Chicontetl, amo tichtequiz amo ticylehuiz in teçiahuiliz—

Luçifer = Auh ca huel yez tecalotica in oanaloque in oquitzquiloque[63] Camo tiquimiztlacahuia—

S.n Mig.l = Ynic Chicuetetl, amo titetentlapiquiz amo tetech tictlamiz tlatlacolli—

Luçifer = Ca huel teixpa inic oquintētlapique in inhuanpohuan inic tetech oquitlamique in tlatlacolli—

S.n Mig.l = Ynic Chiucnauhtetl, amo tiquilehuiz in teçihuauh yhuan tenamic—

Luçifer = Ca miequintin Oquinmahuizpoloque in ica mani in intētlaximaliz aic Omitzmomauhcaittilique = amo oquimauhcaittaque in moteotenahuatiltzin Ca çan Oquihuetzquiliaya ca zan ahuilcamanalli ypan quimatia in motetlatzomtequililitzin manel moyolcuitizque Ca niman amo ic momaquixtizque in mo=[64][49v]tlatocaixpantzinco totecuiyoyen Diosē,—=

S.n Mig.l = Ynic matlactetl, amo tiquilehuiz in teaxca tetlatqui—

Luçifer = Auh quenin amo quilehuizque ca in mimicque in imaxca in intlatqui ca mochi Oquixpachoque Camo, oquinpalehuique in ixquichtin Animas, Ca amo oquinquixtilique in Bula in manel zan = MiSsa = anoço ReSponso, anoso RoSario, ic quintepotztocani amo oquiChiuhque Auh yn iquac otzilinia = Animas, in imilnamicoca, çan innemecatiliztica onenque, in aic Oquimilnamicque Auh ma xiquinmotlatzomtequililitzino—

S.n Mig.l = Yzcatqui in itenahuatiltzin in tonantzin S.ta Ygl.a ca macuiltetl = Ynic Çentetl in Domingo, yhuan ylhuitl ipā huel Çentetl MiSsa mocaquiz

Luçifer = Aic inyollocacopa oquittaque MiSsa, momoztlae Vinonamacoyan moçentlaliaya amo otlateomatia in motlatocaixpantzinco—

S.n Mig.l = Ynic ontetl, neyolmelahualoz yn ipan in axcan tlamaçehualizCahuipan Quaresma—

Luçifer = Ca niman aic Omoyolmelauhque yn iquac onemia in tlalticpac amo ic omoyolcocoque in tlamaçehualiztli = = [50r]

S.n Mig.l = Ynic yetetl, Çeliloz in itlaçomahuiznacayotzin in totecuioyo[65] Jesu xp̄o. yn iquac huey pasqua anoço Xochipasqua.—

---

62. tlaticpac: here and below, read as standard *tlalticpac*.
63. oquitzquiloque: appears to be scribal error; we read as *otzitzquiloque*.
64. In anticipation of the next page: *tla*.
65. totecuioyo: standard *totecuiyo*. The same item can be found above on 40r.

SAINT MICHAEL: Fifth, no one's spirit shall die at your hands.

LUCIFER: In what way did no one die at their hands? They ruined the souls of many people, [49r] they caused people to take up sin, so that it would seem on earth that they had good lives.[20] Many times they desired the death of others.
SAINT MICHAEL: Sixth, you shall not live licentiously on earth.
LUCIFER: Right at this moment they were seized in their carnal delights and their sins of concubinage.
SAINT MICHAEL: Seventh, you shall not be a thief, you shall not covet the labor of others.
LUCIFER: They were seized and taken hold of right on the path to someone's house.[21] We are not deceiving them.
SAINT MICHAEL: Eighth, you shall not slander others nor impute sin to them.
LUCIFER: Right in public they slandered their neighbors and imputed sin to others.

SAINT MICHAEL: Ninth, you shall not covet someone else's wife and someone else's spouse.
LUCIFER: Those here defamed many people with their adulteries. They never looked at you with fear nor your sacred commandments with fear. They just laughed at them, regarding your judgments as just frivolous jokes. O our lord, O God, even if they confess they will absolutely not thereby be saved in your [49v] royal presence.
SAINT MICHAEL: Tenth, you shall not covet the goods and property of others.
LUCIFER: And how did they not covet the goods and property of the dead? They hid it all, they did not help all the souls [in purgatory], they did not take out for them the [papal] bulls and would not even follow up for them with just a mass or prayer for the dead or a rosary. They did not do it. When the bells rang in remembrance of the souls [in purgatory] they just lived in their illicit unions and never remembered it. Judge them.
SAINT MICHAEL: Here are the five commands of our mother holy church. First, on Sundays and feast days an entire mass will be heard.
LUCIFER: They never willingly heard mass. Every day they used to gather together in the place where wine is sold. They did not occupy themselves in spiritual matters in your royal presence.
SAINT MICHAEL: Second, all will confess now in the time of penance, Lent.

LUCIFER: They absolutely never confessed when they lived on earth and they were not repentant with penance. [50r]
SAINT MICHAEL: Third, the precious honored body of our lord Jesus Christ will be received when it is great Easter or the flowery Pasch.[22]

---

20. Tentative translation.
21. Tentative translation.
22. These terms for Pasch are discussed in Burkhart 1996, 172–73.

Luçifer = Ayc inyollocacopa otlaçelique Ca mochipa tlatlacolpan Omitzmoçeliliaya, Auh in quemanian intla otlaçelique niman ye connamiqui otlica mahuiltia teixylehuia nepohualiztica quichihuaya inic oomoqualnextiaya[66]—

S,^{n} Mig,^{l} = Ynic nauhtetl, neçahualoz in iquac motenahuatilia in S,^{ta} Ygl,^{a}

Luçifer = Quenin moçahuazque momoztlae atlitica = tlaqualtica mocohuanotzaya moçentlaliaya yn ica in micCatlatquitl oquinenquixtiq.^{e}—

S,^{n} Mig,^{l} = Ynic macuiltetl, tlamanaloz in tlamatlactetilia inic motenahuatilia in S,^{ta} Ygl,^{a}—

Luçifer = Ca niman, atle qualli oquichiuhque quenin tlamanazque tlahuenchihuazque ca manel temachtiltica nonotzaloya çan quihuetzquiliaya = in inteopixcahuan Ca quitohuaya Cuix nelli melahua^c ca çan ic techmamauhtia Auh ynin Ca zan Xolopitli aic oquimahuiztiliaya in neçahualiztlaquemitl in Luto = mochipa ocnamacoyan tecohuanotzaloyan[67] [50v] tlacatlatolli ypan quichihuaya ypan teca tlatohuaya ipan tetlanximaya aquetztinemia yn iuh momatia azo catle tetlacuiltiliztli[68] ytech ca auh ca tiquinmoçenquizcaitztiliticatqui in timelahuac Jues = Camo tlen tiquintetlapiquia Ca oc çequi in nican yn iCuiliuhtica yn intlatlacol ma yÇiuhcā Xintechmomaquili macamo nican mixpantzinco neçican in tlahueliloque—

Xp̄o = Ca çemicac inpan nixtoçotica in ixquichtin notlaChihualhuan camo niquincahua ca mochipa niquimitztica in tlatlacohuanime Ca yn iquac tlatlacohua in tlapilchihua Ca nictamachiuhtica in intlachihual ynic niquintlacuiltiz[69] niquinçenmanaz niquintzitzquiz niquinchichinatzaz = auh in yehuantin quenin zan tlaelpaquiliztica Oquinenpoloque in teaxca tetlatqui auh in amoyolia in amaniman quenin oanquinenquixtique Ca inic onicyocox onicChiuh Ca çemicac notloc nonahuac nochantzinco oannemizquia oannechmotlayecoltilizquia = Auh çannimac[70] in Çemicac Zentetlayohuiltianime oanquicauhq.^{e} ynic çemicac quitonehuacapolozque anchichinatzazque in ompa = Çentlani mictlan apochquia[71][51r]huayocan oanmomomayauhque = Auh canpa oanquicauhque in miccatlatquitl inic amotech omocauhq^e in ompa tlayohuia = Purgatorio = quenin amo anquinpalehuique ma xinechnanquilican = Auh in axcan, ma xiquinhuicacan in oanquītequipanoque ma amechtlaxtlahuilmacacan in amehuantin in mictlan anchaneque ma xiquinhuicacan Canel Oamechtlayecoltique—

1,^{o} Dem,^{o} = Otlacauhqui, in motlaçoyollotzin otitechmocnelilitzino ma niman tiquinhuicacan in ompa Çentlani, mictlan, oamotlahueliltic tlacentelchihualtinen ma tihuian in ompa toçenchan xitotocacan ca amechhualchie in totlatocauh in Luçifer, Ca amechmottiliz—

---

66. oomoqualnextiaya: standard *omoqualnextiaya*.
67. In anticipation of the next page: *tla*.
68. tetlacuiltiliztli: read *tetlatzacuiltiliztli* (see footnote immediately below).
69. niquintlacuiltiz: read *niquintlatzacuiltiz*.
70. çannimac: read *çan imac*.
71. In anticipation of the next page: *hua*.

LUCIFER: They never willingly took communion for they always took you in sin. If at times they took communion they later met on the road wasting time, desiring women, and pridefully trying to make themselves look beautiful.

SAINT MICHAEL: Fourth, all will fast when the holy church orders.

LUCIFER: In what way did they fast? Every day they invited themselves to feasts, gathering together with drink and food [obtained with] the property of the dead that they squandered.

SAINT MICHAEL: Fifth, offerings of a tenth will be made as the holy church orders.

LUCIFER: They did absolutely nothing properly. In what way did they give and make offerings? Even though they were admonished with sermons they just laughed at the priests, saying: "Is it true and correct? They are just frightening us with [all that talk]." And as for this one, he is just an idiot. He never honored the fasting garments, the mourning clothes. He was always in the place where pulque is sold, the place where people are invited to feasts, [50v] doing bad things in vulgar words, speaking out against others, being adulterous and going about with his head held high, thinking that no punishment attaches to it.[23] But you the true judge had a perfect view of them. We bring no false testimony against them for their other sins are written here [too]. Give them to us promptly. Do not let the[se] scoundrels appear here before you.

CHRIST: I keep eternal vigil on all my creatures. I do not abandon them. I am always looking at sinners.[24] When they sin and commit failings I am measuring their deeds so that I will punish them, rule them, take hold of them and make them suffer pain. As for them, how did they just squander the goods and property of others through filthy carnal pleasures? And how did you uselessly use up your spirits and souls? I created and made them so that you would eternally live next to and with me in my home, and so that you would serve me. But you have left them in the hands of the eternal torturers of everyone so that they will always torment them. You will suffer pain over there in the depths of hell, [51r] you flung yourselves down into the place without a chimney. And where did you leave the property of the dead that they who suffer over there in purgatory entrusted to you? How did you not help them? Answer me! And now, take those on whom you have worked. Let them make restitution to you residents of hell. Take them for they served you [well].

FIRST DEMON: We give you many thanks for the favor you have shown us. Let us take them right away there to the depths of hell. O accursed ones, woe to you! Let us go there to our eternal home. Run along, for our ruler Lucifer is waiting to see you.

---

23. Tentative translation.
24. ca mochipa niquimitztica in tlatlacohuanime: this might also be translated as "I always dwell/live with sinners." See Molina 1977, 72r: "Niquimitztica. biuir, o morar en compañia de algunos."

S.ⁿ Mig.^l = Motlanahuatilia, Yn melahuac Jues, inic tlequauhtemalacatitech anquintlalizque auh tlepopochatitla anquinmayahuitihue yhuan tleapas:calco anquinmayahuitihue tletemazcalco anquin:calaquizque huel anquintonehuacapolozque inic tlatzomtequililo ma xiquinhuicacan—

Quinhuicazque, motzaquaz in Ylhuicatl————[51v]

1,^oAlbaçea = Ay ay ay omochiuh ototlahueliltic ma oc tic=tecuepiliani ~~in teaxca~~ in teaxca tetlatqui yn imaxca in mimicque, Ay Ay Ay omochiuh ototlahueliltic macamo titlacatini Campa tica in titlacatecoloteta macamo xinechtlacatiliani yn tlaticpac—

Viuda = Yehica omochiuh onotlahueliltic tlein onechonquixti in notlaelpaquiliz Auh catlique in oticçenpopoloque in teocuitlatl ma xinechpalehuiqui ma xinechmaquixtiqui—

1º Dem,º = Acmo onca inic antzatziticate axcan anquimetizque in oanquixpachoque in miccatlatquitl ma tihuian ca huel ye antechhuecahua Xitotocacan tlahuelilloque—

v Yazque niman quintlalizque quauhtemalacatitech in animatin tlachichihualtin yezque auh in condenados tlatic tzatzizque quinmalacachozque Cueponiz bonbas oc çecppa quinhualquixtizque quintlayahualochtizque mopi⁷²[52r]tzaz trompeta cuacuauhomitl

2º Albaçea = Ay Ay Ay in timictlan calli ma ça çepa Xitechtolo macamo timitzittacan auh in amehuāntin in antlatlacatecolo ma ça çecpa Xitechtzatzayanacan inyoyahuen ototlahueliltic ma totech ximixcuiticā in antlalticpactlaca ma xictecuepilican in teaxca tetlatqui inic amo no yuhqui amopan mochihuaz = yn iuh topan omochiuh in tehuantin—

Viuda = Ay. Ay. Ay. in amehuantin in anquipiezque in neçahualiztlaquemitl, luto camo ahuilli camanalli ypan anquimatizque ca ynic tinahuatillo tlamaçehualiztica tlatlatlauhtiliztica neçahualiztica yhuan Çeçenmetztica tlaçeliloz Auh camo yuhqui onicChiuh ca yehuatl nictzaqua in axcā ma mochi tlacatl notech mixcuitican yn annoÇihuapohuan macamo yuhqui anquichihuazque ay ay ay ay ay ay—

3º Dem,º = Ça ye Xiquintotoquiltican tocnihuanen aocmo oncan in manel tlein mach anquitozque Xicalaquican tlatelchihualtinen axcan anquittazque = = =

---

72. In anticipation of the next page: *tzaz.*

SAINT MICHAEL: The true judge orders that you place them on a wheel of fire. You will go casting them down into the place of fire-blackened water, into the house with tubs of fire.[25] You shall enter them into the sweatbath of fire. You will greatly torment them. That is the judgment. Take them.
(They take them. Heaven closes up.) [51v]

FIRST EXECUTOR: Oh! Oh! Oh! Woe is us! Would that we could still return the goods and property of others, the property of the dead. Oh! Oh! Oh! Woe is us! Would that we had not been born! Where are you, you demonic father? Would that you had not caused me to be born on earth.

WIDOW: Wherefore, O woe is me, what did my filthy carnal pleasures avail me? And what has become of all the gold we spent? Come help me! Come save me!

FIRST DEMON: There is nothing to cry about. Now you will make yourselves heavy [with] the property of the dead you concealed. Let us go for you have greatly detained us. Hurry along, scoundrels!
(They go. Then they attach to wheels the effigies of souls. The condemned cry out from inside. They turn them. Fireworks go off. Again they bring them out and parade them around. [52r] *A trumpet, [that is,] a horn trumpet,[26] is blown.)*

SECOND EXECUTOR: Oh! Oh! Oh! You who are the house of hell, swallow us up once and for all. Let us not look at you. As for you devils, just rip us to shreds once and for all. Alas, woe is us! You people of the earth, take an example from us. Return to others their goods and property so that what befell us will not also befall you.

WIDOW: Oh! Oh! Oh! You who will have fasting garments, mourning clothes, do not regard them as frivolous for you are ordered to it through penance, prayers, and fasting, and communion will be taken each month. I did not do this and now I am paying the penalty. Let everyone take an example from me. You who are women like me: Do not do likewise! Oh! Oh! Oh! Oh! Oh! Oh!

THIRD DEMON: O our friends, make them run along now. There is nothing for it now no matter what you say. Enter, O accursed ones! Now you shall see!

---

25. Tentative translation.
26. horn trumpet: literally, "head-stick-bone," from a colonial Nahuatl circumlocution for European horned animals, *quaquahueque,* "head-stick owners."

Present Location
Library of Congress
Washington, D.C.

[1r]
+
Nexcuitilmachiotl. motenehua Juiçio final—
tlapitzalos motlapoz yIħ.^{c} hualmotemohuiz S.^{n} mig.^{l} =

S.^{n} miguel = <u>v</u> Dios ytlachihualtzitzinhuane. ma xicmatican. yhuan Ca tel ye anquimati. Ca ypan Ca yn iteotenahuatiltzin ȳ tt.^{o} D.^{s} Ca quimotlamilliz quimopo^{l}huis yn oquimochihuilitzino. yn itlaçomahuiztatzin Dios. ȳ Senmanahuactli. Ca quimopolhuis. quimotlamilliz. yn ixquich yn oquimochihuilitzino. ȳ nepapan totome. y nepapā yoyolime. yhuan yn amehuantin. Ca hamechmopolhuis. yn ansemanahuac tlaca. auh ma yuh ye yn amoyollo. ca moscalizque y mimicque. y qualtin yecti. yn oquimotlayecoltilique. ȳ melahu^{a}caJuez motlatzontequililiani D.^{s} Ca quinmohuiquiliz yn onpa yn itlatocachantz.^{co} ȳ Semicac neSentlamachtiloyan. y gloria. yn inneSentlamachtiaya. yn ixquichtin S.^{tos} S.^{tas} auh yn amo qualtin. yn amo hoquimotlayecoltilique yn tt.^{o} D.^{s} ma yuh ye yn inyollo. Ca quimomasehuizque. yn mictlan tla^{i}yohuiliztli. auh ynin ma xichocaca. ma xiquilnamiquiCan. xiquimaCasiCan. ximauhCamiquiCan. Ca hamopan mochihuas. y tetlatzontequililizylhuitl. y senca temamauhti. y seca teiysahui. temauhcamicti. temauhcaçotlahualti. auh ynin ma ximonemiliz[yectilican?^{1}] [1v] ye amopan mochihuas. ȳ tetlatzontequililizcahuitl. ca ye ocan. ca ye hinma yn axcan—
Tlapitzalos Tlecos S.^{n} miguel hualquisas. Tlamasehualiztli.
Cahuitl: Sta ygl.^{a} : Tlachpanaliztli: miquistli—

Tlamasehualiztli = Ȳ niman ayoc huel mitos: anoçe motenehuas: yn innetlapololtiliz: yn ixquichtin çemanahuac tlaca: y çenca huel yhuicopa oquayxihuitique:^{2} nepapan tlatlacoltica: tlei mach ohuaxque: tlei mach yn quichihua Ȳ niman ahuel quicahua: yn intetzauhtlatlacol: yn inyollo:tepitzahuilliz: yn imixpopoyotilliz: oycen^{tzon}tlahueliltic: aca nel ypam miquisque: yn intlatlacol: y nacatzonteme: y nacastapaleque: yn ixpopoyome: yn atlachianime: huel mitos tlatlacoltica: oyxtepapatzauhque: huel oquitzopelicamatque: ~~oquiya~~cahuiyacamatque: yn tlatlacolli: yuhquima oquimocaltique: oquimoquentique: yn ahuilnemilliztli: Ça yuhqui yn imauh yn intlaqual: ypan quimati: auh yn inteotzin yn intlatocatzin D.^{s} ye omolcahuillique^3: oyçentzotlahueliltic: Ca ye tlami yn innemilliz: yn tlp̄c:—

---

1. This part of page torn and missing. Could also be read as *ximonemilizcueppan*.
2. oquayxihuitique: originally read *oquayxihuiteque*.
3. omolcahuillique: read *oquimolcahuilique*.

Final Judgment
Translated by Louise M. Burkhart, with assistance from Barry D. Sell

[1r]
+

Exemplary model called Final Judgment.
(Wind instruments are played. Heaven opens. Saint Michael descends.)

SAINT MICHAEL: O creations of God! Know, and indeed you already know, for it is in the sacred commands of our lord God, that he will finish off, he will destroy the world that his precious and honored father, God, made. He will destroy, he will finish off all that he made, the various birds, the various living creatures, along with you. He will destroy you, you people of the world. But be certain that the dead will revive. The good and proper ones who served the just judge, the sentencer, God, he will take to his royal home, the place of eternal and utter bliss, glory, the place of utter bliss of all the male and female saints. But the bad ones who did not serve our lord God, may they be certain that they will merit suffering in the place of the dead.[1] So then, weep, remember it. Fear it, be scared to death, for the day of judgment will happen to you. It is very frightening, it is very shocking, it scares people to death, it makes people faint with fright. So then, emend your lives. [1v] The day of judgment is about to happen to you. It is the time, it is the moment, now.

(Wind instruments are played. Saint Michael ascends. Penance enters [along with] Time, Holy Church, Sweeping, [and] Death.)

PENANCE: It is still impossible to say or declare the confusion of all the people of the world. They are thoroughly dizzy in the head from the various sins. Whatever is wrong with them, whatever is the matter with them, that they are in no way able to abandon their ominous sins, their hard-heartedness, their blindness? They are four hundred times[2] unfortunate. Some will die in their sins. The recalcitrant, the deaf, the blind, the unobservant: it can be said that with sin they have destroyed people's eyes. They have considered sin to be quite sweet, they have considered it to be pleasing to the nose. It is as if they housed themselves and dressed themselves with lustful living. It is just as if they consider it to be their drink, their food.[3] And they have already forgotten their deity, their ruler, God. They are four hundred times unfortunate! For their life on earth is about to end.

---

1. mictlan: here and below translated as "the place of the dead" (locative senses such as "in" or "at" are already contained in the Nahuatl term), it was usually rendered by colonial translators as *infierno* (hell).
2. Four hundred times: here and below, *four hundred* is a common idiom in the vigesimally based traditional counting system for "countless, innumerable."
3. drink, food: here and below, this common diphrase often carries the sense "daily sustenance."

Cahuitl: v Ȳ nehuatl y nicahuitl: y niçemilhuiteotlatoltillizcahuitl: yn onechmomaquilitzino: onechmixquechillitzino: yn tt.º D.ˢ ynic momostlaye: niquinpixtica niquinnoCuitlahuitica: niquintzatzilitica: niquintlalnamictiti[ca y çeçem?⁴]ilhuitl: y çeçeyohual: yn amo achitō cahuitl: [2r] nonnotencahua: yn innacastitla nitzatzitica: ynic quimolnamiquillizque: yn inteyocoxcatzin: yn intechiuhcatzin ȳ teotl: tlatohuani D.ˢ niquinCuitlahuiltia ma quimotzatzililican: ma quimoyectenehuilica: ma quimotlayecoltilican: ma quichihuacan: yn iuh quimonequiltia yn tt.º D.ˢ ca niquintzatzillia: ma huian yn ichatz:ᶜᵒ ma quimoyectenehuillica ma quimotlaytlanilililitin: ynic quinmomaquilliz: yn itlaçograçiatzin: auh ⁱⁿ yehuantin çan quinenquixtia: ȳ nonemilliz: ȳ notlatequipanolliz: yeçe tel niquitoa: ca ye yc ninoquixtia: yn inhuicopa atle notechcopa: yc moᵗᵉmapatlasque yn ixpantz:ᶜᵒ yn D.ˢ yniᶜ çeçēme notzalosque: tlatemolilosq̄ yehuantin quimati: yn tleyn ic tlananquilizque: auh ȳ nehuatl: ca Cuenta nicnomaquilliz: yn D.ˢ tetatzin: yn ixquich yhuellitzin: yn otechmoyocolili: auh ynin atle yc notech motlamizque: Ca ye ynman yn notzalosque =

S.ᵗᵃ ygl.ᵃ = v Yn nehuatl. ȳ nitetlaocoliliztenantzin: yn onechmixq̄.chilli: y notlaçotelpotzin Jesu xp̄o: ynic nican ȳpampa yn tlp̄c̄ tlaca: Ca mochipa ypampa ninochoquilitica: oc çenca yn iquac yn ˢᵉme momiquilia: ypampa nicnoquia: ȳ nixayo nicnotlatlauhtilia: ȳ notlaçoçenpapaquilliztea̅meyalnantzin: ȳ ma quinmotlaocolili: ma quinmotlanextilili: yn itlachihualtzitzinhuan: macamo nenquisas: yn chicontetl:[2v]tetl⁵ SaCram.ᵗᵒ y niquinpialitica: yn iuhqui quenmanian conelehuisque: quiteoçihuisque ca niquintlaqualtiz niquimatlitis: yntla a̱miquisque: auh ca yn axcan ca niquinchixtica: ynpampa nitlaocoxtica: ma hualhuian: ma monemilizyectilliqui: ma tlatlatlaᵘʰtican: ca tlaocolilosque: yhuan ma chocacan: yhuan ma tlaocoyacan: ypampa yn intlatlacol: yn intlapilchihual

Tlachpanaliztli = v yn tiçenquiscaçentlaneltoquiliztenantzin: ca mochi melahuac: yn ticmitalhuitzinoa: Camo quilnamiqui ynontzin: amo quelehuia: çan ye quinequi ȳ ma çan ontlatlacocan: Cuix amo tel yxquich notlapal nicchihua: yn nehuatl ca mochipa niquintzatzilia: momostlaye: niquinCuitlahuiltia: ma tlachpanacan: ma yxtoçocan. ma yohuatz.ᶜᵒ mehuᵉcan: ma tlaᵗˡᵃmaçehuacan ma çecmiquican: quitosnequi ma teoyotica quitlachpanilican: yn inyollia yn imanima: ma moçahuacan: ma tlaCuallizcahuaca: ynic huel tlaocollilosque tlapopolhuililosque: auh yntlacamo ca niman amo huel calaquisque: yn itlatocachantz.ᶜᵒ yn tt.º Dios: ca hahuel tlapopolhuililosque: yntlacamo oc achtopa tlamaçehuasque: ca yn tlamasehualoni niqualhuiCa: Ca quimicmic[3r]nellia:⁷ ca ypan pohui yn ilh̄.ᶜ Ecahuastli: ynic huel calaquisque yn ilh̄.ᶜᵗˡ itec: Ca tel ayocmo huecauh Ca ye notzalosque yn ixpantz.ᶜᵒ yn tt.º Dˢ: ynic çeçenmē quimomaquilizque Cuenta yniᶜ onenque yn tlp̄c̄: macamo toteᶜʰ motemapatlasque yn ixpantz.ᶜᵒ yn D.ˢ—

---

4. Corner of document is torn off here.
5. chicontetltetl: read *chicontetl*.
6. mehuᵉcan: read *mehuacan*.
7. quimicmicnellia: read *quimicnelia*.

TIME: I am time. I am one day's time[4] of the sacred word. Our lord God gave and assigned to me the charge that every day I be guarding them, taking care of them, calling out to them, reminding them of things day and night. Not for an instant do [2r] I close my lips. I am crying out into their ears so that they will remember their creator, their maker, the deity, the ruler, God. I induce them to cry out to him, to praise him, to serve him, to do as our lord God wants. I cry out to them to go to his home, to praise him, to ask him to give them his precious grace. But they just waste my life and my work. Even so, I say, I have thus fulfilled my obligations toward them. There is nothing in regard to me with which they will defend themselves before God, as they each are called and examined. They know how they will answer. And as for me: I will give an accounting to God the father, the all-powerful one, who created us. So then, there is nothing for which they will excuse themselves by blaming me. It is time that they be called.

HOLY CHURCH: I am the compassionate mother of the one who appointed me, my precious son Jesus Christ, so that here on account of the people of earth I am always weeping, especially when one of them dies. Therefore I spill my tears. I beseech my precious mother, sacred fountain of utter happiness, to have compassion for them, to illuminate his[5] creatures. May the seventh [2v] sacrament, which I am keeping for them, not come to naught. Sometimes it is as if they will desire it, they will hunger for it. I will feed them, I will give them drink if they are thirsty. And now I am waiting for them. I am sad for their sakes. May they come, and may they come to emend their lives, may they pray. They will receive compassion. And may they weep and be sad because of their sins, their defects.

SWEEPING: You are his mother of perfect and complete faith. It is all correct, what you say. They do not remember what they do not desire; they just want to go on sinning. Do I not exert all my effort? I always cry out to them, every day. I induce them to sweep things, to keep vigil, to arise in the morning, to do penance, to suffer cold, that is, in a sacred way[6] to sweep their spirits, their souls, to fast, to abstain from food so that they will receive compassion and be pardoned. And if not, there is no way at all that they will be able to enter the royal home of our lord God. They will not be able to be pardoned if they do not first do penance. I bring the instrument of penance.[7] It does them favor, [3r] for it is considered the ladder of heaven, by which they will be able to enter into heaven. For it will not be long until they are called before our lord God so that each of them will give him an accounting of how they lived on earth. May they not use us to defend themselves before God.[8]

---

4. Perhaps "an entire lifetime" is meant.
5. "His" is probably intended rather than "her" as it is God/Christ who is the creator.
6. teoyotica: used by priests and their native aides as an equivalent for "spiritual," means "through divinity" or "by means of sacredness." In actual usage it tended to confer not divine instrumentality as much as a broader sense of holiness or an association with Christianity. Translated here and in "How to Live on Earth" as "in a sacred way"; as the more traditional "spiritual" in "The Merchant."
7. Perhaps this refers to an actual broom that Sweeping is supposed to be holding.
8. That is, as Time stated above, humanity cannot blame anything on us.

Miquistli = v Yn nehuatl ȳ nitopilecatzin: ȳ nitlayxquetzaltzin: ȳ nitititlatzin: yn ilh̄.ᶜhuicac⁸ mehuiltitica yn ixquich yhuelitzin yhuan y nican tlp̄c̄: nohuian tentimani ynic motonameyotitzinotica yn ilh̄.ᶜtl itec: yhua nohuian çemanahuac auh ma yuh ye yn inyollo yn tlp̄c̄ tlaca: ca sa mostla huiptla yn hualmotemohuis: yn D.ˢ hitlaçopiltzin ȳ quinmotlatzontequililiquiuh yn yol⁹ yhuan yn mimicque: auh y qualtin Ca quinmohuiquiliz yn itlatocachantz.ᶜᵒ yn ilhuicatl îtec auh yn amo qualtin yn amo oquimotlayeColtilique y nican tlp̄c̄: Ca quinmotlaxiliz y çentlan ȳ mictla: auh ma yuh ye yn inyollo yn tlp̄c̄ tlaca: Ca ynpan mochihuas yn tetlatzontequililizylhuitl: y çenca temamauhti yn inpan mochihuas: auh ynin ma monemilizyectilica yehica Ca ye oCan Ca ye ynma yn tlatzontequililosque: ynic tlatemolilosq̄. ynic oquimotlayeColtilique yn tt.ᵒ D.ˢ =

Santa yglᵃ = v Ca huel melahuac yn oticmotenehuillitzino: yn oticmotenquixtillitzino: Canel amitetlayecolticatzitzin[3v]huan yn amitlatequipanocatzitzinhuan: ȳ notlaçoneyolalilizçenteconetzin: ȳ notlaçonamictzin teoyotica Jesu x̄p̄o: yn ohuamechmixquechillitzino: ynic anquimotzatzililizque: anquinmotlayxpantililizque: yn itlamaquixtitzitzinhuan: yn tlp̄c̄ tlatlacohuanime: y huel çenca tlatlacoltica: oquixtlalteuhpachoque oquiçoquineloque yn inyolia yn imanima: auh yn axcan ma tihuian: ma tiquimontzatzilitin: ynic hualasque teoyotica moçencahuaquihue:¹⁰ choquistica yxayotica: auh yn nehuatl: ca niquinchixtica ynic niquinchipahuas: niquimaltis teoyotica niquinchipahuas: yca yn chiContetl SaCram:ᵗᵒ nenamictiliztli: ca niquinpialitica—

Cahuitl = v Ca niman axcan ye niauh: niquintzatzililiz: niquintlalnamictis: yn ipan çeçen ora quilnamiquisque: yn tley quichihuasque: ynic amo quinenpolosque: amo quinēquixtisque: ȳ nemilizcahuitl: yn onechmopialtilitzino ȳ tt.ᵒ D.ˢ:
Calaquiz cahuitl çan içel—

S.ᵗᵃ yglᵃ = v Ȳ niçentlaneltoquilizteotlanextli. Ca niquintlanextilia: teoyotica niquintlahuillia: yn ixquichtin x̄p̄.tianome: ynic hualasque yniquinchipahuas:¹¹ ca çenca tlatlacoltica oCuayxihuitique: ca yntla chocasque tlaocoyasque: Ca quinmotlapopolhuililiz: ȳ notlaçotelpotzin Jesu xp̄o. Ca quinmomaquiliz yn ilh̄.ᶜ tlatocayotl:—[4r]
Calaquis Santa ygl.ᵃ çan içel

Miquistli = v Ca huel tetlaocoltique yn tlp̄c̄ tlaca: yxpopoyome yn amo quilnamiqui yn iquin quenman tlatzontequililosq̄. çā yehuatl yn ahuilnemiliztli: tlatlacoltica quicatzahua yn imanima: tel niquitoa yehuantin quimati: yn tlp̄c̄: tlaca yxpopoyome: yn atlachianime: ȳ huel tlatlacoltica omixtlilmatoCaque: auh yn īyollia yn imanima: amo quintequipachoa: ma mopapacacan. ma maltican Cualtilizteotlanextiliztica: Cuix quin iquac yn inpā mochihuas yn tetlatzontequililizylhuitl: yn molnamiquisque ᶜᵘⁱˣ quin iCuac yn chocasque Ca nelli melahuac Ca niman ayocmo huel tlaocolilosque oyçentzontlahueliltic: yn tlp̄c̄ ⁱ ᵗˡᵃᶜᵃ. ca ça mostla yn ipan mochihuas ȳ tetlatzontequililizylhuitl: Ca ye oCan Ca ye iman =
Tlapitzaloz Calaquiẓ̄: miquistli Tlachpanaliztli: hualquisas Luçia hualmotequipachotas =

---

8. ilh.ᶜhuicac: read *ilhuicac*.
9. yol: scribal error; in context (and as elsewhere in this play) read *yolque*.
10. moçencahuaquihue: the final vowel appears to be an *i* corrected to *e*.
11. yniquinchipahuas: read *ynic niquinchipahuaz* or perhaps just *yn niquinchipahuaz*.

DEATH: I am the constable, I am the appointee, I am the messenger of the all-powerful one who is seated in heaven and here on earth. He is sending out sunbeams, filling up everywhere in heaven and everywhere in the world. And may the people of the earth be certain that tomorrow or the day after[9] the precious child of God will come down. He is coming to judge the living and the dead. And the good ones he will take to his royal home in heaven. But the bad ones, who did not serve him here on earth, he will throw into the depths of the place of the dead. And may the people of the earth be certain that the day of judgment will happen to them. What will happen to them is very frightening. And so, may they emend their lives because it is time, it is the moment when they will be judged, when they will be examined as to how they served our lord God.

HOLY CHURCH: It is fully correct what you have declared, what you have uttered, for you are the servants, [3v] you are the workers of my precious consolation and only child, Jesus Christ, who in a sacred way is my beloved spouse. He appointed you so that you would cry out to, you would reveal to those he has rescued, the sinners of the earth, that through sin they have thoroughly covered their spirits, their souls, with earth and dust, they have filled them with mud. And now let us go, let us go cry out to them so that they will come, they will come to prepare themselves in a sacred way, with weeping, with tears. And as for me, I am waiting for them so that I will purify them, I will bathe them, in a sacred way I will purify them with the seventh sacrament, marriage, which I am keeping for them.

TIME: Right now I am going. I will cry out to them, I will remind them each hour [so that] they will remember what they will do so that they will not squander and not waste the lifetimes that our lord God entrusted to me.

(Time exits alone.)

HOLY CHURCH: I am the sacred light of the complete faith. I illuminate, in a sacred way I shed light for all Christians, so that they will come and I will purify them. They are very dizzy in the head with sins. If they will weep and be sad my precious son, Jesus Christ, will pardon them and give them the kingdom of heaven. [4r]

(Holy Church exits alone.)

DEATH: The people of the earth are really piteous. They are blind. They do not remember that one day, sometime, they will be judged. It is just lustful living. They dirty their souls with sin. But I say the people of the earth, the blind ones, the unobservant ones, know that with sin they have really masturbated themselves black in the face.[10] And their spirits, their souls do not worry them. May they scrub themselves, may they bathe themselves with the sacred light of goodness. When the day of judgment happens to them, will they remember then? Will they weep then? It is true and correct that there is no longer any way that they can receive compassion. Four hundred times unfortunate are the people of the earth! For tomorrow the day of judgment will happen to them. It is time, it is the moment!

(Wind instruments are played. Death and Sweeping exit. Lucía enters. She comes anxiously.)

---

9. tomorrow, the day after: here and below, a common diphrase that often means "soon, in the near future."

10. Although this may seem graphic, the root verb is *matoca*, which means "to masturbate" (see Molina 1977, 53v: "Matoca. nino. palpar o tocar sus partes vergonçosas").

Luçia = v O noteotzin notlatocatzin Jesu xpō: omochiuh onotlahueliltic: yn axcan tlei nopan mochihua: yn iuhqui ye patzmiqui: y nanima yn iuhquin ye mextitlan i calaqui auh tlei nicchihuas yn axCan: ma niyauh ma ninoyolCuiti [4v] aço tepitzin yc çehuis y nanima: ma niyauh ma nicnotemoli: y noteyolCuiticatzin: Ca huel tonehua ȳ nix noyollo =

yaz Luçia contzotzonas puerta hualquisas teopixq̄:

Luçia: = v Ma motlaçonahuactz.^{co} moetzinotie: yn tt.^o D.^s notlaçotatzin:—

hualquisas teopixqui tlatos = v teopixqui = Ma mitzhualmoyacanilli yn tt.^o D.^s notlaçopiltzine: ma nican timohuicatz: tlein ticmonequiltia—

Luçia = v Ma xicmomachiltitzino: notlaçotatzin y tlein ic onihualla: macamo yc nimitz-noCualanilliz: notlaço^{ta}tzin—

Teopixqui = v Tlein ticmonequiltia: no^{tlaço}piltzine ma xicmitalhui ca yc otechmix-quechillitzino: y tt.^o D.^s ynic tamechyolmelahuasque: yn ansemanahuac tlaca—

Luçia = v Notlaçotatzin: Ca nicnequi nimoyolmelahuas:[12] yxpantz.^{co} yn tt.^o D.^s yhuan yn tehuatzin notlaçotazin—

Teopixqui = v Notlaçopiltzine: Ca Senca tinechhueltlamachtia:[13] ȳ nicaqui mitztequipachoa: mitzyolpatzmictia: ȳ motlatlacol ma tihuian: yn iteopan-chantz.^{co} yn tt^o D.^s—

Niman moyolCuitiz Luçia auh yntla ye moyolCuititica niman moquetztehuas teopixqui huel momauhtis

---

12. nimoyolmelahuas: standard *ninoyolmelahuaz*.
13. tinechhueltlamachtia: standard *tinechhuellamachtia*.

LUCÍA: Oh, O my deity, O my ruler, Jesus Christ! How unfortunate I am! What is happening to me now? It is as if my soul is now oppressed. It is as if it is now entering among the clouds![11] And what am I to do now? Let me go, let me confess. [4v] Perhaps thus my soul will be a bit calmed. Let me go, let me look for my confessor. For my face, my heart are really aching![12]

(Lucía goes and knocks on a door. Priest enters.)

LUCÍA: May our lord God be lovingly with you, O my beloved father.

(Priest enters. He speaks.)

PRIEST: May our lord God guide you, O my beloved child. Be welcome here.[13] What is it that you want?

LUCÍA: Know, O my beloved father, what I have come for. Let me not make you angry with it, O my beloved father.

PRIEST: What is it that you want, O my beloved child? Say it. For our lord God appointed us to straighten the hearts of you people of the world.[14]

LUCÍA: O my beloved father, I want to straighten my heart before our lord God and you, O my beloved father.

PRIEST: O my beloved child, what I hear pleases me greatly. Your sins worry you, they oppress you. Let us go into the temple-home of our lord God.

(Then Lucía confesses. And as she is confessing, then Priest stands up. He is very frightened.)

---

11. That is, into sinful and/or terrifying darkness or maybe just a state of confusion?

12. The possessed metaphorical diphrase -*ix*, -*yollo* (face, heart) has many connotations. The first "by itself often has to do with presence, perception, wisdom" while the second "is associated with emotion and volition" (Karttunen and Lockhart 1987, 54). In combination they often refer to one's "spirit, spirits, mood, state of morale" (54), which is the sense present here (for a more extended discussion see 54–55).

13. ma nican timohuicatz: see Carochi 1983, 67v: "mā nicān timohuīcatz, venga V.m. en hora buena," as well as Arthur J. O. Anderson's rendition of same in Sahagún 1997, 296.

14. Here and below, "to heart-straighten" was commonly used in colonial Nahuatl texts to mean "to confess." The more literal gloss is used here in order to distinguish between this and *yolcuitia* (to acknowledge one's failings), which is translated as "confess" (or sometimes "profess," depending on context).

Teopixqui = v Jesus: Jesus: Tlein tiquitoa: tleyn oticchiuh: Cuix amo tixpāna:[14] Cuix amo ticmati ca çentzonpa huey tlatlacolli [5r] yn oticchiuh: omochiuh omoçentzontlahueliltic: ma xicmaquixtiani ma ᵒxicchipahuani yn manima: Tle yca yn aic oticcelli yn teoyotl: yn çā diablo otichuicalti: yn chicontetl S.ᵗᵒ SaCram̄.ᵗᵒ yn teoyotica nenamictiliztli: omochiuh omoçentzontlahueliltic: yn axcan yn aic oticnec yn timonamictis yn tlpc̄: auh ma yuh ye ȳ mix ȳ moyollo: Ca timonamictitiuh: yn onpa y çentlan yn mictlan: Ca momasehual mochihuas: yn mictlan tlayyohuilliztli: auh yn axcan tlei Cuenta ticmomaquiliz ȳ moteotzin motlatocatzin ca niman ahuel timopalehuis yn axcan: yehica ca ye yman ca ye ohuaçic: yn itetlatzontequililitzin: yn D.ˢ axcan ticmahuiçoz: ynic hualmotemohuis: yn tla D.ˢ ytlaçopiltzin: ȳ quinmotlatzontequililiquiuh: y yolque yhuan yn mimicque ynic çeçenyacan Cuenta quimomaquillizque: yn intechiuhcatzin D.ˢ Auh no yhuan tehuatl: tinesis yn ixpantz.ᶜᵒ yn ᵐᵒmelahuacatetlatzontequililiani hin D.ˢ hitlaçopiltzin: Jesu xp̄ō =

Calaquis teopixqui mocahuas Luçia—
Luçia = v A yoyahue Diose: omochiuh onohueyçentzontlahueliltic: yn tlpc̄. tleyn onicac tleyn onechmolhuilli: yn itlaçotzin D.ˢ quenin çenca temamauhti: tetequipacho. yn iuhqui quimitalhuia yn itlaçotzin D.ˢ ma noçᵒ honicaquini: onicneltocani yn tleyn onechmonahuatiliaya: y nodios[15] yhuan y notatzin y nonantzin: yhuan yn ixquichtin nohuanpohuan: yn ix[5v]n ixquich[16] ynic onechyolmaxiltiaya: y ça notlahuel omoCuepaya: y çan onictlatelchihuiliaya: y S.ᵗᵒ SaCram.ᵗᵒ teoyotica nenamictiliztli: omochiuh onoçentzontlahueliltic yn axcan: ma sentelchihualo yn atlamachiliztli: tlen onax tleyn onechonquixti: yn atlamachiliztli: ma sentelchihualo yn tlpc̄tli: yhuan i cahuitl: yn axcan ye tzonquisas ye tlamis: yn çemanahuactli: omochiuh onohueyçentzontlahueliltic ȳ nihueytlatlacohuani—
Tlapitzalos hualquisasque yolque motlallizque tlaltitech: yhuan Luçia mocamachalpachotiesque: hualquisas amtex̄p̄ō: tlatec quitlaliz tlahuelilocatilmatli: pani quitlaliz tunica quihualquetztas[17] yn iopochmapil: TlaCueponiz ynic hualquisas—
Amtex̄p̄ō= v Notlaçopilhuane: Cuix amo annechiximati: ca nehuatl: yn amopampa ᵒⁿitotoneuh tlpc̄. amopampa onitlayyohui: auh yn axcan ma yuh ye yn amoyollo ca nictlamis: nicpopolos yn tlpc̄tli: ma xinechneltocacan notlachihualhuane: ca namechpopolhuis: yn amotlatlacol: yn amotlapilchihual: ma xinechneltocacan: ma xiquitacan y noᵗˡᵃezⁱᵒyotzin[18]: yʰᵘᵃ noᵗˡᵃçᵒnacayotzin—[19]
1ᵒ yolqui = Camo tehuatl. yn ticmitzchia[20]: ca hualmohuicas yn toteotzi yn totlatocatzin: ca huel yehuatzin topampa omotlayyohuihuiltitzino omo[6r]omomiquillitzino:[21] Cruztitech oquimomāmaçohualtillique: ypampa yn toʰᵘᵉⁱçentzontlatlacol:[22]—

14. tixpāna: read *ticristiana*.
15. nodios: it is extremely rare for the Spanish loanword *Dios* (God) to be possessed.
16. yn ixn ixquich: read *yn ixquich*.
17. quihualquetztaz: read *quihualquetzaz* unless *quihualquetztiyaz* was meant.
18. noᵗˡᵃezⁱᵒyotzin: read *notlaçoezyotzin*.
19. The superscript in the preceding lines is in a slightly different hand.
20. ticmitzchia: read *timitzchia*.
21. omoomomiquillitzino: read *omomiquilitzino*.
22. toʰᵘᵉⁱçentzontlatlacol: the superscript characters are in a different hand.

PRIEST: Jesus! Jesus! What are you saying? What have you done? Are you not a Christian? Do you not know that four hundred times you have done great sins? [5r] Four hundred times unfortunate are you! If only you had saved, if only you had purified your soul! Why did you never receive the sacrament of marriage?[15] Just to the Devil you sent the seventh holy sacrament, marrying in a sacred way. Four hundred times unfortunate are you! Now you never wanted to get married on earth. But be certain that you are going to get married there in the depths of the place of the dead. What you will merit will be suffering in the place of the dead. And now what accounting will you give to your deity, your ruler? For in no way can you help yourself now, because it is already time, God's judgment has already arrived. Now you will marvel at how God's beloved child will come down. He is coming to judge the living and the dead, such that they each will give an accounting to their maker, God. And you, too, will appear before the just judge, God's beloved child, Jesus Christ.

(Priest exits. Lucía remains.)

LUCÍA: Ah, alas! O God! Four hundred times greatly unfortunate am I on earth! What did I hear? What did God's precious one say to me? How very frightening and worrying it is, what God's precious one says. If only I had listened, if only I had believed what my God was commanding me, along with my father, my mother, and all my neighbors. All of this, [5v] which they used to certify to me, used to just turn into my indignation. I used to just scoff at the holy sacrament, marrying in a sacred way. Four hundred times unfortunate am I now! May presumptuousness be despised! What have I done? What did presumptuousness avail me? May the earth and time be despised! Now the world is about to come to an end, about to be finished off. Four hundred times unfortunate am I! I am a great sinner!

(Wind instruments are played. The living enter. They sit on the ground, along with Lucía. Their jaws hang open. The Antichrist enters. On the inside he wears a cloak of wickedness; on top he wears a tunic. He raises the fingers of his left hand. Things explode as he emerges.)

ANTICHRIST: O my beloved children, do you not know me? It is I, who endured pains on earth on your behalf, who suffered on your behalf. And now, be certain that I will finish off, I will destroy the earth. Believe me, O my creations, for I will pardon you your sins, your defects. Believe me. Look at my precious blood, and my precious body.

FIRST LIVING PERSON: It is not you whom we are awaiting. Our deity, our ruler will come. It is he who suffered and died on our behalf. [6r] Because of our four hundred great sins they stretched him out by the arms on the cross.

---

15. teoyotl: this abstract collective noun can be rendered in many ways depending on context. For the single best explanation of this specific item, see the celebrated grammar of Father Horacio Carochi of 1645, 52v–53r (in Carochi 1983). He specifically states on 52v that Nahuatl speakers use *teoyotl* as meaning "el Sacramento del matrimonio" (the sacrament of marriage) and that they use it "quando dan palabra à vna muger de casarse con ella" (when they promise a woman that they will marry her).

Luçia = v̱ Ca quemecatzin. Ca tehuatzin yn timitztochialia: noteotzin notlatocatzin: ma xitechmopopolhuililitzino: yn totlatlacol =

Amtexp̄.ᵗᵒ = v̱ Ca quemaca namechpalehuis: Cuix amo anquimati ca yxquich nohuelitzin: y çemanahuac—

MoCuicaehuas christos factus es: motlapos ylh̄.ᶜ hualmoquixtiz xp̄o Cualmoyacanilliz San miguel Cualmohuiquilliz pexotli: auh yn xp̄o quihualmohuiquilis Crus: ylh̄.ᶜuicatenpa²³ moquetzinos: auh yn amtexp̄o calactehuas tlaCueponiz—

xp̄o: = v̱ ma xihualmohuica: yn tinoyaotlayacancatzin yn tiS.ⁿ migel: y nican ylhuicatl itec: yn axCan Ca ye ynman y nictlamiz nicpolos yn cahuitl: yn motenehua Juicio final: yn tetlatzontequililizylhuitl: Ca yuhqui ypan onictlalli: y noteotenahuatiltzin: Ca nitlachpanas: Ca nicchipahuas yn ylh̄.ᶜ yhuan yn tlp̄ctli: ca huel otlaCatzauhque: yn tlp̄c. tlaca: yn yolque yhuan yn mimicque: ypampa yn imaCualnemiliz: auh yn axcan ma xiquinmixitilli:²⁴ yn yolque yhuan y mimicque: y qualtin yhuan yn amo Cualtin: auh y~n~ ~amo~ Cualtin: ca niquinomaquiliz yn ylh̄.ᶜ yn inxochinetlamachtil: yn ylh̄.ᶜ chalchihuitl: neapantli: yn ylh̄.ᶜ çoyatl: auh yn amo Cualtin ma yuh ye yn inyollo: ca ymaxcā mochihuas: y mictlan calli: yhuan y mictlan tlayyohui[6v]liztli: yehica camo huel oquipixque: ȳ noteotenahuatiltzin = hualmotemohuis xp̄o. S.ⁿ migel motlalitzinos xp̄o =

xp̄o: v̱ Ca ye onimitznonahuatillitzino: yn tlein ticmochihuillitzinos: yn tinoyaotlayacancatzin

S.ⁿ miguel = v̱ Ca ye Cuallitzin notlaçotemachticatzine: ma yolican yn mimicque: ma mosCallican yn yolque: ma quiCuican yn inmomio: yhuan ma quinechicocan: yhuan ma conanacan: yn intlalo yn inçoquio: ma xiquinmomaquillitzino: ȳ nescaliliztli: yn espiritu S.ᵗᵒ yhuan yn imanima: ynic huel mitzmonanquililizque: ynic quitosque yn tley qualli: oquichiuhque yhuan yn tlen amo qualli: oquichiuhq̄. yn intlachihual =

xp̄o = v̱ Ca ycan y nohuellitzin: ca moscallizque ⁱᵒˡⁱᶻq̄.²⁵ ca niquinmaca: ȳ nescaliliztli: yn iuhqui onimoscallitzino:²⁶ yn yeilhuitica çan no yuhqui ma moscallican: y notlachihualhuan—

Tlapitzalos. mocalaquis xp̄o: oc çe puerta ayocmo motlecahuis ylh̄.ᶜ niman motlapichilliz Sn. mig.ˡ =

1ᵒ Angel = v̱ Ximoscallican yn anyolque: Ca ytencopatziᶜᵒ: yn D.ˢ xicCuiCan yn amonaCayo—

Oc çepa motlaPichiliz S.ⁿ miguel y canin yesque mimicque quinmotzatzililiz—

2ᵒ Angel = v̱ Surgite mortui benite a yudiçio: ximosCallican yn anmimicque: xihualquisacan: yn tlalan ancate xicCuiCan yn amonacayo: Ca ytenCopatz.ᶜᵒ yn tt.ᵒ D.ˢ

Ni[can²⁷ h]ualquisasque yn mimicque: nacateme²⁸ [7r] oc çepa motlaPichiliz San miguel—

---

23. ylh̄.ᶜuicatenpa: read *ilhuicatenpan*.
24. xiquinmixitilli: originally read *xiquinmexitilli*.
25. The superscript characters are in a slightly different hand.
26. onimoscallitzino: standard *oninozcalitzino*.
27. Torn corner; text in brackets may be all that is missing.
28. nacateme: while *nacatzonteme* suggests itself as a written possibility (see 1 verso above), it is not a logical choice given the context.

LUCÍA: Yes, it is you whom we are awaiting, O my deity, O my ruler. Pardon us our sins.

ANTICHRIST: Yes, I will help you. Do you not know that I am all-powerful in the world?

(Christus factus est[16] is raised in song. Heaven opens. Christ enters. He leads forth Saint Michael, who brings scales. And Christ brings forth a cross. He stands at the edge of heaven. And the Antichrist rushes in. Things explode.)

CHRIST: Come, my war leader, Saint Michael. Here in heaven it is now high time that I bring time to an end, that I destroy it. It is called Final Judgment, the day of judging people. As I set down in my sacred commands, I will sweep things, I will purify heaven and earth. The people of earth, the living and the dead, have greatly dirtied things because of their bad lives. And now, awaken them, the living and the dead, the good and the bad. And to the good ones I will give their heavenly flowery riches, heavenly jades and garments, heavenly palm fronds. But as for the bad, may they be certain that the house of the place of the dead and the sufferings of the place of the dead will become their possessions, [6v] because they were not able to keep my sacred commands.

(Christ descends; [also] Saint Michael. Christ sits down.)

CHRIST: I have already given you orders as to what you will do, my war leader.

SAINT MICHAEL: Very well, O my beloved teacher. Let the dead come to life, let the living rouse themselves. Let them take their bones and collect them, and let them take on their earth, their clay.[17] Give them reviving, [through] the Holy Spirit, along with their souls, so that they will be able to answer you, so that they will say what they did that was good and what they did that was bad, their deeds.

CHRIST: Through my power they will revive, they will come to life. I give them reviving, as I revived on the third day. In just the same way let my creations revive.

(Wind instruments are played. Christ exits by another door; he will no longer ascend to heaven. Then Saint Michael plays a wind instrument.)

FIRST ANGEL: Rouse yourselves, you living ones! By order of God take your bodies.

(Saint Michael again plays a wind instrument. He cries out to the dead where they will be.)

SECOND ANGEL: Surgite mortui venite ad judicium.[18] Revive, you dead ones! Come out, you who are underground! Take your bodies, by order of our lord God!

(Here enter the dead, fully fleshed.[19] [7r] Saint Michael again plays a wind instrument.)

---

16. *Christus factus est*: short for *Christus factus est pro nobis obediens usque ad mortem* (Christ became for us obedient even unto death). Antiphon sung on Holy Thursday, Good Friday, and Holy Saturday in the reformed breviary (see *Breviarium romanum* 1961, 1:837, 842, 859, 861, 873).

17. earth, clay: a standard diphrase (often found in testaments) that means "earthly body/bodies."

18. Surgite mortui venite ad judicium: Arise, O dead, and come to judgment. Apparently not a biblical passage; provenience unknown. This passage is inscribed on a relief sculpture of the Final Judgment at San Andrés Calpan, Puebla.

19. Tentative translation of *nacateme*.

S.ⁿ Miguel = v̱ yn axcan Ca ye ⁰anmosCallique: ma ximosentlallican ca axcan anquichihuasque Cuenta: yn ixpantz.ᶜᵒ yn momelahuacatetlatzontequililiani Jues: macayac motlapololtiz xicmochialican: yn amoteotzin yn amoteyocoxcatzin D.ˢ = Tlapitzalos mocalaquis S.ⁿ mig:ˡ hualquisas antexp̄o quincacayahuaquiuh yn yolque yhuan mimicque: achi huecauh hualmoquixtiz xp̄.ᵗᵒ—

Antexp̄o = v̱ Ca ye onihuala ma xicneltillican: ȳ notlaçotlatolltzin²⁹ = Mehuas te deū laudamos calactehuas antexp̄o: tlaCueponiz. niman hualmoquixtiz xp̄o: hualahuitiasque ⁰1 Angel y ⁰2 Angel: motlayacanilliz S.ⁿ miguel—

xp̄.ᵗᵒ = v̱ xihualmohuica yn tehuatzin: yn ylh̄.ᶜ tiepyollotzintli ȳ tiSan mig.ˡ arcangel: ma xiquinmonochilli: yn yolque yhuan yn mimicque: oCatCa ma niCan nixpan: moçentlalican: ynic niquinchihuilliz Cuenta yn oc onenque ȳ tlp̄c =

S.ⁿ mig.ˡ = v̱ ma yuh quimochihua: notlaçotemachticatzine: ma niquintzatzilli =—
Motlapichilliz S.ⁿ mig:ˡ niman çeçenyacan yasque yn ixpantz.ᶜᵒ ȳ xp̄o: motlalitzinos auh yn angel tlapexohuis motlanquaquetzas primero micqui—

xp̄o: v̱ xihualauh yn tehuatl: Cuix oticchiuh y notenahuatiltzin [7v] yn oc tlp̄c. otinemia: otipapatlātinenca: ma xitlato xinechnanquilli: yn iuhqui otitlatohuaya: yn tlp̄c: San no yuhqui xitlato yn axcan—

⁰1 micqui = v̱ noteotzine notlatocatzine: Ca onicchiuh onictequipano: onicneltilli ȳ moteotenahuatiltzin: Ca onicchiuh ȳ motlanahuatiltzin: ma xicmotlatlanilli y noangeltzin: notlaçotemachtiCatzine—

xp̄o = v̱ Otinechmocnelili: ca ylh̄.ᶜ timoçentlamachtiz timoCuiltonos yn aic tlamiz tzonquisas: yn mopapaquilliz—
quimoteochihuilliz: conmotopehuiliz yn S.ⁿ miguel ymayecācopatz.ᶜᵒ yn xp̄o—

xp̄o = v̱ xihualauh yn tehuatl: yn tiyolqui aquin oticmahuistilli yn tlp̄c: yhuan aquin otictlaçotlaya—

⁰1 yolqui = v̱ Ca tehuatzin yn tinoteotzin: yn tinotlatocatzin—

xp̄o = v̱ Yntla nelli nimoteouh: nimotlatocauh Cuix oticchiuh ȳ noteotenahuatiltzin: Cuix oticneltilli—

⁰1 yolqui = v̱ Camo onicchiuh noteotzine: ma xinechmotlapopolhuililitzino ȳ nitlatlacohuani—

xp̄o = v̱ yn axcan Ca niman ayocmo ōca ᵗᵉtlapopolhuiliztli xiyauh—
Conmotopehuilliᶻ yn S.ⁿ mig:ˡ yn yolqui oc çentlapal niman³⁰ motlaCuaquetzas 2 micqui yxpantz.ᶜᵒ yn xp̄o =

xp̄o = v̱ xihualauh yn tehuatl: yn timicqui otiCatca: Catli yn oticchiuh yn oᶜ tlp̄c.tzᶜᵒ: otinenca: Cuix otinechtequipano Cuix otinechtlayeColti yn tlp̄c ma xinechnanquilli = [8r]

2⁰ micqui = v̱ Ca niman amotzin: ma xinechmotlapopolhuililitzino: notlatocatzine: notemachticatzine Diose—

xp̄o = v̱ yn axcan Cayocmo onca yn ipan yn tetlatzontequililiztli: cayocmo onca yn tetlapopolhuililiztli: xiyauh—
Conmotopehuilliz San mig:ˡ ȳ micqui auh yn demonios contilanasque quinmanasque. oc çentlapal motlāquaquetzas 2 yolqui Luçia—

---

29. notlaçotlatolltzin: read *notlaçotlatoltzin*.
30. Something illegible follows in superscript.

SAINT MICHAEL: Now you have revived. Gather together. Now you will make an accounting before the just sentencer of people, the judge. Let no one be confused. Wait for your deity, your creator, God.
(Wind instruments are played. Saint Michael exits. The Antichrist enters. He comes jeering at the living and the dead. In a little while Christ enters.)
ANTICHRIST: Now I have come. Fulfill my precious words.
(The Te deum laudamus[20] is raised [in song]. The Antichrist rushes in. Things explode. Then Christ enters. First Angel and Second Angel enter. Saint Michael leads the way.)
CHRIST: Come, you heavenly pearl, Saint Michael the Archangel! Summon the living and those who were dead. Let them gather together here before me so that I will make an accounting of them, of when they still lived on earth.
SAINT MICHAEL: May it so be done, O my beloved teacher. Let me cry out to them.
(Saint Michael plays a wind instrument. Then they each go before Christ. He sits down. And the angel weighs things on a scale. First Dead Person kneels.)
CHRIST: Come, you! Did you carry out my commands [7v] while you were still living on earth, you were flitting about? Speak. Answer me, the way that you used to speak on earth. Speak in the same way now.
FIRST DEAD PERSON: O my deity, O my ruler, I carried out, I worked at, I fulfilled your sacred commands. I carried out your orders. Ask my [guardian] angel, O my beloved teacher.
CHRIST: Thank you. In heaven you will be utterly happy, you will prosper. Your joyfulness will never be finished or come to an end.
(He blesses him. Saint Michael pushes him to Christ's right-hand side.)
CHRIST: Come, you living one. Whom did you honor on earth, and whom did you love?
FIRST LIVING PERSON: You, you who are my deity, you who are my ruler.
CHRIST: If it is true that I am your deity, I am your ruler, did you carry out my sacred commands? Did you fulfill them?
FIRST LIVING PERSON: I did not do it, O my deity. Pardon me. I am a sinner.

CHRIST: Today there no longer is any pardon at all. Go!
(Saint Michael pushes [First] Living Person to the other side. Then Second Dead Person kneels before Christ.)
CHRIST: Come, you who were dead. What did you do while you still lived on earth? Did you work for me? Did you serve me on earth? Answer me! [8r]

SECOND DEAD PERSON: Not at all. Pardon me, O my ruler, O my teacher, O God!

CHRIST: Today in the time of judgment there is no longer any pardon. Go!

(Saint Michael pushes [Second] Dead Person away. And the demons drag him off. They lay him on the other side. Second Living Person, Lucía, kneels.)

---

20. *Te deum laudamus*: "'We praise you as God.' This is the famous hymn simply known as Te deum. It was used in ceremonies of thanksgiving" (personal communication, Stafford Poole, C.M.).

x̄p̄.to = v xihualauh yn tiyolqui Cuix oticchiuh y noteotenahuatiltzin: yn matlactetl: Cuix otiquintlaçotlac yn mohuanpohuā yhuan y motatzin yn monantzin—

o2 yolqui Luçia Ca quemacatzin ca oc achtopa tehuatzin: yn tinoteotzin tinotlatocatzin: onimitznotlaçotilli: ca çatepan y notatzin y nonātzin—
x̄p̄.to = v yntla nelli nimoteouh yhuan otinechtlaçotlac: achtopan çatepan yn motatzin yn monantzin: Cuix oticchiuh y notenahuatiltzin: yhuan yn itenahuatiltzin: y notlaçomahuiznantzi yn ipan chicontetl: S.to SaCram̄.to teoyotica nenamictilliztli: Cuix teoyotica otimopix: ynic otine yn tlp̄c̄: catli yn otiqui^{x}nexti =

Luçia = v Ca hamotzin Camo onimitznotequipanilhuitzino: yhuan amo honicmiximachilli:[31] yn motlaçonantzin: ma xinechmotlapopolhuililitzino: noteotzin notlatocatzin—
x̄p̄o = v Yn axcan Canel ayc totechcacopa otlato: yn moyollo yn tlp^c: yn san yehuatl: yn mahuilnemilliz: otictequipanohuaya - ma xiyauh ma xicchihua: aço hoquitla[32] tiquilcahua: yn mahuilnemilliz: ma xictequipano: ma yuh ye yn moyollo: Catle ic timotemachiz: yn ylh̄.^{c} omotlahueliltic yn axcā [8v] yn aic oticnec otimonamicti: yn tlp̄c̄. Ca otictlan yn mictlan calli: momasehual omochiuh: ma xiyauh ma xiquimita: yn aquiquen otiquintlayecolti: camo nimitzyximati =
Conmotopehuilliz ynhuicopa yn Demonios =
x̄p̄o[33] = v xihualauh yn tehuatl: yn tiyolqui oticatca yn tlp̄c̄: Tlein huel omitzyolcocohuaya: Cuix yehuatl y noteotlatoltzin: Cuix otinechtzatzilitinenca: ȳ mocochia ȳ monenemia =

o3 yolqui = v Ca niman ayc onimitznolcahuilli: y notlaCuayan ȳ natlian: y nonenemiyan: yhua nocochia: notlaçotemachticatzine:—
x̄p̄o = V Ca hotinechmocnelili: notlachihualtzine: ca çā no yuhqui yn nehuatl: ca semicac onimitzylnamictinenca: auh ca nimitzpialitica: yn moxochicoscauh =
Conmotopehuilliz S.n mig.l yntlan yn qualtin =
x̄p̄o = v xihualhuian: yn mictlan anchaneque: ma xiquinhuicacan: yn amotetlayecolticahuan: yn sentlani mictlan: auh ȳ çihuantlahueliloc: ma onpa xichuicaca: yn itec—yn tletemascalli onpa xictoneuhcapolocan—
o2 Demo: v ttoE: otitechmocnellillitzino: Ca ye yuh ca yn toyollo: Ca san oticchixticnemi:[34] yn mohuanlalilitzin: otomasehualtic otlaçotlacauhqui: yn motlaçoyollotzin: ma tiquintomasehuican: yn motlachihualtzitzinhuan = Ma xoconCuitihuetzin: yn tletepozmecatl: yhuan yn tletepoztopinlli:[35] yc tiquinhuitequisque: yhuan xicmolhuilli: yn totlatocatzi[9r]catzin[36]: Lusifer ca ye onpa tiquinhuica: yntetlayecolticatzitzinhuā ma yçiuhcan quihualmotitlanilli: yn tletepostzatzastli: yn ocan tiquinhuicasque: yn itetlayecolticatzitzinhuan—
Calaquis Satanas: canatiuh tletepostzatzastli: =

---

31. honicmiximachilli: standard *oniciximachili*.
32. hoquitla: read *oc itla*.
33. It appears that someone first wrote *yolqui*, crossed it out, and then put an x before the y, changed the y to p and added an overbar, with the intent of creating the x̄p̄o we show in this transcription.
34. oticchixticnemi: perhaps to be read as either *oticchixtinenque* or *ticchixtinemi*.
35. tletepoztopinlli: read *tletepoztopilli*.
36. totlatocatzicatzin: read *totlatocatzin*.

CHRIST: Come, you who are a living person! Did you carry out my sacred commands, the ten of them? Did you love your neighbors, and your father and your mother?

SECOND LIVING PERSON, LUCÍA: Yes. It is you, my deity, my ruler, whom I loved first, afterwards my father and my mother.

CHRIST: If it is true that I am your deity and you loved me first and afterward your father and your mother, did you carry out my commands, and the command of my beloved honored mother, in the seventh sacrament, marrying in a sacred way? Did you guard yourself in a sacred way[21] when you lived on earth? What have you accomplished?

LUCÍA: No. I did not work for you and I did not recognize your beloved mother. Pardon me, O my deity, O my ruler!

CHRIST: Now, truly your heart never spoke to us on earth. It was only your lustful living that you used to work at. Go, do it. Perhaps you are forgetting something else of your lustful living. Work at it. Be certain that you may hope for nothing in heaven. How unfortunate you are now, [8v] that you never wanted to get married on earth. You have won the house of the place of the dead. You have merited it. Go! See those whom you served. I do not know you.
(He pushes her toward the demons.)

CHRIST: Come, you who were a living person on earth. What is giving your heart such pain? Is it my sacred word? Did you go about crying out to me when you were sleeping and when you were going about?

THIRD LIVING PERSON: I never ever forgot you, in my eating, in my drinking, in my going about, and in my sleeping, O my beloved teacher.

CHRIST: Thank you, O my creation. It is just the same with me: I always went about remembering you. And I am keeping your flowery necklace for you.
(Saint Michael pushes him among the good ones.)

CHRIST: Come, you residents of the place of the dead. Take your servants to the depths of the place of the dead. And the wicked woman, take her into the sweatbath of fire. Torment her miserably there!

SECOND DEMON: O our lord, we thank you. We are certain that we have just been going about waiting for your coming. We are fortunate! Your precious heart has been very generous. May we merit your creations. Grab up the fiery chains and the fiery metal staff with which we will beat them and tell our ruler, [9r] Lucifer, that we are taking his servants over there. Let him quickly send the fiery metal warping frame[22] there where we will take his servants.

(Satan enters. He goes along grasping the fiery metal warping frame.)

---

21. That is, practiced chastity.
22. yn tletepoztzatzaztli: see Sahagún 1997, 278.

Satanas = v Ca ye nican niqualhuica mochi ynic tiquimilpizque: ynic amo çe tomac cholotehuas: axcan ye ticpia tauh totlaqual: yn onpa y sentlani mictlan: yn ixquich totlapal oticchiuhque: ynic tomac ohuetzque: yn totetlayecolticahuan =

Mochtin quitosque tt.ºE ma xi^{te}chmopalehuilli =
xp̄o = v Ayoquic anmotemachizque: ma yuh ye yn amoyollo: ca semicac amechtoneuhcapollosq̄: yc çenmayan yn onpa y sentlani mictlan—
Oc çepa mochintī quitosq̄: ttºE: Diose ma San xitechmomaquixtilli: yn titlacohuanime[37] = <u>niman</u> quincalaquisque TlaCueponiz tzatzitasque: auh ȳ qualtin quimaquisque xochicoronaçoyatl: motlecahuis xp̄o: ylh̄.^c nepantla escalera quinmolhuiliztin[38]—
xp̄o = v NotetlayeColticahuane: ma xihualmotlecahuican: xicmoCuilliqui: ȳ namechpialia yn amonetlamachtil yn ayc tlamis: yn ayc tzonquisas—
Tlapitzalos tlecosque yn angeles ^{xp̄o} yhuan yn Cualtin niman quihualquixtizque Luçia: tlepapalome yn ipipilouh: çe cohuatl ycozqui yhuan ç^e yc quicuitlal[9v] pisque: hualtzatzitias quinanquilizque Demonios =
º1 Demº: v xinenemi tlahueliloque: Cuix amo tiquilnamiqui yn tlein oticchiuh yn tlp̄c̄. axcan timitztlaxtlahuisq̄. yn onpa y sentlani mictlan: xinenemi xitotoca =

Luçia = v omochiuh onoçentzontlahueliltic: ȳ nihueytlatlacohuani: o nomasehual omochiuh yn mictlan <u>calli</u> =
Satanas = v Cuix quin axcan yn titzatzin: yn titlahueliloc axcan timitzpapaquiltisque yn onpa y sentlani mitlan[39]: axcan timitznamictisq̄. yn onpa yn totecpanchan ypampa yn ayc otimonamitin: yn tlp̄c̄. xitotoca xine^{ne}mi: Ca mitzhualmochialitica yn totlatocauh Luçifer—
Luçia Ay: Ay: omochiuh onotlahueliltic: ȳ nitlatlacohuani: o nomasehual omochiuh yn mictlan yyohuiliztli:[40] ma noço camo onitlacatini yn tlp̄c̄: ay: ay: ma çentelchihualo yn tlp̄c̄^{tli}: yhuan yn Cahuitl, yn ipan onitlacat: ma no çentelchihualo y nonantzin yn quinin onechiuh: ay. ma sentelchihualo yn chichihualayotl, ynic oninohuapauh: ma no çentelchihualo yn tlein oniCuaya: yhuan yn tlein oniquiya yn tlp̄c̄: ay ma sentelchihualo yn tlalli yn onictelecçaya: yhua yn tlei tzotzomatli onicnoquentiaya Ca mochi tletl: omecuep.[41] ay. çenca ye nechtlatia: yn ⁿⁱcan nonacaztitech pilcatihuitze: yn tlepapalome: Ca quinescayotia ynic oninoqualnextia[10r]tiaya:[42] y nopipilol auh ȳ nican noquechtlan teCuixtihuitz: çenca temamauhti tlecohuatl, ca quinescayotia y noquechcozqui onictlaliaya: auh y niCan ic niCuitlalpitihuitz: çenca temamauhti tlecohuatl: yyollo yn mictlan calli: ca yehuatl quinescayotia ynic oninotlamachtiaya yn tlp̄c̄: ay ay. ma noço onino^{na}mictiani ay. omochiuh onotlahueliltic—
º1 demº: v axcan mochi tictzacuaz ticyxtlahuas: yn amo tlen ipan otiquimitaya: yn mohuanpohuan yn tlp̄c̄. = quihuitequisque =

37. titlacohuanime: read *titlatlacohuanime*.
38. quinmolhuiliztin: perhaps *quinmolhuilitzinoz* was meant.
39. mitlan: read *mictlan*.
40. yyohuiliztli: read *tlayhiyohuiliztli*.
41. omecuep: read *omocuep*.
42. oninoqualnextiatiaya: read *oninoqualnextiaya*.

SATAN: I am bringing everything right here with which we will tie them up so that not one will flee from our hands. Now we have our drink and our food, there in the depths of the place of the dead. We exerted all our efforts so that our servants fell into our hands.
(All of them say "O our lord, help us!")
CHRIST: Never again will you be hopeful. Be certain that they will torment you miserably forever, eternally, there in the depths of the place of the dead.
(Again they all say "O our lord, O God, just save us sinners!" Then they make them go in.[23] Things explode. They go crying. And the good ones put on flowery crowns of palm fronds. Christ ascends. In the middle of the ladder he says to them:)

CHRIST: O my servants, come on up! Come and take what I am keeping for you, your riches which will never be finished, which will never come to an end!
(Wind instruments are played. The angels, Christ and the good ones ascend. Then they bring out Lucía. Fire butterflies are her earrings, a snake her necklace, and they tie one around her waist. [9v] *She comes crying out. The demons answer her:)*
FIRST DEMON: Get moving, O wicked one! Do you not remember what you did on earth? Now we will repay you there in the depths of the place of the dead. Get moving, run along!
LUCÍA: Four hundred times unfortunate am I! I am a great sinner! Oh, I have merited the house of the place of the dead!
SATAN: Not until now do you cry out, you wicked one? Now we will make you joyful there in the depths of the place of the dead. Now we will get you married, there in our palatial home, because you never got married on earth. Run along, get moving! Our ruler, Lucifer, is waiting for you.
LUCÍA: Ah! Ah! How unfortunate I am! I am a sinner. I have merited suffering in the place of the dead. If only I had not been born on earth! Ah! Ah! May the earth be entirely cursed, and the time in which I was born. May my mother who made me also be despised! Ah! May the breast milk with which I was nurtured be despised! May that which I used to eat and that which I used to drink on earth be despised. Ah! May the earth I used to kick be despised, and the rags I used to wear, for they all have turned into fire! Ah! Greatly do they burn me, the fire butterflies that come hanging here from my ears. They signify how I used to beautify myself [10r] with my earrings. And here, wound around my neck, is a very frightening fire serpent. It signifies my necklaces that I used to put on. And here I come girded with a very frightening fire serpent, the heart of the house of the place of the dead. It signifies how I used to enjoy myself on earth. Ah! Ah! If only I had gotten married! Ah! How unfortunate I am!
FIRST DEMON: Now you will pay a penalty, you will make restitution for everything. You had no esteem for your neighbors on earth.
(They beat her.)

---

23. That is, take them offstage.

Sathaz = v xinenemi tlahueliloq̄. Cuix quin axcan yn tiquilnamiqui ma oximonamictiani: quenin amo otiquilnamic yn oc tlp̄c. otinemia: Ca tel axcan mochi tictlaxtlahuas: yn motlahuelilocayo Xitotoca xinenemi = Quihuitequisque Ça ic quicalaquisque: TlaCueponiz. quitlapichilitasque Demonios niman hualquisas teopixqui—

teopixqui = v Notlaçopilhuane x̄p̄tianomeE: D.s ytlachihualtzitzinhuane: Ca ye ohuanquimotillique yn tetzauhtlamahuiçolli: Ca melahuac Ca teoamoxpan yCuiliuhtoc: ma ximimatican ximosCalica ximotesCahuiCan: yn iuhqui ypan omochiuh yn amoanpo auh macamo no yuhqui amopan mochihuas. Ca machiotl: octacatl. techmomaquilia yn tt.º D.s Ca mochihuatiuh yn mostla yn huiptla yn tetlatzonquililizylhuitl:[43] ma cā xicmotlatlauhtilican: yn tt.º Jesu x̄p̄o: yhuan yn yehua [10v]tzin yn çihuapilli S.ta m.a ynic quimotlatlauhtiliz yn itlaçomahuiconetzin[44] Jesu x̄p̄o ynic çatepan anquimomasehuisque anquicnopilhuisque yn ylh̄.c papaquiliztli: yn gloria ma y mochihua =

Abe maria[45]

---

43. tetlatzonquililizylhuitl: read *tetlatzontequililizylhuitl* (as above).
44. itlaçomahuiconetzin: read *itlaçomahuizconetzin*.
45. Abe maria: in a different hand. This is actually at the bottom of 10v, with approximately three-fourths of the space on the page separating it from the last line of this drama.

SATAN: Get moving, O wicked one! Not until now do you remember that you should have gotten married? How is it that you did not remember it while you were still living on earth? But now you will make restitution for all your wickedness. Run along! Get moving!

(They beat her. Just thus they make her go in. Things explode. The demons play wind instruments. Then Priest enters.)

PRIEST: O my beloved children, O Christians, O creations of God! Now you have seen an ominous marvel! It is correct. It is written in the sacred book. Be prudent! Rouse yourselves, look at yourselves in the mirror, the way that it happened to your neighbor.[24] And may it not happen to you the same way. It is a model, a measuring stick,[25] which our lord God gives us. Tomorrow or the next day, the day of judgment is going to happen. Just pray to our lord, Jesus Christ, and to the [10v] noblewoman, Saint Mary, that she pray to her beloved honored child, Jesus Christ, so that afterward you will merit and obtain joyfulness in heaven, glory. May it so be done.

Ave Maria.[26]

---

24. The implication is that the play is the mirror. What happened to Lucía is what they are supposed to see in the mirror, applied to themselves.

25. model, measuring stick: metaphorical diphrase for example after which one should pattern oneself.

26. *Hail Mary.*

Present Location
Library of Congress
Washington, D.C.

[11r]

tlatolpepechtli:[1]
~~Ma moCenquizcayecteneuhtzinno yn Cenquizmahuiztilli~~[2]

---

v. Ma huel yehuatzin ȳ. cenquizCamahuiztililoni ȳ teotl tlatohuani Dios amotlantzinco quimotlalili ȳ teyollalilitzin[3] ȳ toçihuanpillatoCatepatlatoCatzin yn axCa techmotintilia techmomaquillia ȳ tlaçōmahuiztlaoncoyalizCahuitl ȳ nōhuia çenmañahuac tentimani tlaōCoxtimani y tlaçomahuizCahuitli yn axCa ȳpā tiCate tlaçomahuiztlaCaye Ca niCan aquihualmotepotztoquilia ȳ cenCa Chipāhuac ȳ cēCa tlanextia y nohuia Cenmanahuac yn itlāçonmahuizteoxayaCatzin ytech quiçan y[?]tech meiya y teoyotiCa neÇentlalinliztli ȳ teoyotiCa netlaçontlaliztli yn iuhquin techmonahuatilia y tonāntzin Sancta yCleçia y niCa quimotepehuillia yn iuhqui tlaçochalchihuitl CozCatl y costic yn istac teocuitla.tl yn çenCa penpetlaCa yn inpenpenyocyo yuhqui tlaçoatl: ye chipinniz auh yn tehuantin Ca çan ticnequixtia ticnepollohuan yuhqui xochitli yntla oCuitlahuix[4] tixpā oquiztiquiçan Ayocmo totech moneq̄ auh ynin Cuix çan xochitli y ticnepollo y ticnequixtiz y tixpa quimotlalilia yn dios ytlaçonnatzin yn itlaocoyallitzin nepeñchtequiliztiCa necnomachilliztiCa y tixpa quimotlalilia yn itlaocoyallitzin yn inChoquizçotlanhuallitzin: Auh y tehuatin Ca çan ticnequixtia yn itlaçonmahuizyxayotzin niCan tlal^(tic)pac no ñonquihtoc ypampa y totlatlaCol Auh no çan io y niCa tlal[11v]-tlalticpāc[5] yn onepolliuhCa yhua yn intlaçoezyotzin y totlaçomahuiztemaquixtiCatzi tt⁰ x⁰ yn axCa tēchmōmaquillia tēchmotintinlia yn itlaçomahuizpaçiōntzin y tinmochitin y titlatlacohuame[6] Auh yn aqui quimotlaçōtlayecoltilli y çenCa mochinpahuaCanemitia y niCa tlalticpac y çenCa quimomahuiztillilia Ca quimomaquilliz yn cenmicactli panpaquilliztli yn iuhqui axCa anquimotinlilizque tlatlaçomahuiztlaCaē[7] ma oC achitzin Cahuitl xonmotlapaCayoca^(tili)+Ca—

tlapitzaloz hualquiçaz lurenso yhua yçihuauh yhua Agel y nepan^(tla) moq̄z[8] tlantozque—

---

1. tlatolpepechtli: practice letters to the left and the right.
2. ~~Ma moCenquizcayecteneuhtzinno yn Cenquizmahuiztilli~~: read *ma mocenquizcayecteneuhtzino yn cenquizcamahuiztililoni*.
3. teyollalilitzin: read *iteyollaliliztin*.
4. oCuitlahuix: read *ocuetlahuix*.
5. tlaltlalticpāc: read *tlalticpac*.
6. titlatlacohuame: read *titlatlacohuanime*.
7. tlatlaçomahuiztlaCaē: read *tlaçomahuiztlacae*.
8. moq̄z: read *moquetzaz*.

How to Live on Earth
Translated by Louise M. Burkhart, with assistance from Barry D. Sell

[11r]

Prologue

~~May he who is utterly honorable be utterly praised~~

v May the one who is utterly honored, the deity, the ruler, God, place among you the consolation of our queenly advocate, the precious and honored time of sadness that she now shows to us, gives to us. The precious and honored time that we are in now swells and spreads sadly through the world everywhere. O beloved honored people, here you attend to the very pure one whose precious and honored sacred countenance greatly illuminates things everywhere in the world. From it comes out, from it flows, the meeting together in a sacred way, the loving of one another in a sacred way,[1] as our mother holy church commands us. Here she scatters them as if they were precious jades, jewels, gold and silver, their pendants shimmering greatly like precious water about to drip. But we, we just waste them and squander them, as if they were flowers that have withered, that have fled from before us, that are no longer necessary for us. So then, is it just flowers that we squander and waste? God's beloved mother places before us her sadness. Reverently, humbly she places before us her sadness, her weeping swoon. But as for us, we just waste her precious and honored tears, which here on earth lie flowing on account of our sins. And likewise here on earth [11v] the precious blood of our beloved honored savior, our lord Christ, has been wasted. Today he gives and shows to all of us sinners his precious and honored passion. And to whomever serves him lovingly, lives very purely here on earth, honors him very much, he will give eternal joyfulness, as you will see today. O beloved honored people, be patient for a little while.

(Wind instruments are played. Lorenzo enters, along with his wife and an angel who stands in the middle. They speak.)

---

1. See Lorenzo's speech, below.

Lureso y tla xihualmohuiCa notlançonāmictzinne tlaçonçihuapille yn axca huel nictequipachoz ȳ motlaçonyollotzin ȳ techcacopā ȳ nic titonemitizque ȳn itlalticpactzinco ȳn ontechmochihuilli ȳ totechiuhcatzin y dios Ca ye Cuel yzquilhuitl ȳn otechmoçentililitzinno ȳ tt⁰ dios huel yc notequipachohua⁹ y niquilnamiqui y tle ticchihuazque yn axCa Cuix çan yehuatl y toaxCa y totlatqui y tictequinpanozque¹⁰ ȳ tictoCuitlahuizqᵉ ynic tlapihuiyaz ynic miyequi yaz maCamo yehuatl tictoCuitlahuica ma ça yehuātzin ȳ tt⁰ dios ytetzinco titopiloCa ynic techmomaquilliz y neyollaliliztli yn chicahualiztli ma momoztlaye tiCalaquiCa yn ichantzinco ma tictotlatlauhtiliCa y dios ytlaçonātzin Ca yehuatzin topanpa quimotlatlauhtiliz yn itlaçoconetzin Auh ȳ toaxCa y totlatqui ytlanel oyezquiȳa Cuix yehuatl tictlatlauhtizque Auh āC oquichiuh aqui OquiyoCox Cuix amo yehuatzin y dios yn iuhqui tehuatin ontechmochihuilli y niCa tlalticpac auh yn axCa yn tochan y tocallitic maCamo çeCa techteōpachoz Ca çan quezquilhuitzintli onCa tocotochiēlizque [12r] y dios yc tomotlatequipānilhuiz¹¹ ticmotlachpānililiz timotlaCuiCuilliz ynic oCa moquixtia ȳ çençenyohual çençemilhuitl techmomaquillia yn iteyollalilitzin ȳ dios maCamo ticmolcahuiliz yn ixquich onimitztenehuili ynic tictotequipanilhuizque y dios notlaçonnāmictzinne—

Çihuatl y notlaçonamictzin ynon ticmotenehuilia Ca çenCa mahuiztic ȳ motlatoltzin yc ninoyollalia y niCaqui ma yuhqui quimonequiltitzinno ȳ dios Ca mochi yc paCaçenlia¹² y quexquich ticmonequiltintzinnoz Ca mochi mochihuaz y motlatoltzin Ca nocochixtica—

Lureso y notlaçonamictzinne ÇeCa nictlaçocamati ȳ motlatoltzin y nicaqui y motemahuiztililiztlatoltzin ma mochipa yuhqui quimonequiltitzinno ȳ dios ynic techmomaquiltzinnoz¹³ yn iteyollalilitzin yn igrāçiatzin yⁿⁱc teOyotiCa netlaçotlaliztiCa titonemiltizque Auh yn axᶜᵃ ma Oc tictotlatlauhtillitin yn itlaçoñatzin dios ȳpampa yn otechmoCahuiltehuaque y tonātzin ȳ totatzin y capā quimotlalilia y dios Cuix Otiquimonitaque Cuix yuhqui ȳ telpilloa Caten tiquimonitatihui tiquitlapalotihui tiquimotlamaCatihui Ca nelli anyocmo tiquimitazque tiquinotzazque y tt⁰ dios¹⁴ ma Otiquimitani ma otechnotzani ma otechylhuiyani tle yc quimotlatzaCuiltilia y dios Cuix ytla quitehuiquilia y niCa tlalticpac ma ypapa Otiquixtlahuani y tlatquitli y teoCuitlatl yn iztac [?] ȳ y coStic tlaçotli chalchihuitl Ca ça niCā tlami tlalticpac Auh yn iteycnoytanlitzin y dios y tlapaCayihiyohuiliztli y necnomachiliztli yn itlaçotlalloCa y tohuapohua Ca yehuatl tochimal yn ixpatzinco ȳ dios notlaçoñamictzinne ma oc tihuiya—[12v]

---

9. notequipachohua: standard *ninotequipachohua* as in the second version of the play.
10. tictequinpanozque: read *tictequipanozque*.
11. tomotlatequipānilhuiz: read *ticmotlatequipanilhuiz* as in the second version of this play.
12. yc paCaçenlia: read *nicpaccacelia* as in the second version of this play.
13. techmomaquiltzinnoz: read *techmomaquilitzinoz* as in the second version of this play.
14. tt⁰ dios: tt.⁰e d.e in the second version of this play.

LORENZO: Do come, O my beloved spouse, O beloved noblewoman! Now I shall greatly worry your precious heart in regard to how we will live on the earth of him who made us, our maker, God. Some days ago our lord God joined us together [in marriage]. It worries me greatly when I think about what we will do now. Will we just work for and occupy ourselves with our possessions, our goods, so that they will increase, so that they will become many? Let us not occupy ourselves with that. Let us rely on our lord God to give us consolation and health. Let us enter his home every day. Let us pray to God's beloved mother that for our sake she pray to her beloved child. And as for our possessions, our goods, if truly there should be any, are we to pray for them? And who made them, who created them? Was it not God, just as he made us here on earth? And now, in our home, in our house, let it not worry us very much, for it is just for a few days that we will await God there. [12r] You will work, you will sweep, you will tidy up, so that the consolation God gives us issues therefrom every night and every day. Do not forget all that I have declared to you, so that we will work for God, O my beloved spouse.

WOMAN: O my beloved spouse, those words of yours that you declare are very admirable. I am consoled by what I hear. May God wish it so. I receive it all joyfully, whatever you will want. Your words will all be carried out. I am awaiting them.

LORENZO: O my beloved spouse, I am very grateful for your words. I hear your respectful words. May God always wish it so, so that he will give us his consolation, his grace, so that with loving each other in a sacred way we will live. And now let us pray still to God's beloved mother on behalf of those who have left us behind, our mother, our father.[2] Where God places them, have we visited them? Is it as if they are in prison, [where] we are going to visit them, we are going to greet them, we are going to give them things? It is true that we will see them and call to them no longer. Our lord God,[3] if only we had seen them, if only they had called to us, if only they had told us why God punishes them. Do they owe something to someone here on earth? If only we had for their sake repaid the goods, the silver and gold, precious things, jades, for here on earth they come to an end. But the pity of God, patience, humility, loving of our neighbors, those are our shield before God. O my beloved spouse, let us go. [12v]

---

2. mother, father: in variant order, this common diphrase often means "parent."
3. In the second version of the play both terms are in the vocative: O our Lord, O God.

Cihuatl v Ma mochihua y motlanahuatiltzin ma tiCallaquiCa ȳn ichatzinco ȳ dios ma tictotlatlauhtilitin yn ipā yn ānimaz y Capa quimoyeyamaquillitzinnohua y dios ma quimotlanextililitzinno ȳhua y tehuati ma techmomaquiliz yn itechi-Cahualitzin yhua yn ixquich totech monequiz y tiquazque yn tiquizque ynic ticchi-Cahuazque y totlallo y toçonquiyo ma tictintlanililitin[15] y dios notlançoñamictzin[16]— Auh nima yazque y teopa quimotlatlauhtilizque y dios tlapitzaloz[17] itlaçoñatzin quiyaCatiaz y Agel auh ytla oÇique[18] teopaCalteco Calaquizque yn agel OnoCa moCahuaz teopaCalteco tlatoz—

1º Agel v dios ytlachihualtzintzinhuane ma huel ximochiCahuaca maCamo amexiCoz y mictla tzintzinmitli maCamo amechCoto^{n}iliz yn ilh̄icac tlaçomeCatl ȳ çencam pēnpetlaCa y teOmatzantzaztli yniC oAnmechnomaylpillitzinno yn ātle quinenehuiliz y niCa tlalticpa^c yn iuhqui yc tlaçotli yniC amilpitinCate ylh̄cac hualehuatinCac maCamo Aquitlacozque ma huel xicmahuiztinliCa Ca yc amomaquixtizq^e yn ixpatzinCo y dios yhua ytetzinco ximopilloCa ximotzantzinliCa Ca yehuatzin amechmopalehuilliz yhua Ca niCa niCa Amotlatzinco ninemiz amo namechnoCahuiliz maCamo aquitlaCoz yn iuhqui Oanahuatiloque Ca ye niCa huitz yn amoyauh ȳ tlaCatecolotl yn amechyaochihuaquiuh Ca huel yehuatl ynic motlahuelpolohua amotechCacopa—

1º dem^o v y tiAgel yn ayc tinechCahuaz ytlan ipac tinemiz y tlalticpac tlaCa ça tehuatl ticxixinia ȳ [13r] notzohuaz y notlatequipanoliz y notetlayecoltiCahua tinechyCuilhuillia Auh ye amo mitzylnamiqui Ayc mitzatzalia[19] Ayc mitztenehua ytla nehuatl yuhqui on ACa nechonpohua Auh tle niquimilhuizquia yn itla ninemizquia yn in ātle yc nechtlaçotla Cuix amo ça niquiCahuazquia Cuix notequihua[20] Amo tiquiCahua ~~y tehuatl~~ y tiAgel xinechiCahuilli y nōtetlayecoltiCahua—

1º Agel v y tehuatl y timictlatletzintzimitl ȳ timictlacohuatl yn ayc tlamiz y moztlac y motēquallac yn ipa ticnōnoquitinemi ytlamaquixtiltzintzinhua y notechiuhCatzin dios ynon tictenehua yn amo netzatzinlia yn amo nechylnamiqui Ca tehuatl tiquiCahualtia. yn āmo quilnāmiquin ȳn aqui ypāpa tlaOcoxtinemi ChoCatinemi ma xiquiCahua—

---

15. tictintlanililitin: read *tictotlanililitin*.
16. In the second version of this play it is (incorrectly) in the male vocative: notlaçonamictzinem.
17. tlapitzaloz: added later in the left margin in a different hand.
18. oÇique: read *acique*.
19. mitzatzalia: read *mitztzatzilia*.
20. notequihua: read *notequiuh*.

WOMAN: Let your command be carried out. Let us go into God's home. Let us pray for their souls, where[ver] God has placed them. May he illuminate them. And as for us, may he give us his health and all that is necessary for us, that which we will eat, that which we will drink, so that we will strengthen our earth, our clay.[4] Let us ask God for it, O my beloved spouse.[5]

(And then they go to the church. They pray to God's beloved mother. Wind instruments are played. The angel leads them. And when they reach the entrance of the church they go in. The angel remains there at the entrance of the church. He speaks.)

FIRST ANGEL: O creations of God, strengthen yourselves well! May the Tzitzimitl[6] of the place of the dead not deceive you! May he not cut the precious cord of heaven on you! Greatly does it shimmer, the sacred ring with which he tied your hands together. Nothing here on earth will equal in preciousness that with which you are tied together; it comes from heaven. Do not ruin it! Honor it well, for with it you will be rescued before God. And importune him, cry out to him, for he will help you. And I am here. I will live with you; I will not abandon you. Do not ruin it, as you were commanded. Here comes your enemy, the demon. He is coming to make war on you. He is lost in anger against you.

FIRST DEMON: You angel, you never will leave me. You will stay with the people of earth. You just tear down [13r] my snares, my work. You take my servants from me. But now they do not remember you, they never cry out to you, they never mention you. If it were me, would someone consider me like that? And what would I have said to them with whom I would have lived, who love me for nothing? Would I not just have abandoned them? Is it my business? You do not leave them, you angel. Leave me my servants!

FIRST ANGEL: You fire Tzitzimitl of the place of the dead, you serpent of the place of the dead, your drivel, your slaver[7] will never end. You go around spilling them all over those whom my maker, God, has saved. You declare that they do not cry out to me, that they do not remember me. It is you who makes them leave him. They do not remember the one who for their sake goes about sad, goes about weeping. Leave them!

---

4. earth, clay: here and below, a standard diphrase often found in testaments referring to the body.
5. In the second version of this play it is (incorrectly) in the male vocative.
6. In pre-Columbian religion, the Tzitzimime were monstruous female or androgynous numens of the western sky, the twilight, and world destruction. They came to be equated with devils.
7. drivel, slaver: this common diphrase means "lies, falsehoods."

1º demº v queni niquiCahuaz y tiAgel xihuanlauh xiCaqui y yehuati Ahuel nechoCahua achito Cahuitl. ȳ tla ytlaquaya nechtzatzinlia ynic melçimazque ytla ycochia Amo quilnamiqui y Cruz yē nechtzatzinlia y manel y çan ~~qui~~ amo quitzatzinlia y dios. ça huel ye nehuatl ȳCamac niCa ytla mehuaz[21] ytla tlacuazque ytla no çen ȳconeuh oqui[13v]quallani yçiuhCa nechmaCatihuetzin ytla noço ontliCa moteCuinizque Amo quitzatzinlia y dios çannoC[22] achi motlahuelpollotihuiuh Auh y nehuatl.[23] oC achi yCa nināhuiltia yCa nihuehuentzCan yhua miyectlamantli ypā nicchihua y xolopinli yn amo mozCalilia queni niquiCahuaz ytla yehuatin amo nechoCahuazquina ȳ tiquintohua niquiCahuaz ytla yehuatin amo nechopolozquin—

1º Agel v Auh tla xinechylhui tlen iC otihualla y niCan tlateochihuallalpā yCaltepatzinco y Jerosalle Cuix ticmati mochi titlatlacohuanime y niCa ohualCalque[24] Ca quimopalehuilitzinnoz y dios y mohuiCacopan—

1º Demºº v queni mopalehuizque y tiAgel huel xicmati ynic onihualla y niCa Onhuallaque ȳ çan ic millacatzotinemi yn itlahuel motlahuelpollotinemi tlahuelmictinemin momoztlaē y manel hualhui teopa Ca çan itech yetihuitz yn iqualla yn ihuetzquiz yn inepolliz[25] yn imatlamachilliz yn ihuēCapaniliz yn itepanahuiltoquiliz yn icnotlaCa yCa motopeuhtehua [14r] Amo quiyehuayta y manel tle ȳlhuillo ȳ niCa amo quiyehuaCaqui yn intemachtiCahua cānmo yehuatl i yn inemiliz y tlalticpac tlaCa—

1º Agel v Oyhitlahuelliltic ȳ tlalticpāc tlaCa ac tehuatl yn amo titlaOcoya tla ˣⁱᶜCaqui y monepohualiz yn ātle ypa tiqtta yn itlatoltzin y motechiuhCatzin dios yn āyc tichoCa yn āyc titlaOCoya onmoçentzontlahuelliltic ȳ çan tihuallanequixtia tihuallanepollo yCa ychātzin[26] y moteotzin y motlatoCātzi dios xiquitta xitlachia xitlaCaquin—

tlapitza[27] OCa hualquiztihuetzizque Çen Cihuatzintli quihualhuillatiaz yn iConeuh quihuiCaznequi y teopā ça quimictitehuaz yñ inatzin[28]

Çihuatzitli v xihualauh Cuix amo Onimitztitla ȳ teopa tiCaquitiuh ȳ Salue yhua ticpohuatiuh yñ itlacorosanriotzin[29] ȳ [14v] ȳ çihuapilli Santa maria Cuix onimitztitla ~~ti~~timaānhuiltiz y tixolopintli xinenemi niCa xitotoca—

quixtlatlatzinnitehuaz yn ināt~zī~ y piltotli yatehuaz—

---

piltotli v Xinechcahua diablo amo nimotequiuh ytla nimitztzonanaz diablo mitzhuicaz Cuix oc motequiuh ye otinechyzcazti[30] ye nihuey[31]

---

21. mehuaz: read *mehuazque*.
22. çannoC: read *çan oc*.
23. nehuatl: in the second version of this play y[e]huatl.
24. ohualCalque: read *ohualcalaque*.
25. inepolliz: read *inepohualiz* as in the second version of this play.
26. Yca ychātzin: read *nican ychantzinco* as in the second version of this play.
27. tlapitza: in a different hand.
28. Following this in the second version of this play: quixtlantlatzinintehuaz.
29. itlacorosanriotzin: read *itlaçorosariotzin*.
30. otinechyzcazti: read *otinechyzcalti*.
31. Added in superscript in the second version of this play: izca yn icolinechhuapauh.

FIRST DEMON: How am I to leave them? You angel, come here. Listen. It is they who are unable to leave me for a moment. If it is their time of eating they call out to me, so that they will choke. If it is their time of sleeping they do not remember the cross. They cry out to me, even though they do not cry out to God; it is really I who am in their mouths. If they are getting up, if they are eating, or if one of their children makes them angry, [13v] immediately they give it to me. Or if they stumble on the road they do not cry out to God. They just become still more lost in anger. And as for me, I make fun of them still more. I laugh heartily at them and I do many things to the fools, who do not catch on. How am I to leave them if they will not leave me?[8] You say that I am to leave them if they will not overcome me?[9]

FIRST ANGEL: But do tell me why you have come here to the blessed place, the entrance of Jerusalem. Do you know that all the sinners who have entered here God will help against you?

FIRST DEMON: How are they to help themselves? You angel, know well what I have come here for. They who have come here just go about wrapped up in their anger, they go about lost in anger, they go about dying of anger. Every day even though they come to church they just bring along their rage, their laughter, their pride, their presumption, their exaltation, their sense of superiority. The poor people just go off making fun of it [that is, what happens at church]. [14r] They do not esteem it, even though something is said to them. They do not pay attention to their teachers. This is not the [proper] life of the people of earth.

FIRST ANGEL: Oh how unfortunate are the people of earth! Who are you who are not saddened? Do hear your pride! You consider as nothing the words of your maker, God. You never weep, you never feel sad. Four hundred times[10] unfortunate are you! You just waste things, you just squander things here in the home of your deity, your ruler, God. See! Look! Listen!
(*Wind instruments are played.* Then a woman rushes there dragging her child whom she wants to take in the church. His mother just beats him up.)[11]

WOMAN: Come! Didn't I send you to the church? We are going to hear the Salve[12] and you are going to count the precious rosary of the [14v] noblewoman, Saint Mary. Did I send you to play, you fool? Move along here. Run along.
(*His mother quickly slaps his face. Little Child goes forward.*)

LITTLE CHILD: Leave me, devil! I am not your business. If I seize you by the hair the devil will take you. Is it still your business? You have already raised me. I am big now.[13]

---

8. The second version of this play reads: How am I to leave them if they do not want to leave me?
9. Tentative translation. The pragmatic thrust seems to be that the demon would leave only if they overcome him or drive him away. The second version of this play reads: You say that I will leave them if they do not want to overcome me?
10. Four hundred times: here and below, *four hundred* is a common idiom in the vigesimally based traditional counting system for "countless, innumerable."
11. The second version of this play adds: *She slaps his face.*
12. Salve Regina: Hail [Holy] Queen. A popular Catholic prayer.
13. Some text in superscript (izca yn icolinechhuapauh) follows in the second version of this play.

Çihuatztli v ma mitzmoyollali y dios y tinoconeuh maCamo moztla huiptla mopampa nechmotelchihuilitzinnoz y dios Ca ye yc ninoquixtia yn ixpatzinco Ca ye niyauh mopanpa nicnotlatlauhtilitiuh y dios—

Calaquiz y teopa ȳ çihuatzintli

1º Demōō v tla xiq̄ta y tiAg^el moyollo Opachiuh ^mixipā oquiz ȳ piltotli yn atle ypa quita ynātzin yxquich teto³² Auh ye huel atle ypa tlachia auh tiquitohua niquinCahuaz amo ytla ninemiz Cuix amo ticmati Ca huel ypiltia ȳ yehua yn amo nechCahuaznequi huel niq.pactia yn iquac amo nechtenehua amo pactiCate yñotlacoycnihua³³ [15r]

1º agle v Ca yCa yn itlatoCahuelitzin y ÇenmiCac moetztiCa yn Jesu x̄ō ca timiquaniz y timictla miztli y titequani yn ayc tipachihui yn ayc tixhui ma xiCuitlaxitini Ca ypampa ontihuala monexiColiztiCa ynic tiquita quimotlaçotlayeColtilia ȳ dios yn amo quitlaCohua yn SaniCrameto yn onquimonahuatilitzino ~~yn tonatzin~~ Sancta ygleçia yniC amo quitlaCohua mochipahuaCanemitia yn ixpatzinCo y dios momoztlaye moCalaquiya y teonpa quimotlatlauhtilia y dios yntlaçonatzin quipohua yn itlaçomahuizroSanriotzin yn icpacxochitzi maCamo ytzala ynepatla xiCalaqui Ca quimoyollalili y Espirito Sanctu ma ximiquani—

Choloz hueCa moquetzaz y demoniō³⁴ yn iquac quimotenehuiliz y Jesu xº³⁵ yn Aḡle teonpaCalteCo moquetztiyez—

1º demoni v y manel tinechtotoCa amo ninoxiCoz niCa nēmiz³⁶ ytla y manel oc quexquich Cahuitl quilCahuazque y dios ynic motlaçotla momahuiztilia mococolizque momictizque yñ adan onC achi huel chiCahuacque tlanpaltique oniquixiCo oniquihualquixti yn iparāySo yn iyecxochitlalpā y dios yn oquinequia quimotlamachtiz quimoCuiltonozque auh ye yCa ononoCaCayauh auh yehuāti niquiCahuaz yn i manel huel chipahuaque: ynnoc³⁷ çequiti huel tlateomati y manel huel mimati ynic Calaqui y teonpa³⁸ amo quimatizque ȳ [15v] tleyn ipa nicchiuhtihuetzin niquimilnamictitihuetzin y manel ayemo tlami y miSsa y çermo ye Cuel oquilnamic y Capa yc nichuiCaz pampaquitihui motlamachtitihui ye Cuel oquinequixti onquinepolo oC achi qualli OquiCahuazquia amo onyazquiya y teopa onequiz onepoliuh yn itlatlauhtiliz yhua yn ixquich quimilhuiya quinōtza quimachtia ayocmo quiCaquiznequi auh y nehuatl ye huel quitlaçoyta³⁹ ynic niquiyaCana ynic niquipachohua y nōtlaçopilhua niCa niquichixtinemi amo niniquaniz y manel tinechtoCa Ca huel nechmotlaço.tilia—

---

32. teto: scribal error; the same appears in the second version of this play. Given the context we feel that *quito* "she said" or *tlato* "she spoke" was probably the original intention.
33. yñotlacoicnihua: read *yn notlaçoicnihuan*.
34. In the second version of the play: 1.º demonio.
35. Jesu xº: only xº appears in the second version of this play.
36. nemiz: read *ninemiz*.
37. ynnoc: read *yn oc*.
38. tiompa: read *teopan*.
39. quitlaçoyta: appears to be a scribal error; perhaps to be read *niquintlaçoitta*.

WOMAN: May God console you, my child. May God not scorn me tomorrow or the next day because of you. I have now fulfilled my obligations before him. Now I am going. I am going to pray to God for your sake.

(The woman enters the church.)

FIRST DEMON: Do look, you angel. You are satisfied with what has passed before you. The little child considers as nothing everything his mother said, and she has no consideration for him. But you say I am to leave them, I am not to live with them. Don't you know that it is right from their childhood that they do not want to leave me? I make them very happy. When they do not mention me, my beloved friends are not happy. [15r]

FIRST ANGEL: By the royal power of eternal Jesus Christ you will go away, you puma of the place of the dead,[14] you fierce beast who is never full, never sated. May your belly burst! You have come because of your envy, as you see that they serve God lovingly, they do not violate the sacraments ordered by ~~our mother~~ holy church, such that not breaking them they live purely before God. Every day they enter church, they pray to God's beloved mother, they count her precious and honored rosary, the chaplet. Do not enter among them, amid them.[15] The Holy Spirit has consoled them. Go away!

(The demon[16] flees, he stands far off, when the angel mentions Jesus Christ.[17] [The angel] stands at the church entrance.)

FIRST DEMON: Even though you chase me away, I will not be envious. I will live here among them however long a time it is until they forget God, so that those who love and honor one another will hate each other, will kill each other. They are stronger and more robust than Adam whom I deceived, whom I made leave paradise, God's good flowery land, which he wanted him to benefit from and enjoy. And I have already fooled him. And I am to leave them? Even though others are very pure, very devout, even though they are very prudent as they enter the church, they will not know [15v] what I will suddenly do to them, suddenly make them remember. Even before the mass and the sermon are finished, already they have remembered where I will take them, [where] they will go to be joyful, they will go to enjoy themselves. Already they have wasted and squandered it. It would have been better if they had neglected it, if they had not gone to the church. Their prayers have been wasted and squandered. And they no longer want to hear all that they say to them, that they announce to them, that they teach them. And as for me, now I look very lovingly at my beloved children, as I lead them, as I govern them. I go about here waiting for them. I will not go away, even though you chase me away, for they really love me.

---

14. mictlan: here and below translated as "the place of the dead" (locative senses such as "in" or "at" are already contained in the Nahuatl term), it was usually rendered by colonial translators as *infierno* (hell).

15. This may be a traditional idiom that in this context means "Do not be a troublemaker." See Molina 1977, 81r on the Spanish-Nahuatl side under "Malsin," and on 111r on the Nahuatl-Spanish various entries beginning with "Tetzalan." See also Carochi 1983, f. 20, under *"Nepantlâ."*

16. In the second version of this play: *First Demon.*

17. *Jesus Christ*: this is only *Christ* in the second version of the play.

y demoni⁰ moteCaz quauhtzintla Auh y teopa OCatCa hualquiçazque OCa qui^(nchi)xtiyez⁴⁰ y aḡle oc tlatoz⁴¹—

1⁰ aḡle v̱ dios ytlaçohuane ma huel yxquich amotlanpal xicchihuaCa yniC amo amexiCoz yn tlaCateColotl Ca huel amechyahualotinemi amechtoCatinemi ynic amechmotlaCauhtiznequi ynic moxiCohua ynic amechita ynic anquimotlaçotilia yn dios

nima hualquiçazque quiya^(ca)tiyaz ^(tla)pitzalos⁴² Aḡle yazque yn incha motlalizq^(e 43)

---

lureso v auh yn axCa notlaçonamictzine huel yc tequipachohua⁴⁴ y mix y moyollotzin yn o[16r]quic ayemo tictomaÇehuia yn itetlaçotlalitzī y dios y çetetl tlaxCaltzintli oC ach^(to)pa nimitznonahuatilia y moztla ypanpa tictotlatlauhtilizque y dios yn ānimaz y Capa oquimotlalilitzinno y tt⁰ dios Cuix qualCa Cuix nōçe amo huel tetlaoColti yn imomiyotzin yn intetepo yn opa cemātoc tepeuhtoc yn ichatzinCo y dios y teopan nōtlaçonanmictzine çihuapile—

Çihuantl v̱ maCamo ximotequipachotzino Cuix amo ye ticmomachitia y çeçexihuitl. yc timachtilo yn iquac tiCui y nextli ynic techmomachtilia yn itlatequixtiCatzitzinhua y dios yn tlaçonteOnpixCatzitzinti ynic oCa titolnamiquizque⁴⁵ Ca titomiquilizque Ca tinexti Ca titlalti = ti=toCuepazque maCamo ximotequipachotzinno notlaçonamictzin ma tictomaçenhuiCa yn itetlaçotlalitzin y dios ma ximoçehuitzinon—motlalizque⁴⁶ tlaquazque yn aḡle⁴⁷ OCa mo^(tla)pitzaloz⁴⁸ Etztiyez tlatoz

Aḡle 1⁰ v̱ ma mochipa amotzala amonepatla moyetztiye yn iteyollalilintzin y dios Esp.ritu S.tu ynic aquimomahuiztililizque y dios ytlaçonatzin y çihuapili Sancta maria maCayc xiquilCahuaCa yn tla[16v]çoxochiCozCatzin⁴⁹ yn ilhuiCac tlatoCaçihuapilli Sancta maria C̶a̶ y̶e̶h̶u̶a̶t̶z̶i̶n̶ Ca y yehuatzin ayc tlami yn intepātlatolitzi yn intlatlauhtilitzin yn ixpatzinCo yn itlaçoConetzin yn oamechmochihuili yn anmotechiuhCatzin dios ma ytetzinCo ximoCahuaCa Ca huel moyolCoCohua yn amechyta y tlaCateColotl huel amechyahualotinemi y moxiCohuani Auh y nehuatl Ca nanhmechnopiyelitiCa⁵⁰ amo namechnoCahuilia amotlatzinCo ninemi

---

40. qui^(nchi)xtiyez: superscript material apparently added later in a different hand.
41. The stage directions are somewhat different in the second version of this play: [t]lapitzaloz = hualquisasque. Lorenço. yhuan iCihuauh = yn itec teoCalli. h̶u̶a̶l̶q̶u̶i̶z̶a̶z̶q̶u̶e̶. Ocatca = auh yn. 1.⁰ angel. Oncan quichiztiez. Auh yn. 1.⁰ Dem.⁰ moteCaz. Cuauhtzintla. tlantoz. 1.⁰.
42. tlapitzalos: in a different hand.
43. The stage directions are somewhat different in the second version of this play: tlapitzalos =. yc hualquiÇa. yn teopa. Lurenço. Çihuatl yc yasque. yn incha motlalizque. Auh yn 1.⁰ angel quinyacantiyaz.
44. huel yc tequipachohua: read *huel nictequipachohua* as in the second version of this play.
45. titolnamiquizque : perhaps to be read either as *tictolnamiquiltizque* or *tiquilnamiquizque*.
46. motlalizque: in the second version of this play: ^(tla)pitzalos.
47. yn aḡle: in the second version of this play: 1.⁰ Angel.
48. Added in a different hand.
49. tlaçoxochicozcatzin: read *itlaçoxochicozcatzin*.
50. nanhmechnopiyeliti: standard *namechnopielitica*.

(The demon lies down under a tree. And they who were in the church enter. There the angel waits for them. He still speaks.[18])

FIRST ANGEL: O God's beloved ones, exert all your effort lest the demon deceive you! He goes about surrounding you and following you in order to enslave you, as he is envious when he sees how you love God.

(Then they enter. The angel leads them. Wind instruments are played. They go to their home. They sit down.)[19]

LORENZO: And now, O my beloved spouse, I must disturb your face, your heart,[20] [16r] since we still do not yet merit one little tortilla of God's charity. First of all I command you that tomorrow we will pray to God on behalf of the souls who are there where our lord God has placed them. Perhaps it is a good place, or perhaps it is not so consoling. Their bones, their tibias[21] lie all spread about, lie all scattered there, in the home of God, in the church, O my beloved spouse, O noblewoman.

WOMAN: Do not worry. Do you not yet know how we are taught each year, when we take the ashes, how God's spokespersons, the precious priests, teach us, so that we will then remember that we will die, that we will turn into ashes and earth? Do not worry, O my beloved spouse. May we merit God's love. Rest yourself.[22]

(They sit down to eat. The angel is there. Wind instruments are played. He speaks.)

FIRST ANGEL: May God the Holy Spirit's consolation always be among you, amid you, so that you will honor God's beloved mother, the noblewoman Saint Mary. Never forget the precious [16v] flowery necklace[23] of the heavenly royal noblewoman, Saint Mary. For never ending are her advocacy and her prayers before her beloved child, he who made you, your maker, God. Entrust yourselves to her. She feels very sick at heart; she sees that the demon goes about surrounding you, the envious one. And as for me, I am guarding you, I do not leave you, I live with you.

---

18. The second version of this play has somewhat different stage directions at this point: *Wind instruments are played. Lorenzo and his wife enter. Those who were in church enter. And First Angel awaits them there. And First Demon lies down under a tree.*

19. The second version of this play has somewhat different stage directions at this point: *Wind instruments are played. Thus Lorenzo and the woman enter from the church, thus they go to their home. They sit down. First Angel leads them.*

20. face, heart: The possessed metaphorical diphrase *-ix, -yollo* (face, heart) has many connotations. The first "by itself often has to do with presence, perception, wisdom" while the second "is associated with emotion and volition" (Karttunen and Lockhart 1987, 54). In combination they often refer to one's "spirit, spirits, mood, state of morale" (54), which is the sense present here. For a more extended discussion see Karttunen and Lockhart (1987, 54–55).

21. bones, tibias: here and below, a traditional metaphorical diphrase has been used whose precise pragmatic thrust is not entirely clear.

22. The second version of the play includes stage directions that are somewhat different than those immediately following, as well as a speech by Lorenzo that is entirely missing from the first version but that seems to refer to the end of the drama. Note that in this variant the person who speaks next is Lorenzo, not the First Angel.

Wind instruments are played. They eat. And First Angel is there. He speaks.

LORENZO: May it so be done, O noblewoman. May it be that we merit it [that is, God's love]. O people of earth, now you have seen the exemplary model, and how our lord God judges people. And admonish your children. May it not happen to you as it happened to him [that is, the condemned youth, at the end of the play?].

23. This alludes to the rosary.

Auh y demonio çan opa yez y quauhtzitla quihualytztiyaz auh ytla atle tlatohua yn aḡle nima hualmeuhtehuaz tlatoz huel qualaniz yn quimitaz—

1º demoº v huel ninontlahuelpalahua⁵¹ y niquimita ȳ tlaCatotli yhua y çihuātotli huel ye nechçotlahua yn ichiCahualiz ye nechhuihuiyotza ynic tlapaltique ynic yoltepitztique Ca huel chiCahuac yn intlaneltoquiliz Ca huel yuh nicmati Ca ahuel niquinxiCoz ahuel niquihuiCaz nicnepolohua nicnequixtiya y nontlatequipanoliz Ca ye cuel yxquich Cahuitl yn intla ninemi niquinonepachihuitinemi Ca ahuel niquixiCohua onC achi huel motlapaltiliya yn imaḡlel auh yeçe onC achi huel nechyoltonehua nechchichinatza y missa ȳ çermō huel quihuelCaqui y tle ylhuilo nonotzalo: huel ytech quitlaliya yn iyollo oc çeCa yn ihuāpohua yn ōmique. yn opoliuhque yn opa tepeuhtoc yn imomiyon yn intetepo y teopa yn iquac: qui[17r]quimita⁵² huel quitlaoColtia ypampa: choCa: tlatlatlauhtia momoztlaye Calaqui y teopa huel OC achi yc nechtlahuelCuitia yc nipatzmiqui: auh niquitohua ytla yehuati momaquixtizque Cuix mochi quihuiCazque yn ixquichti tlaltipcac Onoque Cuix amo yehuati niquihuiCaz yn amo ça tlapohualti yn itla ninemi yn manel huel mamahuiztique⁵³: yn atle yntech maxitlani y moyecchichihua y momahuiçolani yn imixCo yn imicpac nemi yn icnontlaCa atle ypa quimita yn ihuapohua Ca nehuatl niquiCuitlahuiltia y niCa ytla ninemi amo niquiCahua achito Cahuitl Cuix nel ninoxiCoz tla Oc niquimochiya yn antlamatque yn atle ypa tlachiya yn atle ypa teyta auh yn axCa tla Oc niqualyahualotihuetzin ȳ çenmanahuantl tla ninotlalotihuetzin ye nihuecahua y niCa—

---

nima yaz y demonioº hualmotlaloz auh y lureSo moquetzazque yn itlaquaya huel quitlaçonCamatiz

lureso v auh yn axCa notlaçonamictzinne ma yehuatzin y ttº dios otechmotlaqualtilitzinno auh y moztla Cuix no yuhqui tictomaçehuizque yn itetlaçotlalitzin y dios Cuix noçe ytla topa oquihualmihuanliz yn itetlaçotlalitzi: ma [17v] ma⁵⁴ çā ytetzinCo titoCahuaCa Ca yehuatzin techmopalehuiliz y tocochiya y totlaquanya y tonenemiya ma techmopalehuili ȳ dios ytlaçonatzin Auh yn axCa ma Oc tihuia ticçetlaliti yn totlatlacol ynic otictoyollitlaCalhuique yn totechiuhCatzin dios Ca ye yma y titochipahuazque titoyollitizq̄.⁵⁵ ma moztla tihuiya yxpatzinco y dios yxiptlatzintzinhua y tlaçoteopixCatzintziti—

Çihuatl v notlaçonāmictzin ma yuhqui mochihua: Ca ye ima y totichipahuazque⁵⁶ ma yçiuhca tihuiya
tlapitzalos⁵⁷

Calanquizque nima hualquiçaz y demonioº—

---

51. ninontlahuelpalahua: perhaps to be read *ninontlahuelpolohua*.
52. quiquimita: read *quimitta*.
53. mamahuiztique: although it reads the same in the second version of this play, read *momahuiztique*.
54. ma ma: read *ma*.
55. titoyollitizq̄.: read *titoyolcuitizque*.
56. totichipahuazque: read *titochipahuazque*.
57. tlapitzalos: in a different hand.

(And the demon is just there under a tree. He goes on watching them. And if the angel says nothing[24] then he gets up, he speaks, he is very angry. He looks at them.)

FIRST DEMON: I really lose myself in anger when I see the miserable little man and woman. Their strength really makes me feel faint. They make me tremble, they are so robust and firm–hearted. Their belief is very strong. Thus I know well that I will not be able to deceive them, I will not be able to take them. I waste and squander my work. Already all the time that I have lived with them, I have gone about lying in wait for them in vain. I am unable to deceive them. Their angel strives harder. And moreover, what pains me and hurts me more is the mass and the sermon. They really approve of what is said to them and what they are admonished. They set their hearts on it. Especially when they see their neighbors who have died, who have perished, whose bones and tibias lie scattered there at the church, [17r] then they really make them grieve. They weep and pray for their sake. Every day they go into the church, by which they anger me much more, by which I am oppressed. But I say, if they will be saved, will they take along all who dwell on earth? Am I not to take those without number among whom I live? Even though they are highly honored, unapproachable, well dressed and want to be esteemed, they have no respect for the poor, they have no esteem for their neighbors. I induce them [to do bad things], I live here among them. I do not leave them for a moment. Am I, truly, to be envious? Let me yet wait for the presumptuous ones, the inconsiderate ones, the disrespectful ones. And now let me yet make a quick circle about the world. Let me quickly run off. I have now tarried here a long time.

(Then the demon goes. He runs. And Lorenzo [and his wife] arise from their meal. He gives thanks.)

LORENZO: And now, O my beloved spouse, it is our lord God who has fed us. And tomorrow, will we likewise merit God's charity? Or will he send something of his charity to us? Let us [17v] just entrust ourselves to him. He will help us in our sleeping, in our eating, in our going about. May God's beloved mother help us. And now, let us yet go and gather together our sins with which we have offended our maker, God. It is now time that we purify ourselves, that we confess. Tomorrow let us go before God's representatives, the precious priests.

WOMAN: O my beloved spouse, may it so be done. It is now time that we purify ourselves. Let us go quickly.

(Wind instruments are played. They go in. Then a demon enters.)

---

24. That is, when he stops speaking?

2 demō v̱ huel niçiyauhtihuitz yn onnicyahualoto ȳ. çenmanahuactli ypapa y niCa onihuala. huel miyequiti Omoçentlalique yn telpopochtoti yn ichpopochti ~~tiCa~~ axCa moyolCuitizque huel miyec quilCahuazque ymauhCaConpa ypīnahuilizticA amo quitozque yn intlatlacol yc teyxco teycpac oneque amo quiteCuepilizque y temahuizyo yhua yn itahua yn ināhua. y ⁿᵘⁱmixtlatzinniya amo quimoCuitizq̄. ȳmixpa⁵⁸ yn iteyolCuitiCauh quitlatizque y momati aço ye yC opoliuh yn ixpa y dios tla Oc niquimochie

Motlatiz y demō. y Cani yez quauhtlatli⁵⁹ nima hualquiçazque yeyti telpopochti: ȳ. [18r] tlapitzalos⁶⁰ quechtla quihualhuiCaz Rosanrio y çen yc momaquixtiz y Cru̅z yn iquac moteCaz yn oc çen amo moteonchihuaz yni moteCaz quauhtla Cochtiyezqᵉ.

1º telpochtli v̱ notlaçoycnihuane ma niCa toçehuiCa ȳ quauhtla Ca ye Otlayohuaz: Ca oc hueCa y taçizque yn itic altepetl Ca tel oC moztla: ȳ titoyolCuitizque—

2 telpochtli v̱ ma yuhqui mochihua ma niCa techmoçehuilitzinno y ttº dios notlaço-ycniuhtzitzihuane yn oquic ayemo huel tlaquauhtlayohiā⁶¹ ma ytla toconamicti niCa: Ca huel OhuiCa ȳ quauhtla—

3 telpochtli v̱ y nehuatl huel oniçiyauh ma yçiuhca titoçehuiCa Ca huel nicochiznequi nocninhuane—

Calaquizque quauhtla huel onhuiCa yez motlalizque mononotztiyezque

---

1º telpochtli v̱ nocniuhtzitzinhuane huel yuhqui queni mochihua y noyollo ȳ niquil-namiqui y queni yxpatzinCo nonaçiz y noteyolCuitiCatzi y moztla—
San hueCa hualtzatziz y Snᵗᵃ agl̅e—iCa mitzmopalehuiliz y dios ytlaçonatzin xiᶜmotlatlauhtilitzino—[18v]

2 telpochtli v̱ ça ño yuhqui niquitohua huel neᶜʰtequipachohua y niquilnamiqui amo niteoçihui yn axCa ma techmopalehuilitzinno y ttº dios—

2 agl̅e v̱ yn āquin quichoctiya quitlaOnColtia yn itlatlacol ca quimotlapopolhuililiya yn ttº dios—

3 telpochtli v̱ y nehuatl tle nechmauhtiz y ninonomamauhtiz y niCa ~~huel~~ amo OnāmechhualiCazquiya Cuix huel melahuac y niCa mononotza yn amoneyol-Cuitiliz y nehuatl ma ninoyolCuiti maCamo Cuix tequitli Cuix aCa ye nechahuaz—

Opa quihualtzatziliz y demoniº hueCa yez

2º demonī v̱ huel mahuiztic yn ōtiquilnamic amo ticmolCahuiliz ca oc titelpochtli—

1º telpochtli v̱ nōtlaçonycniuhtzinne cuix tiCamanalti cuix nocen monel⁶² y tiquito-hua—

---

3 telpochtli v̱ huel ypaltzin⁶³ y dios Ca melahuac y niquitohuan—

---

58. ȳmixpa: read *yn imixpan*.
59. quauhtlatli: standard *quauhtla* (as below).
60. tlapitzalos: added in a different hand.
61. tlaquauhtlayohia: read *tlaquauhtlayohua*.
62. monel: probably the intent was *amo nel*.
63. ypaltzin: read *ypaltzinco*.

SECOND DEMON: I have come in a big hurry. I have gone around the world. I have come here because many youths and maidens have gathered together. They are to confess today. They will forget quite a lot through their fear, through their shame. They will not tell their sins, with which they offended people. They will not restore honor to people. And they will not confess before their confessor that they were slapping the faces of their fathers and their mothers. They will hide it. They think that perhaps now it is thereby pardoned before God. Let me yet wait for them.

(The demon hides where there is a forest.[25] Then three youths enter. [18r] Wind instruments are played. One wears a rosary around his neck. He saves himself with the cross[26] when he lies down. The others do not bless themselves when they lie down. They sleep in the forest.)

FIRST YOUTH: O my dear friends, let us rest here in the forest, for it is about to get dark. It is a long way till we will reach the city. So, we will confess tomorrow.

SECOND YOUTH: May it be done so. May our lord God give us rest here, O my dear friends. As long as it is not entirely dark yet, let us put something together here, for it is quite dangerous in the forest.

THIRD YOUTH: As for me, I am really tired. Let us rest right away. I really want to sleep, O my friends.

(They enter the forest. It is very dangerous. They sit down addressing each other.)

FIRST YOUTH: O my friends, my heart is troubled as I think about how I will arrive before my confessor tomorrow.

(From a ways off the holy angel cries out:) God's beloved mother will help you! Pray to her! [18v]

SECOND YOUTH: I say the same. It really worries me when I think about it. I am not hungry now. May our lord God help us.

SECOND ANGEL: Our lord God will pardon anyone whose sins make him weep, make him sad.[27]

THIRD YOUTH: As for me, what will frighten me? What will I be afraid of? I would not have woken you up here.[28] Is it really correct, what is being admonished here, your confessions? As for me, whether I confess or not: is it a requirement? Will someone scold me?

(At that point the demon cries out; he is far away.)

SECOND DEMON: What you have thought of is very splendid. You will not forget that you are still a youth.

FIRST YOUTH: O my dear friend, are you joking? Or do you not speak truly?

THIRD YOUTH: By God, what I say is correct.

---

25. The second version of this play adds a preceding stage direction: *Winds instruments are played.*
26. That is, he will make the sign of the cross.
27. Although the Nahuatl is gender-neutral, this translation specifies "him" because the statement is addressed to a male.
28. That is, he is complaining that his friends are keeping him awake with their pointless chatter [?].

1º telpochtli v Jesuz tle tiquitohua Cuix amo ticminmaCaxilia y motatzin yhua y monatzin—

3 telpochtli v tle niquimaCaxiliz ȳ notatzin y nonātzin Cuix mozCalia yquac niquimonana yquechtlan oquequetza⁶⁴ niquimixtlatlatzinnia amo tle nechilhuizque—

2 demoniº v ximiçihuiti oc çenqui xicmitalhui

[19r]

2 telpochtli v maCamo quimonequiltiz y dios yn iuhqui ticchihuazque y tehuati: Ca amo techmoCahuilia ytzinco⁶⁵ titlachiyazque y totatzi yn ōtechmozCaltili topapa moçiamiquititinemi techmotemolilia y tocochCa y toneyeuhCa yhua y᷿n iz cuellaCa⁶⁶ huel tinahuatilo ytic timaCaxilizque tictenamiqui yn imatzin yn iquac yxpatzinCo taçi maCamo quimonequilti y dios yn iuhqui ticchihuazque y ticmochihuilia—

1º telpochtli v ma techmoçenhuilitzinno y ttº dios ma titoCochitica xihualmohuica nocniuhtzīne ma niCa tomexti titoçenhuiCa xicmoCahuili ȳ tocniuhtzin Canel atle quimauhtiya y nica quauhtla—

moteCazque⁶⁷ quitlalcahuizque yn imicniuh achi tlanahuac yçenl⁶⁸ yez

1º telpochtli v ma techmoçenhuilitzinno yn iteyollalilitzin y dios espīritu S.tu—
2 telpochtli v ninōmachiyotia ȳCa y Crūz ma techmopalehuilitzinno.—
Ytla ye Cochticate nima mehuaz Ave mariztellā hualmoquixtiz yn totlaçonatzin ynhua āgles nahui quihualhuiCazque Cadela⁶⁹

Virgē v ā y tilhuiCatl y ticemanahuactli y tintlalticpactli yn tantl ȳ titepetl yn̄ omitzmochihuili ȳn ōmitzmoyoColili ȳ [19v] notlaçoConetzin ȳ motech meya ȳ motech i quiça ynnin ixquich⁷⁰ yn onmitzmonemactili y nōtlaçoConetzin maçonelihui yn atle motlatlaCol Ca huel no titetlaoColti no timomauhtia no tihuihuiyoca ~~timomauhtia~~ y timolnamiqui⁷¹ yn iquac hualmohuicaz yn nōtlaçoConetzin yn ipa moquixtiquiuh yn ipanpa Omotlayȳyohuilti y tlachiya ȳ tlaCaqui auh ye amo momauhtiya amo huihuiyoCa auh ȳ tehuatl atle monācaz atle motlachiyeliz timomauhtiya tihuihuiyoCa y tiquilnamiqui yn ipā tihuetziz yn ipā tixitiniz Onyhçentzotlahueliltic ma huel tlachiyaCan ma huel tlaCaquiCa.. ma huel quitaCa ȳ notetlaçotlaliz huel ymixpa nictlalia nicnēxtia yn ipalehuiloCa y niCa yxtlahuaCa choCohuaya—

---

64. oquequetza: perhaps scribal error; maybe the intent was *niquinquequetza*.
65. ytzinco: read *ixtzinco* as in the second version of this play.
66. yn iz cuellaCa : the intent here is not clear; perhaps *yn iz cuel tlaca* is meant.
67. moteCazque: this is not in the second version of this play.
68. ycenl: read *ycel* as in the second version of this play.
69. Following this in the second version of this play: hualtlahuintiyazque.
70. ynnixquich: read *yn ixquich*.
71. timolnamiqui: perhaps to be read *ticmolnamiqui*.

FIRST YOUTH: Jesus! What are you saying? Don't you fear your father and your mother?

THIRD YOUTH: What shall I fear from my father and my mother? Do they wake up when I seize them by the neck? I beat them, I slap their faces. They will say nothing to me.
SECOND DEMON: Hurry up! Say more! [19r]

SECOND YOUTH: May it not be God's will that we do this, for our father, who raised us, does not allow us to gaze into his face. He goes about wearing himself out for our sake, searching for our dinner, our breakfast. And we are ordered to fear him.[29] We kiss his hand when we arrive before him. May it not be God's will that we act like you do.

FIRST YOUTH: May our lord God give us rest. Let us go to sleep. Come, O my friend. Let the two of us rest ourselves here. Leave our friend, for he is afraid of nothing here in the forest.
(They lie down. They leave their friend, who is by himself a little to the side.)

FIRST YOUTH: May the consolation of God the Holy Spirit give us rest.
SECOND YOUTH: I sign myself with the cross. + May it help us.
(When they sleep then the Ave Maris Stella is raised.[30] Our beloved mother enters along with four angels. They bring candles.)[31]

VIRGIN: You heaven, you world, you earth, you water, you hill, my beloved child made you, created you. [19v] From you flows, from you emerges all that my beloved child bestowed on you. Even though you have no sins, you also arouse compassion, you also are afraid, you also tremble. You think about when my beloved child will come, will come to appear to those for whose sake he suffered. They look, they listen. And yet they are not afraid, they do not tremble. But you, who have no ears, who have no vision, you are afraid, you tremble, you think on the time that you will fall and crumble. Oh four hundred times unfortunate are they! May they look well, may they listen well, may they see my love, which I place right before them. I show them what helps them here on the plain, in the place of weeping.[32]

---

29. We left "iz cuellaca" untranslated.
30. *Ave Maris Stella*: Hail, Star of the Sea. A very popular Catholic prayer and hymn to the Virgin Mary. It is used for all the Marian feasts in the reformed (Tridentine) breviary (see the *Breviarium romanum*, 1961, 1:1122–23, 1202, 2:748, 840–41, 878–79).
31. In the second version of the play is added: *They go along providing illumination.*
32. The phrasing here is reminiscent of Nahuatl renditions of the Salve Regina prayer's "vale of tears."

nima hualquiztehuaz y demonio y quauhtla motlatitiyez yxpatzinCo motlaquaquetzaz ça hueCa quihualhuiCaz yn imacpal yquimixtlatzinniya[72] yn itahua ȳn ināhuan

_____[20r]

2 demō. v dios ynatzinne ma xinechymomaquili y niCa CoCochtiCate y telpochtototi Ca omitzmolCahuilique yCochiya ma huel xicmotili yn itlahueliloCayo Ca huel mitzmolCahuilia yn iquac pactiCate atle quitequipaChohua amo mitzmolnamiquiliya mitzmolCahuiliya[73] auh tlapanahuiya yn inpa timeȳehuitia çan iquac yn itla ypa hualauh netoliniliztli CoColiztli quin iquac y mitzmoteteuhtzatzinlilia tla xicmotili yn inemiliz amo mitzmomahuiztililia yhua yn itāhua yn ināhua quimictiya quimixtlatzinnia atle ypā quimita Ca niCa niqualhuiCa yn inmacpal yn quimixtlatzinnia yn itahua yn inahua y manel oc tlalticpac nemi pāctinemi Ca ye nichuiCa yn imacpal ȳ momati amo tlatlaColi yn quichihua yhua yn īteyolcuitiCahua quiCahualtia amo quineltoCa çannoC[74] achi tlahuelCui amo quintequipachohua ȳ tle ylhuilo auh yni ma çā xinechimomaquili y niCa CoCochtiCate Ca huel ye ypa mozCaltia yn atle ypa tlachiya—

_____[20v]

Virgē v xihualauh y huel timoxiCohuani yn ayc tlamiz yn ayc tzoquiçaz y monexiColiz Canel yehuatl yniC otihualtemoc yniC otihualaçaloc y monexiColiz y monepohualiz y matlamachiliz auh yn axCa ytech timotlahuelpolohua timotlahuelquixtiya yn itlamaquixtiltzintzinhua y notlaçoConetzin Ca y yezyyotiCatzinCo ytlapalotiCatzinCo onqui^{mo}maquixtili y tlatlacohuanime auh atle yxtlauhCa yCuepCa yn itlayhiyohuilitzin y notlaçoConetzin yn i.miquilitzin atle yc quixtlahua atle yc quiCuepCayotia auh ȳ notlaçonConetzin Ca quihualmonochilia qui.hualmotzatzinliliticCa yn āmo tlacaqui yn āmo tlachiya Onyntlahueliltic y tlalticpac tlaCa yn amo quimaCaçi y miquiztli—

agel 1º v Çihuapile tonechixCaylitzinnen mixpatzinCō tixtlapachtlaçan timitztotlatlauhtilia ma xiquimopalehuili ma xiquimomaquixtili y tlatlaCo.[21r]huanime yn imacpa y tlacatecōtl[75] y quimitlaniya y niCa CoCochtiCate ma çan ipampa xicmochihuilitzinno y motlaçoRonSanriotzin y moxochiCoronatzin Ca yquechtla quihualhuica ma ça yehuatl ymaquixtiloCa mochihua y tlatlacohuanime—

2 agel v y çenmiCac timotemiltitiCa yn ilhuiCatl ytic yhua y niCa tlalticpac y nohuiya çenmanahuac tetimani y moçihuapillatoCateycnelilitzin y motepalehuilitzin yn ixpatzinCo y motlaçoConetzin Ca yehuatl ypalehuiloCa mochihua yn iSanta Crůztzin ma çemiCac quilnamiquiCa Ca ytech: Onquimomaquixtili y tlatlaCohuanime: maCayc quilCahuaCa yn iCochiya yn ineyehuaya Ca yehuatl yc momaquixtia y momoztlaye mitzmoyectenehuilia yn mitzmotzatzinlilia yn amo achito Cahuitl mitzmolCahuilia yhua y motlaçoConetzin—[21v]

72. yquimixtlatzinniya: perhaps to be read *yc quimixtlatziniya*.
73. amo mitzmolnamiquiliya mitzmolCahuiliya: this passage is not in the second version of this play.
74. çannoC: read *çan oc*.
75. tlacatecōtl: read *tlacatecolotl*.

(Then the demon quickly comes out from the forest where he is hiding. He kneels before her, just at a distance. He holds the hand of the one who slaps his fathers, his mothers, in the face.) [20r]

SECOND DEMON: O mother of God, give me the little youths who are sleeping here, for they have forgotten you in their sleep. Observe well their wickedness. They really forget you when they are having a good time. Nothing worries them. They do not remember you; they forget you. And you protect them extremely well.[33] Only when some affliction or sickness comes upon them, then do they cry out strongly to you. Do look at their lives. They do not honor you and they beat their mothers and their fathers, they slap their faces. They have no esteem for them. Here I come bringing by the hand one who slaps the faces of his fathers and his mothers, although he still lives and goes around happy on earth. I bring by the hand one who thinks that what he does is not a sin and he restrains his confessors [from correcting him?]. He does not believe them. He just becomes more irritated; what is said to him does not worry him. And so, just give me those who are sleeping here. They have no consideration now for the way they were raised. [20v]

VIRGIN: Come, you very envious one! Never will your envy be finished, never will it come to an end, for it is through your envy, your pride, your presumption that you went down, that you were cast out.[34] And now you vent your anger, you take out your anger, on those whom my beloved child has saved. With his blood, with his dye[35] he saved the sinners. But there is no payment, no return for my beloved child's suffering and death. They pay nothing for it, they return nothing for it. And my beloved child just calls to them, he is crying out to them; They do not listen, they do not look. Oh, how unfortunate are the people of earth, who do not fear death.

FIRST ANGEL: O noblewoman, O our hope, before you we humble ourselves, we pray to you. Help me! Save the sinners [21r] from the hands of the demon who is asking for those who are sleeping here. Do it just for the sake of your precious rosary, your flowery crown, which they are wearing around their necks. Let this just become the salvation of these sinners.

SECOND ANGEL: Forever you are filled up[36] [with grace], in heaven and here on earth. Your noblewomanly and royal favor, your help, spreads about filling everywhere in the world, in the presence of your beloved child. His holy cross + becomes what helps them.[37] May they always remember that it was on it that he saved the sinners. May they never forget, in their sleep and in their rising, that through it they are saved. Every day now they praise you, they cry out to you. Not for a moment do they forget you and your beloved child. [21v]

---

33. Due to the lack of several words in the second version of this play, the last two lines would read a little differently if based on that alternate text: They were not remembering you. And you protect them.

34. An allusion to the expulsion from heaven of Lucifer and his followers.

35. blood, dye: this can also be translated "blood, blood," which makes it boringly repetitive in English. Perhaps there is a double meaning here for this is a common diphrase, necessarily possessed, for "[someone's] offspring."

36. This Nahuatl verb often refers to the Virgin being filled "with grace" as in the Hail Mary prayer.

37. Alternate translation: becomes their salvation.

3 agel v̄ y çenmiCac timitztoyectenehuilia y tineçetlamachtilitzi yn tihuiCactli mixpatziCo ninotlaquaquetza ma xiquimotlaonColili maçihui y tlachiya ȳ tlaCaqui Camo quita amo quiCaqui y motlatlatlauhtilitzin yn ixpatzinCo y motlaçoConetzin amo achito Cahuitl tiquimoCahuilia auh y yehuati Ca mitzmolCahuilia amo quimati ytla ypa timoquixtia y çençenmilhuitl y çeçenyohuali tiqui^{mo}maquilia yn ixquich y moteyectililizgraçiatzin

4 agle v̄ çihuapile toneyollalililitzine Ca mixpatzinCo nicnoCuitia ynin tlatlaCohuani Ca yxquich yc nictzatzinlintinemi. ninōchoquilitinemi y nitlaOnCoxtinemi yCapa ninōtzatzintitinemi amo nechCaqui auh yn axCa amo nicmati y tley yc nicnicnomaquiliz[76] Cueta ȳ motlaçoConetzin auh yn axCa tle nel oc niquitoz Ca mochi mela[22r]huac neltiliztli y tlen ic motelhuia[77] y tlaCatecolotl[78] y mixpātzinco auh yn axCa Ca momactzinco niCahua y huel yollotepitztli yn amo tlaCaquini—

Virge v̄ auh yn axCa xihualauh ma xichuiCa y tictlatlani Canel yehuati ^{quiti}telchihua yn iximachoCatzin y notlaçoConetzin yn amo quimotzatzinlilia yn iCochiya yn inenemiya Cuix amo quimati yn itech Omaquixtiloque y Sancta Crūz

tlatzotzonaloz moCalaquiz y totlaçonatzin quimohuiquiliza̅q̃^e y agelez mochiti auh y demō. oquic tlatzotzonaloz quichichihua y queni quimamatiquiçaz—
3 telpochtli v̄ nocniuhtzitzihuane ma xinechmopalehuiliquiCa Ca ye nechhuiCaznequi y te[22v]quani yn amo onicneltoCaya Ca huel ohuica y quauhtla

tlaCueponiz OCa polihuizque nima hualiçazque yn oc Ome monotzazque

1º telpochtli v̄ ma yehuatzin tt͞o dios Ontechmotlathuiltilitzinno notlaçoycnicniuhtzinne[79]

2 telpochtli v̄ ma ça no yuhqui y tehuatzi—

2 telpochtli v̄ y tocniuhtzin Cuix oquimotlathuilti y dios—

1º telpochtli v̄ Ca āyoCac onC achi quali Oquichiuh ytla OmoCuep̄ nincha[80] Ca huel tequallani yn itlatol—
2 telpochtli v̄ nocniuhtzinne huel OnnechCanCayauh y Cochiztli Oniquitac Onhuala çen tequani huel temamauh^{ti} yuhqui ye techquaznequi—[23r]
1º telpochtli v̄ notlaçoycniuhtzinne amo xicmoneltoquiti y Cochiztli yn techintitia Ca çan toCa moCaCayahuan Ca amo neltoquiztli ma ye yhciuhCa titotoCatihuentziCa ma^{ca}mo ypa tonançiti y neyolCuitiliztli—

---

76. nicnicnomaquiliz: read *nicnomaquiliz*.
77. y tlen ic motelhuia: perhaps to be read *yn tlein quimotalhuia*.
78. y tlaCatecolotl: not in the second version of this play.
79. notlaçoycnicniuhtzinne: read *notlaçoycniuhtzine*.
80. nincha: read *ichan*.

THIRD ANGEL: Forever we praise you, who are utter bliss, who are heaven. Before you I kneel. Have compassion for them. Even though they look and listen they do not see, they do not hear the prayers you make before your beloved child. We do not leave them for a moment. But as for them, they forget you. They do not know what you attempt for them. Every day and every night you give them all your restoring grace.

FOURTH ANGEL: O noblewoman, O our consolation, before you I acknowledge that this sinner does not hear me, for all that I go about crying out to him, I go about weeping, I go about sad, I go about crying out behind him. And now I do not know how I will give an accounting to your beloved child. And now what else am I to say? It is all correct, [22r] it is the truth, what the devil[38] says before you. And now I leave in your hands the very hard-hearted one who does not listen.

VIRGIN: And now come. Take what you ask for, since he scorns the knowing of my beloved child. He does not cry out to him in his sleeping, in his going about. Does he not know that they were saved on the holy cross?

(Instruments are played. Our beloved mother exits. All the angels accompany her. And the demon, while the instruments are playing, arranges how he will carry him off.)
THIRD YOUTH: O my friends! Come help me! A fierce beast is about to carry me off! [22v] I did not believe it was so dangerous in the forest!

(Things explode. They disappear. Then the other two wake up. They call to each other.)

FIRST YOUTH: May our lord God get us up, O my dear friend.

SECOND YOUTH: May it be the same for you.

SECOND YOUTH: As for our friend, has God gotten him up?

FIRST YOUTH: He is no longer there. He would have done better if he had returned home, for his words were really provocative.
SECOND YOUTH: O my friend, sleep has really deceived me. I saw a fierce beast come. It was very frightening. It was as if it was about to eat us. [23r]
FIRST YOUTH: O my dear friend, do not believe what sleep shows us. It just deceives us. It is not believable. Let us run quickly, lest we not get to confession on time.

---

38. the devil: not in the second version of this play.

2 telpochtli v Ca ye otonaçiCo Ca ye niCa yn Can y teonCali ma toCalaquiCa aço ye neyolCuitilo ma yçiuhCa tonaçiCa nocniuhtzine—

tlapitza[81] Calaquizque yn Cani yez teoCanli tlapitzaloz hualquiçazque yn loreso yhua yçihuauh yhua agel

Loreso v nonamictzinne[82] yn axCan Ca tel ye toyollo pachiuhtiCa yn itechpa yn toneyolCuitiliz auh ynnaxCan[83] Cuix nel nimitznotlatililiz huel chiCahuac yn nechCoCohua y nōma y nocxi y notzoteCon auh ma Oc tepitzin ninocenhui aço achitzi nechtlalCahuiz qui^moneltiz[84] yn dios—

Çihuantl v nontlaçonamictzin: tle ticmitalhuitzinnohuan maCamo que quimonequiltitzinno ȳ dios ytla mopatzinCo quihualmihuanliz Ca tinnoteyollaliCatzin ma ximoçehuitzino—

MoteCaz yn iCochiya auh yn āgel ȳtzotla yez tlapitzaloz ynhua yn içihuauh—

Çihuatl v notlaçonamictzin huel niquita y moCoColitzin ma ti[85] huel timotlanahuitia—[23v]

Loreso v Macamo nimitztequipacho y nehuatl ytla ninomiquiliz onC achi huel titetequipacho Ca tēCal^tepan timomiquilitiuh ayac mitzmoCuitlahuiz ayac mitzyntaz auh y nehuatl Ca nicnomaçenhuia y motetlaçontlalintzin amo ximotequipachontzinno aço quimonequiltitzinnoz y dios anchitzin niçehuiz—

tlapitzalos[86] hualquiÇaz y miquiztli quiminaz achtopa yn içihuauh Çatepa yn inamic

Miquiztli v huel onihualiçiuhta ypampa yçiuhCa namechtlatlaliz yeyCa huel oñquimotlaçotlayeColtilique onhuāquimohuelamachtilique yn amoteyoCoxCatzin y dios ypanpa amo atlayhiyohuizque ȳ niCa tlalticpāc huel yçiuhCa namechponponloCo namechtlatlantico quemach huel amehuati yn onamechchocti yñ oamechtlaOColti yn omitl yn opa tepeuhtoc ȳn opa chayauhtoc yñ ayocmo tlatohuā ȳn ayocmo molinia huetzCa motlalohua ayocmo tepampanahuitiquiça ayoctle yh in ichiCahualiz ayoctle y yn intepozmaquauh yn imac ayoctle y çenCa mahuiztic yn itlaque OCatCan auh yn axCa onCa hueztoc onCa ponpoztectoc xaxamatoc auh yn oc yoltiCate ypan chocholohua ynpa moquequetza ayocmo qualani ayocmo [24r] tlatohua ayocmo moliniya ayocmo tlachiya auh yn iquac tlalticpac oneCan ayac huel yxpa onquiçaya ayac huel onquitlatolpanāhuiya yuhqui teotl ypa ^amomatia tla xinechhuallita Ca nehuatl y nicnechiCohua ȳn amochiCahualiz na^mechq̄xtilia xiquitaCa yñ amonemiliz ma āmechchocti amechtlaonColti Ca moztla huiptla amopa niquiztihuetzinquiuh Ca ye niyauh—

---

81. tlapitza: added in a different hand.
82. nonanmictzinne: in the second version of this play: notlaçonamictzine.
83. ynnaxCan: read *yn axcan*.
84. qui^moneltiz: read *quimonequiltiz*.
85. ma ti: either scribal error or a sentence was started but never completed.
86. tlapitzalos: added in a different hand.

SECOND YOUTH: We have already arrived. Here is the church. Let us go in. Perhaps people are already confessing. Let us arrive quickly, O my friend.
(Wind instruments are played. They go in where the church is. Wind instruments are played. Lorenzo and his wife and an angel enter.)

LORENZO: O my spouse, now we are satisfied regarding our confession. And now, can I truly hide from you that which very strongly hurts my hands, my feet, my head? But let me rest for a little longer. Perhaps in a little while God will want it to leave me.
WOMAN: O my beloved husband, what are you saying? May God not want to send something upon you. You are my consolation. Rest yourself.

(He lies down in his sleeping place. And the angel and his wife are at his head. Wind instruments are played.)
WOMAN: O my beloved spouse, I can see your sickness. You are gravely ill. [23v]

LORENZO: Let it not be I that cause you worry if I die. Better you worry that you are going to die in the street, that no one will take care of you, that no one will see you. But as for me, I benefit from your love. Do not worry. Perhaps God will want me to rest a little.

(Wind instruments are played. Death enters. He shoots arrows first at his wife and afterward at her spouse.)

DEATH: I have really come in a hurry so that I will quickly get you set up,[39] because you have very lovingly served and well pleased your creator, God. Therefore you will not suffer here on earth. Very quickly I have come to obliterate you, I have come to hide you. How fortunate are you whom the bones that lie scattered there, that lie dispersed there made weep, made sad. No longer do they speak, no longer do they move, laugh, run. No longer do they go passing people by. No longer do they have any strength, no longer do they have swords in their hands, no longer is what was their clothing very splendid. And now they lie fallen there, they lie broken up and shattered there. And those who are still alive jump around on them and stand on them. They no longer get angry, no longer [24r] speak, no longer move, no longer look. But when they lived on earth no one could pass before them, no one could surpass them in speech. They considered themselves to be like gods. Do look at me, for I am gathering up your health and taking it away from you. Look at your lives. Let them make you weep and make you sad for tomorrow or the next day I will suddenly come to find you. I am going now.

---

39. That is, prepare them for death.

tlapitzalos[87] Calaquiz y miquiztli tlapitzaloz

Çihuatl v notlaçoñamictzi huel nechCoColhuia y nōtzoteco y moCoColitzin ynic motlatzinCo nehuatiCa huel neçi ȳ Ca huel chiCahuac timococotzinnohua—
loreso v çihuapile nonāmictzinne huel quimati y noyollo Camo ninehuaz ytla oninomiq̄li çan ixquich nictlatlani yxpatzinCo y dios huel hueCatla tlali ytzintla tinechmaquiliz—
Çihuatl v maCamo ximotequipachotzinno Can mochihuaz y motlañahuatiltzin ytlaCamo hualtotoCaz yn itetlaçotlalitzin ȳ dios Ca huel quimati ȳ noyollo Ca ye onnōnipeuh Ca huel acmo huelti yn nōtlalo y noçoquiyo çannixquich[88] nechtequipachohua aqui techitaz aqui techaCoCuiz [24v] Otoçetzotlahuelliltic y titlatlacohuaniem[89]—
Loreso v noñamictzinne ma oC achitzin xinechmotlalCahuili maCamo OC achi ximoCoColizeuhtzinno—
Motecaz oc çecni y cihuantzitli auh yn agel OCa moetztiyez ȳ tlan

---

1º aḡel v dios ytlachihualtzintzinhuane Ca ye yxquich Ca ye ontlamiCo yn amonemiliz Ca ye anmechhualmonochilia yn amotantzin dios yncenmactzinco xomocahuaca—
demoniº hualquicaz[90] motlaCachichihuaz hualaz ytla y CoCoxque quinotzaz—

2º demō v yxquich amotlapal notelpotztzine ynhua yni tehuatzin nochpotzinne maCamo ximoçotlahuaCa ytla xinetlamatiCa aço apantizque aCa xicnotzaCa amechpatiz amotolinia namechyoyollalico—
Loreso v aqui tehuatzin amo timitztiximachilia y titechmolhuilia tictemozque yn aqui techpatiz Ca ye oninonyollCuiti[91] yhua y nonamic ~~yea~~ ye teoyotiCa ontitopatique neyolCuitiliztiCa otictoçelilique y totechiuhCatzin dios Ca ça ticchixtiCate y queni [25r] quimonequiltiz Ca yehuatzin çeuhtzintli pātzintli[92]—

1º aḡēl v Yn timictlatlentexcali ma opa xihuetzin ȳ çenCa ohuiCa yn āyc tlamiz yn anyc tzoquiçaz ma ºpa xitleCoCotonCa monexicoliztiCa axCa ticmahuiçoz yn imicneliloCa xiquitlalCahui y timictlacuitlamiztitli—

quihuihuitequiz quichololtiz y demō

Loreso v nontlaçonāmictzinne nictlatlani y nontlapōpōlhuililoCa ynpanpatzinCo ȳ dios ma nimitznōnahuatequili—

---

87. tlapitzalos: added in a different hand.
88. çannixquich: read *çan ixquich*.
89. titlatlacohuaniem: read *titlatlacohuanime*.
90. hualquicaz: read *hualquiçaz*.
91. oninonyollCuiti: read as standard *oninoyolcuiti*.
92. Stage directions follow in the second version of this play: *quihuinhuitequiz. yn demonio—yn angel quichololtiz*. This anticipates (with relatively minor differences) the stage directions that immediately follow First Angel's lines.

(Wind instruments are played. Death exits. Wind instruments are played.)

WOMAN: O my beloved spouse, my head really hurts me. Your sickness, as I sit beside you, really appears very strong; you are ill.

LORENZO: O noblewoman, O my spouse, my heart knows well that I will not get up. When I have died, all I ask for before God is that you will bury me deeply under the ground.

WOMAN: Do not worry. Your command will be carried out, if I do not die right away myself.[40] My heart knows well that I have already begun [to die]. My earth, my clay is no longer strong. All that worries me is, who will see us, who will lift us up?[41] [24v] Oh, we are four hundred times unfortunate, we sinners!

LORENZO: O my spouse, leave me for a little longer. Do not become more sick.

(He lies down, and in another place the woman. And the angel is there with them.)

FIRST ANGEL: O creations of God, that is all, your lives have already come to an end. Your father, God, is calling you now. Leave yourselves entirely in his hands.

(The demon enters. He dresses himself as a human being. He comes close to the sick ones. He calls to them.)

SECOND DEMON: Give it all your effort, O my son, and you, O my daughter. Do not faint! If you are discontented, perhaps you will recover. Call someone who will cure you. You are afflicted. I have come to console you.

LORENZO: Who are you? I do not know you. You tell us that we are to seek someone who will cure us. I have already confessed, along with my spouse. Already through confession we have healed ourselves in a sacred way. We have received our maker, God.[42] We are just awaiting what [25r] he will want, for he is repose and medicine.

FIRST ANGEL: You, who are the fiery crag of the place of the dead, fall in the very dangerous place that will never be finished, never come to an end. Be broken up by the fire there, through your envy. Now you will behold how they are favored. Leave them, you puma of the place of the dead!

(He repeatedly beats and drives away the demon.)

LORENZO. O my beloved spouse, I ask that I be pardoned for the sake of God. Let me embrace you.

---

40. Literally, "if God's love does not come rushing." Death is often spoken of as "God's love" in Nahuatl wills.
41. That is, carry them for burial?
42. That is, we have also taken communion.

Çihuatl v notlaçonamictzi. ma ypanpa yn dios ytlaçonatzi ylh^c çihuapilli Sancta maria ma xinechmotlaponpolhuilili ma yctenamiq̄[93] y momatzin—

Ytla omotlaponpolhuique ȳ CoCoxque nima hualquiçazque ȳn añimaz huel miyequiti[94] hualyaCanaz~~que~~ on ome oquihualhuicazque ome Candela huallalatiyaz[95] ymac tlatlaz y momiquilizque yhua motlapoz yn ilhuiCaC huel pampaquizque yn agelz—quipalehuizque yn animaz ynic momiquilizque[96]—[25v]

1º añimaz v Ca otiquixtlahuaCo y motetlaçotlalitzin totlaçoycniuhtzinne—

2 añimaz v Ca oticCuepCayotiCo ynic topanpa OtimoChoquilitineCa—

3 animaz v Ca otimitztopalehuiliCo yn iuhqui Ontitechmopalehuili yn ixpatzinCo y dios—

4 animaz v Ca ontiquixtlahuaCo yniC omitztlaonColti yn tomiyotzin ȳ totetepontzin—

5º animaz v Ca otamechtanniliCo yteCopatzincon yn dios yciuhCa tiyazque—

6 anīmaz v yñayolliliztin ma yçiuhCa xictlalCahuica yn amotlalo yn amoçōquiyo Camechhualmonochilia[97] amechhualmotzatzinlilia y toyolilinçenCatzin dios ȳ tloctzinco amopaCançenhuizque—

huel çençenyaCa hualquiztiyazque yñ animaz ynic quitlatlauhtizque ȳ CoCoxque ymac momiquilizque ȳn ānimaz çan ye tlapochtiyez yn ilhuiCac—

agel v xihualmoquixti animā amo ximomauhti tle mitzmauhtiya y niCa Ca mopampa y pampacohua yn h^c[98] ytic [26r] y çenCa ohuaquimotlaçotlayecoltillique y tt^o[99] dios y niCa tlaticpa Ca niCa motlatzinCo ninemini amo nāmechnocahuila—

Onpa y quitoz yn itlatol yn agel nima momiquilizque yçiuhCa quihuiCazque yn progatoriō yn imanima mochichihuazque ome huel tepītzitzin yn piltzintzi Cololhuitiyazque yñ animaz ni[100] hualquiçazque Ometi telponpochti tlapitzaloz[101]—

1º telpochtli v nocniuhtzinne mach ye oquimopolhui y dios y Loresotzi yhuan içihuauhtzin qui huel achitoCa yn onniquimitac yxquich tlaCatl ōpa hualquiquiça tla toyollo onpachihui aço ytla totlamatlanizque[102] yc motoCatzinozque—

2 telpochtli v ma dios quimotlanexmaquili ca huel mahuiztique tlaCa OCatCan ma onpa tonaçitihuetzinCa[103]—

1º telpochtli v ma dios amotlatzinco moyetztie nōtlaçoyCauhtzinne yhua y tehuatzin çihuapile—

---

93. iyctenamiq̄: probably to be read *nictennamiqui*.
94. huel miyequiti: in the second version of this play: 6.
95. huallalatiyaz: read *huallatlatiyaz*.
96. Additional text follows in the second version of this play: yn lorenço—yhua yn içihuauh.
97. Camechhualmonochilia: read *Ca amechhualmonochilia*.
98. h^c: read *ilhuicatl*.
99. tt^o: this superscript addition is not present in the second version of this play.
100. ni: read *niman* as in the second version of this play.
101. tlapitzaloz: added in a different hand. Another addition (not sure where it goes) is the following, in tentative transcription: motzaquaz yn [ih^c?].
102. totlamatlanizque: perhaps to be read *tontlamactlanizque*.
103. In the second version of this play stage directions follow: *niman ic yazque. yn icha. LorenÇo*.

WOMAN: O my beloved spouse, for the sake of God's beloved mother, the heavenly noblewoman, Saint Mary, pardon me. Let me kiss your hand.
(When the sick ones have pardoned each other, then a lot[43] of souls enter. The two who lead the way come carrying two candles which are burning. They burn in the hands of those who will die and heaven opens.[44] The angels really rejoice. The souls help them[45] to die.)
[25v]
FIRST SOUL: We have come to repay your love, O our beloved friend.
SECOND SOUL: We have come to make return for the way you went about weeping for our sake.
THIRD SOUL: We have come to help you as you helped us before God.

FOURTH SOUL: We have come to repay the way our bones, our tibias made you sad.

FIFTH SOUL: We have come to take you, by order of God. We will go quickly.
SIXTH SOUL: You lives, quickly abandon your earth, your clay. The owner of our lives, God, is calling you, is crying out to you. With him you will rest happily.

(One by one the souls come passing by to address the sick ones. In the hands of the souls they die. Heaven remains open.)
ANGEL: Come out, soul, do not be afraid. What frightens you here? For your sake there is rejoicing in heaven. [26r] You have served our lord God very lovingly here on earth. I live here with you. I do not leave you.[46]
(At that point the angel makes his statement. Then they die. They quickly take their souls to purgatory. Two very small children are dressed up. The souls go surrounding them. Then two youths enter. Wind instruments are played.)
FIRST YOUTH: O my friend, they say that God has now destroyed Lorenzo and his wife. Barely a moment ago I saw all the people coming out of there. Do let us satisfy ourselves. Perhaps we will order that something be given so that they can be buried.[47]
SECOND YOUTH: May God give them light. They were highly esteemed people. Let us get there quickly.[48]
FIRST YOUTH: May God be with you, O my dear friend, and you, O noblewoman.

---

43. The second version of this play specifies the number of souls: *Six*.
44. We interpret the preceding to mean that the souls place the candles in the hands of Lorenzo and his wife who are probably lying on their backs, holding the lit candles on their chests.
45. The second version of this play clarifies this referent: *Lorenzo and his wife*.
46. The second version of this play reads: I will not leave you.
47. Tentative translation.
48. The second version of this play adds the following stage directions: *At that point they go to Lorenzo's house.*

2 telpochtli v̄ auh Can oyaque yn ixquich tlaCatl y niCa ONCatca Ca huel tetzahuitl yn axCa tiquita yn oquimochili[104] dios ma yçiuhca titenotzāti ximohuiCa nocniuh-tzine [26v] ma yçiuhCa hualhuilohua ȳnic motoCatzinnozque—

1º telpochtli v̄ ma ninōtlalotihuetzin ynic ȳçiuhCa motoCatzinnozque—
Mochiti hualquiçazque tetoCazque mēhuaz rezponso ytla omotoCaque nima tlapitztzaloz motlapoz yn ȳtĥ.Cac—tlapitzaloz[105]

Vrigē[106] v̄ notlaçōconetzi: noyezyotzin nōtlapālotzin çenCa mitzmetiçihuitilia yn itla-tlacol yn tlalticpac tlaCa ma nalquiça y moJustiçiatzin yn itechcacopa yn ōpa caten y motletenchipahuayatzinco[107] y progāturio Ca ye mixpatzinCo Onnictlali y nochoquiz y notlaOCol ma xiquimotlamachtili ȳ motloctzinCo y monahuactzin[108] yn ilhuiCatl ytic y motlachihualtzintzihua—

pōx[109] no~~ne~~tlaçomahuiznatzinne Ca mochihuaz Ca tzoquiçaz y motlanequilitzin Ca yehuatl niquilnamiqui ynic oyetiçiuh y motlaçomatzin ynic otinechmonāpal[27r]-tineCa yhua Ca anmo çan iyo y ñopampa oticmiyhiyohuilti nopampa Ontimo-choq̇ˡlitinenCa yn iquac Onechtlayhiyohuiltique y noteCoColiCahuan auh amo quitlaçoCamati y tlalticpac tlaCa yn ixqᶜch[110] ypāpa ticmochihuilia auh ma qui-hualquixtiti y ñotlaçontzitzinhua y çenCa onechCuiltononque yCa y motlaçōma-huizroSanriotzin—

Vrige v̄ ytecopatzinCo y nontlaçōconetzin xiquihualquixtiti yn opa Cate y progātorio yhua yn onnechylcauh yn inenemiya yhua yn iCochiya yn anmo Onquitlali yn ixquac y Crū̇z yñ opa quauhtla OquihuiCac y huey tequanni y çan[111] [?] niCa yn inaCayo yn oquihuiCaᶜ ma niCa yxpatzinCo neçi y notlaçoConetzin[112]—

tlapitza[113] # nima quihualquixtitihui y progatorio Caten auh ytla oquihual-huiCaque y Cani yez ylhuiCatl—nima quitzatziliz y diayablome .3. [27v] yn agel mochiti yazq̄ y agelz

---

1º agel v̄ xihualmoquixtiCa y çenCa ohuāquimotlaçotlayecoltilique y dios ȳtlaçon-natzin—
y nima quitzatzinliz y demoñios yn agel ytla ohuaçico yxpatzincon y pōxo—
1º agel v̄ xihualquiçan Ca y mictla amilpitoque xiqualqnixtiCa[114] yn oāquihuiCaque y tlatziuhqui[115]

---

104. oquimochili: read *oquimochihuili*.
105. tlapitzaloz: in a different hand.
106. Vrigē: here and below, read *virgen*.
107. motletenchipahuayatzinco: in the second version of this play: motetlechipahuayatzinco.
108. monahuactzin: read *monahuactzinco*.
109. pōx: here and below in various nonstandard variants, this usually appears in Nahuatl church texts as xp̄o.
110. ixqᶜch: read *ixquich*.
111. çan: something follows that is crossed out and illegible.
112. Following this is in the second version of the play: 2.º angel = ma nima ticchihuati yn motlato-catla[nahua]tiltzin toteyoCoxcatzine Diose xpo.e.
113. tlapitza: added in a different hand.
114. xiqualqnixtiCa: read *xichualquixtican*.
115. Immediately following, in superscript, is an additional item in the second version of this play: mol-cahuani. There are also what appear to be doodles, for the purpose of practicing writing.

SECOND YOUTH: But where did all the people go who were here? It is very ominous. Now we see what God has done. Let us quickly call people. Go, O my friend. [26v] Let people come quickly so that they may be buried.

FIRST YOUTH: Let me run off in a hurry so that they may be buried quickly.

(All enter. They perform the burial. The responsory is raised [in song]. When they have been buried, then wind instruments are played. Heaven opens. Wind instruments are played.)

VIRGIN: O my beloved child, my blood, my dye,[49] the sins of the people of earth weigh very heavily upon you. May your justice reach unto those who are there in your place of fiery purification of people, purgatory. I have already placed before you my weeping, my sadness. Make your creations happy next to you, beside you, in heaven.

CHRIST: O my beloved honored mother, what you desire will be done, will be carried out. I remember how your precious hands were heavily weighted as you carried me about in your arms, [27r] and it was not solely for my sake that you suffered, for my sake that you went about weeping when those who hated me tormented me. But the people of earth are not grateful for all that you do for them. And let them bring forth my beloved ones, who pleased me very much with your precious and honored rosary.

VIRGIN: By order of my beloved child, go bring out those who are there in purgatory, along with the one who forgot me, who in his going about and in his sleeping did not place the cross on his forehead, whom the great beast carried off there in the forest. Right here is his body, which it carried off. Let him appear here before my beloved child.[50]

(Wind instruments are played. Then they go to bring out those who are in purgatory. And when they have brought them out to where heaven is then the angel cries out to the three demons. [27v] All the angels go off [to purgatory].)

FIRST ANGEL: Come out, you who lovingly served God's beloved mother.

(Then the angel cries out to the demons who have come before Christ.)

FIRST ANGEL: Come out, you who lie tied up in the place of the dead. Bring out the one you carried off, the lazy one.[51]

---

49. blood, dye: see above footnote on the same diphrase. In this context not only is the pragmatic thrust "my offspring" but there are also connotations of noble birth.

50. The second version of this play has another speech following this one by the Virgin: SECOND ANGEL: Let us then carry out your royal command, O our creator, O God, O Christ.

51. The second version of this play adds in superscript: the forgetful one.

cētlapal[116] momanazq̄ qualti yhua yn agelz çentlapal yez y codenadon—

3º[117] demō. v Ca ye otiqualhuiCaque ȳ nantle[118] ypa tlachiya

p̄ox v xihualauh notlachihuale xinechnaquili tle yCa yn ōmitzychteq̄to y quauhtla y tlacatecolotl [28r] tlen ic omitzmoxicti Cuix amo onñamechhualCahuilitia yn āmomaq̄xtiloca yn tlalticpac +—
codenado v Ca ytlatlacol ȳ notatzin[119] amo onechyximachti y motoCatzi yhua çan onechpaCayhiyohui yn oniquixtlatzinyaya yn ixCo ycpac onine ytla onechtlaCahualtiyani aço ᵃmo yuhqui nopā omochihuazquiya onoçētzōtlahuellitic—

2 agel v noteotzinne notlatoCatzinne tlen ec[120] niquitoz y mixpatzinco Ca anmo onnechCac yn i Capā OnotzatzintitineCa y niCa mixpatzinco quiteyxpahuiya—

3 demō v y tehuāti Cuix amo ça çentetl yniC otitechhualmotelchihuili auh yni Cuix ça çenpa yn ixCo ycpac one yn itantzi yn inantzin yhua y motoCatzin ça oquitlapic[28v][121]tenehuaya ytla onxicmoCahuiliani y tlalticpac Ca amo ça tlapohualti yn oquimictizquiya yn ihuapohua yninC[122] omitzmopanahuilizquiya—
p̄xo v xihualhuiya xichuiCan Ca onpa yn tletexCalCo xicpiloCa Opa xichuitequiCa xictzatzayaCa ypanpa Ca nehuatl yn ōnechyxtlatzini y nixCo nocpac one—
3 demōno v Otitechmocnelili ma yçiuhCa ticchihuati y motlatocatlanahuatiltzin—
Vrige v auh yn amehuantzitzin y huel ōhuamotlaçontlaque y tlalticpac ma huel pampaqui yn ilhuicatl xihualmotlecahuiC—Cuicō[123]

codenado v yn ātlacahuapahua yn atlaCazCaltia maCamo ça xixoxolopititiCa yuhqui yn amo amozCalia xictlapoCa yn amonaCaz xicCaquiCa ȳ y çermo yhua y nexCuitilmachiyᵒtl amo ahuetziti^(hui) y tletexCalCo ȳ yn iuhqui axCa ye niauh—

---

116. Preceding these stage directions in the second version of this play: hualquiztehuazque. yn demonios.
117. 3º: in the second version of this play: 2.º.
118. yȳ nantle: read *yn atle*.
119. In the second version of this play is added in superscript: i nonantzin.
120. ec: standard *ic*.
121. Something illegible immediately precedes these characters *tenehuaya*.
122. yninC: read *ynic*.
123. Cuicō: Cuicos in the second version of this play.

(On one side are spread about the good ones and the angels. On [the other] side is the condemned one.)[52]

THIRD DEMON:[53] We have brought the disrespectful one.

CHRIST: Come, O my creation. Answer me. Why did the demon steal you in the forest? [28r] Why did he disdain you? Did I not leave you your means of salvation on earth?

CONDEMNED ONE: It is my father's[54] fault. He did not make your name known to me, and he just patiently put up with me when I used to slap his face, when I offended him. If he had stopped me, perhaps it would not have happened to me like this. Oh, four hundred times unfortunate am I!

SECOND ANGEL: O my deity, O my ruler, what will I say before you? Wherever I went about crying out to him, whom they bring to justice here before you, he did not listen to me.

THIRD DEMON: As for us, was it not just one thing that you scorned us for?[55] And was it just one time that he offended his father and his mother? And he would just pronounce your name in vain. [28v] If you left him on earth innumerable are his fellows whom he would have killed, by which he would have surpassed you.[56]

CHRIST: Come. Take him there to the fiery crag. Hang him, beat him, rip him apart there, because it is I whom he slapped in the face, I whom he offended.

THIRD DEMON: Thank you. Let us quickly go to carry out your royal command.

VIRGIN: And you who have loved one another well on earth, rejoice much in heaven. Come on up.
(There is singing.)

CONDEMNED ONE: You who bring up children, you who raise children, do not be idiotic, as if you were not rational. Open your ears! Listen to the sermon and the exemplary model. You are not going to fall into the fiery crag like I am now about to do!

---

52. The second version of this play adds at the beginning of these stage directions: *The demons hurriedly enter.*
53. The second version of this play marks this character: SECOND DEMON.
54. The second version of this play adds in superscript: and my mother's.
55. That is, the devils were cast out of heaven for committing only one sin.
56. That is, disregarded you?

Present Location
Library of Congress
Washington, D.C.

[44r]

NeyxCuintilli yntechpa tlantohua yn pochtecatl Auh axcan NiquiCuilohua nehuatl notlatqui Notoca .d. Joseph gaspar y nica Nocha S. Juā bap.^ta Tolatzin.^co auh nictlalia yn tonali. ynhua y xihuitl Axcan sabado a 15 de nobienbre de 1687 años.

Tlahtolpepechtli

v̄ Ma yehuatzin. Amotlantzico quimotlalili yn itetlamatcanemitiayatzin y dios espū sancto y nica Oanhualmohuicaque anquimoCuilico anquimocaquiltico yn ihiyotzin yn itlahtoltzin y tlacatl tlatohuani dios Ca nican amixpantzin.^co Tocōtlalizque Toconchihuazque Centlamātli neyxCuitilmachiyotl yn Cenca temamauhti yn queni OquimotlatzaCuiltili yn tt.^o dios yn Cen tlacatl moCuiltonohuani motlacamatini tetech tlayxpanani yhuan teaxca tetlatqui quixpachohuaya. auh macihui yn omoyolCuiti. yhuan OquimoCenlili yn itlaçomahuiznacayotzin yn itlaçomahuizezotzin yn totemaquixticatzin Jesu X͞p͞o. Ca amo yc otlaocoliloc Ca oc Cenca ye yc otelchihualoc ypanpa Amo oquiteCuepili. y. teaxca yn tetlatqui yc Cenca temamauhti. teCueCuechmicti. yn ipā omochiuh yn inacayo yhua yn ianima ma huel y^tech ximixCuintica yn tetech antlaxitlapanani¹ macamo yuhqui Amopā mochihuaz yn iJusticiatzin yn tt.^o dios yn āmochinti y nican Amonoltitoque ma yc ximomauhtican ynic amo ypa ahuetzizque y huey tlatlancolli y tetech tlayxtlapānaliztli y tetech tlamiyecaquixtiliztli auh ynī ma huel ypaltzin.^co yn dios yntech tictlalica yn toyollo ynin neyxcuitilmachiyotl. Auh ytla ytla toconitlacozque ma ça yehuantzin yn tlacatl tlantohuani dios atechmotlapopolhuililyzque²—

OnCan hualquiçaz yn poChteCatl—

Quitoz—[44v]

Pochtecatl v̄ yn ipā yn ixquich y nohuelitiliz Ayac huel nechaçiz yn ipa yn ixquich noaxca notlatqui yn Coztic teoCuitlatl yn iztac teoCuitlatl yn chalchihuitl yn quetzalitztli ynnepyollotli³ auh yn ixquich y nepanpa tlaçotli y nopapāquiliz yn tlaçotilmātli yn tlaçotlaquemitl ayac huel nechaçiz aquin yacachtopa tenehualo hitolo yn iquac. teCohuanotzaloyā amo çā ye nehuatl auh yn iquac yn nenamictilo yn Cuico aqui yacatopa notzalo temolo: Amo çan ye nehuatl Ca huel nolhuil nomaCenhual Oc nocotimalotinemi yn tlalticpac auh Cenca nechpanpaquiltia yn icnotlaCantototi y nohuicpa ytztihui ynic niquintlatlaneuhtia auh yn iquac amo yciuhca quixtlahua auh oc cenca nichuecapanohua ynic nechtlaxtlahuilia yehica ynic amo polihuiz y noaxca notlatqui amo ye huitze tla oc niquimōchie. Oncan hualquiças huehuentzin ~~yhuā~~ ylamatzin⁴

---

1. antlaxitlapanani: read *antlaixtlapanani*.
2. atechmotlapopolhuililyzque: read *techmotlapopolhuililitzino*.
3. ynnepyollotli: read *yn epyollotli*.
4. Oncan hualquiças huehuentzin ~~yhuā~~ ylamatzin: added later in a different hand, with lines above and below.

The Merchant

Translated by Barry D. Sell, with assistance from Louise M. Burkhart

[44r]

Edifying example that speaks about a merchant. I am writing it today; it is my property. My name is Don Joseph Gaspar and I am a resident here in San Juan Bautista Tollantzinco. I am setting down the day and year: today is Saturday, 15 November, of the year 1687.

Prologue.

May God the Holy Spirit set down among you the peace of our lord.[1] You have come here to grasp and hear the fine words of God, lord and ruler. Here before you we will set down and perform a model edifying example, very frightening, [concerning] how our lord God punished a person who was happily rich. He was a moneylender and hid other people's goods and property. Even though he confessed and had received the precious honored body and precious honored blood of our savior, Jesus Christ, he was not therefore shown mercy but was especially despised because he had not returned to others their goods and property. Thus what happened to his body and his soul was very frightening and very terrifying. You who are moneylenders, really take an example from it, let not the same justice of our lord God happen to you. Be frightened by it, all of you who are assembled here, so that you will not fall into the great sin of moneylending and usury. Now then, for the sake of God[2] let us set our hearts on this model edifying example. But if [in spite of this moral instruction] we should err in something may God, lord and ruler, pardon us.

(At that point Merchant enters. He says:) [44v]

MERCHANT: No one can equal me in all my power, in all my goods and property, the gold and silver, the jades and emeralds, the precious pearls. No one can equal me in all the diverse precious things that are my pleasures, the expensive cloaks and expensive garments. When it is time for banquets: who is first mentioned and spoken of? Is it not I? When there are weddings and singing: who is the first summoned, who the first spoken to? Is it not I? I go about increasing my rewards and fortunes here on earth. The miserable little poor people give me great pleasure when they go looking to me to make them loans. And when they don't quickly pay them back I especially increase what they are to repay me so that my goods and property will not perish. Are they not coming now? Let me await them.

(At that point Old Man enters ~~with~~ Old Woman.)

---

1. Molina 1977, 42v: "Itetlamatcanemitiaya in dios. la paz de nuestro señor" (see also 74r, 108v). Abbreviations in the original Nahuatl and Spanish have been resolved here and in the other footnotes to this translation.

2. While these and similar constructions (with a few exceptions) have been translated here as "for the sake of," translators sometimes have used the phrasing "for the love of." For "ypaltzinco," consult Molina 1565, 7r: "ypaltzinco Dios" / "por amor de Dios"; see also Carochi 1983, 17r. For "ypampatzinco" see Molina 1984, 116r: "ypampatzinco totecuiyo Dios" / "por amor de nuestro señor dios." See also Arenas 1982, 35: "*hazlo por amor de Dios*—ma ipampatzinco yn toTecuiyo Dios xicchihua." For "icatzinco," see Siméon 1988, 53: "*icatzino in totecuiyo,* por el amor de nuestro Señor, o gracias a nuestro Señor."

huehuetzin v Nopiltzintzine tlacatle tlatohuanie mixpātzin[co] ninopechteca Cenca nimitznotlatlauhtilia ypaltzinco yn tt.[o]. dios ma Xinechmotlaneuhtilitzinno matlactli pesos ynic niquixtiz nopiltzin ilpitica ynic amo tzauhcan quicahuazque Ca çan nimā yciuh[5] nimitznocuepililiz Axcan Caxtolilhuitl.

Pochtecatl. v Ye nicaqui y motlatol yn tehuatl. Auh Cuix çan amehuanti Amopanpa y nictemotinemi yn teoCuitlatl. ynic namechtlatlaneuhtiz Ca ahuelitiz nimitzmacaz XimohuiCatiuh Auh ytla ylpitiCa mopiltzin Cuix noteq̄uh ma ça quinamācacan ma tzauhcan quicahuacā Cuix namechyximati Cuix anezohuan Anotlapalohuan. Ximohuicatihuiya Amo namechmaCaz—[45r]

Ylamatzin ynamic v Noquichpiltzin NoteCuiyotzin ma çan ipanpatzin.[co] yn tt.[o] d. ma ça Xitechmotlaneuhtili y motomintzin Auh ca toCotlapehuizque yn ipa y cen pesso Tehuatzin ticmomachiltia yn quexquich ypā toCotlalizque.

Pochtecatl. v Ca tel ye qualli Ca tel ye melahuac y tiquitohua y tehuatl. y tilamatlacatl. Ca namechmacaz y notomin Auh ca ye anquimati yn çe peso. nahui tomi ypan anquitlalizque Ca ye qualli ma namechmaca auh çan caxtolilhuitl. AquiCueppazque auh ytla quipanahuiz caxtolilhuitl ytla oc quezquilhuitl aquipiezque ca cenpohualli pessos anechmacazq̄ue ytla yuh aquinequi Ca namechmacaz y notomī.

huehuentzin v. Ca tel ye qualli nopiltzintzine ma yuh mochihuaz ȳ motlanequilitzin yn iuh ticmonequiltitzinohua Ca nican cā y nonamic yhua y nehuatl ca nima yçiuhcan timitztoCuepililizq̄. Ca amo quipanahuiz y caxtolli tonatiuh ca nima yçiuhca timitztoCuepililizque Caxtolli peso ynic ocan tocotlalizque totlahuecahuaya maCuilli peso—

Pochtecatl. v. Ca yzcatqui ye namechmacan y matlactli pesos. auh ça caxtolilhuitl. annechCuepillizque yc āquiCuepazq̄ Caxtolli pesos—

ylamatzin v Ca çenca tocōtlaçocamati y motepalehuillitzin otlacauhqui y moyollotzin otitechmocnelili Ca ye tiyatihui—

huehuentzin v Ma mitzmochicahuili yn tt[o] dios ma oc timitztotlalcahuilican—

Pochtecatl v Ximochuicatihuia ma dios Amechmohuiquili—

Tlapitzaloz oca hualquiçaz ychpochtli motlatlanehuiz—[45v]

---

5. yciuh: read *yciuhca*.

OLD MAN: O my nobleman, O personage, O ruler, I humbly bow low before you. I greatly implore you: for the sake of our lord God lend me ten pesos so that I will free my child who is in custody, so that they will not deliver him to a textile manufacturing shop.[3] I will straightaway return it to you fifteen days [from] now.

MERCHANT: I hear your words but is it on your account I go about searching for gold and silver[4] to lend you? I will not be able to give it to you. Be going along. If your child is in custody, is it my responsibility? Let them sell him off, let them deliver him to a textile manufacturing shop. Do I know you? Are you my offspring? Be going along. I will not give it to you. [45r]

OLD WOMAN (his spouse): O my son, O my lord, let it just be for the sake of our lord God. Lend us your money. We will pay interest on each peso; you can decide how much interest we will pay.

MERCHANT: Very well, old woman, what you are saying is true. I will give you my money. But you already know that you will add four tomines for each peso you borrow. Very well, let me give it to you. You will return it within fifteen days. But if more than fifteen days pass, if you have it a few days more, you will give me twenty pesos. If that's the way you want it I will give you my money.

OLD MAN: O my nobleman, very well, may your will be done as you want it. Here are my spouse and I. We will straightaway restore it to you; it will not exceed fifteen days. We will extremely quickly repay you [a total of] fifteen pesos. We will put down five [additional] pesos in a second part [to pay] for our grace period.[5]

MERCHANT: Here are the ten pesos I am giving you but you will return it to me in just fifteen days. As [agreed] you will return fifteen pesos.

OLD WOMAN: Thank you very much for your help. We give you many thanks for the favor you have shown us.[6] We are going now.

OLD MAN: May our lord God give you health. Let us leave you now.

MERCHANT: Be going along. May God go with you.

(Wind instruments are blown. At that point Young Woman enters to ask for a loan.) [45v]

---

3. Izaulican: while the neutral term "textile manufacturing shop" has been used here and below, modern pejorative "sweat shop" may more accurately capture the tone of this colonial institution. For the term itself, see Pérez 1713, 179: "obraxe" / "tzaccan."

4. gold and silver: here and below, Nahuatl *teocuitlatl* (literal meaning probably "divine/god excrement" but general thrust is "precious metal[s]") with the modifiers *coztic* (yellow) and *iztac* (white) that refer, respectively, to "gold" and "silver." Since the more specific meanings are given in the merchant's first speech, with all the following references being to generic *teocuitlatl*, I have interpreted the latter as meaning (in the context of this play) "gold and silver." Note, however, the following two entries in Arenas 1982, 141: "Coztic teocuitlatl—*Oro*," followed immediately by plain "teocuitlatl—*plata*" (that is, the unmodified form means "silver").

5. totlahuecahuaya / our grace period: see related terms in Molina 1977, 144r.

6. The fortuitous phrasing here and below can be found in Molina 1984, 118v: "¶ Notecuiyoe tlatohuanie, otlacauhquin moyollotzin otinechmocnelili" / "¶ Señor mio, hagoos muchas gracias, por los beneficios que me aueys hecho."

ychpochtli v̲ Ma mitzmotlaçochicahuili y motlaçotatzin dios Noquichpiltzin note-Cuio mixpātzin.^co cenca ninopechteca ȳ nehuatl y nimocnomaÇenhualtzin ma ypaltzin^co yn tt̲.^o Jesu X p̄ o. Ma xinechmopalehuilitzino Ca y nonātzin yhuan y notatzin Çencan motoliniticate huel huey cocoliztli ypā quimochihuilia ȳ tt.^o dios auh ynic tiquimopalehuiliz Ca yehuatl ynic nica Onihuanla mixpātzin^co Aço nitlac-nopilhuiz tinechmotlaneuhtiliz Çenpohuali pesos Ca nima niCueppaz Cenpohua-lilhuitl. auh can icatqui[6] Prenda ticmopieliz y notlapac y notlapāchiuhcan yhua y nohuipilli.[7] Cencan nimitznotlatlauhtilia ypaltzin^co y. tlaçoychpochtli Sta m.^a—Chocaz yn ichpochtli

Pochtecatl. v̲ Tle ticnequi ychpochtle ynic nixpā tichoca auh macihui yn qualli mitz-momaquilia yn dios y moxayac Ca anmo yehuatl nictemohua. Ca çenca nicnequi ynic miyec yez motlapehuiz y noteoCuitl auh ȳ tla ticnequi ynic nimitztlaneuhtiz noteoCuitl Ontlamātli ticchihuaz ynic Çentlamātli yn ipanpa Cenpohualli pesos nimitztlaneuhtia Ca Açiz cenpōhualomālactli ynic tinechcueppiliz auh ytla tic-nequin ynic ontlamātli ticchihuaz ynic çan achintzin nictzinquixtiz ynic amo miec ypā tictlaliz Ca tinechtlacamatiz. Ca nican notlan ticoChiquiuh auh ytlacamo tic-nequi ma xiyauh amo nimitzmacaz y notomin—

ychpochtli v̲ Ca nimā Amo huelitiz yn tle ticmitalhuia Ca y nehuatl. Ca amo neli-huiztlancatl. Ca amo nicnānamaca y nonācayo yntlacamo ticmonequiltia ynic tinechmotlaneuhtiliz motomintzin macamo Ma nimitznotlalcahuili—.

Niman Calaquiz hualquiçazque Omenti Cocoxque Motlatlayehuizque. [46r]

1.º Cocoxqui v̲ Ma ycatzin^co y motlaçotatzin dios ma ytlatzin xitechmotlaocolili por amor de dios.

2 Cocoxqui. v̲ Ma çan icatzin.^co yn ilhuicac tlatocaychpochtli Sta m.^a Ma ytlatzi. xitechmocnoytilli Ca ça no yuh mitzmotlaocoliliz y yehuantzin y motlaçotantzin dios.

Pochtecatl v̲ Notlacahuanē Amo aquicaqui yn ōpa Calten^co tzatzatzitimani Cocoyo xiquintocacan[8] ma huiya yn ilihuiztlacan yxpopōyome Cuix yehuantin Niquitla-tlayecoltia ynic niquimacaz y naxca notlatqui Xiquitocacan[9] Ma huian = ma quiça-can Auh xiquimamauhtican Amo nica hualazque.

Ocā quitoCazque[10] Y Cocoxque

Tetlānequi v̲ Xihuian xiquiçancan Amo nican xitzatzintimāca Aquimotzoteconehuilia yn tlatohuani ytla oc çenpa nican Ahualazque huel nican Tamechquatzatzan-yanazque.

1.º Cocoxqui v̲ Yyoyahue diose tlatohuanie melahuacantetlatzōte=quiliyanie ma huel xicmomelauhcaytili yn ineyolpololiz yn ixhuintiliz y motlachihualtzin Ma xicmo-tlachieltili = Macamo xicmotelchihuili.—

OnCan Calaquizque Yn Cocoxque hualq.çaz yyolloco toquichti—

---

6. auh can icatqui: read *auh ca izcatqui*.
7. nohuipilli: read *nohuipil*.
8. xiquintocacan: read *xiquintotocacan*.
9. Xiquitocacan: read *xiquintotocacan*.
10. quitoCazque: read *quintotocazque*.

YOUNG WOMAN: May your beloved Father, God, give you precious health. O my son, O my lord, I humbly bow very low before you. I am your humble subject. For the sake of our lord Jesus Christ, help me. My mother and my father are suffering greatly. Our lord God has worked a very great sickness upon them. The reason that I have come before you is so that you will help them. Perhaps I will be so fortunate that you will lend me twenty pesos. I will return it right away to you [in] twenty days. Here are the pledges you will keep: my clean clothes, my headdress and my blouse. I greatly implore [this] of you, for the sake of the precious maiden Saint Mary. *(Young Woman cries.)*

MERCHANT: What do you want, O young woman, that before me you cry? Although God has given you a pretty face that is not what I am searching for. What I very much want is for my gold and silver to be greatly increased. You will do two things if you want me to lend you my gold and silver. The first thing is that on account of the twenty pesos I will lend you, the amount you will return to me will total thirty pesos. If you want, the second thing you will do so that I will knock a bit off the price, so the interest you pay is not so great is you will obey me [by] coming here to sleep with me. If you don't want to, go, I will not give you my money.

YOUNG WOMAN: What you say is absolutely impossible. I am not an improper person.[7] I am not selling my body. If you do not want to lend me your money, don't. Let me leave you.

(At that point she exits. Two sick people enter to beg for things.) [46r]

FIRST SICK PERSON: For the sake of your beloved Father, God, have mercy on us with a little something. For the love of God!

SECOND SICK PERSON: For the sake of the heavenly royal maiden, Saint Mary, have mercy on us with a little something. Your beloved Father, God, will likewise be merciful to you.

MERCHANT: O my servants, do you not hear the howling of the coyotes there outside the house? Run them off! Let them go, those who are the frivolous people, the blind! Do I serve them such that I will give them my goods and property? Run them off! Let them go, let them leave. Frighten them [so that] they will not come here.

(At that point they run off the sick people.)

LOWLY SERVANT: Go, leave! Do not howl here. You are giving the ruler a headache. If you come here again we will really crack open your heads!

FIRST SICK PERSON: Alas, O God, O ruler, O righteous judge, look very clearly and directly at the doubts and confusion of your creature. Make him see. Do not despise him.

(At that point the sick people exit. Mature Man enters.)

---

7. Ca amo nelihuiztlacatl: here and below, I am here following what I consider to be the general thrust of the entries regarding *ilihuiz* in Molina's *Vocabulario* of 1571 (see Molina 1977, 37v). Nonetheless, note the following entry in Arenas 1982, 48, repeated (in reverse) on p. 145: "*embustero*—ilihuiztlacatl" (that is, an "ilihuiz" person is a "liar" or "trickster").

yyolloco toᵭchti. v̲ Nopiltzintzine tlahtohuanie Ma motlantzinᶜᵒ Moetztie yn dios Çencan nimitznotlatlauhtilia Mixpantzinco Ninopechtecan Ac. nimitznomaChiltitzinohuan Can izcatqui notomin Ma oc mopaltzinᶜᵒ Xinechmopielili. Ca amo niCa niez. Ca oc nipa niyauh Onpa onaçitiuh y quauhtenmālan niCanatiuh y nonāmic. auh ca ypanpa nimitznotilia. Ca timahuiztic tlancatl. tihuey X͞piano: ca nican catqui Ontzontli ypan matlacpohualli pesos—. [46v]

Pochtecatl v̲ Tla yuhqui yn Ca tel ye qualli Ma huallauh yn tomines ⁿⁱᵐⁱᵗᶻᵖⁱᵉˡⁱ;¹¹ auh yn iquac in tihualmoCueppaz yn iquac tinechytlaniliz. Ca nima yçiuhcan nimitzCueppilliz—ha ye onicÇenlli Ontzontli = ypan Matlactli¹² pesos y nimitzpieliz.

—hualquiçazque huenhuetzin yhua ylanmatzin Ynamic—yas yn iyolloco toquichtin¹³

ylamātzin v̲ Notlaçonamictzin Noquichpiltzin Ca ye ticmotilia Ca oaçico y Caxtolilhuitl ynic tiCuepilizque yn itlatqui yn poch=tecatl. Ca yalhua oniCac tiyaquizco quilmach Ayamo huenCauh çe oquichtli yhua çen Çihuatl. tzauhcan Oquincahuato: Onpan OquinamaCato yn ipanpa yn itomin Macamo = no yuhqui topa moChihuaz auh ypanpa yn ma xocomotemoli y mAçican moChihuaz ca nica nicpiya chicomē pesos Auh yn ChiCuey pesos ma yçiuhca xocomotemoli: ynic noconaxiltizque¹⁴ yn Caxtolli macamo ypan tihuetzizque yn·iqualan Ca anmo tlancatl ca çenca huey tlahuelliloc—.

huehuentzin v̲ Ca ye qualli Cihuapille ma nocotemotihuetzin Ma yçiuhca ticmacanca ca ye ohuaçico y caxtolli tonatiuh—.

Pochtecatl v̲ Xihuallauh yn tinonecauh: Ca ye ticmatin: Ca ye otzonquiça.ᶜᵒ y caxtoli tonatiuh: yn ipa motlatlalilinque ynic quixtlahuazque notomines nima yCiuhca xiyauh xiquimitlānili ytlacamo nima yciuhca mitzmacazque Telpiloyan xiquitlalli. nima amo mitztlaocoltizque y manel mixpan chocazque tlaocoyazque Xiquita Amo tiquitlacoz ytla tiquintlaocoliz ca tehuatl nimitzChoctiz nimitztequipachoz— Yaz ytlan i huehuentzin quitlanitiu quito¹⁵

Tetlāneᵭ. v̲ Ca ye qualli tlatohuanie ma niquimita ma niyauh Ca nica Onihualla ca nica niquitlanico y caxtolli pesos ytlacamo ni=ma yciuhca xinechmacancan: namechtlaliz Teylpiloya [47r] anoço namechhuiquiliz yn amoaxca yn amotlatqui—

huehuetzin v̲ Notlaçopiltze ca nican ca yn itlatquitzin y yehuatzin yn topiltzin y tlacatl tlantohuani macamo yc ximoteᵭpachotzino—

+ Onca hualquiçaz Teuctli—

Teuctli v̲ Notlaçopiltzintzine Ma ximehuiltitie nican mixpantzinᶜᵒ Onihualla nictenamiquico y momātzin y mocxitzin tinechmopalehuiliz: notech monequi matlactzontli pesos tinechmotlaneuhtiliz yn ipa. Çen metzli Ca nima nimitznoCueppililiz Ma xinechmotlacamachititzino ma çan ica y motocatzin—

---

11. nimitzpieli: probably to be read *nimitzpieliz* as below; in a different hand.
12. Matlactli: scribal error; read *matlacpohualli* (as above and below).
13. yas yn iyolloco toquichtin: in a different hand.
14. noconaxiltizque: read *toconaxiltizque*.
15. Yaz ytlan i huehuentzin quitlanitiu quito: added at the end of this dialogue; in a different hand.

MATURE MAN: O my nobleman, O ruler, may God be with you. I greatly implore you, I humbly bow low before you. I hold you in great esteem.[8] Here is my money. Guard it for me out of respect for who you are. I am going to be absent for I am going all the way to Guatemala to get my spouse. The reason I am seeing you is because you are an honorable person, a great Christian. Here are one thousand pesos. [46v]

MERCHANT: Very well, let it be so. Let the money come that I will guard for you. When you return then ask me for it and I will promptly return it to you. Ah, I have now received the one thousand pesos I will guard.

(Old Man and his spouse, Old Woman, enters. Mature Man exits.)

OLD WOMAN: O my dear spouse, O my son, you now see that the fifteen days when we will return the merchant's property have passed.[9] Yesterday I heard them say in the marketplace that not long ago they took a man and woman to a textile manufacturing shop. They sold them off there because of his [i.e., the merchant's] money [not being repaid on time]. Let the same not happen to us. Because of this [latest development] see that it is thoroughly taken care of. I have seven pesos here. Quickly go on to search for the [other] eight so that we can make it reach the fifteen. Let us not incur his wrath for he is inhuman and very wicked.

OLD MAN: Very well, O noblewoman, let me quickly search for it. Let us quickly give it to him for the fifteen days have already passed.

MERCHANT: Come, you who are my servant. You already know the fifteen days in which they obligated themselves to repay my money have come to an end. Go quickly then and ask them for it. Put them in jail if they do not give it to you straightaway. Do not let them inspire the slightest pity in you, even though they cry and grieve before you. See to it. Make no mistakes. If you have mercy on them I will make you weep, I will inflict pain and worry on you.

LOWLY SERVANT: Very well, O ruler, let me see them. Let me go.

(He goes to Old Man. He goes to ask him, saying:)

LOWLY SERVANT:[10] I have come here to ask for the fifteen pesos. If you do not quickly give them to me I will put you in jail [47r] or perhaps take your goods and property away from you.

OLD MAN: O my beloved child, here is the property of our child, the lord and ruler. Do not worry yourself over it.

(At that point Lord enters.)

LORD: O my beloved nobleman, do remain seated. I have come here before you, come to kiss your hands and your feet. You shall help me. I need four thousand pesos. You will lend it to me. I will return it to you in one month. Heed me just out of respect for your name.

---

8. See Molina 1977, 2v.
9. Literally, here and below, "arrived."
10. The last several lines had to be rearranged to make sense. Otherwise there is confusion between the statements of the Lowly Servant to the Merchant and the Old Man as well as in the stage directions.

Pochtecatl. v Oticmihiyohuiltitzino yn titlacatl onicac y mihiyotzin yn motlantoltzin auh yn ticmonequiltia ynic nimitznotlaneuhtiliz: yn notomines Ma yuhqui mochihua auh ca ye ticmomachitia. Ca yc ninotlayecoltia auh ytla nimitznotlaneuhtiliz Matlactzontli pesos: yn ipa Çen metztli Ca oncan hualmantiaz Centzontli pesos yn ipan Ce metztl.[16]

Teuctli v Ca tel ye qualli Ma yuhqui mochihua yn iuh ticmonequiltia—
+ Niman MacoS y tomines Conceliz Nima yas

Yyolloco toq̄ch v Nopiltzintzine tlacatle tlatohuanie que timoyetzinnotica = Cuix anchitzin omitzmomaquilli yn itechicahuallitzin y. motantzin dios Çeca nimitznotlatlauhtilia Ma Xinechmomaquili y nimitznopieltili Notomines ca ye oniqualhuicac y nonamic auh yc nocotlacocohuiz.

Pochtecatl. v Ca nipactica Ma mitzmochicahuili yn dios ca qualli ynic otihualmocuepp.auh[17] tle tomines yn tinechytlanilia amo nicmati yn tle tinechylhuia.

Yyolloco toq̄ch v Tlacatle tlantohuanie Acaçomo ticmolnāmiquilia Ma = huel xicmolnamiquilitzino Ca ye axca nahui metzli yn onimitznopieltilitzinno Ontzontli ypā Matlacpohualli pesos. Ma ça ypaltzin^{co} yn dios Xinechmaquilli—[47v]

Pochtecatl. v Ye nimitzilhuia Amo tle nicmati Aço otitlahuan Anoçen tiyolloCocoxqui xinechcahuan xiyauh—

yyolloco toq̄chti v Ca nima Amo nitlahuanqui. Amo niyollopoliuhqui Ca huel melahuac Ca onimitznomaquili yn iuhqui ticmitalhuitzinohua Ma xicmoqueChili Crus Juramento xicmochihuili—

Pochtecatl. v Ca melahuac y nimitzilhuia ca huel neltiliztli nicchihua mixpan Juramēto niquentza Crus nictenamiqui ypaltzinco dios ca amo tle nicmati ca amo tle Otinechmacac y motomin Atle nimitzpielia.

Yyolloco toq̄chti v Ca tel ye qualli Axcan pachihui y noyollo ynic tinechyxpachilhuia y notomines. Ca tel moetztica yn dios nococacahua Ma yehuantzin Mitzmotilili y motetlayxpachilhuilliz amo nica axcan ninotlahuelquixtiz—

Pochtecatl. v Xiyauh xinechtlalcahui ytlacamo yçiuhca tinechtlalcahuiz Ca nican Cante y notlacanhuan huel nican mitzhuihuitequizque Xihualhuian Nonencahuane xiquixtican i.y loco yn tlahuaquin—
+ OnCan quitoCazque quihuihuitequizque: hualquiçaz Nātli yhuā Ypilhuan

nātli v Noquichpiltzin noteCuiyotzin Ma motlatzin^{co} motztie yn igraciatzin dios Spū S.^{to} timitztotlapalhuico y timocnomaÇenhual=tzintzinhuan y nehuatl yhua y nopilhuan Auh ma ycnoyohua y moyollotzin Ca huel ninotolinia yhua huel motolinia y nopilhuan Ma Xinechmomaquilitzinno yn inTestanmēto y nonāmictzin yhua yn ixquich yn imaxca yn itlatq̄. yn itlal yn imil yn iteoCuitl. yn ichalchiuh Ca ye ticmomaChitia ynic Amo nixpan Omomīquili altepetl ypa onihuia ōniquintlayecoltito y nopilhua Ma ypaltzin^{co} yn tt.^{o} dios Ma xiquimocnoytili ȳ mocnotlancantzintzinhuan—[48r]

---

16. metztl: read *metztli*.
17. otihualmocuepp.auh: read *otihualmocuep auh*.

MERCHANT: Greetings, lord. I have heard your fine words. As to you wanting me to lend you my money: let it be done. You already know that that is how I earn my living. But if I lend you the four thousand pesos for one month you will pay interest of four hundred pesos.

LORD: Very well. Let it happen as you want.
(He is given the money right away. He accepts it. Then he exits.)

MATURE MAN: O my nobleman, O personage, O ruler. How are you? Has your Father, God, given you a bit of his health? I greatly implore you to give me the money I entrusted to you for now I have brought my spouse here. I want to buy her things with it.

MERCHANT: I am healthy. May God grant you health. It is good that you have returned but what money are you asking me for? I do not know what you are telling me.

MATURE MAN: O personage, O ruler, perhaps you do not recall. Remember well that it is now four months [since] I entrusted the one thousand pesos to you. For God's sake, give it to me! [47v]

MERCHANT: I am telling you now I know nothing of it. Perhaps you are drunk or a madman. Leave me; go.

MATURE MAN: I am absolutely not a drunk, not deranged. Truly indeed I gave it to you. The way you are talking: hold up a cross and make an oath on it.

MERCHANT: What I am saying to you is correct, it is the very truth. I make an oath before you [by] raising up the cross, kissing it [and affirming that] by the love and respect of God I know nothing. You gave me none of your money. I have nothing of yours.

MATURE MAN: Very well, now I am satisfied that you are hiding my money from me. But God exists [as does] my property. Let him see you are hiding people's things from them. It is not here and now for me to vent my anger.

MERCHANT: Go, leave me. If you do not quickly leave me I have servants right here who will severely beat you. Come, my servants, eject this crazy drunkard.

(At that point they pursue him, severely beating him. Mother enters along with her children.)

MOTHER: O my son, O my lord, may the grace of God the Holy Spirit be with you. My children and I, your humble subjects, have come to greet you. May your heart be compassionate. I am very poor and my children are very poor. Give me the testament of my spouse along with all his goods and property, his fields, his gold and silver, and his jades. You already know that he did not die in my presence [because] I went to work in the altepetl[11] to support my children. For the sake of our lord God have pity on your humble servants. [48r]

---

11. altepetl: Nahuatl term applied to various kinds of sovereign sociopolitical units; most of those existing in central Mexico at this time were of approximately city-state dimensions. During colonial times it was translated in many ways including *ciudad* (city) and *pueblo* (people, settlement).

Pochtecatl. v. Tle tiquitohua Cihuatzintle Acaçomo huel tiquilnanmiq̄. acaçomo nehuatl. aço çan timotlapololtia ca y nehuatl. amo tle nicpian testamento auh yno tlalli yn milli y tictenehuan Ca notlacohual ca ye huecauh yn onicohuilli ȳ monāmic auh y teoCuitlatl. y chalchihuitl amo tle nicmati yn tictenehuan aço tehuatl Oticpōpolo: anoçe amo Oquichiuh yn itestamēto anoço aca motlahuical: amonehua Onaquipōpoloque[18] yn tlatquitl. Ximohuicatiuh amo tle nicmati. y tle tiquitohuan yntla otitlahuan: xiyauh xicochi amo xinechtequipacho ÷

Nantli. v̲ Ca nelli: melahuac y niquitohua ca amo nitlahuanqui: ca huel neltiliztli y nimitznolhuilia. ca tehuantzin ticmopielia Ma çan icatzin[co] yn dios ma xicmochihuili yn itetlaçotlalitzin Ma xiquimotlaocolili y nopilhuantzintzin—

Pochtecatl. v̲ Ca ye nimitzilhuian y tiÇihuatl amo nic[c]aqui y tle ti.quitohuan xiyah[19] amo xinechamāna tinetzonteconehua xiyauh xiquitemoli yn intech monequiz y mochtacanpilhuan amo notequiuh xiyauh ayocmo nica nimitzintaz—Xihuallauh y tinonencauh xinechnochili yn Escriuāno y notlaçoycniuh—

Tetlanenqui v̲. Ca ye qualli tlatohuanie Ma nicnonochili—

   + OnCan hualquiçaz Escriuano—

Escriuano v̲ Ma mitzmochicahuili yn dios tlatohuanie. aço ytla motenahuatiltzin: Ca onihualla nicaquico—

Pochtecatl. v̲ Nocniuhtzine tla nica timohuicatz nima yçiuhca Xocomochihuili Cen Amatl. Oncan ticmotlaliliz OniCouh y calli: yhua y tlalli Xochimilcopa ytzticac auh y milli huel huey tepeyaca[c]copan ytztimani auh onicouh. Ontzontli ypan Matlacpohualli Onnicten. auh huel yuh xictlali ypan yñamatl.[20] ca yei xihuitl y nicouh ypan [48v] ypan[21] 1627 años xiquita huel qualli ticchihuaz amo tiquitlacoz Ca ye ticmati ca tinotlaçoycniuhtzin auh ca çenca nimitztlaçotla yhua Ca nimitztlaxtlanhuiz—

Escriuano v̲ Notlaçopiltzine macamo ximotequipachotzino Ca nicneltiliz y motlaçotlatoltzin Ca ye ticmomachitia Ca nimocnomaCenhualtzin auh ca çenca nimitznotlatlauhtilia Ma achintzin xinechmotlaocolili ȳ mocococantzin ynic niquitlacohuiz y nopilhuan—

Pochtecatl v̲ ynon macamo mitztequipachon Ca nimitzmacaz: ça ye yçiuhca xiquiCuillo yn amatl.—

   + Hualquiçaz yn alCalde

---

18. Onaquipōpoloque: read *oanquipopoloque*.
19. xiyah: read *xiyauh*.
20. yñamatl: read *yn amatl*.
21. ypan ypan: read *ypan*.

MERCHANT: O woman, what are you saying? Perhaps you do not properly remember. Perhaps it was not I or you are just confused, for I have no testament. That land and the fields you mention are my purchases for I bought them from your spouse long ago. As for the gold and silver and the jades that you mention, I know nothing. Perhaps you squandered it or he did not make a testament or you and some companion of yours wasted the property. Be going along. I know nothing of what you are saying. If you are drunk, go, sleep it off. Do not bother me.

MOTHER: What I am saying is true and honest. I am not a drunkard. What I am saying to you is the very truth. You have it. Let it just be for the sake of God that you perform [an act] of his loving charity. Have mercy on my poor little children.

MERCHANT: What I am telling you, woman, is I do not understand what you are talking about. Go, do not disturb me. You are giving me headaches. Go, search for what your bastard children need. It is not my business. Go, I will no longer see you. Come, you who are my servant, summon my dear friend the notary.

LOWLY SERVANT: Very well, O ruler, let me summon him.

(At that point Notary enters.)

NOTARY: O ruler, may God give you health. Perhaps you have some order? I have come to hear it.

MERCHANT: O my friend, please be welcome here.[12] Make a document right away. There you will put down that I bought the house and lands facing Xochimilco and the very big fields lying toward Tepeyacac. I bought them for one thousand [pesos]. In the document you are to put precisely that I bought them three years ago in [48v] the year 1627. See to it that you do it well and do not make a mistake. You already know you are my dear friend and I greatly love and esteem you; in addition, I will make it worth your while.

NOTARY: O my beloved child, do not worry yourself for I will carry out your precious words. You already know I am your humble subject. I greatly implore you to favor me with a little of your property so that I [can] buy things for my children.

MERCHANT: Do not let that bother you for I will give it to you. Quickly write the document.

(Alcalde enters.)

---

12. tla nica timohuicatz: see Carochi 1983, 67v, 80r, and Sahagún 1997, 296. The command/optative particle *tla* can sometimes indicate a more pleading or, at least, less imperious request than its much more frequently seen counterpart *ma*; see Carochi 1983, 25r–v.

nantli y tlacatl tlatohuani Ca nica mixpantzin^co onihualla ma xicmomachiltitzino aço ye chiCuaçemetztli yn omomiquili noñamic ahuitech[22] oquicauh y yehuantzin Pochtecatl yn ipalehuilocan yn ianima. yhua yn ixquich yn axca yn itlatquin[23] yn totech Oquipouh y nehuatl yhua y nopilhuantzintzin auh yn axca ayocmo quimoCuitia y nocal y nomil ye mochi quimaxcatia quimotlatquitia auh yn axcan. y.panpa y Ca çencan mixpantzin^co ninopechtecan nimitznotlatlauhtilia ma quinotzacan ma mixpantzinco neçiquin ma mixpātzin^co quimoCuitiqui ma çan ipaltzin^co. yn tt.^o ma xinechmopalehuilli ca çenca ninotolinicantzintli amo tle ma ytla nicpia yc niquihuanpanhuaz y nican caten mocnomaçēhualtzintzinhuan Ma çan ipāpatzin^co yn tt.^o yhuan ypāpatzin^co y tlaçoçinhuapili xicmochihuillitzin[24] ca huel çenca nimitznotlatlatilia.[25] [49r]

Alcalde. y Ca tel ye qualli Çihuantzintle ca nimitzpalehuiz macamo ximotequipachon—Topile xiyauh xicnotza y yehuatl y pochtecatl yn oncan on tiyanquiztēco ychan—

Topile y Ca ye qualli tlantohuanie ma nicnochinli—

+ Niman yaz quinotzatiuh y pochtecatl.

Topile y Nopiltzintzine ȳ yehuatzin alcalde mitzmonochilia Onpā tomaxitiz centlamantli yc mitzmononochiliznequi yçiuhca timohuicaz amo huel nimitznocahuiliz—+ quihuicaz—

Pochtecatl y Onticmihiyohuiltitzinno tlacantle tlantohuanie tle ticmonequiltitzinnohua Ca nica nica Aço ytla yc nimitzōnotlayecoltiliz ca nicChihuaz—

alcalde. y Ontihualmohuicac Xicmatin Ca nican ca y çihuatzintli mitzteyxpāhuia ca motech oquicauhtia yn iaxca yn itlatquit[26] yn iquac omomiquili ynāmic auh yn axca Ayocmo ticmocuitia xicquetza Crū̄s nican teyxpan xictlali moma ma xiquitta y tle motech ȳtlacauhtica yn ixquich yn iaxca yn itlatqui yn ical yn imil Cuix oticcouh

Pochtecatl y Ca nictenamiqui Nican can Sta Crū̄s Auh ma quimonequilti. yn tt.^o dios Ma diablo nechhuican Ca amo neltiliztli y quitohuan y nican can Çihuantzintli auh ca nica moetztica yn escriuano = ca yxpantzin^co yn onicCohuili yn itlal yn imil yhuan yn ical auh ca amo tle nicpielia yni Cihuantl—

alcalde y Cuix ye nelli Melahuac yn quitohuan y nican ca topiltzin auh catli yn ezCrituran—

---

22. ahuitech: read *auh itech*.
23. yhua yn ixquich yn axca yn itlatquin: read *yhuan yn ixquich yn iaxca yn itlatqui*. Here as in many other places in the manuscript are abundant examples of intrusive and omitted characters, especially *n*; the orthographic loss of possessive prefixes like *i-*, however, is uncommon.
24. xicmochihuillitzin: read *xicmochihuilitzino*.
25. nimitznotlatlatilia: read *nimitznotlatlauhtilia*.
26. itlatquit: read *itlatqui*.

MOTHER: O lord and ruler, I have come here before you. Know that about six months ago my spouse died. He left the merchant what would be of help to his soul along with all his goods and property, which he assigned to me and my children. Now he no longer admits he made my house and my fields his own goods and property. Wherefore now I greatly and humbly bow low before you, imploring you to summon him to appear before you. Let him come to acknowledge it in your presence. Let it just be for the sake of our lord. Help me, for I am very poor. I have absolutely nothing with which to raise your humble little subjects here. Let it just be for the sake of our lord and for the sake of the high-born noblewoman [Saint Mary]. I very greatly implore you, do it! [49r]

ALCALDE: Very well, O woman, I will help you. Do not worry yourself. Constable, go summon the merchant. His residence is over there at the edge of the market.

CONSTABLE: Very well, O ruler, let me summon him.
(He goes right away to summon Merchant.)
CONSTABLE: O my nobleman, the alcalde summons you. You are to go. He wants to consult with you concerning something. You are to go quickly. I must accompany you.[13]
(He accompanies him.)
MERCHANT: Greetings, O lord, O ruler, what do you want? Here I am. Can I serve you in some way? For [if so,] I will do it.
ALCALDE: Welcome.[14] Know that the woman here makes an accusation about you before the law. When her spouse died he left his goods and property with you but now you no longer admit to it. Hold up the cross, set it down here in public with your [own] hands. Look: what do you wrongly hold[15] of all her goods and property, her house and fields? Did you buy them?
MERCHANT: I kiss the holy cross here. Let it be the will of our lord God that the devil take me [if I lie but] what the woman here is saying is not true. Here is the notary. I bought her land and her fields along with her house in his presence. I owe nothing to this woman.
ALCALDE: Is what our child[16] here saying true and honest? What has become of the document [in question]?

---

13. Literally, "I will not be able to leave you."
14. Literally, "you have come (rev.)" but the thrust seems to be "welcome."
15. tle motech ytlacauhtica: these and variants are tentative translations.
16. That is, Merchant.

EScriuano v Ca nica catqui yn Escritura Ca huel melanhuac ynic oquinamacac yn ical yn imil y nican ca çihuantzintli yn ināmic Ca nixpan yhua ymixpan y teStigos Ca oquimacac Ontzontli ypā Matlactzontli pesos Oquicenli y teoCuitlatl huel oquicuic nixpā [49v] nixpan[27] Oquihuicac auh ynteztamento Ca no nixpan y quichiuh Ca amo tle ma ytla Onquicauh ça quezquitzin yn oquicauh ynic motocaz yn inācayo auh ca melahuac ynic amixpantzinco mitohua Cuix ypanpan iztlancatiz y nican ca Pochtecatl—

Quinextiz Testamento =

alcalde v Cihuantzintle ye otiquittac Ca ye mixpan Onmopouh yn amatl: Ca āmo tle ytech ytlacahui y nican ca Pochtecatl. Ma ximohuicatiuh—

Hualquiçaz Teopixqui =

Teopixqui v Nopiltzine ma motlantzin[co] moetztie yn dios Espū sancto macamo nimitzte=quipachoz Macamo nimitzamanaz auh yzcatqui Ca timahuiztic titlancatl. Ca dios tipiltzin auh ca omitzmomaquili yn tt.º dios yn axcantzin[28] yn itlatquitzin Ca ticalpixcatzin yn tt.º dios ypanpa y ma xicmocnelili ma xicmotlaocolili: y cihuantzintli yn otiCuili yn ical yn imil yn inamic Ca ye ticmomachitian Ca anchitzin miyec yn ipatiuh ȳ calli ma xicmopalehuili yhuan yn ipilhua Auh ȳ tle ticmo.maquiliz Ca mochi quimoÇenliliz yn dios Ma çan ipanpatzinco Xicmochihuilitzino notlaçopiltzine—

Pochtecatl v Tlaçoteopixque Ca ye onicac y mihiyotzin y motlatoltzin = Ca melanhuac y nimitznolhuilia Ca huel ninotolinia yn axca—Ca miec yn tetech ytlacauhtican notomin ayamo nechmaca. auh ytla ye oniCuixano ytech nicpōhuaz auh ynin ma tzanhuan ma yquitti aço quemanian niquilnāmiquiz auh yn axcan ma oc xinechmotlalcahuili: ca oca notequiuh—

Teopixqui. v Ma Xicmomachiti nopiltze ca yn ixquich y moaxcan y motlatqui Ca anmo tiquitquiz yn iquac timiquiz Ca çan çentzontzomantzintli ynic moquimiloz y motlallo y moçoquiyo [50r] auh y quenin atl. quiçenhuia yn tletl. Ça no yuhqui y tetlaocoliliztli quiçenhuia y tlatlancolli auh ynin ma xicpalehui y moyollia ȳ manima yc achitzin tepintzin mitzmopalehuilliz yn dios ma ximonoṁapalehui. ayac aquin mitzpalehuiz Ca ye nimitztlalcahuia—

Calaquiz yn Teopixqui

Pochtecatl. v ha. notlanecahuane Ca huel ninococohuan axcan çenyohual nimā amo achitzin onnicoch cenyohual huel nechcocohuan y notzontecō yuhquin acan quixtlanpanā Ma xinechnochilican Tiçitl—

Tetlanequi v Ca ye qualli Nopiltzintzine tlantohuanie ma niqualnonochili yn Tiçitl—. Yaz quinotzatiuh yn ticitl Contzontzonaz yn poertan.

Tiçitl v Oticmihiyohuilti: Notelpotzine tle ticmonequiltitzinnohuan—

Tetlaneq̄. v Notlaçopiltzintzine mohuic[co]patzin[co] Onechhualmihuanli yn yehua=tzin Pochtecatl ynic ticmopalehuiliz mococotzinnohuan—

27. nixpā nixpan: read *nixpan*.
28. yn axcantzin: read *yn iaxcatzin*.

NOTARY: Here is the document. It is very true that the spouse of the woman here sold him his house and fields for he gave him one thousand pesos in my presence and in the presence of witnesses. He received the gold and silver, he really took it, in my presence he took it [off with him]. [49v] He also made his testament in my presence. He left not a thing, just a little something with which his body would be buried. What is said in your presence is true. Would the merchant here lie about it?

(He produces the testament.)
ALCALDE: O woman, you have already seen and heard read before you the document. The merchant here holds nothing wrongly. Be going along.
(Priest enters.)
PRIEST: O my child, may God the Holy Spirit be with you. Let me not bother or disturb you. Look, you are an honorable person, a child of God. Our lord God has given you his goods and property. You are the steward of our lord God. Because of that have pity and mercy on the poor woman from whose spouse you took her house and fields.[17] You already know the value of the house was a bit considerable; help her and her children. What you give to her will all be received [on behalf of] God. O my beloved child, just do it for his sake.

MERCHANT: O dear priest, I have heard your fine words. I am telling you the truth. I am very poor now for much of my money is wrongly in the hands of other people who have not yet given it to me. If I had it in my care I would assign it to her. But as for this one, let her spin and weave;[18] perhaps sometime I will remember her. Now leave me, for I have work [to do].
PRIEST: O my child, know that when you die you will not take any of your goods and property with you, just a little piece of worn-out clothing with which your earthly body will be enshrouded. [50r] As water snuffs out fire likewise compassion snuffs out sin. And as for this matter at hand, help your spirit and your soul and God will thus help you a bit. Help yourself [for] no one else will help you. I am leaving you now.
(Priest exits.)
MERCHANT: Ah, O my servants, I am very sick. Last night I did not sleep at all. All last night my head hurt me a lot as though someone were breaking it. Summon the doctor for me.
LOWLY SERVANT: Very well, O my nobleman, O ruler. Let me summon the doctor.
(He goes to summon the doctor. He knocks on the door.)
DOCTOR: Greetings, O my young man. What do you want?
LOWLY SERVANT: O my beloved nobleman, the merchant sent me to you so that you will help him. He is ill.

---

17. her house and fields: alternatively, this could easily be rendered "his house and fields."
18. The thrust of this reference to gender-typed tasks may be a thinly disguised idiom that means "let her attend to her female responsibilities." This remark also seems especially dismissive if seen from a Hispanic perspective (and this is, after all, a Church-inspired effort). Perhaps it carries the added implication that she should be too busy doing women's work to waste a man's time with her frivolous claims.

Tiçitl. v̲ Ca ye qualli Notelpotzine ma tihuian Ma nicnotili tle quimococolhuintzinnohua—
Quihuicaz: Ynhuan yn pilli—
Tiçitl. v̲ Notlaçopiltzintzine tlahtohuanie. Ma mitzmochicanhuili ȳ motlaçontatzin dios quen timomatzinnohua tle mitzmotequipachilhuian—
Cocoxqui. v̲ Otinechmocnelili Otlacauhqui yn moyollotzin Çenca ninoCocohuan Ca huel nohuian moCocohua y notlallo y noçoquiyon tlantohuanien—[50v]
Tiçitl. v̲ Notlaçopiltzintzine Ma Ximochicauhtzinno: Ma mitzmochicahuili yn motlaçotatzin dios Ma Ximohuican yn iChantzin^{co} dios ma XimoyolCuiti Ma XimoCencanhuan Ma Xicmoçenlili yn itlaçomahuiznācayotzin y motlaçotemaquixticatzin Jesu Xp̄o. ca yuhcan tonahuatil ynic yacachtopan MoyolCuitizque yn cocoxque ynic çatepa palehuillozque yn itlallo yçoquiyo—
Cocoxqui v̲. Xicahua ynon yn tiquitohua ma quitepan mochihuaz ma ça oque²⁹ yçiuhca xinechpalehui ca cenca huel nimiquizneque³⁰ yn axca—
Tiçitl. v̲ tlē ticmitalhuitzinohuan Nopiltzinne ca amo qualli y ticmolnanmiquilia Ma çan ye nima yciuhcan Mitzmohuiquilica yn ichantzin^{co} dios Ca yn tanimā ca ytech quiça yn cocoliztli—
pilli v̲ Notlaçopiltzintzine tlantohuanie Ca huel melanhuac y mitzmolhuilia y nica moetztica y ticitl ca cenca motetzin.^{co} neçi Ca çenCan totocaznequi ȳ Justiciatzin³¹ dios Ma nimā yciuhca ti:mitztohuiquilican Ca huel monequi yn achtopa titoyolCuitizque ma ximoyolCuititzino ma ximoçencauhtzinno ynnic çatepa palehuiloz yn tlalli çoquitl. ca huel yuh qui[?]monequiltia yn dios auh yni ma timitztohuiquilicā—
Cocoxqui v̲ Huel anechtzonteconehuan huel Antetzonteconeuhque Ma ça tel niyauh Auh ye çen huel yuh oquinequia y noyollo yniquiçiuhcan³² nipantiloz auh yni ma tel niyauh—[51r]
+ oncan quihuicazque yn teopan: quicalaquizque = Auh yn oquic: quicalaquiya hualquiçazque 3 dem.^{o}
1° dem.^{o} v̲ Ha Omochiuh Ototlahueliltic Ca ye moyolCuitiznequi yn totetlayecolticauh yn tetech tlayxtlapananin—ytla mochi quimoCuitiz yn itlatlacol ca nima atle yez yn totlapalihuiz yn totiyacauhyan ca mochi nequi–çaz nepolihuiz yn ye hixquich cahuitl yn ye techtlayecoltia—
2 dem.^{o} v̲ Ca niman Amo huelitiz y nequiçaz nepolihuiz yn totlateq̄.panoliz auh y tehuatin tle ypan techmati Cuix amo cenca tiChicahuaque titlapaltique: Ca nima Amo huel tic^{c}anhuazquen ca y nehuatl ca nicmacaz y nemauhtiliztli yhuan y pinanhuiliztli ynic Amo huel quimoCuitiz ynic teca Omocancayuh³³ yhua ynic otetlayxpachilhui auh cuix yequiCa³⁴ Ocan comoCuintiz ye ixpan Justiçian amo quimoCuintia amo quimomaChitocan nimā yztlancanJurāmēto: Onquichiuh ynic Otlaneltili ynic Oquixpancho Teaxca Tetlatquin—

---

29. oque: read *oc ye*.
30. nimiquizneque: read *nimiquiznequi*.
31. ȳ Justiciatzin: read *yn iJusticiatzin*.
32. yniquiçiuhcan: read *ynic içiuhca in*.
33. teca omocancayuh: read *teca omocacayauh*.
34. yequiCa: scribal error; perhaps to be read *yequene* or even *ye ic nican*.

DOCTOR: O my young man, very well. Let us go. Let me see him. What is hurting him?

(He accompanies him along with Nobleman.)

DOCTOR: O my beloved nobleman, O ruler, may your beloved Father, God, give you health. How do you feel? What is bothering you?

SICK MAN: I give you many thanks for the favor you have shown me. I am very sick. O ruler, my earthly body hurts absolutely everywhere. [50v]

DOCTOR: O my beloved nobleman, take heart, may your beloved Father, God, give you health. Go to the home of God, confess, prepare yourself, receive the precious honored body of your beloved savior, Jesus Christ. Such is our [that is, doctors'] obligation that first the sick will confess so that afterward the earthly body will be helped.

SICK MAN: Leave it, let what you say be done later. Just quickly help me for I am very much and really about to die now.

DOCTOR: What are you saying? O my child, what you are thinking about is bad. Let them just take you straightaway to the home of God, for it is out of our souls that sickness comes.

NOBLEMAN: O my beloved nobleman, O ruler, what the doctor here is saying to you is very true. It is very apparent in you that the illness, the justice of God, is about to greatly worsen. Let us immediately take you for it is very necessary that we first confess. Confess, prepare yourself, so that afterward the earthly body will be aided for that is the very will of God. Now then, let us take you.

SICK MAN: You are giving me a big headache, you are really a pain, let me just go. I am very desirous that I be quickly restored to health. Now let me go. [51r]

(They take him to the church and put him inside. While they are putting him inside three demons enter.)

FIRST DEMON: Ah, woe is me! Our servant the moneylender is about to confess. If he confesses to all his sins our help and effort will be for naught. All the time he served us would be futile and uselessly spent.

SECOND DEMON: It is absolutely impossible that our work should be futile and uselessly spent. As for us: what does he think we are? Are we not very powerful and strong? We will absolutely not abandon him for I will give him fright and shame so that he cannot admit to deceiving people and to hiding their property from them. Will he confess there what he would not admit to and acknowledge before the officers of the law? Then it was a false oath he made when he verified that he had [not[19]] concealed other people's property and goods.

---

19. A necessary and logical addition missing from the original text.

3. dem.º v̄ Ma ça ye yçiuhca tihuian ylhuiz tohuecahuan ma ça nimā Onpan titlamelahuancan yn ōpan Oquihuicaque Ma ylhuiz OnmoyolCuitin Ma tonequiztin tlen aquimati Ma titoChicahuacan tocnihuanne—

+ Calaquizque Auh yn iquac ocalaq̄. hualquiçaz [51v] ȳ cocoxqui quihualhuicazquen: ȳ tlatlacatecolo yhua Angle: Sa quihualhuelcapahuitizq.ᵉ quitlalizque yn itlapechco =

Cocoxqui v̄ Ha Omochiuh Onotlahueliltic tlen onicchiuh tlen onax: Ca y noyollo Ca çenca tonehua: chichinanca nima amo achitzin Cenhui tlen onechoquixti tlen itechcopa Onoconittac yn tlalticpaccayotl tlen itech Onicnexti: ha onotlahueliltic—

ynamic v̄ Notlaçonamictzin tlen ic Cenca timomoçihuitzinnohuan tlen ic Cenca timotequipachotzinnohua Cuix ytla ticmonequiltia Cuix onquitla³⁵ ticmolnanmiquilia ytla mitzmotequipachilhuia Ma xicmitalhui: Canel yuh ca. yn itlalticpactzinco dios Ca tlaanlanhuan Ca tlapetzcahuin Ca anmo çan quexquich ynic ytzinco ycpactzinco tinemi y tlancatl tlanto=huani dios. Ma xinechmolhuilli—

Cocoxqui v̄ Otinechmocnelilitzinno Otlacauhqui y moyollotzin Ca melahuac yn ticmitalhuian—

oncan hualquicaz³⁶ teopixqui =

Teopixqui v̄ Ma moçenquizcanyectenehuan yn itlaçomahuiztocatzin Jesu X͞p͞o—que timoetztica Notlaçomahuizpiltzine—

Cocoxqui v̄ Notlaçomahuiztatzine Otlaçotic ȳ moyollotzin Otinechmocnelilitzino Ca çenca Onocuiltono³⁷ Oninotlamachtin ypaltzinco yn dios: ca ye polihuiznequi ynānima³⁸ Ca cencan huel Oçoquiyac y tlalli yn çoquitl.—[52r]

Teopixqui. v̄ Notlaçomahuizpiltzine Ma ximochicahua ximotlapaltili yhuicopatzinᶜᵒ y moteºuh y motlantocatzin dios Ma xicmocnelilmachiti ynic mitzmocnelilia yn oc Achitzinca mitzmocahuilia Ca amo mitzmotelchihuilia Ca quimonequiltitzinohuan yn timomaquixtiz ynic mocnopil Momaçenhual mochihuaz yn itlantocanchantzinᶜᵒ Ca amo monemachpan. C̶a̶ ̶a̶m̶o̶ Otimomicquiliyani auh yn axcan: Ca mitzmomacahuililia yn cahuitl. yn ipan ynic timomaquixtiz ynic timoyoloCuintiz Mochi tiquitoz = y motlatlacol maçonelihui ȳn otimoyolCuiti: Açoquitla³⁹ Oticpinahuizcauh Ma xiquito Ca ye timomicquiliznequi—

1º dem.º v̄ Macamo mitztequipancho Macamo yc xinetlamati: Camo cenca timococohuan Cuix amo ye quezquipan y timococonhuan ça nima yçiuhca tipanti yece mitzmochicahuilia yn dios: Ca çan o yuh mopā mo=chihuaz yn axcan Ca tipatiz—

---

35. onquitla: read *oc itla*.
36. hualquicaz: read *hualquiçaz*.
37. Onocuiltono: read *oninocuiltono*.
38. ynānimā: read *yn naniman*.
39. Açoquitla: read *aço oc itla*.

THIRD DEMON: Let us go quickly; we are uselessly wasting time. Let us go right there to where they took him. Let him especially not confess, let us not be in vain. Pay attention![20] O our friends, take heart!

(They exit. After they have exited Sick Man enters. [51v] Devils accompany him along with [Guardian] Angel. They just follow him from a distance. They will place him on his litter.)

SICK MAN: Ah, woe is me! What oh what have I done? For my heart suffers great burning pain. It is not a bit rested and cooled off. What did it avail me? What earthly thing did I get out of it? What did I gain from it? Ah, woe is me!

HIS SPOUSE: O my beloved spouse, what are you so greatly disturbed by? What are you so bothered about? Do you want something? Are you still thinking of something else? Something troubling you? Speak, for that is how it is on God's earth, it is slippery and slick[21] and we offend the lord and ruler, God, in countless things. Speak to me.

SICK MAN: I give you many thanks for the favor you have shown me. What you are saying is true.

(At that point Priest enters.)

PRIEST: Perfectly praise the beloved honored name of Jesus Christ. O my beloved honored child, how are you feeling?

SICK MAN: O my beloved honored father, I give you many thanks for the favor you have shown me. I have become rich and have enjoyed myself through the agency of God [but] my soul is about to perish and my earthly body is very mired down.[22] [52r]

PRIEST: O my beloved honored child, take heart and [seek] comfort in your deity and ruler, God. Be grateful that he shows you favor. What he gives to you in a short while [shows] that he does not despise you [but rather that] he wants you to save yourself so that you merit and attain his royal home, for you are likely to die when you least expect it. And now he concedes to you time to save yourself by confessing. You are to say all your sins. Even though you have [already] confessed perhaps you left out something because of shame. Say it, for you are about to die.

FIRST DEMON: Do not let it worry you, do not be discontented for you are not extremely ill. Have you not already been sick many [other] times and then quickly recovered? In any case God will grant you health. You are just going through bad times now; you will recover.

---

20. See the following related items in Molina 1977, 17r: "Cenca tle anquimati. mirad mucho en este negocio" and "Cenca tle ticmati. mira mucho y ten gran cuidado desto que te encomiendo. &c."

21. This is an obvious allusion to a well-known traditional Nahuatl metaphor. It appears on the idiom list included in book 6 of the *Florentine Codex*: "TLAALOA, TLAPETZCAVI IN JXPAN PETLATL, ICPALLI: AQUJNEUHIAN, AQUJXOAIAN: qujtoznequj: amo vel nemaqujxtiloian: aiac vel ixpan momaqujxtia in tlatoanj," which is translated by the editors as "IT IS SLICK, IT IS SLIPPERY BEFORE THE REED MAT, THE REED SEAT: IT IS THE PLACE OF NO DEPARTURE, THE PLACE OF NO EXIT It means, it cannot be a place of refuge; no one can escape the presence of the ruler" (Sahagún 1950–1982; 6:254). The accompanying Spanish gloss is also of interest: "Dize esta letra. Resbalan y deslizanse muchos en presencia del trono y del estrado y nadie se escapa. Por methaphora qujere dezir: el que caye en la yra del señor o reyno, [no] se puede escapar de sus manos."

22. Evidently a play on words. Literally, "the earth, the mud is very greatly stuck in the mud."

Angel tepixq̄. v Dios ytlaneltocācatzinne Macamo xicneltocan y moyaouh yn tlacatecolotl Ca ça moca mocacayahuazne⁴⁰ Mitzponpololtiznequi ynic çan ipa timicquiz y motlatlacol ynic Onpa mitzhuicaz yn mictlan Cuix amo tiquitta Ca tetlanpololtiyani teyxcueppani Motenepachinhuiyani Ca amo ça quexquichtin yn oquitlapololti yn inca Omocancanyuh⁴¹ ye mictlan tlanyhiyohuitoque yn opa Cemicac chi=chinantzallo ma yçiuhca ximoyolCuiti Ca ayocmo tiçemilhuitiz Ma yehuatzin Jesus mitzmopalehuiliz—

2 dem.º v Yztlancati Amo axcan timiquiz Ca tipactica Cuix ye tihuehuen ca titelpochtli: Oc ocan yn tinemi Ayamo axcan y timiquiz—

Teopixquin v Ma huel xiquitztimotlali Ca y tlacantecolotl ca yxquich ytlapal quichihuan ynic mitztlapoloztiznequin mitzyollomalacanchoznequi ynic amo melahuac ticmoCuintiz Motlatlacol Macamo xic=neltocan Ma xiquito Ma xicmomachitoca yntla ytla otic[52v]tipināhuizcauh⁴² Ca axcan qualcan Ca nemaquixtilizpan auh = ytla ça ticmauhcancahuaz yn anoçe ticpināhuizcahuaz y motlatlacol ma yuh ye y moyollo ca yn iquac timiquiz ca nima Onpa titlamelanhuaz yn mictlan Onpa çemicac titonehualoz tichinchinatzaloz yn intlan tlantlacatecolo · yc motechpa ni=noquixtia ypaltzinᶜᵒ yn dios—

Cocoxqui. v Otinechmocnelili Notlaçotatzine Otlacauhqui y moyollotzin ma niquinto y niquilnamiqui: Ca çan Onitechicoytohua teca Oninhuetzcac⁴³ Onitequalacanytac Ca ça ye ixquich notlaçotatzine—

Teopixqui v Notlaçopiltzen Ma mitztlapollolti Ma moca mocacanyuh⁴⁴ yn diablo yn tlacatecolol⁴⁵—

Angel tepixq̄ v Ma ximocnelli ximocnoytta Ca ye timiquiz ye tipolihuiz = xiquitta Ca ytla otimic yn amo moch ticmoCuititiyaz yn motlatlancol yn amo mitzchoᶜtiz mitztlaocoltiz Ca çemincac tipolihuiz Ma tt.º dios mitzmotlachieltili Ma mitzmotlanextilili—

Cocoxqui v Ca niman Atle nicahuan Notlaçotatzine Ca mochi oniquinto yn notlatlancol—

Teopixqui v Ca ye qualli tehuatl ticmati: ye ninoquixtian yn ixpantzinᶜᵒ ȳ dios Ma yehuantzin mitzmotlaçopiel⁴⁶ Ca ye niyauh—

Cocoxqui v Ca ye qualli ma tel ximohuica Ha huel namiqui ma xinechmomaquilican achitzin Atzintli Ca huel çenca namiqui ye notehuahuanq̄—

Angel tepixqui. v Yntla ça tepiton Cocoliztli: yc çenca titehuāhuanqui yn cenca tamiqui queni huel tiquiyhiyohuiz: yn mictlan tletl. yhuan yn mictlan tehuanhuanquiliztli yn atle Oc centlanmātli = [53r] yc tipatiz ytlacamo tletepozchapōpoatl y cencan tōtoquin: y cenca techichinatz yn cenca teyolCuitlantzaya mitzintizque—

Cocoxqui v Cuix huelitiz yn nechmocneliliz yn dios yn axca—

---

40. mocacayahuazne: read *mocacayahuaznequi*.
41. yn inca Omocancanyuh: read *yn inca omocacayauh*.
42. otic[52v]tipināhuizcauh: read *oticpinahuizcauh*.
43. Oninhuetzcac: read *oninohuetzcac*.
44. Ma moca mocacanyuh: read *ma moca mocacayauh*.
45. tlacatecolol: read *tlacatecolotl*.
46. mitzmotlaçopiel: read *mitzmotlaçopieli*.

GUARDIAN ANGEL: O believer in God, do not believe your enemy the devil for he just wants to mock and confuse you so that you will die right in your sins and he will take you to hell. Do you not see he is a confounder of people, an ambusher of people? He has confused innumerable people, mocked them. Now they suffer in hell, are made to suffer eternal pain there. Quickly confess for you will no longer last an entire day. Let Jesus help you.

SECOND DEMON: He lies. You will not die today for you are healthy. Are you an old man? [No,] you are a young man. You will yet live there, you are not about to die.

PRIEST: Ponder well for the devil is exerting all his effort in order to confuse and pervert you so that you will not correctly confess your sins. Do not believe him. Speak, acknowledge if there is something you left out because it was shameful, [52v] for now is a good time to save oneself. If you leave out your sins just because of fear or shame be sure [that] when you die you will go straight there to hell. There you will be eternally tormented and made to suffer pain among the devils. For the sake of God I thus fulfill the obligation I have to you.

SICK MAN: O my beloved father, I thank you very much for the favor you have shown me. Let me say what I remember: I have just lied about others, I laughed at people, I looked angrily at others. O my beloved father, that is all.

PRIEST: O my beloved child, do not let the devil confuse and mock you.

GUARDIAN ANGEL: Do yourself a favor, have mercy on yourself for you will die and perish. Look, when you have died and you pass on without confessing all your sins and they have not made you weep and sad, then you will perish forever. May our lord God make you see, may he give you a revelation.[23]

SICK MAN: O my beloved father, I have left absolutely nothing out. I have said all my sins.

PRIEST: Very well, you already know I have fulfilled my obligations before God. May he dearly guard you for I am going.

SICK MAN: Very well, go. I am very thirsty. Give me a little something to drink for I am extremely thirsty and my lips are dried up.

GUARDIAN ANGEL: If your lips are so dry with just a little illness, if you are so thirsty, how can you suffer the fires of hell and the dried cracking of lips in hell, which have no other cure? [53r] They will make you drink molten lava, which is very hot, very painful, and very heartrending.

SICK MAN: Is it possible that God will show me favor now?

---

23. ma mitzmotlanextilili / may he give you a revelation: see related forms on the Spanish-Nahuatl side of Molina 1977, 104v, and on the Nahuatl-Spanish side, 128v.

Angel tepixqui v Ca quemacan Ma xicmotzatzinlili Ca nimitzmopalehuiliz[47]—
+ yas yn Angel
3. dem:º v Macamo xicneltocan Ca çan iztlacati yn angel Ca ye titonemac: Ca ye omitzmocentelchihuili yn dios yehica yn amo otitlamaceuh =
Cocoxqui v Ca ye nelli: Ca mictlā nipouhqui yehica Ca cenca miec y notlatlancol Ca nima ahuel mopohuaz ay ma monotzanca y pipiltin yn tlantoque ytech nicanhuaz yn ixquich: noaxca notlatqui =
+ Oncan hualquiçazque Omentin pipiltin =
1º pilli. v Tle mitzmotequipachilhuian tlantohuanie. ynic titechmonochilia: ca otihuallaque Ma ximochicauhtzinno: Ma mitzmochiCanhuilli yn tlancatl tlantohuan[48] dios Xicmotzatzinlili Macamo Ximotlapololti: yçemactzin^{co} ximocauhtzinno = Ca tlatlancantzintli Ca moteycnoytiliyani Ca mitzmocneliliz: Ca mitzmotlaocoliliz yhua yehuatzin tlatocanychpōchtzintli Sancta M.ª ma mopā motlatolti yn ixpantzinco yn itlaçoconetzin ynic mitzmotlaocoliliz auh tle ticmonenquiltia Ca otihuallaque—
Cocoxqui v Notlaçopiltzintzine Cenca ayocmo nichuelmati y noñacayo huel niçontlanhua ye huel nimiquiznequi. ayocmo huel nitlaCuiloz Ca yehuatl yn ixquich noaxca notlatqui amotetzin.^{co} nicahuan Amehuantzintzin: aquimochihuilizque y Noteztanmēto aquimoxexelhuizque amotetzinco nicauhtiuh: yn ixquich noaxcan notlatqui—[53v]
2 pilli v Ca ye qualli Ca ticneltilizque y motlanequilitzin Ca timitztopalehuilizque yn tlen ic titechmonahuatilitiuh ma yxquich y motlapaltzin ma ximochicauhtzino Ma oc timitztotlalcanhuilican Ca cencan timitztomocihuilia—
+ Canlaquizque auh. y dem.º nimā quiquechmateloz
2 dem.º v Ma xicquechmatelocan xicquechpachocan ma tichuicancan yhua y tlanhuelliloc y huey tlatlancohuani yn ianimā—
+ Onca quiquixtilizque yn ianima auh ytla omic nima hualquiçaz tliltic yn iam̄a miec Coetes ytech =
ynami. v Onocentzotlahuelliltic Ca ye omomiquili y notlaçonamictzin Ca amo huel nicmati y tlen ipa Omochiuh y çan içiuhcan Miquiliztli ypan Oquihualmihuali yn iteuh yn itlantocatzin Ma yçiuhca ypa motlatoltican yn ixquichti nohuayolque ynic motocaz yn iñacayo Ma tzillinin y micantepoztli ma quinotzancan y Cuihcanimē yhua yn ixtlanmatque yn teopixquen ynic quimotoquilizque—
+ Onca hualquicazq̄.[49] y tetocanime mehuaz Rezponso yc calaquizq̄. Quitocazq̄. nima hualq̄.çazque. Angeles

---

47. nimitzmopalehuiliz: standard *nimitznopalehuiliz*.
48. tlantohuan: read *tlatohuani*.
49. hualquicazq̄: read *hualquiçazque*.

GUARDIAN ANGEL: Yes. Cry out to him. I will help you.
  ([Guardian] Angel exits.)
THIRD DEMON: Do not believe him for the angel just lies. You already belong to us for God has entirely despised you because you have not done penance.
SICK MAN: It is true that I belong to hell because I have a great many sins that are absolutely uncountable. Ah! Let the nobles and rulers be summoned. I will assign to them all my goods and property.
  (At that point two noblemen enter.)
FIRST NOBLEMAN: O ruler, what is troubling you that you summon us? We have come. Take heart. May the lord and ruler, God, give you health. Cry out to him. Do not be confused. Leave yourself entirely in his hands, for he is humane and compassionate. He will befriend you and have mercy on you along with the royal maiden Saint Mary. May she intercede for you before her beloved son so that he will have mercy on you. What do you want? We have come.

SICK MAN: O my beloved noblemen, I no longer feel my body is healthy. I am very faint and I am really just about to die. I will no longer be able to write. I leave all my goods and property with you. You will make my testament. You will divide all my goods and property I am leaving you into discrete parts. [53v]

SECOND NOBLEMAN: Very well, we will carry out your will. We will help you in what you go ordering us [to do]. Be of good cheer, take heart. Let us leave you for we are greatly upsetting you.
  (They exit. The demon then strangles him with his hands.)
SECOND DEMON: Strangle him with your hands, squeeze his neck. Let us take him along with the soul of the scoundrel and great sinner.
  (At that point they take his soul out of him. After he has died his blackened soul emerges. Many rockets are attached to it.)
HIS SPOUSE: I am four hundred[24] [times] unfortunate! My beloved spouse has just died and I do not know what happened to him. His god and ruler just quickly sent death upon him. May all my relatives speak quickly on behalf of him so that his body will be buried. Let the bells[25] be rung, let them summon the cantors and the prudent ones, the priests, to bury him.
  (At that point the gravediggers enter. A responsory for the dead is said.[26] They bury him. Then angels enter.)

---

24. This is an idiomatic usage that means "countless, innumerable."
25. miccatepoztli / bells: see Lockhart 1992, 221, where he points out that the term is an early circumlocution that literally means "'dead-person metal,' that is, the metal object sounded to announce someone's death." Chimalpahin also uses this circumlocution and the Spanish loanword, sometimes in tandem and sometimes each term by itself, in speaking of church bells (see Chimalpahin 1965, 2:39, 40, 44, 48, 50, 87, 100, 101, 104).
26. Literally, "raised," often used in expressions like "raised up in song."

Angel tepixqui v̲ Ha yyoyahuen Omochiuh Onotlahuelliltic yn atle nolhuil y̲n̲ atle nomacenhual y nimotlachihualtzin quemachameque: yn oc cenquintin y notlaço-ycniuhtzintzinhuan Angeles y nican = yn itlapielhua y qualli yn ipan monemitia yn tlalticpac = auh y nehuatl Omochiuh Onotlahueliltic yn atle nolhuil: no:macenhual: Cuix amomoztlaye y tiquinnotzan yn tiquitzatzinlian yn tiquiyollotia y qualli yectli y tiquimilnanmictia auh y yenhuantin amo quimocacannenequi: ye ylhuicen quitlacamatin yn diablo yn tlacatecolotl: huel quinacātzatzantilia quinnontilia: quimixtlapachohua: ha yyoyahuen Ca quin onpa y mictlan: quimixtlapohuan quinaCaztlan̲pohua auh Cuix oc onca Ca nimā ayocmo Oncā Ca nica tlalticpac yn ocomixcahualtique yn Cencan tlaçotli yn inemac omochihuazquia—

GUARDIAN ANGEL: Ah, woe is me! I am a creature of yours, undeserving and without merit. How fortunate are the others, my beloved friends the angels, whose charges live in good[ness] on earth. But as for me, woe is me! I am undeserving and without merit. Do we not talk to them every day, cry out to them, inspire them to what is good, remind them of what is proper? But they do not want to hear it; [rather] they want to obey the devil much more. He makes them very deaf and mute and covers up their eyes. Ah, alas! Afterward, over there in hell, he opens their eyes and opens their ears. Do they still exist? In no way do they still exist for here on earth they lost by their faults and negligence what is very precious, what would have been bestowed on them.[27]

---

27. What this inheritance means could refer to so many things mentioned in the play, from God's mercy and loving charity to his royal home in heaven, that perhaps this is shorthand for all the specific points raised in this play.

Present Location
Graduate Theological Union Library
Academy of American Franciscan History Collection
Berkeley, California

[1]
Loa en nahuatl

De oastepec

[2] [blank] [3]

Prologo

Yn amixquichtin Yn nican oamechmocentlalili Yn tona.tzin Sta Yg.^{a} Yn oamechmoquanochili Ynic anhuallazque anConanazq.^{z} Yn ocuhtacatl, machiotl Yn nican, in Campa amixpan quimotlalilia Yn neixcuitil,machiotl Ynic amontlachiesque amicampa Yhuan anmotlâtlanizque SeseYâca, amoYollo ihtec ancontlazasque Yn amotlalnamiquiliz anquitlâtlanizque Yn amoYollo Cuix huel chipahualiztica Ynic annemi, Cuix huel anquimohuellamachtilihtinemi, in Dios, quallachihualiztica? Cuix nocê âmo? Yntlacamo itla qualli tlachihualiztli anquinextia amotechCopa ma xihualmotocahuican, itech niin[1] neixcuitilmachiotl Yn amechmotitilia Yn tonantzin Sta Yglecia Yn campa Ytechcopa tlatohua Se tlâtohuani Yn San Cemihcac omoxochipolotinenca Ytechcopa Yn itecâcayahualiz Yn tlalticpactli Yn aic, itla oquimocahuali[?]Co Yn Dios San mochipa oquitlacaq[ui?] Yn ixtlacat[i?]liz[2] San no Yuhqui Yn tlacatecolotl Yn tlein oquiti[o?]aya, ânoce oquilnamictiaya mochi oquichihuayâ ca niman aic omotlacahualti Ytechcopa Yn quexquich YYolihtlacolocatzin Yn tt.^{o} D.^{s} Auh Yn inamic San no Yuhqui mochipa oquipâpaquilti atliliztica tlaqualiztica Yhuan nechihchihualiztica nican tlalticpac oquipix Yn pâpaquiliztli, auh Yn ihquac oyac onestito Yxpantzinco, Yn momelahuacatetlatzontequililiani Juez Yn tt.^{o} JeSu xp̄o otlâtoltiloc Ytechcopa Yn iteotenahuatiltzin D.^{s} Yn manel san ce quallachihualiztli âtle oquichiuh, auh Yn ihuanpohuan aic oquintlazôtlac Yn motolinihcatzitzinti aic oquintlaocolili San no iuhqui Yn Cihuapilli Ynic onecia huel mahuiztic Yn inemiliz oyaya teopan oquittaya Missa oquiCaquia temachtilli, Auh Yn manel ocalaquia teopan San oncan ohualaya oteixelehuiaya, San ohualaya mononotzas Yn onca^n teiztlacohuaya,[3] oquimpinahuiaya Yn icnotlaca Yn âmo quimopielia Yn tlein ic quimopachosque Yn intlalo, Ynsoquis[4]; Auh Ypampa on ocentelchihualoc Mictlan oya Yn ianiman Yn Campa anquitztimotlalizque Yn ihquac ancalaquizq.^{z} [4] Yn ichantzinco Dios achtopa mochi anquitelchihuazque Yn ixquich âmo qualli

---

1. niin: read *inin*.
2. ixtlacat[i?]liz: perhaps to be read *iztlacatiliz*.
3. teiztlacohuaya: perhaps to be read *teiztlacahuiya*.
4. Ynsoquis: read *ynzoquio*.

The Life of Don Sebastián
Translated by Barry D. Sell, with assistance from Louise M. Burkhart

[1]
Praise Play in Nahuatl

From Huaxtepec

[2] [blank] [3]

Prologue[1]
Our mother holy church has gathered you all together here. She has invited you to come to grasp the measuring stick, the model,[2] here where she places before you the exemplary model so that you each will look behind you and examine yourselves, cast it into your hearts, examine your memories and your hearts. Do you live very purely? Do you really go about pleasing God with good deeds, or not? If you do not discover some good deeds concerning yourselves, follow this exemplary model that our mother holy church shows you, where it talks about a ruler who always went about indulging himself with delicacies, and about the deceptions of the earth. He never abstained from anything [prohibited by?] God. He always listened to the lies, likewise, of the demon. He used to do everything that [the demon] would say to him or make him think. He absolutely never restrained himself concerning whatever was an affront to our lord God. And likewise he always delighted his spouse with drink, with food, and with adornments; here on earth he had pleasures. But when he went to appear before the true sentencer of people and judge, our lord Jesus Christ, he was made to talk about the sacred commandments of God. He had not done even just one good deed. And as to his neighbors, he never loved them. As for the afflicted, he never had pity on them. Likewise the noblewoman appeared to have a very honorable life. She used to go to church to see mass[3] and hear the sermons,[4] but even though she used to enter church she just went there coveting people, she just came to chat. She used to deceive people there, she used to shame the poor people who had nothing with which to cover their earth, their clay.[5] And because of that his soul was completely despised; it went to the place of the dead. From that you are to contemplate, when you enter [4] the home of God, that you are, first, to despise all bad

---

1. Parts of this prologue are tentatively translated.
2. measuring stick, model: here and below, a common diphrase that means "[sound] moral advice" (as opposed to that given by the demons to don Sebastián later in the play).
3. see mass: an early colonial idiom whose pragmatic thrust is "hear mass."
4. temachtilli: here and below translated as "sermon(s)" as it almost invariably was in contemporary ecclesiastical Nahuatl texts, it has the more general meaning of "teaching(s), doctrine."
5. earth, clay: here and below, a standard diphrase (often found in testaments) that means "earthly body/ies."

tlalnamiquiliztli huel mochi iCa Yn amoYollo anquimotlanililizque Yn noma amechmihquanilili mochi Yn ipan amotlalnamiquiliz Yn quexquich Yn âmo yhuellamachtilocatzin ma San Yêhuatl Yn tlein ic motolinia Yn amoanima Yhuan Yn amonacayo ixpantzinco xictlalican Yehica ca in quenin amotechiuhcatzin Yhuan amoteyocoxcatzin amechmomaquilis mochi Yn tlein anquimihtlanililizque intla huel huey tlateomatiliztiCa, necnomatiliztica Yhuan nepechtequiliztica antlaihtlanizque No ihuan huel monequi anquineltilizque Yn iteotenahualtiltzin D.[s] Cmc amixpan, ihuan amotlalnamiquilisp[n] anqualhuicatinemizque[5] Ynic âmo amechtlapololtiz Yn tlacatecolotl; Auh yntla quemmanian, itla iC amechmoyeyecoltiz ma xiquilnamiquican Ca in Yehuatl âmo Ytla qualli Yn amechmacas Yn ompa Mictlan ca san Yehuatl Yn cemicac tlatlaliztli Yn campa, ic cemmayan tlayohuaYan Anyesque Yn niman ayc cepa anquimotililizque Yn itlasôxayacatzin Yn D.[s] Ypampa Ynon ma huel ximimmatinemican macamo Ytla amopan mochihuas in tlein Ympan omochiuh Yn tlatlacohuanime Yn nican amechmotililia tonantzin Sta Yg.[l] ipan, i ocuhtatcatl machiotl ca intla chipahualiztica annemizque Yntla anquimotlazôtilizq.[z] Yn D.[s] Yhuan in amohuanpohuan Ca ic anquimomâCehuizque Yn iteyecnemitiayatzin Yn tt.[o] D.[s] nican tlpc Auh Yn iquac anmomiquilizque Ca amechmomaquiliz Yn cmc netlamachtiliztli Gloria

Amen Jesus M,[a] Y Joseph
Joaquin i + Anna

---

5. anqualhuicatinemizque: read *anquihualhuicatinemizque*.

thoughts with absolutely all of your heart. You are to ask God to take away from you everything that is in your thoughts that is not pleasing to him. Just set before him that which troubles your souls and your bodies. Because, as your Progenitor and your Creator, he will give you everything you ask for if you ask with very great devotion, humility, and reverence. And it is also necessary that you carry out the sacred commands of God that are always before you, and that you go about taking them in your memory so that the demon will not confuse you. But, if he tempts you with something sometime, remember that what he will give you there in the place of the dead will be something bad; it will just be eternal burning where, once and for all, you will be in darkness. Absolutely never again will you see the precious face of God. Because of that, live very prudently. Do not let something bad happen to you [as] happened to the sinners whom our mother holy church shows to you here in the measuring stick, the model. For if you live with purity, if you love God and your neighbors, you will earn here on earth our lord God's instrument of causing people to live properly.[6] And when you die he will give you eternal riches, glory.

Amen. Jesus, Mary and Joseph.
Joachim and Anne[7]

---

6. the instrument of causing people to live properly: this and similar Nahuatl terms are often paired with the Spanish loanword *gracia*, "grace."

7. That is, Mary's father and mother.

[5]

v̲ Neyxcuitilli Ytechpa tlatohua Ynemilis D^n Seb,^{n}—hualquisas D^n Seb.^{n} Yhuan D^a Juana Yhuan 1° Dem.^{o} Yhuan OMentin Pajes Yhuâ 1° Ang.^{L}—

hualMoquixtis Yn Miquistli Motlatoltiz—

v̲ Tlalticpac tlacaye D,^{s} Ytlamaquixtiltzitzinhuane Yn nican anCenquistoq.^{z} Yn teOyotica amechmotetlalilia AmechmoCohuanochilia Yn Sta Yglesia ma xicmatican Yhuâ ma huel xiquilnamiquican Y niYo Y notlatol, Yn axcâ niCan amixp.^{n} niCac, aquipa.[1] anechita: aquipa: anechmati. anoso tlen notoCa. Yn iuh âquimati. xinechilhuiCan xinechnâquiliCan xiquitocan Cuix nitlaltp.^{c} nitlaCatl, Cuix nitlatohuani: ~~Cuix noso niRey anoso niRoq.^{z} Cuix noso niConde: anoso niMarquez: Cuix noso niemperador: Cuix noso nehuatl ni[?] anoso Cuix niarsoBispo anoso:~~ Cuix noço ~~aca~~ niteopixCatlatohuani: Ye neltilistli: Y naMechilhuia: Ca niman amo Ca Yn nehuatl, Ca nitlachihualtzin Yn D,^{s} Nititlantzin nitopileCatzin: niJustiÇiatzin nitetlatzaCuilticatzin Yeyca Yn ixquichtin Oniquinteneuh: Ca mochintin: nomac cate. Yn iquac Nechmonahuatilya Yn D,^{s} Yn saso ac Yehuatl Y nictlatlatis nicpoctlatilis Yn iYolia, Ca iuhqui mochihuas Yuhqui nicneltilia Ca amo Yuh niCahua. Yn manel amo S.^{n} queXquich Ytlatqui ō ca Yn manel: Amo S^n tlapohuali Yn ialtepeuh âmo. Yc momaquixtis Yn aquin tlatlaCohuani Yno.^{n} Yn axcan nican Onechmotitlani Yn tlatohuani D,^{s} Yn itechpa Yn tlatohuani Yn nican Yn moxochitlamachtitica moxochipolotica Yuhqui nicneltilia Yn itenahuatiltzin Yn iÇel teotl D,^{s} Ca ye yxquich otlami[6]co Yn iCahuiuh Yhuan huel oquimamanili huel itzinco Ycpactzinco one AYomo[2] quimopaCayohuiltzia[3] Ca çeca Oquimotequipanilhui Yquip.^{n}pa[4] Yn axcan nictlatlatis nicpopolos; Auh Ompa tlasalos: Ompa tlatzaCuiltilos, Yn ompa Sentlanin mictlan, Ypampa Yn ixquich Yn iaqualnemilis; Yn niCan Oquichiuhtinenca Yn niCan Ytlaltp.^{c}tzinco; Yn D,^{s} Ypampa Yn tlaltp.^{c} tlaCae ma ytech ximixCuitican, Yn tlahuelilocatlatohuani Ca Yasq.^{z} Yn Centlani mictlan, Yhuan Yn tlahuelilocaSihuatl ca ytencopantzinco Yn tt.^{o} D,^{s} macamo San camanali Ypan xicmatican ma huel xiquilnamictinemican Yn iYotzin Yn itlatoltzin tlaltp.^{c} tlacaYe

tlapitzalos moCalaquiz Yn miquistli—

v̲ hualquiCas[5] Don Sebastian yhuan D.ª Juana yhuan 1° Demonio yhuan Omentin PaJes ~~Yhuan 1° agel Don Sebastian~~

D^n Seb,^{n} Tla XihualMohuica notlasotatzine Yn axcan Ca oc tepitzin techmochicahuilia Yn D,^{s} Ca oc tlaltp.^{c} Yn ticate Ca atle CoColistli totech ca ca Atle techcocohua Auh niquitohua Yn axcan ma tiquintonochilican Yn tocniuhtzitzinhuan ma titoSep.^{n}Yolalican Yn manel quaresma ticate ma tonpapaquican Canel Oc tlaltp.^{c} Yn ticate—

---

1. aquipa: here and below, read *ac ipan*.
2. AYomo: read either as *aocmo* or *ayamo*.
3. AYomo quimopaCahuiltzia: perhaps to be read *ayamo quimopaccaihiyohuiltitzinoa*.
4. Yquip.^{n}pa: read *yc ipampa*.
5. hualquiCas: read *hualquiçaz*.

[5]

Moral example which speaks about the life of don Sebastián.
(Don Sebastián enters along with doña Juaña and First Demon and two pages and First Angel.
Death enters. He speaks.)

[DEATH:] O people of the earth, O God's saved ones, you who are all here together, whom the holy church spiritually detains and invites, know and remember well my breath, my words.[1] Now I stand here before you. Who do you see me as? Who do you think I am? What is the name you know me by? Tell me, answer me, say it. Am I a person of the earth? Am I a ruler? ~~Or am I a king, or a rook, or a count, or a marquis, or an emperor, or a [?], or an archbishop?~~ Or am I someone who is a priestly ruler [that is, bishop or pope]? I tell you the truth, that is absolutely not me, for I am a creature of God, I am his messenger, I am his constable, I am his officer of justice, I am his castigator. Because all those whom I have mentioned are all in my hands. When God orders me, whoever it is, I will burn him, I will burn his spirit up like smoke. For such will be done, I will carry it out in that way, for I spare none even though he has great wealth, even though his realms are countless, for he[2] who is a sinner will not save himself with that. Now the ruler, God, has sent me here concerning the ruler here who enjoys delicacies, indulges himself with delicacies. Thus I carry out the commands of the sole deity, God. That is all. [6] His time has come to an end, and he really disturbed, he really offended him; he no longer has patience with him. He worked hard at [offending God], wherefore now I will burn him, I will destroy him. And he will be cast there, he will be punished there, there in the depths of the place of the dead,[3] because of all his bad living he went around doing here, here on God's earth. Wherefore, O people of the earth, take an example from the wicked ruler and the wicked woman who will go to the depths of the place of the dead, by order of our lord God. Do not regard it as a joke. Remember his breath, his words, O people of the earth!

(Wind instruments are played. Death exits.)
(Don Sebastián enters along with doña Juana and First Demon and two pages ~~and First Angel. Don Sebastián~~:)

DON SEBASTIÁN: Do come, O my beloved father. Today God is keeping us alive a bit longer, for we are still on earth, there is no sickness in us, nothing makes us ill. And I say now let us summon our friends, let us console one another. Even though we are in Lent, let us enjoy ourselves, since we are still on earth.

---

1. breath, word: a common diphrase that means "message" or "command," sometimes "fine and elegant speech."
2. Or she; list of titles suggests male frame of reference.
3. mictlan: here and below translated as "the place of the dead" (locative senses such as "in" or "at" are already contained in the Nahuatl term), it was usually rendered by colonial translators as *infierno* (hell).

1.º Dem.º v̱ Auh Ynon Ca huel Oc quali Yn tiquilnamiqui Ca huel oc YmonecYan Yn timoyolalis cuix oc tipiltontli tiConetontli Ma Oc xipapaqui Cuix ye tihuehue Ma yquin Yquac Yntla Ye tihuehue titlamasehuas ma timomecahuitequis Cuix amo ye tiquimita Ynin Ca huel miequintin Yn telpopochtin quipactitinemi Yn telpochYotl ca quitotinemi quilnamictinemi Yn inpapa[7]quilis Ca S,^{n} quitohua Ma yquin YCuac Yn tihuehuetisq.^{z} titocahuasq.^{z} Yn titlateomatisq.^{z}—

D,^{n} Seb,^{n} v̱ Notlasomahuistatzine Ca huel teYolali Yn motlatoltzin Auh yn tehuatzin Notlasonamictzine tleyn ticMitalhuia Canel oc tiuhq.^{z} Yn Canel oc tipipiltotontin ma oc ticpapaquiltican Yn tlaltp.^{c}CaYotl Yn necuYLtonolistli Yn papaquilistli ma Oc motelchihua Yn teop.^{n}nemilistli ma Oc motelchihua Yn neYolCuitilistli Ma Yquin quesquilhuitl Yn ticchihuasq.^{z} Yn qualnemilistli—

D^{na} Juana v̱ Notlasonamictzin notelpotzin Ca Yn otzintic Yn ticmitalhuia Ca noma Amo niCualita Yntlacamo timoYolCuititzinosnequi Ca Yn nehuatl Ca niYauh in ichantzinco D,^{s}—

D^n Seb,^{n} v̱ Ninomati tinechtlahuelnanquilia tle Yca Yn amo tinechtlacamati ^{in} tleYn nimitzilhuia Ca ticchihua Ca tinechtlacamatis Ca ticneltilis Yn notlatol—

1,º Dem.º v̱ Tla xihualMohuica nochpochtzine macamo ximoqualanalti tla xicmo-Caquiltitzino Ca Yntla timohuicas Yn teop.^{n} manoso iquin Ycuac Yn timoCoCo-tzinos Auh Yn axcan ma xicmotlacamachilti Yn motlasonamictzin ca huelitis Yntla moqualanaltis Ca mitzmomictilis Auh Ynin tlasosihuapile ma no xinechmotlaca-machilti Ca amo nipiltontli Ca ye niuhqui Ca Ye nihuehue tlacatl Yn nimotatzin—

D,^{na} Juana v̱ Notlasotelpochtzin NoteCuyo ma xinechmotlapòpolhuilitzino Ca niman amo huel nicchias^6 Yn nehuatl Yn tleyn ticMitalhuia Ca Yn axcan Ca quaresma Yn ticate Ca ticneltilisq.^{z} Yn itenahuatiltzin Yn D,^{s}—

Yaz Yn D,^{na} Juana hualquisas 1º # Angel [8]

D^n Seb.^{n} v̱ Notlasomahuistatzine macamo tlen xicmolhuiliz Yese mochihuas Yn tleYn ticmitalhuis Ca nicchihuas Auh Yese niquitohua Ca Yntla nechqualanis Ca niquichtacamictis Ca tinechmopalehuilis Ca Yn tleyn nicchihuas—

1.º Dem.º v̱ Notelpotze noxocoyohue macamo mitzmotequipachilhuis Ca nimitz-palehuis Amo ximomauhti—

1.º Ang.^{l} v̱ Nopieltzine tleyn ticchihuasnequi Cuix ticochi ma axcan ma mitztequipa-cho Ym motlatlaCol Cuix amo ticmati Yn ca axcan tlamasehualisCahuip.^{n} Yn ticate ma ximoCuitihuetzi ma xitlachie—

D^n Seb,^{n} v̱ Tla xihualhuian Yn amehuantin Yn tehuatl Yn ti[PaJe?] ma xonaci Yn ichantzinco Yn Do^n alberto~~tzin ma xicmonochili Auh Yn tehuatl Yn tiMig.^{l} ma xic-monochili Yn D^n Sebastiantzin~~ Ma nican hualmohuica Ca niCan niquinnochielitica Ca nican tôtoYolalisq.^{z} Ytlauctzinco Ynahuactzinco Yn mahuistlatlacatzintli Yn huehue tlacatzintli Canel ~~Domingo [?]~~^{7}

2.º PaJe. v̱ Ca Ye qualitzin tlacatle tlatohuanie ma tiquintonochilitin—

Mig^l v̱ Ma ticneltilitin Yn miYotzin motlatoltzin—

Callaquizque Yn PaJes

---

6. nicchias: read *nicchihuaz*.
7. There are words in super- and subscript: [?] yehuatzin ang^l hualmohuicas Yn nica[n?] [?].

FIRST DEMON: And that, what you are thinking, is very good, for it is a very opportune time for you to console yourself. Are you still a little kid, a baby? Enjoy yourself for now. Are you an old man already? Do penance and whip yourself when you are an old man. Do you not see the multitude of young men who go about enjoying the things of youth, who go about speaking of and thinking of their pleasures? [7] For they just say, "when we are old men we will stop, we will engage in spiritual activities."

DON SEBASTIÁN: O my beloved honored father, your words are very consoling. And you, O my beloved spouse, what do you say? Since we are still this way, since we are still little kids, let us for now enjoy the things of the earth, wealth and pleasures. Let hanging around at church be despised for now, let confession be despised for now. Let us work at the good life for a few days.

DOÑA JUANA: O my beloved spouse, O my son, as to what you have just finished saying, I myself do not approve if you do not want to confess. As for me, I am going to the home of God.

DON SEBASTIÁN: I think you are answering me in an angry way. Why do you not obey me? What I say to you, you are to do. You will obey me; you will carry out my words.

FIRST DEMON: Do come, O my daughter, do not be angry. Do listen. If you go to church perhaps then you will become ill. But now, obey your beloved spouse for it could be, if he gets angry, that he will kill you. And so, O precious noblewoman: obey me also for I am not a little kid. My nature is that I am an old person, I am your father.[4]

DOÑA JUANA: O my beloved young man, O my lord, pardon me for I absolutely cannot do what you are saying, for we are now in Lent and we will carry out God's orders.

(Doña Juana leaves. First Angel enters.) [8]

DON SEBASTIÁN: O my beloved honored father, do not say anything, yet what you say will be carried out. I will do it. And yet I say, if she makes me angry I will secretly kill her. You will help me do it.

FIRST DEMON: O my son, O my youngest, let it not trouble you for I will help you. Do not be afraid.

FIRST ANGEL: O my charge, what are you about to do? Are you sleeping? May your sins trouble you now. Do you not know that we are now in the time of penance? Come to your senses, see!

DON SEBASTIÁN: Do come. You, page, go to the home of don Alberto; ~~summon him. And you, Miguel, summon don Sebastián~~; may he come here. I await them here, for here we will console ourselves next to and alongside the honored humane person, the old man, since it is ~~Sunday [?]~~.

SECOND PAGE.: Very well, O lord, O ruler, let's go summon them.

MIGUEL: Let's go carry out your breath, your words.

(The pages exit.)

---

4. That is, he belongs to the same generation as her father and demands the same respect and obedience she would give him.

D^n Seb,^{n} v Notlasomahuistatzine tla nimitznotlatlanili tleYn nicchihuas Yn itechcopa Yn nonamic q.^{z} huel nicchihuaz Yn ip^{n}pa Yn amo huel nechtlamati[8]—

1.º Dem.^{o} v Notelpotze noxoCoYohue macamo mitztequipacho^s ca nehuatl nicmati Ca nimitzpalehuis Ca nimitzilhuis Yn q^n huel ticchihuas Ca nimitzilhuis Ca Yn Campa tiquitas Ca nimitzYecanas Yese Ca nimitzmacas Yn tleYn Yc ticmictis Yn mosihuauh ma notech ximochicahua macamo ximomauhti Ca nimitzpalehuis—[9]

Dn Seb,^{n} v Ynontzin Ca Cenca ninoYolalia Yn nicCaqui Yn motlatoltzin Nopiltzintzine tlatohuanie ma Oc tepitzin titoSehuitin Yn oquic hualMohuica Yn tocniuhtzitzinhuan Ynic titoYolalisq.^{z} timochintin—

      # Calaquisq.^{z} hualquisas D^{na} Juana Yhuan 2° Ang.^{l}
      2.º Demo san huel quisas ~~Dem~~ nepantla quisasqz.

D,^{na} Juana v Noteotzin notlatocatzin D,^{s} campa nias Yn mohuitzin Yn nictocas Ynic nias Yn motheop.^{n}Chantzinco—

2° Ang.^{l} v Cihuatzintle Campa Yn timohuiCasnequi ma xinechmolhuili—

D,^{a} Juana v NotlasoConetzin Ca Ompa nonasisnequi Yn ichantzinco D,^{s}—

2.º Ang^l v Tla nimitznotlatlanili tleyn timaYlis Cuix itla mitzmotequipachilhuia Ma xitechmolhuili—

D,^{na} Juana v Tla xicmoCaquilti Ca Ynic nias Ca ninoYolCuitis Yn axcan Canel motenahuatilia Yn tonantzin Sta Yglecia Ynic neSenCahualos Ynic nealtilos Yn ixp.^{n}tzinco D,^{s}—

2° Ang.^{l} v Ca senca mahuistic Yn ticmolnamiquilia Auh Yn nehuatl Ca nimitznonahuatilia macamo Ytla ticmopinahuiscahuilis Ynic timoYolCuititzinos ma huel mochi ticmoSenquixtili Yn motlatlaCol huel huey yn iteycnoytalistzin Yn tt.^{o} Dios—

2° Demo v Macamo xicneltoca Yn itlatol Yn piltontli Yn tleyn mitzilhuia Ca San mitzitztlacahuia[9] amo xicneltoca—Yas mictlan

D^{na} Juana v Onomasehualtic Otinechmocnelilitzino Ca huel mahuistic Yn motlatoltzin Auh ma xinechMohuiquili Yn teop.^{n} ma xinechmoYecanili Ynic quali nictocas Yn iYotzin yn tt.^{o} D,^{s}—

      # Yazq.^{z} yn teop.^{n} hualquisasq.^{z} Lucifer Yhuâ omentin Demonios

Luçifer tla xihualhuian Yn annotetlaYeColtiCahuan tleyn amay tleYn anquichihua Cuix ancochi Ca Ye Ynma Ca Ye oncâ Yn ticate ma anquichihuasq.^{z} Yn amotequiuh ma xicte[10]tecacan Yn amotzohua Yhuan Yn amomatl Yn anmochimal Yn amotlahuis Cuix amo Yn teopixcatotontin Ca huel monequi Yn techpanahuisq.^{z} Yn ica Yn inNeYolCuitilis Yn tlaltp.^{c} tlacatotontin ma yxquich Amotlapal xicchihuacan ca ye Anquimati Ca huel teoCruztica Yn Mictlan—

---

8. nechtlamati: read *nechtlacamati*.
9. mitzitztlacahuia: read *mitziztlacahuia*.

DON SEBASTIÁN: O my beloved honored father, let me ask you: What am I to do about my spouse? What can I do about the fact that she does not obey me?

FIRST DEMON: O my young man, O my youngest, let it not trouble you, for I know about it and I will help you. I will tell you what you can do, I will tell you where you will find her, I will lead you [there]. Moreover I will give you what you will kill your wife with. Rely on me. Do not be frightened, for I will help you. [9]

DON SEBASTIÁN: I am very content to hear your words, O my nobleman, O ruler. Let us rest a little more while our friends are coming so that we will all be consoled.[5]

(They exit. Doña Juana enters along with Second Angel.)
(Second Demon [likewise] enters. They enter in the middle.)[6]

DOÑA JUANA: O my deity, O my ruler, O God, where am I to go? I will follow your road so that I will go to your temple.

SECOND ANGEL: O woman, where do you want to go? Tell me.

DOÑA JUANA: O my beloved child, I want to reach the home of God.

SECOND ANGEL: Let me question you. What's the matter? Is something troubling you? Tell me.

DOÑA JUANA: Do listen. I am going to confess now since our mother holy church orders people to prepare themselves, to bathe themselves in the presence of God.

SECOND ANGEL: What you are thinking is very worthy of esteem. But I order you: do not omit something for shame. When you confess, gather together absolutely all your sins, for the mercy of our lord God is very great.

SECOND DEMON: Do not believe the words of the little kid, what he is saying to you, for he is just lying to you. Don't believe him!

(He goes to the place of the dead.)

DOÑA JUANA: I am fortunate. Thank you, for your words are very splendid. And accompany me to church, lead me so that I will properly follow the breath of our lord God.

(They go to the church. Lucifer and two demons enter.)

LUCIFER: Do come, you who are my servants. What's wrong with you? What's the matter with you? Are you sleeping? For it is the time, it is the moment[7] for us to be [up and about]. Do your job, lay [10] your snares and your nets, your shields, your insignia. Is it not the miserable little priests who find it very necessary to overcome us with the confessions of the miserable little people of the earth? Exert all your effort, for you already know that it is really through the sacred cross [that people avoid?] the place of the dead.[8]

---

5. Tentative translation.
6. The physical setting is not specified.
7. Ca Ye Inma Ca Ye oncâ: translated here as "it is the time, it is the moment," its general thrust is "it is high time that something happen or be done." See Carochi 1983, 103v.
8. This sentence tentatively translated.

1.º Demº v̄ Tlacatle tlatohuanie macamo mitzmotequipachilhuis Ca Yn nehuatl Ca niman ayc nictlalcahuis[10] Yn tlaltp.ᶜ tlacatotontin Ca momostlaYe Yn inp.ⁿ niquistinemi Yn niquintoCatinemi Auh tla xicmocaquiltitzino tlatohuanie ca se tlacatl tlatohuani nictlapololtitinemi huel momahuistiliani huel mos.totocatinemi. Yn teYxp.ⁿ Ynic nemi Auh amo San iCel Ca huel miequintin Ca oc Cequintin onCan cate Yn totetlaYecolticahua Yhuan Yn Cihua no miequintin Yn moSihuapilYtotinemi Yn atle Yp.ⁿ teYtztinemi Ca mochintin maxcatzitzinhua Yesq.ᶻ macamo ximotequipachotzino tlacatle tlatohuanie—

Luçifer v̄ Axcan huel Senca nipapaqui Yn nicaqui Yn motlatol Ynic tinechnanamiqui huel Senca ninoYolalia ninotlamachtia Auh Ca ayemo tel quitequipaChohua Yn ineYolCuitilis Ca Yquin iquac Yn asisq.ᶻ Yn Semana S,ⁿᵗᵃ Yxtomahuasq.ᶻ Ca ymahuililp.ⁿ quimatisq.ᶻ Yp.ⁿpa On acmo mochi quitosq.ᶻ Yn intlatlaCol tla xiquitocan[11] Yn Ye ce xihuitl ca huel Miequintin Yn oquilcauhq.ᶻ Yn intlatlaCol nel cequintin Amo OmoYolCuitiq.ᶻ Auh Yn nehuatl Ca huel ic nipaqui ninotlamachtia Auh Ynin nopilhuane noCoscahuane ma huel Yxquich Amotlapal xicchihuacan macamo xiquincahuacan Yntla Calaquisq.ᶻ Yn teop.ⁿ ma xiquintzaCuilican Yn otlica ma ximotlacanextitinemican Ynic amo quicaquisq.ᶻ Yn temachtilli—[11]

2º Dem.º v̄ Auh Yn nehuatl tlacatle tlatohuanie [?] [Yc?] tlaYhuali[12] nicnonahualtia Yn manel pipiltotontin Ca huel miequintin niquinmamauhtia Ynic amo quilnamiquisq.ᶻ Yn inneYolCuitilis Yhuan Yn tlatquihuaq.ᶻ huel Yⁿpapac Ynic huel quiⁿtequipachos Yn inⁿetlaYeColtilis Ynic amo Ysiuhca quiⁿtequipacho Yn inⁿeYolCuitilis Ye Oc Senca quiⁿtequipachohua Yn inⁿechichihual Ynic mochi tlacatl quiⁿmahuistilis Auh Yntla quitos Se achi Ytzotzomatzin Ytatapatzin Aucmo quimoucniuhtia Sᵃn ica huetzca Yca no topehua Auh Ynon Acmo quitlatlaColmati Oc Senca Yehuâtin[13] Yn mochpoch tlapiquitinemi Ca mochintin maxcatzitzinhuâ Yesq.ᶻ maCamo ximotequipachotzino Ca yxquich totlapal ticchiuhtinemisq.ᶻ tlacatle tlatohuanie—

Lucifer v̄ Notlasopilhuane Ca senca Yc nipapaqui Yn nicaqui Yn amotlatol Ca huel mahuistic ma huel ximochicahuacan macaYac techpanahui maCaYac techpinauhti tla xiquimitaCan ca yn teopixcatotontin Ca huel mochiCahua Ca huel techpanahuisnequi maCamo Yuhqui mochihuas Yn polihuis Yn totenyo in tomahuiso Ynic amo Aquin toCa huetzcas maSihui Yn asi Yn amotequiuh ma Oc tepitzin ninoSehui—

1.º Dem.º v̄ Ma iuhqui mochihua ma oc ximoSehuitzino Yn motlatocaYecYantzinco— Calaquisqᶻ hualMoquixtis Yn xpº Yuhqui Ecce homotzin Yhuan home Angeles se quihualhuicas Cruz Yn oc cequih Qualhuicas[14] lanza—

---

10. nictlalcahuis: read *niquintlalcahuiz*.
11. xiquitocan: probably scribal error for *xiquittacan*.
12. tlaYhuali: read *tlayohualli*.
13. Yehuâtin: read *yehuatzin*.
14. Qualhuicas: read *quihualhuicaz*.

FIRST DEMON: O lord, O ruler, let it not trouble you. I will absolutely never abandon the miserable little people of the earth, for I pass by them every day and follow them around. And do listen, O ruler, for there is a certain ruler whom I go about confusing who really glorifies himself, really goes about imagining he is a saint; that is how he lives in public. But it is not just him, for there are a great many other [men] who are our servants as well as many women who go about calling themselves noblewomen, who are of no account. They will all be your property. Do not be troubled, O master, O ruler.

LUCIFER: Now I am very happy to hear your words with which you help me. I am very consoled, I am enjoying myself greatly. And their confessions do not yet give them concern. When they reach Holy Week they will act stupid, they will regard it as a time of entertainment. Because of that they will no longer say all of their sins. Do see that now it has been a year. A great many have forgotten their sins. In truth, some did not confess [at all]. But as for me, I am very happy about it, I am enjoying myself greatly. So then, O my children, O my jewels, exert absolutely all your effort. Do not relinquish them. If they [try to] enter church, detain them on the road. Go around putting on a [good] act so that they will not hear the sermon. [11]

SECOND DEMON: And I, O lord, O ruler, [?[9]] I hide myself in dark places. Even if it is little kids, I frighten a great many so that they will not think about their confessions. And it is the pleasure of the wealthy that their making a living is what worries them, so their confessions do not soon distress them. What especially worries them is their adornment, so that everyone will honor them. But if he will say "[so-and-so] had [only] a bit of rags and worn-out clothing," he will no longer make friends with him. He just laughs at him, and also pushes him away. And they no longer regard that as sin, especially your daughter who goes about making things up. They will all be your property. Do not worry for we will go about exerting all our effort, O lord, O ruler.

LUCIFER: O my beloved children, I am very happy to hear your words for they are very splendid. Really exert yourselves. Let no one overcome us, let no one shame us. Look at the miserable little priests: they really exert themselves, they really want to overcome us. Let it not thus happen [that] our fame and our honor will perish, so that no one will laugh at us although your task is achieved.[10] Let me rest a bit.

FIRST DEMON: May it so be done. Rest for now in your royal quarters.

(They exit. Christ enters as the Ecce Homo along with two angels. One brings a cross and the other brings a lance.)

---

9. Text is mostly illegible in this section.
10. maSihui Yn asi Yn amotequiuh: literally, "although your task arrives." Tentative translation.

xp̄o v̲ Tla xihualmohuicacâ Yn annotitlantzitzinhuan ca huel Senca ninotequipachohua Yn inp.ⁿpa Yn tlaltp.ᶜ tlaca niman aOcmo nechtlaCamati Yn aOcmo YnYolotica [12] Ynic Calaqui Yn nochantzinco Yn aOcmo quitlasotla Y noteoyotzin amo quitlasocamati Ynic oniquinmaquixti Yn inp.ⁿpa Onicnonoqui Y notlasoYessotzin Auh Yn amehuantzitzin. Yn annotititlantzitzinhuan ma Yxquich Amotlapal xicmochihuiliCan ma ximohuiCaCâ Ynic anquinYaOchihuasq.ᶻ Yn notlatelchihualhuan Yn tlatlaCatecolo Ynca Yehuantin Yn tlaltp.ᶜ tlaca nechtelchihuasq.ᶻ Ca no nehuatl niquintelchihuas niquintlaSas Yn onpa sentlani mictlan Yn aOquic Oc Cepa niquimicnoYta—

        MOtlanquaq.ᶻtzaz Yn Ang.ˡ—

1.º Ang.ˡ v̲ Noteotzine notlatocatzine Ca huel melahuac Yn ticmotalhuitzinohua Auh Ca yxquich totlapal ticchiuhtinemi Yn inhuiCopa Yn tlaltp.ᶜ tlaca Oc Cenca Yehuantzitzin Yn motlatenquixticatzitzinhuan Yn teopixq.ᶻ Yn motemachticatzitzinhua Ca niman Aic quincahua Yn quintzatzilia Yn imixpa Yn quitlalia Yn motonehuilistzin Yn motlasohuilitzin Ynic onoquiuh Yn motlaSoesotzin Yhuan Yn quexquich moteYcnoYtalitzin Ynic senca titlatlaCatzintli Yn ticnohuaCatzintli Auh Ca san mixCoYan monomatelchihua Ca san Yehuatl quitlacamati Yn motlasentelchihualtzitzinhuan Yn tlatlaCatecolo—

xp̄o v̲ OYtlahueliltic Yn tlaltp.ᶜ tlaca niman acmo quilnamiquisnequi Yn q.ᶻnin Oquinmomaquixtili Yese niquitohua Ca Yn aquiq.ᶻ amo nechtemosnequi Yn amo nechilnamicquisnequi Ca in iCuac Yn niquinnotzas Yn nixp.ⁿ hualasq.ᶻ ca niquincemixnahuatis Ynic aOquic quitasq.ᶻ Yn notlasoxaYaCatzin Ca semicac Mictlâ tlalohuasqᶻ—motlanquaq.ᶻtzas

2.º Ang.ˡ v̲ Yo noteotzine notlatoCatzine canel otiquinmochihuilitzino Ca motlachihualtzitzinhuan Auh Ca motetlaYecolticatzitzinhuan OtiquinMomaquixtilitzino macamo ticmone[13]quiltitzino Ynic polihuisq.ᶻ Ca Ye ticmomachiltitzinohua Yn niCan Catqui Yn tepostlachichtli Ca Yehuatl Yc omotlapo Yn ilhuicatl Yn motlasoYomotlantzin Ynic otiquinmotlasotilitzino Auh macamo polihuis Yn imanima Ca huel nimitznotlatlauhtilitzinohua ttᵒᵉ Diose—

xpo v̲ Ca huel Senca nichuelcaqui Yn amotlatol Yn amehuantin innannotlachihualtzitzinhuan¹⁵ Yese Yehuantin Amo Yuh quimati—Tla xihualauh Yn tehuatl ma xiyauh ma xicnotza Yn ~~toPile~~ Ma nican nixp.ⁿ hualauh—

1.º Angˡ v̲ Ca Ye qualitzin noteotzine notlatocatzine ma niYauh ma nicnotza—

      # Yaz quinotzatiuh Yn Miquistli Ytopil quihualhuicasque—

1.º Angˡ v̲ Ma nican timohuicatz tlatohuanie Ca nican moetzinotica Yn Jesus Yn Dˢ Ypiltzin YsRael—

---

15. innannotlachihualtzitzinhuan: read *in annotlachihualtzitzinhuan.*

CHRIST: Do come, you who are my messengers, for I am very much troubled by the people of the earth. They absolutely no longer obey me, no longer willingly [12] enter my home, no longer love my sacraments, are not thankful that I saved them and spilled my precious blood for their sake. And you, who are my messengers, exert all your effort. Go to make war on those whom I despise, the demons, through whom the people of the earth will despise me. I will also despise them. I will cast them into the depths of the place of the dead. Never again will I have pity on them.

([First] Angel kneels down.)

FIRST ANGEL: O my deity, O my ruler, what you are saying is very true. We go about exerting all our effort towards the people of the earth, especially those who are your spokespersons, the priests, your teachers. For they absolutely never abandon them. They cry out to them, they set before them your torments and your suffering when your precious blood was spilled, and how much pity you have, how very humane and compassionate you are. But they just despise their very selves, they just obey those whom you have entirely cursed, the demons.

CHRIST: How unfortunate are the people of the earth! They absolutely do not want to think any longer about how he[11] saved them. But I say, as to those who do not search me out, who do not want to remember me, when I summon them, when they arrive before me, I will completely condemn them so that they will never again see my precious face, for they will flee to the place of the dead forever.
([Second Angel] kneels.)

SECOND ANGEL: Ah, O my deity, O my ruler, since you made them, they are your creations. And they are your servants; you saved them. May it not be your will [13] that they will perish. You already know that here is the nail[12] with which heaven, your precious side, was opened, [demonstrating] that you loved them. And may their souls not perish, I greatly implore you, O our lord, O God.

CHRIST: I listen very approvingly to your words, you who are my creations, but they do not see it way. Do come, you. Go, summon the ~~constable~~, may he come here before me.

FIRST ANGEL: Very well, O my deity, O my ruler, let me go summon him.
(He goes to summon Death. They bring his staff.)

FIRST ANGEL: Please be welcome here,[13] O ruler, for here is Jesus, God, child of Israel.

---

11. That is, Christ. Evidently a scribal error since Christ is talking about himself and should say "I."
12. *tepostlachichtli*: see Bautista 1606, 114, where this is paired with a Spanish term: "ce clauo tepuztlaxichtli."
13. *Ma nican timohuicatz*: here and below in variants it has been translated as "Please be welcome here." See Carochi 1983, 67v, 80r, and Sahagún 1997, 296.

xp̄o v Tla xihualmohuica notopileCatzine ma ximohuica Yn câpa moSentlalisq^z Yn tlatoq^z ma huel iCuac Yn pa[n?]t[i?]sq.^{z} Ca timoteYtilis Yhuan xichuica home tzonteComatl Oncâ Yxp.^{n} tictlalis Yn D^n Seb.^{n} tiquilhuis Ca niCan Ca Yn motatzin Yn monantzin Ca Yehuatl Yn intzonteco Cuix tiquimiXimati—

Miquistli v Noteotzine notlatoCatzine ma niYauh ma nicchihua Yn moteotenahuatiltzin ma niquimita ma niquintzatzili Ma san tehuatzin Motencopatzinco Ynic moYolehuasq^z Ynic monemilisCuepasq.^{z} Ca miequintin Yn tlalp.^{c} tlaca Yn Cuac[16] nechita Ca niman Mitzmotzatzililia mitzmolnamiquilia momauhtia Ca niman monemiliscuepa Yn mixp^{n}tzinco—

xp̄o v Auh Yn amehuantin ma xichuicaca Yn notopilecatzin sese tzontecon yn AnquihuiCasq^z Ce Yn tatli Se Yn nâtli ma xicmohuiCaCâ xicneltilitin Yn noteotenahuatiltzin—[14]

2° Ang.^{l} Ca Ye Cualitzin noteotzine notlatoCatzine ma ticneltilitin Yn moteotenahuatiltzin—

Mocalaquis Yn xp.^{o} Yhuan Miquistli Yhuā Ang.^{l} quiCas[17] D^n Seb.^{n} Yhuâ D^n Alberto D^n Fabian homêtin Pajes Yhua. 1° Dem,^{o}—

D,^{n} Seb.^{n} v Ma nican anmohuicatze notlasoteachcauhtzitzinhuane AnmoSianmiquiltitzinohua Ma niCan tepitzin ximohuetzititzinoCan telpochtle ma xiCualmoquixtili ~~Yn huehuetl ma~~ ~~moYolalitzinocan~~ ~~tlein intetzinco monequis Yn~~ Yn mahuistiq.^{z} tlaca—

1.º PaJe v Ca Ye qualitzin tlatohuanie ma niCan huitz Yn hue~~huetl yn yntetzinco monequis yn tlatoq.^{z}~~

Calaquisq^z quihualquixtisq^z YnMessatlaCuau[18] Yhuan Yn ~~huehuetl~~ vino

D,^{n} Fab,^{n} v Otomasehualtic Yn motetlasotlalitzin Ca amo ticpia Ynic tiquixtlahuasq.^{z} Yn ixquich tetlasotlalistli tlacatle tlatohuanie—

D,^{n} Seb,^{n} v Notlasotatzine ma xiquinmoYecanili Yn mopilhuantzitzinhuan ma ximohuetzilticâ—

D^n Alberdo v Ma ximohuetziltican ma ximoSehuitzinoCan—

1° Dem^o v Notlasopilhuane macamo namechnotequipachilhui Ma ximosehuitzinoCan—

Motlallisq^z Mochintin

D^n Alberdo v Nopiltzintzine ma ximotlateochihuilitzino Canel YaCachtopa homitzmochihuilitzino Yn tt,^{o} D,^{s}—

1° Dem^o v Notlasopilhuane Ca niman Amo nihuelitis Ca nica nichane Yhuan tla xicmoCaquiltiCan Ca Ye anquimomachiltia Yn Cuac titehua yn tihualquisa quiYahuac Cuix amo niman titoteoChihua Yhuan niman no Yquac Motlateochihuilia yn Dios mochi quimoteochihuiliaya Yn quechquich Yn quechquich[19] totech monequis Yn tiquisq^z Yn tiquasq.^{z} Auh Ynintzin ma ximotlaqualtican Nopilhuane—[15]

---

16. Yn Cuac: here and below, read *yn icuac*.
17. quiCas: read *quiçaz*.
18. YnMessatlaCuau: perhaps to be read *ynmesatlacahuan*.
19. Yn quechquich Yn quechquich: so written in the original text.

CHRIST: Do come, O my constable. Go where the rulers will gather. Right when you come upon them you are to show yourself.[14] And bring the two skulls. You are to place them there in front of don Sebastián. You are to say to him: "Here is your father, your mother. There are their heads. Do you recognize them?"

DEATH: O my deity, O my ruler, let me go, let me carry out your sacred commands. Let me see them, let me cry out to them. May they just be inspired by your orders to change their lives. For there are many people of the earth who, when they see me, cry out to you, remember you, and are afraid. Then they change their lives in your presence.

CHRIST: And you, bring my constable each skull. You are to bring them to him. One is the father, one is the mother. Bring them to him. Carry out my sacred command. [14]

SECOND ANGEL: Very well, O my deity, O my ruler, let us carry out your sacred command.

(*Christ exits along with Death and [Second] Angel. Don Sebastián enters along with don Alberto, don Fabián, two pages, and First Demon.*)

DON SEBASTIÁN: Please be welcome here, O my beloved older brothers. You are most welcome. Sit here for a bit. O young man, bring out ~~the drum~~ what ~~Let~~ the honored people ~~be consoled~~ need.[15]

FIRST PAGE: Very well, O ruler, let ~~the drum~~ what the lords need be brought here.

(*They exit. Those serving at the table bring it along with ~~a drum~~ wine.*)[16]

DON FABIÁN: We are so fortunate [as to be enjoying] your hospitality but we do not have anything with which to repay all the hospitality, O lord, O ruler.

DON SEBASTIÁN: O my beloved father, lead your children [to their seats], sit down.

DON ALBERTO: Sit down, rest yourselves.

FIRST DEMON: O my beloved children, let me not trouble you. Rest yourselves.

(*All sit down.*)

DON ALBERTO: O my nobleman, make the blessing, since our lord God made you first [for that purpose].[17]

FIRST DEMON: O my beloved children, I absolutely cannot for I am a resident here. And listen, for you already know that when we get up and come out of the door: are we not then blessing ourselves? And also at that time God blesses things. He blesses everything, whatever we need to drink and to eat. And now, eat, O my children. [15]

---

14. Tentatively translated.
15. To avoid confusion: the original read "O young man, bring out the drum. Let the honored people be consoled." The emended version reads "O young man, bring out what the honored people need."
16. Tentative translation.
17. That is, as the eldest in the party he should say grace before their meal. A demon, of course, must decline the privilege. His excuse is that he resides there and thus should defer to the guests, and anyway the blessing is not necessary.

D.n Seb.n v Notlasotiachcauhtzitzinhuane Ca melahuac Yn quimitalhuia Canel yxe naca[20] Cenca momachtiani Yn tlasopilli macamo Ximotequipachotzino ma Ximotlaqualtican Auh Yn nehuatl, Ma Oc namechnoYollaliliz—

~~OCa tlatzotzonalos tlapitza~~quasq.z—

D.n Fabiâ v Ma oquichquich[21] Yn ~~tinotlatzotzo[ca]huan~~ tlein amechmolnamiquilia nocniuhtzine Ca amo axcan monequi ho Yn paquilistli Ca axcan monequi Yn tlamasehualistli Yn neyolCuitilistli Ca ye axcan Yn motenahuatilia Yn tonantzin S.ta Yglesia Ynic tiaAltisque[22] titopapaCasq.z—

D.n Alberto v tleyn ticmitalhuia Cuix titemiqui Cuix tiCochi Yn tehua OnCan moyolalitzinosnequi Yn tlatoq.z Yn pipiltin ca tenepntla timaquitinemi xitechcahua Oc titoYolalisq.z Cuix ticmati Yntla mostla Yntla huiptla titomiquilisq.z Ma xitechCahua—

1.º Dem.º v Telpochtle Yn tiquitohua XiquinmoCahuili ma Oc mopapaquiltican, Yn tlatoq.z Canel oc telpopochtin pipiltzitzintin ma Oc xicahua Yn teopn huel ohicalistli

D.n Fab.n v Tla nimitznotlatlanili Auh Yn Yehuatzin tlasoCihuapilli Can omohuiCac tlaCatzintli nicnotilia—

D.n Seb.n v MaCamo xicmotenehuili teotzin tlatohuanie Ca Ye omomiquili Ca Ye nahui metztli Axcan Yn otictotlalaquiliqz—

D.n Alberto v Nomati Amo titlaCaquisnequi Yn amo molnamiqui Auh Yn tehuatl Oncan tleyn ticteYlnamictia tla xitechcahua Yntla noso Diablo techhuicas Cuix motequiuh xitechcahua nose xitechtlalcahuis—

hualquisas Miquistli Yhuan Ang.l moquetztehuas Yn Demº quitlasq.z

Messaquac Yn tzōtecontin—

1.º Ang.l v D,s Ytlamaquixtiltzitzinhuane maCamo Ximomauhtican Ca ytêcopatzinco Yn D,s YniC ohualMohuicac Yn topiletzin—

1.º Dem.º Macamo xicneltocacan Ca Sn amechmamauhtia Ca San Ypan asiz Yn temictli—

1º Ang.l v tleYn tiquitohua tlatelchihualpol Ynin ca notlamamal Ca nop[iel?] [Ca amo?] huel tichuicas MoxiCohuanie—

1.º Dem.º Ca nichuicas Ca ye naxca Ca ye notlatqui—[16]

---

20. naca: read *nacace*.
21. oquichquich: here and below, read *oc ixquich*.
22. tiaAltisque: read *titaltizque*.

DON SEBASTIÁN: O my beloved older brothers, what he is saying is true since he has eyes and ears,[18] he is very learned, a high-born nobleman. Do not be troubled. Eat. And as for me, let me console you.

(~~At that point drums are beaten, wind instruments are played~~.)

DON FABIÁN: Let that be all, ~~my musicians~~. What are they making you think of? O my friend, those pleasures are not necessary now, for today penance and confession are necessary, for today our mother holy church commands that we bathe, that we wash ourselves.

DON ALBERTO: What are you saying? Are you dreaming? Are you sleeping? The rulers and noblemen want to console themselves along with others there, [and] you are interfering. Leave us, while we console ourselves. Do you know if we will die tomorrow, or the day after?[19] Leave us!

FIRST DEMON: O young man, what are you saying? Leave them alone. Let the rulers enjoy themselves since they are still young men, little children. Leave the church. [It is dangerous?].[20]

DON FABIÁN: Let me question you. And as to that high-born noblewoman, where did she go? I see her as a human being [alive?].

DON SEBASTIÁN: Do not mention the deity, O ruler, for she has already died. It has been four months now since we buried her.[21]

DON ALBERTO: I think you do not want to hear what is not being remembered. And you there, what are you reminding people of? Leave us. If the devil should take us, is it your business? Leave us or abandon us.

(Death enters along with [First] Angel. [First] Demon protests. They cast the skulls on top of the table.)

FIRST ANGEL: O God's saved ones, do not be frightened, for it is by God's orders that the constable has come.

FIRST DEMON: Do not believe him for he just frightens you. It just comes to him in dreams.

FIRST ANGEL: What are you saying, miserable despised one? This one is my burden [of responsibility], my charge. You can[not] take him, O envious one.[22]

FIRST DEMON: I will take him away for he is already my goods, he is already my property. [16]

---

18. to have eyes, to have ears: a common diphrase that means "to be acute, alert, sharp."

19. tomorrow, the day after: here and below, a common diphrase that often means "soon, in the near future."

20. huel ohicalistli: perhaps read *huel ohuicaliztli*. .

21. Perhaps the woman being discussed is don Sebastian's mother, whose skull Death is about to deliver. Why don Sebastián says "Do not mention the deity" is not clear.

22. Tentative translation.

Miquistli = Tla xihualauh Yn tiD.ⁿ Seb.ⁿ tlen tay tlen ticchihua Cuix ticochi ma xisa Cuix aYac tictemohua Cuix aYac ticpolohua Campa Yn otiquis Cuix itec quahuitl hanoso y tetl ma xinechnanquili tla xiquita Yn is ca Cuix tiquiximati Yhuan Yn nehuatl Cuix tinexiximati²³ Yhuan Yn is cate Cuix amo tiquimiximati aquiq.ᶻ Auh ac nehuatl Cuix amo tiquilnamiqui Ca nihualas Yn amop.ⁿ niquisaquiuh tla xiquita Yn nican ca Ca Yehuatl Yn motatzin catca Yn huel motlaCamatia Ca huel miec tlaca Yn quitequipanohuaya Auh Yn is ca Ca yehuatl Yn monantzin ocatca Auh Catli Yn iAxca Yn itlatqui hi catca Yn inechichihual Yn oquitlaliaya huel xiquimita Yntech ximixCuiti Ca mostla Ca huiptla Yuhqui timotas ma xicahua Yn tlaltp.ᶜCaYotl Yn papaquilistli ma xiquilnamiquica tipolihuis Ca titzonquisas xiquilnamiqui Ca Onca Yn gloria papaquilistli Yhuan Ca Onca Yn mictlan tla-Yohuilistli tla xiquilnamiqui Ca mop.ⁿpa Omotlacatili Yn D.ˢ Yhuan Camop.ⁿpa homotlaYohuilti ᶜAmop.ⁿpa Omomiquili amop.ⁿpa OtoCoc hoc cepa homozcali yn Omotlec[ahui?] Yn ilhuicac Omotlalitzinoto YmaYecCampatzinco Yn itlasotatzin D,ˢ Ca mitzhualmotztilitica ma xicmaquixti Yn manima ma mitztequipacho Yn motlatlaCol—

1º Dem.º v Notelpotze D,ⁿ Seb,ⁿ Macamo mitztequipachos notech xicahua Yn manima Ca nehuatl nimitzmaquixtis Ca mopapa nitlaMAcehuas—

Dⁿ Seb,ⁿ v Yo notehotzine notlatoCatzine Ca onimitznoYolitlacalhuitzino Ca mohuiCopatzinco ninoCuepa Ynic nicaqui Yn motlasotlatoltzin Ca yn aquin mohuiCopatzinco MoCuepaz Ca ticmotlaOcolilis ticmopopolhuililis Auh ma xinechmotlapopolhuiliilitzino ca huel onitlatlaCo—Chocas ho ca tehuatzin notlasotatzine Yhuâ in tehuatzin yⁿ tinotlasonantzin Canel otinechmotlacatilili Auh Campa Yn oamechMoYeYanmaquili Yn tt.º D,ˢ Ca aYac huel quimati—

Miquistli v Yhuā xicaqui xicmati tleYn mitztlapololtitica [17] Yn ticmictisnequi Yn monamic Cuix amo OmitzMomaquili yn tonantzin S.ᵗᵃ Yglesia Cuix amo Ypⁿ Ca yn iteotenahuatiltzin Ynic Sentetl ticmotlasotilis Yn D,ˢ Yn Contetl²⁴ tiquintlasotlas Yn mohuanpohuan Yn iuh timotlasotlas Auh Ynin ma xictlasotla Yn monamic xiquita Ca tiMiquis tipolihuis—

Dⁿ Fab,ⁿ v Ca Yn nehuatl ca huel nicnalquixtis Yn motlanahuatiltzin Canel Ytlatoltzin Yn tt.º D.ˢ—

D,ⁿ Alberto v NotlasoYcniuhtzitzinhuane nomati Anmomauhtia maCamo Ximomauhtican Ca san amechnenmamauhtia huel neli Ca sa amotonal Yn amechmamauhtia—

Calaquis yn miquistli Yhua Angˡ—

Dⁿ Sb,ⁿ v [?] onotlahueliltic tleyn nop.ⁿ mochihua D,ˢ Cuix nitemiqui Anoso niCochi Ca amo Onisatoc tleYn nicchihuas Ca huel ninotequipachohua = tla xoConita Aquin hualasi aquin quitzotzona Yn puerta—

2º Demº v Macamo ximomauhtitzinocâ Ca San namechnomamauhtilia Yn amotlalnamiquilistzin—

Yaz quitatiuh Yn PaJe Calitic monotzazque—

---

23. tinexiximati: read *tinechiximati*.
24. Yn Contetl: read *ynic ontetl*.

DEATH: Do come, don Sebastián. What is wrong with you? What is the matter with you? Are you sleeping? Wake up. Is there no one you are looking for? Is there no one you have lost? Where did you come from? From inside wood or stone? Answer me. Do look. The one who is here: do you know him? And I: do you know me? And those who are here: do you not know who they are? And who I am? Do you not remember? For I will come, I will come among you. Do see that the one who is here was your father, who was very rich; a great many people used to work for him. And she who is here was your mother. And what has come of her goods, her property, her adornments she used to put on? Look at them well, take an example from them, for tomorrow or the day after you will see yourself in this condition. Abandon the things of the earth, the pleasures. Remember that you will perish, you will come to an end. Remember that there in glory is happiness and there in the place of the dead is suffering. Do remember that for your sake God was born and for your sake he suffered, for your sake he died, for your sake he was buried [and then] he again revived, he rose to heaven, he went to sit down at the right hand of his beloved father, God. He is watching you. Save your soul; may your sins trouble you.

FIRST DEMON: O my young man, don Sebastián, don't let it trouble you. Leave your soul to me for I will save it for you. I will do penance on your behalf.

DON SEBASTIÁN: Ah, O my God, O my ruler, I have offended you. I turn to you to hear your precious words for you will have mercy on him who turns to you. You will pardon him. And pardon me for I have sinned greatly.

(He cries.)

O you, O my beloved father, and you are my beloved mother, who truly gave birth to me. And where has our lord God placed you? No one can know.

DEATH: And listen, know what is confusing you. [17] You want to kill your spouse. Did not our mother holy church give her to you? Is it not the first of his sacred commands that you will love God, the second that you will love your neighbors as you love yourself? Well then, love your spouse. See [to] it, for [otherwise] you will die, you will perish.

DON FABIÁN: I perfectly understand[23] your commands since it is the word of our lord God.

DON ALBERTO: O my beloved friends, I think you are afraid. Do not be afraid, for it just uselessly frightens you. Truly indeed it is just your fate[24] that frightens you.

(Death exits along with the angel.)

DON SEBASTIÁN: Unfortunate am I! God, what is happening to me? Am I dreaming or perhaps sleeping? I am not awake. What will I do, for I am very anxious and afflicted. Do go see who has come, who is knocking at the door.

SECOND DEMON: Do not be afraid, for I am just frightening your minds.

(He goes to see the page, who is inside the house. They talk to each other.)

---

23. nicnalquixtis/I perfectly understand: perhaps scribal error for *nicnalquizcamatiz*.
24. That is, death, as represented by the skulls.

2º Demº v tla xihualmohuica telpochtle tla nimitznotlatlanili Cuix OnCan moetztica Se huehue tlacatl Ytocatzin Bercebo—

1º PaJe v Jesus tleyn ticmitalhuia Ca ynon ca tlacatecolotl Yn ticmotenehuilia Ca xpianome Yn niCan motlalia Ca ayac niCan ca tlacatecolotl—

2º Dem.º v Macamo ximomauhti telpochtle Ca san Yahuiltocatzin Cuix aYc ticmoCaquiltia Yn ixquichtin tlaca tleY mach quimahuiltocaYotia ca San no Yuhqui Yn tehuantin—

1,º PaJe v Auh Yn tehuatzin tley mahuiltocatzin YniquinYolo pachihuis [25]—

2º Demº v Ma xicmomachilticâ Ca nican quimonochilia Satanas niCan nimitznochielia—

  hualquisas Yn PaJe quinotzaz Yn 1º Demonios—

1.º PaJe v Notlasotatzine Ca niCan mitzmotemolia ce tlacatl quimahuiltocaYotia Satanas mitzmonochilia quiYahuac—

Dⁿ Seb,ⁿ v Tlein tiquitohua sequi [?] masehualic [26] tlanotzale Yn notlasotatzin. Yuhqui Onechmolhuilico—[18]

1º Demo v Macamo ximomauhtitzinocan ca nahuiltoca Auh Yn techmotemolia YahuiltoCatzin berebo Ca Oc tipipiltotontin Yn otechtoCayotiqᶻ ma Yca Yn amotlasohuelitzin ma oc noConnotili aso Ytla quimotequipachilhuia—

Dⁿ Seb,ⁿ v Ca niman ahuel mochihuas Yn quiYahuac timoquixtis Cuix amo mochantzinco Yn timoetztica ma moCalaqui Yn aqui mitzmotemolia Nopiltzintzine—

1º Dem.º v telpochtle ma xicmonochili ma hualmocalaqui—

2º PaJe v Ca Ye Cualitzin ma nicnonochili = Ma nican timohuicatz tlatohuanie ma ximocalaqui—

2º Dem.º v Ma ximehuiltitiecan tlatoq.ᶻ Ye ma namechonnotlapololtili Ac Yehuatzin Yn D,ⁿ Seb,ⁿ Ca yehuatzin Yn nicnotemolia Centlamantli nicnolhuilis—

D,ⁿ Fab,ⁿ v Ca nican moetztica ma Oc ximononotzinocan Auh Yn tehuatzin ma Oc tamechtotlalCahuilican—

  Yasq.ᶻ D.ⁿ Fab,ⁿ D,ⁿ Alberto mochintin PaJes mocahuas D,ⁿ Seb,ⁿ
  Yhuan Dem.ᵒˢ—

D,ⁿ Seb,ⁿ v Tla nican timohuicas tlatohuanie tleyn ticmitalhuia ma niccaqui Yn motlatoltzin—

2.º Dem.º v Notelpotze ma xicmoCaquiltiCan Ca Ya ticpolohua ano[?]so ticmotemohua Anoso ticmolnamiquilia—

Dⁿ Seb,ⁿ Ca qᶻmacatzin Ca niquinnotemolia Yn onechnochililiq.ᶻ Campa Yn oquinmoYeanmaquili Yn tt.º D,ˢ auh Yn oniquinnotili Ca Sa Omitzitzintin Yn intzonteContzin—

---

25. YniquinYolo pachihuis: read *ynic in noyollo pachihuiz*.
26. masehualic: read *macehualli ic*.

SECOND DEMON: Come, O young man, do let me question you. Is there an old man there named Beelzebub?

FIRST PAGE: Jesus, what are you saying? For that is a demon you are talking about. Those seated here are Christians; nobody here is a demon!

SECOND DEMON: Do not be afraid, O young man, for it is just his nickname. Have you never heard the [sorts of] names all the people give themselves? We do likewise.

FIRST PAGE: And you, what is your nickname? It is so I will be satisfied.

SECOND DEMON: Know that Satan here summons him [that is, Beelzebub]. I await you here.

([First] Page enters. He talks to First Demon.)

FIRST PAGE: O my beloved father, a person whose nickname is Satan is here looking for you. He summons you from the entrance.

DON SEBASTIÁN: What are you saying? It [must] be some vassal of my beloved father who is thus called [Satan] who has come to speak to me. [18]

FIRST DEMON: Do not be afraid; it is my nickname. And the nickname of the person looking for us is Beelzebub. We were still little kids when they named us. Let me have your precious permission to see him. Perhaps something is bothering him.

DON SEBASTIÁN: It certainly shall not happen [that] you should go out to the entrance. Are you not in your home? Let him who seeks you come in, O my nobleman.

FIRST DEMON: O young man, summon him. Let him enter here.

SECOND PAGE: Very well, let me summon him.

Please be welcome here, O ruler. Come in.

SECOND DEMON: Remain seated, O rulers, let me not distract you. Who is don Sebastián? For it is he whom I am seeking. I have something to say to him.

DON FABIÁN: Here he is. Talk to each other. And let us leave you.

(Don Fabián, don Alberto, and all the pages leave. Don Sebastián remains, along with the demons.)

DON SEBASTIÁN: Please be welcome here, O ruler. What do you have to say? Let me hear your words.

SECOND DEMON: O my young man, listen, for now you are losing what you are ~~perhaps~~ looking for or thinking of.

DON SEBASTIÁN: Yes, I am searching for those who called to me from where our lord God has placed them. And I have seen them; their heads are pitiful bones.

2º Dem.º v̱ Nopiltzintzine macamo xicmolnamiquili hotzin aso san itla moCatzinco mocacaYahua Ca Ye tiuhq.ᶻ Yn titlaca ca San totonal Yn techmamauhtia tla Oc ticahuacati tla Ye Oc xicmoCaquilti Ca amo Yehuatl o YniC onihuala Ca Oc Sentlamantli Yn onimitznolhuilico Ca yp.ⁿpa Yn monamictzin Ca huel moca mocacaYahua ca huel paqui Yn moYolia Yn iCuac Calitic timetztica Auh Yn Yehuatl. ca san tlapic Yn mitzmolhuilia Ca ye niauh Yn teop.ⁿ auh amo Yauh çan otlica telpochtotontin quintocatinemi. Cahuiltitinemi ca huel moca mocacaYahua Ynic âhuel mitzpinauhtia timotolinia notelpotze Ca Yehuatl [19] YniC onihuala Yn nimitznolhuilico tleyn quitohua Yn moYolotzin—

Dⁿ Seb,ⁿ v̱ Tleyn tinechmolhuilia notlasotatzine Ca mochi nicneltoca Yn motlatoltzin Ca Yn axcan nicChihuas Yn tleYn niquilnamiqui Auh Ca OniquitoAia ninonemilisCuepas ninoYolcuitis nitlamasehuas. Auh Yn axcâ Aucmo nicnequi ca huel axcan Ypⁿ Yn tonali Ca nicpopolos Yn noCihuauh Ca niman amo nictlapopolhuis Auh Ca namechnotlatlauhtilia ma annechmopalehuilisq.ᶻ Ynic amo temac nihuetzis canel Annotatzitzinhuan—

1º Demº v̱ Macamo ximotequipachotzino telpochtle Ca nican ticate Ca amo tipipiltotontin Ca Ye ticmati Yn tleYn ticchihuasqᶻ Ca yn iuh titelpopochtin ticatca qᶻchquich[27] Oticchiuhq.ᶻ Cuix san tlapic Yn tleYn Otechahu[?]tiq.ᶻ Ca huel tiloCotin Oticatca Auh Ynin nimitzilhuia Amo niCan Ytec Yn altepetl Yn ticmictis Yn monamic cana hueca texcalco Yn tichuicas Ca ticnahualhuicas tel timitzYecanasq.ᶻ Yn Campa moChihuas Yn tlamahuisoli amo ximotequipacho ximoYolChicahua—

Dⁿ Seb,ⁿ v̱ Ca Yehuatl on Yn Cenca Yc ninoYolalia ma yuhqui mochihuas ma namechnohuiquili Yese Yn tleYn anquimonequiltisq.ᶻ Ca nicchihuas Ca nicneltilis Ca namechnotlacamaChiltis ma tihuian ma nictemo Yn nosihuAuh—

2º Dem.º v̱ Ca Ye Cuali ma tihuian tictemosq.ᶻ—Calaquisq.ᶻ Mict.ⁿ
quisas Yn Ang.ˡ quinotzaz Dⁿ Seb,ⁿ—

1.º Angˡ v̱ Otimotlahueliltic Ca Ye mictlan tipouhqui Yese ca huel tinechtolinia Ynin Cuenta nicnomaquilis Yn tt.º D,ˢ in amo timonemiliscuepasnequi Ca huel senca tinechpinauhtia Yn ixp.ⁿtzinco Yn D,ˢ Onotlahueliltic—[28]

Chocas Yaz hualquisas Miquistli Yhuâ home Ang,ˡ quihualhuicasq.ᶻ espada
Mictlan hualquisas Lusifer Yhuan Omentin Demonios—

Miquistli v̱ Tla xihualauh Yn timictlantlatelchihualpol tla xinechilhui tle Yca tle Yp.ⁿpa Yn huel timoxicohua Yn huel tiquinmoYahotia tlaltp.ᶜ tlaca tleyn huel mohueli xiquito xinechilhui—[20]

Lusifer v̱ Tla xiᶜaqui Omitl Ca Y nehuatl Ca onca nohueli Yn mictlâ ca no nitlatohuani YeYca Ca Yn tlaltp.ᶜ tlaca Ca momostlaye Yn intenco niCan Ytla mahuasq.ᶻ Semicac nechtenehua nechtzatzilia Auh Yn itech Yn D,ˢ Ca q.ᶻmanian Yn quinotza San iquac temoCoCohua Anoso YCuac Yn itla Ynnetequipachol [?] Ca—

---

27. qᶻchquich: read *quexquich*.
28. There are stage directions in the margin: Calaq.ᶻ D.ⁿ Seb.ᵃⁿ mocuepatiuh condenado.

SECOND DEMON: O my nobleman, do not think of that. Oh, perhaps they are just mocking you in something. For we people are like that. Our fate just frightens us. Do let us get away from them [the skulls]. Leave it. Do listen now, for that is not why I came, for there is something else I came to tell you concerning your spouse. She is really mocking you, she is really having fun. She is content when you are in the house. But she just tells you falsely, "I am going to the church." But she does not go but, rather, follows after young boys on the road, who go around giving her a good time. She really mocks you. You are in bad shape, as it does not cause you shame. O my young man, that is what [19] I have come to say to you. What is your heart saying?

DON SEBASTIÁN: What are you saying to me, O my beloved father? For I believe all your words. Today I will do what I was thinking. And I was saying I would change my life, I would confess, I would do penance. But now I no longer want [to do] it for right now, during this day, I will destroy my wife for I absolutely cannot pardon her. And I implore you, since you are my fathers, help me so that I will not get caught.

FIRST DEMON: Do not be troubled, O young man, for here we are. We are not little kids. You already know what we will do, for we did things in that way when we were youths. Is it just false what they [scolded?] us with? For we were really crazy! And I say this to you: you will not kill your spouse here in the altepetl [but rather] you will take her, secretly take her, somewhere far away to a crag. But we will lead you where the marvelous deed will be done. Do not be troubled. Be stronghearted.

DON SEBASTIÁN: I am very content with that. May it so be done. Let me accompany you. What[ever] you want me to do, I will carry out, for I will obey you. Let us go. Let me search for my wife.

SECOND DEMON: Very well, let us go search for her.
(They enter the place of the dead.

[First] Angel enters. He talks to don Sebastián.)

FIRST ANGEL: Unfortunate are you! You already belong to the place of the dead. Nevertheless you are really bothering me [with] this accounting I will give to our lord God that you do not want to change your life. You shame me very greatly before God. Unfortunate am I!

(Don Sebastián enters; he turns into the condemned one.[25]

He weeps. He leaves. Death enters along with two angels. They bring a sword from the place of the dead. Lucifer enters along with two demons.)

DEATH: Come, you despised one of the place of the dead. Do tell me, why and for what reason are you so envious? You make war on the people of the earth. By what authority? Say it, tell me! [20]

LUCIFER: Do listen, bones, for I have authority in the place of the dead. I am also a ruler. Because the people of the earth quarrel over things every day they always mention me, they cry out to me. But they only call to God sometimes, only when people are made ill or when they have some care.[26]

---

25. That is, he changes costume to appear as the condemned one. These stage directions are actually in the margin; see transcription.

26. This entire paragraph is tentatively translated.

1.º Ang.l v̱ Tla xihualauh Yn tibersebo ma xiquito tleyn huel mohueli moxicohuanipole tle yca Yn huel titechpanahuisnequi tla xitechilhui—

2º Ang.l v̱ Yn tehuatl Yn tiSatanas tle ica Yn tinechCuilis Yn nopiel Cuix amo nican nica tle yca Yn iuhqui ticchihua tlatelchihualpole—

2º Dem.º v̱ Tle yca Yn amo nimitzCuilis Ca tiquitos Ca nimitzCuilis Ca nicchihuas Yn notequi^uh macamo mitztequipacho—

Miquistli[29] v̱ Nocniuhtzine tleyn a[?] [?] ma tiquintocacan Yn tisentelchihualtin—

quintocasq.z Mictlan Calaquisq.z mocahuas Yn Miquistli Yhuan Angeles—

Miquistli v̱ NotlasoYcniuhtzitzinhuane ma Oquixquich Amotlapaltzin xicmochihuilican maCamo xiquinmoxicCahuilican Y tlaltp.c tlaca Auh Yntlacamo amechmotlacamachiltiq.z Ca tel YmixcoYan motepexihuisq.z Atle amotlatlacoltzin Yez—

2º Ang.l v̱ Cuix amo ticmomachilti Yn niman Aic tiquincahua Ca CmC Ynnahuac tinemi Yn sesemilhuitl Yn seseYohual Auh Yn iCuac Amo Cuali quichihua Ca tiquintlacahualtia Auh amo techtlacamati Ca Oc achi quintlacamati Yn tlatlacatecolo—

1º Ang.l v̱ Ma Oc Yxquich ma Oc Ynp.n tiquisatin Yn oc cequintin topielhuan nocniuhtzitzinhuane ma xoConmanilican Yn amocxitzin—

      # Calaquisq.z hualquisasq.z D.n Fab,n D.n Alberto—[30]

D.n Fab,n v̱ Quenin in q.zn omochiuh Cuix oticmomachilti tlatohuanie D.n Albertotzine Yn itechcopa Yn telpochtli Yn D.n Seb,n tleyn Oquichiuh YniC oquichtacamictito Yn inamic Cuix Ye neli Yn huel hueca OquihuicaC Yn texCalco Yn atlauhco Yn oquimictito ho tt.e D,e tleYn oquichiuh tleYn Oquitlapololti Ca huel mahuistiq.z tlaca Oncatca Ca huel mochipa Ynahuactzinco OtitoYolaliaya Ca Ye ticmomachiltia ca OquitaYa netolinilis[21]tli Auh tleYn Yp.n Omochiuh Camo huel ticmati—

D.n Alberto v̱ Tleyn nimitznolhuilis Ca huel melahuac Yn ticmitalhuia Yese Yn nehuatl niquitohua Ca huel Yehuatl Yn itlan onenca in huehuenton Ca huel oquitlatolmacaya Yn tleyn mach Oquilhuiaia OquiYolcocoltiaia Ynic ten Oquichiuh San onicac Yn iquac Oquimicti niman Ocholo Yn huehuenton Yhuan Yn oc se YhuehueYcniuh Oquicalquixtico Auh niquitohua Yn manel Ye huehuentoton san amo Cuali tlaca San ahuilhuehuetq.z mach ce tlaCatl Yahuiltoca bersebo Auh Yn oc se tlaCatl Yahuiltoca Satanas Ynin Cuix ticmoqualitilia Yn tleYn nimitznolhuilia tlatohuanie—

D.n Fab,n v̱ Jesus tleyn ticmitalhuia Jesus Ca huel temauhti Ynon tlatoli aquin christiano quimotoCayotis Auh Yese niquitohua yn aquin Amo quimimaCaxilia Yn D,s ca quimotoCaYotico Ca san no qui Yn iahuil Yp.n quimati Auh Yese Yn tlahueliloc Ca huel ic papaqui Ototlahueliltic Yn itlaltp.ctzinco Yn tt.º D,s Yhuan niquitohua Amo quali Yn aquin tochan tictlalisque ca San no Yehuatl techtlatlatos techcocolis Ca San no Yehuatl Yp.n mixehuas Yn tlacatecolotl Yehuatl quipehualtis Yn amo quali Yn amo Yectli—

---

29. This should probably be Lucifer talking. If so, scribal error.
30. There are additional stage directions that are difficult to read: Auh Yno mictla [?] in 2o ——— Ylhcac Yn Ang.l

FIRST ANGEL: Do come, Beelzebub, say what is your real authority, O wretched envious one. Why do you want to completely overcome us? Do tell us.
SECOND ANGEL: You, Satan, why do you take my charge from me? Am I not here? Why do you do such, O wretched despised one?
SECOND DEMON: Why will I not take him from you? You will say that I am taking him from you. I will do my job. Don't let it bother you.
DEATH[27]: O my friend, what [?]. Let us who are completely accursed pursue them.
(They pursue them. They enter the place of the dead. Death remains along with the angels.)
DEATH: O my beloved friends, exert all your effort. Do not abandon the people of the earth. But if they will not obey you, well, they will cast their own selves down from the precipice.[28] It will not be your fault.
SECOND ANGEL: Do you not know we absolutely never abandon them? We always go about among them each day and each night. And when they do something that is not good, we restrain them. But they do not obey us; they obey the demons more.
FIRST ANGEL: Let that be all. Let us pass by our other charges. O my friends, make haste.
(They exit. Don Fabián and don Alberto enter.)
DON FABIÁN: How oh how did it happen? Do you know, O ruler, O don Alberto, about the young man, don Sebastián, what he did? He went to kill his spouse in secret! Is it true? He took her far away to a crag, a ravine. He went to kill her. Ah, O our lord, O God, what has he done? What confused him? For he was [one of] the very honored people with whom we always used to console ourselves. You already know he experienced troubles. [21] And what happened to him? We really do not know.
DON ALBERTO: What am I to say to you? For what you are saying is true, yet I say it was the little old man from his household who led him on, that whatever he used to say to him, he would make him angry at her so that he did something. I heard that after he killed her, the little old man ran away along with the other old man, his friend; he came to get him out of the house. And I say, even though they were little old men they were really bad people, just corrupt old men. They say the nickname of one person was Beelzebub, and the nickname of the other was Satan. Do you approve of what I am saying to you, O ruler?
DON FABIÁN: Jesus! What are you saying? Jesus! Those words are very frightening. What Christian would take [such] names? But nevertheless I say, he who does not fear God will come to name himself [such] for likewise he will regard [his name] as a plaything. But nevertheless a scoundrel takes great joy in it. Unfortunate are we on the earth of our lord God! And I say, it is not good that we would put someone [like that] in our home. Likewise he will harangue us, he will hate us; likewise he will be possessed by the demon, he will undertake bad and improper things.

---

27. This should probably be Lucifer talking. If so, scribal error.
28. to cast oneself from the precipice: common idiom meaning "place oneself in danger [through immoral acts]."

D^n Alberto v Ca huel melahuac Yn ticmitalhuia Yn iuhqui Oomochiuh yn axcan Auh cuix no Oticmomachilti Yn tleyn ip.^{n} Omochiuh Yn D^n Seb,^{n} cuix neli mach çan oquiCuatepachoq.^{z} amo OmoYolcuiti YniC omomiquili Yhuan amo nican Yp.^{n} Altepetl hueca hoYa Ca ocholotinenca ypanpa Yn inamic axcan Ye Otlapopoluis Yn axcan ho tt,^{e} D,^{se} Ca niman amo ticmatin Yn tlalp.^{c} San iuhqui tixpopoYome Ototlahueliltic—

D^n Fab,^{n} v Motolinia Yn nohuanpotzitzinhuâ Yn tley Yp^n Omochiuh campa Yn oquimoYeYanmaquilitzino Yn D,^{s} ma ympanpa tictoYectehuilican[31] aso quinmocnelilis aso quinmotlaOcolilis Yn inYolia Yn imanima ma oc tihuian Yn teop.^{n} aso Ye pehuas Yn temachtili ma ticaquitin—

D^n Alberto v Ca Ye Cualitzin ma tihuian nopiltzintzine—

Calaquisq.^{z} niman motlapos ilhuicatl Auh cosamalotl Yp.^{n} mehuiltitiez xp.^{o} Yhuan Sta M.ª Yhua Ome [22] Angles xp̄o Yecancopatzinco xochitl YopochCopatzinco espada—

xp̄o v Ma nican xihualauh nican xinesi topilletzine Ca nimitzonnotza = # Tlatzintla hualquisas Yn Miquistli—

Miquistli v Ca Ye onihuala noteotzine notlatoCatzine tleyn ticmonequiltitzinohua—

xp̄o v Yn axcan ma ximohuica Yn onpa mictlan tiquinmanilitiuh Yn omentin tlaca Ynon Ymac Omic Yn inamic Yhuan Yehua Yn San oquittaq.^{z} YniC omic Auh Ca Ompa Ylpiticate Yn mictlan ma xiquinnotza Yhuan Yhuan[32] yn tlatlacatecolo ma nican nixp.^{n} nesiqui Ca niquinnotza—

Miquistli v Ca Ye Cualitzin ma nicchihua Yn motlanahuatiltzin—

Yaz Yn mictlan Caltenco quixopehuas

Miquistli v tlatelchihualtine ma nican xihualquisacan ca amechmonochilia Yn melahuac motetlatzontequililiani Jues—

hualquistihuetzq^z 2° Demonio—

2° Dem.^{o} v Tleyn ticmonequiltia Yn titechmotzatzililia Ca Oncan tiquintlatzaCuiltia Yn Yolpoliuhque Yn tlatlacohuanime—

Miquistli v Ma xiquinnotza Yn motlacatecoloYcnihuan Ca amechmonochilia melahuac Yn motetlatzontequililiani—

Ontzatzis yn Demonio—

2.º Dem.^{o} v Ma xihualquisacan nocnihuane ma tictotilitin Yn huey tlatohuani D,^{s} Ca techmonochilia—

quisas Lucifer Yhuan 2° Dem.^{o}—

Lucifer v Ma tihuian tocnihuane ma tictotilitin tleyn quimonequiltitzinohua—

Yasq.^{z} Yxp.^{n}tzinco xp̄o—

Miquistli v Noteotzine notlatocatzine Ca Ye oniquinhualhuiCac—

Motlanquaq^{z}tzazque

xp̄o v Xihualhuian xicaquican Yn amehuantin Yn annotlasentelchihualhuan namechnahuatia ma niCan xiquinhualhuicaca Yn onpa Anquinpie Çe Sihuatl Se tlatohuani ma nican nixp.^{n} nesican—[23]

---

31. tictoYectehuilican: read *tictoyectenehuilican*.
32. Yhuan Yhuan: so written in the text.

DON ALBERTO: What you are saying is very true. That is how it happened now. But did you also know what happened to don Sebastián? Did they really break his head with rocks? He did not confess when he died and it was not here in the altepetl. He went far away, he was going about fleeing because of his spouse. Now he will be obliterated. Now, ah, O our lord, O God, we do not know at all [how things are faring] on earth, for it is just as though we are blind people. Unfortunate are we!

DON FABIÁN: What has happened to my suffering neighbors? Where has God placed them? Let us praise him for their sakes. Perhaps he will favor them; perhaps he will have mercy on their spirits, their souls. Let us go to church. Perhaps the sermon will begin soon. Let us go hear it.

DON ALBERTO: Very well, let us go, O my nobleman.

(They exit. Then heaven opens. And Christ sits on a rainbow along with Saint Mary and two [22] angels. To the right of Christ a flower and to his left a sword.)

CHRIST: Come here, show yourself here, O constable, for I summon you.

(At the bottom Death enters.)

DEATH: I have now come, O my deity, O my ruler. What do you want?

CHRIST: Go now there to the place of the dead. You will go to seize the two people. That one whose spouse died at his hands and those who just saw how she died. And they are tied up there in the place of the dead. Summon them along with the demons. Let them come to appear here before me. I summon them.

DEATH: Very well, let me carry out your command.

(He goes to the house at the edge of the place of the dead. He gives it a disdainful kick with his foot.)

DEATH: O despised ones, come out here for the true sentencer and judge summons you.

(Second Demon quickly enters.)

SECOND DEMON: What do you want, you who cry out to us? For there we punish the confused, the sinners.

DEATH: Summon your demonic friends, for the true judge summons you [all].

(The demon cries out.)

SECOND DEMON: Come out, O my friends. Let us go see the great ruler, God, for he summons us.

(Lucifer enters along with Second[29] Demon.)

LUCIFER: Let us go, O my friends, let us go see what he wants.

(They go before Christ.)

DEATH: O my deity, O my ruler, I have brought them now.

(They kneel down.)

CHRIST: Come, listen, my accursed ones. I command you: bring here those whom you have over there, a woman and a ruler. Let them appear here before me. [23]

---

29. This is evidently a scribal error for *"First"* since Second Demon is already onstage.

Lucifer v Ca Ye qualitzin tt.ᵒᵉ Diose ma ticneltilican Yn motlatoltzin ma tiquimanati—

xp̄ō v Yhuan tehuatl xiyauh topille—

Miquistli v Ca Ye Cualitzin ttᵒᵉ Diose = # Yasq.ᶻ quimanatihue Omentin animas tliltiq.ᶻ Yesque—

Miquistli v Ca Ye Otiquimanato Ca ye nican cate ttᵒᵉ Diose—

xp̄ō v tla xihualauh Yn tehuatl Yn tiD̄ⁿ̄ Seb,ⁿ̄³³ ma xinechilhui xinechnanquili tleyn motlachihual ma nicCaqui tleyn Oticchiuh Yn tlaltpᶜ tleYn motetlasotlalis Oticchiuh Yn tehuatl Yn tiD,ᵃ Juana Cihuapilli Catli Yn moCualachihualis huel otimoCualitohuaya titlateomattinenca Axcan xiquitocan xitlananquilican xihualauh ~~topille~~ in tinotitlan xiquintlatlani Yn notenahuatiltzin Cuix oquichiuhque Cuix oquineltiliq.ᶻ Yn tlaltp.ᶜ ma nicaqui—

Miquistli v Ma nicchihua Yn moteotenahuatiltzin ttᵒᵉ Diose tla xihualauh Cuix Oanquichiuhq.ᶻ Yn iteotenahuatiltzin Yn iCel teOtl, D,ˢ Ynic Centetl Cuix Oanquimotlasotiliq.ᶻ Yca mochi moYolo—

Motlanquaqᶻtzas Yn Demᵒ quimolhuilis Yn xp̄ō,

1º Dem.ᵒ v Ca niman amo Omitzmotlasotiliq.ᶻ Yn ⁱca mochi Yn inYolo—

Miquistli v Auh YniC ontetl Cuix Oanquitlapicteneuhq.ᶻ Yn itocatzin Yn D,ˢ YeYca OanmoYolCuitiqᶻ Cuix mochi Oanquitoq.ᶻ Yn amotlatlaCol—

2.º Dem.ᵒ v Ynontzin Ca huel itequiuh Ocatca Yn tlaltp.ᶜ Yn San tlapic ConanaYa Juramento—

Miquistli v Auh Ynic Yetetl Yn Domingo Yhuan Ylhuitl ip.ⁿ Cuix Oantlateomatiqᶻ—

Lucifer v Ca niman A³⁴ Otlateomatq.ᶻ ca San quixcahuiaya Yn ahuilnemilistli Yhuan tlahuanalistli—

Miquistli Auh Ynic nauhtetl Cuix Oanquimahuistiliq.ᶻ Yn amotahuan Yn amonahuan—

1.º Dem.ᵒ v Ca amo Oquichiuhq.ᶻ amo Oquinmahuistiliq.ᶻ San imixco Ymicpac Onenq.ᶻ Yn intahuan Yn innahuan—

Miquistli v Auh Ynic macuiltetl Cuix aca Amomac Omic—[24]

2.º Dem.ᵒ Ca Oquimicti Yn inamic Yn nican ca Auh Yn nican ca Cihuatl Ca yp.ⁿpa Otemictiloc—

Miquistli Ynic ChiCuasentetl Cuix oamahuilnenq.ᶻ—

1.º Dem.ᵒ v Ca Semicac hoahuilnenq.ᶻ Yn Yehuâ Yn iquac tlalp.ᶜ Onenca—

Miquistli v Auh Ynic chiContetl Cuix Oamichteq.ᶻ—

Lucifer Ca Ynin Ca Yc³⁵ Oquichiuhq.ᶻ—

Miquistli v Auh Ynic chiCuetetl Cuix Oantetentlapiquiq.ᶻ Cuix tetech Oanquitlamiq.ᶻ Yn tlatlaColli—

Lucifer v Ca Ynin cihuatl Ca huel itequiuh Ocatca Yhuan Yn nican catqui ca no Yuhqui Ocatca—

---

33. Something written over this, perhaps *tlatohuani*.
34. A: read *amo* or *aic*.
35. Yc: perhaps *ye* was meant.

LUCIFER: Very well, O our lord, O God. Let us carry out your words, let us go seize them.
CHRIST: And you, go, constable.
DEATH: Very well, O our lord, O God.
(They go to seize them. The two souls are black.)
DEATH: We have now gone to seize them. Here they are, O our lord, O God.
CHRIST: Do come, you, ~~you who are don Sebastián~~. Tell me, answer me: what are your deeds? Let me hear what you did on earth, what [works of] charity you performed. You, ~~you who are doña Juana~~, noblewoman, what are your good deeds? You praised yourself a great deal while you went about engaging in spiritual exercises. Now say it, answer. Come, ~~constable~~, my messenger, examine them concerning my commandments. Have they done them? Have they carried them out on earth? Let me hear it.
DEATH: Let me carry out your sacred commands, O our lord, O God. Do come. Have you carried out the sacred commands of the only deity, God? The first: have you loved him with all your heart?
(The demon kneels down. He speaks to Christ.)
FIRST DEMON: They absolutely did not love you with all their heart.
DEATH: And the second: did you take the name of God in vain because of your confession? Did you declare all your sins?
SECOND DEMON: That was his very task on earth, that he took false oaths.

DEATH: And the third: did you engage in spiritual exercises on Sundays and feast days?
LUCIFER: They absolutely did not engage in spiritual exercises but occupied themselves exclusively in lustful living and drunkenness.
DEATH: And the fourth: did you honor your fathers and your mothers?

FIRST DEMON: They did not do it. They did not honor them. They just offended their fathers and their mothers.
DEATH: And the fifth: did someone die at your hands? [24]
SECOND DEMON: The one here killed his spouse. And someone was killed on account of the woman here.
DEATH: The sixth: did you go about living lustfully?
FIRST DEMON: They always lived lustfully earlier, when they lived on earth.
DEATH: And the seventh: did you steal?
LUCIFER: That they did.
DEATH: And the eighth: did you give false testimony about others? Did you falsely impute sin to others?
LUCIFER: It was the very occupation of this woman and the [other] one here was the same.

Miquistli v Auh Ynic chiucnauhtetl Cuix otiquinteCuili Yn tecihuauh Yn tehuatl Cuix otiq.ᶻlehui Yn tenamic—

2.º Demº v Ynontzin Ca huel itequiuh OCatca Yn tlatohuani auh Yn Sihuapilli ca San tlapiC Yn oYaYa Yn teop.ⁿ Auh San nopa³⁶ teyxilehuitica³⁷—

Miquistli v Auh Ynic matlactetl Cuix Oanqᶻlehuiq.ᶻ Yn teaxca Yn tetlatqui—

Lucifer v Ca Ynontzin Ca semicac hoq.ᶻlehuiaya Yn tetlatqui Yn teaxca yhuan huel Miec Miccatlatquitl Oq.ᶻlehuiqᶻ Oquixpoloqᶻ—

Miquistli v Ynic matlactetl teotenahuatilli Yn anquimotlasotilisq.ᶻ Yn iÇel teotl D,ˢ Yhuan Yn amohuanpohuan Cuix Oanquichiuhque—

Lucifer v Ca niman atle Oquichiuhq.ᶻ Yn tlaltp.ᶜ Yn motenahuatiltzin Ca mochi Oquitlacoq.ᶻ Auh Yn iCuac moteop.ⁿchantzinco Ocalaquiya Ca amo YnYolotica Yn oquitaYa Missa ca San nopo³⁸ Omonono[?]catca Auh San no yuhqui Yn ihuanpohuan Ca amo quintlasotlasnequi ma xitechmoCahuililitzino ttºe D,ˢᵉ—

Miquistli v Ca ye onicneltili Yn motenahuatiltzin noteotzine notlatoCatzine Catle Cuali YniC omitzmotequipanilhuiq.ᶻ Auh ca amo Oquineltiliq.ᶻ Yn moteotenahuatiltzin tleYn nel tiquitosq.ᶻ ca tehuatzin ticmomachiltitzinohua [25]

xp̄o v OAnmotlahuelilticq.ᶻ Ca niman atle qualli Oanquichiuhqᶻ Auh Yn amehuantin Yn antlasentelchihualtin Ca huel namechtlaquauhnahuatia ma huel Ompa Yn ixico Yn mictlantli XiquinmaYahuiCan XiquintlaSatin huel xiquintlatzaCuiltican Yn aYc tlamis Yn aYc polihuis tzonquisas Yn notlatoltzin—

Sᵗᵃ M.ᵃ v Yn tinotlasomahuizConetzin Ca senca huel miec tlamantli Ynic mitzinco mocpactzinco nemi Yn tlaltp.ᶜ tlaca Auh ca nican mixp.ⁿtzinco ninixtlapachtlasa nonopechteca ma huel xicmonep.ⁿtlaYtilitzino Yn moJusticiatzin Ca Ye ticmomachiltitzinohua Cemicac mixp.ⁿtzinco nocontlalia Yn nochoquis Yn nixayo Ymp.ⁿpa Yn tlatlacohuanime Canel motlachihualtzitzinhuan macamo nenpolihuis macamo nenquisas Yn motlasoYessotzin Yn inp.ⁿpa Oticmononoquilitzino notlasoconetzin nochalchiuhtzin nomaCuetzin Ca Senca tonehua Yn noYolo Yn iCuac se tlacatl tlaltp.ᶜ tlacatl ticmotelchihuilitzinohua—

xp̄o v Notlasonantzine Ca melahuac Yn ticmitalhuitzinohua Ca Senca miec Yn moChoquilistzin Yn miXayotzin Yn inp.ⁿpa ticmonoquilia Yn tlaltp.ᶜ tlaca Auh Yn Yehuantin [?] yuh quimati Oytlahueliltic Auh in nican cate Yn tlatlaCohuanime Ca huel oquipanahuiq.ᶻ Yn noteotenahuatiltzin Yn iuhqui Oticmitalhuitzino Yn niman atle manel centetl Oquichiuhq.ᶻ Auh Yntla tehuatzin mitzmotlatlauhtilisquia mitzmotequipanilhuisquia Yn tlaltp.ᶜ Ca mop.ⁿpatzinco nicchihuasquia Canel tinotlasonantzin Auh Yn ip.ⁿ Yn tetlaOcolilistli Yn oRra de MiSeriCordia³⁹ Yn nop.ⁿpa Oquichihuasquia Ca amo Oquichiuhq.ᶻ Ca miecpa Yn caltenpa ninoqᶻtzaYa ninotlaYtlaYtlaniaya ca niman aic OnechtlaOcoliq.ᶻ Ca san OnechhualtotoCaYa ca San niquintlayeltiYaYa Auh ca san [26] Yehuantin Yn intlatocaYcnihuan Yn quinCohuanotzaYa Auh Ca nican ca yn angel ma Yehuatl quito motlaneltili Yntla Ytla quali Oquichiuhque—

---

36. nopa: read *onpa*.
37. teyxilehuitica: read *teixelehuitica*.
38. nopo: read *onpa*.
39. oRra de MiSeriCordia: read *obras de misericordia*.

DEATH: And the ninth: did you take others' wives from them? You, [woman,] did you desire the spouses of others?

SECOND DEMON: That was the very job of the ruler. And the noblewoman just went to church on false pretenses; she just coveted people there.

DEATH: And the tenth: did you desire the goods and property of others?

LUCIFER: That is it. They always desired other people's goods and property along with desiring and wasting a great deal of the property of the dead.

DEATH: The tenth sacred commandment: you are to love the only deity, God, and your neighbors. Did you do it?

LUCIFER: They carried out absolutely none of your commandments on earth for they broke them all. And when they used to enter church they did not willingly see mass for there they just talked to each other. And likewise they did not want to love their neighbors. Leave them to us, O our lord, O God.

DEATH: I have carried out your commands, O my deity, O my ruler. What is the good that they labored at for you? They did not carry out your sacred commands. What will we truly say [in their defense] for you know [the truth]? [25]

CHRIST: Unfortunate are you! For you did absolutely nothing good. And you, who are completely accursed, I very firmly order you: hurl them and cast them right there in the navel of the place of the dead, really punish them. My words [that is, sentence?] will never finish, never perish, never come to an end.

SAINT MARY: You, my beloved honored child, the people of the earth offend you in a great many things. And here before you I cast myself face down, I humbly bow low. Show your justice among them for you already know I always set down my weeping and my tears before you for the sake of the sinners. Since they are your creatures, let the precious blood you spilled for their sakes not be uselessly wasted, not be in vain. O my beloved child, O my jade, O my bracelet, my heart is very hurt when you despise a person of the earth.

CHRIST: O my beloved mother, what you are saying is true. Very abundant are the weeping and tears you spill on behalf of the people of the earth. And they know it is so. They are unfortunate! And here are the sinners who have violated my sacred commandments. As you said, they carried out none of them at all. But if they had prayed to you and served you on earth, I would do it [that is, save them] for your sake, since you are my beloved mother. But they did not do the acts of compassion, the works of mercy, that they could have done for my sake. For I stood begging outside their houses many a time. They absolutely never had pity on me; they just ran me off for I disgusted them.[30] And [on the contrary] [26] they just invited their royal friends to eat. And here is the angel. Let him say it, and verify if they did something good.

---

30. The fourteen works of mercy (*obras de misericordia*) were part of the standard Catholic catechism; as here, they were called *tetlaocoliliztli*, "having compassion for others," in Nahuatl. They include feeding, clothing, and sheltering the needy.

1.º Ang.¹ v̠ Noteotzine notlatocatzine tleyn niquitos tleyn nimitznolhuilitzinos ca Yn tehuatzin Ca nohuian timotztilitica Yn tetl Yn quahuitl Ytic Ca niman maYac tleyn mitzmolhuilitzinos Yese Ca Ye ticmomachiltitzinohua Ca Ye Yxquich notlapal Onicchiuh Canel amo Onechtlacamatq.ᶻ Auh Yn axcan Ca tehuatzin ticmomachiltitzinohua ma mochihua Yn motlasotlanequilistzin—

chocas Yn Angel—

2º Demº v̠ Ma mochihua Yn moteotenahuatiltzin—

xp̄o v̠ Ma xihuian ma xiquinhuicacan Canel amotech pouhque Yn atle Ymilhuil Yn atle Ynmasehual Canel YmixCoYan Omotelchiuhq.ᶻ Ca ye yxquich ca Ye oniquinmaCauh—

Lucifer v̠ hotitechmocnelilitzino melahuac motetlatzontequililiani Diose ma ticneltilican Yn motlatocatlanahuatiltzin—

Motzacuas Ylhuicatl—

1.º Dem.º Ma tihuian ma tiquinhuicacan ca Ye tomalhuan Ca Ye totech pouhque Canel totetlaYecolticahuan OCatca—

Condenado v̠ Ay otoSentzontlahueliltiq.ᶻ tleYn Oc ticchihuasqᶻ Yn tlaltp.ᶜ ttºe Diose Catli in papaquilistli catli Yn neYolalilistli ma nechpalehuiqui Omochiuh Onotlahueliltic—

2.º Dem.º v̠ Aucmo xitlato ximocahua AOcmo honca axcâ ompa tiquitas Yn tochan Yn mopapaquilis Ompa timitzmacasq.ᶻ xinenemi ma tihuian—[27]

Condenado v̠ OnoSentzontlahueliltic Yn nehuatl Yn nitechouhti Yn nitetlaOcolti nehuatl ma notech ximixcotican⁴⁰ Yn annohuanpohuan maCaYac Moqualitas macaYac MoYequitos yn tlaltp.ᶜ Ca huel nicnoCoytia Yn tleYn Onicchihuaya Yntla ninonemilisCuepani asocamo Ymac nimiquisquia Yn nonamic aso OninoYolCuitisquia YniC onimiquisquia Ay OnoSentzontlahueliltic ma sentelchihualo Yn Cahuitl Yn ip.ⁿ OninemiYa—

Lucifer v̠ Ma Yxquich Yn tleYn mach tiquitohua ma ysiuhca ma tihuian ma tiquinhuicacan ma xiquinnenemiltican—

1.º Demº v̠ Xitotocacan xinenemican ximotlalocan Yn amochan Yn mictlan—

Calaquisq.ᶻ Mictlan tzatzitiasq.ᶻ Cueponis bonbas Yc tlamis nexcuitilli finis Laus Dᵉº Amen Axcan hotla Ynin nexcuitilli A 1 de Abril del Ano de 169i2 Anos [simple rubric]

---

40. ximixcotican: read *ximixcuitican*.

FIRST ANGEL: O my deity, O my ruler, what will I say? What am I to say to you? For you see everywhere, into stone and wood. Absolutely no one can say something to you for you already know about it. I have exerted all my effort but they did not obey me. And now you know. May your precious will be done.

([First] Angel cries.)
SECOND DEMON: May your sacred commands be done.
CHRIST: Go, take them for they belong to you. They are undeserving and without merit since they condemned themselves. That is all, for I have given them permission.
LUCIFER: Thank you, true judge, O God. Let us carry out your royal command.

(Heaven closes.)
FIRST DEMON: Let us go, let us take them for they are already our captives, they already belong to us since they were our servants.
CONDEMNED MAN: Oh, we are four hundred [times][31] unfortunate. What will we do on earth? O our lord, O God. What has come of joy? What has come of contentment? May they come to help me! O, unfortunate am I!
SECOND DEMON: Speak no more. Be quiet. They no longer exist. Now there you will see our home, there we will give you your joy. Get walking! Let's go! [27]
CONDEMNED MAN: I am four hundred [times] unfortunate! I provoke weeping, I provoke sadness. May you who are my neighbors take an example from me. Let no one be pleased with himself, let no one praise himself on earth. I finally confess what I used to do. If I had changed my life perhaps I would not have died at the hands of my spouse, perhaps I would have confessed when I died. Ah! I am four hundred [times] unfortunate! Let the time in which I lived be despised.
LUCIFER: Let that be all of whatever it is you're saying. Let it be quick, let us go, let us take them, let us get them walking along.
FIRST DEMON: Hurry, get walking, run along to your home in the place of the dead.
(They enter the place of the dead. They cry out. Bombs explode.) Thus comes to an end the moral example. Finis. Laus Deo.[32] Amen.

·This moral example was finished today, the first of April of the year one thousand, six hundred, ninety and two.[33]

---

31. Four hundred [times]: here and below, *four hundred* is a common idiom in the vigesimally based traditional counting system for "countless, innumerable."
32. *Finis. Laus Deo*: The end. Praise God.
33. A simple rubric follows.

[27]

D.ⁿ Seb.ᵃⁿ Condenado = YYô Omochiuh, otocentzontlahueliltic Yn niman aic otitosCalizq.ᶻ Yn tlp̄c Ca nelli melahuac atle ipan pouhqui Yn tlp̄c pâpaquiliztli têhuatl motlatlacol, Yn titlahuelilocaCihuatl: Yntla oxinechtlacahualtiani YtechCopa, Yn nâqualnemiliz asocamo Ymmac onihuetzquiaya Yn nican cate Yn Mictlan tequanime Yn cenca temâmauhtique Ynic tlachie Yhuan Yn amêhuantin Yn antlatlacatecolo q.ᶻnin oannechcâcaYauhque, Ca oannechilhuiaya annechpalehuizque Yn YtechCopa nonemaquixtiliz q.ᶻnin cenca nitlaihYohuia Yn axcan, Ynic nitlatla Yn âmo YhYohuiliz, Yn âehualiztli Yn Mictlan tletl Ca huel neci Ca nica Yn amo tenêecoltiliztli: Yn oan¹ [28] Yn oannechcacayauhq.ᶻ Ai Omochiuh oninotlahueliltic Ym manel nimauhcatzatzi san niman ayc acmo ic ninomaquixtiz. Auh Yn axcan cenca tlatla Yn noYollo in iquac niquilnamiqui Yn acmo nicnotiliz Yn Dios! Ay, ay, oc achi qualli oyezquia Yn macamo onitlacatini. Yn tlp̄c manoso san onechcochpachohuani Yn nonantzin, Yn ihCuac ocuh nitetepiton; tlein onax Yn tlp̄c, Yn Dios Oquimonequilti Ynic monahuac Onechmixnamictili, inic tonehuantin, otictotequipanilhuizquia: Auh Ye san no têhuatl, ica in moteixCuepalliz otimonômaCauh Ynmac Yn nican Cate Yn nexiColizti Ca tel axcan tonehuan Ye techhuica Yn aquique anq.ⁿtlacamatque; Yn Dios miecpa Yn otechmixnamicnamictiliaya, inic tiquallachihuasque Auh Yn nican Cate Yn nexiColizti YCa, in intecanecâcaYahualiz otechmonêecoltiliq.ᶻ ic achpa² Yn âquallachihualiztli. O! [?] ticholiloni titetlaocolihque Yn san quinempoloq.ᶻ Yn Cahuitl, in ipan otinenq.ᶻ tlp̄c = Auh Yn[in?] Mochintin Yn ocuh annemi tlp̄c macamo xicnempolocan Yn Cahuitl Yn ipan annemi ma xiquilnamiquican ca San Sen [?]ixcueyonalizt[?] Yn ontlantihuetziz in amonemiliz: Yn manel huel anhuehuetizq.ᶻ Yntlacamo anquallachihuazque Ca san niman aic anquimotililizque Yn itlazomahuizxayacatzin Yn tt.º Jesu xp̄o. ma totech ximixCuitican Yn tehuanᵗⁱⁿ Yn aic otiquallachiuhque Yn san c̄m̄c otictoYolîtlacalhuilitinenca Yn D.ˢ Ca Ye techhuica Yn ompa centlani Mictlan Yn campa aoquic ceppa tictoᵗⁱlizque Yn D.ˢ Yhuan, in campa acmo tihuelitisque, tiquallachizq.ᶻ³ Yn amêhuantin. Ca huelitiz Yn antlacnopilhuizque Yntla oanquimoYolihtlacalhuihq.ᶻ Yn D.ˢ ammomaquixtizq.ᶻ Cualla[29]Chihualiztica, tlamâcehualiztica Ynic anYaque Anquimotilitihui Yn D.ˢ huelitiz Auh Yntlacamo, ca in quename axCan antechita Ca san no Yuhqui amopan mochihuaz Yn ihquac anmiquizque Ca amechmoCentelchihuiliz Yn D.ˢ Yn ompa Mictlan.

Fin del [?]

1. Yn oan: repeated on the following page.
2. achpa: perhaps to be read *achtopa*.
3. quallachizq.ᶻ: read *quallachihuazque*.

[27]

DON SEBASTIÁN, CONDEMNED MAN:[1] Oh, four hundred [times] unfortunate are we who never educated ourselves on earth! For truly and honestly the pleasures of the earth are of no account. It is your fault, you wicked woman. If you had restrained me concerning my evil life, perhaps I would not have fallen into the hands of the fierce beasts that are here in the place of the dead, who look so very frightening. And you, who are demons: how did you deceive me? For you used to tell me you would help me concerning my salvation. How greatly I suffer now. I am burning with the breathless and unbearable fire of the place of the dead. It is clear that there is no temptation here; [28] you deceived me. Ah, unfortunate am I! Even though I cry out in a frightened way I will absolutely never save myself with it. And now my heart greatly burns when I remember I will never again see God! Ah, ah, it would have been better not to have been born on earth, or if my mother had just smothered me to death in my sleep when I was still little. What did I do on earth? It was God's will to match me with you so that we would work for him together. And likewise you, with your deceptions, left yourself in the hands of the envious ones here. But today those whom you obeyed are taking us away together. Many times God provoked us so that we would do good things. But here are the envious ones who, through their deceptions, tempted us from the first with bad deeds. Oh! We inspire weeping and sadness, who just wasted time while we lived on earth. And all of you who still live on earth, do not waste the time in which you live. Remember that in just one blink of an eye your lives will quickly come to an end. Even though you grow very old, if you did not do good deeds, you will absolutely never see the precious and honored face of our lord Jesus Christ. Take an example from us who never did good deeds but rather always went about offending God. Now they are taking us away to the depths of the place of the dead, where we will never again see God. And there we will no longer be able to do good deeds. It will be possible for you to obtain favor if you have offended God; it will be possible for you to save yourselves with good deeds, [29] with penance, so that you can go to see God. But if not, the way you see us now is the same that will happen to you when you die, for God will completely condemn you to the place of the dead.

End of the [?]

---

1. Some of what follows is tentatively translated.

Appendixes

Appendix 1

SPANISH AND LATIN SPOKEN LOANS IN SEVEN NAHUATL PLAYS IN MODERN ORTHOGRAPHY AND IN ALPHABETICAL ORDER

1. 1627 años "the year 1627"
2. Abrahán "Abraham"
3. alcalde "city council member/judge"
4. amén "amen"
5. ángel "angel"
6. ángeles "angels"
7. ánima "soul"
8. ánimas "souls"
9. arzobispo "archbishop"
10. Ave Maria "Hail Mary"
11. Balaán "Balaam"
12. Belcebú "Beelzebub"
13. Belén "Bethlehem"
14. bula "[papal] bull"
15. capítulo "chapter [of a book]"
16. chicharrones "pork rinds"
17. conde "count"
18. corona "crown"
19. cristiana "[female] Christian"
20. cristiano "[male] Christian"
21. Cristo "Christ"
22. cruz "cross"
23. cuaresma "Lent"
24. cuenta "accounting"
25. David "David"
26. diablo "devil"
27. Dios "God"
28. domingo "Sunday [unit of time]"
29. Egipto "Egypt"
30. emperador "emperor"
31. escribano "notary"
32. escritura "document"
33. Espíritu Santo "Holy Spirit"
34. gloria "glory [religious]"
35. gracia "grace [religious]"
36. Herodes "Herod"
37. hora "hour [unit of time]"
38. incienso "incense"
39. Isaac "Isaac"
40. Isaías "Isaiah"
41. Israel "Israel"
42. Jacob "Jacob"
43. Jerusalén "Jerusalem"
44. Jesucristo "Jesus Christ"
45. Jesús "Jesus"
46. Jesús, María y José "Jesus, Mary and Joseph"
47. Joseph "Joseph"
48. Judea "Judea"
49. judiazos "lousy/rotten Jews"
50. judios "Jews"
51. juez "judge"
52. Juicio Final "Final Judgment"

53. juramento "oath"
54. justicia "justice"
55. loco "crazy person [male]"
56. Lorenzo "Lorenzo"
57. Lucifer "Lucifer"
58. luto "mourning clothes"
59. maitines "matins"
60. marqués "marquis"
61. mesa "table"
62. Mesías "Messiah"
63. mirra "myrrh"
64. misa "mass"
65. misericordia "mercy"
66. Moab "Moab"
67. Moria "Moria [mountain]"
68. obra de misericordia "work of mercy"
69. paje "page [low status servant]"
70. paraíso "paradise"
71. pasión "passion [religious]"
72. Pater Noster "Our Father"
73. patriarcas "patriarchs"
74. Persia "Persia"
75. peso "peso [unit of money]"
76. pesos "pesos [units of money]"
77. por amor de Dios "for the love of God; for nothing"
78. prenda "pledge; security"
79. profetas "prophets"
80. puerta "[Spanish-style] door"
81. purgatorio "purgatory"
82. responso "responsory"
83. rey "king"
84. reyes "kings"
85. Roma emperador, César de Agusto "Cæsar Augustus, Emperor of Rome"
86. roque "rook"
87. rosario "rosary"
88. sacerdote "priest"
89. sacramento "sacrament"
90. Salve "Hail [Holy Queen]"
91. San Miguel "Saint Michael"
92. San Miguel arcángel "Saint Michael the Archangel"
93. santa bula "holy [papal] bull"
94. santa cruz "holy cross"
95. santa iglesia "holy church"
96. Santa María "Saint Mary"
97. santas "[female] saints"
98. Santísima Trinidad "Most Holy Trinity"
99. Santo Joseph "Saint Joseph"
100. santos "[male] saints"
101. santo sacramento "holy sacrament"
102. Satanás "Satan"
103. semana santa "Holy Week"
104. sermón "sermon"
105. Set "Sheth"
106. surgite mortui venite a judicium "Arise, O dead, and come to judgment"
107. testamento "testament [last will]"
108. testigos "witnesses"
109. tomín "unit of money"
110. tomines "units of money"
111. vino "[Spanish-style] wine"

Appendix 2

SPANISH AND LATIN SPOKEN LOANS IN SEVEN NAHUATL PLAYS, IN DESCENDING ORDER OF FREQUENCY AND DATE OF FIRST APPEARANCE

Loans	Frequency	First Appearance
Dios	317	1548
ánima	35	1550
misa	22	1550
Jesucristo	19	1545
Lucifer	19	1552
ánimas	17	c1607–1629
Herodes	17	c1607–1629
pesos [money]	17	1548
santa iglesia	14	1553
tomín	13	1545
cruz	12	1560–1570
purgatorio	11	1552
ángel	10	1552
diablo	10	c1562–1569
Jesús	9	1552
Santa María	9	1552
cuenta [accounting]	8	c1607–1629
Isaac	8	
Jerusalén	8	1631
juez	8	1548
cristiano	7	1560
Espíritu Santo	7	1566
Abrahán	6	1631
judíos	6	1552
rosario	6	1552

310—APPENDIXES

Loans	Frequency	First Appearance
tomines	6	1547
domingo [unit of time]	5	1553
gracia	5	1586
juramento	5	1547
justicia	5	1548
testamento	5	1552
Belcebú	4	
Belén	4	1631
Cristo	4	c1607–1629
gloria	4	c1607–1629
Israel	4	1637
peso [money]	4	1548
responso	4	1570
reyes	4	c1607–1629
Satanás	4	
sermón	4	1611
cuaresma	3	1550
David	3	1631
Joseph	3	1605
Judea	3	c1607–1629
luto	3	1574
misericordia	3	
santa cruz	3	c1607–1629
santo sacramento	3	1550
vino	3	1553
amén	2	1550
capítulo [chapter of a book]	2	c1607–1629
chicharrones	2	
escribano	2	1547
escritura	2	1553
judiazos	2	
patriarcas	2	c1607–1629
profetas	2	c1607–1629
sacramento	2	1549
San Miguel arcángel	2	c1607–1629
1627 años	1	
alcalde	1	1547
angeles	1	1548
arzobispo	1	c1562–1569
Ave Maria	1	1570
Balaán	1	c1607–1629
bula	1	1570
conde	1	c1607–1629
corona	1	c1607–1629

Loans	Frequency	First Appearance
cristiana	1	1658
Egipto	1	c1607–1629
emperador	1	1550
hora [unit of time]	1	c1607–1629
incienso	1	c1607–1629
Isaías	1	
Jacob	1	1631
Jesús, María y José	1	1695
Juicio Final	1	
loco	1	c1607–1629
Lorenzo	1	1550
maitines	1	1552
marqués	1	c1540
mesa	1	1550
Mesías	1	
mirra	1	c1607–1629
Moab	1	
Moría [mountain]	1	
obra de misericordia		
paje	1	c1607–1629
paraíso	1	
pasión [religious]	1	1614
Pater Noster	1	
Persia	1	c1607–1629
por amor de Dios	1	1608
prenda	1	1654
puerta	1	1581
rey	1	1550
Roma emperador, César de Agusto	1	
roque	1	
sacerdote	1	1552
Salve	1	
San Miguel	1	1549
santa bula	1	
santas	1	
Santísima Trinidad	1	1588
Santo Joseph	1	c1607–1629
santos	1	c1607–1629
semana santa	1	1570
Set	1	
surgite mortui venite a judicium	1	
testigos	1	1548
TOTAL	784	

Legend:
   Loans = all 111 spoken Spanish and Latin loans in the seven translated plays.
   Frequency = total number of occurrences in all seven translated plays.
   First Appearance = first appearance in a Nahua-generated text. (See Sell 1993, 312–15, 328–40; Karttunen and Lockhart 1976, 53–84; Chimalpahin 1965, 37–146; Chimalpahin 1997, 2:130–83; Solís et al. 139–229; and Anderson et al. 1976.)

Appendix 3

SPANISH AND LATIN SPOKEN LOANS IN SEVEN NAHUATL PLAYS, IN DESCENDING ORDER OF FREQUENCY WITH OCCURRENCE IN OTHER ECCLESIASTICAL NAHUATL AND DATE OF FIRST APPEARANCE

Loans	Saha	Moli	Anun	Baut	León	Mija	First Appearance
Dios	X	X	X	X	X	X	1548
ánima	X	X	X	X	X	X	1550
misa	X	X	X	X	X	X	1550
Jesucristo	X	X	X	X	X	X	1545
Lucifer	X	X	X	X	X	X	1552
ánimas	X	X	X	X		X	c1607–1629
Herodes	X	X	X	X		X	c1607–1629
pesos [money]		X		X	X		1548
santa iglesia	X	X	X	X	X	X	1553
tomín	X	X	X	X	X	X	1545
cruz	X	X	X	X	X	X	1560–1570
purgatorio	X	X	X	X	X		1552
ángel	X	X	X	X	X	X	1552
diablo	X	X	X	X	X	X	c1562–1569
Jesús	X	X	X	X	X	X	1552
Santa María	X	X	X	X		X	1552
cuenta [accounting]				X			c1607–1629
Isaac	X			X	X	X	
Jerusalén	X		X	X	X	X	1631
juez	X		X	X	X	X	1548
cristiano	X		X	X	X	X	1560
Espíritu Santo	X	X	X	X	X		1566
Abrahán	X		X	X		X	1631
judíos	X	X	X		X	X	1552

Loans	Saha	Moli	Anun	Baut	León	Mija	First Appearance
rosario	X		X				1552
tomines	X	X	X	X	X	X	1547
domingo [unit of time]	X	X	X	X	X	X	1553
gracia	X	X	X	X	X	X	1586
juramento		X	X	X	X	X	1547
justicia	X	X	X	X	X	X	1548
testamento		X		X	X	X	1552
Belén	X		X	X		X	1631
Belcebú						X	
Cristo	X		X	X	X		c1607–1629
gloria		X	X	X	X	X	c1607–1629
Israel	X	X	X	X	X	X	1637
peso [money]		X		X	X		1548
responso					X		1570
reyes	X	X	X	X		X	c1607–1629
Satanás	X			X			
sermón		X		X			1611
cuaresma	X	X	X	X	X		1550
David	X	X	X	X		X	1631
Joseph	X	X		X		X	1605
Judea	X		X			X	c1607–1629
luto							1574
misericordia							
santa cruz	X	X	X	X	X		c1607–1629
santo sacramento	X	X	X	X	X		1550
vino	X	X	X	X	X	X	1553
amén		X		X	X		1550
capítulo [chapter of a book]	X	X	X	X		X	c1607-29
chicharrones							
escribano		X			X		1547
escritura							1553
judiazos							
patriarcas	X	X	X	X		X	c1607–1629
profetas	X	X	X	X	X	X	c1607–1629
sacramento	X		X	X	X	X	1549
San Miguel arcángel		X	X	X			c1607–1629
1627 años							
alcalde		X	X	X			1547
angeles	X		X		X		1548
arzobispo			X	X	X		c1562–1569
Ave Maria	X	X	X	X		X	1570
Balaán	X			X		X	c1607–1629

Loans	Saha	Moli	Anun	Baut	León	Mija	First Appearance
bula				X	X		1570
conde							c1607–1629
corona	X	X	X	X		X	c1607–1629
cristiana			X				1658
Egipto	X	X	X	X		X	c1607–1629
emperador	X	X	X	X		X	1550
hora [unit of time]		X		X		X	c1607–1629
incienso	X			X			c1607–1629
Isaías	X			X	X	X	
Jacob	X		X	X	X	X	1631
Jesús, María y José							1695
Juicio Final							
loco							c1607–1629
Lorenzo	X		X				1550
maitines	X			X			1552
marqués							c1540
mesa		X		X		X	1550
Mesías				X			
mirra	X		X				c1607–1629
Moab				X		X	
Moría [mountain]							
obra de misericordia							
paje							c1607–1629
paraíso	X	X	X	X	X		
pasión [religious]	X	X		X		X	1614
Pater Noster	X	X	X	X			
Persia	X		X				c1607–1629
por amor de Dios							1608
prenda							1654
puerta	X			X	X		1581
rey	X	X	X	X		X	1550
Roma emperador, César de Agusto							
roque							
sacerdote	X	X	X	X		X	1552
Salve							
San Miguel	X		X				1549
santa bula			X		X		
santas							
Santísima Trinidad		X	X	X	X		1588
Santo Joseph	X			X			c1607–1629
santos	X	X		X	X	X	c1607–1629
semana santa							1570

Loans	Saha	Moli	Anun	Baut	León	Mija	First Appearance
Set							
surgite mortui							
venite a judicium							
testigos		X		X		X	1548

Legend:
- Saha = Sahagún 1548 (in Sell 1993) and Sahagún 1583.
- Moli = Molina 1984 and Molina 1578.
- Anun = Anunciación 1575 and Anunciación 1577.
- Baut = Bautista 1599, Bautista 1600b, Bautista 1605, and Bautista 1606.
- León = León 1611.
- Mija = Mijangos 1607 and Mijangos 1624.
- First Appearance = first appearance in a Nahua-generated text. Taken from Sell 1993, 312–15, 328–40; Karttunen and Lockhart 1976, 53–84; and Chimalpahin 1965, 37–146.

Appendix 4

SPANISH AND LATIN SPOKEN LOANS IN SEVEN NAHUATL PLAYS, IN DESCENDING ORDER OF FREQUENCY WITH FREQUENCY OF OCCURRENCE IN EACH OF THE SEVEN TRANSLATED PLAYS

Loans	3Kings	Isaac	Souls	Final	How to	Merchant	Don Sebastián
Dios	21	24	39	36	83	50	64
ánima	7	3	3	8	2	6	6
misa			18		2		2
Jesucristo			5	7	1	4	2
Lucifer			1	2			16
ánimas			15		2		
Herodes	17						
pesos [money]			1			16	
santa iglesia	1		4		2		7
tomín			3			10	
cruz	3		1	1	3	3	1
purgatorio			9		2		
ángel			1	1	6	1	1
diablo	2			1	3	3	1
Jesús			1	2	1	1	4
Santa María			1	1	4	3	
cuenta [accounting]				6	1		1
Isaac		8					
Jerusalén	7				1		
juez			4	2			2
cristiano			2	2		1	2
Espíritu Santo				1	3	3	
Abrahán	1	5					
judíos	6						

318—APPENDIXES

Loans	3Kings	Isaac	Souls	Final	How to	Merchant	Don Sebastián
rosario			2		4		
tomines						6	
domingo [unit of time]			3				2
gracia	1			1	2	1	
juramento			1			3	1
justicia						3	2
testamento						5	
Belén	4						
Belcebú							4
Cristo			4				
gloria			2	2			
Israel	3						1
peso [money]						4	
responso			4				
reyes	4						
Satanás							4
sermón			1		3		
cuaresma			1				2
David	3						
Joseph	3						
Judea	3						
luto			3				
misericordia			3				
santa cruz					2	1	
santo sacramento				3			
vino			3				
amén	2						
capítulo [chapter of a book]	2						
chicharrones	2						
escribano						2	
escritura						2	
judiazos	2						
patriarcas	2						
profetas	2						
sacramento				2			
San Miguel arcángel			1	1			
1627 años						1	
alcalde						1	
angeles						1	
arzobispo							1
Ave Maria			1				
Balaán	1						

Loans	3Kings	Isaac	Souls	Final	How to	Merchant	Don Sebastián
bula			1				
conde							1
corona					1		
cristiana				1			
Egipto	1						
emperador							1
hora [unit of time]				1			
incienso	1						
Isaías	1						
Jacob	1						
Jesús, María y José	1						
Juicio Final				1			
loco						1	
Lorenzo					1		
maitines	1						
marqués							1
mesa		1					
Mesías	1						
mirra	1						
Moab	1						
María [mountain]		1					
obra de misericordia							
paje							1
paraíso				1			
pasión [religious]				1			
Pater Noster			1				
Persia	1						
por amor de Dios						1	
prenda						1	
puerta							1
rey							1
Roma emperador, César de Agusto	1						
roque							1
sacerdote	1						
Salve					1		
San Miguel				1			
santa bula			1				
santas				1			
Santísima Trinidad		1					
Santo Joseph	1						
santos				1			
semana santa							1

Loans	3Kings	Isaac	Souls	Final	How to	Merchant	Don Sebastián
Set	1						
surgite mortui venite a judicium				1			
testigos						1	
	37	7	32	25	24	28	30
TOTAL	113	43	140	86	132	135	135

Legend:

Loans = all 111 spoken Spanish and Latin loans in the seven translated plays.

3Kings = the frequency of occurrence of a particular loan in the play "The Three Kings."

Isaac = the frequency of occurrence of a particular loan in the play "The Sacrifice of Isaac."

Souls = the frequency of occurrence of a particular loan in the play "Souls and Testamentary Executors."

Final = the frequency of occurrence of a particular loan in the play "Final Judgment."

How to = the frequency of occurrence of a particular loan in the play "How to Live on Earth."

Merchant = the frequency of occurrence of a particular loan in the play "The Merchant."

Don Sebastián = the frequency of occurrence of a particular loan in the play "The Life of Don Sebastián."

Total = top number in plain font is total entries for that play and bottom number is total occurrences for that play.

REFERENCES

Adorno, Rolena. 1990. "Iconos de persuasión: La predicación y la política en el Perú colonial." In *Iconografía política del Nuevo Mundo,* ed. Mercedes López-Baralt, 27–49. Puerto Rico: EDUPR.
Anderson, Arthur J. O., Frances Berdan, and James Lockhart, eds. and trans. 1976. *Beyond the Codices: The Nahua View of Colonial Mexico.* Berkeley and Los Angeles: University of California Press.
Andrews, J. Richard. 1975. *Introduction to Classical Nahuatl.* Austin: University of Texas Press.
Anunciación, fray Domingo de la. 1565. *Doctrina christiana breve y compendiosa por vía de diálogo entre un maestro y un discípulo.* Mexico: Pedro Ocharte.
Anunciación, fray Juan de la. 1575. *Doctrina christiana muy complida.* Mexico: Pedro Balli.
———. 1577. *Sermonario en lengua mexicana.* Mexico: Antonio Ricardo.
Arenas, Pedro de. 1982. *Vocabulario manual en las lenguas castellana y mexicana.* Photoreproduction of the 1611 edition, with an introduction by Ascensión H. de León-Portilla. Mexico: Universidad Nacional Autónoma de México.
Arróniz, Othón. 1979. *Teatro de evangelización en Nueva España.* Mexico: Universidad Nacional Autónoma de México.
Augustine, Saint. 1950. *The City of God.* Translated by Marcus Dods, D.D. New York: Modern Library.
Bataillon, Marcel. 1966. *Erasmo y España.* Translated by Antonio Alatorre. Mexico: Fondo de Cultura Económica.
Baudot, Georges. 1976. *Utopie et histoire au Mexique: Les premiers chroniqueurs de la civilisation mexicaine (1520–1569).* Toulouse: Privat.
Bautista, fray Juan. 1599. *Confesionario en lengua mexicana y castellana.* Mexico: Melchor Ocharte.
———. 1600a. *Advertencias para los confesores de los naturales.* Mexico: Melchor Ocharte.
———. 1600b. *Huehuehtlahtolli: Pláticas morales de los indios para doctrina de sus hijos, en mexicano.* Mexico: [Melchor Ocharte?].
———. 1604. *Libro de la miseria y brevedad de la vida del hombre y de sus cuatro postrimerías, en lengua mexicana.* Mexico: Diego López Dávalos.
———. 1605. *Vida y milagros del bienaventurado San Antonio de Padua.* Mexico: Diego López Dávalos.
———. 1606. *Sermonario . . . en lengua mexicana.* Mexico: Diego López Dávalos.

Bazarte Martínez, Alicia. 1989. *Las cofradías de españoles en la Ciudad de México (1526–1860)*. Azcapotzalco: Universidad Autónoma Metropolitana.

Berceo, Gonzalo de. 1980. *Signos que aparecerán antes del Juicio Final*. Edited by Arturo M. Ramoneda. Madrid: Castalia.

Bevington, David. 1975. *Medieval Drama*. Boston: Houghton Mifflin.

Bhabha, Homi K. 1994. *The Location of Culture*. London: Routledge.

Bierhost, John. 1985. *Cantares Mexicanos: Songs of the Aztecs*. Stanford: Stanford University Press.

Braswell, Mary F. 1983. *The Medieval Sinner: Characterization and Confession in the Literature of the English Middle Ages*. Rutherford, N.J.: Fairleigh Dickinson University Press.

Breviarium romanum ex decreto SS. Concilii Tridentini. 1961. 2 vols. New York: Benziger Brothers.

Buber, Martin. 1968. *On the Bible*. New York: Schocken Books.

Burkhart, Louise M. 1989. *The Slippery Earth: Nahua-Christian Moral Dialogue in Sixteenth-Century Mexico*. Tucson: University of Arizona Press.

———. 1993. "The Cult of the Virgin of Guadalupe in Mexico." In *South and Meso-American Native Spirituality: From the Cult of the Feathered Serpent to the Theology of Liberation*, ed. Gary H. Gossen, 198–226. New York: Crossroad.

———. 1996. *Holy Wednesday: A Nahua Drama from Early Colonial Mexico*. Philadelphia: University of Pennsylvania Press.

———. 1999. "'Here Is Another Marvel': Marian Miracle Narratives in a Nahuatl Manuscript." In *Spiritual Encounters: Interactions between Christianity and Native Religions in Colonial America*, ed. Nicholas Griffiths and Fernando Cervantes, 91–115. Birmingham, England: University of Birmingham Press.

———. 2001. *Before Guadalupe: The Virgin Mary in Early Colonial Nahuatl Literature*. Albany: Institute for Mesoamerican Studies, State University of New York at Albany.

Carochi, Horacio. 1983. *Arte de la lengua mexicana*. Photoreproduction of the 1645 edition, with an introduction by Miguel León-Portilla. Mexico: Instituto de Investigaciones Filológicas, Instituto de Investigaciones Históricas, Universidad Nacional Autónoma de México.

Carrasco, David. 1990. *Religions of Mesoamerica: Cosmovision and Ceremonial Centers*. New York: HarperCollins.

Carrasco, Pedro. 1997. "Indian-Spanish Marriages in the First Century of the Colony." In *Indian Women of Early Mexico*, ed. Susan Schroeder, Stephanie Wood, and Robert Haskett, 87–103. Norman: University of Oklahoma Press.

Cartas de Indias. 1980. 3 vols. Mexico: M. A. Porrúa.

Chimalpahin Quauhtlehuanitzin, Don Domingo de San Antón Muñon. 1965. *Die Relationen Chimalpahin's zur Geschichte México's*. Edited by Günter Zimmermann. 2 vols. Hamburg: Cram, De Guyter.

———. 1997. *Codex Chimalpahin*. Volumes 1 and 2. Edited and translated by Arthur J. O. Anderson and Susan Schroeder. Norman: University of Oklahoma Press.

———. 1998. *Las ocho relaciones y el memorial de Colhuacan*. Edited and translated by Rafael Tena. 2 vols. Mexico: Consejo Nacional para las Culturas y las Artes.

Cilveti, Angel. 1977. *El demonio en el teatro de Calderón*. Valencia: Albatros.

———. 1989. "Teología dramatizada y teología dramática en los autos de Calderón," *Boletín Bibliográfico Menéndez y Pelayo* 45:139–77.

Clendinnen, Inga. 1991. *Aztecs: An Interpretation*. Cambridge, England: Cambridge University Press.

Cline, S. L., and Miguel León-Portilla, eds. and trans. 1984. *The Testaments of Culhuacan*. UCLA Nahuatl Studies Series No. 1. Los Angeles: UCLA Latin American Center Publications.

Cline, Sarah. 1986. *Colonial Culhuacan, 1580–1600: A Social History of an Aztec Town*. Albuquerque: University of New Mexico Press.

———. 1993. *The Book of Tributes: Early Sixteenth-Century Nahuatl Censuses from Morelos*. Nahuatl Studies Series No. 4. Los Angeles: UCLA Latin American Center Publications.

———. 1998. "Fray Alonso de Molina's Model Testament and Antecedents to Indigenous Wills in Spanish America." In Kellogg and Restall, 13–33.

———. 2000. "The Spiritual Conquest Reexamined: Baptism and Christian Marriage in Early Sixteenth-Century Mexico." In *The Church in Colonial Latin America*, ed. John F. Schwaller, 73–101. Wilmington, Del.: Scholarly Resources.

Códice franciscano, siglo XVI: Informe de la provincia del Santo Evangelio al visitador Lic. Juan de Ovando. 1941. Mexico: Salvador Chávez Hayhoe.

Córdoba, fray Pedro de. 1988. *Doctrina cristiana y cartas*. Santo Domingo: La Fundación Corripio.

Cornyn, John H., and Byron McAfee. 1944. "Tlacahuapahualiztli (Bringing Up Children)." *Tlalocan* 1:314–51.

Cortés y Zedeño, Jerónimo de Tomàs de Aquino. 1967. *Arte, vocabulario y confesionario en el idioma mexicano*. Photoreproduction of the 1765 edition. Guadalajara, Jalisco: Edmundo Aviña Levy.

Cotarelo y Mori, Emilio. 1904. *Bibliografía de las controversias sobre la licitud del teatro en España*. Madrid: Revista de Archivos, Bibliotecas y Museos.

Cuevas, Mariano. 1928. *Historia de la iglesia en México*. 3 vols. El Paso, Texas: Editorial "Revista Católica."

Cuevas García, Cristóbal. 1982. "Introducción." In fray Luis de León, *De los nombres de Cristo*, 13–129. Madrid: Cátedra.

Daniélou, Jean. 1964. *The Theology of Jewish Christianity*. Vol. 1. Translated by John A. Baker. Chicago: Henry Regnery.

Dávila Padilla, fray Agustín. 1955. *Historia de la fundación y discurso de la provincia de Santiago de Mexico, de la orden de predicadores*. Photoreproduction of the 1595 edition. Mexico: Editorial Academia Literaria.

Díaz Balsera, Viviana. 2001. "A Judeo-Christian Tlaloc or a Nahua Yahweh? Domination, Hybridity, and Continuity in the Nahua Evangelization Theater." *Colonial Latin American Review* 10:209–27.

Doctrina, evangelios y epístolas en nahuatl. N.d. Manuscript in the John Carter Brown Library, Brown University, Codex Indianorum 7.

Doctrina cristiana en lengua española y mexicana, por los religiosos de la orden de Santo Domingo. 1944. Photoreproduction of the 1548 edition. Madrid: Ediciones Cultura Hispánica.

Doctrina cristiana en lengua mexicana. 1548. Mexico: Juan Pablos.

Durán, fray Diego de. 1971. *Book of the Gods and the Ancient Calendar*. Edited and translated by Fernando Horcasitas and Doris Heyden. Foreword by Miguel León-Portilla. Norman: University of Oklahoma Press.

Duverger, Christian. 1978. *L'esprit du jeu chez les Aztèques*. Paris: Mouton Editeur.

Eire, Carlos M. N. 1995. *From Madrid to Purgatory: The Art and Craft of Dying in Sixteenth-Century Spain*. Cambridge, England: Cambridge University Press.

Enders, Jody. 1999. *The Medieval Theater of Cruelty: Rhetoric, Memory, Violence*. Ithaca. Cornell University Press.

Escalona, fray Alonso de. N.d. *Sermones en mexicano*. Manuscript in the Biblioteca Nacional de México, Fondo Reservado, no. 1482.

Farmer, David Hugh. 1992. *The Oxford Dictionary of Saints*. Oxford: Oxford University Press.

Feijóo, fray Benito Jerónimo. 1958. *Teatro crítico universal*. Vol. 6. Madrid: Espasa-Calpe, S.A.

Fernández del Castillo, Francisco, ed. 1982. *Libros y libreros en el siglo XVI*. Reedition. Mexico: Fondo de Cultura Económica. Originally published 1914 in Mexico by the Archivo General de la Nación.

Fernández de Oviedo y Valdés, Gonzalo. 1959. *Historia general y natural de las Indias y Tierra Firme*. Edited by Juan Pérez de Tudela. Madrid: Atlas/B.A.E.

Flowers Broswell, Mary. 1983. *The Medieval Sinner: Characterization and Confession in the Literature of the English Middle Ages*. Rutherford, N.J.: Fairleigh Dickinson University Press.

Flynn, Maureen. 1994. "The Spectacle of Suffering in Spanish Streets." In *City and Spectacle in Medieval Europe,* ed. Barbara A. Hanawalt and Kathryn L. Reyerson, 153–68. Minneapolis: University of Minnesota Press.

Furst, Jill Leslie McKeever. 1995. *The Natural History of the Soul in Ancient Mexico.* New Haven: Yale University Press.

Gante, fray Pedro de. 1981. *Doctrina cristiana en lengua mexicana.* Photoreproduction of the 1553 edition. Edited by Ernesto de la Torre Villar. Mexico: Centro de Estudios Históricos Fray Bernardino de Sahagún and Editorial Jus.

García Icazbalceta, Joaquín. 1877. "Representaciones religiosas en México en el siglo XVI." In Fernán González de Eslava, *Coloquios espirituales y sacramentales.* Mexico.

———. 1954. *Bibliografía mexicana del siglo XVI.* Mexico: Fondo de Cultura Económica.

———. 1968. "Representaciones religiosas de México en el siglo XVI." In *Obras de D. J. García Icazbalceta,* vol. 2. New York: Burt Franklin.

Garibay K., Angel María. 1953–1954. *Historia de la literatura náhuatl.* 2 vols. Mexico: Editorial Porrúa.

Gibson, Charles. 1964. *The Aztecs under Spanish Rule.* Stanford: Stanford University Press.

Graef, Hilda. 1963–1965. *Mary: A History of Doctrine and Devotion.* 2 vols. New York: Sheed and Ward.

Grijalva, fray Juan de. 1624. *Crónica de la orden de N. P. S. Augustin en las provincias de la Nueva España.* Mexico: Juan Ruiz.

———. 1985. *Crónica de la Orden de N.P.S. Agustín en las provincias de la Nueva España.* Original edition 1624. Mexico: Porrúa.

Gruzinski, Serge. 1988. *La colonisation de l'imaginaire: Sociétés indigènes et occidentalisation dans le Mexique espagnol, 16e–18e siècle.* Paris: Editions Gallimard.

Gurevich, Aron. 1993. *Medieval Popular Culture: Problems of Belief and Perception.* Translated by Paul A. Hollingsworth. Cambridge, England: Cambridge University Press.

Harris, John Wesley. 1992. *Medieval Theatre in Context: An Introduction.* London and New York: Routledge.

Hill, Jane H., and Kenneth C. Hill. 1986. *Speaking Mexicano: Dynamics of Syncretic Language in Central Mexico.* Tucson: University of Arizona Press.

Homza, Lu Ann. 1999. "The European Link to Mexican Penance." In Sell and Schwaller, 33–48.

Horcasitas Pimentel, Fernando. 1948. "Piezas teatrales en lengua náhuatl." *Boletín Bibliográfico de Antropología Americana* 11:154–64.

———. 1962. "Textos de Xaltepoxtla, Puebla." *Estudios de Cultura Náhuatl* 2:83–91.

———. 1967. "Los xoxocoteros: Una farsa indígena." *Estudios de Cultura Náhuatl* 7:225–32.

———. 1968. *De Porfirio Díaz a Zapata: Memoria náhuatl de Milpa Alta.* Foreword by Miguel León-Portilla. Mexico: Universidad Nacional Autónoma de México.

———. 1972a. "El entremés del Señor de Yencuictlalpan, una farsa en náhuatl." *Anales de Antropología* 9:125–41.

———. 1972b. *Life and Death in Milpa Alta: A Nahuatl Chronicle of Díaz and Zapata.* Norman: University of Oklahoma Press.

———. 1974. *El teatro náhuatl: Épocas novohispana y moderna.* Mexico: Universidad Nacional Autónoma de México.

———. 1977. "Para la historia de Tlalocan." *Tlalocan* 7:11–19.

———. 1980. "La danza de los tecuanes." *Estudios de Cultura Náhuatl* 14:239–86.

Horcasitas Pimentel, Fernando, and Bente Bittmann Simons. 1974. "Anales jeroglíficos e históricos de Tepeaca." *Anales de Antropología* 11:225–94.

Horcasitas Pimentel, Fernando, and Wanda Tommasi de Magrelli. 1975. "El Códice de Tzictepec, una nueva fuente pictórica indígena." *Anales de Antropología* 12:243–72.

Horcasitas Pimentel, Fernando, and Sara O. de Ford. 1979. *Los cuentos en náhuatl de doña Luz Jiménez.* Mexico: Universidad Nacional Autónoma de México.

Horn, Rebecca. 1997a. "Gender and Social Identity." In *Indian Women of Early Mexico*, ed. Susan Schroeder, Stephanie Wood, and Robert Haskett, 105–22. Norman: University of Oklahoma Press.

———. 1997b. *Postconquest Coyoacan: Nahua-Spanish Relations in Central Mexico, 1519–1650*. Stanford: Stanford University Press.

———. 1998. "Testaments and Trade: Interethnic Ties among Petty Traders in Central Mexico (Coyoacan, 1550–1620)." In Kellogg and Restall, 59–83.

Hunter, William H. 1960. *The Calderonian Auto Sacramental El Gran Teatro del Mundo: An Edition and Translation of a Nahuatl Version*. In *Middle American Research Institute Publication 27*, 105–202. New Orleans: Tulane University.

The Interpreter's Bible. 1952. Edited by Nolan B. Harmon. 12 vols. New York: Abingdon.

Israel, Jonathan I. 1975. *Race, Class, and Politics in Colonial Mexico*. Oxford, England: Oxford University Press.

Karttunen, Frances. 1982. "Nahuatl Literacy." In *The Inca and Aztec States, 1400–1800: Anthropology and History*, ed. George A. Collier, Renato I. Rosaldo, and John D. Wirth, 395–417. New York: Academic Press.

———. 1983. *An Analytical Dictionary of Nahuatl*. Austin: University of Texas Press.

———. 1985. *Nahuatl and Maya in Contact with Spanish*. Texas Linguistic Forum 26. Austin: Department of Linguistics, University of Texas.

———. 1992. *An Analytical Dictionary of Nahuatl*. Norman: University of Oklahoma Press.

Karttunen, Frances, and James Lockhart. 1976. *Nahuatl in the Middle Years: Language Contact Phenomena in Texts of the Colonial Period*. University of California Publications in Linguistics 85. Berkeley and Los Angeles: University of California Press.

———, eds. 1987. *The Art of Nahuatl Speech: The Bancroft Dialogues*. Nahuatl Studies Series No. 2. Los Angeles: UCLA Latin American Center Publications.

Kellogg, Susan. 1998. "Indigenous Testaments of Early-Colonial Mexico City: Testifying to Gender Differences." In Kellogg and Restall, 37–58.

Kellogg, Susan, and Matthew Restall, eds. 1998. *Dead Giveaways: Indigenous Testaments of Colonial Mesoamerica and the Andes*. Salt Lake City: University of Utah Press.

Klor de Alva, Jorge. 1982. "Spiritual Conflict and Accommodation in New Spain: Toward a Typology of Aztec Responses to Christianity." In *The Inca and Aztec States, 1400–1800: Anthropology and History*, ed. George A Collier, Renato I. Rosaldo, and John D. Wirth, 345–65. New York: Academic Press.

———. 1993. "Aztec Spirituality and Nahuatized Christianity." In *South and Meso-American Native Spirituality: From the Cult of the Feathered Serpent to the Theology of Liberation*, ed. Gary H. Gossen, 173–97. New York: Crossroad.

Krickeberg, Walter. 1961. *Las antiguas culturas mexicanas*. Translated by Sita Garst and Jasmín Reuter. Mexico: Fondo de Cultura Económica.

Kuschel, Karl Josef. 1995. *Abraham*. Translated by John Bowden. New York: Continuum.

Lachowski, Joseph Michael. 1967. "Guilt (in the Bible)." In *New Catholic Encyclopedia* 6:850–52. New York: McGraw.

Las Casas, fray Bartolomé de. 1967. *Apologética historia sumaria*. 2 vols. Edited by Edmundo O'Gorman. Mexico: Universidad Nacional Autónoma de México, Instituto de Investigaciones Históricas.

———. 1995. *Historia de las Indias*. 3 vols. Edited by Agustín Millares Carlo. Mexico: Fondo de Cultura Económica.

Launey, Michel. 1979. *Introduction à la langue et à la littérature aztèques*. Paris: L'Harmattan.

León, fray Martín de. 1611. *Camino del cielo en lengua mexicana*. Mexico: Diego López Dávalos.

———. 1614a. *Manual breve y forma de administrar los Santos Sacramentos a los indios universalmente*. Mexico: Imprenta de María de Espinosa.

———. 1614b. *Primera parte del Sermonario del tiempo de todo el año, duplicado, en lengua mexicana.* Mexico: Imprenta de la Viuda de Diego López Dávalos, por C. Adriano César.

León-Portilla, Ascensión H. de. 1988. *Tepuztlahcuilolli / Impresos en náhuatl / Historia y bibliografía.* 2 vols. Mexico: Instituto de Investigaciones Históricas, Instituto de Investigaciones Filológicas, Universidad Nacional Autónoma de México.

León-Portilla, Miguel. 1974. "Testimonios nahuas sobre la conquista espiritual." *Estudios de Cultura Náhuatl* 11:11–36.

———. 1982. "Fernando Horcasitas Pimentel en la historia de Tlalocan." *Tlalocan* 9:11–40.

Leyva, Juan. 2001. *La pasión de Ozumba: El teatro religioso tradicional en el siglo XVIII novohispano.* Mexico: Universidad Nacional Autónoma de México.

"The Life of Don Sebastián." 1 April 1692. Nahuatl manuscript held by the Academy of American Franciscan History. 29 pages. Berkeley, California.

Llaguno, José A. 1962. *La personalidad jurídica del indio y el III Concilio Provincial Mexicano (1585): Ensayo historico-jurídico de los documentos originales.* Mexico: Editorial Porrúa.

———. 1983. *La personalidad jurídica del indio y el III Concilio Provincial Mexicano (1585): Ensayo histórico-jurídico de los documentos originales.* Mexico: Editorial Porrúa.

Lockhart, James. 1991. *Nahuas and Spaniards: Postconquest Central Mexican History and Philology.* Stanford: Stanford University Press.

———. 1992. *The Nahuas after the Conquest: A Social and Cultural History of the Indians of Central Mexico, Sixteenth Through Eighteenth Centuries.* Stanford: Stanford University Press.

———. 1999. *Of Things of the Indies: Essays Old and New in Early Latin American History.* Stanford: Stanford University Press.

Lockhart, James, Frances Berdan, and Arthur J. O. Anderson. 1986. *The Tlaxcalan Actas: A Compendium of the Records of the Cabildo of Tlaxcala (1545–1627).* Salt Lake City: University of Utah Press.

Lopétegui, León y Félix Zubillaga. 1965. *Historia de la Iglesia en la América Española.* Madrid: Biblioteca de Autores Cristianos.

López Austin, Alfredo. 1977. *Tamoanchan, Tlalocan.* Translated by Bernard R. Ortiz de Montellano and Thelma Ortiz de Montellano. Niwot: University Press of Colorado.

———. 1984. *Cuerpo humano e ideología.* 2 vols. Mexico: Universidad Nacional Autónoma de México.

———. 1988. *The Human Body and Ideology.* Translated by Thelma Ortiz de Montellano and Bernardo Ortiz de Montellano. Salt Lake City: University of Utah Press.

Lorra Baquío, Francisco de. 1634. *Manual mexicano de la administración de los santos sacramentos conforme al manual toledano.* Mexico: Diego Gutiérrez.

Mansfield, Mary C. 1994. *The Humiliation of Sinners: Public Penance in Thirteenth-Century France.* Ithaca, N.Y.: Cornell University Press.

Matos Moctezuma, Eduardo. 1984. "The Templo Mayor of Tenochtitlan: Economics and Ideology." In *Ritual Human Sacrifice in Mesoamerica,* ed. Elizabeth Hill Boone, 133–64. Washington, D.C.: Dumbarton Oaks.

McAfee, Byron, and Robert H. Barlow. 1947. "Un cuaderno de Marqueses." *El México Antiguo* 6:392–404.

McGinn, Bernard. 1994. *Antichrist: Two Thousand Years of the Human Fascination with Evil.* San Francisco: Harper.

McMillen Villar, Susan. 1993. *Drama and the Theater in the Millenarian Project of the Franciscans in New Spain.* Ph.D. diss.: University of Minnesota.

McNeill, John T., and Helena M. Gamer. 1990. *Medieval Handbooks of Penance.* New York: Columbia University Press.

Mendieta, fray Gerónimo de. 1980. *Historia eclesiástica indiana.* Edited by Joaquín García Icazbalceta. Third edition. Mexico: Editorial Porrúa.

———. 1988. "Informe biográfico y lingüístico del P. Jerónimo de Mendieta, OFM, sobre los 238 franciscanos pertenecientes a la provincia del Santo Evangelio de Méjico." *Archivo Ibero-Americano*, segunda época, 48:557–68.
Mijangos, fray Juan de. 1607. *Espejo divino en lengua mexicana*. Mexico: Diego López Dávalos.
———. 1624. *Sermonario*. Mexico: Juan de Alcázar.
Miller, Mary, and Karl Taube. 1993. *The Gods and Symbols of Ancient Mexico and the Maya: An Illustrated Dictionary of Mesoamerican Religion*. London: Thames and Hudson.
Molina, fray Alonso de. 1552. *Ordenanzaz para aprovechar los cofradias que han de servir en estos hospitales*. Manuscript no. M-M 455 in the Bancroft Library of the University of California, Berkeley. Included in full transcription and translation in Sell, Barry D., ed. and trans. 2002. *Nahua Confraternities in Early Colonial Mexico: The 1552 Nahuatl Ordinances of fray Alonso de Molina, OFM*. Academy of American Franciscan History, pp. 82–141.
———. 1555. *Vocabulario en la lengua castellana y mexicana*. Mexico: Juan Pablos.
———. 1565. *Confesionario breve*. Mexico: Antonio de Espinosa.
———. 1578. *Doctrina cristiana en lengua mexicana*. Mexico: Pedro Ocharte.
———. 1977. *Vocabulario en la lengua castellana y mexicana y mexicana y castellana*. Reedition of the 1571 edition. With a preliminary study by Miguel León-Portilla. 2nd edition. Mexico: Editorial Porrúa.
———. 1984. *Confessionario mayor, en lengua Mexicana*. Photoreproduction of the 1569 edition. Mexico: Universidad Nacional Autónoma de México.
Most, W. G. "Grace (in the Bible)." 1967. In *New Catholic Encyclopedia* 6:672–74. New York: McGraw.
Motolinia, fray Toribio de Benavente. 1951. *History of the Indians of New Spain*. Translated by Francis Borgia Steck. Washington: Academy of American Franciscan History.
———. 1979. *Historia de los indios de la Nueva España*. Edited by Edmundo O'Gorman. Mexico: Editorial Porrúa.
———. 1985. *Historia de los indios de la Nueva España*. Edited by Georges Baudot. Madrid. Castalia.
———. 1996. *Memoriales*. Edited by Nancy Joe Dyer. Mexico: El Colegio de México.
Muñoz Camargo, Diego. 1981. *Descripción de la ciudad y provincia de Tlaxcala de las Indias y del mar océano para el buen gobierno y ennoblecimiento dellas*. Edited by René Acuña. Mexico: University Nacional Autónoma de México.
———. 1986. *Historia de Tlaxcala*. Edited by Germán Vázquez. Madrid: Historia 16.
Nacar Fuster, D. Eloino, and Alberto Colunga, O. P. 1961. *Misal ritual latino-español y devocionario*. Barcelona: Vallés.
Nalle, Sara T. 1999. "Printing and Reading Popular Religious Texts in Sixteenth-Century Spain." In *Culture and the State in Spain: 1550–1850*, ed. Tom Lewis and Francisco J. Sánchez, 126–56. New York: Garland.
The New International Dictionary of New Testament Theology. 1975. 3 vols. Edited by Colin Brown. Grand Rapids, Mich.: Zondervan.
Nicholson, Henry B. 1971. "Religion in Pre-Hispanic Central Mexico." In *Handbook of Middle American Indians* 10:395–446. Austin: University of Texas Press.
Nietzsche, Friedrich. 1956. *The Genealogy of Morals*. New York: Doubleday Anchor.
Offutt, Leslie S. 1992. "Levels of Acculturation in Northeastern New Spain: San Esteban Testaments of the Seventeenth and Eighteenth Centuries." *Estudios de Cultura Náhuatl* 22:409–43.
Ortiz de Montellano, Bernard R. 1990. *Aztec Medicine, Health, and Nutrition*. New Brunswick: Rutgers University Press.
Paso y Troncoso, Francisco del. 1890. *Invención de la Santa Cruz por Santa Elena*. Mexico: Museo Nacional.
———. 1899. *El sacrificio de Isaac*. In *Biblioteca Náhuatl I*. Florencia: Tipografía de Salvador Landi.

———. 1900a. "Comedies en langue nahuatl: Une petite vieille et le gamin, son petit fils." Congres International des Americanistes (Paris), 309–16.

———. 1900b. *La adoración de los Reyes*. In *Biblioteca Náhuatl II*. Florencia: Tipografía de Salvador Landi.

———. 1902. *La comedia de los Reyes*. In *Biblioteca Náhuatl VI*, cuaderno 3. Florencia: Tipografía de Salvador Landi.

———. 1907. *La destrucción de Jerusalén*. In *Biblioteca Náuatl I*, cuaderno 4. Florence: Tipografía de Salvador Landi.

Potter, Robert. 1986. "Abraham and Human Sacrifice: The Exfoliation of Medieval Drama in Aztec Mexico." *New Theater Quarterly* 2:306–12.

Procesos de indios idólatras y hechiceros. 1912. Directed by Luis González Obregón. Mexico: Publicaciones del Archivo General de la Nación.

Ramoneda, Arturo M., ed. 1980. "Introducción." In *Signos que aparecerán antes del Juicio Final*. Madrid: Clásicos Castalia.

Ravicz, Marilyn Ekdahl. 1970. *Early Colonial Religious Drama in Mexico: From Tzompantli to Golgotha*. Washington, D.C.: Catholic University of America Press.

Read, Kay Almere. 1998. *Time and Sacrifice in the Aztec Cosmos*. Bloomington and Indianapolis: Indiana University Press.

"Las representaciones teatrales de la Pasión." 1934. In *Bolétin del Archivo General de la Nación*, 332–56. Mexico: Talleres Gráficos de la Nación.

Reyes García, Luis, Eustaquio Celestino Solís, Armando Valencia Ríos, Constantino Medina Lima, and Gregorio Guerrero Díaz, eds. and trans. 1996. *Documentos nahuas de la ciudad de México del siglo XVI*. Mexico: Centro de Investigaciones y Estudios Superiores en Antropología Social and Archivo General de la Nación.

Ricard, Robert. 1966. *The Spiritual Conquest of Mexico: An Essay on the Apostolate and the Evangelizing Methods of the Mendicant Orders in New Spain: 1523–1572*. Translated by Lesley Byrd Simpson. Berkeley and Los Angeles: University of California Press.

———. 1991. *La conquista espiritual de México*. Translated by Ángel M. Garibay. Mexico: Fondo de Cultura Económica.

Rojas Garcidueñas, José J. 1935. *El teatro de Nueva España en el siglo XVI*. Mexico: Published by the author.

Román Bellereza, Juan Alberto. 1987. "Offering 48 of the Templo Mayor: A Case of Child Sacrifice." In *The Aztec Templo Mayor*, ed. Elizabeth Hill Boone, 131–43. Washington, D.C.: Dumbarton Oaks.

Rouanet, Léo, ed. 1979. *Colección de autos, farsas y coloquios del siglo XVI*. 4 vols. Hildersheim, N.Y.: George Olms.

Rubial García, Antonio. 1997. "Los santos milagreros y malogrados de la Nueva España." In *Manifestaciones religiosas en el mundo americano*, ed. Manuel Ramos Medina and Clara García Ayluardo, 51–87. Mexico: Universidad Iberoamericana.

Sahagún, fray Bernardino de. 1563. *Sermonario de dominicas y de sanctos en lengua mexicana*. Manuscript no. 1485, Ayer Collection, Newberry Library, Chicago.

———. 1583. *Psalmodia cristiana*. Mexico: Pedro Ocharte.

———. 1950–1982. *Florentine Codex, General History of the Things of New Spain*. Edited and translated by Arthur J. O. Anderson and Charles E. Dibble. Santa Fe, N.M.: School of American Research and University of Utah.

———. 1986. *Coloquios y doctrina cristiana*. Edited and translated by Miguel León-Portilla. Mexico: Universidad Nacional Autónoma de México.

———. 1989. *Historia general de las cosas de la Nueva España*. 2 vols. Edited by Alfredo López Austin and Josefina García Quintana. Mexico: Alianza Editorial Mexicana.

———. 1990. *Historia general de las cosas de la Nueva España*. 2 vols. Edited by Juan Carlos Temprano. Madrid: Historia 16.

———. 1993a. *Adiciones, apéndice a la postilla, y ejercicio cotidiano*. Edited by Arthur J. O. Anderson. Mexico: Universidad Nacional Autónoma de México.

———. 1993b. *Psalmodia Christiana (Christian Psalmody)*. Edited and translated by Arthur J. O. Anderson. Salt Lake City: University of Utah Press.

———. 1997. *Primeros memoriales: Paleography of Nahuatl Text and English Translation*. Completed and revised, with additions, by H. B. Nicholson, Arthur J. O. Anderson, Charles E. Dibble, Eloise Quiñones Keber, and Wayner Ruwet. Norman: University of Oklahoma Press.

Schroeder, Susan. 2000. "Jesuits, Nahuas, and the Good Death Society in Mexico City, 1710–1767." *Hispanic American Historical Review* 80:43–76.

Schwaller, John Frederick. 1989. "Constitution of the Cofradía del Santissimo Sacramento of Tula, Hidalgo, 1570." *Estudios de Cultura Náhuatl* 19:217–44.

———. 1991. "Nahuatl Manuscripts in the John Carter Brown Library (Providence, Rhode Island)." *Estudios de Cultura Náhuatl* 21:311–24.

———. 1999. "Don Bartolomé de Alva, Nahuatl Scholar of the Seventeenth Century." In Sell and Schwaller, 3–15.

Sell, Barry D. 1988. "Linguistics as a Tool of Historical Analysis: Loanwords in Colonial Nahuatl Religious Plays." Unpublished paper.

———. 1993. *Friars, Nahuas, and Books: Language and Expression in Colonial Nahuatl Publications*. Ph.D. diss.: University of California at Los Angeles.

———. 1999. "The Classical Age of Nahuatl Publications and Don Bartolomé de Alva's Confessionario of 1634." In Sell and Schwaller, 17–32.

———. 2000. "Our Lady of Solitude of San Miguel Coyotlan, 1619: A Rare Set of Cofradía Rules in Nahuatl." *Estudios de Cultural Náhuatl* 31:331–58.

Sell, Barry D., and Susan Kellogg. 1997. "We Want to Give Them Laws: Royal Ordinances in a Mid-Sixteenth Century Nahuatl Text." *Estudios de Cultural Náhuatl* 27:325–67.

Sell, Barry D., and John Frederick Schwaller, with Lu Ann Homza, eds. and trans. 1999. Don Bartolomé de Alva, *Guide to Confession Large and Small in the Mexican Language*. Critical edition of the 1634 edition. Norman: University of Oklahoma Press.

Sermones y santoral en mexicano. N.d. Manuscript no. 464 in the Bancroft Library, University of California at Berkeley.

Siker, Jeffrey S. 1991. *Disinheriting the Jew*. Louisville: Westminster/John Knox Press.

Siméon, Rémi. 1977. *Diccionario de la lengua nahuatl o mexicana*. Translated by Josefina Oliva de Coll. Mexico: Siglo Ventiuno.

———. 1988. *Diccionario de la lengua nahuatl o mexicana*. Mexico: Siglo Ventiuno.

Solís, Eustaquio Celestino, Armando Valencia R., and Constantino Medina Lima, eds. and trans. 1985. *Actas de cabildo de Tlaxcala, 1547–1567*. Mexico: Archivo General de la Nación, Instituto Tlaxcalteca de la Cultura, and Centro de Investigaciones y Estudios Superiores de Antropología Social.

Sousa, Lisa, Stafford Poole, C.M., and James Lockhart, eds. and trans. 1998. *The Story of Guadalupe: Luis Laso de la Vega's Huei Tlamahuiçoltica of 1649*. Stanford: Stanford University Press.

Soustelle, Jacques. 1955. *La vie quotidienne des aztèques à la veille de la conquète espagnole*. Paris: Hachette.

Sten, María. 1982. *Vida y muerte del teatro náhuatl*. Xalapa, Mexico: Biblioteca Universidad Veracruzana.

Sten, María, Oscar Armando García, and Alejandro Ortiz Bullé-Goyri, eds. 2000. *El teatro franciscano en la Nueva España: Fuentes y ensayos para el estudio del teatro de evangelización en el siglo XVI*. Mexico: Universidad Nacional Autónoma de México and Consejo Nacional para la Cultura y las Artes.

Stern, Charlotte. 1996. *The Medieval Theatre in Castille*. Binghamton, N.Y.: Center for Medieval and Renaissance Studies, SUNY.

Sullivan, Thelma D. 1987. *Documentos tlaxcaltecas del siglo XVI en lengua náhuatl*. Mexico: Universidad Nacional Autónoma de México.

Sumario de las Indulgencias concedidas a los cofrades del sanctissimo sacramento. 1584. Mexico: Pedro Balli.

Taix, Hieronimo. 1576. *Institucion, modo de rezar, y milagros e indulgencias del rosario de la Virgen Maria, nuestro Señora*. Edited by Domingo de Salazar. Mexico.

Taylor, William. 1996. *Magistrates of the Sacred*. Stanford: Stanford University Press.

Tentler, Thomas N. 1977. *Sin and Confession on the Eve of the Reformation*. New Jersey: Princeton University Press.

"Three Indian Dramas." Manuscript owned by the Clements Library, University of Michigan. 52 folios. Contains three plays: "The Three Kings," "The Sacrifice of Isaac," and "Souls and Testamentary Executors." The last concludes with the date 1 February 1760. Ann Arbor, Michigan.

"Three Plays." Manuscript owned by the Library of Congress. 53 folios. Contains three plays: "Final Judgment," "How to Live on Earth" [two copies], and "The Merchant." The last begins with the date 15 November 1687. Washington, D.C.

Torquemada, fray Juan de. 1986. *Monarquía indiana*. 3 vols. Introduction by Miguel León-Portilla. Mexico: Porrúa.

Vetancurt, fray Agustín de. 1982. *Teatro mexicano, Crónica de la provincia del Santo Evangelio de México, Menologio franciscano*. Photoreproduction of the 1698 edition. Mexico: Editorial Porrúa.

Vollert, C. 1967. "Transubstantiation." In *New Catholic Encyclopedia* 14:259–61. New York: McGraw-Hill.

Weckmann, Luis. 1984. *La herencia medieval de México*. 2 vols. Mexico: El Colegio de México.

Williams, Jerry. 1992. *El teatro del México colonial: Época misionera*. New York: Peter Lang.

Wood, Stephanie. 1991. "Adopted Saints: Christian Images in Nahua Testaments of Late Colonial Toluca." *The Americas* 47:259–294.

———. 1998. "Testaments and Títulos: Conflict and Coincidence of Cacique and Community Interests in Central Mexico." In Kellogg and Restall, 85–111.

Zumthor, Paul. 1972. *Essai de poétique médiévale*. Paris: Éditions du Seuil.

INDEX

Abraham, 12, 16, 86–88, 90–101, 103–108, 108n3, 109n8, 109n10, 110n19, 110n20, 136–37, 146–61
Academy of American Franciscan History, 4, 26n11, 268
Accounting (made at judgment), 13, 46, 52; in plays, 63, 164–65, 192–93, 198–99, 202–203
Actopan, 34, 39
Adam, 33, 81n18, 83n33, 219
"Adoración de los reyes." *See* "Three Kings, The"
Adorno, Rolena, 78
Advent, 42, 71, 97, 109n15
Afterlife: Nahua concepts of, 30, 32, 71; Spanish/Christian concepts of, 30
Akedah, 85–111
Alcalde, 5, 21; character in "The Merchant," 21, 66, 254–57
Alcohol. *See* Drunkenness
Alfonso X, King, 59
Altepetl, 5, 16–18, 25n4, 28n41; in plays, 118–33, 137n44, 141n56, 154–55, 224–25, 250–51, 290–91, 294–95
Alva [Ixtlilxochitl], don Bartolomé de, confession manual of, 18, 21, 22, 33, 48
Andrew, Saint, 97
Angels, 31, 63; as characters in "Final Judgment, 200–203; as characters in "How to Live on Earth," 210–41; as characters in "The Life of Don Sebastián," 274–87, 290–93, 300–301; as characters in "The Merchant," 262–65; as characters in "The Sacrifice of Isaac," 12, 92, 93, 148–49, 160–63; as characters in "Souls and Testamentary Executors," 172–75; guardian angel, 45, 174–75, 202–203, 262–65
Antichrist, 72; as character in "Final Judgment," 75, 198–203; *Play of Antichrist*, 72
Anunciación, fray Domingo de la, 50
Anunciación, fray Juan de la, 32, 33, 36, 37, 38, 41–42, 48
Aranda, Council of, 59
Arróniz, Othón, 74, 83n36
Ars moriendi, 48–49
Articles of Faith, 39
Ash Wednesday, 33, 220–21
Augustine, Saint, 88, 92, 97, 98, 104, 110n18, 111n26
Augustinians, 50, 71
Augustus, Caesar, 126–27

Balaam, 124–25
Balak, 125n18
Balthasar, 12, 119n2, 132–33, 142–43
Bancroft Dialogues, 14, 119n6, 137n42
Baptism, 37–38, 48

Baudot, Georges, 79n6
Bautista (Viseo), fray Juan, 13, 15, 26n13, 96–97, 115; "Book of the Misery and Brevity of the Life of Man" of, 38, 43; confession manual of, 22, 24; *contemptus mundi* of, 38; "Life of Saint Anthony of Padua" of, 13; *Sermonario* of, 15, 18, 27n36, 42–43, 96–101, 110n21, 137n48
Bells, rung for dead, 47, 50, 176–81, 184–85, 264–65
Berceo, Gonzalo de, 73
Bevington, David, 66, 78, 81n21
Bhabha, Homi, 108
Bloodletting, 68, 69
Body: Nahua concepts of, 31, 44; Spanish/Christian concepts of, 33
Bones, 30, 31, 200–201, 220–23, 232–33, 236–37, 282–89
Braswell, Mary F., 81n19
Burials, 36, 43–47, 50, 238–39, 264–65

Cabildo (town council), 5, 14, 17, 24
Calpan, San Andrés, 12, 23, 39, 201n18
Calpolli, 16
Cantares mexicanos, 135n40
Carochi, Horacio, 14, 27n33, 165n1, 199n15
Casper, 12, 118–19, 130–31, 136–39
Cauli, Giovanni da, 106
Chalco, 60, 61
Charles V, King, 61
Chichimecs, 62
Chimalpahin Quauhtlehuaniztin, Don Domingo de San Antón Muñon, 13, 79n2
Christ: in Calpan sculpture, 12; as character in plays, 76, 180–81, 186–87, 200–207, 238–41, 278–83, 295–301; as judge, 39–43, 52, 64; Passion of, 34–35, 60, 103–105, 106, 111n26, 228–29; as redeemer, 101–102
Cipactonal, 102
Clements Library, 4, 26n11, 118, 146, 164
Clendinnen, Inga, 92
Cline, Sarah, 47–48
Commandments of the Church, 32, 66, 82n26, 184–87
Communion, in the plays, 172–73, 184–89, 234–35, 258–59
Confession, 32, 36, 48, 50, 53n6, 63, 64, 69, 73, 81n19; in the plays, 51, 65, 196–99, 222–25, 32–35, 258–63, 274–79, 284–85, 296–97; preconquest rite of, 64, 69

Confession manuals, 4, 18, 21, 22, 24, 28n44, 57. *See also* Alva, Bautista, Molina
Confraternities, 49–51, 53n17, 60–61; confraternity of the rosary, 49–50; confraternity of souls in purgatory, 50, 61
"Conquest of Jerusalem, The," 74
Córdoba, fray Pedro de, 90
Cornyn, John H., 4, 81n16, 109n6
Cortés, Hernando, 61, 62, 81n18
Cortés y Zedeño, Jerónimo Tomás de Aquino, 25
Council of 1642, 58
Culhuacan, 22, 23, 24, 32, 45, 48

Dances, 59
David, King, 128–29, 136–37
Dead, as characters in "Final Judgment," 200–203; service to, 51–52, 63, 68–69, 164–89
Death: as character in "Final Judgment," 75, 82n29, 194–95; as character in "How to Live on Earth," 232–33; as character in "The Life of Don Sebastián," 31, 82n29, 272–73, 280–83, 286–87, 290–99; as character in plays, 30, 52; friars' teachings on, 32–39; Nahua views of, 29; Nahuas' visions of, 32; Nahuatl guidebooks for, 48–49; Spanish/Christian views of, 29, 30, 33–39
Demons and devils, 29, 32, 34, 70, 75, 77, 262–63, 268–69; as characters in "Final Judgment," 32, 63, 76–77, 202–207; as characters in "The Sacrifice of Isaac," 148–51; as characters in "Souls and Testamentary Executors," 166–77, 180–81, 186–89; as characters in "How to Live on Earth," 214–29, 234–35, 240–41, 258–65, 274–79, 282–301; as characters in plays, 51, 70. *See also* Lucifer, Satan, Tzitzimitl
Disease. *See* Epidemics, Sickness
Dominicans, 26; *Doctrina cristiana* of, 9, 35, 36, 39, 81n18
Drunkenness, 22, 51, 176–79, 182–83, 268–69, 296–97
Duverger, Christian, 68

Eden, 76
Eire, Carlos, 29
Enders, Jody, 64
Epidemics, 18, 29, 62, 73, 101
Escalona, fray Alonso de, 32, 33
Eschatology, 61, 70, 71–72, 83n33

Eve, 33, 81n18, 83n33, 83n34
Extreme unction (last rites), 47–48, 53n14

Farmer, David Hugh, 119n2
Fasting, 69, 186–89, 192–93
Feijóo, fray Benito Jerónimo, 80n11
Fernández de Oviedo, Gonzalo, 74
Final Judgment, 12, 64, 71, 73, 77, 78, 190–209; in Indo-Christian art, 39; in Nahuatl doctrinal literature, 39–43
"Final Judgment," 39–43, 71–78, 82n28, 83n32, 83n36, 190–209; angels as characters in, 200–203; Antichrist as character in, 72, 198–203; authorship and date, 6, 10, 15; calque in, 13; characters in, 73, 74–76, 82n22, 82n30; Christ as character in, 200–207; confession in, 196–99; the dead as characters, 200–203; Death as a character in, 31, 194–95; demons as characters in, 202–207; eternal punishment given in, 51; fasting in, 192–93; fireworks in, 75, 198–203, 206–209; loanwords in, 12, 13; Lucifer/Satan as a character in, 32, 204–209; manuscripts and transcriptions of, 4, 7–8, 9; marriage as sacrament in, 192–95, 198–99, 204–209; orthography of, 26n14; Penance as character in, 190–91; priests as characters in, 18, 75, 196–99, 208–209; restitution in, 206–209; resurrection of dead in, 31; Saint Michael as a character in, 73, 74, 76, 190–191, 200–203; Sweeping as character in, 192–93; Tlatelolco performance of, 60, 74, 79n2, 83n36; violence in, 22, 76
Fiore, Joachim de, 73
Fireworks: used in plays, 31, 67, 69, 75, 180–81, 198–203, 206–209, 230–31, 264–65, 300–301
Fiscales, 47
Flynn, Maureen, 82n27
Francis, Saint, 18
Franciscans, 5, 9, 14, 50, 66, 71, 73, 74, 78, 93; first twelve missionaries in Mexico, 61, 62, 91, 108n5
Fuente, Agustín de la, 13, 18, 24, 26n13, 27n36, 38, 96, 115
Funerals. *See* Burials
Furst, Jill, 30

Gante, fray Pedro de, *Doctrina christiana* of, 39, 48–49

Gaona, Juan de, 110n23
García Icazbalceta, Joaquín, 81n18, 83n36
Garibay Kintana, Ángel María, 83n36, 89, 96
Gaspar, Don Joseph, 5–6, 242–43
Genesis, Book of, 33, 86, 93, 98
Gerona, Council of, 59
Gilberti, fray Maturino, 80n10
Good Death Society, 50–51
Gregory, Saint, 32
Gregory of Nisa, 104
Guilt, 65, 67, 82n27, 111n27
Gurevich, Aron, 56–57, 60, 80n7

Hagar, 12, 90, 108n3, 150–155
Hail Mary prayer, 35, 176–77, 208–209, 229n36
Hebrews, Book of, 88, 92
Hell, 35, 36, 43, 53n9, 71, 72, 76, 186–87. *See also* Mictlan
Herod, 12, 13, 27, 118–31, 144–45
Holy Sacrament, confraternity of, 61
"Holy Wednesday," Nahuatl play, 89
Horcasitas, Fernando, 4, 6–8, 72, 79n2, 81n16, 81n18, 81n20, 82n28, 83n36, 83n39, 90, 93
Horn, Rebecca, 19
"How to Live on Earth," 62–64, 210–41; angels as characters in, 210–41; authorship and date, 6, 9, 10, 15; bones in, 31, 220–23, 232–33, 236–37; calque in, 13; characters in, 33, 62–64; Christ as character in, 238–41; Death as a character in, 31, 232–33; deaths in, 51; demons as characters in, 214–29, 234–35, 240–41; fireworks in, 67, 230–31; loanwords in, 12; manuscripts of, 4; Mary as advocate in, 35, 62, 210–13, 220–21, 224–25, 236–37; Mary as character in, 226–31; orthography of, 26n14; service to dead in, 36; souls as characters in, 236–37; violence in, 22, 64
Huaxtepec, 5, 6, 268–69
Huehuetlatolli, 14, 21, 27n36, 101, 110n23
Huitzilopochtli, 76
Human sacrifice, 86, 90, 91–92, 93, 95, 96, 103, 105, 107, 108, 109n5

Idolatry, 28n40, 37–38
Ihiyotl, 53n1
Indulgences, 35, 49–50, 53n17; plenary, 38
Inquisition, 50, 60, 70
Ipalnemoani (deity title), 124, 132, 136, 138, 142

Isaac, 12, 87, 88, 90–94, 97–101, 103–104, 106–107, 109n9, 146–63
Isaiah, 128–29
Ishmael, 12, 90, 108n3, 148–55

Jacob, 124–25
James, Epistle of, 87, 93
Jerome, Saint, 73
Jesse, 129n29
Jesuits, 50–51
Jesus. *See* Christ
Joel, Book of, 53n7
John, Gospel of, 87
John Carter Brown Library, 38
Joseph, Saint, 135n38, 144–45
Judaism, 87–88, 91, 104
Judgment Day. *See* Final Judgment
Judgment, of souls after death, 33, 34–35, 38–39, 45, 46, 65, 164–65, 180–89, 202–203, 238–41, 296–303
"Juicio Final." *See* "Final Judgment"

Karttunen, Frances, 10, 14

Land titles, 67
Las Casas, Bartolomé de, 64–65, 79n2, 81n18
Laso de la Vega, Luis, 57
Last Supper, 60
Lent, 33, 60, 272–73
Leo the Great, 104
Léon, fray Luis de, 110n23
León, fray Martín de, 43, 44, 48, 49, 105–106
León-Portilla, Ascensión H. de, 96
León-Portilla, Miguel, 71, 85
Library of Congress, 4, 26n9, n11, 190, 210, 242
"Life of Don Sebastián, The," 268–303; angels as characters in, 274–87, 290–93, 300–301; authorship and date, 5, 6, 9–10, 15; calque in, 13; Christ as character in, 278–83, 295–301; dead reproaching living in, 42; Death as character in, 31, 82n29, 272–73, 280–83, 286–87, 290–99; deaths in, 51; demons as characters in, 32, 274–79, 282–301; fireworks in, 300–301; hell represented in, 35; loanwords in, 12, 27n38; Lucifer as character in, 32, 82n29, 276–79, 290–91, 294–301; manuscript of, 4; Mary as character in, 298–99; orthography of, 26n21; violence in, 22; works of mercy in, 298–99

Limbo, 35, 38
Loanwords, 6, 10–15, 27nn27–29, 27n38, 307–20
Lockhart, James, 6, 8, 10, 14, 16, 18, 28n41, 56, 57, 80n7, 89, 102
López Austin, Alfredo, 68
Lucifer, 11, 32, 53n2, 68, 77, 82n29; in plays, 166–67, 180–87, 204–207, 276–79, 290–91, 294–301
Luke, Gospel of, 42, 72

Mansfield, Mary C., 82n27
Marriage, sacrament of, 73, 192–95, 198–99, 204–209
Mary, Virgin, 106, 143n61, 246–47; as character in plays, 35, 62, 178–81, 226–31, 298–99; as sinners' advocate, 35, 45, 48, 62, 178–79, 208–209, 210–13, 220–21, 224–25, 236–37, 264–65, 298–99
Mary Magdalene, 106
Mass, 102, 103, 105, 166–67, 184–85, 222–23, 268–69; for dead, 36, 38, 46–47, 49, 50, 51, 52, 82n28, 111n24, 164–65, 168–75, 178–79, 184–85
Matthew, Gospel of, 53n8, 72, 87, 97, 119n2, 127nn21–22, 131n30, 131nn33–34, 133n37, 143n62, 145n65
Mayas, 3
McAfee, Byron, 4, 81n16, 83n36
McGinn, Bernard, 72
Melchior, 12, 119n2, 124–25, 132–35, 138–41
Mendieta, fray Jerónimo de, 14, 133n36
"Merchant, The," 66–67, 242–67; angels as characters in, 262–65; authorship and date, 6, 10, 15; characters in, 17, 66–67; confession and penance in, 67, 70, 258–63; demons as characters in, 258–65; fireworks in, 264–65; loanwords in, 11, 12, 27n38; manuscript of, 4; moneylending in, 19–21, 66, 242–51; priests as characters in, 18, 256–57, 260–63; realistic setting of, 16–25; similarity to medieval dramas, 65; swearing of oaths in, 250–51, 254–55, 258–59; testaments in, 20, 43, 250–53, 256–57, 264–65; violence in, 21–22, 66
Mexico City, dramas enacted in, 79n2, 83n36
Michael, Saint: as character in "Final Judgment," 73, 74, 76, 190–91, 200–203; as character in "Souls and Testamentary Executors," 82n29, 180–89

Mictlan (Nahua underworld), 30, 33, 34, 35, 38, 42, 52, 53n2, 67, 73, 75, 76; mentioned in plays, 154–55, 174–75, 180–81, 186–91, 194–95, 198–201, 204–207, 214–15, 218–19, 234–35, 238–39, 262–73, 276–77, 286–87, 290–95, 300–303. *See also* Hell

Mictlantecuhtli, 53n2

Mijangos, fray Juan de, 101–105, 110n22, 110n23, 111n24, 111n25

Mixtecs, 3

Moab, 124–25

Molina, fray Alonso de, 14, 44, 50, 80n10, 83n41, 143n59; confession manual of, 21, 38, 43

Moneylending and borrowing, 23–25, 51; in "The Merchant," 19–20, 66, 242–51; in "Souls and Testamentary Executors," 166–67

Morality plays: medieval, 65, 66; as Nahuatl genre, 30

Motolinia (fray Toribio de Benavente), 64, 69, 71, 79n2, 81n18, 90, 91

Muñoz Camargo, Diego, 71, 72, 77, 82n31

Nahuatl: literacy in, 3; stages of linguistic change, 10–11, 13, 14

Neixcuitilli, neixcuitilmachiotl (Nahuatl terms for plays): used in plays, 118, 162, 190, 240, 242, 268, 272, 300

New Fire ceremony, 76

Nietzsche, Friedrich, 67

Oaths, swearing of, 18; God's oath to Abraham, 93, 98; in "The Merchant," 21, 66, 250–51, 254–55, 258–59; in "Souls and Testamentary Executors," 182–83

Oaxtepec, Morelos, 26n8

Obraje (textile manufacturing shop), 19, 22–23, 244–45, 248–49

Ocharte, Pedro, 50

Olmos, Andrés de, 27n36, 83n36, 97

Origen, 104, 119n2

Orthography, 7–10

Ortiz de Montellano, Bernard, 68

Otomis, 19

Our Father prayer, 176–77

Oxomoco, 102

Ozumba, 60, 80n13

Paredes, Father Ignacio de, 27n30

Paso y Troncoso, Francisco del, 4, 7

Passion plays, 60, 79n2, 80n13

Paul, Saint, 87, 91, 104, 110n20

Pedraza, fray Bermúdez, 110n23

Penance, 33, 35, 65, 68, 69, 81n19; as character in "Final Judgment," 190–91; in plays, 63, 150–1, 170–71, 184–85, 188–89, 192–93, 274–75, 284–85

"Penitential of Silos," 81n19

Pérez, fray Manuel, 25

Philo of Alexandria, 87, 93

Polygamy, 90, 108n3

Potter, Robert, 93, 109n8

Priests: attendance at death, 47–48; as characters in plays, 18, 75, 174–77, 196–99, 208–209, 256–57, 260–63

Provincial Council (Mexican): First, 58; Third, 53n15, 59

Purgatory, 33–34, 35–38, 51, 76; in plays, 30, 62, 68, 82n28, 164–65, 168–81, 184–87, 238–39

Ravicz, Marilyn Ekdahl, 81n16, 82n30, 109n7

Responses, prayers for dead, 46–47, 50, 164–65, 168–89, 174–75, 178–79, 184–85, 238–39, 264–65

Restitution, 64, 66, 69, 70, 206–209

Ricard, Robert, 79n6, 110n23

Romans, Book of, 99

Rosary, 13, 178–79, 184–85, 216–21, 228–29, 238–39; confraternity of, 49–50

"Sacrifice of Isaac, The," 82n30, 85–96, 146–63; angel as character in, 12, 93, 94, 148–49, 160–63; authorship and date, 5, 6, 10, 15, 90; demon as character in, 148–51; God as character in, 156–57; *huehuetlatolli* in, 14; loanwords in, 11, 27n38; manuscript of, 4, 9; orthography of, 26n16; penance in, 150–51; personal names in, 12; violence in, 22, 91, 93, 94; works of mercy in, 150–51

Sahagún, fray Bernardino de, 15, 26n17, 26n20, 70, 80n10, 81n15, 83n40; *Adiciones* of, 109n12; *Apéndiz* of, 97; *Arte adivinatoria* of, 89; *Florentine Codex* of, 14–15, 137n42, 137nn45–46, 139n53, 140nn36–37, 141nn57–58, 261n21; *Historia General* of, 69, 75, 76; *Psalmodia christiana* of, 26n20, 33, 135n40; sermons of, 33, 34, 42

Salamanca, Council at, 58

Sarah, 146–49, 152–55

Satan: as character in "Final Judgment," 204–209; as character in "The Life of Don Sebastián, 288–89, 292–93. *See also* Demons, Lucifer
Sermons, 4, 18, 56. *See also* Bautista, León, Mijangos, Sahagún
Sexual transgressions, 20, 51, 178–79, 184–89, 190–91, 198–99, 204–205, 246–47, 290–91, 296–97
Sheth, 124–25
Sickness, 36, 44, 48, 68, 232–35, 246–47, 256–65. *See also* Epidemics
Siete partidas, 59
Siker, Jeffrey, 88
Sin, 32, 64, 81n19, 102–103, 111n27; in plays, 62, 63, 70, 172–73, 182–83, 186–87, 190–209, 260–65; original, 63, 104
Souls: at death, 48; as characters in plays, 31, 51, 52, 63, 172–73, 176–81, 236–37; Nahua concepts of, 30–32; in purgatory, 33, 164–89; Spanish/Christian concepts of, 30–31; treatment in testaments, 43–47
"Souls and Testamentary Executors," 67–70, 82n28, 164–89; angels as characters in, 172–75; authorship and date, 5, 6, 10, 15; characters in, 18, 51–52, 68, 69, 82n30; Christ as character in, 180–81, 186–87; commandments in, 182–87; communion in, 172–73, 184–89; deaths in, 51; demons as characters in, 32, 166–77, 180–81, 186–89; fireworks in, 180–81; fasting in, 186–89; judgment in, 180–89; loanwords in, 12; Lucifer as character in, 166–67, 180–87; manuscript of, 4, 9; Mary as character in, 178–81; mass in, 174–75, 184–85; moneylending in, 166–67; orthography of, 26n16; penance in, 170–71, 184–85, 188–89; priests as characters in, 174–77; punishment of negligent executors in, 49, 180–89; purgatory in, 168–81, 184–87; realism in, 17–18; responses chanted in, 46; service to dead in, 36, 70; souls as characters in, 172–73, 176–81; testaments in, 43, 164–67; tolling of bells in, 47, 176–81, 184–85; violence in, 22, 69
Sousa, Lisa, 57
Sten, María, 79n2
Stern, Charlotte, 59–60
Sweathouse (temazcalli), 76, 83n41, 188–89, 204–205

Sweeping, 212–13; as character in "Final Judgment," 192–93

Taix, Hierónimo, 50
Tarascans, 3
Taylor, William, 108
Tecalco, 70
Tecamachalco, 50
Ten Commandments, 22, 23, 24, 32; in plays, 18, 21, 66, 68, 82nn28–29, 109n10, 182–85, 202–205, 268–71, 296–99
Tepeyacac, 5, 252–53
Testaments, 4, 19, 28n43, 43–47, 51, 67, 164–67; Culhuacan collection of, 22, 23, 24, 45, 48; dispute over, in "The Merchant," 20, 250–53, 256–57, 264–65
Tezcatlipoca, 76, 93, 94, 95, 108
Thirst, 68, 262–63
"Three Kings, The," 118–45; authorship and date, 15; *huehuetlatolli* in, 14; loanwords in, 11, 13, 16; manuscript of, 4; orthography of, 26n16; relationship to *Florentine Codex* and *Bancroft Dialogues*, 14, 137n42, 137n45, 139n53, 141nn57–58; *tlatoque* equated with *reyes* in, 16, 17, 27–28n39; use of personal names in, 12; violence in, 22
Tlacatecolotl. *See* Demons
Tlalmanalco, 60
Tlaloc, 91, 92, 94, 95, 108
Tlalocan, 76
Tlatelolco, performance of Final Judgment play in, 60, 74, 79n2, 83n36 79n2
Tlatoani, 14, 16, 17, 27n39, 92; equated with *rey*, 16, 17, 27–28n39
Tlaxcala, 21, 44, 77, 81n18, 90; town council *Actas*, 23, 28n42, 28nn48–49
Tlaxilacalli, 16, 17, 28n47
Tlazolteotl, 69
Tloque nahuaque (deity title), 122, 124, 132, 136, 138, 140, 142
Toledo, Council of, 58, 59
Tollantzinco, San Juan Bautista, 5, 18–19, 24, 25n7, 242–243
Tonalli, 31, 53n1
Torquemada, fray Juan de, 81n18
Trent, Council of, 58, 111n24
Tula, 49, 50
Tuxpan, 61
Tzitzimitl, 62, 70, 76, 77, 214–15. *See also* Demons

Ucelo, Martin, 70, 84n42
Urban VIII, Pope, 58, 59
Usury. *See* Moneylending

Valadés, fray Diego, 36
Valencia, fray Martín de, 61
Valeriano, don Antonio, 137n48
Vázquez, Bernabé, 5, 162–63
Veracruz, Alonso de la, 110n23
Vetancurt, fray Agustín de, 18, 38
Villar, Susan McMillen, 83n36
Violence, 23, 106; in medieval drama, 64; in the plays, 21–22, 64, 66, 69, 91, 93, 94; in preconquest ritual, 94
Virgin of Guadalupe, 57

Weckmann, Luis, 79n5
Williams, Jerry, 83n36, 109n7
Wills. *See* Testaments
Works of mercy, 36, 41–42, 150–51, 298–99

Xochimilco, 5, 26n20, 60, 252–53
Xochiquetzal, 83n34

-Yolia (spirit), 30, 33, 44, 52, 52n1

Zapotecs, 3
Zárate, fray Jerónimo de, 13
Zumárraga, fray Juan de, 108n5
Zumthor, Paul, 77, 84n43